The History of the

MEDIEVAL
WORLD

ALSO BY SUSAN WISE BAUER

The History of the Ancient World:
From the Earliest Accounts to the Fall of Rome
(W. W. Norton, 2007)

The Well-Educated Mind:
A Guide to the Classical Education You Never Had
(W. W. Norton, 2003)

The Story of the World: History for the Classical Child
(Peace Hill Press)

Volume I: Ancient Times (rev. ed., 2006)

Volume II: The Middle Ages (rev. ed. 2007)

Volume III: Early Modern Times (2004)

Volume IV: The Modern Age (2005)

The Complete Writer: Writing with Ease
(Peace Hill Press, 2008)

The Art of the Public Grovel: Sexual Sin and Public Confession in America
(Princeton University Press, 2008)

WITH JESSIE WISE

The Well-Trained Mind:
A Guide to Classical Education at Home
(rev. ed., W. W. Norton, 2009)

The History of the
MEDIEVAL
WORLD

From the Conversion of Constantine
to the First Crusade

SUSAN WISE BAUER

W · W · Norton   New York   London

For information about permission to reproduce selections from this book,
write to Permissions, W. W. Norton & Company, Inc.,
500 Fifth Avenue, New York, NY 10110

For information about special discounts for bulk purchases, please contact
W. W. Norton Special Sales at specialsales@wwnorton.com or 800-233-4830

Maps designed by Susan Wise Bauer and Sarah Park and created by Sarah Park.

*Since this page cannot legibly accommodate all the copyright notices,
page 719 constitutes an extension of the copyright page.*

Manufacturing by RR Donnelley, Harrisonburg
Book design by Margaret M. Wagner
Production manager: Julia Druskin

Library of Congress Cataloging-in-Publication Data

Bauer, S. Wise.
The history of the medieval world : from the conversion of
Constantine to the First Crusade / Susan Wise Bauer. — 1st ed.
p. cm.
Includes bibliographical references and index.
ISBN 978-0-393-05975-5 (hardcover)
1. Middle Ages. 2. Civilization, Medieval. I. Title.
D117.B34 2010
909.07—dc22

2009038978

W. W. Norton & Company, Inc.
500 Fifth Avenue, New York, N.Y. 10110
www.wwnorton.com

W. W. Norton & Company Ltd.
Castle House, 75/76 Wells Street, London W1T 3QT

1 2 3 4 5 6 7 8 9 0

For Ben

Contents

Part Four
STATES AND KINGDOMS
317

Part Five
CRUSADES
539

Maps

—

Illustrations

———

Acknowledgments

—

MY EDITOR at Norton, Starling Lawrence, first suggested this project and has kept it on the rails with expert advice, ongoing encouragement, and the occasional exhortation to come down off the ledge and get back to the manuscript. I continue to be grateful to both Star and Jenny for providing me with a place to work and think whenever I show up in New York.

The good people at Norton amaze me with their skill, dedication, and (above all) good humor. I'm grateful to all those who have so kindly and cheerfully worked on my various projects with me; thanks especially to Molly May, Nydia Parries, Golda Rademacher, Dosier Hammond, Eugenia Pakalik, Bill Rusin, and Jenn Chan.

I am most indebted to the librarians and staff at my home library, the Swem Library of the College of William & Mary. Thanks also to the tolerant staff at the University of Virginia's Alderman Library, Columbia University's East Asian Reading Room, and the London Library.

Gratitude also goes to my agent, Richard Henshaw, for continuing to manage an increasingly complicated set of commitments.

Here in Virginia, Sarah Park did an extraordinary job of creating complicated maps which could show the multiple shifting kingdoms in the medieval landscape; thanks to her for her patience with my ever-changing instructions. Justin Moore's eye for detail caught an amazing number of embarrassing mistakes before they reached the reading public; his skill at fact-checking continues to amaze me. (And any embarrassing mistakes that remain are solely my responsibility.)

At Peace Hill, Kim Norton, Jackie Violet, and Mollie Bauer kept the office running, answered phone calls and e-mail, fielded questions, and made it possible for me to get away and write. Suzanne Hicks kept my travel schedule running without a hitch.

Zhe Quan, Kevin Stilley, and Tom Jackson read early drafts of this manuscript and provided valuable feedback. Jonathan Gunderlach found answers to obscure questions and began the laborious task of clearing permissions.

My Korean publisher, Theory & Praxis, hosted my two oldest sons and me in Korea and allowed me to do on-site research in Korean history. Many thanks to them for their generous hospitality; thanks also to Yeonglan Han of the Corea Literary Agency for her capable assistance and her friendship.

Boris Fishman came on board near the end of this project, when I was at my most exasperated, and worked magic on the remaining snarls in the permissions.

My family and friends have not only survived another world history project, but have done their best to make sure I emerged alive at the end of it. Thanks to Mel Moore, Diane Wheeler, and Susan Cunningham for keeping me (relatively) sane. Bob and Heather Wise took on the burden of my other publishing commitments when the medieval world swallowed my life.

Without my parents, Jay and Jessie Wise, my household would have ground to a halt a long time ago. As they've grown, my children—Christopher, Ben, Dan, and Emily—have become partners in helping Mom get her work done. It seems inadequate to say *thank you* to any of them: but thank you.

My deepest gratitude goes to my husband, Peter, who continues to make it possible for me to do work I love and have a real life, all at the same time. *Sumus exules, vivendi quam auditores.*

Part One

UNITY

Chapter One

—∎—

One Empire, Under God

Between 312 and 330,
Constantine imposes his will on the Roman empire
and gives the Christian church a hand with its doctrine

ON THE MORNING of October 29, 312, the Roman soldier Constantine walked through the gates of Rome at the front of his army.

He was forty years old, and for six years he had been struggling to claim the crown of the *imperator*. Less than twenty-four hours before, he had finally beaten the sitting emperor of Rome, twenty-nine-year-old Maxentius, at the Battle of the Milvian Bridge. Constantine's men had fought their way forward across the bridge, toward the city of Rome, until the defenders broke and ran. Maxentius drowned, pulled down into the mud of the riverbed by the weight of his armor. The Christian historian Lactantius tells us that Constantine's men marched into Rome with the sign of Christ marked on each shield; the Roman* writer Zosimus adds that they also carried Maxentius's waterlogged head on the tip of a spear. Constantine had dredged the body up and decapitated it.[1]

Constantine settled into the imperial palace to take stock of his new empire. Dealing at once with Maxentius's supporters, he ordered immediate but judicious executions: only Maxentius's "nearest friends" fell victim to the new regime.[2] He dissolved the Praetorian Guard, the standing imperial bodyguard that had supported Maxentius's claim to the throne. He also packaged Maxentius's head and shipped it south to North Africa, as a message to the young man's supporters that it was time to switch allegiances. Then he turned to deal with his co-emperors.

His victory over Maxentius had given him a crown but not the entire

---

*Histories of the later Roman empire usually identify its citizens as either Christian or pagan, with "pagan" generally meaning "not Christian." There are two problems with this approach: first, the religious landscape of the early Middle Ages was far more complicated than this simple division implies; second, the label "pagan" has been resurrected in recent years with an entirely different set of associations. I have chosen to avoid the word altogether. Zosimus, often called a "pagan historian," was a follower of the old Roman religion, so I have called him "Roman" instead.

empire. Thirty years earlier, his predecessor, Diocletian, had appointed co-rulers to share the job of running the vast Roman territories—a system that had spawned multiple lines of succession. Two other men currently held parts of the empire. Licinius, a peasant who had risen through the army ranks, had claimed the title of *imperator* over the central part of the empire, east of the province Pannonia and west of the Black Sea; Maximinus Daia, who had also clawed his way up from peasant birth, ruled the eastern territories, which were constantly threatened by the aggressive Persian empire.*

Diocletian, an idealist, had designed his system to keep power out of the hands of any one man; but he had not reckoned with the drive to power. Constantine had no intention of sharing his rule. Nevertheless, he was too smart to open two wars simultaneously. Instead he made a deal with Licinius, who was not only closer than Maximinus but also less powerful: Licinius would become his ally. In return, Licinius, now nearing sixty, would marry Constantine's half-sister, the eighteen-year-old Constantia.

Licinius accepted the deal with alacrity. In his first gesture of good faith towards his brother-in-law-to-be, he met Maximinus Daia in battle on April 30, 313—six months after Constantine entered Rome. Licinius had fewer than thirty thousand men, while Daia had assembled seventy thousand. But Licinius's army, like Constantine's, marched under the banner of the Christian God. It was a useful rallying point; Maximinus Daia had vowed, in Jupiter's name, to stamp out Christianity in his domains, and the presence of the Christian banner pointed out that the battle for territory had become a holy war.

The armies met on the poorly named Campus Serenus, outside the city of Adrianople, and Licinius's smaller army outfought Maximinus's. Maximinus Daia fled in disguise, but Licinius followed him across the province of Asia and finally trapped him in the city of Tarsus. Seeing no escape, Maximinus Daia swallowed poison. Unfortunately, he indulged in a huge last meal first, which delayed the poison's action. The historian Lactantius writes that he took four days to die:

> [T]he force of the poison, repelled by his full stomach, could not immediately operate, but it produced a grievous disease, resembling the pestilence.
> . . . Having undergone various and excruciating torments, he dashed his forehead against the wall, and his eyes started out of their sockets. And now, become blind, he imagined that he saw God, with His servants arrayed in white robes, sitting in judgment on him. . . . Then, amidst groans, like those of one burnt alive, did he breathe out his guilty soul in the most horrible kind of death.[3]

---

*This included the administrative districts of Pannonia, Dacia, Thracia, and Macedonia.

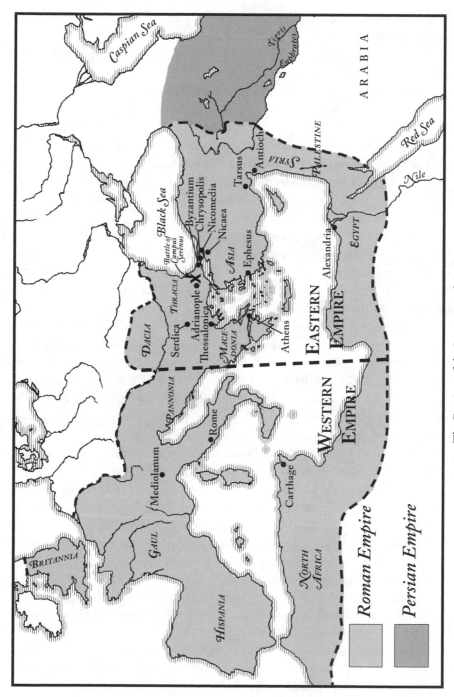

1.1: *The Empires of the Romans and Persians*

Roman Empire

Persian Empire

Nor was it the last horrible death. Licinius then murdered Maximinus Daia's two young children, both under the age of nine, and drowned their mother; he also put to death three other possible blood claimants to the eastern throne, all children of dead emperors.

Constantine found it prudent to ignore this bloodshed. The two men met in Mediolanum (modern Milan) to celebrate Licinius's marriage to Constantia and to issue an empire-wide proclamation that made Christianity legal, which was highly necessary given that both men had now wrapped themselves in the flag of God in order to claim the right to rule.

In fact Christianity had been tolerated in all parts of the empire except the east for some years. But this proclamation, the Edict of Milan, now spread this protection into Maximinus Daia's previous territories. "No one whatsoever should be denied the opportunity to give his heart to the observance of the Christian religion," the Edict announced. "Any one of these who wishes to observe Christian religion may do so freely and openly, without molestation. . . . [We] have also conceded to other religions the right of open and free observance of their worship for the sake of the peace of our times, that each one may have the free opportunity to worship as he pleases." Property which had previously been confiscated from Christians was supposed to be returned. All Christian churches were to be turned over to Christian control. "Let this be done," the Edict concluded, "so that, as we have said above, Divine favor towards us, which, under the most important circumstances we have already experienced, may, for all time, preserve and prosper our successes together with the good of the state."[4]

The "good of the state." In Lactantius's accounts, Constantine is a servant of the Divine, and his enemies are brought low by the judgment of God Himself. Eusebius, the Christian priest who wrote Constantine's biography, reflects the same point of view: Constantine is the "Godbeloved," bringing the knowledge of the Son of God to the people of Rome.[5]

Eusebius was Constantine's friend, and Lactantius was a starving rhetoric teacher until Constantine hired him as court tutor and changed his fortunes. But their histories are motivated by more than a desire to stay on the emperor's good side. Both men understood, perhaps before Constantine had managed to articulate it even to himself, that Christianity was the empire's best chance for survival.

Constantine could deal with the problem of multiple emperors; he had already eliminated two of his three rivals, and Licinius's days were numbered. But the empire was threatened by a more complex trouble. For centuries, it had been a political entity within which provinces and districts and cities still maintained their older, deeper identities. Tarsus was Roman, but it was also an Asian city where you were more likely to hear Greek than Latin on the streets. North Africa was Roman, but Carthage was an African city with an African population. Gaul was a Roman territory, but the Germanic tribes who populated it spoke their own languages and worshipped their own gods. The Roman empire had held all of these dual identities—Roman and *other*—together, but the centrifugal force of the *other* was so strong that the borders of the empire were barely containing it.

Constantine didn't put the cross on his banner out of an attempt to gain the loyalty of Christians. As the Russian historian A. A. Vasiliev points out, it would have been ridiculous to build a political strategy on "one-tenth of the population which at that time was taking no part in political affairs."[6] Nor did Constantine suddenly get religion. He continued to emboss Sol Invictus, the sun god, on his coins; he remained *pontifex maximus*, chief priest of the Roman state cult, until his death; and he resisted baptism until he realized, in 336, that he was dying.[7]

But he saw in Christianity a new and fascinating way of understanding the world, and in Christians a model of what Roman citizens might be, bound together by a loyalty that transcended but did not destroy their own local allegiances. Christianity could be held side by side with other identities. It was almost impossible to be thoroughly Roman and also be a Visigoth, or to be wholeheartedly Roman and African. But a Christian could be a Greek or a Latin, a slave or a free man, a Jew or a Gentile. Christianity had begun as a religion with no political homeland to claim as its own, which meant that it could be adopted with ease by an empire that swallowed homelands as a matter of course. By transforming the Roman empire into a Christian empire, Constantine could unify the splintering empire in the name of Christ, a name that might succeed where the names of Caesar and Augustus had failed.

Not that he relied entirely on the name of Christ to get what he needed. In 324, Licinius provided Constantine with the perfect excuse to get rid of his co-emperor; the eastern ruler accused the Christians in his court of spying for his colleague in the west (which they undoubtedly were) and threw them out. Constantine immediately announced that Licinius was persecuting Christians—illegal, according to the Edict of Milan—and led his army east.

The two men met twice: the first time near Adrianople, the site of Licinius's own victory against the former eastern emperor Maximinus Daia, and the final time two months later, on September 18, at Chrysopolis. In this last battle, Licinius was so thoroughly defeated that he agreed to surrender.[8] Constantine spared his life when Constantia pleaded for him, instead exiling him to the city of Thessalonica.

Constantine was now the sole ruler of the Roman world.

HIS FIRST ACTION as solitary emperor was to guarantee the unity of Christian belief. Christianity would not be much help to him if it split apart into battling factions, which it was in danger of doing; for some years, Christian leaders in various parts of the empire had been arguing with increasing stridency over the exact nature of the Incarnation, and the quarrel was rising to a crescendo.*

The Christian church had universally acknowledged, since its beginnings, that Jesus partook in both human and divine natures: "Jesus is Lord," as J. N. D. Kelly remarks, was the earliest and most basic confession of Christianity. Christ, according to the earliest Christian theologians, was "indivisibly one" and also "fully divine and fully human."[9] This was a little like simultaneously filling one glass to the brim with two entire glassfuls of different liquids, and Christians had wrestled with this paradox from the very beginning of their history. Ignatius of Antioch, who died in a Roman arena sometime before AD 110, laid out the orthodox understanding in a series of balanced oppositions:

> There is one Physician who is possessed both of flesh and spirit;
> both made and not made;
> God existing in flesh;
> true life in death;
> both of Mary and of God. . . .
> For "the Word was made flesh."
> Being incorporeal, He was in the body;
> being impassible, He was in a passible body;
> being immortal, He was in a mortal body;
> being life, He became subject to corruption.[10]

But other voices offered different solutions. As early as the second century, the Ebionites suggested that Christ was essentially human, and "divine" only in the sense that he had been selected to reign as the Jewish Messiah. The sect known as Docetists employed Greek ideas about the "inherent impurity of matter"[11] and insisted that Christ could not truly have taken part in the corruption of the body; he was instead a spirit who only *appeared* human. The Gnostics, taking Docetism one step further, believed that the divine Christ and human Jesus had formed a brief partnership in order to rescue humankind from the corrupting grasp of the material world.† And while

---

*The Incarnation is the central doctrine of Christianity: that God came to earth in the person of Jesus Christ.

†A dizzying number of religions and practices can be classified as "gnostic": generally a gnostic religion is one that requires its followers to search out a high level of knowledge (gnosis) which only a select few can ever truly attain. Interested readers may want to consult Karen King's *What*

Constantine and Licinius fought over the crown, a Christian priest named Arius had begun to teach yet another doctrine: that since God was One, "alone without beginning, alone true, alone possessing immortality, alone wise, alone good, alone sovereign," the Son of God must be a created being. He was different from other created beings, perhaps, but he did not share the *essence* of God.[12]

Arius, who served in the Egyptian city of Alexandria, had been gathering followers and vexing his bishop,* who had finally excommunicated him. This created a potentially serious and major breach, one that might well separate a large group of Christians from the main body of the Christian believers. Constantine, learning of the split, sent a letter to Egypt strongly suggesting that the two men sit down and work out their differences: "Restore me then my quiet days, and untroubled nights, that the joy of . . . a tranquil life may henceforth be my portion," he wrote.[13]

But neither the bishop nor Arius was willing to yield, and in desperation Constantine called together a council of church leaders to settle the question. He first intended to have the council at the city of Nicomedia, but a severe earthquake unsettled the city while the bishops were on their way to the meeting; buildings collapsed, hundreds died where they stood, and flames from hearths and braziers were flung into the dry frames of the houses, where the blaze spread so rapidly that the city became, in the words of Sozomen, "one mass of fire."[14]

Such a sudden and disastrous event suggested to many that God was not pleased with the coming council, and the travelling bishops halted in their tracks and sent urgent inquiries to the emperor. Would he call off the council? Should they proceed?

Reassured by the churchman Basil that the earthquake had been sent not as judgment but as a demonic attempt to keep the church from meeting and settling its questions, Constantine replied that the bishops should travel instead to Nicaea, where they arrived in late spring of 325, ready to parley.

Settling theological questions by way of council was not a new development for Christianity; since the time of the apostles, the Christian churches had considered themselves smaller parts of a whole, not individual congregations. But never before had an emperor, even a tolerant one, taken the step of summoning a church council on his own authority.[15] In 325, at Nicaea, the Christian church and the government of the west clasped hands.

Is Gnosticism? (Belknap Press, 2005), particularly the first chapter, "Why Is Gnosticism So Hard to Define?"

*Since the earliest days of Christianity, each Christian church had a senior leader, an "overseer" (*episkopos*) or "bishop" who assumed ultimate responsibility for the flock. By the fourth century, each city containing a Christian church had a bishop who represented all of the Christians in that particular geographic area.

One might wonder why Constantine, who didn't have any trouble reconciling his belief in Apollo with his professed Christianity, cared about the exact definition of Christ's Godness. In all likelihood, his interest in this case wasn't theological but practical: to keep the church from splitting apart. A major breach would threaten Constantine's vision of Christianity as a possible model for holding together a disparate group of people in loyalty to an overarching structure. If the overarching structure cracked, the model would be useless.

Which probably explains his decision to be anti-Arian; taking the temper of the most influential leaders, he realized that the most powerful bishops disagreed with Arius's theology. Arianism essentially created a pantheon of divinities, with God the Father at the top and God the Son as a sort of demiurge, a little lower in the heavenly hierarchy. This was anathema to both the Jewish roots of Christianity and the Greek Platonism which flourished in most of the eastern empire.*

Directed by their leading bishops and by the emperor himself to be anti-Arian, the assembled priests at Nicaea came up with a formulation still used in Christian churches today: the Nicene Creed, which asserts the Christian belief in "one God, the Father almighty, maker of all things visible and invisible":

> And in one Lord Jesus Christ,
> the only-begotten Son of God,
> begotten of the Father before all worlds,
> God of God,
> Light of Light,
> Very God of Very God,
> begotten, not made,
> being of one substance with the Father
> by whom all things were made.

It was a formulation that, in its emphasis on the divinity of Christ, shut the door firmly on Arianism.

And it had the imperial stamp on it. In laying hold of Christianity as his tool, Constantine had altered it. Constantine's ineffable experience of the divine at the Milvian Bridge had proved useful in the moment. But ineffable experiences are notoriously bad at binding together any group of people in common purpose for a long time, and the empire, now tenuously held

---

*Platonic philosophy had no place for ranked divinities, all of whom belonged to the divine realm (the realm of the Ideal), but some of whom were less ideal than others.

together by a spider-web linkage, needed the Christian church to be more organized, more orderly, and more rational.

Christians, in return, would have had to be more than human to resist what Constantine was offering: the imprint of imperial power. Constantine gave the church all sorts of advantages. He recognized Christian priests as equal to priests of the Roman religion, and exempted them from taxes and state responsibilities that might interfere with their religious duties. He also decreed that any man could leave his property to the church; this, as Vasiliev points out, in one stroke turned "Christian communities" into "legal juridical entities."[16]

Further tying his own power to the future of the church, he had also begun construction of a new capital city, one that from its beginning would be filled with churches, not Roman temples. Constantine had decided to move the capital of his empire, officially, from Rome and its gods to the old city of Byzantium, rebuilt as a Christian city on the shores of the pass to the Black Sea.[17]

All at once Christianity was more than an identity. It was a legal and political constituency—exactly what it had not been when Constantine first decided to march under the banner of the cross. The church, like Constantine's empire, was going to be around for a little while; and like Constantine, it had to take care for its future.

After his condemnation at the Council of Nicaea, Arius took to his heels and hid in Palestine, in the far east of the empire. Arianism did not disappear; it remained a strong and discontented underground current. In fact, Constantine's own sister became a champion of Arian doctrines, rejecting her brother's command to accept the Nicene Creed as the only Christian orthodoxy.[18]

She may have been motivated by bitterness. In 325, within months of the Council of Nicaea, Constantine broke his promise of clemency to her husband Licinius and had him hanged. Unwilling to leave any challengers to his throne alive, Constantine also sent her ten-year-old son, his own nephew, to the gallows.

Four years later, he officially dedicated the city of Byzantium as his new capital, the New Rome of his empire. Disregarding the protests of the Romans, he had brought old monuments from the great cities of the old empire—Rome, Athens, Alexandria, Antioch, Ephesus—and installed them among the new churches and streets. He ordered Roman "men of rank" to move to his new city, complete with their households, possessions, and titles.[19] He was re-creating Rome as he thought it should be, under the shadow of the cross. The emblem of Daniel in the lion's den, the brave man standing for his God in the face of a heathen threat, decorated the fountains in the public squares; a picture of Christ's Passion, in gold and jewels, was embossed on the very center of the palace roof.[20]

By 330 Constantine had succeeded in establishing one empire, one royal family, one church. But while the New Rome celebrated, the old Rome seethed with resentment over its loss of status; the unified church Constantine had created at Nicaea was held together only by the thin veneer of imperial sanction; and Constantine's three sons eyed their father's empire and waited for his death.

T I M E L I N E   I

ROMAN EMPIRE

Diocletian (284–305)

Maxentius (306–312)
    Licinius (308–324)   **Maximinus Daia** (308–313)

Battle of the Milvian Bridge (312)
Constantine (312–337)
Battle of Campus Serenus (313)   Edict of Milan (313)

Council of Nicaea (325)

Chapter Two

—∎—

Seeking the Mandate
of Heaven

Between 313 and 402,
the Jin cling to the Mandate of Heaven,
while the northern barbarians aspire to seize it

A s Constantine was uniting his empire in the west, the eastern empire of the Jin* was disintegrating. Its emperor, Jin Huaidi, had been forced into captivity and servanthood. In 313, at the age of twenty-six, he was pouring wine for his masters at a barbarian feast, and his life hung by a thread.

The Jin empire was a young one, barely fifty years old. For centuries, the old Han dynasty had held the Chinese provinces together in one sprawling and unified whole, the eastern parallel to the Roman empire in the west. But by AD 220, the Han had fallen to rebellion and unrest. The empire fractured apart into thirds, and the Three Kingdoms that took over from the Han—the Cao Wei, the Shu Han, and the Dong Wu —were unstable, shifting and battling for control.

The northernmost of the Three Kingdoms, the Cao Wei, was controlled by

*The Jin dynasty is sometimes transcribed "Chin"; "Jin" is the Pinyin transcription. As in the first volume of this series, I have chosen to use Pinyin transcription for Chinese characters unless another transcription for a particular name is so familiar that use of the Pinyin might cause confusion (i.e., the Yangtze river becomes Chang Jiang in Pinyin, but I have chosen to retain the better-known romanization for clarity's sake).

I have also used only one name for each emperor. Typically, a Chinese emperor was known by his birth name until his accession, when he took an imperial name. He was then awarded a posthumous name, and after the Han dynasty, emperors were often given a temple name as well. Some emperors were also known by courtesy names (adopted later in life to indicate maturity). This is confusing for the general reader, so in most cases I have chosen to use the imperial name to refer to each emperor even before his accession. For clarity's sake, I have given each emperor his dynasty's name for a prefix, even though this is not customary for some of the dynasties and emperors we will encounter later. Emperor Huaidi of the Jin dynasty thus appears as Jin Huaidi; Emperor Ruizong of the Tang dynasty will be referred to as Tang Ruizong.

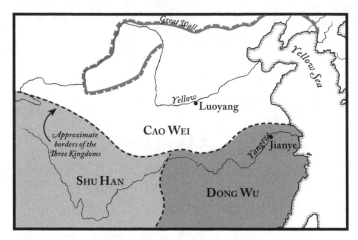

2.1: The Three Kingdoms

its generals; the kings who sat on the Cao Wei throne were young and easily cowed, and did as they were told. In 265, the twenty-nine-year-old general Sima Yan decided to claim the Cao Wei crown for himself. His entire life he had watched as army men pulled the puppet-king's strings. The commanders of the Cao Wei army, including his father and his grandfather, had led in the conquest of the neighboring kingdom of the Shu Han, reducing the Three Kingdoms to two; Cao Wei dominated the north, but its generals remained crownless.

Unlike them, Sima Yan did not intend to spend his career as puppet-master. He already had power; what he craved was legitimacy, the *rightful* power to command—the title that accompanied the sword.

According to the *Three Kingdoms*, the most famous account of the years after the fall of the Han, Sima Yan buckled on his sword and went to see the emperor: the teenager Wei Yuandi, grandson of the kingdom's founder. "Whose efforts have preserved the Cao Wei empire?" he asked, to which the young emperor, suddenly realizing that his audience chamber was crowded with Sima Yan's supporters, answered, "We owe everything to your father and grandfather." "In that case," Sima Yan said, "since it is clear that you can't defend the kingdom yourself, you should step aside and appoint someone who can." Only one courtier objected to this; as soon as the words left his mouth, Sima Yan's supporters beat him to death.

The *Three Kingdoms* is a romance, a fictionalized swashbuckling account written centuries later; nevertheless, it reflects the actual events surrounding the rise of the Jin dynasty. Wei Yuandi agreed to Sima Yan's plans; Sima Yan built an altar, and in an elaborate, formal ceremony, Wei Yuandi climbed to the top of the altar with the seal of state in his hands, gave it to his rival, and then descended to the ground a common citizen.

That day the entire body of officials prostrated itself once and again below the Altar for the Acceptance of the Abdication, shouting mightily, "Long live the new Emperor!"[1]

The ceremony had transformed Sima Yan into a *rightful* ruler, a divinely ordained emperor, holder of the Mandate of Heaven. Wei Yuandi, stripped of the Mandate, went back to ordinary life. He died some years later in peace.

Sima Yan took the royal name "Jin Wudi" and became the founder of a new dynasty: the Jin. By 276, he was confident enough in his grasp on his empire to launch a takeover bid against the remaining kingdom, the Dong Wu.

The power of the Dong Wu had been dwindling under an irrational king who had become unbearably cruel; his favorite game was to invite a handful of palace officials to a banquet and get them all drunk, while eunuchs stationed just outside the door wrote down everything they said. The next morning he would summon the officials, hungover and wretched, to his audience chamber and punish them for every incautious word.[2] By the time the Jin armies arrived at the Dong Wu capital of Jianye, his subjects were ready to welcome their conqueror.

This story, which comes from the Jin's own official chronicles, probably tells us more about Jin Wudi than about his opponent. Jin Wudi, desperate for legitimization, knew his history. He knew that for thousands of years, dynasties had risen through virtue and fallen through vice. Emperors ruled by the will of Heaven, but if they grew tyrannical and corrupt, the will of Heaven would raise up another dynasty to supplant them. Jin Wudi wanted a greater justification than force to help him dominate the Dong Wu.

Nevertheless, force brought him into the city. The Jin armies, planning on making the final push into Jianye by river, found their way blocked by barriers of iron chain. So they sent flaming rafts, piled high with pitch-covered logs, floating down into the barriers; the chains melted and snapped, and the Jin flooded into Jianye.[3] The tyrannical emperor surrendered. The era of the Three Kingdoms was ended; by 280, all of China was united again under the Jin.[4]

This was the empire which lasted barely half a century.

Jin Wudi died in 290, leaving as heir an oldest son who was, in the words of his disgusted subjects, "more than half an idiot." Unwisely, he also left behind twenty-four other sons (he had overindulged himself in wives and concubines), all of whom had been awarded royal titles of one kind or another.[5] At once, war broke out. Wife, father-in-law, step-grandfather, uncles, cousins, and brothers all jockeyed to control the half-wit who sat on the throne.

The chaos that swallowed up the Jin empire from 291 to 306 was later known as the Rebellion of the Eight Princes. In fact, far more than eight royal relatives were jockeying for control, but only eight of them managed to rise

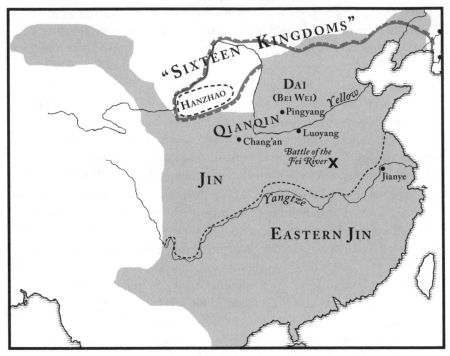

2.2: *The Jin*

to the position of regent for the idiot emperor, a position that gave them the crown de facto. In the middle of all this, the emperor himself survived until 306. Finally, an unknown assassin brought his miserable life to an end with a plateful of poisoned cakes.[6]

After his death, a faction supporting his youngest half-brother managed to get its candidate crowned. The new emperor, Jin Huaidi, was an intelligent, educated, and thoughtful young man, not particularly interested in self-indulgence or tyranny. But he was fighting against rough odds. The Rebellion of the Eight Princes had moth-eaten his empire into fragility, and various claimants to the throne were still lurking nearby, with their own personal armies behind them. There was also danger to the north, where a slew of tiny states ruled by warlords aspired to conquer the greater kingdom below them. The Chinese to the south gave these the collective name "Sixteen Kingdoms," although their number was fluid.

In the end, it was one of the Sixteen Kingdoms, the Hanzhao, that brought the frayed Jin empire down. Hanzhao armies pushed constantly south, raiding Jin land. By 311, they had reached the walls of the Jin capital Luoyang itself.

Luoyang, stripped and wrecked by civil war, was not well equipped to withstand siege. The Jin armies fought a dozen desperate engagements with the Hanzhao invaders outside the walls; but the people inside were starving, and the gates were finally thrown open. Jin Huaidi fled, hoping to reach the city of Chang'an and take refuge there. Instead, he was captured on the road and hauled back as a prisoner of war to the new capital city of the swelled Hanzhao kingdom, Pingyang.[7]

There, the Hanzhao ruler, Liu Cong, dressed him as a slave and forced him to serve wine to officials at royal banquets. Jin Huaidi spent two miserable years as a palace slave, but visitors to the court were shocked to see the man who held the Mandate of Heaven forced into servitude. That the Mandate had come to him by way of threat and manipulation made no difference; its mantle still covered him. An upswell of feeling that Jin Huaidi should be freed began to trouble Liu Cong's court. Liu Cong, who had already proved that his sword was stronger than Jin Huaidi's mandate, responded by putting the Jin emperor to death.[8] Three years later, he marched down to Chang'an, where the surviving Jin court had gathered, and conquered it.

The brief dominance of the Jin had ended. But the Jin name itself survived. Sima Rui, another Jin relative, was in command of a sizable Jin force quartered at the city of Jianye. He was the strongest man around, and in 317, after a gap in the Jin emperorship, his soldiers pronounced him emperor. He took the imperial name "Jin Yuandi," and although his reign was short, he was succeeded by his son and grandsons in an unbroken imperial line that ruled from Jianye over a shrunken southeastern domain.*

Neither the Hanzhao nor any of the other Sixteen Kingdoms tried to bring a final end to the Jin, possibly because the land south of the Yangtze didn't lend itself to fighting on horseback (the preferred method of northerners, inherited from their nomadic ancestors). As far as the Jin were concerned, the river now marked the boundary between *real* China and the northern realm of the barbarians. Despite the short history of their empire, the Jin emperors attempted to prove that the Mandate was theirs by keeping the torch of ancient Chinese civilization burning. The court at Jianye modelled itself on the old traditions of the Han, bringing back rituals of ancestor worship that had faded during the chaotic decades of civil war and playing host to Confucian scholars who taught, in the traditional manner, that the enlightened man was he who recognized his duties and carried them out faithfully. Holding on to Confucius's promise that a virtuous ruler will gain more and more authority over his people (moral authority, Confucius taught, would roll out from the righteous ruler like wind, bending his subjects to obedience as wind bends

---

*Jianye is also known as Jiankang. The Jin dynasty held power from 265 to 420; the latter half of the Jin rule, when Jin power was pushed to the southeast, is known as the period of the Eastern Jin (317–420). Sometimes the earlier part of the dynasty (265–316) is called the Western Jin to distinguish the two eras.

grass), the Jin emperors struggled to live rightly and follow the ancient rituals. "Guide the people by virtue," the *Analects* had promised, "keep them in line by rites, and they will . . . reform themselves."⁹ The promise that virtuous government would always triumph held the Jin court together, even in the face of defeat by the northern barbarians.

"BARBARIAN" was a moveable term; the harder the Jin fought to distinguish themselves from the uncivilized warriors to the north, the more those uncivilized warriors wanted to be just like the Jin.

In the latter half of the fourth century, the most ambitious of the northern "barbarians" was Fu Jian, chief of the Qianqin. Fu Jian had aspirations to be truly Chinese. He had founded Confucian academies in his state and had reformed the government of his kingdom so that it was run along Chinese lines; his capital city was the ancient Chinese capital of Chang'an; his chief minister, the ruthless Wang Meng, was Chinese.¹⁰

As soon as he inherited the rule of the Qianqin, in 357, Fu Jian began to launch attack after attack on the nearby Sixteen Kingdoms. After twenty years of fighting, he had absorbed most of them, almost uniting the north of China under a single crown; and he intended to absorb the Jin as well.

In 378, the northern army of the Qianqin marched south against the Jin borders. The Jin emperor, Jin Xiaowudi, fought back, but over the next few years he lost his border cities, one at a time. By 382, Fu Jian of the Qianqin was ready to make a final assault. He marched south with an enormous force: according to the chroniclers of his day, 600,000 foot-soldiers and 270,000 cavalry, historical hyperbole that nevertheless points to an army of unprecedented size.¹¹

With a much smaller force, Jin Xiaowudi came north to meet him and put up a desperate defense of the core of the Jin empire. The armies clashed at the Fei river (now dry), in an epic encounter that became one of the most famous in Chinese history: the Battle of the Fei River. "The dead were so many," says one account, "that they were making a pillow for each other on the ground."¹²

To the shock of both kings, the smaller Jin force triumphed. With that defeat, Fu Jian's bid to reunify China was over. His fledgling Chinese-style government had never been firmly established; his empire was held together with the sword, and each war of conquest strained the existing government a little bit more. "You have had so many wars lately," one of his advisors had warned him before the invasion of the Jin, "that your people are becoming dissatisfied, and hate the very idea of fighting." Once defeated, Fu Jian began to lose territories to rebellion and revolt, one at a time. Two years after his loss at the Fei river, Fu Jian was strangled by one of his own subordinates.¹³

The strangler was named Tuoba Gui. Like Fu Jian himself, he was of northern stock; his ancestors were nomads of the Xianbei tribe, and the Tuoba family name testified to his "barbarian" origins. His own native state, the Dai state, had been conquered by Fu Jian ten years earlier; his grandfather had been its prince until Fu Jian annexed the state as part of his growing northern empire.

Now Tuoba Gui declared Dai's independence. He changed its name from the Xianbei "Dai" to the Chinese "Bei Wei,"* and he changed his own family name from the Xianbei "Tuoba" to the Chinese "Yuan." With his Chinese identity firmly in place, he then began his own campaign to conquer and unify the north.

Meanwhile the Jin army faced another challenge on its other frontier. Around 400, a pirate named Sun En began to recruit a navy, finding his crew among the sailors and fishermen who lived along the coast.[14] For two years, the pirate fleet sailed along the shore, raiding, burning, and stealing, earning the name "armies of demons" from the shore-dwellers. The Jin emperor put the duty of crushing the rebellion into the hands of his generals, who managed to defeat the demon army in 402—and who, in the process, gained more and more power for themselves.

The weakness of the eastern Jin throne, the increasing chaos along its northern frontiers, and the constant shifts in power in the north: China was in constant flux. A monastic movement began to gather force, giving those who followed it a way to remove themselves completely from the disorder that surrounded them.

The monastic impulse in Buddhism went all the way back to the Buddha himself, who is said to have established the first community of monks so that the "path of inner progress" could be followed without distraction.[15] The monasticism of the early fifth century was centered around the teachings of the newly developed Amitabha sect. By 402, two revered monks—the native Hui-yuan and an Indian monk named Kumarajiva—were spreading teachings of the Amitabha, the "Buddha of Shining Light," who lived in the Western Paradise, the Pure Land, "a sphere without defilement where all those who believed in the Buddha were to be reborn."[16]

Compared with the nasty uncertain present, the Western Paradise was a particularly lovely place; and just as the Western Paradise was far, far away from the battling northern kingdoms and the failing Jin, so the monastic communities that began to grow in the early fifth century were far, far removed from any involvement in court politics. To join a monastic community was to renounce the world and give up all ownership of private property: to cut all

*Or "Northern Wei," to distinguish it from an earlier kingdom also known as "Wei."

ties of interest and ambition that bound you to the culture, the society, or the kingdom on the outside of the monastery. But monasticism also provided a refuge. You might give up the chance of bettering yourself—but in exchange, you gained peace.

The followers of the Amitabha had nothing to do with earthly power; Hui-yuan rarely even left the monastery, and his students joined him in escape from the world.[17] Their practice was entirely different from that of the Christians in the west. There, Christianity had begun to serve the needs of the emperor; but in the land of the Jin, Hui-yuan argued, successfully, that Buddhist monks should be exempt from the requirement to bow to the emperor. They had chosen to exist in a different reality, where neither the battles in the north nor the warring in the south had any real importance.

TIMELINE 2	
ROMAN EMPIRE	CHINA
	Fall of Han (220)/Rise of Three Kingdoms: Shu Han, Cao Wei, Dong Wu
	Wei Yuandi (260–265) Destruction of Shu Han (263) Fall of Cao Wei/Rise of Jin (265) **Jin Wudi** (265–290)
	Destruction of Dong Wu (280) Unification under the Jin (280–316)
Diocletian (284–305)	Rebellion of the Eight Princes (291–306)
Maxentius (306–312) **Licinius Maximinus Daia** (308–324) (308–313)	**Jin Huaidi** (307–313)
Battle of the Milvian Bridge (312) **Constantine** (312–337) Battle of Campus Edict of Serenus (313) Milan (313)	**Liu Cong** of the Hanzhao (310–318)
	Fall of unified Jin (316) **Jin Yuandi** (317–323)
Council of Nicaea (325)	
	Fu Jian of the Qianqin (357–385)
	Battle of the Fei River (383)
	Rise of Bei Wei (386) **Tuoba Gui** of the Bei Wei (386–409)

Chapter Three

—▪—

An Empire of the Mind

Between 319 and 415,
the Guptas of India conquer an empire
and resurrect Sanskrit to record its greatness

WHILE THE JIN were trying to re-create themselves in their shrunken domains, while Constantine ruled from his new city on the Black Sea, India was a sea of battling subkingdoms and tribal states. No religion, or idea, or emperor united the patchwork of tiny countries. The Mauryans, the last dynasty to claim a large part of the subcontinent as their own, were long gone. The north of India had been conquered and reconquered by wave after wave of foreigners: Greeks, central Asians, Parthians.[1]

Unified rule had lasted a little longer in the south, where a dynasty called the Satavahana had managed to keep control over the Deccan, the desert south of the Narmada river. But by the third century, the Satavahana empire too had collapsed, giving way to a series of competing dynastic families. Even farther south, a line of kings called the Kalabhra was slowly building a more lasting dynasty that would hold power for more than three hundred years and swallow the entire southern tip of the subcontinent; but this kingdom left few inscriptions and no written history behind it. Throughout the rest of India, small states stood elbow to elbow, none of them claiming much more territory than the next.[2]

In 319, a very minor king of one of those small jostling states passed his throne to his son. We know the name of the father, Ghatokacha, but it is not entirely clear where his original territory lay—possibly in the ancient kingdom of Magadha, near the mouth of the Ganges, or perhaps a little farther to the west.

Ghatokacha's single most important accomplishment in life was to make a match between his son, Chandragupta, and a royal princess from the Licchavi family, which had once ruled a small kingdom of its own and still controlled land to his north.[3] So when Chandragupta inherited the throne from his father in 319, he had a little bit more than most other petty Indian kings: he had not only his own kingdom but also the alliance of his wife's family. This proved just enough. He began to fight, and over the next years he conquered his way from Magadha through the ancient territories of Kosola and Vatsa, building himself a small empire centered on the Ganges. As a reward he gave himself the title *maharajadhiraja,* "Great King of Kings" (a claim that somewhat anticipated the reality).[4]

In 335, Chandragupta died and his crown went to his son Samudragupta. In Samudragupta's hands, the little empire reached the critical mass that it needed in order to spread across the Indian countryside. Over the forty-five years of his reign, Samudragupta expanded his empire outwards in an irregular circle from his father's possessions, encompassing almost all of the Ganges river in his kingdom. He also campaigned his way south, into the land of dynasties that had not yet come to their full strength. These dynasties (the Pallava on the southeastern coast, the Satavahana in the Deccan, the Vakataka, just to the west) were not quite powerful enough to keep Samudragupta out, and were forced one by one to pay him tribute.

Ruling from his capital city Pataliputra, at the great fork in the Ganges river, Samudragupta carved the names of his conquests on one of the ancient stone pillars erected long ago by Asoka the Great himself. Asoka had scattered these pillars around his own empire, using them for inscriptions later known as the Pillar Edicts; Samudragupta inscribed his own victories right over top of Asoka's words.

Samudragupta *needed* to connect himself, explicitly, with the glorious past. He was facing an enormous challenge: holding together a geographically far-flung empire populated by lots of minor warleaders, kings, and tribal chiefs who were stubbornly holding on to their own power, their own bloodlines, their own identity. Constantine had tackled this same problem by gathering his empire together under the banner of the cross, but Samudragupta had a two-prong strategy instead. First, he did not insist on the same power and control that Constantine asserted for himself. He called himself "conqueror of the four quarters of the earth,"[5] but the larger the boast, the smaller the truth. Samudragupta did rule over more land than any Indian king before him, but he was not the master of his empire. Most of the "conquered" land was not folded into his empire; to the north and the west, he wrung tribute money out of the "conquered" kings and then pulled his armies back and let them rule their territories, as before, with only nominal acknowledgment of his victory. He did not even attempt to conquer the stubbornest of the independent strongholds: the lands of the Shaka, which lay in western India and were governed by the descendents of Scythians, roaming nomadic tribes from north of the Black Sea.

The land directly under Samudragupta's rule was nothing to sneeze at;

it was, in fact, the biggest Indian empire since the collapse of the Mauryans four centuries earlier. But in the days of their most powerful king, Asoka the Great, the Mauryans had controlled almost the entire subcontinent. By contrast, Samudragupta's empire, barely a fifth of the land south of the Himalaya mountains, was a pale shadow of former glory.

Once Samudragupta counted his tributaries though—the surrounding kingdoms that had agreed to pay him off on an annual basis—his kingdom tripled in size. So he found it simplest to ignore the difference between empire and tributary land. As far as he was concerned, he had conquered his neighbors to the south and west. Had India been facing imminent outside invasion, this would not have worked. But, guarded for the moment by the mountains, Samudragupta had the luxury of lifting his hands away from the "conquered" lands. He could have a form of emperorship without the headaches thereof.

Thus, under the Gupta rule, India arrived at what is sometimes called a golden age, and sometimes the classical age of Indian civilization. The label points us towards the second part of Samudragupta's strategy, already hinted at by his use of Asoka the Great's old pillar: he made conscious use of nostalgia, trying to create from the past a core that would exert a gravitational pull on the far edges of his empire.

The Gupta kings had been turning towards the past for their power for some years already. In the decades leading up to Samudragupta's reign, the ancient language Sanskrit had become more and more widely recognized as the language of scholarship, court, government, and even economics. Sanskrit had come down into India long ago, trickling across the mountains from the central Asian war tribes that had seeped into India (their relatives had gone east into Persia and become Persian). It had, as languages do, mutated, changed, and mingled with other languages: it had given birth to simplified "languages of everyday use" such as Magadhi and Pali, both so-called *prakrits*, or "common tongues."[6] But, well into its mutation, the original archaic form of the language had made an unprecedented comeback. By AD 300, Sanskrit was the language of public record; by the time of Samudragupta's conquests, Sanskrit was also the language of the court and the preferred speech of philosophers and scholars.[7] The Hindu scriptures known as the Puranas, the law codes, the epic tales of the Ramayana and the Mahabharata: all were written in Sanskrit.

The keepers of Sanskrit were the *brahmans*, the educated Hindu upper class of Gupta society. Buddhism was alive and well in India: Buddhists were building monuments and carving caves, leaving their mark on the Indian landscape. But Sanskrit's dominance shows that the brahmans were firmly at the top of the world, at least in northern India.

Which goes a long way to explain why the Gupta age, inaugurated by

Chandragupta and brought to its peak by Samudragupta, is so often looked back upon as a golden age and the classical period of Indian culture. Romila Thapar points out that both of these terms are suspect, implying as they do an entire structure of historical understanding. A "golden age" is when "virtually every manifestation of life reached a peak of excellence," and a "classic period" implies a certain height from which a culture declines. To discover either in the past first requires that historians define excellence and height: Hindu chroniclers defined them as both Hindu and Sanskritic. In those terms, the Gupta age was indeed golden.[8]

In fact, the Guptas themselves were not exactly "Hindu," since this is a name that encompasses an elaborate later system. They built Hindu temples and wrote their inscriptions in Sanskrit, but they also erected Buddhist stupas and supported Buddhist monasteries. Hinduism and Buddhism, both systems for understanding the world, were not yet enemies, and Samudragupta, content with nominal rule over his outskirts, had no pressing political need to enforce a rigid religious orthodoxy.

But the official inscriptions of the Gupta court were Sanskrit, and Samudragupta used Hindu rituals in conquest, in victory, as tools of his royal power. It was useful to him to ally his reign with a glorious past: a learned past, an honorable past, a past of victory. Nostalgia and conservatism marked Samudragupta's reign.

And like so many movements of nostalgia and conservatism, his was based on a total misunderstanding of what had come before. The inscriptions of his victories are a case in point. Asoka's conquests had pushed the Mauryan empire outwards to its greatest extent, but his campaigns had killed hundreds of thousands (particularly in the south), and once his kingdom was secure he had been overwhelmed with remorse and regret. Turning away from war and victory, he had spent the remainder of his rule pursuing virtue and righteousness. And as part of his penance, he had carved his guilt in Pillar Edicts throughout his land: "The slaughter, death and deportation of the people is extremely grievous," he mourned, ". . . and weighs heavy on the mind."[9]

Samudragupta too wanted to be a great king; he hoped to set himself in line with Asoka the conqueror, carving his own accomplishments side by side with the victories of the Mauryan emperor. But he seems to have used the pillar without understanding the faint traces of the edict already on it. Unwittingly, he set his triumphs and his boasts of victory next to Asoka's regrets and repentance.[10]

WHEN SAMUDRAGUPTA DIED, sometime between 375 and 380, a brief struggle for the throne followed. Coins from the period show, not an orderly progression from father to son, but the interpolation of another royal name: one Prince Ramagupta. Two centuries later, the play *Devi-Chandra-gupta* (from

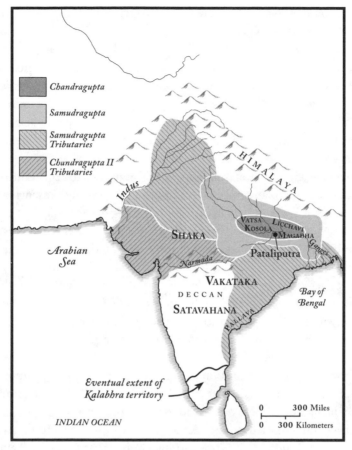

3.1: The Age of the Gupta

which only a few paragraphs survive) suggested that Ramagupta schemed to kill his younger brother Chandragupta, namesake of the kingdom's founder. The younger Chandragupta had carried out a daring offensive against the Shaka enemies to the west, infiltrating the Shaka court in woman's dress and assassinating the Shaka king. This made him so popular that Ramagupta decided to get rid of him. Discovering the plot, Chandragupta stormed into the palace to confront his brother and killed him in the heat of anger.[11]

Chandragupta became king as Chandragupta II in 380. Eight years after his accession, Chandragupta II added the Shaka to the list of Gupta tributaries. Like his great-grandfather, he also made an alliance: between his daughter Prabhavati and the Vakataka dynasty of minor kings in the western Deccan. This sideways strategy led to a partial enfolding of the Vakataka into the Gupta empire: Prabhavati's husband died, not too long after their marriage, and Prabhavati became regent and queen, ruling the lands of the Vakataka under her father's direction. Master of two more Indian domains, Chandragupta commemorated his new reach by giving himself the name "Vikra-maditya," "Sun of Prowess."[12]

Like his father, Chandragupta II never tried to assert much more than nominal control over the outlying areas of his empire; like his father, he refused to enforce a strict Hindu orthodoxy. The Chinese monk Faxian, on a pilgrimage to collect Buddhist scriptures for his monastery, arrived in India sometime between 400 and 412. He was struck by the peace and prosperity that this laissez-faire style of government brought:

> The people are numerous and happy; they have not to register their house-holds, or attend to any magistrates and their rules; only those who cultivate the royal land have to pay (a portion of) the grain from it. If they want to go, they go; if they want to stay on, they stay. The king governs without decapitation or (other) corporal punishments. Criminals are simply fined, lightly or heavily, according to the circumstances (of each case). Even in cases of repeated attempts at wicked rebellion, they only have their right hands cut off. The king's body-guards and attendants all have salaries. Throughout the whole country the people do not kill any living creature, nor drink intoxicating liquor, nor eat onions or garlic.

Travelling to Pataliputra, the Gupta capital, he was even more impressed with both the wealth and the spirituality of its inhabitants: "The inhabitants are rich and prosperous," he wrote, "and vie with one another in the practice of benevolence and righteousness." As for the city itself, where Chandragupta II's palace stood, he calls it "[t]he city where King Asoka ruled," and praises Chandragupta II for taking the same position as the earlier king towards Buddhism: "The Law of Buddha was widely made known, and the followers of other doctrines did not find it in their power to persecute the body of monks in any way."[13] Like his father, Chandragupta II had managed to associate himself with the glorious and partly mythical past.

Chandragupta II ruled for nearly four decades. After his death in 415, he became a legend: the wise king Vikramaditya, subject of heroic tales and mythical songs. He left behind him an empire that, though at its core not much larger than in the days of Samudragupta, claimed nominal control over the southeast, west, and north, covering all but the southwest quarter of the subcontinent. It was an empire where control was untested, where orthodoxy was untried, and where loyalty was not needed: an empire of the mind.

TIMELINE 3	
CHINA	INDIA
Fall of Han (220)/Rise of Three Kingdoms: Shu Han, Cao Wei, Dong Wu	
Wei Yuandi (260–265) Destruction of Shu Han (263) Fall of Cao Wei/Rise of Jin (265) **Jin Wudi** (265–290)	
Destruction of Dong Wu (280) Unification under the Jin (280–316)	
Rebellion of the Eight Princes (291–306)	
Jin Huaidi (307–313) **Liu Cong** of the Hanzhao (310-318)	
Fall of unified Jin (316) **Jin Yuandi** (317–323)	**Chandragupta** (319–335)
	Samudragupta (335–c. 380)
Fu Jian of the Qianqin (357–385)	
Battle of the Fei River (383)	**Chandragupta II** (c. 380–415)
Rise of Bei Wei (386) **Tuoba Gui** of the Bei Wei (386–409)	
	Faxian journeys to India

Chapter Four

—•—

The Persian Threat

Between 325 and 361,
Shapur II of Persia challenges the Roman empire,
Constantine plans the first crusade,
and his heirs fight each other for power

N OW THAT HE HAD MOVED his capital city eastward, Constantine was face to face with his most dangerous enemy: the king of Persia.

Shapur II had been king since he was in the womb. His father, Hurmuz, had died a month before Shapur's birth, and the Persian noblemen and the priests of the state religion, Zoroastrianism, had crowned the queen's pregnant belly. Until he turned sixteen, Shapur and his empire were controlled by regents who were more concerned for their own power than for the greater good of Persia. So Persia had been unable, during Constantine's rise to power, to do much in the way of seizing land for itself.

In fact, it had been forced into defending itself from southern invasion: tribes of kingless and nomadic Arabs who had lived in the Arabian peninsula for centuries were now driven northward by a sinking water table. Because of the harshness of their own native land, says the Arab historian al-Tabari, they were the "most needy of all the nations," and their raids were growing more troublesome: "They seized the local people's herds of cattle," al-Tabari laments, "their cultivated land, and their means of subsistence, and did a great deal of damage . . . with none of the Persians able to launch a counterattack because they had set the royal crown on the head of a mere child."[1]

This lasted only until Shapur attained his majority, which he did early. In 325, he told his army commanders that he would now take over the defense of the empire. He selected a thousand horsemen to act as a strike force against the Arab invaders, under his personal command. "Then he led them forth," al-Tabari writes, "and fell upon those Arabs who had treated Fars as their pasture ground . . . wrought great slaughter among them, reduced [others of] them to the harshest form of captivity, and put the remainder to flight." He then pursued them, sending a fleet of ships across the Persian Gulf to Bahrain, landing in eastern Arabia, and shedding "so much of their blood that it flowed like a torrent swollen by a rainstorm."[2] His forces reached as far as the small oasis city of Medina, where he took captives.

Nevertheless, it was not this force at arms that impressed al-Tabari the most. Shapur's wisdom, al-Tabari tells us, was first seen when, as a young man, he watched his people crossing a bridge over the Tigris, pushing against each other on the crowded span. This struck him as inefficient.

> So he gave orders for another bridge to be built, so that one of the bridges could be used for people crossing in one direction and the other bridge for people crossing from the opposite direction. . . . In this way, the people were relieved of the necessity of endangering their lives when crossing the bridge. The child grew in stature and prestige in that single day, what for others would have taken a long period.[3]

Running an empire the size of Persia required more than skill with a sword; it took administrative ability. Inventing a new traffic pattern was an innovation. Shapur II was intelligent and shrewd, and fully able to withstand Constantine's plans to dominate the known world.

Constantine's move to Byzantium was silent testimony that he intended to challenge Persia's hold on the east. But his first approach to Shapur II was relatively polite. As soon as Shapur II shook off his regents, Constantine sent him a letter suggesting in respectful but unambiguous terms that Shapur refrain from persecuting the Christians in Persia. "I commend [them] to you because you are so great," Constantine wrote, tactfully. "Cherish them in accordance with your usual humanity: for by this gesture of faith you will confer an immeasurable benefit on both yourself and us."[4]

Shapur II agreed to show mercy to the Christians within his border, but this tolerance became increasingly difficult as time went on. Not long after Constantine's missive, the African king of Axum became a Christian—an act that proclaimed his friendship with the Roman empire as loudly as it proclaimed his hope of heaven.

THIS KING was named Ezana, and the kingdom he ruled lay just west of the Red Sea.* On the other side of the narrow strait at the sea's southern end

---

*The kingdom of Axum lay in the area also known, in Greek and Latin sources, as Abyssinia and Ethiopia. The Romans had also used "Ethiopia" to refer to Nubia, the southern Egyptian kingdom; and sometimes Axum is simply called "Ethiopia." In the same way, the Himyarite kingdom of Arabia lies in the area also known as Yemen, and sometimes is referred to as Yemen. I have avoided using either Ethiopia or Yemen when talking about the kingdoms of the fourth and fifth centuries, since both terms serve as more general geographic labels.

was Arabia, and in the 330s Arabia was filled with Persian soldiers. Shapur the Great, who had driven the invading Arabs out of his southern realm at the beginning of his reign, had continued an enthusiastic campaign into the Arabian interior. For his entire reign, al-Tabari tells us, Shapur was "occupied with great eagerness in killing the Arabs and tearing out the shoulder-blades of their leaders; this was why they called him Dhu al-Aktaf, 'The Man of the Shoulders.' "* Ezana's conversion assured him of Constantine's support, should Persian aggression move across the water.[5]

For the moment, Shapur left the African kingdom alone. Instead, his soldiers invaded Armenia.

Armenia, which had been a kingdom for nearly a millennium, had long suffered from its position on the eastern frontier of Rome. For centuries, Roman emperors had either allied themselves with the Armenian kings or invaded the kingdom in an effort to make it part of the empire; the eastern kingdoms of the ancient Persians and Parthians had done the same, hoping to make Armenia a buffer against Roman expansion.

At the moment, Armenia was independent, but once again squeezed between two large and expanding empires. It was not at war with either Rome or Persia, but it tended towards friendship with the Roman empire. The king of Armenia, Tiridates, had been baptized by a monk named Gregory back in 303, before Christianity was politically useful.[6] When Constantine made Christianity the religion of the empire, Armenia's ties with its western neighbor grew even stronger.

Agents of Shapur the Great—who was increasingly worried that a Christian Armenia would never again serve as an ally of the Persian empire—managed to convince Tiridates's chamberlain to turn traitor. In 330, the chamberlain poisoned his king. Unfortunately for the Persians, this did not turn Armenia away from Christianity; instead, Tiridates became a martyr (and eventually a saint), and his son Khosrov the Short became king.

Since the indirect approach had failed, Shapur sent soldiers. The 336 invasion of Armenia failed—the soldiers withdrew—but Shapur had conveyed a clear message to Constantine: he didn't intend to relinquish the border areas to Rome, even if those border areas were Christian.

Converting to Christianity had now gained all sorts of fraught political implications, and Shapur decided to crack down on Christianity in his own empire. In Persian eyes, Christians were increasingly likely to be double agents working for Rome. The systematic persecution of Persian Christians, mostly on the western frontier, began early in 337.

---

*The "tearing of the shoulders," a custom that seems to have been peculiar to Shapur II, did not necessarily kill the victim; instead it left the sword-arm, used to fight against the Persian king, useless and dangling.

The attacks were recorded by the Persian Christian Aphrahat, who lived at the monastery Mar Mathai, on the eastern bank of the Tigris river. Shapur, he wrote to a fellow monk who lived outside Persia, caused "a great massacre of martyrs," but the Persian Christians were holding strong; they believed that they would be blessed with a "great reward," while the Persian persecutors would "come to scorn and contempt."[7]

To the west, Constantine was plotting to make those words come true. He was preparing an invasion, but this invasion would be a crusade; his justification was that the Christians of Persia needed his help. He planned to take with him a portable tabernacle, a tent in which bishops (who would accompany the army) would lead regular worship, and he announced that he would be baptized (something he hadn't yet gotten around to) in the river Jordan as soon as he reached it. It was the first time that a ruler had planned to wield the cross against an outside enemy.[8]

But before he could depart on his crusade, he grew sick; and on May 22, 337, Constantine the Great died.

The name of his city was changed from Byzantium to Constantinople, in his honor, and he was buried there in a mausoleum he had prepared at the Church of the Holy Apostles. The mausoleum had twelve symbolic coffins for the twelve apostles in it, with Constantine's as the thirteenth. Later historians called this an act of massive hubris, but the burial had its own logic: Constantine, like the apostles, was a founder of the faith. "He alone of all the Roman emperors has honoured God the All-sovereign," Eusebius concludes, ". . . [H]e alone has honoured his Church as no other since time began. . . . [H]is like has never been recorded from the beginning of time until our day." He had married Christianity and state politics, and in doing so had changed both forever.[9]

As soon as news of Constantine's death spread eastward, Shapur invaded Armenia again. This time he succeeded; Armenia's Christian king, Khosrov the Short, was forced to run for his life towards the Roman border. Shapur installed a Persian puppet in his place. The buffer kingdom was, at least temporarily, his.[10]

The Roman response was not immediate because Constantine's heirs were busy trying to kill each other in Constantinople. Constantine, canny politician in life, had made no definite arrangements for the succession; it was almost as though he expected to live forever. Instead, he left behind three sons and a nephew who had all been given the title of Caesar, who had all ruled for him in various parts of the empire, and who could all claim the right to the throne.

No impartial historian records exactly what happened in the weeks after Constantine's death, but by the time the bloodshed ceased, Constantine's nephew, both of his brothers-in-law, and a handful of high court officials

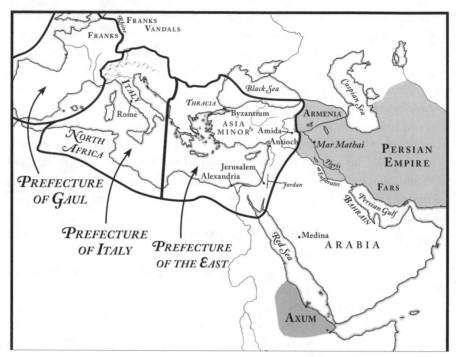

4.1: *The Romans and Persians*

had been murdered. Constantine's three sons—Constantine II (twenty-one), Constantius (seventeen), and Constans (fourteen)—had come to some sort of family agreement that left the three of them alive and all possible competitors or naysayers dead.[11] The only exception was their five-year-old cousin Julian, who was being raised in a castle in Asia Minor, well away from the purge.

In September, the three sons had themselves acclaimed as co-emperors in Constantinople. The empire was again divided, this time into three parts (or prefectures). Constantine II took the Prefecture of Gaul; Constans took the Prefecture of Italy, which included not only Rome but also North Africa; and Constantius took the entire Prefecture of the East along with the region of Thracia, which meant that he got Constantinople. Almost at once, Constantius reinvaded Armenia and put Khosrov the Short back on his throne.

Fourteen-year-old Constans, despite his age, soon showed that he was not to be trifled with. In 340, his brother Constantine II tried to take Italy from him; Constans went to war against his older brother, ambushed him in the north of Italy, and killed him. Now the empire was again divided into two, between Constans in the west and Constantius in the east.

Constans was a staunch supporter of the Christian church; nevertheless, he was unpopular with everyone. His personality was so foul that even the church historians, normally fulsome about any Christian emperor, disliked him. He managed to survive for another ten years, but in 350, at age twenty-seven, he was murdered by his own generals.[12]

Rather than throwing their support behind the remaining brother, Constantius, the generals then acclaimed a new co-emperor: an officer named Magnentius. Constantius marched west to get rid of the usurper, but it took two years of fighting before Magnentius was defeated. He killed himself rather than fall into Constantius's hands. By 352, Constantius (like his father) was ruler of the entire empire.

Meanwhile, of course, Constantius had been away from his eastern border; and Shapur had taken advantage of his absence to reclaim Armenia yet again. The son of Khosrov the Short had been ruling as a Roman ally; Shapur invaded, captured the king, put out his eyes, and allowed his son to ascend the throne only on the condition that he remain subject to Persian wishes.[13]

Constantius did not immediately answer this challenge. He had problems to solve, the most pressing of which was finding an heir. He had no son, so in 355 he appointed his surviving cousin Julian to be Caesar and heir. Julian, now twenty-three, had been squirreled away in Asia Minor, being carefully trained in Christianity by the tutor Mardonius.

Constantius preferred to reside in Constantinople, so he put Julian in charge of affairs on the western side of the empire. Here, the young man campaigned so successfully on the Rhine front that the army became his enthusiastic supporter; when he reduced taxation in the west, the people loved him too.

While Julian's popularity grew, Constantius's waned. Like his father, Constantius was a Christian; unlike his father, he was supportive of Arianism, now officially a heresy. In the same year that he appointed Julian as his Caesar, Constantius wielded his imperial authority to get rid of the bishop of Rome, an anti-Arian churchman named Liberius who disapproved of Constantius's beliefs. In Liberius's place, he appointed a bishop of his own choosing.

This was a serious matter, as the bishop of Rome was probably the most influential priest in the entire Christian church. The bishops of Rome considered themselves the spiritual heirs of the apostle Peter, and they considered Peter to be the founder of the Christian church. For some decades already, the bishop of Rome had claimed the right to make decisions that were binding on the bishops of other cities.*

This privilege was far from unchallenged; the bishops of Alexandria, Antioch, and Jerusalem, all cities that could boast a Christian community as old as the Christian community in Rome, resented the assumption that Rome was the center of the Christian world. Nevertheless, all of the bishops could

---

*This belief was based on Matthew 16:18, where Jesus says to Peter, "Upon this rock I will build my church." The Roman church interpreted this as saying that Peter was the founding apostle of the Christian church; since Peter then went to Rome to preach, the Roman Christians also considered Rome the birthplace of the church.

agree that Constantius ought not to appoint and remove *any* bishop at will. Constantius, paying no attention to their objections, called a church council of his own in 359 and announced at it that Arian Christology was now orthodox. Neither Roman bishop—either the deposed one or the newly appointed one—was invited.

None of the churchmen were pleased with this high-handedness, which seems to have stemmed from real theological conviction (certainly Constantius reaped no political benefits by meddling in church affairs in this way). Constantius fell into disfavor, particularly with churchmen in the western half of the empire, where anti-Arian sentiment was strongest. So when Constantius, alarmed by Julian's swelling popularity, demanded that Julian in the west reduce his armed force by sending some of his troops eastward, Julian banked on his cousin's growing unpopularity in the west and his own stellar reputation and refused. The army on the Rhine, backing him up, elevated him to the post of co-emperor.

This put the empire back under two emperors, a situation that neither man found bearable. But Julian was not anxious to launch an out-and-out attack on Constantius, who (after all) had Constantinople and most of the east on his side. For his part, Constantius didn't dare leave the eastern borders and march west against Julian. The Persian threat was too immediate; Shapur's army was already approaching the Roman borders.

The Roman soldier Ammianus Marcellinus, who later wrote a history of the Roman wars with Persia, had been sent secretly into Armenia (now Persian-controlled) to spy on the Persian advance. From the top of a cliff, he spotted the armies advancing: "the whole circuit of the lands filled with innumerable troops," he remembers, "with the king leading the way, glittering in splendid attire."[14] The Roman army burned the fields and houses in front of the approaching enemy to prevent them from finding food, and made a stand at the Euphrates river; but the Persians, advised by a Roman traitor who had gone over to their side, made a detour north through untouched fields and orchards.

The Romans pursued them, and the two armies finally met at the small walled city of Amida, in Roman territory. The city was good for defense, since (as Ammianus Marcellinus explains) it could only be approached by a single narrow pass, and the Romans took up a defensive position in the gap. But a detachment of Persian cavalry had managed, without the Romans' knowledge, to get around behind the city, and the Romans found themselves jammed into the pass, attacked from both sides. Ammianus, fighting in the middle of the throng, was trapped there for an entire day: "We remained motionless until sunrise," he writes, ". . . so crowded together that the bodies of the slain, held upright by the throng, could nowhere find room to fall, and that in front of me a soldier with his head cut in two, and split into equal halves by a powerful sword stroke, was so pressed on all sides that he stood erect like a stump."[15]

Finally Ammianus and the other surviving Roman soldiers made it into the city. The Persians attacked the walls with archers and with war elephants: "frightful with their wrinkled bodies and loaded with armed men, a hideous spectacle, dreadful beyond every form of horror." Amida withstood the siege for seventy-three days. The streets were stacked with "maggot-infested bodies," and plague broke out within the walls. The defenders kept the wooden siege-engines and the elephants at bay with burning arrows, but finally the Persians heaped up mounds of earth and came over the walls. The inhabitants were slaughtered. Ammianus escaped through a back gate and found a horse, trapped in a thicket and tied to its dead master. He untied the corpse and fled.[16]

Constantius was forced to surrender not only Amida but also at least two other fortresses, a handful of fortified towns, and eastern land. Meanwhile, Julian still threatened in the west. Suspended between two hostile powers, Constantius didn't dare turn his back on one to attack the other.

A fever solved his dilemma. On October 5, 361, Constantius died from a virus, his body so hot that his attendants could not even touch him. Julian was sole emperor, by default, of the entire Roman empire.

INDIA	ROMAN EMPIRE	PERSIAN EMPIRE
	T I M E L I N E 4	
	Diocletian (284–305)	
	Maxentius (306–312)	
	Licinius (308–324) Maximinus Daia (308–313)	
		Shapur II (309–379)
	Battle of the Milvian Bridge (312)	
	Constantine (312–337)	
	Battle of Campus Serenus (313) Edict of Milan (313)	
Chandragupta (319–335)		
	Council of Nicaea (325)	
		Khosrov the Short of Armenia (330–338)
Samudragupta (335–c. 380)	Constantine II Constantius Constans	
	(337–340) (337–361) (337–350)	
	First Council of Constantinople (359)	
	Julian (360/361–363)	
Chandragupta II (380–415)		
Faxian journeys to India		

Chapter Five

—·—

The Apostate

Between 361 and 364,
Julian tries and fails
to restore the old Roman ways

As SOON AS JULIAN took control of Constantinople, it became clear that his Christian education had been entirely unsuccessful. He had been in correspondence for some years with the famous rhetoric teacher Libanius, who guided him in his study of Greek literature and philosophy, and had been in secret sympathy with the old religion of Rome for most of his adult life.

Now he openly announced himself as an opponent of Christianity. His baptism, he said, was a "nightmare" that he wished to forget. He ordered the old temples, many of which had been closed under the reign of the Christian emperors, to be reopened. And he decreed that no Christian could teach literature; since a literary education was required for all government officials, this would eventually have guaranteed that all Roman officials had received a thoroughly Roman education.[1]

It also meant that the Christians in the empire would become chronically undereducated. Most Christians refused to send their children to schools where they would be indoctrinated in the ways of the old Roman religion. Instead, Christian writers began to try to create their own literature, to be used in their own schools: as A. A. Vasiliev writes, they "translated the Psalms into forms similar to the odes of Pindar; the Pentateuch of Moses they rendered into hexameter; the Gospels were rewritten in the style of Plato's dialogues."[2]

Most of this literature was so substandard that it disappeared almost at once; very little has survived.

This was an odd kind of persecution—and one that reveals Julian's essential likeness to his Gupta counterparts, kings he would never meet. Julian was a conservative. He wanted to bring back the glorious past. He wanted to draw a line clearly between Roman and non-Roman; it was a disappearing line, thanks to Constantine's decision to unite his empire by faith rather than by their pride in "Romanness," and Julian wanted it back. He wanted to rebuild the wall of Roman civilization against not only the Christians but all who did not share this same tradition. "You know well," Libanius had written to him, back in 358, "that if anyone extinguishes our literature, we are put on a level with the barbarians." To have no literature was to have no past. To have no past was to be a barbarian. As far as Julian was concerned, Christians were both barbarians and atheists; they had no literature, and they did not believe in the Roman gods.[3]

Julian did realize that the old Roman religion would need updating if it were to compete with the unifying power of the Christian church. So he pursued two strategies. First, he stole the most useful elements of the Christian church for the Roman religion. He studied the hierarchy of the Christian church, which had proved relatively good at holding far-flung congregations together, and reorganized the Roman priesthood in the same way. And he ordered Roman priests to model the worship of the Roman gods on the popular Christian services, importing discourses (like sermons) and singing into the old Roman rituals. Worship of Jupiter had never looked more like worship of Jesus.

His second strategy was more subtle. He allowed all of the Christian churchmen who had been banished at various times for being on the wrong side of the Nicene-Arian debate to return. He knew they were incapable of getting along; and sure enough, serious theological arguments were soon breaking out. It was the flip side of Constantine's methods; Julian was capitalizing on Christianity's power to divide, not its power to unify.[4]

For all of this, he earned himself the nickname "Julian the Apostate."

Ironically, his political problems forced him to recognize the rights of barbarians to Roman privileges at the same time that he was restoring the old ideas of Romanness. Unable to fight simultaneously with Shapur on his east and with invading Germanic tribes to the north, he had no choice but to allow the Germanic tribes of the Franks to settle in northern Gaul as *foederati*, Roman allies with many of the rights of Roman citizens.

With the threat of the Franks averted, Julian launched a Persian campaign. In 363, he marched east with eighty-five thousand men—not only Romans, but also Goths (Germanic tribes who had been *foederati* since the days of Constantine) and Arabs, who were anxious to get their revenge on Shapur for his shoulder-tearing. He also brought traditional soothsayers and Greek philosophers with him, in place of the priests and tabernacle Constantine had planned to use. The two groups complicated the enterprise by falling out with each other; the soothsayers insisted that the omens were bad and the army should withdraw, while the philosophers countered that such superstitions were illogical.[5]

At the Persian border, he divided his forces and sent thirty thousand of his men down the Tigris, himself leading the rest down the Euphrates by means of ships, constructed on the banks of the river where it ran through Roman territory and launched downstream. The idea was that they would meet at Ctesiphon, the Persian capital (on the east bank of the Tigris, a bit south of Baghdad) and perform a pincer move on the Persians.

According to Ammianus, the Roman fleet was an amazing sight: fifty war galleys and a thousand supply ships with food and bridge-building materials. Shapur, alarmed by the size of the approaching army, left his capital city as a precaution, so when Julian arrived he found the king gone. The armies built bridges across the Tigris to the east bank and laid siege to Ctesiphon anyway. The siege dragged on and on. Shapur, safely away from the action, rounded up additional men and allies from the far corners of his empire and returned to fight the besieging army. Julian was forced to retreat back up the Tigris, fighting the whole way and struggling to keep his men alive; the Persians had burned all of the fields and storehouses in their path.

The retreat took all spring. By early summer, the Roman soldiers hadn't yet made it back to their own border. They were starving, wounded, and constantly harassed by the Persians who pursued them. One June day, during yet another Persian ambush, Julian was struck by a Persian spear that lodged in his lower abdomen. He was carried back to camp, where he slowly bled to death: one of only three Roman emperors to fall in battle against a foreign enemy.*

Ammianus Marcellinus, who was with the army, describes a beautifully classical death: Julian, resigned to his fate, carrying on a calm discussion about the "nobility of the soul" with two philosophers until he died. The Christian historian Theodoret insists that Julian died in agony, recognizing too late the power of Christ and exclaiming, "Thou hast won, O Galilean!"[6]

Of these two equally unlikely accounts, the Christian version comes closest to describing the situation. Julian's army was stranded, besieged, and in need of leadership and rescue. After a bit of arguing and milling around, the officers dressed one of their generals, a dignified and kindly man named Jovian, in the imperial robes and proclaimed him emperor.[7] Jovian, aged thirty-three, was a Christian.

From this point on, Christian emperors would rule the empire. The old Roman religion would never again dominate the Roman court. Not that this brought an end to the striving; it simply meant that the battle between past and the present, the old Rome and the new empire, went underground.

Jovian was a pragmatist. Instead of fighting, he put on his crown and asked Shapur for a parley. The treaty, once concluded, allowed the Roman army to go home in peace. In exchange, Jovian agreed to hand over to the Persians all Roman land east of the Tigris, including the Roman fortress of Nisibis. Nisi-

*The other two were Valerian (Persia, 260) and Decius (Goths, 251).

5.1: The Persian Campaign

bis would become the center of Persian assaults against the Roman frontier; it never returned to western control.[8]

The army limped westward under Jovian's command, to face scorn and fury from the Romans back home. The treaty was condemned as shameful, a disgrace to Rome, an unacceptable conclusion to Julian's bold and disastrous campaign.

Jovian himself never even returned to Constantinople. Once he was back in Roman land, he paused at the city of Antioch and started to work at once to chart a middle way. He revoked all of Julian's anti-Christian decrees, but rather than replacing them with equally restrictive decrees against the Roman religion, he declared religious toleration. He was, himself, unabashedly faithful to the Nicene Creed, but he had decided to remove religion from the center of the empire's politics. Christian, Greek, Roman: all would have equal rights to worship and to take part in government.[9]

But it was too late. Religious and political legitimacy—religious and political claims to rule—were intertwined at the empire's center. A very strong and charismatic emperor (which the nice-minded Jovian was not) might have managed to hold on to power and proclaim religious tolerance at the same time, but Jovian's political authority was already weak, thanks to the unpopular treaty with Persia. His only hope for hanging on to power was to use religious authority in its place, establishing a strict religious orthodoxy as the center of his power.

His refusal to do so meant that he had no authority at all. In 364, eight months after his elevation to the imperial crown, he died in his tent while he was still making his slow way back towards the eastern capital. Reports of the cause were suspiciously varied; he was said to have died of fumes from a badly vented stove, from indigestion, from a "swollen head." "So far as I know," Ammianus remarks, "no investigation was made of the death." The Roman throne lay open for the next claimant.[10]

TIMELINE 5		
INDIA	ROMAN EMPIRE	PERSIAN EMPIRE
		Shapur II (309–379)
	Battle of the Milvian Bridge (312)	
	Constantine (312–337)	
	Battle of Campus Serenus (313) Edict of Milan (313)	
Chandragupta (319–335)	Council of Nicaea (325)	
		Khosrov the Short of Armenia (330–338)
Samudragupta (335–c. 380)		
	Constantine II Constantius Constans	
	(337–340) (337–361) (337–350)	
	First Council of Constantinople (359)	
	Julian (360/361–363)	
	Jovian (363–364)	
Chandragupta II (380–415)		
Faxian journeys to India		

—

Chapter Six

Earthquake and Invasion

Between 364 and 376,
natural disaster and barbarian attacks
trouble the Roman empire

JOVIAN'S DEATH MEANT that the Roman empire had three emperors in four years: a "ferocity of changeable circumstances," Ammianus Marcellinus calls it, a time when Rome's religion and Rome's frontiers had shifted as quickly as Rome's chief official.

No one supported the claim of Jovian's infant son. Instead, the army (which had become, without design, representatives for the entire empire) chose another officer to be the next emperor.

Valentinian was forty-three, a lifelong soldier and a zealous Christian, something that makes it slightly difficult to get an accurate portrayal of him from the contemporary sources. The historian Zosimus, a devotee of traditional Roman religion, remarks grudgingly that Valentinian was "an excellent soldier but extremely illiterate"; the Christian historian Theodoret rhapsodizes that Valentinian was "distinguished not only for his courage but also for prudence, temperance, justice, and great stature."[1]

What the empire needed at this point was not a learned leader but an experienced general, and Valentinian's decisions suggest that his army service hadn't necessarily qualified him to be emperor. He was at Nicaea when the army acclaimed him; before setting out for Constantinople to be crowned, he decided to declare a co-emperor. This was a soldier's precaution. Life was cheap along the roads in the eastern provinces, and Valentinian had no heir.

According to Ammianus, he gathered his fellow officers together and asked what they thought of his younger brother and fellow soldier Valens. There was a silence at this, until finally the commander of cavalry said, "Your highness, if you love your kin you have a brother, but if you love the state look carefully for a man to invest with the purple."[2]

It was advice that Valentinian decided to ignore. He gave his brother the imperial title and put him in charge of the eastern empire as far as the province of Thracia; then he travelled to Italy, where he set up his court not in Rome, but in Milan.

This was a brief reorientation to the west, with the senior emperor taking up residence in Italy and the junior emperor in the east, although Valens settled not at Constantinople, but at Antioch, on the Orontes river. And it almost immediately became clear why the commander of cavalry had reservations. The empire had all sorts of military problems. Germanic tribes were invading Gaul and pushing across the Danube; the Roman holdings in Britannia were under attack by the natives; the North African territories were suffering from the hostility of the tribes to the south; and Shapur, claiming that the treaty he had sworn with Jovian was nullified by Jovian's death, was getting ready to attack the east.[3]

But Valens, in the east, was apparently more worried about inner purity than outer threat. His older brother Valentinian held to Nicene Christianity but was tolerant both of Arian Christians and of adherents to the traditional state religion. In fact, one of Valentinian's most aggressive moves was to pass a law restricting evening sacrifices to the gods, but as soon as one of his proconsuls pointed out that many of his subjects held to these ancient customs as a way to define themselves as part of Roman society, Valentinian immediately ordered everyone to disregard his brand new regulation.[4]

But the younger Valens belonged to the Arian branch of Christianity, and he was entirely intolerant of any other form of doctrine. He began a war of extermination against the Nicene Christians in Antioch: exiling their leader, driving out the followers, and drowning some of them in the Orontes. This gave the Persians even more freedom to harass the eastern border, since the inexperienced and preoccupied Valens did little to garrison the fortresses on the east. Valens, Zosimus says, had so little experience with governing men that he could not "sustain the weight of business." The soldier Ammianus puts it even more succinctly: "During this period," he writes, "practically the whole Roman world heard the trumpet-call of war."[5]

And then catastrophe struck.

At dawn on July 21, 365, an earthquake rumbled from deep beneath the Mediterranean Sea, spreading along the seabed and rising up to the Roman shores. On the island of Crete, buildings collapsed flat on their sleeping occupants. Cyrenaica was shaken, its cities crumbling. The shock travelled up to Corinth, shivering its way across to Italy and Sicily on the west, Egypt and Syria to the east.[6]

As Romans all around the coast began to pick their way through the rubble, putting out fires, digging out possessions, and mourning their dead, the water on the southern coast—right at Alexandria, on the Nile delta—was sucked suddenly away from the shore. The people of Alexandria, diverted, went out to the waterfront to see. "The sea with its rolling waves was driven back and withdrew from the land," remembers Ammianus Marcellinus, "so that in the abyss of the deep thus revealed men saw many kinds of sea-creatures stuck fast in the slime; and vast mountains and deep valleys. . . . Many ships were stranded as if on dry land, and many men roamed about without fear in the little that remained of the waters, to gather fish and shells with their hands."

The entertainment lasted a little less than an hour. "And then," Ammianus writes, "the roaring sea, resenting, as it were, this forced retreat, rose in its turn; and over the boiling shoals it dashed mightily upon islands and broad stretches of the mainland and levelled innumerable buildings in the cities and wherever else they were found. . . . The great mass of waters, returning when it was least expected, killed many thousands of men by drowning."[7]

When the tsunami receded, ships lay in splinters all along the shore. Bodies had been tossed into streets and across the tops of buildings and floated face down in the shallows. Several years later, Ammianus, travelling to a nearby city, saw a ship that had been thrown two full miles inland; it still lay on the sand, its seams coming open with decay.

In the wake of the destruction, both Valens and Valentinian struggled to hold their domains together. Valens was challenged by the usurper Procopius, a cousin of the dead emperor Julian, who managed to convince the Gothic soldiers in the army to support his claim to the eastern crown. Valens sent a frantic message west to his brother Valentinian, asking for help; but Valentinian was far away on the battlefield, fighting the Alemanni (another Germanic tribal federation) in Gaul, and he did not have soldiers to spare.[8]

With the help of substantial bribing, which turned Procopius's two chief generals and part of his army against him, Valens managed to defeat Procopius in battle at the city of Thyatira. Once he had the rebel in his hands, he had Procopius torn apart. He also executed Procopius's two chief generals, piously condemning them for their helpful treachery.[9]

Traditional Roman chroniclers, like Ammianus, found in Procopius's usurpation an explanation for the horrible wave; they simply moved the wave forward in time, placing it after the revolt and insisting that the rebellion had caused an upheaval in the natural order of things. Christian historians who write of the tsunami were more likely to blame it on Julian the Apostate; God was punishing the empire for Julian's misdeeds. Libanius, Julian's old friend, suggested that Earth was mourning Julian's death; the quake and wave were "the honour paid him by Earth, or if you would have it so, by Poseidon."[10]

Christian or Roman, they all set out to make sense of the devastation. There had to be a reason for it. There was no place in either the Roman or the Christian world for an event that was not a direct response to human action—no place in either world for random evil.

THE NATURAL DISASTER was followed, in short order, by a series of political catastrophes: barbarian attacks that pushed into Roman territory and chipped away at the edges of Roman power.

Valens initiated the first catastrophe by declaring war on the Goths. The Gothic soldiers in the army had supported the usurper Procopius, and he wanted to punish them.

Up until this point, the Romans and Goths had worked out a means of coexisting; the Goths provided soldiers for the Roman army, and in return were allowed to settle in Roman land with some of the privileges of Roman citizens. And they had become increasingly Christian over the past decades. Their native bishop Ulfilas had invented an alphabet and had used it to translate the Bible into their own language, and Ulfilas, like Valens himself, was a zealously Arian Christian. (Nicene Christianity, he preached, was an "odious and execrable, depraved and perverse . . . invention of the Devil.")[11]

None of this kept Valens from launching his punitive campaign against the Gothic-settled lands. His war of revenge began in 367 and dragged on for three full years without any particular resolution. It was a bad time to start a war against a people who were inclined to be friendly; in the west, Valentinian was already fighting the Alemanni. Late in 367, as Valens fought against the Goths, the Alemanni surged across the Rhine and attacked Valentinian on his own ground. Valentinian managed to defeat them in a pitched battle, but lost so many men that he was unable to push the invaders back out.

Meanwhile, the Roman holdings in Britain were also under barbarian attack.

In this case, the "barbarians" were the tribes who lived to the north. Back in AD 122, the Roman emperor Hadrian had drawn a line between civilization and wilderness by building a wall across the island. Roman Britain—the province of "Britannia"—was south of the wall. Six towns in Britannia had been given the status of full Roman citizenship.* The largest, Londinium, had twenty-five thousand inhabitants and a complex Roman infrastructure: shipping lines, baths and drainage, military installations.[12]

To the north, as far as the Romans were concerned, lay only wilderness.

The tribes who lived north of Hadrian's Wall, as well as on the smaller island west of Britannia, had arrived on British shores as invaders, perhaps in 500 BC. Now *they* were the natives (a thousand years of habitation has a funny way of rooting a people into their land), masters of scores of tribal kingdoms. The strongest tribes were the Picts and Caledones ("red-haired and large-limbed," wrote the Roman historian Tacitus). On the western island,

---

*The six towns were Eboracum (modern York), Verulamium (St. Albans), Glevum (Gloucester), Lindum (Lincoln), Camulodunum (Colchester), and Londinium (London).

which had never been invaded by Romans, the Venii dominated the south from their capital city of Tara, while the Uluti controlled much of the north.[13]

Britannia had been troubled for more than a century by land invasions from northern Picts, as well as piratical raids launched by tribes on the western island.* In the fourth century, these were joined by sea attacks from another Germanic tribe: the Saxons, who came from the lands north of Gaul and sailed across the ocean to plunder the eastern coast of Britannia.

The Roman official who was in charge of defending Britannia from these attacks was the Dux Britanniarum. He was aided by a special commander called the Comes Litori

6.1: Britain and Ireland

("protector of the shore"), whose job was to keep the Saxons away from the southeastern coast. But in late 367, while Valentinian was frantically beating back the Alemanni and Valens was deadlocked with the Goths, the British defenses in Britannia fell apart, and barbarians poured into the country from all four sides.[14]

It was a carefully planned and coordinated attack; Ammianus Marcellinus calls it the *Barbarica Conspirato*, the "Barbarian Conspiracy." Roman garrisons stationed at Hadrian's Wall, who had been fraternizing with the Picts for years, allowed Pictish soldiers to cross over into Roman Britain. At the same time, pirates from the western island landed on the coast, and Saxons invaded both southeast Britannia and northern Gaul. Both the Dux Britanniarum and the Comes Litori were overwhelmed; in the past decades, Roman forces in Britannia had been slowly depleted by transfers to the army over on the mainland.[15]

Although he had his hands full of Alemanni, in 368 Valentinian sent the experienced general Theodosius the Elder over to Britain to try to retake the

---

*These pirates were known to the Romans as "Scoti," from the word in their own language that means "plunderers." This confuses the issue, as the Scoti were not from the modern land of Scotland, but rather from the island now known as Ireland. So technically the "Scots," at this point, were Irish.

Roman provinces. Theodosius the Elder went, obediently, taking with him as vice commander his son Flavius Theodosius. He established himself at Londinium, from where he waged a year-long war that finally restored Roman control of Britannia. "He warmed the north with Pictish blood," one Roman poet wrote, admiringly, "and icy Ireland wept for the heaps of dead." New forts were built along the southeastern coast, with towers where guards could keep an eye out for the approach of Saxon ships.[16]

But all was not well. The invasions had ravaged cities and burned settlements, wiped out entire garrisons, and destroyed the trade that had once existed between Britannia and the northern tribes. The Pictish villages near the Wall had now been burned, their people slaughtered, and along the border the Roman garrisons had shut themselves into crude and isolated fortresses.[17]

Back in the Roman empire proper, the royal brothers were forced to make peace with their barbarian enemies. Valens gave up on conquering the Goths in 369 and swore out a treaty with their leaders; in 374, Valentinian made peace with the Alemanni king, Macrianus. But almost immediately, yet another barbarian war broke out.

The year before, Valentinian had ordered new forts built north of the Danube, in land that belonged to the Germanic tribe known as the Quadi. The Quadi were not much of a threat ("a nation not greatly to be feared," Ammianus calls them), and when the fort-building began, they sent a polite embassy to the local commander, asking that it stop. The complaints were ignored; the embassies were sent again.[18]

Finally the Roman commander, apparently unable to think of a better solution, invited the Quadi king to a banquet and murdered him. This atrocious mishandling of the affair so infuriated the Quadi that they joined together with their neighbors and stormed across the Danube. None of the Roman farmers who lived on the frontier were expecting the attack: the invaders "crossed the Danube while no hostility was anticipated, and fell upon the country people, who were busy with their harvest; most of them they killed, the survivors they led home as prisoners."[19]

Valentinian, furious with the incompetence of the commander who had started the fight, recalled Theodosius the Elder and his son Flavius from Britannia and sent them to the trouble spot. He arrived shortly after, breathing fire and promising to punish his wayward officials. But when he saw the devastation of his frontier with his own eyes, he was horrified. He decided to ignore the murder of the Quadi king and launch a punitive invasion instead. He himself led the attack; Ammianus says, disapprovingly, that he burned villages and "put to death without distinction of age" all Quadi civilians he could get his hands on.[20]

In fact, his behavior suggests that he had lost touch with reality in some frightening way. He cut off a groom's hand after the horse the groom was holding for him reared up as he tried to mount; he had an inoffensive junior secretary tortured to death because of an ill-timed joke. He even ordered Theodosius the Elder, who had served him so well in Britannia, put to death after Theodosius lost a battle, and exiled his son Flavius to Hispania. Finally, the Quadi sent ambassadors to negotiate for a peace. When they tried to explain that they had not been the original aggressors, Valentinian grew so enraged that he had a stroke. "As if struck by a bolt from the sky," Ammianus says, "he was seen to be speechless and suffocating, and his face was tinged with a fiery flush. On a sudden his blood was checked and the sweat of death broke out upon him." He died without naming an heir.[21]

The western empire was temporarily without leadership, and the officers on the frontier hastily suspended all hostilities with the Quadi. Valens sent word that Valentinian's son, the sixteen-year-old Gratian, should inherit the crown and reign as co-emperor with his little brother, four-year-old Valentinian II.

Gratian's first act (one that showed amazingly good judgment) was to recall Flavius Theodosius, son of the dead Theodosius the Elder, from Hispania and to put him in charge of the defense of the northern frontier. Flavius Theodosius had learned to fight in Britannia, and he proved to be a brilliant strategist. By 376, a year after Valentinian's death, he was the highest ranking general in the entire central province.

His skill was needed. The Romans had begun to hear rumors of a new threat: the merciless advance of nomadic enemies from the east, fearless fighters who slaughtered and destroyed, who had no religion, no knowledge of right and wrong, not even a proper language. All the tribes east of the Black Sea were in agitation. The Alans, a people who had lived for centuries east of the Don river, had already been driven from their land. The king of the Goths, himself a "terror to his neighbors," had been defeated. Refugees were crowding to the northern side of the Danube, asking to enter the security of Roman territory.[22]

The Huns had arrived at the distant edges of the western world.

To the Romans, who had never seen them, they were as frightening as earthquake and tsunami, an evil force that could barely be resisted. Historians of the time had no idea exactly where these frightening newcomers came from, but they were sure it was somewhere awful. The Roman historian Procopius insists that they were descended from witches who had sexual congress with demons, producing Huns: a "stunted, foul and puny tribe, scarcely human and having no language save one which bore but slight resemblance of human speech."[23]

The story isn't original; Procopius borrowed it from the book of Genesis, which says that in the times of wickedness before the Great Flood, "the sons of God went to the daughters of men and had children by them." The church fathers believed that this described the union of fallen angels—demons—

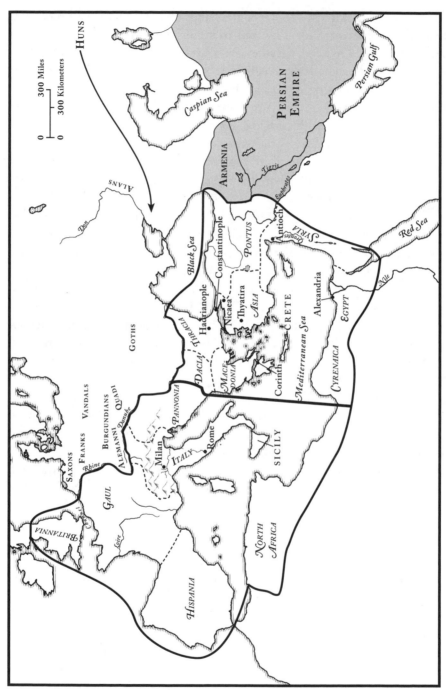

6.2: The Barbarian Approach

who slept with human women and fathered children who brought great evil
to the world. Now the Christian interpretation of history had been married
to the threatening present: the Huns were not just barbarians, but demons
out to destroy the Christians of the Roman empire, the kingdom of God on
earth.[24]

The Huns were still distant, though, and the immediate problem was what
to do with the refugees. Valens received an official delegation of Goths asking
permission to settle in the Roman land on the other side of the Danube. He
had already been forced to make peace with the Goths, and now he decided
to permit the immigration. In return, the newcomers could farm the unculti-
vated land in Thracia and provide additional soldiers for the Roman army (as
other Gothic peoples who had settled in the empire had agreed to do).[25]

With the dam of the Roman border breached, new waves of fleeing Goths
poured across the Danube. The Roman officials who were in charge of the
new settlers were quickly overwhelmed by the paperwork. Taxes were mis-
handled; money was misappropriated; the newcomers wiped out food supplies and began to go hungry. Within two years, Valens's decision led, yet
again, to war with the barbarians. An army of angry Goths stormed through
Thracia, spreading a "most foul confusion of robbery, murder, bloodshed,
and fires," killing, burning villages, taking captives, and heading for the walls
of Constantinople.[26]

Valens set out from Antioch to go to the defense of his city; in the west,
young Gratian started east to help his uncle. Before he could arrive with his
reinforcements, the paths of Valens and the Goths intersected at the city
of Hadrianople, west of Constantinople—a city named after Hadrian, the
emperor who had built a wall against barbarians.

On August 9, 378, Valens plunged into the battle among his men and was
killed. Two-thirds of his army fell with him; the Roman soldiers were thirsty
and starving after their forced march. Valens was not wearing the imperial
purple, and his body was so badly disfigured that it was never identified. The
ground, says Ammianus, was ankle-deep in blood. All during the next night,
the people of Hadrianople could hear coming from the dark the wails of the
wounded and the death rattles of the dying left on the battlefield.

The Goths laid siege to the city, but they had less experience with sieges
than with hand-to-hand combat, and soon withdrew. They tried the same at
Constantinople, and again found that they had no hope of breaking down the
walls. So they withdrew; but the point had been made. The Roman empire
was far from all-conquering. Earthquake and flood could wreck it; a distant
band of barbarians could disrupt it; and a ragged band of exiles could bring
down the emperor.

TIMELINE 6

INDIA	ROMAN EMPIRE	PERSIAN EMPIRE
		Shapur II (309–379)
	Battle of the Milvian Bridge (312) **Constantine** (312–337) Battle of Campus Serenus (313) Edict of Milan (313)	
Chandragupta (319–335)	Council of Nicaea (325)	
		Khosrov the Short of Armenia (330–338)
Samudragupta (335–c. 380)	**Constantine II Constantius Constans** (337–340) (337–361) (337–350)	
	First Council of Constantinople (359) **Julian** (360/361–363) **Jovian** (363–364) **Valentinian** (364–375) **Valens** (364–378) The Gothic War (367–370) **Gratian** (375–383) **Valentinian II** (375–392)	
Chandragupta II (380–415) Faxian journeys to India		

Chapter Seven

———

Refounding the Kingdom

Between 371 and 412,
Goguryeo adopts Buddhist principles and Confucian teachings
and defeats its neighbors

ALL THE WAY to the east—beyond Constantinople, beyond Persia and India, past the empires of the Jin and the Bei Wei—another king struggled to recover from defeat. In 371, the young king Sosurim inherited the crown of the kingdom of Goguryeo, and with it a shattered and demoralized country. He had no firm foundation on which to rebuild; his army had been devastated, his officers killed in battle, his land laid waste.

His answer arrived in 372 in the hands of a monk.

The kingdom of Goguryeo lay on the peninsula east of the Yellow Sea. The ancestors of its people had probably come from the Yellow river valley long before, but the cultures of China and of the peninsula had been separate for centuries.* The people of the peninsula claimed an ancient and distinguished heritage. According to their own myths, the first kingdom in their land was Choson, created by the god Tan'gun in 2333 BC—the era of the oldest Chinese kingdoms.

Before its collapse, the Chinese dynasty of the Han had captured the land across the north of the peninsula and had settled Chinese officials and their families there. In the south, three independent kingdoms formed: Silla, Goguryeo, and Baekje. Meanwhile, on the very southern tip of the peninsula, a fourth set of tribes—the Gaya confederacy—resisted attempts by its neighbors to fold it into the increasingly strong monarchies.

The kingdom of Goguryeo had always been the most aggressive and the most troublesome to the Han, who had hoped to keep the kingdoms south of their colonies from developing too much power: "By temperament," the

---

*Linguistically, the peoples of the peninsula were separate from the Chinese quite early; their language belonged to the "Tungusic" group of languages, which is different from the "Sinitic" group of languages to which "Old Chinese" (or "Archaic Chinese"), the oldest form of written Chinese, belongs.

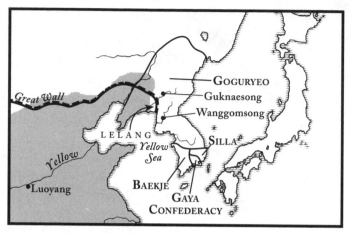

7.1: Goguryeo at Its Height

Romance of the Three Kingdoms remarked, "the people [of Goguryeo] are violent and take delight in brigandage."[1] By the time the Han empire fell, its control over its lands in old Choson had shrunk to a single administrative district: Lelang, centered around the old city of Wanggomsong—modern Pyongyang.

Lelang outlasted its Han parent, surviving until 313. In that year, the ruler of the kingdom of Goguryeo, the ambitious and energetic king Micheon, pushed his way north and captured Lelang, adding it to his own territory and ousting the remaining Chinese forces. This made Goguryeo, under King Micheon, three times the size of any of its neighbors. It was the most powerful, the most dominant of the Three Kingdoms of Korea.

Which made it the biggest target as well. King Micheon died in 331, leaving his son Gogugwon on the throne. King Gogugwon was apparently not a warrior equal to his father; he followed a thirty-year policy of inaction, during which Goguryeo was sacked twice. In 342, armies from the Sixteen Kingdoms took thousands of prisoners and broke down the walls of its capital city, Guknaesong; in 371, the crown prince of Baekje led an invading army all the way up to Wanggomsong.

Shaken out of his withdrawal, King Gogugwon of Goguryeo came out in person to fight his neighbor. He was killed defending the Wanggomsong fortress. Baekje claimed much of Goguryeo's territory as its own; and Sosurim, son of the defeated king, grandson of the great Micheon, was left with the shrunken shambles of Goguryeo.

Not long after he came to the throne, a Buddhist monk travelling from the west arrived at his court. This monk, Sun-do, brought with him gifts and Buddhist scriptures, along with the assurance that the practice of Buddhism would help to protect Goguryeo from its enemies. King Sosurim welcomed

Sun-do and listened to him, and in 372 embraced the faith as his own. The following year, he established the T'aehak: the National Confucian Academy, patterned on Chinese principles.[2]

Buddhism and Confucianism, essentially very different, formed a useful hybrid for Goguryeo. Sun-do taught Sosurim and his court that discontent, unhappiness, ambition, and fear were *samskrita*, conditions of the mind that were nonexistent: the enlightened student recognized that in fact there was no discontent, no unhappiness, no ambition, no fear. The kingdom of Goguryeo was itself *samskrita*, a conception that had no ultimate reality. Should King Sosurim and his officials truly understand this, they would be able to function in the world while recognizing (in the words of the Zen master Shengyan) that "the world and phenomena have no true existence." Their decisions would not be shaped and tainted by the desire for gain, the desire for security, the desire for happiness.[3]

Confucianism, on the other hand, accepted the reality of the physical world and taught its adherents how to live properly, with virtue and responsibility, within it. The principles of Buddhism gave Goguryeo a new unity, a spiritual oneness; the principles of Confucianism gave King Sosurim a tested framework for training new army officers, secretaries, accountants, and bureaucrats—everything a state needed to prosper. Buddhism was the philosophy of the monk, Confucianism the doctrine of the training academy.

And since Buddhism was not a creedal religion—one with a written statement of faith to which its believers assented—the two different ways of thinking existed, harmoniously, side by side. Buddhism, unlike Christianity, was never viewed by its practitioners as exclusive, a system that demanded the relinquishment of all opposing beliefs. So although King Sosurim made Buddhism his own, he did not make it an official state religion; this would have given it an exclusive authority, which made no sense within the Buddhist framework.[4]

Goguryeo was no longer teetering on the edge of dissolution; King Sosurim was hauling it back from the brink, refounding it as a state. But it would be some time before the foundation he was building would be solid enough to support a campaign of conquest and expansion.

Meanwhile, Baekje remained the most powerful state on the peninsula, under the rule of Geunchogo, the king who had launched the invasion that killed Sosurim's father. Baekje's borders had swollen to encompass much of the south, and King Geunchogo (like his northern neighbor) needed to put into place practices that would keep the territory united under a single king. Never before had the crown of Baekje passed from father to son; one warrior after another had claimed it through strength. But a battle over the succession would, in all likelihood, result in Baekje losing territory, thanks to its leaders putting their energy into inside politics rather than outside expansion. King Geunchogo, protecting his conquests, declared that his crown should pass to his son. When he died in 375, his arrangements held firm. The throne passed first to his son and then (after his son's early death) to his grandson Chimnyu.[5]

In 384, the Indian monk Malananda, on a pilgrimage through China, came from the Jin to Baekje. When King Chimnyu heard of his approach, he came out to meet Malananda and took him into the capital city to listen to what he had to say. And, like King Sosurim, he too accepted the teachings of Buddhism.[6]

For both kings, Buddhism held a sheen of antiquity, a flavor of ancient Chinese tradition. Both kings ruled over relatively new kingdoms, and in these kingdoms, all things Chinese were more desirable. Buddhism carried with it the resonance of centuries of inherited authority, a faint echo (by way of the Jin) of the distant and glorious past.

By the time Sosurim's nephew Guanggaeto came to the throne in 391, the foundation laid by his predecessors was strong enough to support conquest; and the spread of Buddhist philosophy did nothing to convince Guanggaeto that he should forgo ambition and earthly gain. Barely a year after his coronation, Guanggaeto organized an attack against Baekje, which just decades before had seemed impregnable.

He had managed to make an alliance with the third kingdom on the peninsula, Silla. In 391, Silla was ruled by King Naemul, a man of forethought. He had already sent diplomats to the Jin court across the sea; now he responded to Guanggaeto's overtures with friendship, happy to have an ally against the constantly encroaching Baekje.

The armies of Silla and Goguryeo joined together and stormed through Baekje. The kingdom was unable to resist for long; Baekje was overwhelmed by the combined armies of its neighbors. In 396, the king of Baekje handed over a thousand hostages to guarantee his good behavior, and agreed to pay homage to King Guanggaeto.

The rest of Guanggaeto's rule was spent in conquests so extensive that Guanggaeto earned himself the nickname "The Great Expander." Between 391 and 412, the Expander conquered sixty-five walled cities and fourteen hundred villages for Goguryeo, recovered the northern land that had been taken away decades before, and made Baekje retreat to the south. His deeds are carved on the stone stele that still stands at his tomb, the Guanggaeto Stele, the first historical document of Korean history: "With his majestic military virtue he encompassed the four seas like a spreading willow tree," it tell us. "His people flourished in a wealthy state, and the five grains ripened abundantly." His own words are preserved in the temple he built to commemorate his victories: "Believing in Buddhism," the dedicatory inscription reads, "we seek prosperity."[7]

ROMAN EMPIRE	PERSIAN EMPIRE	GOGURYEO	BAEKJE	SILLA
		TIMELINE 7		
		Micheon (300–331)		
	Shapur II (309–379)			
Battle of the Milvian Bridge (312)				
Constantine (312–337)				
Battle of Campus Edict of Milan				
Serenus (313) (313)				
Council of Nicaea (325)		Gogugwon (331–371)		
Khosrov the Short of Armenia (332–338)				
Constantine II Constantius Constans				
(337–340) (337–361) (337–350)				
			Geunchogo (346–375)	
				Naemul (356–402)
First Council of Constantinople (359)				
Julian (360/361–363)				
Jovian (363–364)				
Valentinian (364–375) Valens (364–378)				
The Gothic War (367–370)		Sosurim (371–384)		
		The arrival of Buddhism		
Gratian (375–383) Valentinian II (375–392)				
			Chimnyu (384–385)	
		Guanggaeto (391–413)		

Chapter Eight

—

The Catholic Church

Between 378 and 382,
Gratian rejects the old Roman religion,
while Theodosius tries to legislate brotherhood and unity

FIVE MONTHS AFTER the death of Valens, the emperor Gratian appointed a new ruler for the east: Flavius Theodosius, who now became Emperor Theodosius I. Gratian's younger brother Valentinian II, technically his co-emperor, was still only seven years old, and he needed a competent colleague.

The greatest threat to the east, Persian invasion, was diminishing. In 379, Shapur the Great of Persia died after a spectacularly long reign of nearly seventy years and was succeeded by his elderly brother Ardashir II, who was more concerned with hanging on to his crown than with invading foreign parts. Instead, both Gratian and Theodosius turned to ensure that the Roman empire would survive. The Goths to the north were growing steadily more powerful, but the more immediate problem was the ongoing tendency of the Roman coalition to pull apart from the inside; Constantine's hope for an empire held together by faith was still unrealized.

Gratian, a devout Christian, soon found himself at odds with the Roman senators who still held to the traditional Roman state religion. Four years after the Battle of Hadrianople, Gratian made it quite clear to the Senate that he would not allow the Roman gods to undermine the empire's Christian faith. In 382, he removed the Altar of Victory from the Senate building in Rome. It had stood there since Augustus's defeat of Antony and Cleopatra four hundred years before, as tribute to the goddess of victory. The senators protested, but Gratian stood firm. He also removed the title pontifex maximus, high priest of the Roman state religion, from his list of titles; and when the sacred robes were brought to him, as was traditional, for him to put on, he refused to don them. In doing so he was rejecting not just the Roman gods, but the entire Roman past; as Zosimus points out with asperity, the kings of Rome had accepted the title pontifex maximus since the days of Numa Pompilius a thousand years before. Even Constantine had put on the robes. "If the emperor refuses to become Pontifex," one of the priests is said to have muttered at the time, "we shall soon make one."[1] Whether Gratian's power could survive the hostility of the senators remained to be seen.

To the east, Theodosius was forced to deal with the destructive power of Christian division. Arguments about the Arian take on the divinity of Christ, as opposed to the Nicene understanding, had spread to the lowest levels of society. "Everywhere throughout the city is full of such things," complained the bishop Gregory of Nyssa, in a sermon preached at Constantinople,

> the alleys, the squares, the thoroughfares, the residential quarters; among cloak salesmen, those in charge of the moneychanging tables, those who sell us our food. For if you ask about change, they philosophise to you about the Begotten and the Unbegotten. And if you ask about the price of bread, the reply is, "The Father is greater, and the Son is subject to him." If you say, "Is the bath ready?", they declare the Son has his being from the non-existent. I am not sure what this evil should be called—inflammation of the brain or madness or some sort of epidemic disease which contrives the derangement of reasoning.[2]

To restore the empire to the vision of Christian unity that Constantine had seen so clearly, Theodosius turned to law. He used the legal structures of the ancient Roman state to support the Christian religion (never mind that it was diametrically opposed to the ancient Roman traditions); he used the power of the emperor to shape the Christian faith so that the Christian faith could shape the empire. The interweaving of the two traditions continued to change both of them in ways that would prove impossible to undo.

Two years after taking the throne, in the year 380, Theodosius declared that Nicene Christianity was the one true faith, and threatened dissenters with legal penalties. In doing so, he called into being a single, unified, *catholic* (the word means universal, applying to all humankind) Christian church. "He enacted," writes the Christian historian Sozomen, "that the title of 'Catholic Church' should be exclusively confined to those who rendered equal homage to the Three Persons of the Trinity, and that those individuals who entertained opposite opinions should be treated as heretics, regarded with contempt, and delivered over to punishment."[3]

Long before Theodosius, Christian bishops had distinguished the *ecclesia catholica* from the *haeretici*, the heretics, those who were by belief outside of the stream of true Christian doctrine. But never before had "heretic" been defined by law. Now, "heretic" had a legal definition: someone who did not hold to the Nicene Creed. "All of the people shall believe in God within the concept of the Holy Trinity," the law declared, "and take the name catholic

Christians. Meeting places of those who do not believe shall not be given the status of churches, and such people may be subject to both divine and earthly retribution."[4]

Theodosius actually believed that he could legislate his subjects into believing only in a Nicene-defined deity. He was a clever politician, but his theological reasoning was often naive. Sozomen, for example, writes that when Theodosius convened a church council the following year (381), as a follow-up to the issuing of the law, he brought together the "presidents of the sects which were flourishing" so that they could discuss their differences: "for he imagined that all would be brought to oneness of opinion, if a free discussion were entered into, concerning ambiguous points of doctrine."[5]

This was wildly optimistic, and as anyone who has ever been involved in church work could predict, it didn't work. But Theodosius soldiered on. Now that his law had been passed, he could start enforcing uniformity on a practical level. He took all of the meeting places and churches of the non-Nicene Christians and handed them over to the Nicene bishops, a material gain for those fortunate priests. He threatened to expel heretics who insisted on preaching from the city of Constantinople and to confiscate their land. He didn't always carry through on these threats; Sozomen remarks, approvingly, that although he had enacted severe punishments for heresy into law, the punishments were often not applied: "He had no desire to persecute his subjects; he only desired to enforce uniformity of view about God through the medium of intimidation."[6]

Theodosius was finding that it was easier to announce unity than to actually create it. In many ways, the Goths were easier to deal with than heretics; all he had to do was kill them.

While he was convening councils and making doctrine, Theodosius was also directing a fight against Gothic invasion. The Goths had become such a problem that Gratian, in the west, had agreed to transfer the most Goth-infested part of his western empire—three dioceses in the central province of Pannonia—over to the eastern empire so that Theodosius would be responsible for driving the Goths out.

8.1: The Transfer of Pannonia

Unfortunately the army was not quite strong enough to take on this extra task, so Theodosius managed to beef it up with an innovative strategy: he recruited barbarians from some regions to fight against barbarians in other regions. He would hire Goth mercenaries from Pannonia, transfer them over to Egypt, and then bring Roman soldiers from Egypt over to Pannonia to fight other Goths. The definition of "Roman soldier," like the definition of "Roman," was becoming increasingly nebulous, even while Theodosius managed to make the definition of "Christian" more restrictive.[7]

The thinness of the line between Roman and barbarian became more obvious in 382, when, after four years of fighting against the Goths, Theodosius decided that too much energy was going to the war, and made a peace treaty with them instead. The treaty allowed them to exist, within the borders of the Roman empire, under their own king. The Gothic king would be subject to him as emperor, but the Goths themselves would not have to answer to any Roman official; and when they fought for Rome, they would do so as allies, rather than as Roman soldiers in regular Roman army units subject to regular Roman officers.[8]

By 382, Theodosius could claim that he had reduced the chaos in the eastern part of the empire to order. The Christian church was unified, the Goths were at peace, all was right with the world.

But all of Theodosius's solutions had the appearance, not the reality, of victory. In fact, the Goths were not subdued. Arianism (not to mention a score of other heresies) was not dead. The Christians of the empire were not united. And even the leadership of Theodosius's newly created Catholic church was in debate. As part of his church council in 381, Theodosius had announced that the bishop of Constantinople was equal to the bishop of Rome in authority, "because Constantinople is the New Rome."[9] This law might be on the books, but in 382—even as Theodosius celebrated his victories—the bishops of the older cities, the traditional centers of Christianity, were objecting to the exaltation of the relatively young bishopric in Constantinople.

So did the bishop of Rome, who called his own council in Rome in 382 and announced that the bishop of Rome was the leader of all other bishops, including the upstart at Constantinople. The churchmen in Rome agreed, and the bishop of Rome ordered his secretary, a young man named Jerome, to record the decision. The Roman council also agreed that Jerome, who was good with languages, should start working on a new Latin translation of the Scriptures.

This was a direct response to the attempt to make the Greek-speaking east equal to the west; the council at Rome had now declared that Latin, the language of the west, was the proper language for Scripture (and the proper language for public worship as well). Theodosius had declared all Christians to be one, but the eastern and western halves of his catholic church were beginning to pull apart.

TIMELINE 8				

GOGURYEO BAEKJE SILLA	ROMAN EMPIRE		PERSIAN EMPIRE
Micheon (300–331)			
			Shapur II (309–379)
	Battle of the Milvian Bridge (312)		
	Battle of Campus Edict of Milan		
	Serenus (313) (313)		
	Council of Nicaea (325)		
			Khosrov the Short of Armenia (330–338)
Gogugwon (331–371)			
	Constantine II **Constantius** **Constans**		
	(337–340) (337–361) (337–350)		
Geunchogo (346–375)			
Naemul (356–402)			
	First Council of Constantinople (359)		
	Julian (360/361–363)		
	Jovian (363–364)		
	Valentinian (364–375) **Valens** (364–378)		
	The Gothic War (367–370)		
Sosurim (371–384)			
The arrival of Buddhism	**Gratian** (375–383) **Valentinian II** (375–392)		
	Theodosius (378-395)		
			Ardashir II (379–383)
Chimnyu (384–385)			
Guanggaeto (391–413)			

Part Two

FRACTURES

Chapter Nine

—

Excommunicated

*Between 383 and 392,
a Spaniard becomes king of the Britons,
and Theodosius discovers
that he has underestimated the power of the church*

IN 383, THE ROMAN ARMY in Britain rebelled and proclaimed a new emperor: Magnus Maximus, their general.

At first Magnus Maximus possessed only the loyalty of the troops in Britannia; he was, in effect, the king of the Britons—despite being a Roman citizen and a Spaniard by birth. But it seems likely that he had exercised a king-like power in isolated Britannia for some years. His name pops up in Welsh legends, where he is known as Macsen Wledig, a half-legendary figure who stars in the epic *Breuddwyd Macsen*. In the tale, Macsen Wledig is in Rome, ruling as emperor, when he dreams of a beautiful maiden who must become his wife; he searches for her and eventually crosses the water to Britain, where he finds her and marries her. He then spends seven years building castles and roads in Britain—so long that a usurper back in Rome takes his throne from him.

The faint whisper of historical truth in this myth is that Magnus Maximus did in fact claim the title "Emperor of Rome" while still in Britain, and undoubtedly had spent a good portion of his time as a Roman commander building roads and developing the Roman infrastructure on the island. Possibly Magnus Maximus also allowed tribes from the western island (modern Ireland) to settle on the western coast of Britain, a combination of cultures that produced the country of Wales; this would explain his appearance in Welsh tales of the country's origin, where he shows up so often that John Davies calls him a "ubiquitous lurker."[1]

At this point Britain had not yet been Christianized. The Roman army in Britannia was thoroughly committed to the old Roman state religion, discontented that both senior Roman emperors, Gratian and Theodosius, were Christian. Maximus, on the other hand, was unabashedly Roman in his beliefs; when the army acclaimed him, he announced his loyalty to Jupiter

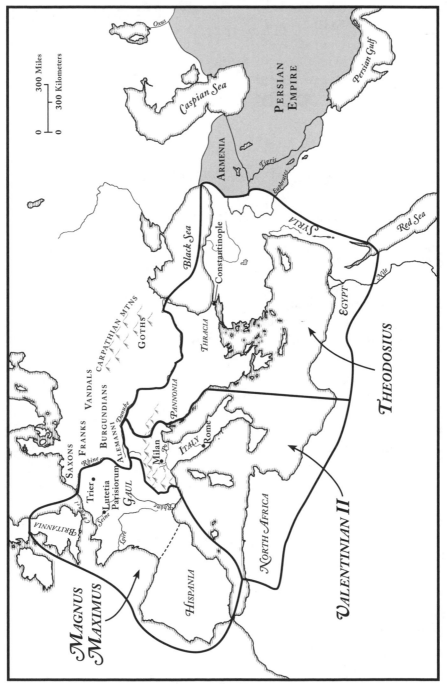

9.1: The Empire in Thirds

and then gathered up his forces and headed for Gaul, hoping to possess the throne of the west in fact and not simply in name.

An echo of this campaign appears in Geoffrey of Monmouth's thoroughly unreliable *History of the Kings of Britain*, in which King Arthur sails with his army to Gaul and fights against the Roman tribune who governs it. In that version of the tale, Arthur triumphs (after laying waste to the countryside) and sets up a royal court at the old Roman fortress town Lutetia Parisiorum, on the Seine. In the real world, Magnus Maximus marched into Gaul and arrived at Lutetia Parisiorum, where Gratian met him in battle. Part of Gratian's army—the part that wanted an emperor who worshipped Jupiter rather than the Christian God—defected to Maximus's side, and the remainder were defeated. Gratian fled and died not long afterwards, either captured and killed by Maximus's soldiers or assassinated by one of his own officers.[2]

This left Maximus in control of Gaul, and he declared himself emperor of Gaul and Hispania as well as Britannia. The empire was divided into three: Magnus Maximus in the far west, Theodosius in the east, and Gratian's younger brother and former co-emperor, Valentinian II, still hanging on to power in Italy and North Africa.

Now that he was in control of part of the western mainland, Maximus sent Theodosius an official message, emperor to emperor, suggesting that they be allies and friends. The invasion had happened too quickly for Theodosius to block it, and now that it was a fait accompli, he decided that it would be prudent to accept Maximus's offer. He and Maximus were old acquaintances, as it happened; they had fought together in Britannia as young men. He agreed to recognize Maximus as a legitimate emperor, and for four years, the three emperors ruled side by side, with Theodosius as the senior Augustus. "Nevertheless," writes Zosimus, "he was at the same time privately preparing for war, and endeavouring to deceive Maximus by every species of flattery."[3]

Preparing for war involved negotiating with the Persians; Theodosius didn't want to head west and immediately find his eastern border under attack. Ardashir II, the elderly brother of the great Shapur, had been deposed by the Persian noblemen at court after four years of inefficiency; now Shapur's son Shapur III sat on the throne. The issue most likely to cause another war between the two empires was control of Armenia, so Theodosius sent an ambassador to Shapur III's court to negotiate a settlement.[4]

The ambassador was a Roman soldier named Stilicho, who had been born in the northern parts of the empire. His mother was Roman, but his father was a Vandal—a "barbarian," a native of the Germanic peoples who lived just north of the Carpathian Mountains. Unlike the Goths, the Vandals were not a present trouble to the Roman empire. Nevertheless, in the eyes of many Romans, Stilicho carried with him the taint of the barbarian. The historian Orosius, who disliked him, used his parentage to condemn him; he was "sprung from the Vandals, an unwarlike, greedy, treacherous, and crafty race."[5]

But Theodosius trusted him, and in return Stilicho—at that time still in his twenties—performed an impressive negotiating feat. In 384, Shapur III agreed to divide the control of Armenia between the two empires. The western half of Armenia would be ruled by a Roman-supported king, the eastern half by a king loyal to Persia. Theodosius was grateful; when Stilicho returned, Theodosius promoted him to general and married him to the fourteen-year-old princess Serena, Theodosius's own niece and adopted daughter.

The treaty with the Persians allowed Theodosius to continue his preparations for war with the western usurper. Meanwhile, Magnus Maximus was making plans to move east, against the court of Valentinian II. Maximus wanted to be true emperor of the west, and as long as Valentinian II was still in Italy, his legitimacy was shadowed.

Valentinian II was only fifteen, and the real power in Italy was held by his generals and his mother, Justina. In 386, Justina gave Maximus the excuse he needed to invade Italy. She was herself an Arian Christian, which put her at odds with the orthodox bishop of Milan, Ambrose. They had quarreled off and on for years, but in 386, Justina (by way of her son) issued an imperial order commanding Ambrose to hand over one of the churches of Milan to the Arians so that they could have their own meeting place. Ambrose indignantly refused, upon which Justina upped her demands and asked for another, more central and more important church instead: the New Basilica.

She sent officials to the Basilica on the Friday before Palm Sunday (the beginning of Holy Week, the most important week in the church calendar), while Ambrose was teaching a small group of converts in order to prepare them for baptism. The officials started to change the hangings in the church; Ambrose carried on, apparently ignoring them.

This invasion of the church by imperial officials infuriated the Nicene Christians in Milan, and they gathered at the church to protest. The demonstrations spread. Holy Week was taken up with riots in the streets, armed arrests of citizens ("The prisons were filled with tradesmen," Ambrose wrote to his sister later), and a larger and larger turnout of imperial soldiers. Ambrose couldn't get out of the Basilica because it was surrounded by soldiers, so he staged an involuntary sit-in with his congregants. He passed the time by preaching that the church could never be controlled by the emperor; the church was in the image of God, it was the body of Christ, and since Christ was fully God (a slap at the Arians), the church was itself one with the Father.[6]

Finally, Valentinian II intervened and ordered the soldiers out. But he was unhappy with Ambrose's power, even more than with the defeat of the Arian takeover: "You would deliver me up in chains, if Ambrose bade you," he snapped at his court officials, and Ambrose was deeply afraid that the next thing coming down the pike would be an accusation of treason.

When Maximus got wind of the unrest, he announced his plans to attack. "The pretext," writes the church historian Sozomen, "was that he desired to prevent the introduction of innovations in the ancient form of religion and ecclesiastical order. . . . He was watching and intriguing for the imperial rule in such a way that it might appear as if he had acquired the Roman government by law, and not by force."[7]

Considering that Maximus had originally campaigned in the name of Jupiter, his new pose as defender of the Nicene faith undoubtedly rang a little hollow. But this shows the extent to which Christianity, in the late Roman empire, had already become the language not just of power but of legitimacy. Maximus didn't merely want to be emperor. He wanted to be a *real* emperor, a lawful emperor, and in order to have any chance to assert this, he had to align himself with the Christian church. Even while Ambrose preached that the church was separate from the power of the emperor, the emperors wielded the church as a weapon against each other.

As Maximus marched across the Alps towards Milan, Theodosius marched west with his own army—and Valentinian II and Justina fled from Italy into Pannonia, taking with them Valentinian's sister Galla and leaving Milan open to Maximus and his armies. When Theodosius arrived in Pannonia, Justina offered to give Theodosius her daughter Galla if he would drive Maximus out. Theodosius accepted; Galla was reputedly very beautiful, but in addition the marriage related him, the rough ex-soldier from Hispania, to the Valentinian dynasty.

He then marched the rest of the way to Milan, sending ahead of him plenty of information about the size and lethal skill of his army. Possibly Maximus had not expected Theodosius to actually leave the eastern border and come all the way west. In any case, by the time Theodosius reached Milan, Maximus's men were so thoroughly intimidated that his own soldiers took Maximus captive and handed him over. The war was resolved without a single battle. Theodosius executed Maximus, bringing an end to the reign of the first king of the Britons. He also sent an assassin, his trusted general Arbogast, to find Maximus's son and heir. Arbogast found the young man in Trier and strangled him.[8]

The whole invasion had worked out pretty well for Theodosius. He now had a whole new level of power over the west; he was Valentinian's brother-in-law and deliverer, and he staged a triumphal procession to Rome in which he took center stage. He then departed, taking his beautiful young wife with him and leaving his general Arbogast (now back from strangling Maximus's son) to be Valentinian's new right-hand man.

Like Stilicho, Arbogast was of "barbarian" descent. His father was a Frank, and so although he could pursue a shining career in the army, he had no hope of ascending to the imperial throne. Theodosius's most trusted aides tended to be half (or more) barbarian; they could not challenge their master for the crown. Arbogast was an experienced soldier by this time, and Valentinian II, accustomed to being dominated, was helpless against him. Arbogast took over the administration of the empire, reporting directly to Theodosius in the east, while Valentinian II sat in his imperial throne as little more than a figurehead.

In essence, Theodosius now had control over the entire empire, and he turned his attention again to the project of unification. On his return to Constantinople, he began to issue the Theodosian Decrees—a set of laws designed to bring the whole Roman realm into line with orthodox Christian practice. The first decree, issued in 389, was a strike at the very root of the relationship between the old Roman religion and the Roman state: Theodosius declared that the old Roman feast days, which had always been state holidays, would now be workdays instead. Official holidays then, as now, were ways of laying out the mythical foundations of a nation, of pointing citizens towards the high points of the past that helped to define the present. Theodosius was not just Christianizing the empire; he was beginning to rewrite its history.

In this he was slightly out of step with the mood of the west. Back in Rome, the senators had already applied three times to the imperial court in Milan, asking that the traditional Altar of Victory (removed by Gratian) be reinstalled in the Senate. The appeals had been led by Quintus Aurelius Symmachus, the prefect (chief administrative officer) of the city of Rome. He begged Valentinian to preserve the customs of the past: "We ask the restoration of that state of religion under which the Republic has so long prospered," he wrote. "Permit us, I beseech you, to transmit in our old age to our posterity what we ourselves received when boys. Great is the love of custom."

But even more central to the argument of Symmachus was his understanding of faith; he could not see why it was necessary, for the triumph of Christianity, to do away with all reminders of the old Roman religion. His appeal continues:

> Where shall we swear to observe your laws and statutes? by what sanction shall the deceitful mind be deterred from bearing false witness? All places indeed are full of God, nor is there any spot where the perjured can be safe, but it is of great efficacy in restraining crime to feel that we are in the presence of sacred things. That altar binds together the concord of all, that altar appeals to the faith of each man, nor does any thing give more weight to our decrees than that all our decisions are sanctioned, so to speak, by an

oath. . . . We look on the same stars, the heaven is common to us all, the same world surrounds us. What matters it by what arts each of us seeks for truth?[9]

This was indeed the question, and Theodosius would have answered that as long as the citizens of the empire searched for truth by many means, they would have no single loyalty to hold them together. Already the division of the empire into two or three parts had sounded the death-knell for any chance that the empire would be held together by any identity as Roman citizens; already the Western Roman Empire and the Eastern Roman Empire had begun to assume different characters.

Ambrose, the bishop of Milan, opposed the applications; his answer to Symmachus laid out the exclusive theology that made Christianity so useful to the emperors.

What you are ignorant of, that we have learnt by the voice of God; what you seek after by faint surmises, that we are assured of by the very Wisdom and Truth of God. Our customs therefore and yours do not agree. You ask the Emperors to grant peace to your gods, we pray for peace for the Emperors themselves from Christ. You worship the works of your own hands, we think it sacrilege that any thing which can be made should be called God. . . . A Christian Emperor has learned to honour the altar of Christ alone. . . . Let the voice of our Emperor speak of Christ alone, let him declare Him only Whom in heart he believes, for the king's heart is in the Hand of God.[10]

Ambrose was a hard and uncompromising man, but he understood what was at stake. *The altar of Christ alone*: it was the only hope for unification that Theodosius had left, and it was a powerful hope.

Yet this power for unity was not without its complications for Theodosius. In 390, the year after the first of the Theodosian Decrees was issued, he ran afoul of the church he was trying to make use of, and Ambrose excommunicated him—the first time that a monarch was ever punished by the Christian church for a political action.

The action was a fairly straightforward, if cruel, act of retaliation. Over in Pannonia, a Roman governor had run into troubles at a tavern; drinking late one night, he had "shamefully exposed" himself, and a charioteer sitting next to him at the bar had "attempted an outrage."[11] The routine drunken pass turned into an incident when the governor, embarrassed, arrested the charioteer and threw him in jail. Unfortunately, he was one of the most popular contestants in a chariot race to be run the next day, and when the governor refused to release him in time for him to compete, his fans rioted, stormed the governor's headquarters, and murdered him.

Theodosius cracked down immediately and put to death everyone who had a hand in the riot—a purge that swept up a number of people who had simply been standing around watching. Ambrose was appalled by this injustice. When Theodosius next arrived in Milan to check on the affairs in the western part of his domain, Ambrose refused to allow him to enter the church either for prayer or for the celebration of the Eucharist, the Lord's Supper, the rite that separated believers from unbelievers.

The Christian historians who record this merely say that Theodosius then confessed his sin, did penance, and was restored. But what passes almost as a footnote is the fact that it took Theodosius eight months to do so. Standing on the steps and looking at Ambrose's unyielding face, Theodosius must have realized that his decrees were having an unintended consequence. The single, catholic church held his empire together because it was greater than the state, greater than any national loyalty, greater than any single man.

It was greater than the emperor.

Theodosius's eight months of reflection were eight months in which, in all likelihood, the future of Christianity hung in the balance. Had Theodosius been able to think of any better strategy, he could simply have refused Ambrose's demands. But in doing so he would have had either to turn his back on the Eucharist—which would have condemned his soul—or to deny Ambrose's authority—which would have revealed that the Christian church was, in fact, not bigger than the emperor. "Educated as he had been in the sacred oracles," concludes the Christian historian Theodoret, "Theodosius knew clearly what belonged to priests and what to emperors."[12]

What belonged to emperors was not sufficient to hold the empire together. Theodosius finally went back to Milan, subjected himself to Ambrose's religious authority, accepted the several months of penance that Ambrose prescribed, and was readmitted to the fellowship of the church. He then ordered all Roman temples closed and abandoned so that Christians could knock them down and build Christian churches instead. He commanded that the fire once guarded by the Vestal Virgins in the Roman Forum be officially dowsed. He announced that the Olympic Games would be held one final time before their permanent cancellation.

Finally he announced that any act of worship made in honor of the old Roman gods would be an act of treachery against the emperor himself. The church might be greater than the emperor, but the emperor could still corral its loyalty and direct it to his own ends.[13]

TIMELINE 9		

GOGURYEO BAEKJE SILLA	ROMAN EMPIRE	PERSIAN EMPIRE
	Constantine II **Constantius** **Constans** (337–340) (337–361) (337–350)	
Geunchogo (346–375) Naemul (356–402)		
	First Council of Constantinople (359) **Julian** (360/361–363) **Jovian** (363–364) **Valentinian** (364–375) **Valens** (364–378) The Gothic War (367–370)	
Sosurim (371–384) The arrival of Buddhism		
	Gratian (375-383) **Valentinian II** (375–392) **Theodosius** (378-395)	
		Ardashir II (379–383)
Chimnyu (384–385)	**Magnus Maximus** (383–388)	**Shapur III** (383–388)
	Theodosian Decrees	
Guanggaeto (391–413)		

Chapter Ten

Cracked in Two

Between 392 and 396,
the eastern and western halves of the empire
find themselves in opposition

Iⁿ 392, ᴀғᴛᴇʀ ғᴏᴜʀ ʏᴇᴀʀs of Arbogast's "help," Valentinian II killed himself in Milan. He was twenty-one.

His death immediately lit the fuse of civil war. Valentinian's sister Galla, now Theodosius's wife, insisted that her brother could not have killed himself. Theodosius was obligated to investigate, and Arbogast realized that the emperor's first action would most likely be to remove him from power. Before Theodosius could act, Arbogast went to the Roman Senate and promised that he would help the senators restore the Altar of Victory and protect the Roman religion from extinction. Together, the senators and Arbogast chose a new western emperor: a harmless and malleable Roman official named Eugenius, who was a Christian but inclined to be supportive of the rights of the old state religion.

Theodosius, receiving news of this action, refused to recognize Eugenius as a valid emperor. Instead, he named his own eight-year-old son, Honorius, to the western throne. He then prepared for battle, hiring additional troops—*foederati*, Gothic troops under the command of their own warleader, Alaric—to beef up his own army. He marched west with Stilicho, his general and son-in-law, and met the army of Eugenius, Arbogast, and the Roman senators at the Battle of the Frigidus, September 5, 394.

Orosius insists that Theodosius gave the sign of the cross just before plunging into battle, and three different Christian historians record that a divine wind blew up and rammed the arrows of the western army back into their own bodies.* Sozoman adds that during the fight, a demon appeared at the church where Theodosius prayed just before the battle, taunting the Christian

---

*The battlefield may have been blasted by a wind known as the "bora," formed when cold air is sucked into a low-pressure area over the Adriatic. Frederick Singleton notes that the bora can gust up to 100 mph and can cause a rapid temperature drop of 40 degrees Fahrenheit. See *A Short History of the Yugoslav Peoples* (Cambridge University Press, 1985), pp. 1–2.

10.1: The Battle of the Frigidus

cause and then fading away as Theodosius's army began to win the victory. Stilicho and Alaric, leading two wings of the attack, were largely responsible for crushing the western Roman army. Eugenius was killed that same day; Arbogast, seeing the destruction of his army, killed himself the next day. It was, says Orosius, a battle of "pious necessity."[1]

The accounts may not be terribly helpful in chronicling the exact progression of the Battle of the Frigidus, but the stories of divine winds and demons show that the historians knew what was at stake. This was more than another battle between competing emperors; it was a battle between two entirely different ways of understanding the world. When the battle ended, Theodosius controlled the entire empire: the east as senior emperor, the west as regent for his young son Honorius. It was the last time the Roman empire would be united under a single ruler.

Theodosius died in 395, the year after the battle. At his death, his two sons from his first marriage divided the rule as co-Augusti. Arcadius, eighteen, took the throne of Constantinople; Honorius inherited the west. As Honorius was only ten, Theodosius left instructions that Stilicho, the half-Vandal general, should act as his guardian. He also left his five-year-old daughter, Placida (daughter of his second wife, the young and beautiful Galla), to be raised by Stilicho and his Roman wife, Serena. Stilicho, too barbarian to be emperor in name, was now emperor in practice.

To the east, Arcadius, mild and easily intimidated, was ruling with the help of the army officer Rufinus. Rufinus was head of the emperor's personal guard, the highest military official in the east and the final decision-maker in the empire. Like Stilicho, he held ultimate power. "The whole empire being vested in Arcadius and Honorius," writes Zosimus, "they indeed appeared by their title to possess the sovereign authority, although the universal administration of affairs was under Rufinus in the east, and under Stilicho in the west." Unlike Stilicho, Rufinus had no barbarian blood; he could nurse the ambition of someday becoming emperor.[2]

Both sides of the empire were now threatened by a previous ally of Theodosius: Alaric, commander of the Gothic regiments at the Battle of the Frigidus. Alaric had hoped to become a regular Roman commander—*magister militum*—after Theodosius's death. Instead, neither emperor offered him this honor. Alaric blamed this, rightly, on his Gothic blood. His troops were already seething with discontent; a disproportionate number of Goths (over ten thousand) had fallen at the Frigidus, and they suspected that they had been used as human shields for the regular regiments.

Rather than continuing to struggle for Roman privilege, Alaric took control of his Gothic army and made himself its supreme commander and leader. In doing so, he managed to create a newborn nation and become its first ruler: king of the Visigoths.[3]

The historians of the late Roman empire (Jordanes and Cassiodorus, most prominently) divided the Goths into two separate groups: the Ostrogoths, who lived to the east, and the Visigoths, farther west. But these names didn't represent nations; they were simply a way to geographically distinguish between the Goths who lived closer to the Black Sea and the Goths who lived farther away. Before the time of Alaric, there was not really a Gothic nation. There was, instead, a shifting collection of Germanic tribes that sometimes fought together and sometimes against each other.

Alaric's Gothic army was united not because the soldiers belonged to a certain tribe (although they all shared the same, vaguely Germanic blood), but because they had drawn together into a cohesive military unit. When Alaric made himself their king, they became for the first time something more than an army. They became a self-constituted nation, bound together not by a single tribal heritage but by a single purpose. This new confederacy took its name from the land where many of them had once lived—the western Gothic land—but it included "Visigoths," Goths from farther east, as well as members from other tribes farther north. Historians call this "ethnogenesis": when a confederacy, united together by necessity or geography, makes itself into a nation by giving itself a name, a history, a royal lineage.[4]

Thanks to the outside pressure of Roman disdain, Alaric's Visigoths had become an independent people who now existed right in the middle of Roman land. They were resentful and hungry, and they had a strong leader with military experience—and so their first act as a nation was to raid the surrounding Roman provinces, taking what they thought they deserved and making a path towards Constantinople.[5]

The eastern emperor Arcadius and his general/puppet-master Rufinus were not well equipped to resist. Most of the Roman army was farther west, with Stilicho. Appealed to, Stilicho provided soldiers to head off Alaric. Either because of the threat of a pitched battle or (more likely) because Stilicho carried on some behind-the-door negotiations with him, Alaric sloped off and instead started to ravage the countryside of Greece.

The Roman soldiers then continued on to Constantinople; apparently Stilicho had ordered them to go join the eastern army, as a favor to the eastern emperor Arcadius. When the troops reached the walls of the city, Arcadius came out to greet them, with the general Rufinus trailing behind him. The contemporary Roman poet Claudian records the events that followed: as Rufinus followed the emperor along the serried ranks of soldiers, the troops

> begin to extend their long lines behind his back
> and to join up the ends so as to form a circle unnoticed by Rufinus.
> The space in the centre grows smaller
> and the wings meeting with serried shields
> gradually form into one lessening circle . . .
> Then one more daring than the rest drew his sword
> and leapt forward from the crowd
> and with fierce words and flashing eye rushed upon Rufinus . . .
> Straightway all pierce him with their spears
> and tear quivering limb from limb. . . .
> They stamp on that face of greed
> and while yet he lives pluck out his eyes;
> others seize and carry off his severed arms.
> One cuts off the foot, another wrenches a shoulder from the torn sinews;
> one lays bare the ribs of the cleft spine, another his liver, his heart,
> his still panting lungs.
> There is not space enough to satisfy their anger nor room to wreak their hate.[6]

The official story from the west was that the soldiers acted out of impulse. But Claudian insists that the Gothic soldier who first stabbed Rufinus leapt forward crying, "It is the hand of Stilicho that smites you." He isn't alone in attributing the plan to Stilicho; Zosimus, who finds the men behind the throne unadmirable on both sides of the empire ("In the respective cities," he complained, "the money from all quarters flowed into the coffers of Rufinus and Stilicho"), agrees that Stilicho ordered the assassination.[7]

If Stilicho did give the order, it was the first step in his attempt to extend his power over the entire empire. However, another courtier of the weak Arcadius immediately rose to fill the power vacuum: the eunuch Eutropius.

According to Zosimus, Eutropius was no more admirable than the dead Rufinus. He was "intoxicated with wealth, and elevated in his own imagination above the clouds." And he was more dangerous than Rufinus because he now knew his enemy. "He recollected," Zosimus says, "that Stilicho was master of every thing in the west; and therefore . . . he persuaded the emperor to convoke the senate, and by a public decree to declare Stilicho an enemy to the empire."[8]

Eutropius was not emperor; he could not attack the western power with armies. He had to use law instead. As he did so he brought the duality of the Roman empire into full view. The empire had held together under dual emperors and twin capitals, and it still existed as a single domain in name. But the crack that would divide it in two had become visible: Stilicho, guardian of the west, was now an outlaw in the east.

TIMELINE 10				
GOGURYEO	BAEKJE	SILLA	ROMAN EMPIRE	PERSIAN EMPIRE
			Julian (360/361–363)	
			Jovian (363–364)	
			Valentinian (364–375) Valens (364–378)	
			The Gothic War (367–370)	
Sosurim (371–384)				
The arrival of Buddhism			Gratian (375-383) Valentinian II (375–392)	
			Theodosius (378–395)	
				Ardashir II (379–383)
			Magnus Maximus	Shapur III
	Chimnyu (384–385)		(383–388)	(383–388)
			Theodosian Decrees	
Guanggaeto (391–413)				
			Eugenius (392–394)	
			The Battle of the Frigidus (394)	
			Honorius (395–423) Arcadius (395–408)	
			Alaric of the Visigoths (395–410)	

Chapter Eleven

— ⋅ —

The Sack of Rome

Between 396 and 410,
the North African province rebels,
the emperor of the west retreats to Ravenna,
and the Visigoths plunder Rome

For the Roman citizens on the North African coast, crosscurrents in authority were nothing new. For centuries they had lived under the double authority of the distant emperor and of his local representative, the Roman provincial governor. North Africa was far from Rome; it was not uncommon for the governor to pay lip service to the emperor while doing the opposite of the emperor's orders.

In 396, while Stilicho and Eutropius were jousting over control of the empire, a new bishop was appointed to watch over the Christian church in the busy coastal city of Hippo Regius. Augustine was a native African, born into Roman citizenship and trained at Roman schools in Carthage. His struggle to explain the nature of the divided authority he lived under would provide an imaginative picture of the world so strong that the entire Christian church—and, eventually, the kings of the western world—would grasp hold of it.

In his twenties, Augustine had lived in Rome as a teacher of rhetoric; in his thirties, he lived in Milan, where the bishop Ambrose became his friend and advisor. For most of this time Augustine was a Manichee, a follower of the religion established by the Persian prophet Mani more than a century before. Manichaeism taught that the universe was made up of two powerful forces, Good and Evil, which were eternally opposed; that matter was intrinsically Evil; and that human beings could only return to the Good by withdrawing from as much contact with matter as possible.[1]

After listening to Ambrose, though, Augustine rejected his Manichee past and, after some thought, decided to become a catechumen (a student) of Nicene Christianity. His new training threw him into increasing uncertainty and distress; one day, as he sat in a garden in Milan, weeping over the misery in his soul, he heard a child's voice chanting, "Pick up and read, pick up and read." This he interpreted as a command to pick up St. Paul's Epistle to the Romans, which lay nearby. When he read from it, he was instantly converted to belief in Christ: "A light of relief from all anxiety flooded into my heart," he wrote in his autobiography, the *Confessions*. "All the shadows of doubt were dispelled."[2]

He went back home and took up a career in the church. But the North African church to which he returned had been almost ripped apart by a dispute peculiar to it. Rather than arguing about the nature of Christ, the North African Christians were struggling with a question that had to do with the nature of his church.

The dispute was rooted in the persecutions by Diocletian, a hundred years before. Diocletian had executed Christians all across the empire, but down in North Africa the local Roman governor hadn't thrown himself behind the persecution. Instead, he told the local clergy that if Christians would just hand over their Scriptures as a symbol of recantation, they could go about their business.[3]

Some did; others refused. When the persecution was over, the Christians who had rejected the governor's offer were incensed to find that one of the priests who *had* turned over his Scriptures to the authorities was about to be made bishop of Carthage. They insisted that any baptisms administered by this man would be a sham, and that his bishopric would contaminate the entire Christian church.[4]

The protesting North African Christians, who became known as Donatists, after their leader Donatus Magnus, believed that the church was a place where the grace of God was conveyed to believers through holy men. For the Donatists, baptisms were effective and Eucharists were real only when the priest who administered them was himself a holy man. "What perversity must it be," asked the Donatist leader Petilianus, "that he who is guilty through his own sins should make another free from guilt?"[5]

To this, Augustine replied, "No man can make his neighbor free from sin, because he is not God." His answer reflected the official position of the bishop of Rome: the church was a place where the grace of God was conveyed to believers because God willed it to be so, not because of the character of the men who occupied its official positions. The Donatists were the first *puritan* Christians, the first to insist that the church was supposed to be a gathering of holy and righteous people, and that the unrighteous and unworthy should be purged from its midst; against them, the orthodox, *catholic* thinkers of the church argued that it was impossible (and just plain wrong) for men to attempt to purify the church of God.[6]

Augustine, forced by the Donatists to define the church, wrote that the church on earth would always be a "mixed body," true believers and hypocrites temporarily united in a single group. "The Church declares itself to be at present both," he concluded, "and this because the good fish and the bad are for the time mixed up in the one net." It was not for man to separate the good and bad; only at the end of time, when Christ returned and all things were set right, would the frauds be winnowed out.[7]

This was not a minor problem. It was a major difference, and from the North African turmoil would eventually spring inquisitions and heresy trials and English Puritans. And although the question was a theological one, it was not unaffected by politics. In a time of chaos, when what it meant to be a Roman was increasingly unclear, the Donatists insisted on creating an identity they could control and a community that was thoroughly well defined—without ambiguity, without uncertainty.

The political chaos only worsened over the next years. In 397, the North African province revolted. The leader of the revolt was Gildo, the Comes Africae—the officer in charge of the defense of the Roman territory in North Africa. Since North Africa was part of the western Roman empire, it belonged under the control of the young emperor Honorius and his guardian Stilicho. But the eunuch Eutropius, Stilicho's enemy and the power behind the eastern throne of the young emperor Arcadius, had convinced Gildo to repudiate his loyalty to Honorius. "He annexed it [instead] to the empire of Arcadius," writes Zosimus, "[and] Stilicho was in extreme displeasure at this, and knew not what course to pursue."[8]

The rebellion caused an immediate problem for Stilicho because the fertile fields of North Africa were the primary supplier of grain to the western part of the empire. Gildo's first move was to hold up the shipments of corn headed for Rome, which very quickly reduced the population of the city to hunger. In response, Stilicho convinced the Senate to declare a war against Gildo. Five thousand Roman soldiers, under the command of Gildo's own brother Mascezel, sailed to Africa to meet Gildo and his seventy thousand men. Mascezel had more than Rome to avenge; Gildo had murdered his two sons, Gildo's own nephews.

What could have been a bloodbath of Roman troops turned into a travesty. Mascezel, meeting one of Gildo's standard-bearers, slashed at the bearer's arm with his sword; the bearer dropped the standard, upon which all of Gildo's standard-bearers down the line assumed that surrender had been called and lowered their standards as well. The soldiers behind them surrendered at once. Mascezel declared victory with barely a death on either side. Gildo tried to flee, but when his ship was shoved back to African shores by the wind, he killed himself.

In declaring Stilicho an enemy of the east, Eutropius had won round one of the battle for power; now Stilicho, reclaiming Africa for the west, had won

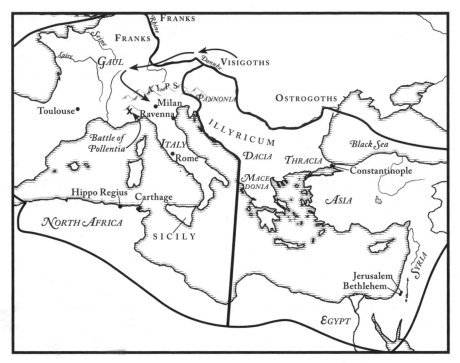

11.1: The Visigoth Invasion

round two. Eutropius's plot had failed, and this made him vulnerable. Soon, he went the same way as his dead predecessor Rufinus; the Goth general Gainas arrived at the court of Constantinople with his army, demanded that the emperor put Eutropius to death, and then took his place as the third puppet-master to control Arcadius. In less than a year, Gainas too lost his head, and another Goth soldier, named Fravitta, became Arcadius's consul and advisor.

Then yet another crisis struck Stilicho and Honorius in the west. In 400, the Visigoth king Alaric—still leading his new nation—invaded the north of Italy. The Visigoths came not just with their fighting men, but also with their women and children. They intended to settle. Alaric had a nation; now he was in search of a homeland.

The Visigoth invasion forced Honorius and his court to flee from Milan and take refuge in the city of Ravenna. Ravenna was ringed with swampland and relatively easy to defend, but it was an impossible place from which to launch a fight against the Visigoths. The western Roman empire was entrenching and shrinking. For two years, the Visigoths spread across the north of Italy.

Meanwhile, in the east, Arcadius had fathered a son: the future emperor

Theodosius II. It had become the custom for emperors to appoint their infant sons as co-emperors; that way, if the father died, a crowned emperor was already in place to succeed. But Arcadius was afraid that declaring his son his co-emperor would sign the child's death-warrant. Should Arcadius die—and Arcadius knew just how precarious his hold on life was—no one would protect his son's power. "Many would inevitably exploit the boy's isolation and make a bid for the Empire," writes the Roman historian Procopius, "and once they had attained it, they would easily usurp the throne and kill Theodosius II, who had no relative to be his guardian. He did not imagine that the divine Honorius would help, for things were now bad in Italy."[9]

Instead, Arcadius turned to the Persians. Persia had been at peace with the east since Stilicho's negotiations on behalf of Arcadius's father, twenty years earlier; the Persian king who had agreed to Stilicho's terms, Shapur III, had been succeeded by his younger son Yazdegerd I. Yazdegerd, says Procopius, "adopted and continued without interruption a policy of profound peace with the Romans."[10] So marked was the friendship Yazdegerd offered that Arcadius, who trusted no one within his own empire, asked Yazdegerd to act as guardian to his baby son.

"THINGS WERE BAD in Italy," Procopius had written, but they were about to get better. In 402, Stilicho managed to halt the Visigoth invasion. He met Alaric and his army on April 6, at the Battle of Pollentia, and defeated them.

It was not an entirely honorable victory; April 6 fell on Easter weekend, and Alaric, barbarian though he may have been, was a Christian who assumed that Easter was a sacred holiday on which fighting was banned. Stilicho, ignoring the prohibition, drew up his troops and (according to the poet Claudian) exhorted them by shouting, "Win a victory now and restore Rome to her former glory; the frame of empire is tottering; let your shoulders support it!"[11]

The fighting that followed was bloody and costly for both sides, but it ended when Stilicho's soldiers stormed into Alaric's camp and captured his wife. The two men negotiated a treaty that returned Alaric's wife to her husband and gave northern Italy back to Stilicho. Alaric retreated back across the Alps, still without a homeland.[12]

But despite the victory in Italy, the empire continued to totter. Roman Britannia was in serious trouble. When Magnus Maximus had crossed over into Gaul to claim the throne, he had taken the best part of the Roman army with him, and for years afterwards the remaining soldiers battled desperately against the "fierce peoples of Britain," invaders from the northern lands and from the sea. In 407, the remnants of the Roman army in Britannia, exasperated with the court politics in distant Ravenna, proclaimed one of their own generals emperor, as Constantine III. Like Maximus, Constantine III wasn't happy merely to be emperor in Britannia, which was still the Siberia of the Roman empire; he set out to conquer Gaul and Hispania as well.[13]

While Constantine III was heading eastward, Honorius made a sudden bid for independence. He was now twenty-three and presumably tired of having his life and his empire run for him by Stilicho. He had begun to hear rumors that Stilicho was planning a match between his own son and Honorius's sister Placida; raised by Stilicho and his wife after Theodosius's death, Placida was now eighteen. This sounded like a play for power: Stilicho might be resigned to never holding the title of emperor himself, but his son, with less Vandal blood and with a royal wife, might well ascend to the imperial throne.[14]

Honorius allowed himself to listen to the Roman officials at his court who accused Stilicho of planning treason; he arrested his former guardian, and on August 23 Stilicho, not yet fifty and with over thirty years of service to Rome behind him, was put to death at Ravenna.

With his formidable old opponent dead, Alaric the Visigoth immediately came back from his wanderings in central Europe and laid siege to the city of Rome. The Roman Senate tried to negotiate a peace, agreeing to pay him gold, silk, leather, and pepper if he would withdraw. Alaric took the ransom and withdrew, but he hadn't been merely seeking wealth. In 409, he sent a message to Honorius, threatening a second siege of Rome if Honorius didn't give him land in Illyricum for his Visigoths to settle on. Alaric was still in search of that elusive homeland.*

Honorius refused, and Alaric fulfilled his threat, marching straight back to Rome. This time the siege dragged on a little longer, until Rome was hungry, exhausted, and beginning to suffer from plague. Alaric refused to leave, promising that he would see the city starve to death unless he was given a place to settle.

No help came from Honorius, safely holed up in Ravenna. He had already received a message from the Roman soldiers left in Britannia after Constantine III's departure, begging for relief, and had sent them back a curt order to cope on their own. He had no soldiers to send either to Britannia or to Rome.

So the Roman Senate offered Alaric a deal. The Roman people would never accept Alaric as emperor, but the Senate would declare one of its own, the senior senator Attalus, to be emperor in place of Honorius. Alaric could then become his *magister militum*, his top military official; like Stilicho before him, he would become ruler in all but name.

---

*"Illyricum" was the name for the larger area in which the provinces of Pannonia, Dacia, Thracia, and Macedonia lay—the modern countries of Austria, Slovenia, Croatia, Bosnia and Herzegovina, Serbia, Bulgaria, Macedonia, and Albania.

To seal the deal, the Visigoths and the senators exchanged hostages, a strategy meant to ensure that each side kept its bargain for fear of its hostages losing their lives. One of the hostages sent by the Romans was a fourteen-year-old boy named Aetius, the son of a high Roman official; he would grow to adulthood among the Visigoths.[15]

Now there were three emperors in the west: Honorius in Ravenna, Attalus in Rome, and Constantine III in Gaul. Not long after, a Roman official in Hispania declared himself to be an emperor as well. Any hope that Christian faith would bind the whole disintegrating mess together had entirely disappeared. Conquest was the only hope that any of the four emperors had of reunifying the western empire.

Very soon, the cardboard emperor Attalus and his *magister militum* Alaric fell out with each other. When the Senate suggested putting a joint army of Visigoths and Romans under the command of a Visigoth officer, Attalus refused indignantly. He argued that putting a Visigoth commander in charge of Roman soldiers would be a disgrace. Incensed at this antibarbarian sentiment, Alaric ordered Attalus to meet him at Ariminum, on the northeastern Italian coast. There, he took Attalus's purple robe and diadem away by force and imprisoned him in his own camp.[16]

Alaric then marched back to Rome. In August of 410, he arrived at the city's gates and forced his way in without difficulty. He was angry; he had been trying for years to get recognition from the traditional leaders of Rome, some sort of admission that his skill and his power compensated for his barbarian ancestry, but the recognition always receded away from him. In his bitterness, he told his soldiers that they could plunder the city, taking by force what they had not been given by right. The Visigoths broke into treasuries, stole coins and riches, and set fire to whatever took their fancy (although Alaric told them to spare the churches). Alaric himself took Placida, Honorius's sister, as his personal captive.

The 410 incident became known as the Sack of Rome, even though it didn't destroy all that much of the city, and even though Rome had suffered much worse attacks. But for the far-flung citizens of the empire, both east and west, it served as a jolting revelation. The Eternal City, the Rome they had assumed would stand forever, was so diminished that a band of Visigoths could overrun it with almost no effort. No band of foreigners had entered the city for almost eight centuries, not since 387 BC, when the city was not yet part of an empire. Jerome, the young secretary to the bishop of Rome, was now a hermit in his fifties, living in the eastern empire near Bethlehem and still working on his translation of the Scriptures into Latin for the use of the west. "My voice sticks in my throat," he wrote later, recalling the dreadful news, "and sobs choke my utterance. The City which had taken the whole world was itself taken."[17]

In North Africa, Augustine too mourned. And in response to Rome's fall, he began to write his great work of history, the *City of God*. It was clear that Rome was no longer—if it had ever been—the Eternal City. It was merely an earthly kingdom that had served the purposes of God in its time, and its time was now past. But what of the bishop of Rome? Did the city's fall mean that the Christian church too would fade?

It took Augustine thirteen years to work out the answers. Once again he drew on the idea of double existence and dual authority. Rome, he wrote, was a city of man; and in all times, at all places, the cities of men exist side by side with the city of God, the true Eternal City, the unseen spiritual kingdom. Men choose which city they will occupy, and although the goals of the two cities may occasionally intersect (and their citizens may find themselves able to cooperate with each other), the ultimate purposes of their citizens diverge. The city of man seeks power; the citizens of God's city seek only the worship and glory of God. Rome had fallen, but the city of God would endure forever.

TIMELINE II		
ROMAN EMPIRE	VISIGOTHS	PERSIAN EMPIRE
Theodosius (378–395)		
Magnus Maximus (383–388)		Shapur III (383–388)
Theodosian Decrees		
Eugenius (392-394)		
The Battle of the Frigidus (394)		
Honorius (395–423) Arcadius (395–408)	Alaric (395–410)	
WESTERN EASTERN ROMAN EMPIRE ROMAN EMPIRE		
Augustine confirmed as bishop of Hippo (397)		Yazdegerd (399–421)
Battle of Pollentia (402)		
Constantine III (407–411) Attalus (409) The Sack of Rome (410)		

Chapter Twelve

One Nature versus Two

Between 408 and 431,
the Persian emperor makes himself unpopular
by protecting the eastern Roman throne,
and a quarrel over theology reveals deeper divisions

THE EASTERN ROMAN EMPEROR Arcadius had expected to die a violent death, but in the end illness brought him down. He died of natural causes in 408, leaving the crown of the eastern empire to his seven-year-old son, Theodosius II.

Thanks to the guardianship of the Persian king Yazdegerd I, Theodosius II ruled in peace. Yazdegerd took the job of preserving the little boy's power seriously. He provided an accomplished Persian tutor for the child; he sent the eastern Senate a letter detailing his intentions to keep Theodosius II safe; and he threatened war on anyone who attacked the eastern empire. "Yazdegerd reigned twenty-one years," the eastern Roman historian Agathias tells us, "during which time he never waged war against the Romans or harmed them in any other way, but his attitude was consistently peaceful and conciliatory."[1]

This attitude did him little good with his own people. The Persian noblemen at his court resented his peaceful policies. By extension, they also loathed his tolerance for Christianity within his domain; to them, Christianity was less a religion than a symbol of loyalty to the Romans. Yazdegerd earned praise from the Christian historians of the Roman empire, but the Persians gave him the nickname "Yazdegerd the Sinner," and he gets a universally black portrayal from Arab historians. The Muslim writer al-Tabari says, "His subjects could only preserve themselves from his harshness and the affliction of his tyranny . . . by holding fast to the good customs of the rulers before his period of power and to their noble characters."

In other words, the Persians looked back with longing at the good old days when they had fought the Romans for dominance. They resisted Yazdegerd's policies and his decrees until he was driven to more and more drastic enforce-

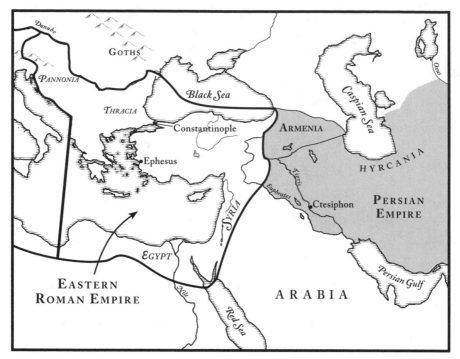

12.1: Persia and the Eastern Roman Empire

ment of his own orders. This only justified their bad opinion of him: "His bad nature and violent temper made him consider minor lapses as great sins and petty slips as enormities," al-Tabari writes, censoriously. [2]

Finally, Yazdegerd buckled. When an overzealous Christian priest in Ctesiphon tried to burn down the great Zoroastrian temple there, Yazdegerd sanctioned a full-fledged persecution of the Persian Christians.

This drove a wedge between Yazdegerd and the eastern Roman court—particularly Theodosius II's sister Pulcheria, two years older than the emperor and a devout Christian. At fifteen Pulcheria, already formidable, had talked the Roman Senate into naming her empress and co-ruler. In 420, when Pulcheria was twenty-one and Theodosius II was nineteen, she convinced him to declare war on his former guardian.[3]

Nor did the persecution do enough to mollify the Persian aristocracy. In 421, Yazdegerd died while travelling through Hyrcania, southeast of the Caspian Sea. The official story was that he had been struck by sudden illness, but an old Persian story suggests a more violent end: Yazdegerd was travelling when a spirit-horse rose from a nearby stream, killed him, and then disappeared back into the water. The horse was the symbol of Persian nobility; *something* undoubtedly was lying in wait for the king.[4]

The crown prince of Persia, raised by Yazdegerd to carry on his policies, was murdered by courtiers almost at once. The king's second son, Bahram, came from Arabia, where he had been exiled by his father, to be crowned Bahram V in his brother's place. Al-Tabari writes that when Bahram came into sight of the palace, Yazdegerd's former chancellor came out to greet him and was so awe-stricken at his handsomeness that he forgot to perform the ritual prostration with which Persians greeted their rulers: the story reflects the Persian belief in the Avesta, the divine "aura" of the appointed king, the "royal glory" that proved he had the right to hold power. Bahram's rule was legitimized, just as Theodosius's had been, by the will of the divine.[5]

Avoiding his father's mistakes, Bahram V carried on the persecution of Christians. He also mounted an aggressive defense against Theodosius II's declaration of war, assembling an army of forty thousand to march against the frontiers of the eastern Roman empire. It was a short war. Within a year, both Theodosius II and Bahram had decided it would be more prudent to swear a truce instead. Neither empire was dominant, and a war would be long and painful. Both sides agreed to refrain from building new frontier fortresses, and also to leave the Arab tribes on the edges of the desert alone (each empire had been actively wooing the loyalty of the Arab tribes, Persia with offers of friendship, the Romans with Christian missionaries).

"When they had concluded this," Procopius sums up, "each side attended to its own affairs."[6] For Theodosius II, this meant getting married to a wife chosen by his sister Pulcheria; all three, brother, sister, and wife, lived together in the royal palace.

Thanks to the Persian-enforced peace of his early years, Theodosius's court had now achieved the sort of stability that made the eastern Roman realm capable of functioning like an actual empire, rather than like a military encampment whose generals were busy killing each other (the current state of the western empire). Theodosius now had the luxury of actually ruling, instead of just fighting for survival. In 429, he appointed a commission to synthesize all the irregular and competing laws in his part of the empire into a single coherent law code, the Codex Theodosianus.* He took credit for the new walls that now protected Constantinople, the Theodosian Walls. And he founded a school in Constantinople for the study of law, Latin, Greek, medicine, philosophy, and other advanced subjects—a school that would eventually gain the name "University of Constantinople," making it one of the oldest universities in Europe.

This university was designed to take the place of the Roman university of

---

*It would be finished in 438 as the Codex Theodosianus, the basis for Justinian's law code; see chapter 28.

Athens, the last remaining bastion of the old state religion. The intellectual center of the empire had begun to shift to the east, a movement bolstered by the relative peace of the east and the chaos in the west. Furthermore, in the University of Constantinople, there were a total of thirteen "chairs," or faculty positions, for teachers of Latin, and fifteen for teachers of Greek—a small but significant gain in Greek language and philosophy over the Latin which, thanks to Jerome's translation of the Bible, continued to be used in the western part of the empire.[7]

In 431, Theodosius also had to deal with another theological controversy, one that came to full blaze at the Council of Ephesus.

Arianism (the doctrine that Christ was created by the Father, rather than coexisting with him from eternity) was still alive, but it had been shoved away from the core of the empire, towards its edges: it was the religion of barbarians, a sign of incomplete assimilation to the Roman identity. But the matter of Christ's exact nature was far from settled. Among those who were orthodox in their adherence to the Nicene Creed, a new division arose: given that Christ was God and also man, just how did these two natures *relate* to each other? There were two schools of thought. The first held that the two natures had become mystically one, united in the person of Christ in a way impossible to tease out by reason; the second, more rational school held that two separate natures, divine and human, were both present but separate, like two different colors of marbles in a jar.[8]

The assertion of a single nature became known as monophysitism, while the argument that Christ had two natures mixed together became known as Nestorianism, after Nestorius, bishop of Constantinople and its most ardent supporter.* Theodosius II himself was a Nestorian, but when the Council of Ephesus met to hash out the issue, it finally rejected Nestorianism and condemned Nestorius as a heretic. Theodosius II was forced to bow to pressure and exile Nestorius to an Egyptian monastery.

This was a defeat for him, and he felt it. The argument was not just theological hairsplitting. For one thing, there were always political dimensions to the theological debates. This particular controversy was partly about the power centers of the empire: the two-natures-mixed school of theology was centered in the city of Antioch while the more mystical one-nature school was centered in Alexandria. The influence and importance of these two cities were at stake. So was the relative power of ambitious men: Cyril, the bishop of Alexandria, was a one-nature man (as was the bishop of Rome), while

---

*The positions were also defined by the way in which they referred to Mary. If, in Jesus, God and man were mystically one, Mary was *theotokos*, the Mother of God; if the divine and human natures were mixed together, she was instead *christotokos*, the Mother of Christ.

the bishop of Constantinople, Nestorius, was a two-nature man. Nestorius's condemnation made clear that the bishop of Rome still sat at the top of the ecclesiastical heap.

Fear of Persian influence sharpened the argument further. Zoroastrianism, the religion of the Persians, was a monotheistic religion like Christianity; nevertheless it was the religion of the enemy, and the Christians of Rome and Alexandria were suspicious of any Christian doctrines that sounded a little too Zoroastrian. Since Zoroastrianism denied that there could ever be any mixing of divine and earthly substances, Nestorius's two-nature theology fit into the Persian schema in a way that the mystical one-nature theology never could. This tainted it further, in the eyes of the bishops farther from the border; they suspected that Nestorius had been influenced by Persian philosophies.[9]

But the theological debates over the nature of Christ's divinity cannot be reduced to politics or nationalism. They were the flashpoint of a bigger war, the symbol that two entirely different ways of thinking were about to come into full conflict.

The arguments over Christology were, in fact, not unlike the modern American debates about creationism. A whole complex of ideas is at stake in the defense of a literal creation: a worldview that has some room in it for the supernatural and inexplicable; the fear that conceding this point will lead to the destruction of a moral code; resentment over the superiority and condescension of what are seen as overeducated intellectuals. On the other side, the sharp rejection of *all* creationist assertions (one thinks of the rhetorical excesses of a Richard Dawkins or Sam Harris) also reveals fears: that accepting a mystical explanation of the earth's beginning will lead to the triumph of irrationality and violence; that concession will boost the earthly power of a particular political group.

And so it was in the fifth century as well. The men who quarrelled over Christology in Alexandria and Rome and Constantinople were also fighting over the place of mysticism and the power of rationalism, the fear of Persian influence and the rejection of all Persian culture—as well as the suspicion that one half of the empire might manage to gain political and practical power over another.

TIMELINE 12		
ROMAN EMPIRE	VISIGOTHS	PERSIAN EMPIRE
Eugenius (392–394) The Battle of the Frigidus (394) **Honorius** (395–423) **Arcadius** (395–408)	**Alaric** (395–410)	

WESTERN ROMAN EMPIRE	EASTERN ROMAN EMPIRE	
Augustine confirmed as bishop of Hippo (397)		**Yazdegerd** (399–421)
Battle of Pollentia (402)		
Constantine III (407–411) **Attalus** (409) The Sack of Rome (410)	**Theodosius II** (408–450)	
		Bahram V (421–438)
	Codex Theodosianus (429–438) Council of Ephesus (431)	

Chapter Thirteen

Seeking a Homeland

Between 410 and 418,
the Visigoths settle in southwestern Gaul

WITH ROME BEHIND THEM, Alaric and his Visigoth army headed south to attack Africa, taking their loot and their captives with them.

It was a short journey. Jordanes tells us that a sudden fierce storm wrecked the ships as they sailed from Sicily, forcing the Visigoths to retreat back into southern Italy. Alaric was deciding on his next course of action when he was struck by illness and suddenly died. His men diverted the path of the nearby river Busentus and "led a band of captives into the midst of its bed to dig out a place for his grave. In the depths of this pit they buried Alaric, together with many treasures, and then turned the waters back into their channel. And that none might ever know the place, they put to death all the diggers." The first king of the Visigoths had never gained the recognition he spent most of his life seeking, but at least he received a hero's burial.[1]

The Visigoth Ataulf became king in his place. Not long after Alaric's death, Ataulf married Placida, in a formal ceremony in a small city in northern Italy (the Visigoths had apparently given up their plan of crossing over to North Africa). He was, says Jordanes, "attracted by her nobility, beauty, and chaste purity." Whether this was a romance of captor and captive or a political move, the result was the same: "the Empire and the Goths," Jordanes concludes, "now seemed to be made one." Alaric's lifetime of fighting had failed either to overcome that persistent Roman identity or to merge his own with it; Ataulf's marriage, blending Visigoth blood with Roman, accomplished much more in a single stroke.[2]

Once married, Ataulf decided that Gaul would provide easier pickings than either southern Italy or North Africa. Gaul was in turmoil. It had been in the hands of the British pretender Constantine III, and while Ataulf was getting married in north Italy, the western emperor Honorius was sending an army over the Alps to get Gaul back. The reconquest succeeded almost at once. Constantine III's soldiers, once in Gaul, had begun to desert him in favor of

life in the countryside; his weakened troops fled in the face of the Roman soldiers, and Constantine III ran to the nearest church and had himself ordained
as a priest.[3]

This blatant attempt to shield himself with the cross was only temporarily
successful. Alaric had refused to burn the churches of Rome, and Honorius
(the nonbarbarian) could do no less. He spared Constantine III's life and
instead took him prisoner. While he was being brought back to Rome, however, an assassin murdered him, and his accomplices were, as Jordanes puts it,
"unexpectedly slain." The supposed unity between fellow Christians was not
strong enough to save the life of a challenger to the imperial throne.[4]

Ataulf's Visigoths inserted themselves into the middle of Gaul while Honorius was busy with Constantine III. By 413, they had conquered land in the
old Roman territory of Narbonensis, in southern Gaul, and Ataulf had made
the city of Toulouse into the capital of a small Visigothic kingdom. He had
finally found a possible homeland for Alaric's nation.

13.1: Visigoth Kingdom

But rather than establishing his kingdom as a Visigothic nation, Ataulf returned to the seductive idea of Roman rule. His marriage to Placida had given him visions of a world in which he controlled not just the ragtag Visigoths but the empire itself. He hoped, says the historian Orosius, to "seek for himself the glory of completely restoring and increasing the Roman name by the forces of the Goths, and to be held by posterity as the author of the restoration of Rome, since he had been unable to be its transformer."[5]

Attalus, the ex-emperor that Alaric had created and then stripped of his title, had been trailing around in the Visigothic army ever since. Now, Ataulf again crowned him, setting him up once more as a rival emperor to Honorius.

He would have done better to throw himself into building up the Visigoths. Honorius sent his right-hand general and *magister militum*, the Roman-born Constantius, against the new emperor. Constantius's army harassed the Visigoths, eventually capturing and beheading Attalus and reducing Ataulf's newborn kingdom to hunger and desperation. Resentment against Ataulf began to simmer among his own people. In 415, one of his own countrymen murdered him and claimed the position of Visigoth king, only to be killed in turn seven days later by another Visigoth warleader named Wallia.[6]

Wallia retrenched and sent word to Constantius that he was willing to make a deal. He would help the western Roman army in Hispania to fight against a coalition of Germanic tribes who had made their way onto the peninsula; and he would send Honorius's sister Placida, the young hostage Aetius (now nineteen), and the other captives taken in Rome, five years earlier, back to Ravenna. In exchange, he wanted southwestern Gaul for the Visigoths.

Honorius agreed to the treaty. After nearly two decades of wandering, the Visigoths finally had a homeland.

The freed captives were soon put back into the service of the state. In 417, two years after her return to Ravenna, Placida was ordered by her brother to marry his general Constantius, the man who had driven her first husband, Ataulf, into desperation and death. We do not know what she said; we do know that she obeyed him.

And in 418, Honorius sent Aetius off in another hostage exchange. The Huns, still hovering on the distant edges of the known world, had agreed to make a temporary peace. The treaty demanded that both sides provide guarantees of goodwill by sending young men to live at the enemy court. Honorius offered the Huns Aetius, who had been home for only a short time. In return, the Huns sent a relative of the Hun warleader Rua: Rua's nephew, a twelve-year-old boy named Attila.

TIMELINE 13		
ROMAN EMPIRE	VISIGOTHS	PERSIAN EMPIRE
Honorius (395–423) Arcadius (395–408)	Alaric (395–410)	
WESTERN ROMAN EMPIRE EASTERN ROMAN EMPIRE		
Augustine confirmed as bishop of Hippo (397)		Yazdegerd (399-421)
Battle of Pollentia (402)		
Constantine III (407–411) Theodosius II (408–450)		
Attalus (409)	Ataulf (410–415)	
The Sack of Rome (410)		
Attalus (415)	Wallia (415–419)	
		Bahram V (421–438)
Codex Theodosianus (429–438)		
Council of Ephesus (431)		

Chapter Fourteen

—

The Gupta Decline

Between 415 and 480,
the Gupta empire fades away,
while Theravada Buddhism encourages the pursuit
of individual enlightenment

WHEN THE INDIAN KING Chandragupta II died in 415, he left behind him an empire of internal contradictions. It was modelled on the ancient glories of Asoka but built on the armed conquests that Asoka had renounced. Sanskrit, the moribund language of nomadic invaders, had become its language of sophistication and education. It boasted a huge expanse, but in much of its territory the king ruled in name only.

To complicate these internal contradictions, an outside threat arose. During the thirty-nine-year reign of his son and successor Kumaragupta, the Hephthalites began to straggle down across the Kush mountains.

The Hephthalites were nomads from the wide steppes of central Asia. The Indians called them *hunas*, not because they were related to Huns in the west, but because the Indians used the general name "Huns" for all roaming nomadic groups north of the mountains.* Rather, the Hephthalites were most likely a branch of the Turkic peoples: Asian tribes that had long ago shared a common language, and began to spread out from their homeland in central Asia during the fifth century. They had been fighting off and on with the Persians for forty years already; the Armenian historian Faustos of Byzantium says that Shapur III fought against "the great king of the Kushans," his term for the Hephthalites.[1]

Roman historians say that the Hephthalites were quite different from other nomadic invaders: "They are ruled by one king," Procopius writes, "and have a lawful government and deal in an upright and just way with each other and with their neighbors, just like Romans and Persians." Later Arab geographers, putting the history of the Persians into the context of their own holy books, record a genealogical tradition that the Hephthalites were descended from Shem, the

---

*Many other sources refer to the Hephthalites as "White Huns," an equally inaccurate designation.

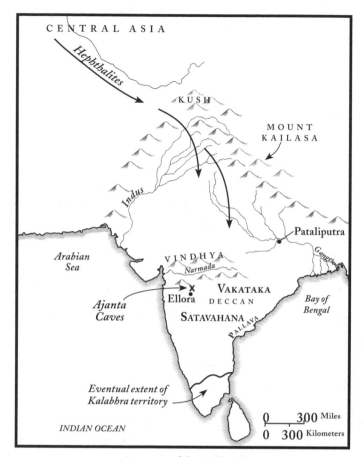

14.1: Invasion of the Hephthalites

son of Noah. But as far as the peoples of north India were concerned, they were simply *mleccha*, speakers of other tongues—barbarians in the classical sense.[2]

Kumaragupta drove them back, preserving the Gupta domain for the time being. Details of his other accomplishments are scarce, but one royal inscription boasts that his fame "tasted the waters of the four oceans." Another inscription lays out the extent of his empire. By 436, it stretched from Mount Kailasa on the north, to the forests on the slopes of the Vindhya Mountains in the south, and was bordered by the oceans on the east and west. This was the largest area that the Guptas ever claimed for their own; Kumaragupta brought the empire to its peak. Legends of his reign reflect his real conquests. He was "lord of the earth," with the "valour of a lion" and the "strength of a tiger," the "Moon in the firmament of the Gupta dynasty."[3]

But the end of his reign seems to have been clouded by troubles. Inscriptions mention fighting in the region called "Mekala"—the land of the Vakataka in the western Deccan, the peoples that Chandragupta II had folded into the Gupta empire by marriage. The new king of the Vakataka was Kumaragupta's own great-nephew, Narendrasena; he came into his throne at just about the time that Kumaragupta was at the height of his power. But despite his great-uncle's fame, Narendrasena rebelled.[4] The fighting seems to have taken place just as Kumaragupta was occupied with the Hephthalite invasions, and so Narendrasena was able to assert his independence.

From this point on, the Gupta fortunes began to decline. A hostile invasion came next: it is not completely clear who the invaders were, but a stone pillar inscription says that they "had great resources in men and money" and "threatened the Gupta kingdom with utter ruin." The fight against them, led by Kumaragupta's son and heir Skandagupta, was long and difficult. At one point Skandagupta was so bereft of men and supplies that he had to spend the night on the bare ground of a battlefield.[5]

Ultimately, the inscriptions tell us, the Guptas won the war against the invaders. But all was not well in the empire. Coins from the last years of Kumaragupta's reign are no longer made from silver or gold; instead they are made of copper, with a thin coating of silver concealing the inferior metal. The royal treasury had been thoroughly drained.

When Kumaragupta died in 455, Skandagupta inherited his troubles. He beat the Hephthalites off once again: "He destroyed at its roots the pride of his enemies," his victory inscription reads. But the battles had taken a heavy toll. In the years after Skandagupta's accession, events become increasingly muddled, but a hazy picture of increasing disorder emerges: poverty, quarrelling officials, rebellions of warlords and minor kings at the edges of the empire, constant war. Skandagupta fought for his entire reign, managing to keep the empire from disintegrating; through most of the 460s, victory inscriptions continue to appear throughout the old Gupta territory.[6]

The last of these inscriptions dates to 467. After that, the evidence is confused. It seems likely that Skandagupta died in this year and a war over the throne broke out, adding internal chaos to the chaos on the outside. First Skandagupta's brother and then a nephew claimed the throne. Ultimately the victor was a second nephew, Budhagupta. He held onto the Gupta throne for thirty years, but he was the last Gupta king to rule over anything that resembled an empire.

The Gupta attempt to hold together an empire of the mind had lasted only as long as no external threat approached. The Hephthalite attacks during the reigns of Kumaragupta and Skandagupta were serious, but they were hardly civilization-ending and not nearly as overwhelming as the Hun threat in the west. But turning to answer even a medium-sized crisis from the outside had strained the empire's cohesiveness to its limits. With the king's attention elsewhere, the states around the empire's edges—states that were receiving no real benefit from being part of the Gupta empire—immediately seized on the opportunity to declare themselves once again free.

In fact, it seems to have been the nature of Indian kingdoms to organize themselves as relatively small, independent entities with shifting borders. In the south, where the Gupta reach never extended, a multiplicity of dynasties claimed dominance over different parts of the subcontinent. Inscriptions and coins give us dozens of royal names, but no clear story emerges from the southern jostle. Towards the end of Budhagupta's reign, there was no political power that seemed capable of uniting even a small part of the subcontinent.

IT WAS A LOW TIME for empires, but a flourishing time for religion. Buddhist monuments known as "stupas" spread across the country, many carved with scenes of worshippers. In the west of India, a series of temples and monasteries were carved into natural chambers, with pillars and prayer rooms, corridors and staircases, rock-hollowed great halls for the use of those who pursued knowledge rather than political power. They were modelled after wooden buildings, with stone rafters and ribs upholding the domed ceilings sculpted into the rock. The largest series of these temples, the thirty or so caves known as the Ajanta Caves, had already been under construction for the last three hundred years, and work on them would continue for three hundred more.[7]

Twelve simpler caves had already been built in Ellora, barely fifty miles south. In this part of India, the Vakataka dominated, and the Vakataka king Harishena celebrated his victories by sponsoring the construction of at least two of these caves. Harishena, rising to the throne around 480 and overlapping the reign of Budhagupta to the north, had acquired a brief empire of his own, but his fleeting kingdom would not outlast his death.[8]

The intersection between Harishena's victories and the cave-temples was an aberration. Most of the caves were excavated simply to provide a place for worship, not to commemorate conquests. They had absolutely nothing to do with politics, and neither did the men who lived there.

Among the cave-temples were other networks of carved rooms: the *viharas*, monasteries complete with individual cells, common rooms, and refectories. Here the monks could devote themselves to the practice of their beliefs without distraction. They did not go into isolation; they lived in community themselves, and since they relied on lay people for clothing and food (items they could not acquire since they had renounced money), they also stayed in touch with the locals. But they took no part in the doings of the empire.[9]

By this time, Buddhism had branched into two major schools: the Theravada school and the Mahayana school. Both taught that all physical things were transient, and that only enlightenment—a "state of mind reached through moral conduct and meditation"—could reveal the world for what it is, an impermanent and unreal place. Theravada Buddhism, dominant in India, taught that reasoning, mindfulness, and concentration would lead the mind to enlightenment; in slight contrast, Mahayana Buddhism, which tended to dominate the Chinese experience, stressed prayer, faith, divine revelation, emotion.[10]

With its greater emphasis on reasoning and thought, Theravada Buddhism placed a higher value on the monastic existence, which allowed the believer to put all of his energies into study and meditation. Certainly Theravada Buddhism gave no help to an army officer or minor king who wanted to conquer an empire. It was diametrically opposed to earthly conquest, and rather than binding its adherents together under one flag, it encouraged them to live side by side while seeking individual enlightenment.

Which is exactly what the landscape of India in the fifth century reflected. Perhaps Theravada Buddhism helped to produce the patchwork profile of India; or perhaps the Indian patchwork made the country particularly suited to Theravada Buddhism. Either way, the result was the same. All across the Indian countryside, kingdoms existed side by side: each pursuing its own individual goals, none of them dominating the rest.

TIMELINE 14			
ROMAN EMPIRE	VISIGOTHS	PERSIAN EMPIRE	INDIA
			Chandragupta II (380–415)
		Shapur III (383–388)	
Honorius (395–423)	Alaric (395–410)		
WESTERN ROMAN EMPIRE Augustine confirmed as bishop of Hippo (397)		Yazdegerd (399–421)	
Battle of Pollentia (402)			
Constantine III (407–411) Attalus (409) The Sack of Rome (410)	Ataulf (410–415)		
Attalus (415)	Wallia (415–419)		Kumaragupta (415–455)
		Bahram V (421–438)	Hephthalite invasion Narendrasena of the Vakataka (c. 435–470)
			Skandagupta (455–467)
			Budhagupta (c. 467–497)
			Harishena of the Vakataka (480–515)

Chapter Fifteen

—∎—

Northern Ambitions

Between 420 and 464,
the Liu Song displace the Jin,
the Bei Wei of the north brew magic potions,
and the first state persecution of Buddhists begins

AFTER ITS EXILE to the south, the dynasty of the Jin barely lasted a century. In an attempt to keep a strong core of aristocratic support, the emperors had begun to grant tax relief, exemption from military service, and other advantages to the descendents of the oldest families that had fled from Luoyang. As a result, the noble families of southern China had developed a keen interest in genealogical tables called *jiapu*, which would demonstrate their right to claim these privileges. These tables were becoming more and more complex as the aristocratic families took more and more pride in tracing real physical connections to the past—something that the ex-nomads of the north would never be able to do.

Privilege led to power, and the power of the aristocrats finally brought an end to the Jin. The general Liu Yu, who had helped put down the pirates of the "demon armies" fifteen years earlier, managed to ingratiate himself with the landowning families whose estates had been threatened by piracy and pillage. He gained their loyalty and their support, and in 420 Liu Yu forced the Jin emperor, Jin Gongdi, to abdicate.

Like his predecessors, Liu Yu chose to make the abdication legal, rather than simply getting rid of the emperor; the myth of the Mandate demanded that he gain the throne by virtue, not force. He sent a letter to Jin Gongdi, ordering the emperor to make an edict proclaiming that since Liu Yu had preserved the empire, it was only just that its rule be handed over to him. His army, standing behind him, gave Jin Gongdi a good reason to comply. A ceremony in a building erected specially for this purpose sealed the transfer of power, and Jin Gongdi retired into private life.[1]

Now the general became emperor under the name Song Wudi, founder

15.1: The Liu Song and the Bei Wei

of a new dynasty: the Liu Song.* The Jin had ended. Now the two strongest powers in China were the Liu Song of the south and the Bei Wei—still one among several states—to the north.

Two years after his accession, Song Wudi removed the living memory of the previous dynasty. He ordered one of the court officials to poison Jin Gongdi, now in his late thirties and living peacefully in the capital city. The official, still loyal to the Jin family, wavered in indecision for some time; finally, deciding that the choice lay between killing the man he still thought of as the rightful king of his country and being put to death by Song Wudi for failing his commission, he drank the poison himself.

Song Wudi sent a second official with another dose of poison. When the deposed Jin Gongdi greeted him at the door, he saw at once what was hap-

---

*The Liu Song (also transliterated as plain Song and as Sung) ruled in the southeast from 420 to 479.

pening. But he refused to be poisoned, something that would have allowed Song Wudi to pretend that Jin Gongdi's death was natural. Instead, the official smothered him—which allowed Song Wudi to carry on the pretense almost as well. According to tradition, he met with his officials the next day to receive news of the death and wept copiously. Then he gave the murdered king a glorious royal funeral, with hundreds of mourners lamenting around the tomb.[2]

Wrapped in the mantle of legitimacy, Song Wudi now reigned as unquestioned emperor of the traditional Chinese realm. But he had been in his late fifties when he took power, and the year after he did away with Jin Gongdi, he took to his bed with his last illness. He passed his throne to his nineteen-year-old son, Shao, a wild teenager who ruled for a little over a year before the throne was taken by Song Wudi's second son (Shao's older half-brother), Song Wendi.

Song Wendi became king in 424 and held onto power for twenty-nine years, bringing the new dynasty to a brief high point. Known as the "Reign of Yuanjia," these twenty-nine years combined successful war (mostly against the nomadic Xiongnu tribes; Song Wendi led a three-year campaign that drove them to the west) and competent administration. In 439, the emperor established four Confucian colleges, each staffed by distinguished Confucian scholars, for the purpose of training the young men of his empire in the principles and precepts of Confucian literature—something that made them better officials and bureaucrats.[3]

Soon the Liu Song kingdom in the south had a northern counterpart. In 440, the Bei Wei king, Wei Taiwu, managed to conquer the remaining northern states to unify the north under his rule. The Bei Wei, which had existed as a kingdom since 386, would rule as a northern empire for the next century.

Now the split between north and south was complete.

THE BEI WEI, like the other northern kingdoms, was made up of people who had not long before been nomadic. Slowly, over the last century, they had begun to settle under a single king, to centralize, to develop laws and regular armies and diplomats. By the time the Bei Wei unified the north, the kingdom had already adopted many of the traditions and ways of the south. The king Wei Taiwu had a Chinese advisor, Cui Hao, who brought Chinese administration and Chinese law into the king's court and helped him to implement it. In their own eyes, the Bei Wei were mostly Chinese.[4]

But Wei Taiwu retained one bit of the nomadic tradition: like a warleader, he kept a harsh and autocratic hand on his people. He organized his kingdom into a strict hierarchy. The countryside was divided into communes, or *dang*, each one with its own administrator. Each *dang* was divided into five villages (*li*), with a leader in each village reporting to the *dang* administrator; each *li* was made up of five *lin*, or neighborhoods; each *lin* consisted of five families.[5]

To this tight structure, Wei Taiwu added something that was new in the north: a state religion.

He had been deeply influenced by his Chinese minister Cui Hao, who followed a weird and idiosyncratic version of Taoism. Classic Taoism taught nonaction, withdrawal from the world of strife and politics in order to focus on personal enlightenment. The mythical Seven Sages of the Bamboo Grove, a group of Taoist philosophers who were said to have lived in the previous century, were the model for perfect Taoist detachment: they "revered and exalted the void, and nonaction . . . drank wine to excess, and disregarded the affairs of this world, which seemed to them like duckweed."[6]

Originally, Taoism had not paid much attention to the afterlife; promises of immortality were not part of its philosophy. But some decades earlier, a Chinese philosopher named Ge Hong had begun to teach a new kind of Taoism. This Taoism encouraged its followers to seek enlightenment through magical elixirs that would lift the drinker to a higher spiritual level and—as a side effect—bring eternal youth. Ge Hong claimed that his family had received three texts from a divine being, the "Scriptures of the Elixirs" (or "Taiqing texts"), with instructions on how to create these magical potions. What earlier Taoists had achieved through philosophy, fifth-century Taoists could achieve with chemical aids; Ge Hong, the Timothy Leary of Chinese Taoism, had turned Taoism into something more like a cult than a philosophy.[7]

In 415, one of the chief teachers of this new kind of Taoism, Kou Qianzhi, left the mountain where he had been living as a hermit and came into the Bei Wei, ending up at Wei Taiwu's court. Wei Taiwu, already enamored with this new Taoism, welcomed him and built him a temple, putting him (and his disciples) up at taxpayers' expense. In 442, Kou Qianzhi gave the emperor a book of charms: "After this," the historian C. P. Fitzgerald writes, "every Emperor of the Wei dynasty used to proceed to the Taoist temple at his accession and obtain a charm book."[8] Taoism had become something completely new: a state religion that lent its magical powers to support the emperors and their claim to power.

Wei Taiwu's enthusiasm for his new religion led him to defend it with the sword. In 446, Wei Taiwu was forced to put down a rebellion led by a guerilla fighter who had stored weapons in Buddhist temples. Wei Taiwu was convinced that Buddhist priests had been part of the conspiracy to overthrow his magically confirmed reign. He began by outlawing the religion: "I am determined to destroy every trace of Buddhism from my kingdom," he announced, in an official edict declaring Buddhism anathema. "I have been appointed by Heaven to establish the right and to sweep away what is false."[9]

He then ordered his men to slaughter all of the Buddhist monks in the empire, starting in the capital Chang'an. The killings began; they were only mitigated, in part, by Wei Taiwu's son, the crown prince Huang. Huang was himself a Buddhist, and when he discovered that his father was about to issue the edict, he sent secret messages to all of the Buddhist priests he could reach, warning them to flee. Many of them did. But not all; many more were captured and put to death, and the Buddhist temples across the entire Bei Wei empire were reduced to rubble.

ONCE HE HAD PUT DOWN the rebellion and killed the (alleged) conspirators, Wei Taiwu suggested to Song Wendi of the Liu Song that the two Chinese empires make a permanent peace, sealed with a marriage alliance. In his own eyes, his empire was just as Chinese as the south. Song Wendi not only disagreed but was so insulted by the barbarian attempt to behave like an equal that he invaded the Bei Wei territory twice.[10]

The invasions damaged his own army and accomplished nothing. And despite its indignation over the barbarian presumption and its own claims to be a legitimate royal family, the Song was weakening while the Bei Wei prospered. Song Wendi's younger son Song Xiaowu became emperor in 454 and ruled for ten years; contemporary chroniclers pointed to his reign as a time when the Mandate began to fade. Song Xiaowu was frivolous and pleasure-centered. He preferred hunting to state business, and instead of addressing his officials and nobles of the court by their proper titles (something in which they placed great stock), he gave them undignified nicknames.

So shallow and worthless was he that when he died, ten years after his accession, his son and heir showed no grief upon hearing the news. His lack of proper sentiment shocked his ministers: "The dynasty will not be long before it perishes," they cried.[11] The natural affection between father and son had been warped; the natural order of things was twisted and distorted; the kingdom would soon follow the same path.

TIMELINE 15

INDIA	CHINA
	Fall of unified Jin (316) **Jin Yuandi** (317–323)
	Fu Jian of the Qianqin (357–385)
Chandragupta II (380–415)	Battle of the Fei River (382)
	Rise of Bei Wei (386) **Tuoba Gui** of the Bei Wei (386–409)
Kumaragupta (415–455)	
	Fall of Jin/Rise of Liu Song (420) **Song Wudi** (420-422) **Song Shao** (422-424)
Hephthalite invasion **Narendrasena** of the Vakataka (c. 435–470)	**Song Wendi** (424-453) **Wei Taiwu** of the Bei Wei (424–452) Establishment of Confucian colleges (439) Unification of the north under Bei Wei (440) First persecution of Buddhists in the north (446)
Skandagupta (455–467)	Song Xiaowu (454–464)
Budhagupta (c. 467–497)	
Harishena of the Vakataka (480–515)	

Chapter Sixteen

—•—

The Huns

Between 423 and 450,
the Vandals build a pirate kingdom in North Africa,
and the bishop of Rome becomes the pope
while Aetius takes control of the western empire
and the Huns approach its borders

WHILE THE EASTERN ROMAN EMPIRE hosted theological councils, the western empire struggled for survival. Britannia had been abandoned; under Wallia and his successor, the Visigoths prospered in southwestern Gaul, allies of Rome but a sovereign state in their own right; and despite the efforts of a combined Roman and Visigothic army, the Vandals had managed to take over much of Hispania, forming their own kingdom there and shaking off all Roman attempts to retake the former province.

The western emperor Honorius died in 423. After a scuffle for power that occupied the best part of a year, his nephew Valentinian III (six years old, son of Honorius's sister Placida and her second husband, the general Constantius) was crowned as emperor. Placida, the little boy's regent, was soon forced to appoint as *magister militum* the Roman soldier Aetius, the hostage who had been sent first to the Visigoths and then to the Huns.

Aetius had been returned by the Huns some time earlier, although we have no record of exactly when. But in his years with the Huns, he had developed a friendship with his hosts. After Honorius's death, Aetius—twenty-five years old, hardened by exile, and accustomed to tricky situations—made it clear to Placida that his Hun friends would descend on Ravenna unless he was given the highest military post in the west. Placida gave him both the title and the authority that went with it.

Meanwhile, another part of the western empire disappeared.

In 429, the king of the Vandals in Hispania, Geiseric, built a fleet of ships and sailed across the mouth of the Mediterranean Sea. He then began to march along the North African coast, conquering his way through Roman provinces and independent African kingdoms alike. By 430, he had reached the Roman city of Hippo Regius. His army laid siege to it while the elderly bishop Augustine lay inside, suffering from his final illness. The siege dragged on for eighteen months; the man who had written of the ultimate triumph of the kingdom of God died with Vandals still surrounding his city and no hope of relief.

When Hippo fell, Geiseric marched on to Carthage. It was defeated and overrun in 431; Geiseric lined up the Roman soldiers who had defended it, forced them to swear an oath that they would never again fight against a Vandal army, and then let them go. North Africa was lost to Rome.

Before long Geiseric decided to concentrate his energies on his North African holdings. He abandoned Hispania and ruled as a North African pirate-king, his headquarters at Carthage, master of a powerful Vandal kingdom that had sprung up as quickly as a mushroom.

Aetius, *magister militum* and now the most powerful man in the western empire, made no effort to fight for the Roman territories across the Mediterranean. He sent the nominal emperor Valentinian III off to visit Constantinople, where Valentinian (now nineteen) married his co-emperor's daughter, creating a blood alliance between the two halves of the empire. While the emperor was away, Aetius went to war in Gaul.

North Africa was lost, the Visigoths were firmly established in southwestern Gaul, and Hispania was too far to recapture; parts of it now fell into the hands of another Germanic tribe, the Suevi, and the Visigoths began to push their way into the land vacated by the Vandals. But Aetius had no intention of losing the land on his northwestern frontier as well. He had already put down a rebellion of the Germanic Franks who lived within the Roman borders as *foederati*; now he mustered his army and marched against the Burgundians, yet another Germanic tribe who had settled in the Rhine valley as *foederati*. Their king, Gundahar, had established his capital at Borbetomagus (later the city of Worms) and was showing worrying tendencies towards independence.

Aetius hired Hun mercenaries to fight with him against the Germanic upstarts. In a brutal battle in 437, the Romans and Huns together destroyed Borbetomagus, crushed the Burgundians, and killed Gundahar. The slaughter survived in the tales of the Germanic tribes, and came down into the *Nibelungenlied*, the Song of the Nibelungs; the Burgundian king Gundahar, whose name is rendered Gunther, welcomes the dragon-slayer Siegfried to his court at the epic's beginning, and at the end travels to the land of the Huns and is murdered by treachery.

Aetius had now used the Huns for years to establish his own power. But the Huns were not tame mercenaries, and Aetius was about to find himself the loser in his dangerous game.

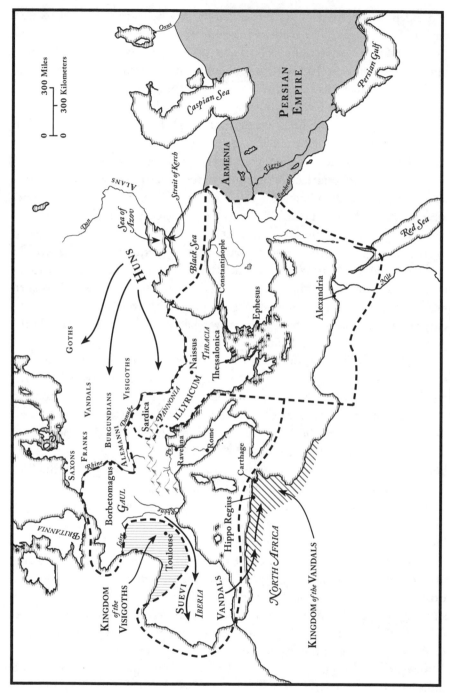

16.1: The Approach of the Huns

Up until this point, the Huns had not launched any sort of sustained assault on the Romans. Stories of their unearthly ferocity and strength had become a staple of Roman history: "They made their foes flee in horror," says Jordanes, "because . . . they had, if I may call it so, a sort of shapeless lump, not a head, with pin-holes rather than eyes."[1] But the Huns were not yet a great threat to the empire; Hun raids, when they troubled the borders, were damaging and scary, but the Huns always withdrew.

The Huns had not been able to sustain an attack because they had never been a single unified force. Like the Germanic barbarians, they were a coalition of tribes with no particular loyalty to each other. "They are not subject to the authority of any king," Ammianus Marcellinus writes, "but break through any obstacle in their path under the improvised command of their chief men." They did not plant or tend crops; instead, they drove cows, goats, and sheep in herds across the countryside, which meant that it took a lot of pasture to feed a group of Huns. So they had remained in small nomadic knots, easier to support, economically more stable than a massive monolithic force. They had no strategy for taking over the world. They were simply trying to survive.[2]

But even while Aetius was hiring those independent bands of Huns to fight for him, Hun society was changing. Over the preceding decades, they had made their way from the bare foraging ground east of the Black Sea, into the relatively rich and cultivated land of the Goths, land that allowed at least the possibility of feeding themselves in a new way and coalescing into a much larger group.

Sometime around 432, the warrior chief Rua—uncle of the young hostage Attila, who had been returned to his own tribe after spending some years at Ravenna—had managed to extend his power over Hun tribes unrelated to his own. By 434, Attila and his brother Bleda had succeeded their uncle as joint chiefs over an expanding Hun coalition. Six years later, Attila and Bleda led their combined Hun army in an attack on a Roman fort on the Danube. They continued to rampage up and down the Roman side of the river, flattening forts and towns, before they withdrew in 441 and agreed to negotiate a truce.[3]

For two years, the Huns kept the truce. Then, in 443, they headed for Constantinople with battering rams and siege towers. Theodosius II, evaluating the approaching force and deciding that it would be prudent to settle rather than fight, paid them off and agreed to a crippling yearly tribute. Once again the Huns retreated, and another temporary silence descended over them.

Not long after the retreat from Constantinople, Attila killed his brother Bleda and proclaimed himself the single, unopposed king of his people. In the breathing space provided by their truces with the eastern and western empires, the Huns were mutating from a loose coalition into a ruthless conquering horde. The Huns, wrote the exiled bishop Nestorius in his lengthy defense of his own beliefs (a book that touches only briefly on outside events), had been "divided into peoples" and were only robbers who "used not to do much wrong except through rapacity and speed." But now they were a kingdom: "very strong, so that they surpassed in their greatness all the forces of the Romans."[4]

WITH THE HUNS on their very doorstep, the emperors of eastern and western Rome occupied themselves with a quarrel over theological power.

In 444, the new bishop of Rome, Leo I, wrote an official letter to the bishop of Thessalonica, informing him in no uncertain terms that the bishop of Rome, as the heir of Peter, was the only churchman with the authority to make final decisions for the entire Christian church. The bishop of Thessalonica had, in Leo's view, overstepped himself by bringing another bishop up before the civil court in his province. No matter what the reason for this arraignment, Leo scolded, only Rome had the right to exert authority over other bishops:

> Even if he had committed some grave and intolerable misdemeanour, you should have waited for our opinion: so as to arrive at no decision by yourself until you knew our pleasure. . . . Though all priests have a common dignity, yet they have not uniform rank; inasmuch as even among the blessed Apostles, notwithstanding the similarity of their honourable estate, there was a certain distinction of power, and while the election of them all was equal, yet it was given to one to take the lead of the rest. From which model has arisen a distinction between bishops also . . . the care of the universal Church should converge towards Peter's one seat, and nothing anywhere should be separated from its Head.[5]

Leo did not depend only on this letter to establish his authority. He appealed to the throne, and in 445, Valentinian III (still dominated politically by his *magister militum* Aetius) agreed to make a formal official decree that recognized the bishop of Rome as the official head of the entire Christian church. Leo the Great, the bishop of Rome, had become the first pope.

His claim to imperially sanctioned power infuriated the bishop of Alexandria. The bishops of Rome and Alexandria had been allies at the 431 council in Ephesus, but since then, the power of Alexandria had grown. Now the bishop of Rome saw the current bishop of Alexandria, Dioscorus, as his primary competition both for theological power and for the ear of the emperor.

Dioscorus was just as suspicious of Leo the Great, and he tried to flex some theological muscle in return. Although both men were monophysites ("one-nature" supporters),* Dioscorus's version of monophysitism was more extreme than Leo's; he insisted that "the two natures of Christ became a single divine nature at the incarnation," an interpretation that almost veered back over into heresy again, since it tended to remove Christ's humanity from view.[6]

In 449, Dioscorus called a hasty church council in Ephesus and talked the bishops who were able to arrive on short notice into signing documents that affirmed *his* version of monophysitism as orthodox. According to later accounts, some of the bishops signed blank papers (the theological content was filled in later), while others who didn't sign simply found that their names mysteriously had appeared at the bottom of pro-monophysite statements. All of this earned the council the title "Robber Council," or the Latrocinium—a term condemning the council as illegitimate.† Dioscorus then wrapped up this performance by declaring the bishop of Constantinople a heretic and by excommunicating the absent bishop of Rome, a clear attempt to usurp the authority of Rome by transferring it to Alexandria. Leo I responded by excommunicating everyone who had been at the council.

Since they had all now excommunicated each other, the struggle for theological power appeared, temporarily, to be at an impasse. And at that moment, while the bishops were declaring each other to be anathema, two of Attila's lieutenants appeared in Constantinople, carrying a threat from their king.

The lieutenants were a mixed pair: one was a Hun, the other a Roman-born man of Germanic blood named Orestes. Their threat was couched in diplomatic terms. Attila accused the eastern empire of breaking the terms of its truce with him, and demanded that ambassadors ("of the highest rank") be sent to meet him at Sardica to resolve the issue.[7] Theodosius II and his advisors, meeting hastily together, organized a small party of ambassadors to travel back to Attila's headquarters. One member of the party, the historian Priscus, later wrote of the Roman journey into Hun-occupied territory. Passing the sacked city of Naissus, where Constantine the Great was born, they saw that it had been reduced to heaps of stones and rubble. So many bones of the dead city's defenders littered the ground that the party was unable to find a clear space to camp for the night.[8]

On the journey, the eastern Roman embassy found its paths intersecting with an embassy from Ravenna, also hoping to negotiate a peace with Attila. Together the representatives of both halves of the empire finally arrived at Attila's headquarters, on the other side of the Danube, a village he had built to be his temporary capital. Priscus was stunned by the workmanship: it was,

---

*Monophysitism held that Christ's divine and human natures were mystically united into an indivisible whole; see chapter 12.
†The same term was later used of Vatican II by some Catholics.

he says, more "like a great city" than a village, built of "wooden walls made of smooth-shining boards . . . dining halls of large extent and porticoes planned with great beauty, while the courtyard was bounded by so vast a circuit that its very size showed it was the royal palace."[9]

The negotiations were difficult; Attila did not intend to come to an easy peace. In the end, the western Roman party sent by Aetius saved the day. Aetius, who knew the Huns better than anyone else, had proposed terms that Attila was willing to accept. By the time the two embassies departed, Attilla had agreed to refrain from attacking either the eastern or western Roman kingdom.[10]

Into this temporary peace, a new complication suddenly intruded itself.

Down in Rome, the emperor Valentinian's sister Honoria had been living in the royal court for most of her life. In 449, she was thirty-one, and her life was growing ever more dull; she was unmarried, and although she had great privilege as the emperor's sister, his daughters were growing up and overshadowing her. The one bright spot in her life was her steward, Eugenius, who became her lover.[11]

16.1: A contemporary portrait of Attila the Hun.
Credit: Alinari/Art Resource, NY

But late in 449, her brother discovered the affair. To him, it seemed an act of treason; if Honoria married Eugenius, the pair could easily become emperor and empress, since Valentinian had no male heir. He arrested Eugenius, put him to death, and ordered his sister to marry a Roman senator named Herculanus, an older man who had a bone-deep loyalty to the emperor and could "be depended upon to resist if his wife attempted to draw him into ambitious or revolutionary schemes."[12]

Honoria was horrified. And so she sent one of her servants on the dangerous journey to Attila's camp, along with money, a ring, and a promise: if Attila would come and rescue her, she would marry him. "A shameful thing, indeed," sniffs Jordanes, "to get license for her passion at the cost of the public good."[13]

But Honoria wasn't indulging her passion for Attila, who (despite his undoubted charisma) was twelve years her senior and universally described as short, squat, small-eyed, and large-nosed. She had seen a way out of her gray and pointless life. If she were to marry Attila, *he* could become emperor of Rome, and she would be empress. And even if he failed to overcome her brother, she would still become queen of the Huns.

Attila at once accepted the offer. He sent a message not to Valentinian, but to Theodosius II—the senior and more powerful of the two emperors—demanding not only Honoria for his wife, but also half of the western Roman territory as her dowry. And Theodosius wrote at once to Valentinian, suggesting that he do as Attila demanded in order to avoid an invasion of the Huns.

Valentinian was apoplectic, both at his sister's plan and at Theodosius's suggestion. He tortured and beheaded the servant who had carried Honoria's message, and threatened violence to his sister as well, but his mother Placida (who had herself been married to the barbarian Ataulf) interceded and protected the princess. He also refused, flatly, to agree to Attila's demands.

It was at this delicate moment that Theodosius II, out riding—he was passionately fond of *tzukan*, an early form of polo, and had laid out a polo ground in Constantinople—fell from his horse and died.[14]

Like Valentinian II, he left no male heir; the most powerful personality in the east was his sister Pulcheria, his co-ruler and empress. Pulcheria chose a husband to help her remain empress: the soldier Marcian, who had been at Carthage when Geiseric took it from the Romans, eighteen years earlier. After swearing the required oath not to fight the Vandals any more, Marcian had been set free and had spent the next two decades rising through the ranks of the army. He had to agree, as a condition of the marriage, to maintain Pulcheria's virginity, which he did. (She was, in any case, fifty-one.)

Their first act as rulers of the east was to defy Attila, refusing to pay him the bribes that Theodosius had been shelling out to keep the Huns from attacking Constantinople. It was a gamble; Attila might turn and attack, but on the other hand, he had just been given the perfect excuse for invading Valentin-ian's domain instead.

The gamble succeeded. Attila assembled his army—the frightened resi-dents of the western empire insisted that he had half a million men at his command—and began to march west.

			TIMELINE 16				
	CHINA		WESTERN ROMAN EMPIRE	VANDALS	VISIGOTHS	HUNS	EASTERN ROMAN EMPIRE
	Tuoba Gui of the Bei Wei (386–409)						
			Honorius (395–423) Augustine confirmed as bishop of Hippo (397)				
			Battle of Pollentia (402)				
			Constantine III (407–411) Attalus (409) The Sack of Rome (410) Attalus (415)	Ataulf (410–415) Wallia (415–419)			Theodosius II (408–450)
Fall of Jin/Rise of Liu Song (420) Song Wudi (420–422) Song Shao (422–424) Song Wendi (424–453)	Wei Taiwu of the Bei Wei (424–452)		Valentinian III (423/425–455)				
			Vandal conquest of North Africa	Geiseric (428-477)		Rua (432–434) Bleda (434–445)/ Attila (434–453)	
Establishment of Confucian colleges (439)	Unification of the north under Bei Wei (440)		Pope Leo the Great (440/445–461)				
First persecution of Buddhists in the north (446)			Robber Council (449)				
							Marcian (450–457)
Song Xiaowu (454–464)							

Chapter Seventeen

—

Attila

Between 450 and 455,
Attila the Hun approaches Rome,
Pope Leo the Great negotiates a political peace,
and the Huns lose their chance at nationhood

RATHER THAN MARCHING straight across the difficult Alps directly towards Ravenna, Attila led his army towards Gaul. By April, he had reached the city of Metz, right in the center of the former Roman province, and captured it for his own. "They came to the town of Metz on Easter Eve," writes Gregory of Tours, "burned the town to the ground, slaughtered the populace with the sharp edge of their swords and killed the priests of the Lord in front of their holy altars."[1]

His territory now stretched almost from the Black Sea to the north of Italy, threatening both Roman capitals. The general Aetius, who for so long had controlled the affairs of the western empire, put together a coalition against him. The western Roman army was joined by the Visigoths of Hispania and southwestern Gaul, under their king Theodoric I, and Aetius also had a new ally: the tribe of the Salians.

The Salians were Franks, the strongest of the tribes who settled into northern Gaul as *foederati*. Now the chief of the Salians led the warriors of the entire Frankish coalition into the Roman camp to help fight against the Huns. He was one of the earliest "long-haired kings" of the Franks; the Salian chiefs wore their hair long to distinguish them from the ordinary Franks, to demonstrate their greater power.[2] The name of this chief is unknown, but later chroniclers would call him Merovech.

Aetius now had Visigoths, Franks, and Burgundians (the Germanic tribe in the Rhine valley, now in full submission to Rome) in his camp. The joint army of former barbarians and Roman soldiers marched towards the western Roman city of Orleans. In June of 451, they met the Huns in battle at Châlons-sur-Marne, halfway between Orleans and the Hun-occupied town of Metz.

Jordanes says that while the Huns put Attila and his strongest warriors in

17.1: Attila's Conquests

the center of their line, with the weaker and less reliable allies on each wing, Aetius and his Romans fought on one wing and Theodoric I and the Visigoths on the other, with the troops in whose loyalty they had "little confidence" in the middle, so that they could not easily flee in the midst of battle.[3] The strategy succeeded. The wings of the Hun attack disintegrated, and Attila was forced to retreat with his core of warriors back across the Rhine.

Gaul had been saved in an expensive victory. Over 150,000 soldiers fell in the battle; the chronicler Hydatius claims that 300,000 men died. The slaughter was so great, says Jordanes, that a brook flowing through the battlefield was swollen and "turned into a torrent by the increase of blood."[4] Theodoric I of the Visigoths had fallen in battle; his son Thorismund led the diminished Visigoths back to Toulouse kingless. The Franks limped home, their numbers slashed.

Attila, on the other side of the Rhine, kept track of the disbanding of the coalition. When the allies were safely away, he made a second attack: this one on Italy itself.

The attack began in early 452, and the north of Italy quickly fell to the Huns. Attila's army destroyed the city of Aquileia, sacked Milan and Ticinum, and laid waste to the countryside. Aetius's reduced army was not strong enough to meet him in full battle again. Instead, the Romans were forced to harass the Huns in small sorties, doing their best to slow the Hun advance.[5]

When Valentinian III left Ravenna with his court and went south to Rome for safety, it became clear that neither the emperor nor the *magister militum* had any chance of halting the Hun advance. So Leo the Great, bishop of Rome and the first pope of the Christian church, took matters into his own hands. He travelled north to intercede with the king of the Huns on his own. Attila agreed to see him, and the two men met at the Po river. Afterwards Leo never wrote or spoke of what had passed between them, but when the audience had ended, Attila had agreed to a peace.

To the terrified Romans (and perhaps to Aetius as well), Leo's success must have seemed like a magic spell. The historian Prosper of Aquitaine thought that Attila was overwhelmed by Leo's holiness; Paul the Deacon insisted that a huge supernatural warrior with a drawn sword, sort of a cross between "Mars and Saint Peter," stood beside Leo and terrified Attila into a truce.[6]

But hints of different motivations can be woven together into a less dramatic interpretation. For one thing, the Huns had lost as many warriors as their opponents; Attila's remaining army could ravage northern Italian towns, but a siege of Rome was probably out of his power. For another, the Huns were already fairly well loaded down with loot and were no longer as dead set on collecting further riches. And for a third, they were becoming very anxious to leave Italy. The summer heat had aggravated an episode of plague, and this "heaven-sent disaster" was decimating their already thinned ranks. Leo's approach gave Attila the chance to retreat with his dignity intact. He left Italy, still breathing fire, insisting that he would come storming back to the west if Valentinian III didn't send him Honoria: "seeming to regret the peace, and vexed at the cessation of war," Jordanes writes.[7]

Leo returned to Rome haloed with victory. For the first time in history, a bishop had taken on the emperor's job. Valentinian's decree, the six-year-old imperial pronouncement that made Leo head of the entire Christian church, had given the pope an extra dimension of power. He was the spiritual head of the church, but the spirit of the church could not survive if its adherents were wiped out. As spiritual leader, he could also claim the right to guarantee the church's physical survival.

Attila would never return to Italy. Back in his headquarters across the Danube, recovering his strength and rebuilding his army, he decided to marry. His choice was Ildico, the daughter of a Gothic chief. She was reportedly young and very beautiful, but the marriage also gave him a closer tie with the Gothic allies he needed to rebuild his weakened army. Attila was not averse to having more than one wife, but he had likely given up hope of gaining the title

"Western Roman Emperor" by way of marriage with Honoria. If he wanted Rome, he was going to have to fight for it.

He celebrated the wedding with an enormous feast, at which he gave himself up "to excessive joy," as Jordanes puts it; he probably drank an enormous amount before passing out in the bridal chamber. "As he lay on his back," Jordanes writes, repeating the lost account of the historian Priscus, "heavy with wine and sleep, a rush of superfluous blood, which would ordinarily have flowed from his nose, streamed in deadly course down his throat and killed him." When his attendants broke down the doors of his rooms, late the next morning, they found Attila dead in his bed and his bride weeping and covered with his blood. His officers buried him late at night, filling the grave with treasure and then (like Alaric's followers decades earlier) executing the gravediggers so that his burial place could never be found.[8]

Attila's sons tried to pick up his mantle, but with their leader dead, the Huns began to disintegrate. Like the Visigoths before Alaric, the Huns before Attila were not a nation. They were barely even a *people*: they were still, simply, a collection of tribes with a distant past in common and a charismatic leader.

Alaric had turned his followers into Visigoths; Attila had united his tribes into a single army of Huns. But when the ambition of a single leader was the driving force behind the emergence of a new people, the death of the leader could mean the death of a newborn national identity.

The Visigoths, perhaps through long association with the Romans, had picked up enough trappings of administration and bureaucracy to hold their confederation together until a new king emerged. The Huns were not so lucky. By 455, they had been thoroughly defeated. Driven back from the Roman borders, they scattered; their chance to become a nation had passed.

T I M E L I N E 1 7				
CHINA	WESTERN ROMAN EMPIRE	HUNS	VISIGOTHS	SALIAN FRANKS
	Tuoba Gui of the Bei Wei (386–409)			
	Honorius (395–423) Augustine confirmed as bishop of Hippo (397)			
	Battle of Pollentia (402)			
	Constantine III (407–411) **Attalus** (409) The Sack of Rome (410) **Attalus** (415)		**Ataulf** (410–415) **Wallia** (415–419)	
Fall of Jin/Rise of Liu Song (420) **Song Wudi** (420–422) **Song Shao** (422–424) **Song Wendi** (424–453)	Valentinian III (423/425–455)		**Theodoric I** (419–451)	
Wei Taiwu of the Bei Wei (424–452)		**Rua** (432–434) **Bleda** (434–445)/ **Attila** (434–453)		
Establishment of Confucian colleges (439) Unification of the north under Bei Wei (440)	Pope Leo the Great (440/445–461)			**Merovech** (?–c. 457)
First persecution of Buddhists in the north (446)				
Song Xiaowu (454–464)	Robber Council (449) Battle of Châlons- sur-Marne (451)	Disintegration of the Huns	**Thorismund** (451–453)	

Chapter Eighteen

Orthodoxy

Between 451 and 454,
both the eastern Roman emperor and the Persian emperor
try to control belief

T HE EASTERN HALF of the empire had not been unconcerned with the affairs in the western half. Attila's invasion, the rising power of the Vandal and Visigothic kingdoms, the rapid turnover in emperors: all of these had registered on the consciousness of the eastern Roman court.

Registered, but not dominated. The Roman court at Constantinople was preoccupied with its own difficulties. Nothing reveals the death of the common Roman cause like the relative prosperity and peace of the eastern Roman empire during the west's struggle for survival.

In fact, while Aetius and his allies were fighting desperately against the Huns in Gaul, the eastern Roman emperor Marcian was presiding over a church council. He had called this council to tackle, once again, the vexed problem of how Christ's two natures, the human and the divine, related to each other. The bishops of Rome and Alexandria were still excommunicated, the bishop of Constantinople had been declared a heretic, and Marcian hoped to straighten the situation out.

This desire was complicated by Marcian's tendency to agree with the bishop of Rome's theology. He wanted to support the power of the bishops in his own part of the empire, but Leo's expression of the relationship between the two natures was much more attractive to him. In Christ, Leo had written, the human and divine natures remained distinct: "not divided in essence, but . . . both natures retain their own proper character without loss. . . . For each form does what is proper to it with the co-operation of the other; that is the Word performing what appertains to the Word, and the flesh carrying out what appertains to the flesh."[1]

It was this formulation that Marcian found closest to his own conviction, and little wonder: Leo had neatly encapsulated the double identity that lay at the core of the empire's existence. It was the same capacity to hold two things together in one that had attracted Constantine back at the Battle of the Milvian Bridge.

But Marcian had to promote Leo's doctrine without admitting Leo's claim to ultimate spiritual power, something the emperor wanted to keep for his own city; Constantinople had to remain equal to Rome. So when he called the church council in 451, he refused to hold it in Italy as Leo suggested. He announced that instead it would be at the city of Chalcedon, right across the water from Constantinople. This was a little too far for Leo to come, particularly since he did not wish to leave the church of Rome leaderless during a Hun invasion; so the bishop of Rome sent several churchmen to be his representatives, along with his own written statement detailing the exact relationship of the two natures.

In Leo's view, the council could be a short one. His delegates should read his statement, and then, "Peter having spoken, no further discussion should be allowed or required." But under Marcian's direction, the bishops instead agreed that the statement was in line with what they had already decided, on their own authority. They also agreed (again prompted by Marcian) that the bishop of Constantinople, while perhaps second to the bishop of Rome himself, nevertheless had more authority than any other bishop. He was not merely a bishop, but a patriarch: a churchman with authority over *other* bishops.[2]

This produced a series of letters between Leo, Marcian, and the eastern bishops in which Leo complained that the east wasn't paying enough attention to his authority and Marcian and the bishops told Leo to mind his own business, with all of this jockeying for position framed in flowery sacred language. "The See of Constantinople shall take precedence," the bishops wrote to Leo. "We are persuaded that, with your usual care for others, you have extended that apostolic prestige which belongs to you to the church in Constantinople, by virtue of your great disinterestedness in sharing all your own good things with your spiritual kinsfolk. But your holiness's delegates attempted vehemently to resist this decision." "I am surprised and grieved that the peace of the universal Church which had been divinely restored is again being disturbed by a spirit of self-seeking," Leo wrote back to Marcian. "Let the city of Constantinople have its high rank and long enjoy your rule. But secular things stand on a different basis from things divine. Anatolius [the bishop of Constantinople] cannot make it an Apostolic See." Hedging his bets, he also wrote to Pulcheria, the emperor's wife: "Anatolius has been inflamed with undue desires and intemperate self-seeking," he complained. "By the blessed Apostle Peter's authority, we do not recognize the bishops' assent [to Constantinople's exaltation]." And to the bishop of Constantinople himself, Leo wrote, "You went so far beyond yourself as to drag in an occasion

18.1: The Battle of Vartanantz

of self-seeking. This haughty arrogance tends to the disturbance of the whole Church!"³

None of this was as bloody as the battles going on in Gaul between Aetius's army and the Huns, but the issue was not all that different. It was an argument over territory, over authority, over legitimacy: a battle for a spiritual crown, but a crown nonetheless.

Leo's protests got him nowhere; the emperor continued to insist on the prestige and independence of the bishop of Constantinople, and the Council of Chalcedon closed on that note. The eastern Roman empire had taken an additional step away from Rome.

The aftereffects of the council would ripple on through the eastern kingdom for years to come. Down in Egypt, resentment ran strong over the demotion of the bishop of Alexandria to a place below the bishop of Constantinople; the resentment continued in a strong underground current that would only grow more destructive. And now that the Council of Chalcedon had confirmed as orthodoxy that Christ's two natures were separate but indivisible, many Christians who disagreed with this formulation began to migrate over into Persia—where they were welcomed by the Persian emperor Yazdegerd II (son of Bahram V, who had died in 438).*

---

*Many of the Christians who went to Persia were Nestorians, who believed that the Council of Chalcedon had not made enough distinction between Christ's two natures. Ultimately, the difference in doctrine would split the Christians of Persia decisively away from both Rome and Constantinople; the branch of Nestorian Christianity thus formed would be known as the Syrian Orthodox Church.

DESPITE HIS WILLINGNESS to disaccommodate Marcian by accepting his refugees, Yazdegerd II was no friend of Christianity. In fact, he had not long before imposed his own sort of orthodoxy: rather than doing this through council, as Marcian had, Yazdegerd simply decreed that Zoroastrianism would be followed in all parts of his empire, including the Persian half of Armenia, which up until this point had remained Christian. The decree is recorded by the Christian Armenian historian Yegishe, who heard it with his own ears. "He alleged that we, the believers in Christ, were his opponents and enemies," Yegishe writes, "and commanded, 'All peoples and tongues throughout my dominions shall abandon their false religions and shall come to worship the sun.' "[4]

Like Marcian, Yazdegerd II had both political and theological motivations. He was devout in his faith, but the decree was motivated more by a desire to root out any sympathy with the eastern Romans—particularly in the less reliably loyal parts of his empire. The Armenians saw the decree both as an abridgment of their freedoms (which it was) and as religious persecution, and refused to give up their Christian faith.

Yazdegerd reacted with force. In 451, the same year as the Council of Chalcedon, he marched into Armenia. Sixty-six thousand Armenians gathered behind their great general Vartan, ready to go into battle as martyrs.

In the fight that followed, the Battle of Vartanantz, Vartan was killed, and both sides suffered heavy losses: "Consciousness of defeat came to both sides," Yegishe says, "because the piles of the fallen bodies were so thick that they looked like craggy masses of stone."[5] Ultimately the Persians were victorious over the smaller Armenian army; Yazdegerd II imprisoned and tortured the surviving leaders and reduced Armenia to a Persian territory, putting a new governor in charge of the country. Meanwhile, Yazdegerd II took preventative measures against other possible dissidents; in 454, he began to enact a series of decrees that kept the Jews in Persia from observing the Sabbath and eventually from educating their children in Jewish schools.[6]

Both emperors were still operating under the belief that one set of religious beliefs would make their empires stronger; that orthodoxy, the enforcement of a single theology and religious practice, would bind the territory together. But in both Persia and the eastern empire, the discontent was merely driven out of sight, where it spread beneath the surface like groundwater.

TIMELINE 18					
WESTERN ROMAN EMPIRE	HUNS	VISIGOTHS	SALIAN FRANKS	EASTERN ROMAN EMPIRE	PERSIAN EMPIRE
Constantine III (407–411)				**Theodosius II** (408–450)	
Attalus (409)					
The Sack of Rome (410)		**Ataulf** (410–415)			
Attalus (415)		**Wallia** (415–419)			
		Theodoric I (419–451)			
Valentinian III (423/425–455)					**Bahram V** (421–438)
	Rua (432–434)				
	Bleda (434–445)/				
	Attila (434–453)				
Pope Leo the Great (440/445–461)			**Merovech** (?–c. 457)		**Yazdegerd II** (438–457)
Robber Council (449)				**Marcian** (450–457)	
Battle of Châlons-sur-Marne (451)		**Thorismund** (451–453)		Council of Chalcedon (451)	Battle of Vartanantz (451)
		Disintegration of the Huns			

Chapter Nineteen

— ◼ —

The High Kings

Between 451 and 470,
Ireland falls under the domination of the Ui Neill,
Patrick brings Christianity to the island,
and Vortigern invites the Angles and the Saxons to Britain

P AST THE BATTLEFIELDS of Gaul, across the water from the growing power of the Visigoths in Hispania, far away from the western throne, the islands of Britain were piecing together their own identity.

The western island of Ireland, never occupied by Roman soldiers or crisscrossed with Roman roads, was taking its own winding path towards nationhood. Like the tribes that surrounded the Roman empire, the peoples of Ireland were a collection of tribes and clans, each boasting a certain local power and led by a warlord and his family. But even without Roman conquest, the Irish tribes were not free from Roman influence. In 451, the strongest tribe in Ireland was the Venii, or Feni, and the strongest clan of the Feni was the Connachta. The leader of the Connachta family was named Niall of the Nine Hostages, and his mother was Roman; Niall's father, Eochaidh, had captured a Roman girl during a raid on Britannia and made her his concubine.[1]

Niall, the youngest son in his family, became clan leader after his father's death. The chronicles of Irish history, most of which come from centuries later, weave his exploits into legend and combine them with the accomplishments of other Irish kings, making it difficult to sift out exactly what Niall accomplished.

But one of the tales hints at a very bloody rise to power. According to "The Adventures of the Sons of Eochaid Mugmedon," Eochaidh sends Niall and his four older brothers (all sons of his father's legitimate wife, unlike Niall) on a quest to determine which one of them deserved to inherit his power. On their journey, the sons grow thirsty and go in search of water. They find a well, but a horrible hag guards it:

[E]very joint and limb of her, from the top of her head to the earth, was as black as coal. Like the tail of a wild horse was the gray bristly mane that came through the upper part of her head-crown. The green branch of an oak in bearing would be severed by the sickle of green teeth that lay in her head and reached to her ears. Dark smoky eyes she had: a nose crooked and hollow. She had a middle fibrous, spotted with pustules, diseased, and shins distorted and awry. Her ankles were thick, her shoulder blades were broad, her knees were big, and her nails were green.[2]

The hag demands that the brothers trade sex for access to the well. The four older brothers refuse, but Niall throws himself enthusiastically on her, ready to sleep with her for the sake of the water. Immediately she transforms into a beautiful maiden in a royal purple cloak. "I am the Sovereignty of Erin," she tells him, "and as you have seen me, loathsome, bestial, horrible at first and beautiful at last, so is the sovereignty; for seldom it is gained without battles and conflicts; but at last to anyone it is beautiful and goodly."[3]

In the tale, Niall's brothers then acclaim him as family leader of their own free will. But Niall's rise, first to power over his clan and then to the kingship of the Feni tribe, was undoubtedly accompanied with violence, forced possession, and bloodshed: bestial and horrible. Only with the crown in one hand and his sword in the other could he claim the beauty of legitimate kingship.

Over the decades of his reign, Niall expanded his power over the Feni into one of the first exercises of high kingship: control over the other minor kings of Ireland, over the other tribes. He earned the nickname "Niall of the Nine Hostages" by taking prisoners from nine of the tribes that lay around him, guaranteeing the loyalty of their tribal leaders. With Ireland more or less united under his rule, he then launched raids on the coasts of Gaul and Britain.

During one of these raids, he captured a Romanized Briton named Patricius and took him back to Ireland as a slave, where Patricius served for six years before stowing away on an Irish raiding ship and escaping into Gaul when it docked. There, he was converted to Christianity and had a vision calling him to return to the land of his slavery and teach the Irish of Christ.

This much we learn from Patricius's own writings, his *Confessio*. By the time he arrived back at the high king's court, Niall of the Nine Hostages had died in battle (either in Britain or in Gaul), and his own sons were battling over his kingdom. While interfamily warfare went on around him, Patricius devoted himself to the spread of Christianity, so successfully that Ireland became Christian long before the British island to the east. Later Christian historians knew him as Saint Patrick, the apostle to the Irish, and credited him with driving the snakes out of Ireland.

In fact, there had been no snakes in Ireland since the end of the Ice Age

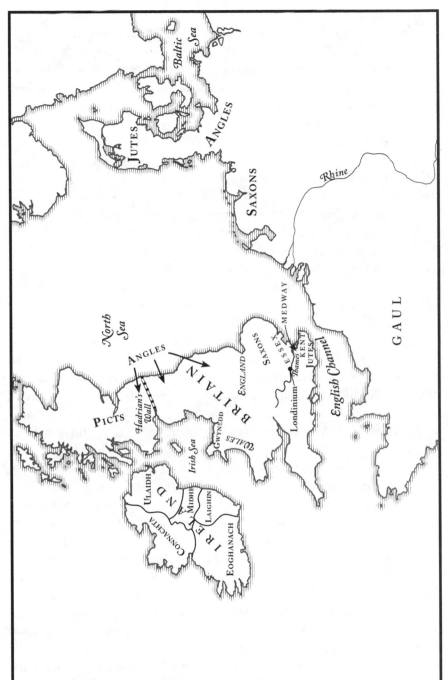

19.1: Ireland and Britain

("No reptile is found there," writes the English church historian Bede, " for although serpents have often been brought from Britain, as soon as the ship approaches land they are affected by the scent of the air and quickly perish"), but for the Christian writer a snake was much more than a snake: Satan had taken the shape of a snake in the Garden of Eden, and serpents (which were sacred to the druids, the practitioners of the indigenous religion of Ireland) symbolized the powers of darkness that were opposed to the Gospel of Christ. The new faith was slowly supplanting the old.[4]

By the time of Patricius's death, sometime before 493, three sons of Niall held power over three kingdoms in the northern half of the island: Midhe, where the ancient city of Tara lay; Ulaidh; and Connachta, the original homeland of the clan. Their descendents would rule as the Ui Neill dynasty for six hundred years, but their influence would stretch far, far beyond the Middle Ages. Niall's particular Y chromosome shows up in as many as three million men worldwide; his sons and their randy offspring managed to sire so many children that one in twelve Irishmen (one in five in the part of Ireland that was once Connachta) can claim Niall of the Nine Hostages as their ancestor.[5]

Despite their dominance, the Ui Neill did not conquer the whole island. In the southwest of Ireland, the clan of the Eoghanach still ruled, resisting the spread of Feni power. To the southeast, the Laighin tribe held onto its land as well. But some of the Laighin left, in the face of ongoing attack from Niall's descendents, and settled on the coast of Britain, in the area that became Wales. There, in flight from the high king of Ireland, they came into direct conflict with the high king of Britain.[6]

This high king was, so far as we can tell, a man named Vortigern, who by 455 had the unenviable task of defending Britain from invaders determined to take the island for their own. Roman Britain, more or less abandoned by its occupiers after the departure of Constantine III in 410, was now a collection of local warlords—mostly Romanized Celt or Celticized Roman—along with a few Saxon settlements which the Romans had allowed along the coast. Raids from Irish pirates, the Scoti, had grown more vicious under the dominance of the Ui Neill: in the vivid words of the sixth-century historian Gildas, the Irish raiders emerged from their ships "like dark throngs of worms who wriggle out of narrow fissures in the rock when the sun is high and the weather grows warm." The northern Picts, meanwhile, were launching ever more vicious attacks down across Hadrian's Wall, aiming to grab the north for their own.[7]

In the face of all this chaos, the minor kings and tribal chiefs of Britain gathered together in council, in which they elected the northern king Vortigern as their warleader. Vortigern sent one of those chiefs, a British warlord named Cunedda, to drive the Laighin out of their new home; Cunedda, his eight sons, and his soldiers did so and founded a kingdom of their own, Gwynedd, in the conquered land.

Vortigern also sent a letter to the Roman *magister militum* Aetius, begging for help against the Picts. But it went unanswered.

In desperation, Vortigern suggested that the remaining British soldiers bolster their ranks with Saxon allies; the British could allow more Saxon settlements in the south (particularly in Essex and in Kent, on the southeastern coast) in exchange for tribute warriors who would help them to fight against the Picts and the Irish. The other chiefs agreed, and so Vortigern sent messages not only to the Saxons on the distant North Sea coast just west of modern Denmark, but also to their allies the Angles, who lived just northeast of the Saxons, on the dividing line between modern Germany and Denmark. This strategy, undertaken in desperation, earned him the hatred of later historians: "They devised for our land," froths Gildas, "that the ferocious Saxons (name not to be spoken!), hated by man and God, should be let into the island like wolves into the fold, to beat back the peoples of the north. . . . How utter the blindness of their minds! How desperate and crass the stupidity!"[8]

But at first the strategy seemed to be working. The Angles and the Saxons accepted the invitation, and around 445 they sailed across the water to join the British in their fight against the Picts. "They fought against the enemy who attacked from the north," Bede writes, "and the Saxons won the victory." In return, Vortigern granted the allies settlement rights in Kent; or, as the inexorably hostile Gildas puts it, the newcomers "fixed their dreadful claws on the east side of the island, ostensibly to fight for our country, in fact to fight against it."[9]

The Saxons and Angles, once established in the green land of Kent, did not stay nicely in the granted land; they had ambitions to spread farther. In a matter of months, new shiploads of their countrymen (along with the Jutes, allies of the Angles who lived on the Danish peninsula just north of them) were arriving on the southeastern shores in longships. "They were full of armed warriors," the British historian Geoffrey of Monmouth says, "men of huge stature." Vortigern had crushed the northern menace, and in doing so had created a southern invasion.[10]

Led by two Saxon brothers named Hengest and Horsa, the Jutes occupied the southern coast, the Saxons moved from Kent farther inland, to the south and southwest of Londinium, and the Angles invaded the southeastern coast just above the Thames. Destruction reigned. "All the major towns were laid low," Gildas mourns. "In the middle of the squares the foundation-stones of high walls and towns that had been torn from their lofty base, holy altars, fragments of corpses, covered (as it were) with a purple crust of congealed blood, looked as though they had been mixed up in some general wine press. There was no burial to be had except in the ruins of houses or the bellies of beasts and birds."[11]

The British tribes, allied behind Vortigern, spent six years fighting fruitlessly against this overwhelming influx. The invaders seemed unstoppable, so fierce that the monk Nennius, writing his *History of the Britons* several centuries later, ascribes magical malice to them. Vortigern, he insists, was unable to build a fortress that would withstand them until his court magicians told him that he would need to find a child born without a father, sacrifice him, and sprinkle his blood over the foundations.

This echo of a druidic ritual suggests that the British were driven to drastic and ancient strategies in desperate defense of their country. But Nennius, a Christian priest constructing a Christian history, adds that the sacrifice never actually happened. Instead, the child, once discovered, showed Vortigern a pool beneath his proposed foundations in which two serpents, one white and one red, slept. "The red serpent is your dragon," he told Vortigern, "but the white serpent is the dragon of the people who occupy Britain from sea to sea; at length, however, our people shall rise and drive away the Saxon race from beyond the sea."[12]

This after-the-fact prophecy was not entirely fulfilled. In 455, Vortigern finally managed to defeat the invaders in a pitched battle at the fords of the Medway river, in Kent.

The *Anglo-Saxon Chronicle* says that Horsa was killed in the fighting. The loss of one of their chiefs forced the invaders to regroup, and for a few brief moments Vortigern must have had wild hopes of victory. But Horsa's son took up his father's mantle, and the balance tipped back. For the next fifteen years, war continued, each year seeing a new and violent conflict between Vortigern, his men, and the newcomers, neither side gaining the advantage, neither willing to come to terms.[13]

TIMELINE 19			
EASTERN ROMAN EMPIRE	PERSIAN EMPIRE	IRELAND	BRITAIN
		Niall of the Nine Hostages (c. 390–c. 455)	
Arcadius (395–408)	**Yazdegerd I** (399–421)		
Theodosius II (408–450)			Departure of **Constantine III** (410)
	Bahram V (421–438)	Patricius returns to Ireland	
	Yazdegerd II (438–457)		
Marcian (450–457) Council of Chalcedon (451)	Battle of Vartanantz (451)		**Vortigern** (450s?) **Cunedda** of Gwynedd (c. 455–c. 460) Invasion of Hengest and Horsa

Chapter Twenty

The End of the Roman Myth

Between 454 and 476,
the Vandals sack Rome,
and the last emperor leaves Ravenna

AETIUS HAD NOT ANSWERED Vortigern's plea for help because he had troubles of his own.

Sentiment against his domination of the western empire had been growing, and the Hun invasion of Italy had given him a black eye. He had powerful enemies at court—most notably Petronius Maximus, a Roman senator who had been prefect of Rome twice. In 454, Aetius made a final misstep when he arranged the engagement of his son to Valentinian III's daughter. It was a clear attempt to put his family in line for the western throne.

Valentinian III, still only thirty-six, had been emperor of Rome for thirty years but had always ruled in the shadow of his general. He had lost much of his empire; Hispania and much of Gaul were gone to the Suevi and the Visigoths, and North Africa to the Vandals, who under their great king Geiseric had already taken Sicily and were eyeing Italy itself. Huns had stormed through Italy almost without check, and the bishop of Rome had done Valentinian's job while he cowered. It was easy for Petronius Maximus to convince the emperor to focus his discontent on Aetius. "The affairs of the western Romans were in confusion," writes the historian John of Antioch, "and Maximus . . . persuaded the emperor that unless he quickly slew Aetius, he would be slain by him."[1]

In 455, Valentinian III was in Ravenna when Aetius came to court on a routine visit to discuss tax collection. He was standing in front of Valentinian III, absorbed in presenting the difficulties of raising money, when Valentinian III leaped up from his seat, shouting that he would no longer put up with treachery, and swung his sword against Aetius's head. The great general died on the floor of the throne room while the stunned courtiers watched.

John of Antioch says that Valentinian then turned in satisfaction to one

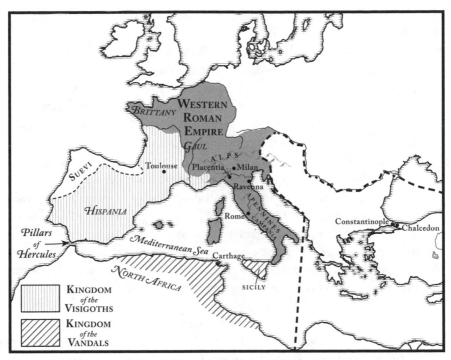

20.1: The Collapse of the Western Roman Empire

of his officers and said, "Was not the death of Aetius well accomplished?" The officer answered, "Whether well or not I do not know, but I do know that you have cut off your right hand with your left." And so it proved. In killing the man who prevented him from claiming full power, Valentinian had destroyed his only chances of retaining any power at all. Just weeks later, Petronius Maximus convinced two old army cronies of Aetius's to assassinate the emperor as he practiced archery in the Campus Martius. They stole the dead man's crown, and fled with it to Petronius Maximus—who took it and declared himself emperor.[2]

Thus began a seven-year cycle of death and destruction. Petronius Maximus tried to head off the Vandals by sending the retired prefect of Gaul, a native of Gaul named Avitus who was living peacefully on his own Gaulish estates, to negotiate an alliance with the Visigoth king at Toulouse. But Avitus had not yet returned with Visigoth allies when Geiseric and his Vandals landed their ships on the shores of southern Italy.

The news was greeted in Rome with panic and riots. Petronius Maximus, seeing the mood of the city grow increasingly ugly, tried to leave, but he was riding away from the walls when a rock thrown by a rioter struck and killed him. Rome was without an emperor and without a general. Three days after

Maximus's death, on April 22 of 455, the Vandals arrived at the city and broke through the gates.[3]

For fourteen days, the North African barbarians roved through the city, plundering and wrecking so thoroughly that their name became a new verb: to "vandalize," to ruin without purpose. In fact, the plundering had a very definite purpose. Geiseric did not intend to try to hold the city. He wanted its wealth, and the Vandals did a thorough job of stealing all the gold and silver of Rome—even tearing the gold plating off the roof of the temple of Jupiter Capitolinus.

The intercession of the pope, Leo the Great, prevented the burning of the city and the large-scale massacre of the people, but even Leo could not prevent Geiseric from kidnapping Valentinian's widow and his two teenage daughters. The Vandals returned to Carthage with the three women and ships full of treasure; one ship, loaded with statues, sank and is still in the Mediterranean mud somewhere, but the others reached North Africa safely. Geiseric then married his son Honoric to the older of the two girls, Eudocia (the same daughter Aetius had chosen for his own son), and sent the other two women, with his compliments, to Constantinople.[4]

In Constantinople, the new eastern Roman emperor, Marcian, welcomed Valentinian's family, but he refused to send eastern Roman soldiers west to avenge the sack of Rome. He had sworn, more than twenty years earlier, never again to fight against the Vandals; it had been a condition of his release after he had been taken prisoner at the capture of Carthage by Geiseric and his invading army.

When the news of Petronius Maximus's death and the sack of Rome arrived in Toulouse, where the Gaulish ambassador Avitus was still negotiating with the Visigoths, the Visigoth king Theodoric II suggested that Avitus declare *himself* emperor. He offered his own Visigoth forces as allies. Avitus accepted and marched south across the Alps, entering Rome in triumph as the third emperor to rule within the year.

By this point, Rome was robbed, wrecked, and hungry. Avitus found himself grappling with a city devastated by famine and plunder. There was so little food that he was forced to send the Visigothic allies away, since there was no way to feed them. First, though, he had to pay them, and since there was no money left in the treasury, he stripped all the remaining bronze off the public buildings and handed it over to them.[5]

This infuriated the people of Rome, who were in a mood to be infuriated by any offense, and Avitus's attempts to rule failed in less than a year. He had appointed as his *magister militum* a half-German general named Ricimer, who had fought under Aetius as a young man. While Avitus was trying to pacify Rome, Ricimer was off south driving the remaining Vandals back from the Italian coast. This made him enormously well liked, in inverse proportion to

Avitus's plummeting popularity. In 456, when Avitus finally fled from the city of Rome in fear for his life, heading back to his estates in Gaul, Ricimer met him on the road and took him prisoner. The early historians disagree on what happened next, but it appears that Ricimer kept him under guard for some months, after which Avitus died of unknown causes.

Ricimer was now the most powerful man in Rome, but he knew that his barbarian ancestry would prevent the Roman Senate from confirming his rule as emperor. So he prepared to appoint a colleague—the soldier Majorian, who now became the western emperor in name and Ricimer's puppet in reality.

Majorian served, usefully, as Ricimer's public face, which meant that Ricimer could shift the blame for failure onto his shoulders. In 460, Majorian and the western Roman army gathered on the coast of Hispania (thanks to the friendship of the Visigoths) with three hundred ships, preparing to attack the Vandal kingdom in North Africa. Procopius writes that the ships assembled at the Pillars of Hercules, the entrance to the Mediterranean, planning to "cross over the strait at that point, and then to march by land from there against Carthage." Geiseric began to prepare for a massive war; the people of Italy, expecting victory, got ready to celebrate.[6]

A sneak attack cut the invasion short. The ships, says the chronicler Hydatius, were suddenly seized from the shore "by Vandals who had been given information by traitors."[7] Some behind-the-scene plot, either carried out with the connivance of the Visigoths or done with the help of someone in the western Roman army, had thoroughly sabotaged the plan.

Majorian began to march from Hispania back towards Italy in disgrace. In the foothills of the Apennines, Ricimer's men waylaid and beheaded him. In his place, Ricimer chose Libius Severus, who became the next emperor of the western Roman empire.[8]

No one seems to have recorded much of anything that Severus did. He was simply another one of Ricimer's faces, and he only remained in place for four years. In 465, he died in Rome, either of sickness or of poison, and for eighteen months Ricimer did not bother to push for the appointment of another emperor. The idea of a legitimate Roman emperor in the west was suddenly revealed for what it was: a myth which helped the Romans pretend that a disintegrating realm, now consisting of little more than the peninsula of Italy, still had some vital connection with the glory of the past; a useful fiction which disguised the truth that to be Roman and to be barbarian were now one and the same.

Finally, in 467, Ricimer roused himself to appoint a new emperor, not because he needed one but because he found it useful in facing his current problem: the Visigoths. In 466, Theodoric II of the Visigoths had been murdered by his brother Euric, who took up the Visigothic flag and started storming around Gaul with it. He was rapidly expanding his reign over land that had once been Roman, and Ricimer needed to fight back. The Visigoths had once been a useful ally; now they were a menace.[9]

But Ricimer did not intend to start an actual war without the figurehead of an emperor to lead it. So in 467 he proposed to the Senate that the Roman general Anthemius, who happened to be married to the daughter of the eastern emperor Marcian, become the new *imperator*.

Anthemius, who was no fool, suggested that Ricimer marry his own daughter Alypia to create an extra layer of loyalty. The marriage was celebrated late in 467, just as the poet Sidonius Apollinaris was arriving in Rome: "My arrival coincided with the marriage of the patrician Ricimer," he wrote to a friend, "to whom the hand of the Emperor's daughter was being accorded in the hope of securer times for the State."

> Though the bride has been given away, though the bridegroom has put off his wreath, the consular his palm-broidered robe, the brideswoman her wedding gown, the distinguished senator his toga, and the plain man his cloak, yet the noise of the great gathering has not died away in the palace chambers, because the bride still delays to start for her husband's house.[10]

Apparently Alypia was not pleased with the marriage; Ricimer was now a soldier in his sixties, fifteen years older than her own father.

TOGETHER, RICIMER and the new emperor Anthemius prepared for war against the Visigoths.

The Visigoths had provided the Romans with soldiers to fight against the Vandals; now the two men looked around for soldiers who could help them fight against the Visigoths. They found a new alliance in the northwestern corner of Gaul. There, a Briton named Riotimus had settled with some twelve thousand men; they were tired of the ongoing battle between the British and the Angles and Saxons and had crossed the channel to find peace.[11]

But peace was hard to come by in the lands of the old empire. Riotimus knew that the spread of Visigothic power threatened his new home, which had become known as Brittany. He agreed to supply twelve thousand men for the fight against the Visigoths, but the Visigothic king Euric did not give the reinforcements time to join up with the main body of the Roman army. "He came against the Brittones with an innumerable army," Jordanes says, "and after a long fight he routed Riotimus, king of the Brittones, before the Romans could join him."[12]

The fight against the Visigoths had failed almost before it began, and the Visigothic kingdom in Hispania spread still farther. Meanwhile Roman

20.1: Castel dell'Ovo, where the last Roman emperor lived out his days.
Credit: Photo by Davide Cherubini

soldiers continued fighting fruitlessly against the Vandals in North Africa. Nothing was going well, and when Anthemius got sick in 470, he decided that his ill fortune had been caused by black magic. He "punished many men involved in this crime," writes John of Antioch, even though the crime itself was unproven sorcery, and started putting men to death.[13]

Ricimer, who was in Milan, heard of the witch hunt with exasperation. He recalled six thousand soldiers from the North African front, marched into Rome, and in 472 defeated Anthemius and put him to death.

The marriage had not saved Anthemius, but Ricimer did not survive much past his father-in-law. He had barely arrived in Rome when he came down with a fever. Two months later, Ricimer was dead.

Without its puppet-master, the empire stumbled even more fatally. Anthemius was followed by four emperors in four years, none of them managing to assert any kind of real power. Finally another barbarian soldier stepped forward to take control. His name was Orestes, and he had already emerged once at a turning point of Roman history: he had been the Roman-born ambassador sent from Attila the Hun to Constantinople back in 449.

After the Hun disintegration he had returned to serve in the western Roman army and had gained an increasing following. In 475, with the title of Roman emperor held by the useless Julius Nepos, Orestes rallied his troops behind him, hired a collection of Germanic mercenaries from various tribes, and marched on Ravenna. Julius Nepos fled without putting up a fight. Rather than taking the throne himself (the myth that Roman emperors were not barbarians had been exposed, but still lived), Orestes appointed his own ten-year-old son, Romulus, to the imperial throne. Romulus, the child of Orestes and his fully Roman wife, was less barbarian by blood than the father.

The court at Ravenna was willing to accept this fiction, which kept the Roman title alive for one more year. Romulus—given the patronizing nickname "Augustulus," meaning "little Augustus," by his subjects—sat on the throne for a single year while the western empire fell apart around him.

In 476, even the fiction failed. Orestes had promised to pay his Germanic mercenaries by giving them land in Italy to settle on. Now their leader, the general Odovacer—a German and a Christian—demanded more land for his followers. Orestes refused, and in the hot days of August, Odovacer and the mercenaries marched toward Ravenna, seeking payment and revenge. Orestes met him in battle at Placentia, in northern Italy. The Roman forces were defeated; Orestes was killed in the fighting.

Odovacer went on to Ravenna unopposed, took little Romulus prisoner, and sent him to live in a castle in Campania: Castel dell'Ovo, a fortress on an island reached only by a causeway. There he spent the rest of his days in obscurity. "Thus the Western Empire of the Roman race," says Jordanes, "which Octavianus Augustus, the first of the Augusti, began to govern in the seven hundred and ninth year from the founding of the city, perished . . . and from this time onward kings of the Goths held Rome and Italy."[14] The old western empire, with its stubborn insistence that Romans must rule in Roman land, was no more.

But the death warrant for the western empire had been signed by Constantine over a century before, when he had decided that *Romanness* alone could hold the empire together. Odovacer's rise to the throne of Italy was merely the final admission of what had already happened: the barbarians had given up on the project of becoming Roman. Italy was largely Christian; Odovacer was a Christian. He took the title "King of Italy," separating himself from the old imperial past. He was a competent soldier, and a decent administrator; and as far as his supporters were concerned, his blood no longer mattered.

		WESTERN ROMAN EMPIRE	VANDALS	VISIGOTHS	SALIAN FRANKS
IRELAND	BRITAIN				
Niall of the Nine Hostages (c. 390–c. 455)					
		Constantine III (407–411) Attalus (409)			
	Departure of Constantine III (410)	The Sack of Rome (410)		Ataulf (410–415)	
		Attalus (415)		Wallia (415–419)	
				Theodoric I (419–451)	
		Valentinian III (423/5–455)			
Patricius returns to Ireland			Geiseric (428–477) Vandal conquest of North Africa		
		Pope Leo the Great (440/445–461)			Merovech (?–c. 457)
		Robber Council (449) Battle of Châlons-sur-Marne (451)		Thorismund (451–453)	
	Vortigern (450s?)			Theodoric II (453–466)	
	Cunedda of Gwynedd (c. 455–c. 460) Invasion of Hengest and Horsa	Assassination of Aetius Petronius Maximus (455) Avitus (455–456) Majorian (457–461) Libius Severus (461–465)	Sack of Rome (455)		
				Euric (466–484)	
		Anthemius (467–472)			
		Julius Nepos (475) Romulus Augustulus (475–476) Fall of western Roman empire (476)			

Part Three

NEW
POWERS

Chapter Twenty-One

—•—

The Ostrogoths

Between 457 and 493,
the Isaurians ascend to the eastern throne,
the Ostrogoths take control of Italy,
and the Benedictines retreat

IN 457, THE EASTERN Roman emperor Marcian died at the age of sixty-five. His wife, Pulcheria, had died four years earlier. The Theodosian dynasty that had ruled in Constantinople since 379 had ended.*

As there was no blood heir available, the army had the greatest say in who would become emperor next. Their commanding general would normally have been a top candidate, but in 457 the army was commanded by a man of barbarian descent: Aspar, who belonged to a tribe known as the Alans (they had once lived east of the Black Sea and had been driven from their own lands by the Huns decades earlier). The eastern empire, still calling itself Roman, clung to its old suspicion of barbarian blood: Aspar could no more become emperor of the eastern Roman realm than the Vandal Stilicho or the Visigoth Ricimer could have become emperor in the west.

Instead, Aspar chose the agreeable fiftyish steward of his household, Leo the Thracian, to be his voice-piece. Leo was crowned emperor by the patriarch of Constantinople—the first time the bishop had taken on this pope-like role in the east.

But once on the throne, Leo the Thracian proved impossible to manipulate. Aspar had the loyalty of the army, so in order to reduce his general's influence, Leo made a new series of alliances with the Isaurians, a mountain people of southern Asia Minor. The Isaurians had been under Roman rule for five hundred years, but they had remained warlike and free-acting, carrying on their own affairs almost independently on the slopes of the Taurus Mountains. They had the advantages of barbarians—the skill at war, the self-directed purpose—

---

*The Theodosian dynasty ruled from 379 to 457; the Leonid dynasty, which followed, ruled from 457 to 518.

without the disadvantages; they were, thanks to the centuries that had passed since their incorporation into the empire, undisputably Roman.

Leo, who had no sons (another reason why Aspar had fingered him for the job of emperor), made a match between his daughter Ariadne and the Isaurian leader Zeno. With the Isaurians behind him, he accused Aspar of treachery and, in 471, executed him.[1]

Three years later, the elderly emperor died of dysentery. His daughter's six-year-old son, Leo II, was crowned as emperor in his place. Leo II's father, the Isaurian warrior Zeno, served as his regent. The child ruled for ten months, rubber-stamped his father's coronation as co-emperor, and then died, leaving the Isaurian on the throne of the eastern Roman empire.

This was a dizzying rise to power for the Isaurians, and it created temporary unrest in Constantinople; Leo the Thracian's brother-in-law managed to raise an army against Zeno and drive him out of the city. The brother-in-law, Basiliscus, then crowned himself emperor. Thanks to his policies of heavy taxation, though, Basiliscus made himself unpopular; meanwhile Zeno had gone home and assembled an Isaurian army of his own, which he marched back into Constantinople eighteen months later. The financially strapped population greeted him with relief, and Basiliscus deserted his throne and fled to a nearby church. Zeno, standing outside the church, got Basiliscus out by promising that he would not shed the usurper's blood; when Basiliscus emerged, Zeno then shut him up in a dry cistern and let him starve to death.[2]

Firmly back in power by 476, Zeno the Isaurian watched from the east as the remnants of the western Roman empire spun apart. Odovacer, the Germanic general who had just removed little Romulus from the throne, was now king of Italy. He had taken Ravenna by force; Jordanes says that his initial strategy was to "inspire a fear of himself among the Romans."[3] But there was a limit to how long he could rule over the larger territory of Italy through terror. To bolster his claim to power, Odovacer sent a message to Zeno suggesting a new strategy: he would acknowledge Zeno as overlord and emperor, and would rule Italy in submission to the eastern empire, if Zeno would in turn recognize him as rightful ruler of Italy.

Zeno accepted the offer and gave Odovacer the title of patrician (not king) of Italy. It was a titular reunification: for a brief time, under Zeno the Isaurian, the empire was again one. But Odovacer, having obtained a legitimacy that made his mastery of the Romans in Italy a little easier, went on to ignore Zeno and do exactly as he pleased. In 477, he conquered Sicily, which had been in the hands of the Vandals; the great Vandal king Geiseric had just died, and the Vandal kingdom declined in power without his leadership. He made treaties, just like an independent king, with the Visigoths (who now ruled a kingdom that stretched from the Loire all the way across Hispania)

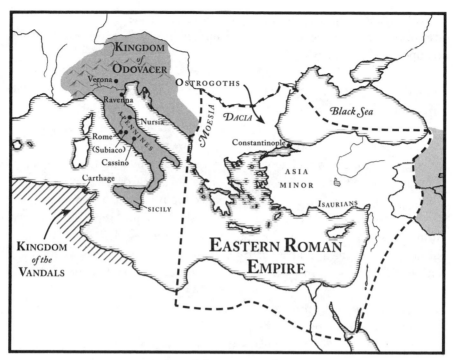

21.1: Odovacer's Kingdom

and with the Franks.[4] By 488, Zeno was seriously worried about Odovacer's growing ambition.

Zeno also had another western problem to solve. A coalition of Ostrogoths was moving from their lands in the west eastwards, towards Constantinople. They were led by a soldier named Theoderic, son of a Gothic chief who had spent ten years as a child in Constantinople, a hostage guaranteeing the good behavior of his father. At eighteen, he had returned to his people and become their leader—which meant that he had the task of finding them more land. The Ostrogoths had too many people and not enough space; they were hungry and overcrowded.*

*This story is complicated by the number of Goths named Theoderic. Theoderic the Ostrogoth should not be confused with Theodoric I or Theodoric II, both of whom were kings of the Visigothic confederation. In addition, there were actually two coalitions of Ostrogoths, each one led by a general named Theoderic. The general referred to here is the first Theoderic: Theoderic the Ostrogoth, who would become known as Theoderic the Great. He commanded Ostrogoths from Pannonia, while his distant cousin Theoderic the Squinter, named after his unfortunate eyes, was from Thracia. The two generals were not automatic allies since they were competing for the same scarce resources. They acted together against Zeno at least once, and Zeno had allied himself with one Theoderic against the other at various times. However, Theoderic the Squinter died around 481, after which Theoderic the Great dominated the Ostrogoths.

Between 478 and 488, the Ostrogoths under Theoderic advanced steadily towards Constantinople, claiming food and territory as they went. Zeno tried to appease Theoderic with the title of *magister militum*, awarded him land in the regions of Dacia and Moesia, and even paid him a substantial amount of money when Theoderic threatened to besiege Constantinople itself in 486. But none of these solutions had pacified the Ostrogoths for long.[5]

Zeno decided to solve the two problems simultaneously: he offered to recognize Theoderic the Ostrogoth as king of Italy and give him the peninsula, as long as Theoderic would go west and get rid of Odovacer. The sources disagree about who first came up with this plan, Theoderic or Zeno, but whoever thought it up, Theoderic liked it. He headed west, marching at the head of a heterogeneous mass of adventurers: Ostrogoths, random Huns, discontented Romans, displaced members of other Germanic tribes. The Gaulish writer Ennodius, who was a child at the time, writes that a "whole world" followed Theoderic to Italy—perhaps as many as a hundred thousand people, in search of a country.[6]

When they marched into northern Italy, Odovacer tried to resist; he assembled an army on the plain of Verona to block the path of the invaders, but Theoderic destroyed it "with great slaughter" and stormed towards Ravenna.

The fight over Italy went on for three years. Jordanes says that Odovacer spent most of those three years holed up in Ravenna: "He frequently harassed the army of the Goths at night," he writes, "sallying forth with his men . . . and thus he struggled." Ravenna grew increasingly shabby and hungry. Finally, in 491, Odovacer suggested a compromise. He would sign a treaty making the two of them co-rulers of Italy if Theoderic would lift the siege.

Theoderic had found the siege frustrating; Odovacer could resupply the city by sea, and Theoderic, with no fleet, couldn't stop him. He agreed to the compromise, but in 493 he ended their joint rule by killing his colleague. The contemporary account of Valensianus says that the Ostrogoth king hewed his co-ruler in two "with his own hands, boasting that his suspicions were at last confirmed—Odovacer had no backbone."[7]

Unlike Odovacer, Theoderic had a spine. He was not interested in being a "patrician" and paying lip service to Constantinople. He was now Theoderic the Great, king of Italy, and as king he had no duty to pay the eastern Roman emperor.

One of his first acts was to declare that only the Romans who had supported him in his takeover of Italy could still claim to be Roman citizens; the rest were deprived of their rights. Roman citizenship, that once-prized distinction, was now connected directly to the person of Theoderic the Great.[8]

UNDER THEODERIC'S RULE, the prestige of Rome, once queen of the world, faded away. Theoderic visited Rome only once, in the year 500, and never bothered to go back. The Senate still met in Rome, but the power of law lay with the king, and ultimately the Senate rubber-stamped his rule.

Roman culture made inroads into Gothic practice; the Goths increasingly spoke Latin, adopted Roman names, married Roman women, and cultivated Roman estates. But while Romans held many of the civil offices in Theoderic's government, high *military* posts were held almost exclusively by Goths. Boys were sent to Rome to study grammar and rhetoric, but Ravenna, dominated by Goths, was the power center of the kingdom.[9]

The conflict between the two races came sharply to the fore when Theoderic died in 526. His heir, his ten-year-old son Athalaric, became the pawn in a struggle for power between his mother Amalasuntha (who served as his regent) and the Ostrogoth nobles who wanted to control the kingdom from behind the throne. Amalasuntha wanted to send her son to school in Rome, to receive the sort of education that "Roman princes" received. The Goths objected that a Roman education would make him a sissy. Procopius writes, "For letters, they said, are far removed from manliness, and the teaching of old men results for the most part in a cowardly and submissive spirit. Therefore the man who is to show daring . . . ought to be freed from the timidity which teachers inspire and to take his training in arms." Apparently Theoderic himself, careful though he was to keep the Romans and Goths in his empire on more or less equal footing, had nurtured misgivings of his own over the value of a Roman education: the Goths claimed that he "would never allow any of the Goths to send their children to school; for he used to say that, if the fear of the strap once came over them, they would never have the resolution to despise sword or spear." Clearly, a literary education in Rome was not the high road to power and influence it had once been, and the lifestyle of young men studying in the once capital grew increasingly dissolute and aimless.[10]

One of the young men sent to school in Rome was Benedict of Nursia, son of a Roman nobleman. Like Augustine, he dabbled in the less respectable pastimes available to him; but finally he grew exasperated with the noise and licentiousness of the city, gave up his studies (which weren't providing him with advantage in any case), and left.

According to Gregory the Great, who provides us with the only early account of Benedict's life, he ended up in a cave in the Apennines about forty miles east of Rome, near the modern town of Subiaco. At some point he had heard the teachings of Christianity and had been converted; now he devoted himself to the lifestyle of a pious hermit, seeking to understand the grace of God in solitude. News of the hermit in the wilderness spread, and several years later monks in a nearby monastery asked him to come and take charge of their community, since their abbot had just died.

Benedict agreed. His chaotic years in Rome and his solitary meditation had given him a vision for community life that was regulated, quiet, and productive: "Having now taken upon him the charge of the Abbey," says Gregory the Great, "he took order that regular life should be observed, so that none of them could, as before they used, through unlawful acts decline from the path of holy conversation, either on the one side or on the other." The monks, unused to such strict supervision, decided to poison his wine; but Benedict got wind of the plan and went back to his cave. There he taught the shepherds who came to see him, converting a number of them to the monastic lifestyle.[11]

Around 529, he led them up a mountain near the town of Cassino. On the mountaintop, an old temple of Apollo had been slowly decaying into ruins. Benedict and his monks burned it and in its place began to build a monastery of their own.

In this monastery, Monte Cassino, Benedict developed the rules by which his community would live: the Rule of St. Benedict. The Rule was the *lex* of a kingdom removed from the political struggles, a conscious attempt to bring Christian practice back to the realm where the Indian and Chinese monks dwelt. "We desire to dwell in the tabernacle of God's kingdom," Benedict wrote, "and if we fulfill the duties of tenants, we shall be heirs of the kingdom of heaven."[12]

He listed those duties: to relieve the poor, clothe the naked, visit the sick, bury the dead, to prefer nothing to the love of Christ. In daily life, silence was preferable to speech, since words so often led to sin; the monks, rising regularly during the night to sing psalms, were to sleep clothed so that they would always be prepared for worship and service; the abbot was to consult the monks over decisions that affected the whole community, but in the end his decisions were final; the "vice of personal ownership" was to be "cut out in the monastery by the very root," so that monks were to own nothing, not even books or writing materials; each monk was to spend a prescribed number of hours per day in manual labor; any monk who persisted in breaking the Rule was to be barred from eating with the community or taking part in worship until he repented. Gregory the Great reports that the "spirit of prophecy" allowed Benedict to know when the monks were breaking the Rule even when they were away from the monastery; when they returned, he would tell them their faults. They repented, and "would not any more in his absence presume to do any such thing, seeing they now perceived that he was present with them in spirit."[13]

As the first abbot of Monte Cassino, Benedict was the ruler that Italy lacked: devoted to a calling higher than his own ambitions, offering a law that was the same for all and was enforced with absolute justice and regularity, providing a clear and straightforward path into happiness. The Benedictine way of life provided the monks with unity, with an identity as members of a community they themselves constituted. And it was, above all, *orderly.* "You who hasten to the heavenly country," the Rule concluded, "perform with Christ's aid this Rule, which is written down as the least of beginnings: and then at length, under God's protection, you will come to the greater things that we have mentioned; to the heights of learning and virtue." Learning and virtue had once been prized in Rome, but now they led nowhere; only in the Benedictine monastery did the exercise of the mind and the discipline of the spirit yield great reward.[14]

TIMELINE 21					
WESTERN ROMAN EMPIRE	VANDALS	VISIGOTHS	SALIAN FRANKS	EASTERN ROMAN EMPIRE	PERSIAN EMPIRE
	Geiseric (428–477) Vandal conquest of North Africa				**Yazdegerd II** (438–457)
			Merovech (?–c. 457)		
Pope Leo the Great (440/445–461)					
Robber Council (449)				**Marcian** (450–457)	
Battle of Châlons-sur-Marne (451)		**Thorismund** (451–453)		Council of Chalcedon (451)	Battle of Vartanantz (451)
		Theodoric II			
Assassination of Aetius		(453–466)			
Petronius Maximus (455) Sack of Rome (455)					
Avitus (455–456)					
Majorian (457–461)				Leo the Thracian (457–474)	
Libius Severus (461–465)					
		Euric (466–484)			
Anthemius (467–472)					
				Leo II (474)	
Julius Nepos (475)				**Zeno** (475–491)/**Basiliscus** (475–476)	
Romulus Augustulus (475–476)					
Fall of western Roman empire (476)				Ostrogoth invasion	
GERMANIC ITALY					
Odovacer (476–493)					
Theoderic the Great (491–526)					
Athalaric (526–534)					
Benedict founds Monte Cassino					

Chapter Twenty-Two

Byzantium

Between 471 and 518,
the Persians object to social reform,
Slavs and Bulgars appear,
and the Blues and Greens fight in Constantinople

PERSIA WAS SUFFERING, and in 471 the suffering was compounded when the Persian king led the empire into war.

Yazdegerd II had died in 457, and his oldest son, Peroz, had taken the throne after a brief struggle with his brothers. Peroz's twenty-seven-year reign was a difficult one; Persia suffered from a severe famine and, according to the eyewitness account attributed to the eastern monk Joshua the Stylite, locusts, earthquake, plague, and a solar eclipse.[1] On the heels of the famine came war with the Hephthalites, the same peoples who had straggled down across the Kush mountains to cause trouble for the Gupta kings of India. They had settled into a kingdom on the eastern side of the Persian empire, but Peroz quarrelled repeatedly with the Hephthalite king over the boundary between their lands.

In 471 he finally marched an army into Hephthalite territory. The Hephthalites retreated in front of them, craftily, and then circled around behind and trapped the Persian army. Peroz was forced to surrender, swear an oath that he would never attack again, and retreat. He also agreed to pay the Hephthalites an enormous tribute, so large that it took him two years to raise it from his people. Meanwhile his oldest son, Kavadh, spent two years at the Hephthalite court as a hostage, a guarantee that the money—thirty mules loaded with silver, according to Joshua the Stylite—would eventually be handed over.[2]

Peroz finally managed to tax the tribute out of his people, and Kavadh returned home. But the defeat simmered in the mind of the Persian king until he could no longer bear it. In 484 he assembled an even greater army and invaded Hephthalite land once more.

Again he was tricked. Procopius says that the Hephthalites dug a pit and covered it over with reeds sprinkled with earth, and then withdrew beyond it to set up their battle line; al-Tabari adds that the Hephthalite king stuck the treaty that Peroz had signed, promising not to invade Hephthalite territory again, on the tip of his spear. The Persians, thundering forward into battle, fell into the pit—horses, lances, and all. Peroz himself was killed "and the whole Persian army with him." It was a shattering defeat, perhaps the worst in the history of Sassanid Persia. The Hephthalites, who up until this point had remained on the eastern side of the Oxus river, now took control of Khorasan (the Persian province on the western side), and the Persians "became subject and tributary to the Hephthalites." Peroz's body, crushed by the twisted mass of men and horses in the battlefield trench, was never recovered.[3]

Back at the Persian capital Ctesiphon, Peroz's son and heir, Kavadh, was driven out by Peroz's brother, Balash. The brief civil war that followed was complicated by the fact that the Persian treasury was empty. Balash sent ambassadors to Constantinople to ask for Roman help, but none appeared. Unable to fight on multiple fronts, he agreed to put an end to the ongoing problem of Armenia by signing a treaty that gave the Armenians independence to run their own affairs.* Meanwhile Kavadh, like Aetius before him, took advantage of the friendships he had formed as a hostage and went to the Hephthalites for help. It took him several years to talk their king into assisting him, but in 488 he was finally able to claim the Persian throne as his own.[4]

Which introduced a brand new complication into Persian attempts to recover from the ill-advised wars with the Hephthalites. Rather than being a follower of the orthodox Zoroastrian religion, Kavadh I was a disciple of a heretical cult led by a Persian prophet named Mazdak. Zoroastrianism, like Christianity, believed that good would ultimately triumph; the Christian savior would return to earth to destroy evil and make all things right, while the Zoroastrian god Ahura Mazda would wipe out his evil competitor, Ahriman, renew the earth, and raise the dead so that they could walk upon it in perfect bliss.[5]

But Mazdak, like the Christian gnostics, taught that the ultimate power in the universe was a distant and uninvolved deity, and that two lesser but equal divine powers, good and evil, struggled over the universe. Men had to align themselves with the good power and reject the evil, choosing light over darkness. Different gnostic religions suggested various ways in which that might be done; Mazdak believed that the primary way of finding the light was to get rid of human suffering by making all men (and to some degree women) equal. He preached that men should share their resources equally, no one owning

---

*This is known as the Nevarsek Treaty; as a result of the treaty, Armenia was able to preserve itself as a nation.

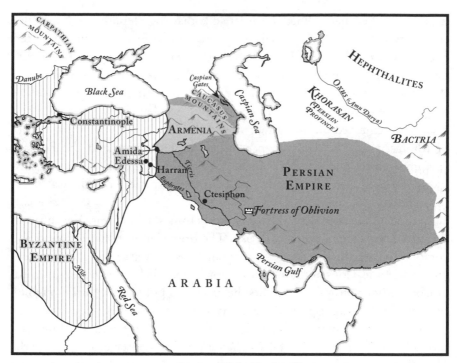

22.1: Persia and the Hephthalites

private property to the detriment of others; that competition be replaced by equality, strife by brother love. Unlike Christian gnosticism, Mazdakism worked itself out as social justice.[6]

Kavadh I began to reform his country in line with Mazdak's ideas. The laws he passed puzzled his contemporaries so deeply that some interpretation is necessary if we are to figure out exactly what he intended. Al-Tabari says that he intended "to take from the rich for the poor and give to those possessing little out of the share of those possessing much," while Procopius writes that Kavadh wanted the Persians to have "communal intercourse with their women." It is highly improbable that Kavadh I was trying to institute full communism in Persia, but it is very likely indeed that he was attempting to redistribute some of the wealth held by the powerful Persian nobles (this would have reduced their power and influence, which could have only helped Kavadh I), and that he lifted some of the oppressive restrictions that forced women to marry men of their own class and allowed them to be shut up in the harems of wealthy noblemen.[7]

The Persian nobles naturally resented the curtailment of their privileges, and Kavadh's social reforms ended in 496 when the aristocrats of his court removed him by force and put his brother Zamasb on the throne of Persia.

Zamasb refused to murder anyone who shared his bloodline, and so Kavadh was hauled away to southern Persia, to a prison called the Fortress of Oblivion. "For if anyone is cast into it," Procopius writes, "the law permits no mention of him to be made thereafter, but death is the penalty for the man who speaks his name."[8]

While Zamasb rolled back his brother's reforms, Kavadh languished in the Fortress of Oblivion for two years. Finally, he managed to make his escape. Al-Tabari says that Kavadh's sister sprung him out of prison by getting visiting privileges (through sleeping with the fortress's warden), rolling Kavadh up in a carpet, and having the carpet carried out; Procopius says that the woman who slept with the warden was Kavadh's wife, and that once she had earned the privilege of seeing her husband, the two switched clothes and Kavadh made his escape under cover of a woman's robe.[9]

Either way, Kavadh made his way to the land of the Hephthalites, where he once again pled for help in regaining his throne. The Hephthalite king not only agreed but also gave Kavadh his own daughter as a wife to seal the bargain. Kavadh marched back to Ctesiphon at the head of a Hephthalite army. The Persian soldiers fled as soon as they saw their opponents, and Kavadh broke into the palace, blinded his brother with a hot iron needle, and imprisoned him.

His second possession of the throne lasted over thirty years, but there was no more flirting with communism and no further attempts to level the Persian playing field through social-justice legislation. He could rule only with the support of the Persian noblemen, and with the help of the soldiers they supplied, and this placed a limit on his power.

What he could do, however, was fight the eastern Romans, and in 502 he declared war on the Roman emperor Anastasius.

Zeno the Isaurian died without a son in 491; a month after his death, his widow married Anastasius, a minor but devout court official who became the new emperor of the eastern Romans. He was undistinguished both in peace and in war, and his most notable feature was a mismatched pair of eyes, one black and one blue, which earned him the nickname "The Two-Eyed."[10]

His attempts to fight off Kavadh were inept and futile. The Persians sacked the Roman half of Armenia and laid siege to the border city of Amida, a siege that went on for eighty days while Kavadh's Arab allies, under the Arab king Na'man of al-Hirah, ranged farther south and sacked the territory around Harran and Edessa. Finally the Persians took Amida; Procopius says that they broke in when the Christian monks who had been given the defense of one of the towers had a religious festival, ate and drank too much, and went to sleep. Once inside the city, they massacred the population—eighty thousand people, according to Joshua the Stylite, who adds that they piled the bodies in two huge heaps outside the city so that the smell of decomposing corpses wouldn't choke the Persian occupiers.[11]

The conquest of Amida would probably have been followed by many more Persian triumphs had Kavadh not found himself dealing with another Hephthalite invasion on his other border; his alliance by marriage had not produced a permanent peace with the eastern enemies. He found himself fighting on two fronts, and although the Persian army continued to devastate the land on the eastern Roman border, by 506 the two empires were ready to negotiate a treaty.

The war was over. Not much had been accomplished, except that the Romans had lost a little more than they had gained. The treaty gave Amida back to the Romans, but the Persians remained in control of their most important conquest: just before peace negotiations opened, they had taken control of the narrow path through the Caucasus Mountains, known to the ancients as the Caspian Gates. The king who controlled the Gates had power to open or close the south to invaders from the north.[12]

THE PERSIAN INVASION was only one of Anastasius's problems. New peoples had appeared on the western border of his empire and were causing unending troubles.

The initial threat came from the Slavs, tribes that were moving south and west towards the eastern Roman borders. The Slavs came from north of the Danube, but they weren't "Germanic"—a name the Romans had applied indiscriminately to anyone from the northern territories. Imprecise though the term was, the Germanic peoples had spoken languages with a common source, which linguists have reconstructed in the form of "Proto-Germanic"— a hypothetical ancestral tongue. This suggests some sort of shared origin, too far back in time to be located with any certainty, but more than likely the far-distant origin of the Germanic peoples was northern European. The Slavic tribes came from farther east, between the Vistula and Dnieper rivers, and belonged to a different language family.*

It isn't always easy to figure out exactly which tribes referred to by ancient historians belong to the Slavic rather than the Germanic language group, but both Jordanes and Procopius describe peoples who seem to be Slavs coming from the Carpathian Mountains, north of the Danube. They were taking up residence in the Danube river valley and threatening to overflow down into the old Roman provinces of Thracia and Illyricum.†

---

*Contemporary historians called the Slavs "Getae" because they first appeared in the territory where the ancient Getae had once lived.
†The "original homeland" of the Slavs is an academic issue, which, like many having to do with ethnicity, is also political in nature.

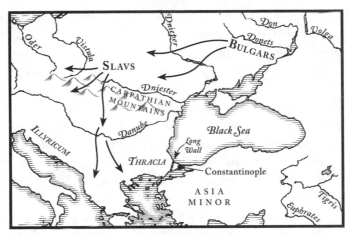

22.2: Troubles West of Byzantium

Anastasius dealt with the problem by exiling the Isaurians, who had shown a tendency to rebel, from their homeland and settling them instead in Thracia. This had the double effect of weakening their sense of national identity and providing him with a barrier against the Slavs. To survive in their new country, the Isaurians had to fight off the Slavs.

The Slavic invasion was joined by yet another influx of wanderers: the Bulgars. They were from central Asia, from the same land as the Huns, and they were governed by khans. The bulk of the Bulgar tribes (not yet coalesced into any kind of a kingdom) were still east of the Slavs, but trailing after them to the west; the later *Russian Primary Chronicle* says that they followed the Slavs into their territory and "oppressed" them there. They crossed the Danube in 499, fought, raided, and then returned back over the river, "gorged with plunder and crowned with the glory of a victory over a Roman army." They invaded again in 502, stealing and destroying.[13]

The eastern Roman domain was shrinking. Not drastically or all at once, but a little at a time. The Persians had chipped away at the eastern border. To the west, invasions of Bulgars and Slavs into Thracia were growing more persistent; so in 512, Anastasius decided to build a wall against them.

Wall-building against barbarians was an old and honorable solution: Hadrian's wall in Britain was only one of many erected in an attempt to keep invaders out. But the building of a wall was also an admission of defeat. It divided land into civilized and uncivilized, Roman and barbarian, controlled and uncontrolled; and Anastasius's wall, the Long Wall, gave Thracia away. It was fifty miles long and stood thirty miles west of the city. "It reaches from one shore to the other, like a strait," wrote the sixth-century historian Evagrius, "making the city [of Constantinople] an island instead of a peninsula."[14]

The Long Wall saved Constantinople, but it temporarily reduced the Roman holdings west of Asia Minor to the capital itself and the land immediately around it. Despite the lingering threat of Persian attack, this reoriented the entire empire towards the east, away from the west. From this point on—with Italy lost to Theoderic and his Ostrogoths, the remnants of the western empire gone beyond recovery, growing hostility between the bishop of Rome and the bishop of Constantinople—the eastern Roman empire began its transformation into something slightly different: Byzantium, an empire that was less Roman than eastern, less Latin than Greek, and increasingly less *catholic* in the eyes of the bishop of Rome.*

IRONICALLY, WHILE ANASTASIUS was building the Long Wall to protect his empire from barbarians on the outside, barbarism on the inside of the wall became a much greater threat.

Since the time of Constantine, the traditional Roman sport of gladiatorial combat had been systematically replaced by chariot-racing, which was not as closely associated with worship of the old Roman gods. In the larger cities of the eastern empire, chariot-racing dominated the sports and entertainment scene: like stock car racing in Charlotte, North Carolina, or hockey in Toronto, it was a citywide phenomenon, part of the background of daily life even for citizens who weren't particularly involved in it. Everyone in a city the size of Constantinople knew who the star chariot-drivers were; everyone had at least a passing acquaintance with the race results; and a good percentage of the city's inhabitants identified themselves, however loosely, with one of the chariot-racing teams.

These teams were not defined by individual drivers and their horses. Different associations and companies in the city sponsored the races, paying for horses and equipment, and each one of these sponsors used as its symbol a color: red, white, blue, green. A number of different horse-and-driver pairs might race under the color blue, and spectators of the races became fans, not of individual performers, but of the color under which they raced. The Blues were one group of fans, the Whites another; and like modern boosters, these fans (largely young men) were fanatical in their devotion to their color.[15]

They also hated each other with a zeal that scholars have tried to explain by finding deeper reasons for the hostility: perhaps the Reds were aristocrats and the Whites were merchants; maybe the Greens were inclined to Chalcedonian Christianity, while the Blues preferred the heresies of monophysitism. None

---

*I have chosen to use "Byzantium" rather than "Byzantine Empire" to refer to the eastern half of the old Roman empire; so far as we know, the term "Byzantine Empire" is a later name, not used by the residents of Byzantium themselves.

of these explanations really hold up. The fans hated each other irrationally, like soccer fans who beat each other senseless at half-time.

By the time Anastasius died of old age in 518, the fans had settled into two opposed factions: the Blues, who had absorbed the Reds, and the Greens, who now encompassed the Whites. They were increasingly violent, always ready to seize any excuse to murder fans in the other faction. In fact, three thousand Blues had been killed at Constantinople in a 501 riot over chariot-race results, and other riots in 507 and 515 had been almost as bloody.[16]

Anastasius left no son, although he had nephews who were anxious to claim the right to rule. In their place, though, the imperial bodyguard elected its own commander, the seventy-year-old career army officer Justin, as the new emperor.

Justin was shrewd, experienced, and had the support of the Blues. He also had the firm support of his nephew Justinian, a soldier in his thirties. In 521, Justin made his nephew consul, the highest official position in Constantinople below that of emperor, and Justinian began to take a greater and greater part in the government of the empire.

He was a competent administrator and an accomplished military leader. But he was also an ardent Blues fanatic who did little to quell the growing violence of the racing fans in the city. Their excesses grew worse and worse. "They carried weapons at night quite openly," writes Procopius, "while in the day time they concealed short two-edged swords along their thighs under their cloaks. They used to collect in gangs at nightfall and rob members of the upper class in the whole forum or in narrow lanes." The people of Constantinople quit wearing gold belts or jewelry, since this was an open invitation to be mugged by a gang of Blues or Greens; they hurried home at sunset so they could be off the street before dark. It was a state of affairs that would persist for the next fifteen years before breaking out into open conflagration.[17]

TIME LINE 22			
WESTERN ROMAN EMPIRE	VISIGOTHS	EASTERN ROMAN EMPIRE	PERSIAN EMPIRE
Majorian (457–461)		Leo the Thracian (457–474)	Peroz (457–484)
Libius Severus (461–465)			
Anthemius (467–472)	Euric (466–484)		
Julius Nepos (475)		Leo II (474)	
Romulus Augustulus (475–476)		Zeno (475–491)/Basiliscus (475–476)	
Fall of western Roman empire (476)			
GERMANIC ITALY		Ostrogoth invasion	
Odovacer (476–493)			
			Balash (484–488)
			Kavadh (488–531)
Theoderic the Great (491–526)		Anastasius (491–518)	
			[Zamasb (496–498)]
		Justin (518–527)	
Athalaric (526–534)			
Benedict founds Monte Cassino			

Chapter Twenty-Three

Aspirations

Between 471 and 527,
the Bei Wei of the north expand to the south,
while Goguryeo continues its conquests,
and Silla moves carefully towards nationhood

THE BEI WEI in the north of China were strong and warlike, the Liu Song in the south fading. Despite the imbalance, the two kingdoms had sworn a temporary truce. They had spent more time fighting over boundaries than figuring out how to strengthen their own states, and both needed to pay attention to neglected domestic matters. "Our ruling ancestors have worked hard to reign," the Bei Wei emperor Wei Xiaowen remarked, "but to establish an internal norm was an uphill task."[1]

Wei Xiaowen was the great-great-grandson of the Taoist emperor Wei Taiwu, who had died barely twenty years before Wei Xiaowen's coronation—an oddity produced by the fact that each of Wei Taiwu's successors had begun fathering sons at the age of thirteen or fourteen. Wei Xiaowen himself was crowned in 471 at the age of four. At first he was under the control of his grandmother and regent, the dowager empress Feng, a woman who only had power because she had managed to defy the traditions of the Bei Wei. The ancient custom of the nomadic Tuoba clan, the not-so-distant ancestors of the Bei Wei royal family, decreed that the mother of each crown prince be put to death so that she could not influence the politics of the court; Feng, who was Chinese by blood, had maneuvered her way out of execution. She then exercised her considerable energy and ingenuity in order to gain as much power as possible, inadvertently proving the point of the bloodthirsty Bei Wei custom.

As her grandson grew, the two managed to work out a power-sharing arrangement that turned them into co-rulers. Together, they began to transform the Bei Wei court into a place that drew more and more from the Chinese heritage of the empress Feng, and more and more shunned the traditions of the Xianbei nomads who had originally formed the kingdom. Chinese officials gained high places in the government; no one was allowed to wear the traditional nomadic dress of the Xianbei; the two even outlawed any use of the Xianbei language, decreeing that only Chinese could be spoken, and forced the great families to adopt Chinese surnames in place of their traditional clan names.[2]

Taoism remained a strong thread in the tapestry of northern Chinese religion; in fact, the peculiarly magical form of Taoism practiced by Wei Xiaowen's great-great-grandfather, focused as it was on the preparing of elixirs (Wei Xiaowen himself had a court alchemist who spent many years trying to make the emperor a potion for immortality), was the bedrock on which medieval Chinese advances in pharmaceutical and chemical formulations were built.[3]

But Confucianism and Buddhism provided the Bei Wei throne with much more useful tools for rule. As it had for centuries in China, Confucianism supplied a model for a state hierarchy; it provided a picture of the world in which properly ordered, properly structured government was an essential part of an orderly and moral universe.

Buddhism offered something else entirely: a model for kingship.

The Buddhism of northern China was Mahayana Buddhism, which (in contrast to the Theravada Buddhism of India and southern Asia) had developed a whole series of deities, each exercising a kind of kinglike power. These deities were not quite a pantheon. Rather, each one of them was Buddha in a different manifestation. These manifestations were called bodhisattvas; they were enlightened ones who had reached Nirvana and "release from the cycle of rebirth and suffering," but who had chosen to turn back and remain in the world, refusing to depart into Nirvana until all were saved.[4]

This was a departure from the intensely individual focus of Theravada Buddhism. Instead of simply honoring those who withdrew into solitude, Mahayana Buddhism praised those greater and more accomplished believers who worked on behalf of the less powerful. The bodhisattvas were the very models of kindly kings, and the Buddhism of the Bei Wei gave the emperor the power of ideology, the sanction of an entire system of doctrine to undergird his claim to extend a wise and benevolent rule over his people. Wei Xiaowen and his grandmother built lavish Buddhist temples, provided land and money, and stamped the imperial sanction firmly on the religion by commissioning enormous Buddhist sculptures to be carved right into the soaring cliffs near the northern Bei Wei capital of Pingcheng.[5]

Under their patronage, scores of Buddhist monks migrated from the south and west into the Bei Wei kingdom, and Buddhist monasteries sprang up all through the country. One of the most famous of these, the Shaolin Monastery on the sacred mountain Song Shan, was established by the Indian monk Batuo; the monks of the monastery were bound, by the terms of their royal endowment, to pray for the emperor and for the peace of the Bei Wei people. As part of their prayer and meditation, the monks followed a set of physical exercises intended to focus the mind. According to legend, Bei Wei generals who visited the monastery saw the monks carrying out their exercises, recognized the value of the systematic movements for fighting, and adopted them. These movements are considered the source for the martial art of kung fu.[6]

In 490, the dowager empress died, leaving Wei Xiaowen, at twenty-three, in sole power. He observed three full years of mourning for her—the traditional period of grief for a mother, not a grandmother (who typically got twenty-seven days).[7]

With the mourning over, he rounded up the clan leaders of the Bei Wei—now doubling as court aristocrats with Chinese names—and led them on what he claimed would be a military reconnaissance into southern China. Instead, he halted the party at the ruins of Luoyang, the old Jin capital that had been starved and sacked into submission in 311. "Pingcheng," he told his men, "is a place from which to wage war, not one from which civilized rule can come." Luoyang, five hundred miles farther to the south, was the pinnacle of his plan to turn the Bei Wei into a fully Chinese kingdom. He intended to rebuild it and to move the entire government from the old capital of Pingcheng; and he planned to recarve the giant Buddhist sculptures on two cliffs overlooking the river that ran through Luoyang, so that the divine eyes would still be watching the new capital city.[8]

The rebuilding took nine years, and Wei Xiaowen did not live to see it finished. He died of illness in 499, at the age of thirty-two, and was succeeded by his sixteen-year-old son, Wei Xuanwu. At its peak, the reconstructed city was home to over half a million people, with walls eighty feet thick protecting them and five hundred Buddhist monasteries inside. Only Chinese was spoken inside, and the Chinese classics had been gathered into a great city library for the education of the future officials of the Bei Wei. The ex-barbarians were coming closer and closer to eclipsing the glories of the Jin.[9]

To THE EAST, the little Korean kingdom of Baekje—worried about the swelling size and power of Goguryeo, to its north—sent an appeal to the Bei Wei court asking for protection and alliance.[10]

The great Goguryeon king Guanggaeto the Expander had been followed by his son Jangsu, who ruled for seventy-nine years and earned himself the epithet "The Long-Lived." For decades, Jangsu had been carefully transforming Goguryeo from a collection of conquered territories into a state.

Twenty years into his rule, he moved his capital city. His father had ruled from the ancient capital city of Guknaesong, on the Yalu river: it was a good and defensible place for a fortress, but with Goguryeo's territory expanded so

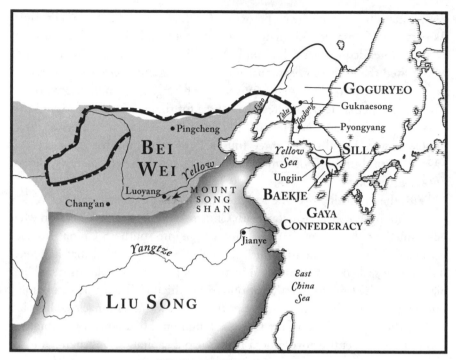

23.1: The East in the Era of King Jangsu

far down the peninsula, Guknaesong was now too far north to act as a center of government. Jangsu decided instead to rule from Pyongyang, farther south, on the broad plains of the Taedong river.[11]

This suggested a new focus on the south and alarmed the two southern kingdoms of Silla and Baekje. Both realized that help would have to come from the northern Bei Wei; the Liu Song were no longer powerful enough to tip the balance of power.

Bei Wei armies were dispatched to help Baekje out, and Silla allied with its neighbor as well. But even this triple defense proved inadequate. In 475, King Jangsu of Goguryeo led his armies against the capital city of Baekje. He captured the king of Baekje in battle and beheaded him, and the remaining Baekje government was forced south to the city of Ungjin.

Baekje had almost been destroyed by the conflict. Meanwhile Goguryeo had expanded its borders to cover a massive territory stretching far up to the north and even over to the west.

But despite the ruination of its neighbor and ally, Silla survived. In part, this was because Goguryeo saw Baekje as a threat and Silla as an afterthought; Silla had lagged behind the other two states. In 500, when the Sillan ruler Chijung came to its throne, Silla still had little industry, almost no foreign trade, rudimentary administration. So unformed was its sense of nationhood that the country did not even have a single accepted name.

Chijung became the catalyst for Silla's awakening as a nation. He took, for the first time, the Chinese title of king (*wang*) instead of the traditional title of *maripkan*, which was closer to "governing noble." He began to outlaw some of the more ancient and unpleasant Sillan customs, such as burying slaves along with their masters. He brought Chinese consultants in to teach the people of Silla how to plow with oxen (something they had never done) and to demonstrate how to construct an underground ice-cellar to preserve food in the hot summer months.[12]

Like the king of Bei Wei, the monarch of Silla saw Chinese government, Chinese technology, even Chinese dress and Chinese names as the keys to strength. With Chinese customs as his tool, he shaped Silla into a nation. His mythical stature as the father of Silla is preserved in the tales about him, which explain that Chijung had trouble finding a wife because his penis measured seventeen inches long.[13]

Chijung's successor, King Pophung, came to the throne in 514; under his direction, Silla's government solidified into a true centralized state with a written code of law (published in 520) and a state religion. It was also during King Pophung's rule that Buddhism finally came to Silla.

Baekje and Goguryeo had been Buddhist for over a hundred years, but in 527 Silla was still unconverted. In that year, the Indian monk Ado arrived in the capital city just in time to help the king of Silla out of an embarrassing dilemma. According to the traditional account *Haedong kosung chon*, the king of the Liu Song, in southern China, had sent an ambassador to Silla bringing gifts of incense, but neither the king nor his court knew what the incense was (or how to interpret the gift).

Ado, who was present in the court, explained that you were supposed to burn it, upon which the Chinese envoy bowed to him and said, "So monks are not strangers in this country after all." Immediately, the story adds, King Pophung "issued a decree permitting the propagation of Buddhism." Not long afterwards, Pophung went a step further and declared Buddhism to be the *state* religion. The story reveals, with unusual openness, a court full of barbarians who know their own shortcomings and are saved from humiliation in front of the infinitely more sophisticated Chinese ambassador.[14]

The only way to prevent further humiliation was to become even more Chinese. Before long, the people of Silla had developed their own version of the past: Yes, Buddhism had come to Silla late, but Pophung claimed that royal builders, while excavating for new foundations, had uncovered Buddhist stupas from long ago and more: "pillar bases, stone niches, and steps," remains of an ancient Buddhist monastery. He was refashioning the tale of

Silla's past: Buddhism had been part of its history for centuries, even longer than it had been a part of the history of the neighboring kingdoms. With a mythical past behind it, Silla was ready to give Goguryeo a run for control of the peninsula.[15]

TIMELINE 23						
EASTERN ROMAN EMPIRE	PERSIAN EMPIRE	CHINA SOUTH	NORTH	GOGURYEO	BAEKJE	SILLA
	Yazdegerd I (399–421)					
Theodosius II (408–450)						
				Jangsu (413–491)		
	Bahram V (421–438)	Fall of Jin/Rise of Liu Song (420) **Song Wudi** (420–422) **Song Shao** (422–424) **Song Wendi** (424–453)	**Wei Taiwu** of the Bei Wei (424–452)			
	Yazdegerd II (438–457)	Establishment of Confucian colleges (439)	Unification of the north under Bei Wei (440) First persecution of Buddhists in the north (446)			
Marcian (450–457) Council of Chalcedon (451)	Battle of Vartanantz (451)					
		Song Xiaowu (454–464)				
Leo the Thracian (457–474)	**Peroz** (457–484)					
			Wei Xiaowen (471–499)			
Leo II (474) **Zeno** (475–491)/**Basilicus** (475–476)						
Ostrogoth invasion						
	Balash (484–488)					
	Kavadh (488–531)					
Anastasius (491–518)	[**Zamasb** (496–498)]					
			Wei Xuanwu (499–515)			**Chijung** (500–514)
						Pophung (514–540)
Justin (518–527)						

Chapter Twenty-Four

—·—

Resentment

Between 479 and 534,
the Liu Song collapses in the south,
and the Bei Wei splits apart in the north

WHILE THE KINGDOMS to the north and west raided the ancient Chinese traditions for themselves, the Liu Song were falling apart. The undignified emperor Song Xiaowu, who had abandoned the principles of Confucian order in favor of pleasure and idleness, had been succeeded by Song Ming, who was nicknamed "the Pig." After seven years, Song Ming was followed by Song Hou Fei, an undisciplined teenager who ruled only three years before his antics (painting a target on the stomach of a dozing official and then shooting blunt arrows at it) became unendurable. The court officials assassinated him and instead elevated his thirteen-year-old brother, Song Shun.[1]

Two years later, in 479, an exasperated aristocrat took the throne by force and declared himself to be Qi Gaodi, first emperor of a new dynasty. The Liu Song dynasty was finished; the Southern Qi dynasty had arrived.

However, the Southern Qi dynasty turned out to be little more than a family grasping at the distant possibility of power. Qi Gaodi, elderly when he came to the throne, died within three years and passed his throne to his son, Qi Wudi. Qi Wudi kept power for ten years, but at his death a family free-for-all ensued; eventually Qi Wudi's brother seized power as Qi Mingdi in 494. He ruled for only four years and then died (or, as a later historian put it, "was compelled to drop the sceptre which he had grasped through bloodshed and murder").[2]

His successor, his son Qi Hedi, was nicknamed "the Idiot King" for his apparent lack of sense (during his father's funeral he fell over laughing at the sight of a bald-headed man), but he was sensible enough to tax his people heavily in order to build a beautiful new palace. The taxes were such a burden on the population that it was not uncommon to see travellers weeping over their ruined fortunes as they walked along the road.

Finally Qi Hedi went one step too far, when he poisoned an official whom he suspected of plotting against him. This official was the brother of the general Xiao Yan, who had the loyalty of the army. When Xiao Yan heard of the murder, he turned his men out in open rebellion, posting public calls for additional troops. He marched on the Southern Qi capital, Nanjing (also known as Jianking), and laid siege to it for two months. At the end of this wretched time, the people of the city—starving and famine-wracked, over eighty thousand of them dead—stormed the palace and murdered Qi Hedi. They preserved his head in wax so that they could show it to the general when he marched into the city.[3]

The Southern Qi dynasty had lasted from 479 to 501, barely a single generation. Xiao Yan, now the most powerful man in the kingdom, lingered before taking power himself; for a little over a year, he called himself prime minister and put his energies behind supporting Qi Hedi's sixteen-year-old brother in *his* claim to the throne. The southern Chinese kingdom was in the grip of an idea: it needed a hereditary ruler. Unlike Rome, China had never been a place where a general could simply take power because of his strength. He had to fit into the dynastic system, the system that lent to its members a sheen of legitimacy because they belonged to a royal family. Even if that family had just taken power, it still had to *define itself* as a royal family.

Less than a year after the death of the Idiot King, the general convinced the teenaged emperor to officially hand power over to him. We do not know what kind of pressure he exerted, but undoubtedly the young man thought that performing a ceremony that officially transferred imperial power to his prime minister would save his life. He was wrong. When the assassins arrived to kill him, they allowed him to drink himself into a stupor before strangling him; they liked him and wanted his death to be an easy one.[4]

Xiao Yan took power in 502 under the royal name "Liang Wudi," as the first king of a new dynasty. This third southern dynasty, the Southern Liang, would hold power for a little over fifty years, forty-seven of those under Liang Wudi himself.

But it would still identify itself as a *dynasty*. Liang Wudi transformed his own undistinguished family into royalty, worthy heirs of the dynastic succession of imperial China. And his strong personality did give the south a temporary anchor. He spent most of his years on the throne trying to rebuild the nation's bureaucracy; he built five new Confucian schools for the training of young officials, declared that all heirs to the throne must be fully educated in Confucian ethics, and even instituted a system for peasants and the poor to complain anonymously about the behavior of the rich so that they would not fear reprisals. He also beat off an attack from the Bei Wei and shored up the frontier defenses.

He was a Buddhist, and in the years of his reign, his devotion to his faith grew. He sponsored the travels of monks from India so that they could come and preach in the capital city; he built temples (by the end of his reign, there were almost thirteen thousand within the Southern Liang borders); he ordered the gathering of the first Chinese Tripitaka, a comprehensive collection of Buddhist scriptures; he did his best to make sure that Buddhist prohibitions against the taking of life were followed, going so far as to order that all sacrifices demanded by Confucian or Taoist rites be carried out with vegetables and flour cakes shaped like animals standing in for the usual sacrificial victims.[5]

He was doing his best to undergird his claim to the crown by displaying his virtue. As a southern ruler, he had placed himself in the ancient royal tradition that stretched back for thousands of years, and that royal tradition offered a way to legitimize his grasp for power. Virtuous emperors were Heaven-blessed, with divine approval giving them a mandate to rule. Since the very first emperors had ruled in the Yellow river valley, historians and philosophers had argued that they held power *because* of their virtue. "They were constantly attentive to ritual," Confucius had said, explaining *why* the first emperors were given the Mandate of Heaven to rule, "exposed error, made humanity their law and humility their practice. Any who did not abide by these principles were dismissed from their positions."[6] A dynasty could lose the right to rule—the Mandate of Heaven—if it became tyrannical and corrupt. Liang Wudi's new dynasty would *earn* the Mandate of Heaven through displaying its virtue.

This strategy proved, in Liang Wudi's case, to have a sting in its tail. As he developed his virtue, he became more and more convinced that Buddhism required him to renounce his ambitions to earthly power. In 527, he took off his royal robes, put on a monk's robe, and entered a monastery, following its rules and disciplines and finding in it, according to his chroniclers, greater joy than he had ever found in his palace.[7]

His ministers begged him to come out and take back his crown; his renunciation had apparently not extended to designating an heir, and they were having difficulty running the country without the authority to make royal decrees. The head of the monastery saw a good thing and refused to release the king from his vows until the ministers had paid a huge ransom out of the royal treasury. With the money handed over, he expelled Liang Wudi from the monastery, and the king went reluctantly back to rule the Liang state.

TO THE NORTH, Wei Xuanwu ruled the Bei Wei from the new capital at Luoyang. His invasion of the south had failed, thanks to Liang Wudi's competent resistance, and although he launched several more attacks, he decided within five years that attacking the Southern Liang was fruitless. Instead, he concentrated on carrying on his father's campaign to sinicize the northern kingdom into complete Chinese-ness.

But the effort to combine the two worlds of the Bei Wei—the dynamic world of the nomadic soldier and the orderly world of the settled kingdom—now began to bear bitter fruit.

In the old nomadic clan system, tribal leaders held more or less equal authority, with one leader granted slightly greater power to oversee the joint efforts of the tribes. The remnants of this system troubled Wei Xuanwu. He was surrounded by local "aristocrats," offspring of the tribal leaders, who claimed the right to control their own portions of land, while collecting taxes from the peasants who lived on this land (taxes that were supposed to be paid over to the royal treasury) and raising armies from the population they governed (armies that were supposed to serve the interest of the royal family). These landowners existed on the thin boundary between two identities—powerful nobleman loyal to the throne and independent petty ruler—and their natural tendency was to lean towards independence.[8]

In an effort to corral their power, Wei Xuanwu continued his father's attempts at land reform. New laws decreed that the land in the Bei Wei kingdom belonged, not to individual families or noblemen, but to the government. The government had the right to assign land to individuals, who would farm it, support their families with it, and pay taxes from it directly to the throne. When a farmer died, the government could then reassign his land to someone else.

This system, called the *juntian*, or "equal-field" system, had been used by previous Chinese dynasties farther south, but never by the northern kingdoms. It kept noblemen from collecting more and more land and passing it on to their sons, something that tended to create independent hereditary kingdoms within the Bei Wei borders. But it also produced huge resentment from the ex-tribal leaders who saw their traditional power under attack.

Furthermore, it deprived those leaders of their private armies. In the old system, they had provided the throne with soldiers, whose first loyalty was to the noblemen who owned their homes and whose *second* loyalty was to the king. In this new, equal-field system, soldiers (like families) were given fields of their own, which they farmed in return for serving in the king's army for a certain number of months per year. This broke their tie to the noblemen and reforged it directly to the king.[9]

These noblemen were caught in the hard press of transition. Like the king himself, they longed to be Chinese. So even while they resented the decrease of their traditional powers, they found themselves forced to protect their new identity by distancing themselves from their rough warrior past.

In the reign of Wei Xuanwu and his successor, this "distancing" took the form of scorn for the soldiers who were posted on the northern border. The

Bei Wei kingdom was under constant attack from the nomadic peoples who had *not* settled into kingdoms, who still roamed in the high grasslands farther to the north. For many years, part of the Bei Wei strategy for dealing with these nomads was to capture them and then integrate them into the garrisons posted along the northern frontier—controlling the threat, in essence, by bringing part of it within the Bei Wei borders and into the Bei Wei army.[10]

This meant that the frontiers were primarily barbarian, and that the northern garrisons remained far closer to their nomadic roots than the aristocrats at court. The move of the capital city south to Luoyang had increased the distance between northern soldiers and upwardly mobile noblemen even more. Assignment to fight on the northern frontier, once an honor, became a punishment. Aristocrats were suspicious of the loyalty of the northern garrisons, always ready to see treachery and revolt in the slightest unexpected movement. In 519, one of the noblemen who served at the royal court suggested that soldiers no longer be eligible to hold government offices—a proposal that reflects the growing aristocratic scorn for a part-barbarian army. It was the same scorn that had kept the great Roman soldiers Alaric and Stilicho, halfway across the world, from rising to the throne.[11]

When word of the proposal got out, the soldiers in Luoyang rioted. Wei Xuanwu had died in 515, leaving his wife the empress dowager as regent for his young son Wei Xiaoming, and the empress quelled the riot by promising that the idea would never be put into practice. But the contempt of the gesture revealed a deep hostility between the border and the court. In 523, the garrisons along the north began to revolt.

Fighting between the Bei Wei and its own border guard dragged on for several years. The empress dowager, who was supposed to be running things in Luoyang, had earned herself the nickname "Inattentive Empress" for her habit of ignoring anything that was happening outside the city, and the northern rebellions were no exception. Apart from dispatching troops under the guidance of the general Erzhu Rong, the *magister militum* of the Bei Wei, she did nothing to solve the deep-seated hatred that was ripping the kingdom apart. By 528, she had given her lover most of the power at court while refusing to grant any to the young emperor Wei Xiaoming.

Wei Xiaoming, now eighteen, was old enough to fight back. He sent messages to Erzhu Rong, asking him to come back from the northern frontier and remove both the empress and her lover from power. Erzhu Rong started south to answer his emperor's plea, but before he could reach Luoyang, the empress dowager poisoned her son.

She and her lover then appointed a two-year-old child to be the figurehead emperor. In response, Erzhu Rong and his army declared a cousin of the dead Wei Xiaoming to be the rightful emperor and crowned him in camp, on the move. When Erzhu Rong arrived at Luoyang, he sacked the city, captured

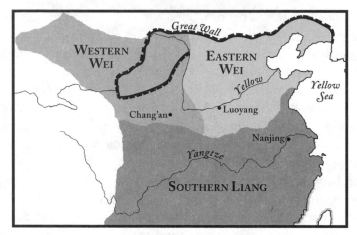

24.1: The Division of the Bei Wei

the empress, and had both her and the child emperor drowned in the Yellow river. He then summoned two thousand of her officials and supporters to his headquarters and had them murdered, in an act that became known as the Heyin Massacre.[12]

Worried about Erzhu Rong's ambitions (to be the figurehead for an ambitious soldier was not a secure position in either east or west), the new emperor, Wei Xiaozhuang, agreed to marry his daughter—which might keep Erzhu Rong from claiming the throne, since his grandchild would theoretically become emperor. But the distrust between the two men deepened. In 530, when Erzhu Rong came to the court of Luoyang to wait for his daughter to give birth to her first child, Wei Xiaozhuang had him assassinated.

This opened a civil war, with Erzhu Rong's relatives and his field army on one side, and the emperor and the army of Luoyang on the other. In 531, Erzhu Rong's nephew Erzhu Zhao captured the emperor in a battle near Luoyang. He broke into the city with his army, sacked it, murdered Wei Xiaozhuang's infant son, and then had the emperor himself strangled.

By 534, the ongoing civil war between the dead emperor's clan, the dead general's clan, and their various claimants to the imperial throne had split the Bei Wei empire into two separate kingdoms: the Eastern Wei and the Western Wei. Luoyang, the center of the conflict, was a ghost town, sacked and almost entirely deserted. The strongest general in each faction placed a puppet-king on each throne, and the two new kingdoms squared off against each other.[13]

Confucian order and Buddhist resignation were a thing of the past. In attempting to make his kingdom Chinese, the emperor Wei Xiaowen had woven into it a thread that, when pulled, ripped the entire construct apart.

TIMELINE 24			
EASTERN ROMAN EMPIRE	**PERSIAN EMPIRE**	**CHINA**	
		SOUTH	**NORTH**
		Song Wendi (424–453)	Wei Taiwu of the Bei Wei (424–452)
	Yazdegerd II (438–457)	Establishment of Confucian colleges (439)	Unification of the north under Bei Wei (440)
			First persecution of Buddhists in the north (446)
Marcian (450–457) Council of Chalcedon (451)	Battle of Vartanantz (451)		
		Song Xiaowu (454–464)	
Leo the Thracian (457–474)	Peroz (457–484)	Song Ming (465–472)	Wei Xiaowen (471–499)
		Song Hou Fei (473–476)	
Leo II (474) Zeno (475–491)/Basiliscus (475–476)		Song Shun (477–479) Fall of Liu Song/Rise of Southern Qi Qi Gaodi (479–482)	
Ostrogoth invasion		Qi Wudi (483–493)	
	Balash (484–488) Kavadh (488–531)		
Anastasius (491–518)	[Zamasb (496–498)]	Qi Mingdi (494–498)	Wei Xuanwu (499–515)
		Qi Hedi (501) Fall of Southern Qi/Rise of Southern Liang Liang Wudi (502–549)	
Justin (518–527)			Wei Xiaoming (515–528)
			Heyin Massacre Wei Xiaozhuang (528–531)
			WESTERN WEI EASTERN WEI (534)

Chapter Twenty-Five

Elected Kings

Between 481 and 531,
Clovis becomes the first king of all the Franks,
Ambrosius Aurelianus of Britain beats back the Saxons,
and the Ostrogoths choose a new king

AFTER THE COSTLY DEFEAT of Attila, the Salian Franks had straggled back westward to their lands west of the Rhine. The battle with the Huns had weakened them; but now they regathered their strength.

The semi-legendary Merovech died, probably around 457, and was succeeded as chief of the Salian Franks by his son Childeric. But although Childeric claimed the title "King of the Franks" and established his court at the northern city of Cambrai, he was merely one chief among many. The other Frankish tribes still kept their independence, even while acknowledging the long-haired Salians as leaders of the coalition. There were minor Frankish kings scattered across the landscape, and Roman kings too; after the Romans had given up full control of Gaul, renegade Roman warleaders had set up their own little domains in the land north of the Loire.

Childeric was forced to battle against these rival kings, against Odovacer of Italy, against Alemanni invaders to the east, and against Saxon pirates sailing into the Loire. When he died in 481, he was merely chief of the Salians despite his royal title.[1]

But he was succeeded by his fifteen-year-old son, Clovis. At twenty, Clovis attacked and defeated a neighboring Roman kingdom and folded its land into his own. This was the first major victory of his reign. Over the next ten years, he took land from the nearby Thuringii, Burgundians, and Alemanni, and his knack for leading the Franks to victory earned him greater and greater authority over the other tribal leaders.[2]

He made alliances by marriage as well, contracting a diplomatic match between himself and the daughter of the king of the Germanic tribe of Burgundy. This princess, Clotild, was a Christian, and the Frankish historian Gregory of Tours tells us that she began to evangelize her husband. "The gods whom you worship are no good," Clotild insisted. "They haven't even been able to help themselves, let alone others. What have Mars and Mercury ever done for anyone?"

It was a pragmatic argument, and in 496, Clovis found it politic to agree with his wife. In Gregory's account, Clovis is on the battlefield, fighting a losing battle against the Alemanni, when he raises his eyes to heaven. "Jesus Christ," he prays, "if you will give me victory over my enemies, I will believe in you. I have called upon my own gods, but, as I see only too clearly, they have no intention of helping me." At once the Alemanni break their ranks and surrender. Clovis returns home a Christian, and he and Clotild summon the bishop of Reims to come and baptize him.[68]

For Gregory, Clovis is the Frankish Constantine. And Clovis was indeed following Constantine's lead. Like Alaric's Goths, the Franks were a confederacy, not a nation: they were held together by custom, by geography, and by necessity. They had lived within Roman boundaries for over a century, and their adoption of Roman practices—the worship of Mars and other Roman gods, the Romanized organization of their army—was the strongest bond holding them together.

But the Roman empire had crumbled in the west, and the bond of *Romanness* was crumbling with it. Like Constantine, Clovis saw that a stronger bond was needed to hold his people together (and to allow him to claim the right of kingship over them all). Christianity would serve as the new glue of the Frankish nation.

Gregory insists on Clovis's sincerity: "Like some new Constantine," he writes, fulsomely, "he stepped forward to the baptismal pool, ready to wash away the sores of his old leprosy and to be cleansed in flowing water from the sordid stains which he had borne so long." And then he adds, without a trace of irony, "More than three thousand of his army were baptized at the same time." The mass conversion of the army was the necessary and politic counterpoint to Clovis's own redemption: the Christian royal family and the Christianized army would be the attractive core of a newly united Christian nation of Franks.[4]

The benefits of conversion were not long in coming. By 507, Clovis, who had been baptized into orthodox Christianity, was confident enough to launch a concentrated attack on the Arian Visigoths of Hispania: "I find it hard to go on seeing these Arians occupy a part of Gaul," he told his ministers. "With God's help let us invade them. When we have beaten them, we will take over their territory."

Reinforced by soldiers lent to him by his father-in-law, the king of Burgundy, Clovis marched towards the Loire river and the Visigothic frontier. The armies met at the city of Vouille, in Visigothic territory on the southwestern side of the Loire. The Visigoth king Alaric II was killed in battle, and

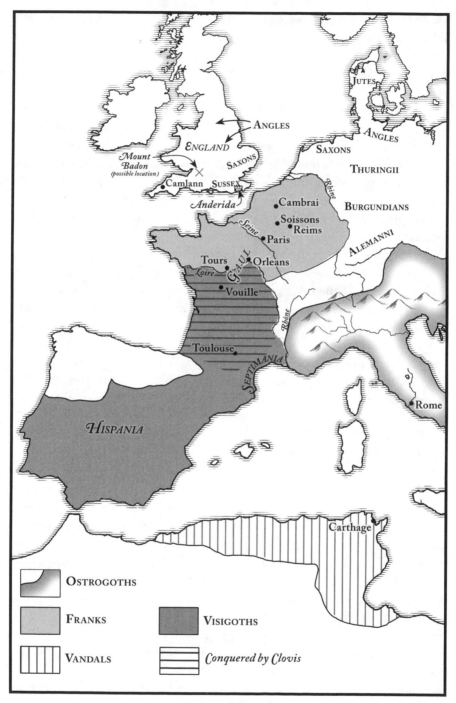

25.1: Clovis and His Neighbors

the Visigoth army was scattered. The Franks stormed southward, invading the city of Toulouse itself, and the remnants of the Visigothic court fled into Hispania with Alaric II's five-year-old son, Amalaric, in tow.[5]

This brought the armies of the Italian Ostrogoths into the fight. Theoderic the Great's daughter had been married to Alaric II, so that young Amalaric— possibly the next king of the Visigoths—was a member of the Ostrogothic royal family. Ostrogothic armies arrived at the Rhône river, in the south, in 508, and forced Clovis to withdraw from the little patch of Gaulish land known as Septimania, right on the coast. But this was a tiny victory. It kept Clovis from establishing himself on the Mediterranean coast, but Toulouse remained in Frankish hands, and Septimania was now the only little patch of Visigothic land in all of Gaul. The Visigoths had been driven almost entirely into Hispania, where they would have to rebuild their shattered kingdom from the ground up.[6]

Returning from his victorious campaign with wagonloads of treasure from Toulouse, Clovis paused in the city of Tours to thank God for his victory. There he found a letter from Constantinople waiting for him. The eastern Roman emperor wanted to give Clovis, his fellow Christian monarch, an honorary title that would recognize him as a shining light in the barbarian west.

Clovis misinterpreted the gesture. He named himself "Augustus, Consul of the West," and put on a purple tunic and a diadem. This is undoubtedly *not* what the eastern emperor had in mind. But he did not object: Clovis was far away; his power would check Theoderic the Great of Italy, who was a much greater problem; and there was no harm in letting him wear a purple cloak over there in the shabby little city of Cambrai.

Clovis did not remain in Cambrai. Now that he was Augustus, victorious Christian and Roman king, he needed a new capital. He settled on the old Roman town Lutetia Parisiorum, on the Seine, and began to reinforce its walls. He issued a set of Latin laws for his domain, the Pactus Legis Salicae; the laws were very specific in forbidding the old Germanic traditions of blood revenge, instead substituting fines and penalties for clan-based revenge killings.[7]

And he killed off the Frankish chiefs who might challenge him for sole power, one at a time. From 509 until his death, Clovis ruled from his new capital, Paris, as the first Christian king of the Franks, the first law-giving king of the Franks, the first king of *all* the Franks. His descendents, taking their name from the legendary warrior Merovech, would occupy the throne for the next two centuries as the Merovingian dynasty—the first royal dynasty of the Franks.

ACROSS THE CHANNEL, another king with a Roman past was struggling to save what was left of his native land. His name was Ambrosius Aurelianus, and his origins were obscure and vaguely royal. In 485, just as Clovis was beginning his decade of conquest, Ambrosius Aurelianus led the rulers of Britain in a great battle against the Saxon invaders.

For thirty years, the native British had been fighting against this invasion. Keeping the Saxons and Angles away had become a way of life for two generations. Vortigern, who had managed to kill one of the original Saxon generals back in 455, had led the resistance for another fifteen years before dying, with the enemy still on his doorstep. Later British historians would charge him with all sorts of imaginary crimes, from killing the rightful king of all Britain and taking his place (even though there was nothing close to a "rightful king of all Britain" in existence in the fifth century) to inviting the Saxons in and handing the country over to them so that he could sleep with the Saxon women. Despite a lifetime of battling the invaders, Vortigern had failed to drive them off, and the bitter memory of his ultimate failure lingered.[8]

At Vortigern's death, Ambrosius had taken up the position of chief British warlord. Ambrosius's background is lost; Gildas's history, the oldest account, calls him a "Roman gentleman" whose parents had "worn the purple" and had been slaughtered by the invaders. William of Malmesbury refers to him as the "sole surviving Roman," while Bede says, mysteriously, that his "parents bore a royal and famous name"; he also calls Ambrosius a *viro modesto*, a discreet, or reticent, man.[9]

What we are to make of this is uncertain, but Ambrosius was likely the son of one of the last Roman soldiers left in Britain, perhaps even a descendent of one of the Roman generals who had claimed the title of emperor in the dying days of the western empire. Whatever his birth (which he did not trumpet), he had inherited the traditions of the Roman army, and he rallied the petty kings of Britain behind him once more.

His initial forays against the Anglo-Saxon invaders were no more successful than Vortigern's; he was badly defeated in 473, and his cause suffered another setback in 477, when yet more Saxon troops landed on the southern coast, near the British fortress of Anderida. They were under the command of a general named Aelle, who claimed the southern land nearby as his own kingdom: the Kingdom of the South Saxons, later shortened to Sussex. He was among the very first Saxons to claim kingship in Britain; the Saxon foothold on Britain was working its way more deeply into the soil.[10]

But in 485, the British struck back. On a hilltop known as Mount Badon (perhaps Solsbury Hill in southeast England, although its exact location is unknown), the British under Ambrosius Aurelianus won a great victory over the Saxons. The stories surrounding the Battle of Mount Badon are varied, confused, and filled with later interpolations. Famous names swirl through them. Ambrosius's brother Uther Pendragon fought by his side; Gorlois, duke of Cornwall, led a wing of the attack; Ambrosius's right-hand general was a soldier named Arthur; Vortigern himself (somehow alive again) joined with the Saxons to fight against his own people. The tales contradict each other, and even the date is not entirely certain. The only constant is British victory.

Thousands of Saxons were killed; hundreds more were driven out of England, back into Gaul and the surrounding areas. A score of legends grew around Aurelianus himself, the last Roman, the last defender of civilization in the face of seemingly unstoppable destruction and death.[11]

The victory at Mount Badon did not end the Saxon takeover. The *Anglo-Saxon Chronicle* records an ongoing round of battles between the British and the Saxons who remained. In 491, the South Saxon leader Aelle strengthened his grasp on his own kingdom by capturing Anderida, the British fortress meant to guard the southern shore, and massacring all of its inhabitants. "There was not even one Briton left there," the *Chronicle* says.[12]

For a time, though, the Battle of Mount Badon ended the influx of *new* armies into the island. For a time, as Irish folklorist Daithi O Hogain puts it, the "erosion of native Britain was checked."[13]

But "native Britain" was weak, welded together as it was only by the necessity of keeping Saxons out. There was no British kingdom and no British high king, no shared religion, no idea of nationhood. At the beginning of the sixth century, to be British was to be *not* Saxon, and the independent kings and tribal leaders were jealous of their power, no matter who threatened it. In 511, twenty-six years after saving Britain, Ambrosius Aurelianus died in battle against another British king, one who previously had been his ally. The battle was at Camlann, near the southwestern coast, and the sword that killed the savior of Britain was British, not Saxon.[14]

Ambrosius became immortal as "Arthur, King of the Britons," a man fighting for civilization and order in a world where neither was natural: always threatened by the power of other warleaders, brought down at the end of his life by the treachery of those he should have been able to trust. The mournful declension of the Arthur story, as it was embroidered by the Welsh bard Taliesin, the English historian Geoffrey of Monmouth, the French poet and crusader Robert De Boron, and ultimately by Thomas Malory, is a glimpse into a time when kingship ended with death. In the dark world of the British—as, indeed, in the world of most Germanic peoples, including the Saxons—the king did not inherit his power. He earned the right to rule through successful leadership of his tribe in battle; his power was given to him, by the men who followed him, because he deserved it. When he died, his power died with him, and his followers banded together to recognize another king.[15]

For the Romans (as for the Persians), kingship was quite different. In the Roman mind, the king represented something immortal and immutable that went on eternally, outlasting any king who might hold it: the idea of the Roman state. A king could pass the right to represent this idea on to his son (thus the possibility of hereditary kingship); his death did nothing to abridge it.

But in Britain, when the king died, his kingdom died with him. The next man to hold the crown re-created it anew. It was a point of view shared by most Germanic peoples, which was why Theoderic the Great had connected the possession of Roman citizenship to loyalty to his own person. Once he had conquered Italy, he *was* the kingdom of Rome.

It is impossible to know whether the old Roman idea of the state had any grasp on the mind of Ambrosius Aurelianus, that British "gentleman" of undetermined Roman lineage who may or may not have had a Roman emperor in his family tree. But Geoffrey of Monmouth, looking back from a much different Britain six hundred years later, reproduces (perhaps without meaning to) a moment when the death of a king did indeed mean the death of his kingdom. Arthur is mortally wounded on the battlefield of Camlann, but he does not die; he hands his crown to his cousin and is taken away to the Isle of Avalon to be healed. His kingdom survives because *he* survives, even though he is far away and mysteriously divided from his people. Arthur *becomes* the idea of the British state, in a time when the state and the king were the same. Like the idea of the state itself, he exists eternally.

IN 511, THE SAME YEAR as the battle at Camlann, King Clovis of the Franks died.

He had ruled as sole king of the Frankish state for only two years and did not name an heir to his crown. Instead, he left his kingdom to the joint rule of his four sons: Childebert, Chlodomer, Chlothar, and Theuderic (not to be confused with Theoderic the Great of Italy; the name, along with its variations, was the Germanic equivalent of the English "Henry"). Clovis had fought to earn his title "King of the All the Franks," and his realm was filled with warlike Franks who still carried with them the old Germanic ideal of kingship: that they had the right to choose their king. They would have bitterly resented any attempt to leave the realm to a single designated heir, one who had not proved himself in battle. Instead, Clovis had left rule of the Franks to his *clan*, which was quite different—and a much more familiar idea to the Franks, who *were* accustomed to recognizing the leadership of the Salian clan over the others.

Each of the four sons chose a different city as the center of his power. The oldest son, Theuderic, went to Reims; Chlodomer claimed Orleans; Childebert stayed in Paris; and the youngest son, Chlothar, took Soissons as his capital. In 524, the first crack appeared in the arrangement. When Chlodomer was killed on an expedition against the Burgundians, his younger brother Chlothar led the other two siblings into Orleans to kill the dead brother's sons before they could lay claim to their father's portion of the crown. The four kings had become three.

The old Germanic clan system was inclined to plunge kingdoms into civil war—but it kept incompetent kings out of the throne room. In 531, the young

Visigothic king Amalaric, who had come into his majority but had failed to prove himself an effective warleader, was murdered by his own men. They elected a new king in his place: an officer named Theudis who was not of royal blood. Nor was he even a Visigoth. He was from Italy, an Ostrogothic soldier-official who had been sent to Hispania some years before by Theoderic the Great of Italy in order to watch over the court while Amalaric was a child.

But his blood mattered less than his strength, and he became the new king of the Visigoths. From this point on, ancestry played little part in the selection of Visigothic kings; the nation had reverted to the old Germanic method of choosing their ruler.[16]

TIMELINE 25						
CHINA		SALIAN		GERMANIC		
SOUTH	NORTH	FRANKS	VISIGOTHS	ITALY	BRITAIN	
					Vortigern	
		Merovech (?–c. 457)			(450s–470)	
Song Xiaowu (454–464)						
		Childeric (c. 457–481)				
Song Ming (465–472)			Euric (466–484)			
	Wei Xiaowen (471–499)				**Aurelius Ambrosius**	
Song Hou Fei (473–476)					(c. 470–511)	
				Odovacer (476–493)		
Song Shun (477–479)					Aelle of Sussex	
Fall of Liu Song/					(477–514)	
Rise of Southern Qi						
Qi Gaodi (479–482)						
		Clovis (481–511)				
Qi Wudi (483–493)			Alaric II (485–507)		Battle of Mount Badon	
				Theoderic the Great (491–526)		
Qi Mingdi (494–498)						
	Wei Xuanwu (499–515)					
Qi Hedi (501)						
Fall of Southern Qi/						
Rise of Southern Liang						
Liang Wudi (502–549)						
			Amalaric (507/526–531)			
		Chlothar (511–561)/			Battle of Camlann	
		Childebert/Theuderic/Chlodomer				
		(511–558) (511–534) (511–524)				
	Wei Xiaoming (515–528)					
	Heyin Massacre					
	Wei Xiaozhuang			Athalaric (526–534)		
	(528–531)					
			Theudis (531–548)			
	WESTERN EASTERN					
	WEI (534) WEI					

Chapter Twenty-Six

—•—

Invasion and Eruption

Between 497 and 535,
the Hephthalites build a kingdom in north India,
and Krakatoa's eruption troubles the world

BUDHAGUPTA, EMPEROR OF the Gupta domain, died in 497 after a thirty-year reign. It is unclear exactly who followed him on the throne, but most likely his brother Narasimha took control of the empire, which had shrunk drastically from its height under their great-great-great-uncle Chandragupta II. Tributaries had wandered away, minor kings had asserted their independence, and the Hephthalite trickle down into the north of India had turned into a flood.

One Hephthalite warrior emerges from the faceless horde: Toramana, a warleader who conquered his way into northern India between 500 and 510, subduing one petty king after another. By 510, he had pushed his way through the empire all the way to the city of Eran, on the southern edge of the Gupta domain.

The governor of this area, Bhanugupta, was himself of royal blood. Together, he and his general, Goparaja, mounted a great defense against the Hephthalites. It proved fruitless; Goparaja was killed in the fighting, while Bhanugupta simply disappeared from the historical record. Narasimha's fate is unknown; Toramana claimed Eran for his own, and Gupta power was forced all the way back into its eastern cradle, while Toramana declared himself king.[1]

Toramana's original domain lay west of the Indus, in land he kept hold of as he pushed south across the mountains. This gave him an empire that stretched from the eastern borders of Persia down across the mountains into India, breaching the physical border between Central Asia and India. He established his capital city at Sakala, and in a brief time Sakala grew into a metropolis, a "great centre of trade." *The Questions of King Milinda* says that Sakala abounded

in parks and gardens and groves and lakes and tanks, a paradise of rivers and mountains and woods. Wise architects have laid it out, and its people know of no oppression, since all their enemies and adversaries have been put down. Brave is its defence, with many and various strong towers and ramparts, with superb gates and entrance archways; and with the royal citadel in its midst, white walled and deeply moated. Well laid out are its streets, squares, cross roads, and market places. . . . So full is the city of money, and of gold and silver ware, of copper and stone ware, that it is a very mine of dazzling treasures. And there is laid up there much store of property and corn and things of value in warehouses—foods and drinks of every sort, syrups and sweetmeats of every kind.[2]

In wealth and glory, the account concludes, Toramana's city was like the city of the gods.

Nevertheless his empire still had some of the qualities of a nomad's kingdom. In the words of historian Charles Eliot, the Hephthalites "overran vast tracts within which they took tribute without establishing any definite constitution or frontiers."[3] Like the Guptas, the Hephthalites did not attempt to enforce laws or tight administrative structures across their domains. A Chinese ambassador who visited Toramana's court remarked that "forty countries" paid tribute to the Hephthalite king, but the payment of goods and money was the only sort of dominion that the empire exerted over the peoples on its edge.

Toramana, building up his great capital city, seemed content with this. But when he died sometime between 515 and 520 and was succeeded by his son, crown prince Mihirakula, the nature of the empire changed.

Mihirakula was a throwback to his nomadic roots: uncouth, rough-edged, and particularly hostile to the Buddhist faith of his new subjects. The Hephthalites had been converted, some decades earlier, to the Manichean and Nestorian Christianity that had filtered eastward through Persia towards them. Perhaps because of the fluidity of his borders, Mihirakula decided to enforce a new kind of orthodoxy: to get rid of Buddhism.*

He did not seem to view Hinduism with the same suspicion. In fact, the Indian historian Kalhana, writing six centuries later, says that Mihirakula's hostility enabled the Hindu brahmans to gain power in his empire: they accepted grants of land from him, making themselves more powerful than their Buddhist countrymen. But he saw Buddhism as the enemy of his power, most likely because it was the religion of the Guptas.[4]

---

*As a reminder: Manicheans tended to see good and evil as equal opposed forces, while Chalcedonian Christianity asserted the omnipotence of the good God and the ultimate subordination of evil; Nestorians believed that Christ had two separate natures, human and divine, while Chalcedonian Christianity argued that the two natures were distinct but mystically combined into one in Jesus, who was thus both God and Man indivisibly. Thus both of the "heresies" tended towards dualism, while Chalcedonian Christianity tended towards unity.

The emperor Budhagupta, whose name gives tribute to the Buddha himself, had been followed by equally devout Buddhist emperors: first by his brother Narasimha and then by Narasimha's son and grandson, each ruling over progressively smaller bits of empire. By the time Mihirakula inherited his father's throne, the Gupta dominion had shrunk to the area of Magadha, in the Ganges valley. Nevertheless, the Guptas remained the most powerful opponent on the Indian frontier, and Mihirakula set out to destroy their religion.[5]

Sometime around 518, a Buddhist mission came to the north of India from China, searching for Buddhist scriptures to collect and preserve. According to their own records, they managed to leave India with 170 volumes. They also met Mihirakula and were unimpressed with him. "The disposition of this king was cruel and vindictive," their account tells us, "and he practised the most barbarous atrocities." Although the Indians he ruled were primarily Hindu ("of the Brahman caste"), they had prized Buddhist teachings—until Mihirakula came to power and began to destroy Buddhist temples, monasteries, and books.[6]

Rather than strengthening his kingdom, Mihirakula weakened it. The Guptas, still trying to drive the Hephthalites out, were joined by local rulers who resented Mihirakula's high-handed rule. In 528, the governor of Malwa—a province that had first belonged to the Guptas and then had earned independence before falling under the control of the Hephthalite king—won a great battle against Mihirakula so decisively that he was able to drive the enemy back up into the northern reaches of the Punjab. Mihirakula lived for another fifteen years in his diminished kingdom, but he was never able to return to the northern Indian lands he had once ruled.

The Guptas were not able to fill the power void. Monasteries and cities had been destroyed in the Hephthalite wars; trade routes had been disrupted. Over the next years, northern India returned to its patchwork condition, filled with little states ruled by independent kings, tribes who migrated from central Asia into the lands with no king, and small communities formed by farmers and shepherds who came down over the mountains and settled in the plains. These small kingdoms and tribes joined together, when necessary, to drive off any Hephthalite attempts to return, but no strong ruler emerged from these sporadic efforts at defense.[7]

In central and south India, a patchwork of kings continued to rule. We know little of them except what we can glean from inscriptions and coins: names and dates of rule. The Indian kingdoms did not aspire to the universal dominion visualized by the kings of the west. Nor did their scholars attempt to write narratives that would tie events together into some sort of huge and meaningful pattern. Scholarship was far from absent: despite the chaos farther north, the astronomer Aryabhata, who had his home in the Gupta domain, had by 499 calculated the value of pi and the exact length of the solar year, and suggested that perhaps the earth was a sphere that moved around the sun while rotating on its axis. This was most certainly an assertion about a universal pattern, but it was an observation, not an attempt to impose meaning on a scattered variety of political events.

THE INDIAN KINGDOMS on the southeastern coast traded across the Indian Ocean with the islands farther east: the large island of Sumatra, and the smaller island of Java. We do not know a great deal about these kingdoms, apart from their ongoing trade with India. On the southern end of Sumatra, a kingdom called Kantoli was in its very early stages (it would develop further in the next century), while on the northern end of Java, the kingdom of Tarumanagara was ruled by King Candrawarman. Between the two islands lay the mountain of Krakatoa: a volcano, slowly building up a head of steam and lava beneath its ice-capped surface.

In 535, Krakatoa erupted.* The explosion hurled pieces of the mountain through the air to land as far as seven miles away. Tons of ash and vaporized salt water exploded upwards into the air, forming a plume perhaps thirty miles high. The land around the volcano collapsed inward, forming a cauldron of rushing seawater thirty miles across. The Indonesian chronicle *The Book of Ancient Kings* describes a tidal wave sweeping across Sumatra and Java, which at the time may have been a single island: "The inhabitants were drowned and swept away with all their property," it reads, "and after the water subsided, the mountain and the surrounding land became sea and the island [had been] divided into two parts."[8]

The Book of Ancient Kings is not entirely reliable, since this account comes from a much later transcription and may reflect more recent eruptions. But the Indonesian records are not the only ones that testify to a 535 disaster. The effects of Krakatoa's eruption rippled across a much wider landscape. In China, where the sound of the explosion was recorded in the *History of the Southern Dynasties*, "yellow dust rained down like snow." Procopius reports that in 536, all the way over in the Byzantine domain, "the sun gave forth its light without brightness, like the moon, during this whole year, and it seemed exceedingly like the sun in eclipse, for the beams it shed were not clear." Michael the Syrian writes, "The sun was dark and its darkness lasted for eighteen months; each day it shone for about four hours, and still this light was only a feeble shadow. . . . [T]he fruits did not ripen and the wine tasted like sour grapes." The ash from the explosion was spreading across the sky, blocking the sun's heat. In Antarctica and Greenland, acid snow began to fall, and continued to blanket the ice for four years.[9]

---

*Probably. David Keys has done an extensive review of the evidence for a disastrous 535 eruption of Krakatoa in his 1999 book *Catastrophe* (Ballantine Books); other dates have been suggested, but tree-ring data seem to make the 535 date most likely.

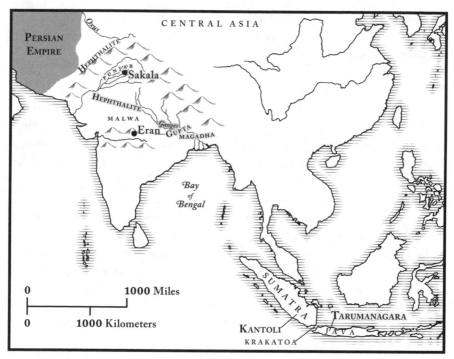

26.1: India and Its Southeast Trading Partners

Two years later, in the early fall of 538, the Roman senator Cassiodorus, serving at the Ostrogoth court in Ravenna, lamented in a letter to one of his officials,

> The Sun, first of stars, seems to have lost his wonted light, and appears of a bluish colour. We marvel to see no shadows of our bodies at noon, to feel the mighty vigour of his heat wasted into feebleness, and the phenomena which accompany a transitory eclipse prolonged through a whole year. The Moon too, even when her orb is full, is empty of her natural splendor. Strange has been the course of the year thus far. We have had a winter without storms, a spring without mildness, and a summer without heat. Whence can we look for harvest, since the months which should have been maturing the corn have been chilled? . . . The seasons seem to be all jumbled up together, and the fruits, which were wont to be formed by gentle showers, cannot be looked for from the parched earth. . . . [T]he apples harden when they should grow ripe, souring the old age of the grape-cluster.[10]

Crop failure was not limited to the east. Tree-ring data from as far away as modern Chile, California, and Siberia show a "drastic drop in summer growth" from around 535 until about 540: this testifies to cold, dark summers. The darkening of the sun was producing plague, hunger, and famine across the medieval world.[11]

And to the east, the civilizations on the islands of Sumatra and Java were destroyed. In Tarumanagara, King Candrawarman was killed; his heir, Suryawarman, moved the capital of his kingdom farther east, away from the site of the catastrophe. But the kingdom had been dealt a death-blow. The once-thriving culture on the island was reduced to shambles; all that is left now are a few inscriptions and the foundations of destroyed temples to the gods of Hinduism and to the Buddha.[12]

TIMELINE 26				
SALIAN FRANKS	VISIGOTHS	GERMANIC ITALY	BRITAIN	INDIA
			Vortigern (450s–470)	Skandagupta (455–467)
Merovech (?-c. 457)				
Childeric (c. 457–481)				
	Euric (466–484)			Budhagupta (c. 467–497)
			Aurelius Ambrosius (c. 470–511)	
		Odovacer (476–493)		
			Aelle of Sussex (477–514)	
				Harishena of the Vakataka (480–515)
Clovis (481–511)				
	Alaric II (485–507)		Battle of Mount Badon	
	Theoderic the Great (491–526)			
				Narasimha (?) (497–c. 510)
	Amalaric (507/526–531)			Toramana (c. 510–c. 520)
Chlothar (511–561)/			Battle of Camlann	
Childebert/Theuderic/Chlodomer (511–558) (511–534) (511–524)				
				Candrawarman of Tarumanagara (c. 515–c. 535)
				Mihirakula (c. 520–528/543)
		Athalaric (526–534)		
	Theudis (531–548)			
				Eruption of Krakatoa (535) Suryawarman of Tarumanagara (c. 535– c. 561)

Chapter Twenty-Seven

The Americas

*Between c. 500 and c. 600,
the cities of Mesoamerica flourish
until drought and famine strike*

THE ASH FROM KRAKATOA, blown by winds far above the earth, circled the globe for five years. On the other side of the world, summers grew cold and gray.[1] Drought struck the forests and fields of the Americas, and for thirty years crop-killing dryness alternated with the vicious flooding brought on by unnaturally frequent El Niño events.*

While the great urban civilizations of Rome, Egypt, and the east were at their height, the peoples who lived on the land in central America were developing complex civilizations of their own. But unlike the Romans, Egyptians, and Chinese, they did not write the histories of their rulers. The archaeologist can trace the rise and fall of cities, the carving out of trade routes and the exchange of goods, but the historian has very little raw material to shape into a narrative. There are statues and carvings but no explanations; there are lists of dates and rulers but no tales of their deeds.

We can start to piece together at least the broad outlines of a story beginning in the sixth century. On the peninsula that jutted out from the central American land bridge into the Gulf of Mexico, a familiar phenomenon was shaping itself. A group of tribal peoples, loosely related by language and culture, building cities that tended to act in alliance, became distinct enough for us to give them a name: the Maya. Southwest of the Mayan territory, in the

---

*An El Niño event occurs when the surface temperature of the Pacific Ocean near the South American coast warms significantly. The change shifts weather patterns, producing violent storms and flooding in some areas of South America. El Niño can also drastically reduce the fish population in heavily fished areas, causing difficulties for peoples who rely on them for food. The drought and flooding in Central and South America between 535 and 593 are well documented by scientists who have examined tree rings, lake deposits, and other physical evidence. Its cause is still debated. The Krakatoa eruption is, in my opinion, the most likely explanation; however, arguments have also been made for the eruption of El Chichón or the impact of a comet in North America.

fertile plain known as the Valley of Oaxaca, another collection of small tribal territories was united (mostly by force) under the leadership of the strongest city among them, Monte Alban: this allows us to see them also as a single people, the Zapotec. Monte Alban became the capital city of their kingdom, a city occupied by over twenty thousand people and extending for fifteen square miles across ridges and valleys.[2]

Both the Maya and the Zapotec wrote. Their records are terse and enigmatic, but the very nature of the writing gives us a glimpse (although indistinct) of a very different world than the kingdoms across the oceans. The development of writing in the east and in Egypt was driven by economics, by the need to keep track of goods and payments. For the Maya and the Zapotec, writing had an entirely different function. It helped them to keep track of time.[3]

And calculating time was no simple matter. The two peoples shared a sacred calendar, one that placed great importance on birth dates and auspicious days; to us, this calendar seems almost unusably complex. It was based on multiples of twenty, not ten (a vigesimal, rather than decimal system), and its core was a series of twenty days, each with a different name. Each one of these days occurred thirteen times during the central American "year," each time paired with a number, from 1 through 13; thus 5 Flower and 5 Deer were different days, as were 5 Flower and 12 Flower. This yielded a total of 260 days before the sequence of names and numbers began to repeat again; if Day 1 of the cycle was Flower 1, the day Flower 1 would not reoccur again until day 261.

This 260-day cycle was the Sacred Round, but it did not coincide with the Earth's rounding of the sun. So it ran side by side with a 365-day calendar, restarting itself a hundred days before the year's end. It took 18,930 days—approximately fifty-two years—for every permutation of the two calendars to play itself out, and each one of those days had significance.[4] The skimpy written records of the Maya and the Zapotec fit each birth and death, each marriage and conquest, the accession of each ruler, into this framework. The passage of time, and the connection between each day and its sacred meaning, were at the center of each kingdom's history. Time was the firstborn of creation; it was born "before the awakening of the world,"[5] so that every creative act, every god, and every human came into being already slotted into the intricate patterns of the calendar.

The third powerful kingdom on the land bridge worked out the passage of time in a slightly different way. This kingdom was centered around the city of Teotihuacan, which in AD 500 was the sixth largest city in the entire world.* It was home to perhaps 125,000 people who spoke a range of languages; many of

---

*"Teotihuacan" is the name given to the city, long after its fall, by the Aztecs (who do not enter the historical record for some centuries yet). The city's ancient name is unknown.

27.1: The Cities of Mesoamerica

them had once farmed the nearby fields and had been moved by force within the city walls in a deliberate attempt by the kings of Teotihuacan to prevent any nearby villages from growing into cities that might challenge their power. The Teotihuacan empire was thus entirely centered within the city walls; like a fried egg, the meat was all in the center, and the edges were almost empty. It had the densest occupation of any central American city (a record it would hold until the fifteenth century), as well as more monuments to the power of its rulers.[6]

With its identity so encircled by its borders, the city built its observation of sacred time directly into its streets and walls. Little in the way of genealogies or calendars survives from Teotihuacan, but the city itself was a matrix in which sacred time met earthly existence. The city was oriented east to west, with the western horizon, the place of the setting sun, at the top of the compass. Its map was not shaped by rivers or the rise of land; it was shaped by sunrise and sunset, the phases of the moon, and the places of the stars. Its greatest structure, the Pyramid of the Sun, stood at its center facing west; a channel dug through the city's center diverted water into an east-west flow. The city's major thoroughfare, the Avenue of the Dead, ran through the city from north to south, with the Pyramid of the Moon on the northern end. At the southern end of the Avenue of the Dead lay the Pyramid of the Feathered Serpent, built in honor of the god who protected mankind.[7]

Details of this god and his worship are known to us only from traditions that were written down hundreds of years afterwards, and it is impossible to know how many of these customs were already followed by the sixth century. He was later known as Quetzalcoatl, and his greatest deed was to restore life to humanity after all men and women had been destroyed in a battle between rival gods. Quetzalcoatl went down into the Land of the Dead, ruled by the Bone Lord Mictlantecuhtli, and retrieved the bones of a man and a woman. He then slashed his own penis, dripped blood over the bones, and restored them to life.

In the religion of Teotihuacan, death was not the end; it was the beginning. Bloodshed generated life. The people of Teotihuacan, like the Maya and the Zapotec to their east, believed in a force called *tonalli*, a sort of radiance or animating heat that brings life. In the words of religion scholar Richard Haly, *tonalli* was "the blood link that binds generation to generation"; it "comes down to humans at the time of their birth, linking the newborn to the ancestors." In return, humans offer blood back to the sky, in order to complete the cycle.[8]

In the countries of the old Roman empire, the growing Christian consen-

27.1: Visitors on the steps of a massive Teotihuacan pyramid.
Credit: Jonathan Kirn/the Image Bank/Getty Images

sus put life and death in opposition; in central America, life and death existed in reciprocity. The Bone Lord himself was the source not just of death but also of life; the Land of the Dead was not merely an underworld but also a place that existed side by side with the earth.[9]

So it is not surprising that the Pyramid of the Feathered Serpent, where the temple to the protector god stood, was erected with blood. Its corners are mass graves filled with over two hundred sacrificial victims, buried in groups that reflect significant numbers in the calendar. The Pyramid of the Feathered Serpent stood for the beginning of time, the beginning of life. And so it was also a re-creation of the Land of the Dead, the place where and when life began.

THE CYCLES OF THE CALENDAR meant that each central American king ruled in the footprints of the king who had come before him in the previous cycle. Each of the milestones of his rule—birth, marriage, coronation, conquest, death—occupied a particular slot on that elaborate calendar. But the slots were already crowded. On the day of his coronation, a king might glance at the written chronologies and see that on that very same day, in the previous cycle, a king had died or been born. Each of the 18,930 days of the cycle was the site of both past and present events.[10]

In this way of thinking, the past was always present; and the rulers of central America kept their power by connecting themselves to the legendary beginnings of their world. Carvings and pictographs hint at complicated bloodletting rituals, echoing the shedding of blood that first gave life back to humanity, carried out by kings. The king who cut himself on top of a pyramid was not simply copying Quetzalcoatl's actions in the distant past; he was with Quetzalcoatl, acting alongside of him, as his representative—and perhaps even as his incarnation.[11]

Declaring yourself the friend of the god (or the god himself) was a time-honored way of keeping control of your people. It was effective, too, when the people shared the same faith—which the residents of the central American kingdoms appear, almost without exception, to have done. And as long as the gods remained powerful and popular, so did the king.

Unfortunately for the kings of the mid-sixth century, the gods they claimed as friends were also the gods of the elements. Quetzalcoatl had the wind at his side; the particular patron god of Teotihuacan, Tlaloc, was the god of rain. The deadly alternating cycle of droughts and storms that began in the 530s could mean only one of two things: either the gods were angry with them or they had simply given up caring for the city. Either way, the representative of the gods on earth was in trouble.

The results of the bad weather can be seen in the cemeteries of Teotihuacan, where skeletons begin to show malnutrition dating back to around 540. The death rate for people younger than twenty-five doubled. And then, sometime around or just after 600 (the exact date is difficult to establish), a riot broke out in Teotihuacan. Along the Avenue of the Dead, the majestic temples and royal residences were vandalized and burned. The staircases leading up to the tops of the temples, where priests and kings met the gods, were broken apart. Statues were smashed, reliefs and carvings slashed and damaged. Excavations reveal skeletons, skulls smashed and bones broken, lying in corridors and rooms of the royal palaces. The fury of the destruction was aimed directly at the rulers, aristocrats, and priests—the elite of the city who had governed it and failed to keep it safe.[12]

Drought and flood affected the entire central American land bridge, but the effects on the Zapotec capital Monte Alban are not quite as easy to trace.

The torching of ceremonial buildings at Teotihuacan tells us that the people who had been moved into the city bore their rulers a fair amount of resentment; they had been living under an autocratic and heavy-handed government and were ready to revolt when famine struck. Like the kings of Teotihuacan, the Zapotecs were not mild and gentle rulers. Reliefs in the remains of ceremonial buildings at Monte Alban show conquered tribal chiefs, probably from the more distant reaches of the Valley of Oaxaca, paraded naked and mutilated by their Zapotec captors.[13] Nevertheless they had not concentrated their populations into a single urban area, something that made Teotihuacan particularly vulnerable to famine and disease when food sources faltered. Their subjects, spread out over a much wider area, were not forced by hunger and misery into a single violent revolt; and the glyphs that we *can* read do not provide us with any chronicle of decline.

But archaeology shows that between 550 and 650, the population of Monte Alban began to bleed out into the surrounding countryside. The villages and farms of the valley continued to be occupied; this was not the death of the Zapotecs, but instead a rejection of the city where its leaders lived and governed. The people survived, but the kingdom died. Like the rulers of Teotihuacan, the kings of Monte Alban had failed to convince their subjects that they were favored by the gods.[14]

What happened to the Mayan cities is even less clear. Unlike their neighbors, the Mayan cities had remained independent of each other. Fiercely autonomous, they fought each other for power as often as they acted in alliance. A few names and deeds survive: the king Sky Witness ruled for ten years over the fifty thousand residents of Calakmul; the king of Caracol, Lord Water, defeated his neighbor, the king of Tikal, and offered him as a sacrifice around 562. Ruins testify to the ingenuity of the Mayan builders: Cancuen still stands out because of the enormous size of its royal palace; Chichen Itza had one of the most elaborate ball courts of any Mayan city, a court where players who represented life and death battled to slam a ball through a stone ring in a sacred ritual that remains obscure to us (although reliefs of decapitated players suggest that bloodshed played a large role).

But most of the Mayan records—the elaborate calendars, genealogies, and chronologies—break off at 534, and the silence lasts for nearly a century. Archaeology must fill the gap: outlying fortresses of the larger Mayan cities were burned, the population dwindled, tree rings show long, cool, wet summers. Hunger stalked the Maya as well. The dearth of official records speaks its own message. When catastrophe struck, divine sanction could not preserve the power of kings—not once their people realized that the kings were helpless in the face of famine, drought, and flood.*

---

*The decades of destruction (the length of the break varied from 60 years at some cities to as long as 120 years at others) are generally considered to be the closing years of the Early Classic Period in Mesoamerican history. The so-called Pre-Classic Period stretches from around 1500 BC to AD 250; after this, archaeologists divide Mesoamerican civilization into Early Classic (c. 250–650), Late Classic (c. 650–900), Early Post-Classic (900–1200), and Late Post-Classic (from 1200 to the Spanish Conquest). See Richard E. W. Adams, *Ancient Civilizations of the New World* (Westview Press, 1997), chapters 2 and 3.

TIMELINE 27			
		CENTRAL AMERICA	
INDIA	MAYA	ZAPOTEC	TEOTIHUACAN
Budhagupta (c. 467–497)			
	Dominance		Height of
	of Mayan cities		Teotihuacan
Harishena of the Vakataka (480–515)			
Narasimha (?) (497–c. 510)			
Toramana (c. 510–c. 520)			
Candrawarman of Tarumanagara (c. 515–c. 535)			
Mihirakula (c. 520–528/543)			
Eruption of Krakatoa (535)			
Suryawarman of Tarumanagara (c. 535– c. 561)	Population begins to leave Monte Alban		
	Sky Witness of Calakmul (c. 560-570)		
	Lord Water of Caracol (c. 560s)		
			Destruction of Teotihuacan (c. 600)

Chapter Twenty-Eight

Great and Holy Majesty

Between 510 and 529,
an Arabian king converts to Judaism,
while the emperor Justinian marries an actress
and claims to speak for God

I N AFRICA, just east of the Nile, the armies of Axum were planning to invade Arabia.

Their target, the Arabian kingdom of Himyar, lay just on the other side of the Red Sea. It had existed in southern Arabia for six hundred years, expanding slowly until it controlled not only its ancient territory on the southwest corner of Arabia but also the central Arabian tribes known as Kindites.

The peoples of Himyar and Axum were not all that different; centuries of migration across the narrow strait between Africa and Arabia had produced African-Arabian kingdoms on both sides of the water. But Axum had been Christian for two hundred years, since its king Ezana had converted and forged a friendship with Constantine, and since then Axum had also been an ally of the Romans.[1]

Most of Himyar, on the other hand, still followed traditional Arab ways—a useful phrase that covers a mass of divergent and contradicting customs. In 510, to be Arab meant nothing more than living on the Arabian peninsula, and even that designation grew fuzzy up towards the north, where the peninsula shaded over into Persian- and Roman-controlled land. Cities populated the coastal areas and the north, while nomadic tribes known collectively as Bedouins roamed the desert; and even though the Bedouins and the urban-dwellers were descended more or less from the same tribal ancestors, they lived in competition for resources and in mutual disdain for each other's lifestyle.

They were further divided by religion. A Nestorian form of Christianity had spread patchily down into some of the northern Arab cities, and even into some of the northern tribes. The Ghassanids, originally nomadic tribes from southern Arabia, had wandered northward in the previous century and settled down as farmers just south of Syria; there they converted to Christianity and

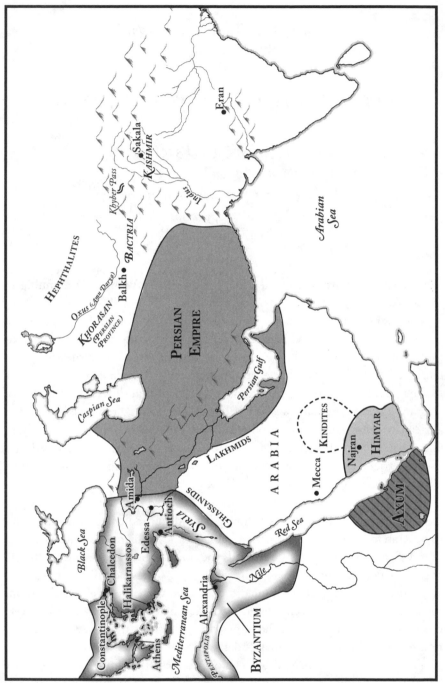

28.1: *Arab Tribes and Kingdoms*

in 502 had agreed to become *foederati* of Byzantium. But most Arabs were loyal to traditional deities who were honored at various shrines and about which we know almost nothing. For many years, the greatest of these shrines was found at the city of Mecca, halfway between Himyar and the Mediterranean Sea. The shrine was called the Ka'aba; it housed the Black Stone, a sacred rock (possibly a meteorite) oriented towards the east. Tribes came from the interior to pay homage at the shrine, and war was prohibited for twenty miles around.[2]

From his corner of the peninsula, the king of Himyar, Dhu Nuwas, could see two great threats looming in the distance. To the northeast was Persia, which had already invaded the Arab peninsula at least once; since Shapur II's expeditions in 325, the Lakhmids (Arab tribes who lived on the southern side of the Euphrates) had served as the Persian arm into Arabia, dominating the tribes nearby with the help of Persian cash and weapons. To the northwest was Byzantium, which had ambitions to spread into Arabia with the help of *its* two allied kings, the rulers of the Axumites across the Red Sea and the Ghassanids south of Syria. Even with the Kindites as a buffer, Dhu Nuwas faced an uncertain future.[3]

So he took a highly unusual step: he converted to Judaism and declared Himyar to be a Jewish kingdom.*

Practically no one in the Middle Ages became Jewish as a way to get ahead. But Dhu Nuwas was already beating off periodic raids launched by Caleb, the Christian king of Axum. He wanted to distance himself from the Christian allies of Byzantium without completely alienating Persia, and the Persian king, Kavadh I, was kindly disposed towards Jews.

As a Jewish monarch, Dhu Nuwas could pronounce the Byzantine and Axumite Christians in his kingdom to be his enemies. He began to arrest the merchants of both nationalities and put them to death. His purge then extended to Himyarite natives whom he suspected of belonging to a fifth column; where Christianity had spread into his country, it had done so in the upper classes, the aristocrats of his society who were the most likely challengers to his power in any case. They were concentrated most heavily in Najran, an oasis city at the intersection of caravan routes from Syria and Persia. Sometime between 518 and 520, Dhu Nuwas massacred the Christians of Najran.

Rather than preserving his kingdom, the massacre destroyed it.[4]

News of the purge reached the Byzantine emperor in 521. Justin had just made his nephew Justinian consul, and the two men were dealing with

---

*Some sources suggest that the conversion took place a century earlier, under the king Karib Asad (ruled 385–420), but the weight of evidence seems to be with Dhu Nuwas. Either way, the motivation of the conversion would have been the same. See Tudor Parfitt, *The Road to Redemption* (Brill Academic, 1996), pp. 7ff.

renewed Persian hostility. Justin's predecessor, the emperor Anastasius, had handed over a yearly tribute to the Persian king Kavadh I, a strategy that had yielded a number of relatively peaceful years; Justin decided to cease the payments, and in retaliation Kavadh I sent an army of Lakhmid mercenaries to attack the Byzantine borders.

In early 521, Justin dispatched an ambassador to the king of the Lakhmids, Mundir, to try to negotiate a peace directly with the Persian-sponsored raiders. Among the ambassador's party was a Syrian churchman named Simeon of Beth Arsham. Afterwards, Simeon wrote to a fellow bishop describing the arrival of the news about the massacre; the Byzantine ambassador and King Mundir were negotiating in the Lakhmid army camp when a call went up from the sentries that another delegation was approaching. It was from Himyar and carried letters from King Dhu Nuwas to his Arab colleague Mundir, telling him that the Christians of Najran were dead.

According to Simeon, the letter described treachery and deceit; Dhu Nuwas had sent Jewish priests to the Christian churches in Najran bearing promises that if the Christians would surrender peacefully, he would send them all across the Red Sea to Caleb of Axum. "He swore to them," Simeon writes, "by the Tablets of Moses, the Ark, and by the God of Abraham, Isaac, and Israel that no harm would befall them if they surrendered the city willingly." But when the Christians surrendered, Dhu Nuwas ordered them slaughtered: men, women, and children were beheaded, their bodies burned in a flame-filled ditch. Dhu Nuwas concluded the letter by offering to pay King Mundir "the weight of 3,000 dinari" if he would convert to Judaism as well, forming an alliance of Arabic Jews who could unite against the Christians and drive Byzantine power entirely from the peninsula.[5]

Simeon's rhetoric is extreme, and his other writings reveal a malicious turn of mind, so his account should be taken with a tablespoon of salt. But his was apparently not the only report of the massacre. When the news reached Constantinople, Justin and Justinian threw the weight of Byzantium behind Caleb of Axum's army, providing him with ships and soldiers and commissioning him to bring the Himyarite kingdom to an end.

Procopius records the expedition: Caleb (whom he calls by the Greek name "Hellestheaeus") crossed the Red Sea with his fleet. Hearing of the approach, the remaining Christians in Himyar tattooed the cross on their arms so that the attacking Axumites would know them and spare their lives. Caleb met Dhu Nuwas in battle and defeated him. Later legends insisted that Dhu Nuwas, seeing his army fall before the Axumite attack, turned his horse towards the Red Sea in despair and rode into it, drowning himself and bringing an end to his kingdom—a baptism with no resurrection.[6]

Caleb of Axum installed a Christian lieutenant of his own as governor, folding the territory into his own; he did not manage to keep control of the land across the Red Sea for long, but the Himyarite kingdom was no more.

But Dhu Nuwas's letter gave birth to a rumor that still lives. The kingdom of Himyar had long ago spread across the old territory once governed by the Sabeans, whose queen had journeyed north to see the great Israelite king Solomon in his capital of Jerusalem. And Dhu Nuwas was said to have sworn his oath to the Christians on the Ark. Perhaps the Ark of the Covenant, lost long ago, had in fact been taken down into Sabea by descendents of the queen, and Dhu Nuwas's oath meant that he *had* the Ark in his possession; and perhaps Caleb, plundering the capital city of Himyar after his victory, took the Ark back across the Red Sea into Axum.

It is still rumored to rest there, in the Church of Our Lady Mary of Zion, in the ancient capital of the Axumites.*

SKIRMISHES BETWEEN Byzantine and Persian armies continued, but for a time neither empire was willing to commit to full war. Kavadh had temporarily lost his Arab mercenaries. After the destruction of Himyar, the Kindites, freed from the dominance of their southwestern neighbors, started a fight with the Lakhmids, which preoccupied the Lakhmid king Mundir for the next few years with the defense of his own people. The emperor Justin was ill with an old army wound that caused him constant pain. And the consul Justinian was in love.

He had fallen for an actress, a profession that in the eastern Roman empire had long combined on-stage performances with the off-stage servicing of male clients willing to pay. The actress who caught Justinian's eye was Theodora; she was barely twenty and had been forced to support herself since childhood in a world where women without the protection of fathers or brothers had little choice of jobs.

Theodora's life is chronicled by Procopius, the Roman historian who gives such a sober and trustworthy chronology of Byzantium's military history in his *History of the Wars*. Procopius was a man's man; he admired strength and force, he scorned uncertainty and compromise, and he believed that a real emperor should be free of female influence. His joint biography of Justinian and Theodora, *The Secret History*, was written after Justinian married his actress, and after it became clear that Justinian—brilliant and mercurial—depended on his wife. It drips with vitriol.

Despite the acidic tone, there is little reason to think that Procopius got his basic facts wrong; Theodora's past was well known to her contemporaries. Her father had been a bear-trainer who worked in the half-time shows given

---

*Other versions of this story have Solomon and the queen of the Sabeans bearing a son together; the son, Menelik, takes the Ark across into Axum. But none of these stories begin to show up until about the eighth century AD, and all of them probably stem from the historical events given above.

by the Greens between chariot races. He had died of illness, leaving his wife with three small girls under the age of seven. The Greens had hired another trainer, and in order to survive, the mother had forced the girls to appear before the Blues as entertainers. Entertainment led to prostitution, and by the time Theodora reached puberty she had already been in a brothel for years. Procopius chalks this up to Theodora's insatiable appetite (he claims that she could sleep with upward of forty men per night without "satisfying her lust"), but a darker picture emerges from even his sharp-tongued account: "She was extremely clever and had a biting wit," he writes, "she complied with the most outrageous demands without the slightest hesitation, and she was the sort of girl who if somebody walloped her or boxed her ears would make a jest of it and roar with laughter." She had, after all, little other choice.[7]

When she was still in her teens, she caught the eye of a Roman official who was heading down to North Africa to take charge of a five-city district known as the Pentapolis. She went with him to his new post, but once in North Africa he threw her out. She made her way along the coast ("finding herself without even the necessities of life," Procopius says, "which from then on she provided in her customary fashion by making her body the tool of her lawless trade") and ended up in the Byzantine city of Alexandria, in Egypt.[8] There, she became a heretic.

In the theological wars of the previous century, Alexandria had lost prestige. Despite the age and size of the city's Christian community, the bishop of Alexandria had been placed below both the bishop of Rome (the pope) and the bishop of Constantinople (the patriarch) in the Christian hierarchy. Resentment over this ordering of church authority made Alexandria a welcome haven for Christians who found themselves out of step with the Chalcedonian Christianity of Constantinople and Rome. In fact, Alexandrian Christians tended to think that the Chalcedonian Creed had not gone far enough in condemning Nestorianism (the belief that Christ had two separate natures, human and divine). The priests at the Council of Chalcedon thought of themselves as monophysitic, and they had carefully rejected language that might make it sound as though Christians worshipped more than one divinity: Jesus and God are "one Person and one subsistence," the Chalcedonian Creed said, "not as if Christ were parted or divided into two persons."[9]

But the creed also maintained that Christ had two natures—and that although those natures were without confusion, division, or separation, the "characteristic property of each nature" was preserved. The Council of Chalcedon had walked as close to the edge of monophysitism as it could without stepping over, and the Alexandrians were unhappy with this phrasing. They were unhappy because it was being imposed on them and also because they wanted no hint of two-ness in their theology. The farther east you lived, the

more aware you were that the Persians believed in a pantheon of deities—
and the more important it became to mark off the differences between you
and your foreign neighbors by insisting that you believed in only one God.
Timothy III, the bishop of Alexandria, not only defended monophysitism
but welcomed into his city churchmen who had been thrown out of Rome,
Constantinople, and Antioch for being insufficiently Chalcedonian. Among
them was Julian of Halikarnassos, who taught that Christ was *so* divine that
even his human body was incorruptible, meaning that the Incarnation was
"real only in appearance."[10]

Theodora was converted to Christianity, and for the rest of her life she held
onto the extreme monophysitism that she had learned in the early days of her
faith. But she did not stay in Alexandria long after her conversion. Even Procopius has to acknowledge that once she had been baptized, she gave up her
livelihood and, having no way to live, went to stay with an old friend, another
actress who was currently living in Antioch.

The friend, Macedonia, had discovered a new way to survive. She too had
given up prostitution, in favor of joining the imperial secret police. Antioch
was the third most important city in Byzantium (just behind Constantinople
and Alexandria), and Justinian apparently had a network of spies and informers to keep him abreast of any unseen developments. Macedonia was one of
these informers; Procopius says that she reported to her boss by writing letters,
but at some point Justinian must have visited the city and asked for a personal
update, because Macedonia introduced him to her friend.

Theodora was no longer in the business of supplying companionship for
cash, and Justinian—twenty years her senior, smitten beyond all reason—
promised to marry her. By 522 she was living in Constantinople, in a house
he provided, and he was trying to talk his uncle and aunt into approving the
marriage. The complication was a law passed by Constantine two hundred
years earlier, meant to guard the morals of his officials: as consul, Justinian
was forbidden to marry an actress. But the greater obstacle appears to have
been his aunt, Justin's wife Euphemia. Euphemia announced that she would
never approve of the marriage—not because the young woman had been in a
brothel, but because she was a monophysite.

Sometime around 524, Euphemia died. Almost at once, the elderly Justin
agreed to pass a law revoking Constantine's ban. "Women who have been on
the stage," he decreed, "but who have changed their mind and have abandoned a dishonorable profession . . . shall be entirely cleansed of all stain."
Legally redeemed by imperial fiat, retired actresses could marry anyone they
pleased, and as soon as the law passed, Justinian and Theodora were married
at the Church of the Holy Wisdom in Constantinople.[11]

The law was Justin's last major act as emperor. He was approaching eighty,
often ill, and weary. On April 1, 527, he crowned Justinian as his co-emperor

28.1: Theodora and a courtier, portrayed on a Constantinople mosaic.
Credit: Scala/Art Resource, NY

and heir. In the hot days of early August, Justin died; his nephew became emperor, and Theodora, still only in her twenties, was crowned empress.

For some decades, the crown of Constantinople had been worn by military men, concerned above all else with protecting the borders of the empire from Persians and Huns, with administration and taxes, treaties and alliances. Justinian was not oblivious to these matters. But he was, above all, a Christian emperor; and he took his duties as God's representative on earth more seriously than any emperor since Theodosius I.[12]

In 528, he appointed a committee to collect and rewrite the unwieldy (and often contradictory) mass of laws passed by eastern emperors over several centuries into a single coherent code. The first volume of this code was completed by the following year, and Justinian's own contributions to it reveal the exact place he occupied in his own ideal universe. "What is greater or holier than the imperial majesty?" he asked, rhetorically, and then decreed,

> Every interpretation of laws by the emperor, whether made on petitions, in judicial tribunals, or in any other manner shall be considered valid and unquestioned. For if at the present time it is conceded only to the emperor to make laws, it should be befitting only the imperial power to interpret them. . . . The emperors will rightly be considered as the sole maker and

interpreter of laws; nor does this contradict the founders of the ancient laws, because the imperial majesty gave them the same right.[13]

"Greater or holier": Justinian claimed for himself the double legitimacy of Roman custom and Christian authority, seeing no contradiction between the two. He was both the heir of Augustus Caesar and the representative of Christ on earth. His code regulated taxes, oaths, land ownership, and matters of belief: "Concerning the High Trinity" was the first regulation in the first book of the code. "We acknowledge," Justinian himself wrote, "the only begotten Son of God, God of God, born of the Father, before the world and without time, coeternal with the Father, the Maker of all things."[14]

Something had happened, almost invisibly, in the eighteen months that Justinian had been on the throne: his word had become law. And not just secular law, but sacred law as well. Despite his claim to wield the ancient Roman *imperium*, Justinian's assertion that his authority was *sacred* was a new assertion. It needed the force of Christian theology behind it, that theology which said there was one and only one right way to God, one and only one Word, one and only one Son, so one and only one man with the final authority to speak for God on earth.

The Roman pantheon could not lend such weight to imperial law; the autocratic Roman emperors of the past had used force and violence as their ultimate justification for carrying out their will. Justinian was not shy about using force, but for him, force was a means. His ultimate appeal to power was the identification between his will and the will of God. No competitors for authority were permitted: the Code of 529 forbade any adherents to the old Greek and Roman religions to teach in public. As a result, the academy at Athens, the last school where Platonic philosophy was taught, shut down. Its faculty emigrated to Persia: "All the finest flower of those who did philosophy in our time," writes the contemporary historian Agathias, "since they did not like the prevailing [Christian] opinion and thought the Persian constitution to be far better . . . went away to a different and pure place with the intention of spending the rest of their lives there."[15]

TIMELINE 28

CENTRAL AMERICA MAYA ZAPOTEC TEOTIHUACAN	PERSIAN BYZANTIUM EMPIRE ARABIA AFRICA
Dominance Height of of Mayan cities Teotihuacan	
	Kavadh (488–531)
	Anastasius (491–518)
	[**Zamasb** (496–498)]
	Mundir of the Lakhmids (c. 504–554)
	Dhu Nuwas **Caleb** of Himyar of Axum (c. 510–525) (c. 510–540)
	Timothy III of Alexandria (517–535) **Justin** (518–527)
	Justinian (527–565)
	Justinian Code, first volume (529)
Population begins to leave Monte Alban	
Sky Witness of Calakmul (c. 560-570) **Lord Water** of Caracol (c. 560s)	
Destruction of Teotihuacan (c. 600)	

Chapter Twenty-Nine

— ■ —

Pestilence

Between 532 and 544,
Justinian and Theodora survive a riot,
Byzantine armies defeat Vandals and Ostrogoths but not Persians,
and bubonic plague docks at the Golden Horn

I N 532, THE PERSIAN AND BYZANTINE emperors decided to forgo any more border spats, long enough to solve their own domestic troubles. They swore a truce with each other called the Eternal Peace. It lasted for eight years.

The emperor Kavadh had just died at the age of eighty-two, naming his favorite (and third-eldest) son Khosru as his heir. Since he wasn't the eldest, Khosru found himself obliged to defend his right to the crown against his other brothers. He also had to put down an opportunistic revolt of the remaining Mazdakites.* When they rioted, Khosru massacred them, chopped off the heads of their leaders, and in an act of poetic justice, shared out all their property among the poor of Persia.[1]

While Khosru was trying to establish his power in Persia, Justinian was on the edge of losing it in Constantinople. His uncle Justin had barely maintained the empire in its present state; Justinian was a reformer, a builder, an energetic hands-on emperor with his fingers in almost every imperial pie. Procopius says that he had little need of rest or food, sometimes sleeping only an hour a night and going for a day or more without bothering to eat. His vast law-code project was just the tip of the iceberg: he had plans for great building projects in Constantinople, for reconquering lost lands in the west, for burnishing the empire into a glorious kingdom of God on earth.[2]

All of this took tax money, and the new taxes Justinian imposed were widely unpopular. To support his policies, Justinian appealed to the loyalty of the Blues, the faction he had supported since his youth. But the factions were inherently unstable: they were armed and ambitious and inclined to pick fights

*See chapter 22.

whenever possible. Factional loyalty was essentially irrational: "They care neither for things divine nor human in comparison with conquering," Procopius wrote, "and when their fatherland is in the most pressing need and suffering unjustly, they pay no heed if only it is likely to go well with their faction."[3]

For Justinian, Blue support was a foundation of sand. In January of 532, two criminals—one of whom happened to be a Blue, the other a Green— were condemned to hanging by the courts at Constantinople. They were marched out for public execution, but the hangman proved incompetent. Twice in a row, the ropes failed to function properly and the criminals hit the ground still alive. Before the hangman could try for a lucky third, monks from a nearby monastery intervened and insisted that the criminals be given sanctuary. It was too late; the torture had already aroused the watchers. Both the Greens and the Blues rioted—not against each other, but joining forces against the government of Constantinople.[4]

With a (somewhat) legitimate grievance fueling them, the factionalists went wild. City employees were indiscriminately slaughtered. Buildings all over Constantinople were set on fire; the Church of the Holy Wisdom, part of the palace complex, the marketplace, and dozens of houses of the wealthy all went up in flames. The rioters began to demand that Justinian turn over to them two city officials who were particularly unpopular, so that they could carry out their own executions. When the officials failed to appear, the fighting grew more violent. Rioters stormed through the streets shouting, "*Nika!*"—Victory!

Meanwhile, Justinian, Theodora, and the high officials of Constantinople "shut themselves up in the palace and remained quietly there." Perhaps they hoped that the rebellion would burn itself out. Instead, the rioters went in search of a new ruler. Hypatius, the nephew of the dead emperor Anastasius, lived in Constantinople with his wife; he had gone home and barred his doors, but the rioters dragged him out of his house against his will and declared him emperor, and then escorted him to a throne they had set up in the Hippodrome (the huge chariot-racing venue in the center of the city).[5]

At this, Justinian decided it would be best to make for the nearest harbor and flee in one of the royal ships docked there. Theodora stopped him. "For one who has been an emperor, it is unendurable to be a fugitive," she told him. "If you wish to save yourself, there is no difficulty. There is the sea, here are the boats. But consider: after you have been saved you may wish that you could exchange that safety for death. For myself, I accept the ancient saying that royalty is a good burial shroud." Theodora had spent all of her earlier years struggling for survival; she had no intention of returning to that life.[6]

The speech snapped Justinian out of his panic, and the besieged emperor and his courtiers decided to hold on a little longer. Justinian's chief general, Belisarius, and the commander of the Illyricum army, who happened to be

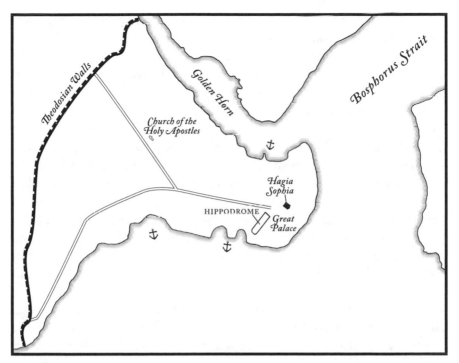

29.1: Constantinople

in Constantinople on business, formed a plan. They had already summoned reinforcements from nearby cities, and those soldiers would arrive at the city shortly. With the new forces behind them, the two men would break in through opposite doors of the Hippodrome with whatever soldiers they could muster, and hope that the surprise attack would panic the crowd into stampeding. Meanwhile one of Justinian's secretaries, posing as a traitor to the imperial cause, passed the news to the leaders of the rebellion that Justinian had fled, which reduced their wariness; another official went to the Hippodrome with a bag of cash and started to pay out bribes, producing dissention between Greens and Blues who had previously been in alliance.[7]

When the reinforcements arrived, the two generals crept through the streets, which now were largely deserted (everyone was in the Hippodrome cheering Hypatius). Belisarius assembled his men at the small door right next to the throne where Hypatius sat, while the Illyricum commander went around to the entrance known as the Gate of Death. When the soldiers barged into the crowd, the hoped-for panic erupted. Belisarius and his colleague mopped up the rebellion; Procopius says that over thirty thousand people were slaughtered in that single night. The next day, Hypatius was captured and assassinated by some unknown and useful member of the army.

The "Nika" revolt was the last challenge to Justinian's power. For the next three decades, he would rule with an autocracy that stemmed partly from his conviction that God had put him in charge of the empire, partly from the determination to keep such a rebellion from ever threatening him again. His partiality for the Blues was markedly diminished, and the factions remained at odds with each other for the rest of his reign.

The revolt left its mark on the city; dozens of public buildings had been burned, and large swathes of the richer neighborhoods had been levelled. Justinian put into place an enormous building program, led by his master-builder Anthemius of Tralles. Enormous glittering edifices rose on the ruins. The Church of the Holy Wisdom, the Hagia Sophia, became the jewel of the restored city; Anthemius, who was also an accomplished mathematician, designed a new dome supported by arches that Procopius found almost magical.* "It is marvellous in its grace, but altogether terrifying," he writes, "for it seems somehow to float in the air on no firm basis, but to be poised aloft to the peril of those inside it." The ceiling was overlaid with gold inset with stones, which added streaks of colored light to the shining yellow surface. The inner sanctuary was lined with forty thousand pounds of silver, and the church was filled with relics and treasures: it was like "a meadow with its flowers in full bloom," Procopius marvels, "the purple of some, the green tint of others, those on which crimson glows, those from which white flashes."[8]

While polishing up the capital city, Justinian also put into play his plans to conquer some of the lost land in the west. The kingdoms of the once-barbarians occupied the former provinces: the Visigoths in Hispania, the Vandals in North Africa, the Ostrogoths in Italy, the Franks in Gaul. But as far as Justinian was concerned, these were not kingdoms: they were overgrowths on Roman land. He intended, not to invade, but to *reclaim*. Justinian still thought of that western land as Roman, and thus as rightfully his.

He settled on North Africa as his first target and put Belisarius at the head of the campaign. Belisarius set sail from Constantinople with five thousand cavalry and ten thousand foot-soldiers. He arrived at the coast of North Africa at an opportune moment: half of the Vandal army was elsewhere, putting down an uprising. The Vandal king Gelimer (a distant relation of Geiseric, the kingdom's founder) had too few soldiers to keep the Byzantines out. Instead he gathered up his bodyguard and fled from his palace in Carthage. Procopius was with Belisarius when the general arrived at the city: "No one hindered us from marching into the city at once," he wrote in his account

---

*Anthemius was both an architect and a mathematician of note; he wrote several treatises covering the properties of cones, parabolas, and ellipses that were studied for centuries afterward. See, for example, "Roman Architects" in *The Architect: Chapters in the History of the Profession*, ed. Spiro Kostoff (Oxford University Press, 1977).

*29.1: The dome of the Hagia Sophia, now the Ayasofya
museum in Istanbul, Turkey.*
Credit: Panoramic Images/Getty Images

of the invasion. "For the Carthaginians opened the gates and burned lights everywhere and the city was brilliant with the illumination that whole night, and those of the Vandals who had been left behind were sitting as suppliants in the sanctuaries."[9]

The Byzantines occupied the city peacefully; Gelimer, finally managing to recall his absent forces, had to attack his own city in an attempt to keep his throne, but his forces were wiped out. In that single battle, fought in mid-December of 533, the Vandals were shattered, their nation destroyed. Ever since the death of Geiseric in 477, they had been declining; Procopius says that by 533, the walls of Carthage were crumbling and dilapidated. Geiseric's fifty-year rule had established the nation, and they had been unable to survive without him; they had never evolved an identity beyond that of "followers of Geiseric."[10]

Belisarius returned to Constantinople in triumph. In 535, Justinian dispatched him on his second western campaign: against Italy, where the symbolic heart of the empire still lay, and where the land was very imperfectly under the control of the Ostrogoth king. Enduring years of bitter quarrelling between his regents and his noblemen, the teenaged king Athalaric had been driven to seek comfort in wine. He had drunk himself to death by the time he was eighteen, and his elderly relative Theodahad had been elected to be the new Ostrogoth ruler.[11]

Belisarius landed on Sicily in late 535 and conquered it without difficulty. He then moved on to the shores of Italy and captured the ancient coastal city of Naples, which had been under Ostrogothic control.

The defeat unseated the elderly Theodahad. The Ostrogoths, displeased by the city's fall and by Theodahad's attempts to make peace by selling part of his land to Justinian, allowed a warrior named Witigis to dethrone and kill him. The old Germanic custom of picking a warleader as king was in full force, as Witigis himself announced in a royal letter to his people:

> We inform you that our kinsmen the Goths, amid a fence of circling swords, raising us in ancestral fashion upon a shield, have by Divine guidance bestowed on us the kingly dignity, thus making arms the emblem of honour to one who has earned all his renown in war. For know that not in the corner of a presence-chamber, but in wide-spreading plains I have been chosen King; and that not the dainty discourse of flatterers, but the blare of trumpets announced my elevation, that the Gothic people, roused by the sound to a kindling of their inborn valour, might once more gaze upon a Soldier King.[12]

While Witigis crowned himself in Ravenna, Belisarius advanced from the coast. In December of 536, he captured Rome itself.

The easy victory in North Africa was not repeated; it took the Byzantine general another four years to advance as far as Ravenna and capture Witigis. But in 540, he took the Ostrogoth king prisoner and declared himself master of Italy.[13]

For the first time in over a hundred years, the empire teetered on the edge of a restoration. But communications between the emperor and his great general had disintegrated. Justinian became convinced that Belisarius intended to set himself up as king of Italy. Rather than allowing Belisarius to consolidate his conquests, he ordered the general to return to Constantinople. Belisarius began to travel back to Constantinople, with Witigis in tow, leaving a skeleton force in Italy to assert Byzantine control. To protect the Byzantine garrisons, Justinian made treaties with three northern tribal confederations (the Gepids, the Lombards, and the Heruls), convincing them to settle along the Italian border northeast of the mountains and act as buffers, should any other wandering peoples attempt to invade.[14]

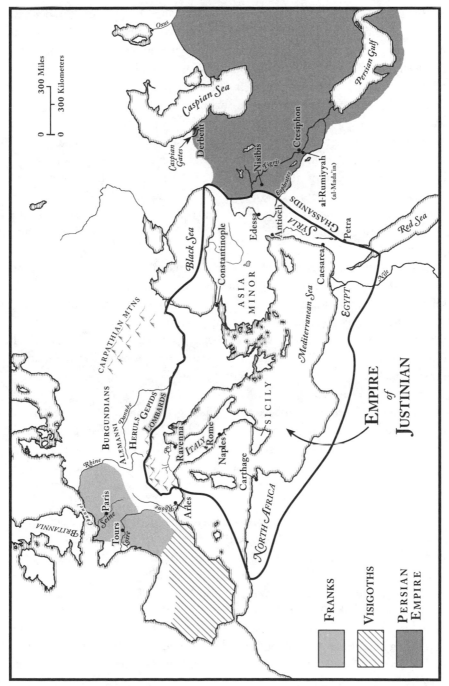

29.2: *The Reconquest of Roman Land*

But as soon as Belisarius was gone, the remaining Ostrogoths elected a new king, a soldier named Totila, and began to fight back against Byzantine occupation. For the next decades, control of Italy would seesaw back and forth between Ostrogoth and Byzantine forces. Witigis died in captivity; Justinian's tribal allies remained along the edges of the territory with their backs to the conflict. No one had enough men to bring the war to a decisive end. "The war has not turned out well to the advantage of either side," an Ostrogothic ambassador remarked, which was an understatement.[15]

The wars in Italy and North Africa, not to mention the enormous building projects in Constantinople, had drained the treasury. The Eternal Peace stipulated that Byzantium would pay the Persian empire a yearly tribute, but Justinian could no longer afford it. The payments went into arrears. In June of 540, Khosru marched into Syria and sacked the ancient city of Antioch in punishment.[16]

Belisarius had not yet arrived back in Constantinople with his men, and without them Justinian simply did not have the manpower to fight back. He sent Khosru messages promising that he would send the tardy tribute just as soon as he was able to raise it; Khosru accepted the offer and began to retreat, very slowly, back through the Syrian province, taking captives from Antioch with him. As he went, he repaid himself for the campaign by demanding ransom money from the Byzantine cities along the way, threatening to burn them if they did not comply.[17]

Meanwhile, Justinian managed to scrape together the tribute. But Khosru insisted on leaving a Persian garrison within Roman territory. He also embarked on a building project designed to irritate the Byzantine emperor: he ordered his architects to construct an exact plan of the sacked city of Antioch, and then built a street-by-street replica of it in his own territory, at al-Mada'in. He settled his captives in it; the Arab historian al-Tabari writes, "When they entered the city's gate, the denizens of each house went to the new house so exactly resembling their former one in Antioch that it was as if they had never left the city." Most of the Persians called it al-Rumiyyah, "Town of the Greeks," but Khosru called it "Built Better than Antioch." Anticipating the beginning of war, he also built walls to fortify the city of Derbent, keeper of the Caspian Gates.[18]

Justinian, not anxious to scrape his bare treasury to fund yet more fighting, had sent a letter of appeal asking for peace to be restored, but Khosru ignored it. He was determined to bring a formal end to the Eternal Peace, and he invaded again in 541.

By this time Belisarius was back in the east, taking command of the Byzantine defense. He won a few smallish victories, but before long the war began to swing the Persian way; Khosru's armies captured the fortress of Petra and the surrounding lands, and Belisarius's attempt to retake the fortress of Nisibis failed.[19]

The fighting had not gone well for the Byzantine army, but a blacker enemy hovered. In 542, just as Khosru was crossing over the Euphrates for yet another assault on the Byzantine frontier, a ship docked at the Golden Horn. It brought much-needed grain from the mouth of the Nile; the cold dark summers of the previous years had reduced food supplies, and the population of the eastern empire was already hungrier and weaker than normal. But not long after the ship threw down its anchor, a sickness began to spread along the waterfront. It was an illness known to the ancients but new to the people of Constantinople: sudden fever, swellings in the groin and armpit, coma, and death.

Physicians, dissecting the bodies of the dead in an effort to find the cause, found strange abscesses filled with pus and dead tissue at the center of the swellings. They were at a loss: nothing seemed to stop the spread of the disease. At first, the deaths from the illness were no worse than from any other epidemic making its way through the crowded suburbs of Constantinople. But within days the mortalities had doubled and then doubled again. This was no mere epidemic. It had become a catastrophe without parallel: a pestilence, writes Procopius, "by which the whole human race came near to being annihilated."[20]

The sickness burned through the city at full force for three entire months. "The tale of dead reached five thousand each day," Procopius tells us, "and then came to ten thousand, and still more than that." Some victims broke out with black pustules, "about as large as a lentil," and died vomiting blood. Others, driven delirious by high fever, died screaming in pain when the swellings grew gangrenous and burst. Some took agonizing days to die. Others walked from their houses healthy and were struck down in the road by fever so sudden that they fell in their tracks and lay on the road until they died. "Nobody would go out of doors without a tag upon which his name was written, and which hung on his neck or arm," writes John of Ephesus, who lived through the plague; that way, their disfigured bodies could be identified and claimed by surviving relatives.[21]

The sickness of Constantinople was bubonic plague (named for the swellings or "buboes"), carried by the fleas that travelled from port to port on ship's rats. Bubonic plague had not struck Constantinople before, but the cold wet summers after 535 had a three-sided consequence: the drop in temperature provided the *Yersinia pestis* bacterium, the active agent of the plague, the perfect environment in which to flourish; years of poor harvests had forced Constantinople to increase its grain imports, bringing ships from all over the Mediterranean to the Golden Horn; and the people of Byzantium were weaker, hungrier, and more vulnerable than ever before. It was only a matter of time before one of those ships brought death to the city.

The population died, and died, and died. The historian Evagrius Scholasticus suffered from the swellings and survived, one of the few to live through the sickness. But he lost his wife, his children, and his grandchildren. "Some were desirous of death," he wrote, in his otherwise dispassionate chronicle, "on account of the utter loss of their children and friends, and placed themselves as much as possible in contact with the diseased, and yet did not die, as if the pestilence struggled against their purpose." The bodies of the dead were at first buried in Constantinople's tombs. When those were filled, mass graves were dug all over the city. Ceremony was nonexistent; the bodies were slung into the graves as fast as possible. When Justinian (who himself suffered from buboes, according to Procopius, but recovered) realized that there was nowhere left to dig new graves, he ordered the tops of the towers just across the Golden Horn ripped off, and the towers themselves filled with bodies. "An evil stench pervaded the city," Procopius writes, "and distressed the inhabitants still more."[22]

Plague brought a temporary end to the war with Persia. The sickness appeared in Ctesiphon, and Khosru himself abandoned the battlefield, retreated back across the Euphrates, and went home to take care of his people. By the following year, plague had spread westward, as far as the lands of the Franks: Gregory of Tours records outbreaks of "swellings in the groin" in Arles in 543.

But the deadliness of the plague was also its weakness. By 543, it had killed so many people (as many as two hundred thousand in Constantinople alone) that it could no longer remain at full strength; it had run out of uninfected hosts, and began to decrease.

Which meant that Khosru was able to return. In 544, he made a great push against the Byzantine fortress of Edessa. If Edessa fell, Khosru could sweep across the Byzantine land all the way into Asia Minor, claiming it for his own. It was a well-defended fortress, and he planned the siege carefully: his men took their time, building a huge circular mound outside the city walls, painstakingly constructing it, layer by layer, from earth and timber. "Elevating it gradually, and pushing it forward towards the town," Evagrius writes, "he raised it to a height sufficient to overtop the wall, so that the besiegers could hurl their missiles from vantage ground against the defenders." The city's defenders, desperate to bring the mound down, tunnelled underneath the city walls, dug a chamber under the mound, and tried to set a fire beneath it, but there wasn't enough air in the underground chamber to feed the flames.[23]

Eventually, using a combination of sulfur and bitumen, they convinced the wood to burn. Smoke started to come up through the pile; to keep the Persians from discovering the fire underneath, the soldiers on the walls of the city shot burning arrows into the top of the mound, using the smoke of the smaller fires to conceal the larger one. Finally the pile of timber and earth went up in flames, and the mound came down.

Khosru sent his armies against the walls in a last attack, but the entire population of the city—women and children included—formed chains up to the walls, passing heated oil for those at the top to pour onto the attackers. The Persian soldiers began to retreat, and Khosru could not keep them moving forward. When an interpreter came out on the walls to offer a treaty, he accepted. The city paid him an enormous ransom in gold; he retreated, and not long afterwards concluded a five-year treaty with Justinian that brought temporary peace to both of the war-ravaged, plague-decimated empires.[24]

Both Procopius and Evagrius attribute the lifting of the siege of Edessa to a sacred object, a relic that had been kept in Edessa for centuries. According to the people of the city, a king named Abgar had ruled Edessa in AD 30. He had fallen ill and had sent messengers to Jerusalem to ask the prophet Jesus to heal him. Jesus had written back, promising healing by means of the letter and the disciple who carried it; when the letter arrived in Edessa, Abgar was made well. Eusebius, bishop of Caesarea, claimed in the early fourth century not only to have seen the letter, but to have translated it from the original Syriac.[25]

Before long, the story had expanded: the disciple was said to have brought not only the letter but also a miraculous cloth with the face of Jesus divinely imprinted on it. It was this cloth, known as the Mandylion, that the people of Edessa treasured. They believed, says Procopius, that the city could never be conquered as long as the Mandylion was inside it; Evagrius insists that the fire under the mound caught only after the Mandylion was washed in water and the water was sprinkled on the timber; the fire burned so hot that Khosru was forced to recognize "his disgraceful folly in having entertained an idea of prevailing over the God whom we worship."[26]

Set beside the accounts of the plague, the story shows a world in which Christianity coexisted uneasily with the sheer power of natural forces. "For this calamity, there is no explanation, except indeed to refer it to God," Procopius writes, baldly, and then later adds, "I am unable to say whether the cause of diversity in symptoms was to be found in the difference in bodies, or in the fact that it followed the wish of Him who brought the disease into the world." Evagrius ascribes the course of the plague to "the good pleasure of God," and for John of Ephesus, the horror was "a sign of grace and a call to repentance."[27] Yet none of the sixth-century historians suggest that Christ, who had lifted the siege at Edessa, might also lift the plague. War was human; plague was something else, something under God's command yet also woven into the fabric of the universe.

TIMELINE 29

ARABIA	PERSIAN EMPIRE	BYZANTIUM	VANDALS	SALIAN FRANKS	VISIGOTHS	GERMANIC ITALY
				Clovis (481–511)		
					Alaric II (485–507)	
	Kavadh (488–531)					
		Anastasius (491–518)				
	[Zamasb (496–498)]					Theoderic the Great (491–526)
Mundir of the Lakhmids (c. 504–554)						
Dhu Nuwas of Himyar (c. 510–525)					Amalaric (507/526–531)	
				Chlothar/Childebert/Theuderic/Chlodomer		
				(511–561) (511–558) (511–534) (511–524)		
		Timothy III of Alexandria (517–535)				
		Justin (518–527)				
		Justinian (527–565)				Athalaric (526–534)
		Justinian Code, first volume (529)	Gelimer (530-534)			
	Khosru (531–579)				Theudis (531–548)	
		"Nika" riots (532)				
						Theodahad (534–536)
		Capture of Rome (536)				Witigis (536–540)
		Capture of Italy (540)				
		Plague in Constantinople (542)				Totila (541–552)

Chapter Thirty

—

The Heavenly Sovereign

Between 536 and 602,
the king of Baekje appeals to the Yamato ruler in Japan,
Buddhism travels eastward to the Japanese islands,
and the Yamato court issues its first constitution

IN 536, NINE YEARS AFTER BUDDHISM came to his country, King Pophung of Silla declared the beginning of a new era: Konwon, the "Initiated Beginning." He had already made Buddhism the state religion, issued a code of law, and given Silla a bureaucracy. The new name marked the birth of Silla as a state just as important as its neighbors, Baekje and Goguryeo.[1]

Now the peninsula was laid out in a three-kingdom opposition of equals. In language, in race, in custom, in shared culture, and now in religion, the kingdoms were the same. Silla's rise to maturity had brought it into line with its companions. All three were Buddhist countries with monarchs, bureaucracies, codes of law, aspirations to be all things Chinese, and ambitions to be the biggest fish in the pond.

Unfortunately there was little room to expand on the peninsula. The sea to the south and east, the Chinese to the west, and the sheer *cold* to the north meant that the three like kingdoms continually pushed back and forth against each other, with power shifting from one side of the peninsula to each other. The Visigoths, the Ostrogoths, and the Franks all had enough space to spread out over a comfortable area without bumping constantly up against each other, but the kingdoms of the peninsula had to fight, and they did so, constantly, without any one kingdom either disappearing or dominating for very long.

Around 540, while Silla was flourishing, the neighboring state of Baekje was also in the midst of a renewal. Pophung of Silla had chosen the idea of time to unify his people, giving them a sense of their place on the vast calendar of Asian peoples; the king of Baekje, King Seong, chose place instead. He moved the capital away from its safe, confined, mountain-protected location at Ungjin and established it instead at Sabi, on the Kum river, in a broad central plain. The message of the move was simple: Baekje would no longer

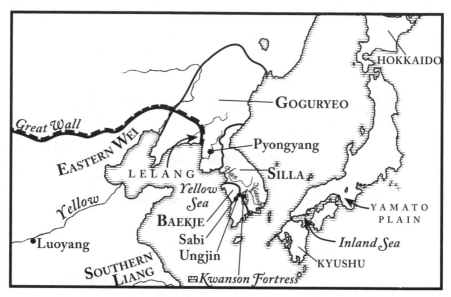

30.1: The Far East in the Sixth Century

be a defensive, wall-building, cowering state protecting its own territory, but an expansive country with ambitions to dominate the peninsula.[2]

In an effort to establish himself as the premier power among the three kingdoms, King Seong of Baekje made an alliance with the Southern Liang of China. Going one better on Goguryeo, which had also allied with the south of China, he made diplomatic contact with the northern dynasties of the Eastern and Western Wei as well; Goguryeo, still the biggest and most powerful of the three kingdoms, was a bitter enemy of the northern Chinese kingdoms, which were near enough to reach threatening fingers into the upper reaches of the peninsula. With water between himself and the mainland, King Seong of Baekje was more willing to make goodwill gestures, particularly those that might put Goguryeo at a disadvantage.

In the 540s, Goguryeo began to suffer through assassination and civil war. It remained powerful, but unrest in the capital Pyongyang meant, inevitably, that less attention was devoted to protecting its borders. At the same time, King Pophung of Silla died and was succeeded by the young and ambitious King Chinhung, who inherited a well-organized and peaceful country ready to expand. The king of Baekje took advantage of both events; he convinced Chinhung of Silla to join with him in alliance and attack the giant Goguryeo.

In particular, Seong of Baekje had his eye on land in the Han river basin that had once belonged to Baekje but had been taken away in the conquests of Guanggaeto the Great a century before. As far as he was concerned, that land was captive: Goguryeo might claim it, but it was Baekje territory kept prisoner.

The distracted armies of Goguryeo were unable to defend the territory, and by 551 the combined armies of Silla and Baekje had driven them out. But Chinhung of Silla had been playing a double game. He now turned against his ally and took the land for himself.

Seong of Baekje hung grimly on to the lower Han for some time, but his troops were soon driven out. He had picked a fight with the giant and gotten nothing for it, and he was enraged. He went home and made a new plan: he sent presents, a statue of the Buddha made of gold and copper, and books of Buddhist scriptures eastward to the island of Japan, and asked its king for help.*

FOR AT LEAST TWO CENTURIES, the kingdoms on the peninsula had known of the inhabitants of the eastern island. Known as the Wa, they appeared occasionally to trade, to buy, and every once in a while to join in a war.

We know very little about the earliest days of the Wa. There is no written history from the ancient cultures of Japan; its oldest historical account, the *Kojiki*, was not written until the seventh century AD. Archaeologists, working from objects rather than stories, speak of the first era of Japanese history as the "Jomon period"; *Jomon* means "cord marked," and during the Jomon period, the inhabitants of the Japanese islands marked their clay by pressing braided cords into it.†

Around 400 BC, a new culture seems to have begun spreading down from the north of the islands, bringing with it new methods of farming, innovations in working bronze and copper, and other advances. These skills were probably brought to Japan by settlers from China, or from the Korean peninsula, or by a mingling of both; the combination of native culture with these new, immigrant skills marks the next historical period, the Yayoi, which ran (after a century or so of transition) from 300 BC to around AD 250.

By AD 250, Japan, like its neighbors to the west, was mutating from a land filled with allied warrior clans into a nation with a monarchy. The warrior clans, known as *uji*, still existed; the geography of the country (four larger islands and a swarm of smaller ones, mountains chopping even the continuous surface of the larger islands into smaller self-contained areas) lent itself to

---

*Although Buddhist statues and books may have arrived in Japan before 552, this is the generally accepted date for the introduction of the Buddhist religion to the island. See Robert Reischauer, *Early Japanese History* (c. 40 BC–AD 1167), part A (Peter Smith, 1967), pp. 134ff, for a brief summary of the debate.

†The Jomon period runs from around 10,000 to 400 BC. Archaeologists further divide the Jomon period into Incipient Jomon (10,000–7500 BC), Initial Jomon (7500–4000 BC), Early Jomon (4000–3000 BC), Middle Jomon (3000–2000 BC), Late Jomon (2000–1000 BC), and Final Jomon (1000 BC–AD 400), each period distinguished by developments in pottery style and advances in farming and other cultural attainments.

multiple independent groups ruling themselves. However, by AD 270, Japan had at least one monarch and one royal family. The Yamato dynasty ruled the flat fertile plain on the largest island: the Yamato plain, which gave easy passage to the Inland Sea.[3]

The first period of Yamato control was marked by the coronation of the semi-mythical ruler Ojin in AD 270. Ojin, the first Japanese monarch in the Kojiki who can be connected with a real historical personage, was seventy when he ascended the throne, and he reigned for an improbable forty years.[*]

In fact, the real Ojin was probably not a king, but a warrior-chief who had managed to subdue his neighbors. For the next few centuries, his family would govern at Yamato; but they were not rulers of their entire domain, let alone the nearby islands. They would become known as *tenno*, "heavenly sovereigns." They did not command world-conquering armies or control trade routes; they provided, instead, a nexus point where the divine could meet the earthly, where the presence of the sacred provided (in a way unclear to us from the contemporary sources) a stable center for the people of the islands.[†]

A mass of tribal chieftains and warleaders spun around the Yamato center. On the island to the south, known as Kyushu, lived clans known as *bambetsu,* "foreign clans"—networks of families whose ancestors had, within living memory, migrated from the Korean peninsula or from the Chinese mainland and settled in a new home. On the northern island, Hokkaido, lived peoples whom the Yamato called the Ezo—the barbarians. It didn't take much of a royal line before a people drew a line between civilization (themselves) and barbarians (the others).[4]

THE 552 ARRIVAL of the gifts from the Baekje presented the Yamato ruler with a decision: to accept and ally, or to reject and isolate.

Japanese chronicles tell us that the heavenly sovereign, Kimmei, summoned the clan leaders loyal to him and asked them whether or not to accept the gifts. The heavenly sovereign may have been the nexus of divine power on earth, but the clan leaders exercised much of the real *political* power in the land of the Wa, and in this case they were divided. The Nakatomi clan, which controlled the worship of the traditional Japanese deities, was opposed,

---

[*]The Yamato dynasty was divided into two parts: the Kofun period (270–c. 538) and the Asuka period (538–715). Both names are designations for types of burial mounds used during these times.

[†]I have followed Joan Piggott in avoiding the use of the terms "emperor" and "imperial" for the power of the Japanese sovereign during this period. Piggott writes, "The term *empire* is strongly associated with a martial political formation founded on conquest. . . . In contrast, the *tenno . . .* did not conquer his realm, he had no standing army save some frontier forces, and the realm remained significantly segmented" (*The Emergence of Japanese Kingship* (Stanford University Press, 1997), p. 8).

as were the members of the Mononobe clan, who objected not so much to the religion as to its foreignness. On the other hand, the leader of the Soga clan, the most powerful in Japan, argued that since every other kingdom now followed the Buddha, it was high time for Japan to follow suit. He had apparently been convinced by the message Seong sent: "From distant India to the three kingdoms of Korea," Seong had written, craftily, "all receive these teachings and there is none who does not revere and honour them." No one east of China wanted to live in a backwater, or to get a reputation as the last hick town out of the mainstream.[5]

Kimmei decided to keep the statue, and in return dispatched an army to help Seong out. King Seong launched an attack against Kwansan Fortress, the keystone to the defense of the Silla frontier; despite the reinforcements, the battle was a disaster. Seong was killed, the Baekje army was driven back, and Chinhung of Silla, elated by his success, kept fighting his way south until he held not only the land around the Han river but also the land along the Naktong river, all the way to the southern coast of the peninsula.

In just a few years, Chinhung had turned his country into the largest and strongest on the peninsula. The map had shifted again. Silla, not Goguryeo, had risen to the top of the heap; and the new king of Baekje, Seong's son Wideok, hastily made an alliance with his previous enemy, the king of Goguryeo, to protect himself against further aggression.[6]

Meanwhile, east of the peninsula, the image of the Buddha was in peril.

The Yamato monarch Kimmei had allowed the Soga chief, Soga no Iname, to build a temple and begin following the ways of the Buddha, but the religion was definitely on probation; the Nakatomi chief had already warned that the old gods of Japan would punish this foreign trespass on their territory. Soga no Iname ignored the warning—until an epidemic broke out in the capital city and intensified. He finally heeded the Nakatomi advice, threw the statue into a canal, and burned down the temple.[7]

But the teachings of the Buddha had already taken hold. It is difficult for us to know exactly what the traditional faith of Japan (later known as Shinto) looked like before the arrival of Buddhism; writing came to Japan along with Buddhism, so all of the descriptions we have were written well after Buddhism had worked its way into the Japanese landscape. But in its earliest forms, Shinto depended on rituals conducted at *kami*, sacred places where earthly existence and the sacred world were thought to intersect; clan leaders were charged with supervising the rituals and keeping the *kami* unpolluted.[8]

Whatever else it encompassed, in the sixth century Shinto was firmly connected to particular places; it was, in the strictest sense, a *local* religion. The universalism of Buddhism meant that the two faiths did not collide. Buddhism, with its global truths, its focus on vast all-encompassing realities, offered answers to questions that Shinto did not ask. The gold and copper Buddha might lie in the mud of a canal bed, but after 552 the Buddha's words spread unstoppably through the islands of Japan.

BY GETTING RID OF THE BUDDHA, Soga no Iname had protected his clan's power; now the dissident Nakatomi couldn't use the new religion as justification to challenge the Soga hold over the emperor. The monarch Kimmei and his dynasty called themselves Great Kings, but their greatness was a tentative and wary affair; they channelled divinity, in their role as heavenly sovereign, but their earthly power was supported by growing reliance on Soga strength.[9]

Of Kimmei's three royal wives, two were of Soga family; Kimmei himself arranged the marriage of his son and heir Bidatsu to one of his own daughters, the prince's half-sister by a Soga wife, tying the clan even more closely to the throne. When he died, the prince Bidatsu came peacefully to the crown; when Bidatsu died after a thirteen-year reign, he was followed by his half-brother Yomei (who reigned for two years) and then his half-brother Sushun (five years). All were children of Kimmei's Soga wives; the Soga had a vested interest in keeping them in power.

Sushun, like his brothers, had been brought to the throne and maintained there by Soga influence. Unlike his brothers, he quarrelled with the kingmakers.

He fell out with the current chief of the Soga clan, Soga no Umako, who was also his uncle. "He hated his uncle for the high-handed way in which he ran the government as Great Imperial Chieftain," the official chronicles tell us. "One day the head of a wild boar was presented to him, and the Sovereign pointedly asked when the head of his hated enemy would be brought in like manner." Soga no Umako got word of this not-so-veiled threat and acted first; he sent an assassin to get rid of his royal nephew. At the same time, he led his clan in a concerted attack on the most powerful rival to Soga power: the anti-Buddhist clan of the Mononobe, allies of the equally anti-Buddhist Nakatomi family. When the dust had settled, the Mononobe had been badly defeated (although not destroyed) and Sushun was dead.[10]

The senior claimant to the throne was a woman named Suiko, triply qualified to rule: she was a daughter of Kimmei and thus half-sibling to the previous rulers; her mother was from the Soga clan; and she had been not only the monarch Bidatsu's half-sister, but also his wife. Soga no Umako wanted her on the throne: "He wanted someone he could control, so chose a woman," the chronicles tell us. Alongside of her, he placed as regent yet another Soga relative: Shotoku Taishi, a Buddhist scholar who became the first true statesman of Japan.[11]

Nineteen at his appointment in 593, the regent Shotoku hit his stride in his thirties. He sent envoys to the Chinese kingdom, demanding that the ambassadors be received as representatives of an equal and sovereign nation; in an attempt to diminish the power of the clan leaders, he instituted a Chinese-style set of government ranks, naming each rank after a cardinal virtue (such as fidelity, justice, and wisdom) in order to remind the officials that they were serving because of their character, not their birth. And he took it upon himself to create a written statement of the principles by which the Yamato dynasty held power. For the first time, the heavenly sovereign would move beyond the vague claim of divine sanction as he grasped his power.

The Seventeen-Article Constitution—the Jushichijo no Kempo—was issued in 602. It is not exactly a constitution in the western sense; it does not lay out a structure for government or restrict the power of the ruler. Instead, it lists the principles by which the Yamato monarchs should be ruling their country—and by which the people should agree to be ruled.

> If the governing harmonize and the governed are hospitable, and matter accords argument, reason will find its way.
>
> Upon the Imperial command, scrupulous obedience should be practised. The Lord is the Heaven, the subject is the earth. Therefore, the Lord speaks; the subjects obey. Disobedience leads to self defeat.
>
> If the people observe decorum, the State will govern itself.[12]

The Constitution reveals, in every line, the conviction that the monarch is the government, that the king is the law. If the king is law, there is no need for a written law to restrict him; there is simply the need, ongoing and prior to all else, that the ruler be moral and virtuous. The Constitution does not try to lay down law; it tries to define the moral character of the king, and also his people. All else should flow harmoniously from this.

It was an elegant and simple point of view: if the occupant of the royal palace was morally and spiritually pure, the country would be at peace. At its core, it was a political philosophy that denied Soga power. If the monarch was not only heavenly sovereign but also the embodiment of earthly law, there was no place in Japan for Soga maneuvering. By appointing Shotoku as regent, the Soga patriarch had inadvertently kicked away the underpinnings of his own power.

Yet, like the Mandate of Heaven, the Seventeen-Article Constitution also had a sting in its tail for the king. Loss of virtue meant that the spiritual power of law no longer inhered, that a heavenly sovereign who was not a righteous ruler was merely masquerading as rightful king. Loss of virtue meant that the ruler could be removed, in full compliance with the Constitution itself.

TIMELINE 30						
ARABIA	PERSIAN EMPIRE	BYZANTIUM	GOGURYEO	BAEKJE	SILLA	JAPAN
			Jangsu (413–491)			
	Kavadh (488–531)					
		Anastasius (491–518)				
	[Zamasb (496–498)]					
					Chijung (500–514)	
Mundir of the Lakhmids (c. 504–554)						
Dhu Nuwas of Himyar (c. 510–525)						
					Pophung (514–540)	
		Timothy III of Alexandria (517–535)				
		Justin (518–527)		Seong (523–554)		
		Justinian (527–565)				
		Justinian Code, first volume (529)				
	Khosru (531–579)					
		"Nika" riots (532)				
		Capture of Rome (536)		Konwon (536)		
				Kimmei (539–571)		
		Capture of Italy (540)		Chinhung (540–576)		
		Plague in Constantinople (542)				
			Wideok (554–598)			Arrival of Buddhism
					Bidatsu (572–585)	
					Yomei (585–587)	
					Sushun (587–592)	
					Suiko (593–628)/ Shotoku (593–621)	
			Seventeen-Article Constitution (602)			

Chapter Thirty-One

—•—

Reunification

Between 546 and 612,
the Sui dynasty brings the north and south back together,
and the Tang dynasty reaps the benefits

ACROSS THE OCEAN, Liang Wudi of the Southern Liang tried again to enter a monastery and devote himself to enlightenment. He had been king of the Southern Liang for forty-five years; he was old, he was tired, and the wars in the outside world brought him no closer to peace. Again, his ministers paid a ransom to get him out, this one even larger. Again, Liang Wudi was forced to leave the monastery and go back to his palace.

Not long after his return to the throne, there was another turnover in power to the north. The general behind the Eastern Wei throne, Gao Huan, died. He had kept alive the fiction that a legitimate Wei ruler still sat on the throne by ruling from the shadows through a puppet-emperor with royal blood. It was a traditional strategy, one that preserved the myth of the heaven-selected emperor, but Gao Huan's son had no patience with it. In 550, he deposed the puppet-emperor and announced that he was emperor, founder of a new dynasty: the Northern Qi. Two years after he took the throne, he had the former puppet-emperor and his entire family murdered.

Now the three dynasties that ruled in China were the Southern Liang, the Western Wei, and the Northern Qi. Of the three, the Western Wei and the Northern Qi were of northern blood, and the Southern Liang continued to view them as foreign.

The old hostility between "Chinese" and "barbarian" was far from dead. Southerns scorned northerners, while northerners were touchy and defensive about their "barbarian past." The northerner Yang Xuanzhi wrote, in the sixth century, of a drunken southerner who says loudly to his friends, in the hearing of the palace master of the north, that the northerners are nothing but barbarians: "The legitimate imperial succession is in the South," he sneers.

The northern palace master retorts that he wouldn't live in the south for the world: "[I]t is hot and humid, crawling with insects and infected with malaria," he snaps. "You may have a ruler and a court, but the ruler is overbearing and his subordinates violent. Our Wei dynasty has received the imperial regalia and set up its court in the region of Mount Sung and Luoyang. It controls the area of the five sacred mountains and makes its home in the area within the four seas. Our laws on reforming customs are comparable to those of the five ancient sage rulers. Ritual, music, and laws flourish to an extent not even matched by the hundred kings. You gentlemen, companions of fish and turtles, how can you be so disrespectful when you come to pay homage at our court, drink water from our ponds, and eat our rice and millet?"[1] This northern defense appealed to ritual, law, custom, learning, and divine sanction—every ancient tradition, bar bloodlines, that the south claimed as its own.

When the Northern Qi dynasty replaced its predecessor, though, one northerner decided to put away that hostility long enough to ally himself with the south. The general Hou Jing, who had served the Western Wei, decided that he had no future in the new regime. He sent a message to Liang Wudi, offering to hand over to the south thirteen former Wei territories and a sizable army in return for a high southern government post.[2]

Liang Wudi accepted the offer, but when the promised promotion came through, Hou Jing found his new rank insufficient. He allied himself with another malcontent: one of Liang Wudi's many sons, Jian, also unhappy with his preferment. Together, the two men assembled an army and marched to the Southern Liang capital, Nanjing (Jianking), where the old king was forced to defend himself against a long and brutal siege. Contemporary chronicles tell of the starving population chasing rats through the streets in hopes of getting a mouthful of meat, of soldiers boiling their own leather armor, trying to make it soft enough to eat.

Finally Liang Wudi surrendered to the inevitable. He opened the gates and let his son and former ally through. Jian deposed his father, sparing his life; but he imprisoned Liang Wudi and allotted him so small a daily allowance of food and water that the old man weakened and died. He was eighty-six years old, and since claiming the crown by force, he had tried to relinquish it on three separate occasions.

Jian, now Liang Jian Wendi, lasted barely a year before his co-conspirator Hou Jing murdered him. The general then fell in turn, when the dead king's younger brother raised a rebellion against Hou Jing and cornered him in the palace. The memory of the horrible siege was still fresh, and the people of Nanjing enthusiastically ripped Hou Jing to pieces.[3]

The younger brother then took the throne himself as Liang Yuandi, third king of the Southern Liang. Liang Yuandi was a scholarly man, a Taoist (unlike his father) with over two hundred thousand books in his personal library. *His* reign was less than three years long; one of his own nephews went north, gathered a northern army, and then came back south and threatened to besiege Nanjing again. Seeing that defeat was inevitable, Liang Yuandi turned on his books and burned them. Buddhism had not straightened his father's path; Taoism had not delivered him.

The instability of the Southern Liang throne continued, with three emperors claiming the crown between 554 and 557. In 557, the short-lived dynasty ended when an army general named himself founder of the new Southern Chen dynasty. This one would last barely thirty years.

The north was in no better shape. The Western Wei also fell when another army officer pursued the same path: he deposed the king and named not himself, but his son, king of the new Northern Zhou. A few decades earlier, the Eastern Wei, Western Wei, and Southern Liang had governed; now the three kingdoms in China were the Northern Qi, the Northern Zhou, and the Southern Chen. In 577, the Northern Zhou absorbed the Northern Qi, and China was once again divided into two: the Northern Zhou and the Southern Chen, occupying almost the same territory as the old Bei Wei and Southern Liang kingdoms forty years before.

Assassination and usurpation had begun to snowball into custom. Legitimacy was clearly a myth on both sides of the Yangtze; for a time it had become clear that divine sanction went to the man with the biggest sword.

THE NORTH AND SOUTH had now drawn themselves together into two separate kingdoms; the fracturing spin-off of separate realms had slowly reversed itself. But the Yangtze, wide and slow, lay between the ancient self-proud south and the ambitious newcomers to the north.

A southerner named Yan Zhitui, serving at the Southern Liang court, was forced to flee north when the Southern Chen deposed his employers. In his northern exile, cut off from his roots, he wrote down a set of rules for his sons to follow so that they would remember southern principles. "Whereas southerners maintain a dignified silence over family affairs due to respect for each other," he warned, "northerners not only discuss these things loudly in public, but even ask each other questions about it. Do not inflict such matters on others. If some one else asks you such questions, give evasive answers." Northerners resent criticism, he points out, while southerners prefer to *be* criticized so that they "can learn their failings and make improvements." Southern women conduct themselves in privacy, but his sons should be cautious of women in the north, who "take charge of family affairs, entering into lawsuits, straightening out disagreements. . . . The streets are filled with their carriages, the government offices are filled with their fancy silks. Those in the North often let their wives manage the family. This," he adds, with the disdain of the Chinese courtier for the barbarian, "may be the remnant of the customs of the Tuoba."[4]

Despite any lingering barbarian practices, Zhou Wu of the Northern Zhou had ambitions to reunite the whole country under his throne—something that had not been done since the collapse of the Jin dynasty, more than two centuries before. He was young, ambitious, sane. But just as he began to plan the conquest, he grew ill. He was on campaign when the sickness killed him at the age of thirty-five.

The honor of reuniting China would fall to one of his officials: Yang Jian, a man of his own age who had fought for him, had given his daughter to be the crown prince's wife, and had been rewarded with the noble title "Duke of Sui." Yang Jian, loyal to his emperor's family, helped the dead king's son—his own son-in-law, Zhou Xuan—ascend the throne of the north in 578.

Zhou Xuan was already nineteen; his father had sired an heir in his early years. Unlike his father, he did not have his eye on long-lasting glory. Instead he proved to be more interested in his immediate power. He began to call himself "The Heaven," designating his courtiers as "the earth"; he forced all of his officials to get rid of any ornaments or decorative clothing so that his own costume would stand out; he began to execute anyone who offended him; he went on lavish royal progresses through the countryside to demonstrate his power, leaving his father-in-law Yang Jian in charge at home. A year after his coronation, he made his own six-year-old son emperor in name, apparently to give himself more freedom to indulge in his pleasures, which included beating and raping the women of the court.[5]

All this time, Yang Jian managed to keep the government running smoothly, which Zhou Xuan both relied on and resented: "As Yang Jian's position and reputation rose ever higher," the contemporary *Sui History* records, "the Emperor more and more regarded him with dislike." He threatened to execute his wife, Yang Jian's daughter, and began to plan the assassination of Yang Jian himself.[6]

Fortunately for the northern Chinese, the wayward emperor had a stroke and died in 579, at the age of twenty. Yang Jian, seeing his old friend's kingdom in danger of falling apart, took immediate steps. He forged a document making him regent for the new emperor, his seven-year-old grandson Zhou Jing, and began to form an inner circle that could help him establish himself as the new ruler of the north.

Among his familiars were a competent general named Gao Ying and a great writer named Li Delin; Gao Ying helped him wipe out opposition to his regency, while Li Delin wrote beautifully convincing political rhetoric about Yang Jian's right to rule. In September of 580, the child emperor signed an edict giving official praise to Yang Jian's worthiness: it acknowledged him as

"Supreme Pillar of State, Grand State Minister, responsive to the mountains and rivers, answering to the emanations of the stars and planets. His moral force elevates both the refined and the vulgar, his virtue brings together what is hidden and what is manifest, and harmonizes Heaven and Earth."[7]

Like so many soldiers before him, Yang Jian was in search of more than just power. Over the last decades, mere conquest had produced short-lived unstable kingdoms. He was after a lasting empire, and that meant he needed the Mandate of Heaven.

The edicts continued. In October, Yang Jian gave his grandfather, father, and great-grandfather posthumous royal titles. In December, he made himself a prince, a higher rank than any other noble at court. In January of 581, an edict of abdication appeared: more of Li Delin's words, again with young Zhou Jing's signature at the bottom. Yang Jian made the customary demur, refusing three times to take the title, but was eventually "persuaded" to ascend the throne as Sui Wendi, emperor of the north. He declared his rule the beginning of a new dynasty: the Sui, rightful rulers of the north.[8]

He then made sure that the Mandate of Heaven would be unchallenged by murdering fifty-nine members of the Northern Zhou ruling family. Among them was his grandson, who died in July "at the will of the Sui."[9]

In 582, the king of the Southern Chen died and was succeeded by a dissolute and extravagant son, and the new Sui emperor saw his chance to begin the reunification.

He spent a careful seven years preparing the ground for invasion. The attack was prefaced with rhetoric: the emperor Sui Wendi (the onetime general Yang Jian) sent agents into the south with three hundred thousand copies of a manifesto listing all of the faults of the new southern emperor, and explaining that vice had deprived the southern dynasty of the Mandate of Heaven.[10]

In 589, the actual war began. Sui Wendi marched towards the southern capital Nanjing; by the time his armies arrived at the city's walls, the power of the Southern Chen had crumbled. With remarkable ease, the Sui forces took control of the city and then of the south. Sui Wendi had restored China to unity with his two-pronged strategy: first words, then swords.

Next he put into place a whole series of quick and effective reforms. He deprived everyone but the army of weapons, thus reducing the possibility of rebellion and eliminating bloody private feuds. He ordered the Great Wall, the barrier against northern invasion, to be rebuilt where it had crumbled. He reorganized the two untidy governments of the north and south into a single, rational, efficient unit, highly structured and hierarchical, each office having its own rank, its own set of privileges, and even its own particular uniform. Like Justinian to his west, he ordered that a new set of laws be drawn up

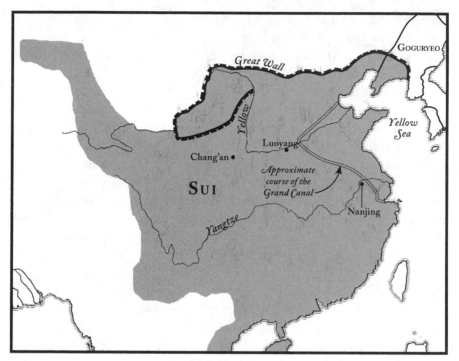

31.1: The Grand Canal

that would apply across the entire empire, replacing the untidy contradictory mass of local regulations: the New Code. To reduce southern hostility to the northern takeover, he married his son and heir, Yangdi, to a southern bride. And, recognizing that the north and south would never hold together without free intercourse between them, he began to build a series of new canals from waterway to waterway that would ultimately link the Yellow and Yangtze rivers. The finished waterway became known collectively as the Grand Canal.[11]

Recognizing that a country gained cohesion in the face of an outside enemy, he began a war with the Korean kingdom of Goguryeo—close enough to be considered a threat, weak enough (Silla still dominated the peninsula) to pose no serious or immediate threat to his power.

This would prove to be a disastrous mistake, one that would bring the Sui down in its infancy, but the scope of the error would not be seen for another decade.

IN 604, THE EMPEROR SUI WENDI died, ruler of a united China. He had single-handedly established China as a newly strong country: new law, new defenses, new canal, new war. Sui Wendi *was* Sui China, acting out his own virtues and vices in its landscape.

Those virtues and vices continued to work themselves out under his son, and the vices proved stronger. For one thing, no matter how great the Grand Canal—and it was indeed a dazzling network of rivers and man-dug channels that ran for over a thousand miles from north to south, with roads and post stations and royal pavilions all along its banks—it had been built with an enormous outlay in manpower. Over five million Chinese were forced to labor on the canal for part of the year, many dying of the hard labor, many more impoverished by the months spent away from their own crops and herds. Tax money had been poured into the water like sand. And, for the last years of his reign, Sui Wendi had been stymied by his war with Goguryeo. The country was proving unexpectedly hard to conquer, thanks to the stiff resistance of the great Goguryeon general Eulji Mundeok.[12]

Wendi's son Sui Yangdi inherited his crown and his problems—which he immediately worsened. Rather than retrenching, Sui Yangdi carried on his father's attempt to build a country in less than one generation. He stepped up on the taxes and labor in order to complete the Grand Canal, and took a victory sail on the completed waterway, with sixty-five miles of royal vessels following stem-to-stern behind him—celebrating the accomplishment while ignoring the human cost. He grew obsessed with completing the conquest of Goguryeo, pouring the remaining treasury into it and sending troops into the Korean peninsula over the bodies of their fallen comrades. The war had now dragged on for nearly twenty years; the standing Sui army of three hundred thousand soldiers had been reduced to less than three thousand.[13]

Sui Yangdi drafted, conscripted, and enslaved enough men for one final push. In 612, he took an army reported to be more than a million men strong into tiny Goguryeo, where Eulji Mundeok made his stand at the capital city Pyongyang. In a fierce, epically bloody battle, the Korean soldiers surrounded and obliterated the Chinese troops.

The embarrassing and horrendous defeat spelled the end for Sui Yangdi. A rebel officer declared himself to be emperor, and Sui Yangdi lost Luoyang to the revolt in 618. He died in the battle for the city, and the rebel officer ascended the throne as the emperor Gaozu, founder of a new dynasty: the Tang.

Tang Gaozu inherited a troubled country. The final years of the Sui had reduced both north and south to unhappy poverty, the king of Goguryeo was on the attack, and the treasury was empty.[14]

But he also inherited a country in which, despite the fatal flaws of the Sui regime, many of the essential difficulties had been solved. He inherited a strong administrative structure, a law code, a north-south trade route, a fortified capital city, a system of governing the far-flung edges, a tax structure. The Tang would rule over China for centuries, but they owed their existence to the bloody and short-lived innovations of the Sui.

TIMELINE 31			

			CHINA	
GOGURYEO BAEKJE SILLA JAPAN		SOUTH		NORTH

	CHINA	
GOGURYEO BAEKJE SILLA JAPAN	SOUTH	NORTH
	Liang Wudi (502–550)	
Pophung (514–540)		
Seong (523–554)		**Wei Xiaoming** (515–528)
		Heyin Massacre **Wei Xiaozhuang** (528–531)
Konwon (536) **Kimmei** (539–571) **Chinhung** (540–576)		Western Wei Eastern Wei (534)
Arrival of **Wideok** (554–598) Buddhism	**Liang Jian Wendi** (550–551) Fall of Eastern Wei/ Rise of Northern Qi (550) **Liang Yuandi** (552–555)	
	Fall of Southern Liang and Western Wei/ Rise of Southern Chen and Northern Zhou (557)	
		Zhou Wu (561–578)
Bidatsu (572–585)		Fall of Northern Qi (577) **Zhou Xuan** (578–579) **Zhou Jing** (579–581) Fall of Northern Zhou/Rise of Sui (581) **Sui Wendi** (581–604)
Yomei (585–587) **Sushun** (587–592)		
Suiko (593–628)/ Shotoku (593–621)	Reunion of China under Sui (589)	
Seventeen-Article Constitution (602)		
Resistance of Eulji Mundeok	**Sui Yangdi** (605–618)	
	Fall of Sui/Rise of Tang (618) **Tang Gaozu** (618–626)	

Chapter Thirty-Two

—

The South Indian Kings

*Between 543 and 620,
the Chalukya kingdom spreads,
a polymathic Pallava ruler fights back,
and Harsha of the north almost captures the south*

IN 543, THE JAGGED LANDSCAPE of small kingdoms in the south of India began to smooth itself into an empire.

The king who took the first step towards conquest was Pulakesi, ruler of the Chalukya. The Chalukya tribe lived in the Deccan; they had probably come down from the north, at some distant period, but now were thoroughly native to central India. For centuries, they had existed more or less in peace, but in the sixth century Pulakesi, charismatic and ambitious, began to create a small empire out of a tribal kingdom.

Pulakesi's capital city was Vatapi, and his conquests pushed the Chalukya empire out from that center against the neighboring tribes. He annexed the kingdom of the Vakataka, which had briefly swelled to power during the last days of the Gupta empire and now crumbled underneath his approach. He conquered land on the western coast, which meant that the Chalukya could now trade unhindered with the Arabs. But he did not rest his whole claim to authority on his sword. Instead, he boasted of having fifty-nine royal ancestors, giving his dynasty an unlikely sheen of antiquity.[1]

Bolstering his authority further, he performed the horse-sacrifice: the ancient Hindu ritual that was intended to bring health and strength to the people by channelling it through the king.

The horse-sacrifice was, in the words of Indologist Hermann Oldenberg, the "highest sacral expression of royal might and splendor." It was an elaborate and time-consuming ritual. The consecrated horse was set to wander free for a full year, under guard, before it was brought back to the king. Priests covered the horse with a golden cloth, and the king killed it with his own right hand at the culmination of a three-day festival. The queen then lay down beside the dead horse, underneath the golden cloth, and acted out sexual congress with the corpse. The strength of the horse and the strength of the king became one; the power of the horse entered the queen and she gave birth to a royal heir, who would also bear the divine strength. Power and sex were interrelated. The crown, and the passing of the crown to a blood heir, were intertwined. It was the sacrifice of an emperor, not a minor king.[2]

Pulakesi's sons built on this assertion, putting their swords behind their insistence that they had the right to rule. When the king died in 566, his son Kirtivarman took his crown and spent the next thirty years expanding the range of Chalukya power still further; inscriptions tell us that among other conquests, he defeated the nearby Mauryans, descendents of the ancient royal house that had once ruled much of India. He also built up the village of Vatapi, filling it with new temples and public buildings, beginning to turn it into a capital city.

In 597, Kirtivarman too died, and was succeeded by his young son Pulakesi II. But Pulakesi II did not at once govern his own people; for thirteen years, Kirtivarman's brother Mangalesa served as regent, controlling the kingdom even after Pulakesi II was of age. He was reluctant to let go of the king's sword, and as regent he carried on the conquests of his father and brother.

Chalukya momentum was rolling across the center of the subcontinent, but the kingdom's advance would soon be complicated by another rising power: the Pallava, on the eastern coast.

In ancient times, the Pallava had lived in Vatapi, the capital city that was now at the center of the Chalukya domain. Two hundred years earlier, the Chalukya had driven them out, and they had been forced to settle in the territory known as Vengi. The long-ago defeat had produced a deep-rooted hatred between the two peoples: the Chalukya, taking the high ground, accused the Pallava of being "hostile by nature," while the Pallava resented Chalukya expansion.[3]

Around 600, the Pallava king Mahendravarman came to power. He too would prove to be a charismatic ruler who lit the fuse of a country's expansion. For the moment, though, he avoided direct conflict with the Chalukya, instead conquering his way through the territory north of the Godavari river. Mahendravarman stands out in the sketchy chronicles of the south Indian kings, not because of his military victories (every south Indian king boasted of military victories), but because he managed to keep an interest in the arts alive, even while directing the inevitable campaigns against bordering states. He gave himself the name Vichitrachitta, which means something like "the man with new-fangled ideas"; he was interested in architecture (pioneering a new method of carving out rock-temples), painting (he commissioned a scholar at his court to write an instructional manual for painters, the Dakshinachitra), town design (he built a number of new towns incorporating his own engineering techniques), music (he is credited with inventing a method of musical notation), and writing (he wrote two plays in Sanskrit, one of them a satire skewering his own government).[4]

Had Mahendravarman lived in the west, with courtiers and monks who were determined to chronicle the exact place he occupied in God's plan for the world, he would stand out in history as a polymathic king, a genius who happened to be born to the crown. Instead, we know of his accomplishments only from single lines of inscriptions.

Meanwhile the Chalukya began to suffer through civil war. The king's ambitious uncle, Mangalesa, had refused to relinquish the throne. He was still ruling as regent but had hopes of installing his own son as king. He had led the Chalukya to victory over one of their strongest enemies, the Kalachuri; like Kirtivarman, he had added buildings and cave-temples to the capital city of Vatapi. He had every quality of a king, including royal blood—except that he was not in the direct line of succession.

In 610, young Pulakesi II rebelled against his uncle's control. An inscription left by Pulakesi II's court poet, Ravikirti, preserves his rationale: Pulakesi II, says the verse, claimed rule as the grandson, namesake, and rightful heir of Pulakesi I, the first of his family to rule the Chalukya as emperor. His grandfather had performed horse-sacrifice, and he alone had the right to rule.[5]

Details of the rebellion are sketchy. All we know is that Pulakesi II was able to win the support of enough soldiers to assemble an army. Mangalesa's able leadership and royal blood apparently were not enough: the tradition of direct succession trumped his strength. He was killed in the fighting, and Pulakesi II claimed the throne.

At once he picked up the sword. The list of chiefs he defeated and forced into obedience is long: Gangas, Latas, Malavas, Gurjaras, and many more. Chalukya power extended across much of the Deccan, and the Pallava and Chalukya armies began to clash. Both of their kings—Pulakesi II of the Chalukya, Mahendravarman of the Pallava—were ambitious men, bounded by sea on either side, setting the stage for an ongoing struggle that would characterize Indian history for decades.

However, a bigger threat than either of them had suddenly ballooned to the north.

After the rule of the Guptas and Hephthalites, the northern part of India had fallen apart into competing tiny kingdoms and states. But around the beginning of the seventh century, an extraordinary boy named Harsha Vardhana inherited from his dying father the rule of the small city of Thanesar, in the north. Again, the charisma and determination of a single man would change the landscape of a country.

Unlike Mahendravarman, Harsha had a courtier who wrote. This man, Bana, left for us a eulogy praising his king's accomplishments: the Harsha

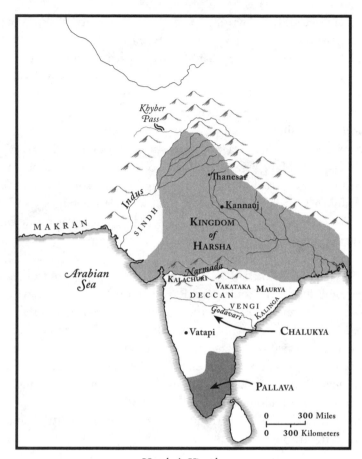

32.1: Harsha's Kingdom

Carita. The Carita describes Harsha's royal ancestry: "a line of kings," Bana writes, ". . . dominating the world by their splendor, thronging the regions with their armies in array." In fact, Harsha's family was not particularly distinguished and had never ruled over much in the way of territory; but Harsha's later conquests demanded that he be destined for glory.[6]

Harsha had no sooner been crowned king than a message came to him, carried by a frantic servant. His sister Rajyasri, who had been married to a neighboring king for treaty-making purposes, had been made a widow by her husband's sudden death. Her adopted kingdom was about to be invaded by enemies, and she herself was facing death by fire on a funeral pyre honoring her husband.

Harsha assembled an invasion force and went in to rescue her; Bana says that he lifted her from the pyramid of wood just before it could be lit. He then claimed the country for himself.

It was the first of many victories. The chiefs he defeated swore loyalty to him one after another, all across north India. As the realm grew, Harsha moved his capital city eastward to Kannauj, closer to the center of his mushrooming realm, and from there he ruled, with his sister as his co-ruler and empress. While she governed, he fought. He united Thanesar and Kannauj and defeated the neighboring tribes in an ever-widening circle around him.[7]

In 620, he turned south and met the Chalukya king Pulakesi II at the Narmada river. To have any hope of holding on to his kingdom, Pulakesi II needed to keep Harsha from crossing the river. But his forces were outnumbered; the Chinese monk Xuan Zang, who spent seventeen years travelling through India during Harsha's reign, estimated that Harsha had a hundred thousand horsemen, as many foot-soldiers, and sixty thousand elephants.[8]

Pulakesi's court poet later wrote that the smaller army prepared for battle by getting both themselves and their war elephants drunk: this made them reckless, dangerous, and overwhelming. The strategy is confirmed by Xuan Zang: "They intoxicate themselves with wine," he writes, "and then one man with lance in hand will meet ten thousand and challenge them. . . . Moreover they inebriate many hundred heads of elephants, and taking them out to fight, they themselves first drink their wine, and then, rushing forward in mass, they trample everything down, so that no enemy can stand before them."[9]

Drunken courage may have played a part in the battle that followed, but Pulakesi II had the easier task: to enter Chalukya territory, Harsha's army had to fight its way through mountain passes that were much simpler to defend than to seize. The mountains, the river, and the desert at the center of India had long militated against any king managing to sweep both north and south India into the same kingdom.

The Chalukya troops were successful, pushing back Harsha's vast invasion force. From that point on, the Narmada was the southern border of his kingdom. This was terribly embarrassing for Harsha; Pulakesi II, great in his own sphere, was a minor ruler compared to Harsha, his kingdom a mere blot against Harsha's vast expanse.

But he had staked out his territory and held on to it. He returned from the battle against Harsha, high with victory, and also defeated the Pallava king Mahendravarman and took away the northern provinces—Vengi, the land where the Pallava had settled after being ejected from Vatapi so many years earlier. For the second time, the Chalukya had driven the Pallava from their homeland.[10]

TIMELINE 32

SOUTH	CHINA / NORTH	INDIA
		Toramana (c. 510–c. 520)
	Wei Xiaoming (515–528)	
		Candrawarman of Tarumanagara (c. 515–c. 535)
		Mihirakula (c. 520–528/543)
	Heyin Massacre Wei Xiaozhuang (528–531)	
	Western Wei Eastern Wei (534)	
		Eruption of Krakatoa (535) Suryawarman of Tarumanagara (c. 535–c. 561)
Liang Jian Wendi (550–551)	Fall of Eastern Wei/ Rise of Northern Qi (550)	Pulakesi of the Chalukya (543–566)
Liang Yuandi (552–555)		
Fall of Southern Liang and Western Wei/ Rise of Southern Chen and Northern Zhou (557)	Zhou Wu (561–578)	
		Kirtivarman of the Chalukya (566–597)
	Fall of Northern Qi (577) Zhou Xuan (578–579) Zhou Jing (579–581) Fall of Northern Zhou/Rise of Sui (581) Sui Wendi (581–604)	
Reunion of China under Sui (589)		
		Pulakesi II of the Chalukya (597/610–642) Mahendravarman of the Pallava (600–630)
	Sui Yangdi (605–618)	Harsha (606–647)
Fall of Sui/Rise of Tang (618)	Tang Gaozu (618–626)	

Chapter Thirty-Three

——

Two Emperors

Between 551 and 579,
the Lombards seize Italy, the Persians push into Arabia,
and both Justinian and Khosru leave their kingdoms to lesser heirs

I N CONSTANTINOPLE, the plague had finally died away. A five-year truce
with the Persians protected the eastern border. At last, Justinian could turn his
attention back to his project of conquering the west.

The Byzantine army in Italy was stretched to its limits and would not be
able to hold out much longer, so Justinian sent the soldier-eunuch Narses
(Belisarius had recently retired from active duty) to Italy with instructions to
hire mercenaries from the Gepids and the Lombards.

Both of these tribes had already agreed to settle along the northern edge of
the country, but the Lombards proved easier to recruit for actual fighting. The
Lombards had probably come, long ago, from the cold northern lands on the
far side of the Baltic Sea, known to ancient historians as Scandia. Their own
oral history (set down by Paul the Deacon in the eighth century, hundreds of
years later) testifies to this origin: "The peoples [of Scandinavia] . . . had grown
to so great a multitude that they could not now dwell together," Paul writes,
"so they divided their whole troop into three parts, as is said, and determined
by lot which part of them had to forsake their country and seek new abodes."
The Lombards, one of those three bands, had been forced by chance to set out
for a new home.[1]

When Narses arrived in Italy around 551, he promised the Lombards new
land in Pannonia in exchange for their help. With the Lombard reinforcements behind him, he picked up the war against the Ostrogoth resistance.
Their king Totila had recaptured Rome and mounted his defense there, rather
than at Ravenna, but Narses's mercenaries numbered almost thirty thousand
men: he had recruited not only Lombards but also a few Gepids and opportunistic Huns. When Narses attacked Rome, six thousand Ostrogoths died in
battle, and Totila was killed.[2]

The Goth nobles elected another king, but he too fell in battle. Narses and his mercenaries recaptured Ravenna and re-established a Byzantine capital there. The Ostrogoth domination had ended; now Italy would be ruled, on behalf of the emperor Justinian, by a Byzantine official called an exarch, a general who also had authority to administer civilian affairs. Constantinople had regained the heart of the empire—but only after years of war that had destroyed the countryside, wrecked the cities, and impoverished the people.[3]

In 552, Justinian also regained control of southern Hispania. The Visigothic king had been murdered, and the court was in disarray; one of the nobles, Athanagild, sent a message to Constantinople, appealing (unwisely) for help in seizing the throne. Byzantine ships arrived to support him and Athanagild got his throne, but by 554, Byzantine armies had captured ports and fortresses all along the southern coast, and Justinian was able to establish a Byzantine province there with Cartagena as its capital.[4]

In the wake of the plague, Justinian was finding victory. He was on the edge of rebuilding the old Roman empire, restoring the old glories; Byzantine administration now reached to the western edge of the Mediterranean; Rome was again his.

But at once new challenges arose in the east.

YET AGAIN, a new nation had formed itself out of a loose and disorganized tribal confederation. Over the previous century, nomads from northern China, known to the Chinese as the T'u-chueh, had made their way westward into central Asia. One of their warchiefs was named Bumin Khan, and in 552 he gathered his tribe and their allies together at a place called Ergenekon, in the Altay mountains, and declared himself their king. This declaration must have followed some years of conquest, although those are invisible to us; he also married a Chinese princess from the former Western Wei royal family, adding the sheen of royalty to his rough grasp of power, and established his capital at the city of Otukan.

The new state formed by Bumin Khan became known as the Gokturk Khaghanate, the first Turkish kingdom. Turkish legends gathered around the mountain stronghold where Bumin Khan created a people: Ergenekon, the ancestral homeland of the Turks, also became a paradise of sorts, a Garden of Eden within living memory.[5]

Not long after the gathering at Ergenekon, Bumin Khan died and his son Mukhan took over the brand-new country. Mukhan began to fight the neighboring tribes to expand the Gokturk state, driving the nearest tribes—the nomadic Avars—westward towards Persia and Byzantium.[6]

In 558, the displaced Avars reached the Byzantine borders, forcing Justinian to buy them off. They kept on going west and finally settled near the Danube, just east of the Gepids. They were not the only peoples disturbed by

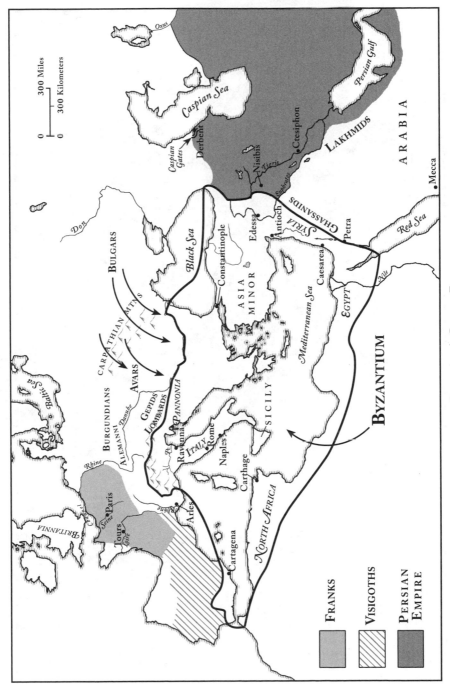

33.1: Byzantium's Greatest Extent

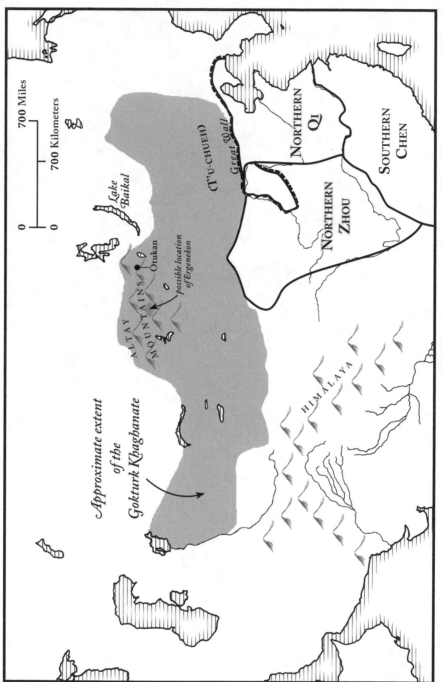

33.2: *The Gokturk Khaghanate*

the new Turkish nation; Mukhan managed to conquer the eastern tribes of the Bulgars, agitating the remaining tribes who lived on the western shores of the Don river. Some of them crossed into Byzantine land, but rather than paying them off as well, Justinian recalled Belisarius from his retirement and sent his most experienced general to drive them away.[7]

He succeeded—which aroused all of Justinian's old suspicions of his lifelong colleague. Even after decades of reign, Justinian must have felt his throne to be insecure. In 562, he accused Belisarius of corruption and jailed him; the following year, he relented, released his old friend, and pardoned him. It was the last skirmish between the two. Both men died in 565; Justinian was eighty-three, Belisarius sixty.

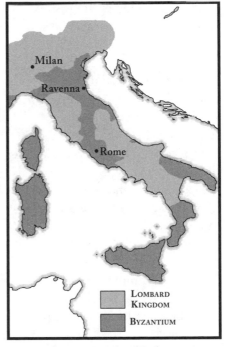

33.3: Lombard Italy

When Justinian drew his last breath, so did any chance that the Roman empire might be revived. Theodora had died childless in 548, probably of cancer, and Justinian had never remarried; he had no sons. His nephew Justin became emperor in his place. Almost at once, the new conquests in the west began to fragment.

In Italy, Byzantine domination was threatened by the arrival of plague in the year after Justin II's accession. Paul the Deacon describes the characteristic swellings in the groin, the high fever, the stacks of unburied corpses, Italy emptied and vulnerable. "The dwellings were left deserted by their inhabitants, and the dogs only kept house," he wrote.

> You might see the world brought back to its ancient silence: no voice in the field; no whistling of shepherds; no lying in wait of wild beasts among the cattle; no harm to domestic fowls. The crops, outliving the time of the harvest, awaited the reaper untouched; the vineyard with its fallen leaves and its shining grapes remained undisturbed while winter came on; a trumpet as of warriors resounded through the hours of the night and day; something like the murmur of an army was heard by many; there were no footsteps of passers by, no murderer was seen, yet the corpses of the dead were more than

the eyes could discern; pastoral places had been turned into a sepulchre for men, and human habitations had become places of refuge for wild beasts. And these evils happened to the Romans only and within Italy alone.[8]

Once the plague had died away, empty lands were left for the taking, and the Lombard king Alboin set his sights on them.

The territory in Pannonia had not been enough for his people. Their numbers had grown, in part because he had conquered both of the neighboring tribes, the Heruls and the Gepids (Paul the Deacon tells us that he killed the Gepid king in battle, married his daughter by force, and made a drinking goblet out of his head, a throwback to a much more ancient warrior custom). Now the Lombards numbered over a quarter of a million, and they needed more space.[9]

By 568, Lombards were crossing en masse into Italy. In 569, Alboin and his Lombard warriors conquered Milan and began to storm southward. The Byzantine territory in central Italy fell quickly. Only the southern coasts and a strip of land from Ravenna down the coast, cutting across to Rome (where the pope, Benedict I, claimed the protection of the Byzantine emperor) remained in Byzantine hands. Italy had changed hands once again.

Meanwhile the Visigothic king Leovigild, brother and successor to Athanagild, had come to the throne of Hispania and was busy reconquering the land his predecessor had lost. Justin II was unable to organize a decent defense, let alone retake the disputed land. The Byzantine attempt to claim the old Roman lands had ended.*

EAST OF CONSTANTINOPLE, the Persian Khosru was having exactly the opposite experience. His conquests to the east (he had destroyed the Hephthalites some years earlier) had brought Persia to a high-water mark of power.[†] Khosru reorganized the now vast expanse of his land, dividing it into quadrants and placing a military commander over each: the far eastern land won from the Hephthalites, the central area of the kingdom, the lands to the west near the Byzantine border, and the southern Arabian territories.[10]

In 570, Khosru was presented with the opportunity to expand his hold over those Arabian lands.

---

*The Byzantine hold on patches of land in Italy would persist for centuries, with the relationships of the Byzantine-loyal cities to the throne at Constantinople growing more and more complex, but the empire would never again dominate the peninsula.

†This high-water mark applies to the medieval Persian empire, often known as "Sasanian Persia" to distinguish it from the ancient Persian empire, which lay in the same general area but lost its independence to Alexander the Great. Persia did not regain its existence as an independent kingdom until a man from the Sasanian clan declared himself Ardashir, emperor of a revived Persia, in AD 224.

The kingdom of Axum was planning to cross the Red Sea and attack the Arabian city of Mecca.* Once again, the attack would take the form of a religious crusade: the king of Axum, Abraha, was Christian, and Mecca was the center of traditional Arabic religion. It was also vulnerable. There was no king in Mecca, no one able to organize and lead an effective defense. Arabs were loyal to the tribe of their birth; the tribe was their ethical center, which meant that loyalty did not extend outside of tribal boundaries. Raiding another tribe for food, animals, and women was a constant that bore no stigma of moral wrong. Arabia was a dry land of ever-colliding micro-nations. Mecca itself was governed by a council made up of heads of the leading families, all of whom had equal authority; the convention that no one was to draw a weapon in the sacred territory of the Ka'aba was the only acknowledgment that some greater force might bind the tribes together. There was no common law, no central authority, no acknowledged warleader. Even the strongest tribe in Mecca, the Quraysh, was divided, with three clans within it struggling for dominance.[11]

Abraha of Axum assembled not only his armies and ships but also at least one elephant—the first time this beast had ever been used in Arabian warfare. He moved his forces across the Red Sea and prepared to lay siege to Mecca. But before he could bring the city down, his forces were felled by plague and he was forced to withdraw. His failure in the Year of the Elephant appears in the Qur'an, half a century later, as an intervention of God:

Didn't you see how your Lord treated the troops with the elephant?
Did not God foil their strategy,
sending against them flocks of birds
pelting them with rock-hard clay,
making them like stubble of grain that's been consumed?[12]

Swords had played little part in the defeat.

Hoping to avoid a repeat attack, the tribes of southern Arabia asked Khosru for aid. In 575, he came south with both foot-soldiers and a fleet of ships, into the land Abraha had hoped to conquer.

The Persian intervention halted Abraha's attempts to organize a second invasion. There was no chance now that Christianity would spread eastward into the Arabian peninsula. Mecca would not be converted; the Quraysh tribe would continue to worship at the Ka'aba; and the children of the Quraysh tribe, including a six-year-old boy later known simply as Muhammad, would not grow up under the cross.[13]

Justin II made no effort to challenge Khosru's meddling in Arabian poli-

*See map 28.1.

tics. In fact, he appears to have been losing his mind. John of Ephesus says that he used to bite people when he was angry with them, and that he was only soothed when his courtiers let him sit in a little wagon and pulled him around the palace in it.[14]

It had been a long time since the empire had suffered from an insane emperor: for decades, the throne had been held by the fit and the shrewd. Justin's wife Sophia, niece of the legendary Theodora, convinced Justin to name the able courtier Tiberius to be his Caesar. Justin II agreed, and until the emperor died in 578, she and Tiberius controlled the empire together. After Justin's funeral Tiberius was crowned emperor; Sophia offered to marry him if he would divorce his wife, but he declined.[15]

In 579, one year later, Khosru of Persia died after a forty-eight-year reign. Despite his abandonment of the Mazdakite creed, Khosru had worked hard to make his empire just.* The later historian al-Tabari, eulogizing him, lists Khosru's reforms: children with questioned paternity must nevertheless be given their fair inheritance; women married against their will could choose to leave their husbands if they wished; convicted thieves should make restitution, not merely suffer punishment; widows and orphans must be provided for by relatives and by the state. He had also conquered new territory and equipped Persia with a strong infrastructure of canals and irrigation conduits, rebuilt bridges and restored villages, well-maintained roads and well-trained tax officials and administrators, and a strong army.[16]

But the deaths of the two great emperors, Justinian and Khosru, closed an era for both empires. Byzantium had already begun a downward slide; whether Persia could remain strong without its great king at the helm remained to be seen.

*See chapter 22.

TIMELINE 33

INDIA	AFRICA	BYZANTIUM	PERSIAN EMPIRE	VISIGOTHS	LOMBARDS TURKS
Harishena of the Vakataka (480–515)					
				Alaric (485–507)	
			Kavadh (488–531)		
		Anastasius (491–518)			
			[Zamasb (496–498)]		
Narasimha (?) (497–c. 510)					
				Amalaric (507/516–531)	
Toramana (c. 510–c. 520)	Caleb of Axum (c. 510–540)				
		Timothy III of Alexandria (517–535)			
Mihirakula (c. 520–528/543)		Justin (518–527)			
	Abraha of Axum (525–c. 553)				
		Justinian (527–565)			
		Justinian Code, first volume (529)			
			Khosru (531–579)	Theudis (531–548)	
		"Nika" riots (532)			
Eruption of Krakatoa (535)		Capture of Rome (536)			
		Capture of Italy (540)			
		Plague in Constantinople (542)			
Pulakesi of the Chalukya (543–566)					
		Death of Theodora (548)			
					Bumin Khan of the Gokturk Khaghanate (552)
					Mukhan Khan (552–572)
				Athanagild (554–567)	
Kirtivarman of the Chalukya (566–597)		Justin II (565–578)			Alboin (565–572)
		Leovigild (569–586)			
		Tiberius (578–582)			
			Hurmuz (579–590)		
Pulakesi II of the Chalukya (597/610–642)					
Mahendravarman of the Pallava (600–630)					
Harsha (606–647)					

Chapter Thirty-Four

The Mayors of the Palaces

Between 558 and 656,
the lands of the Franks divide into three realms,
and the Merovingian kings slowly give up their power

B Y 558, THE FOUR-WAY RULE of the Franks had once again become a single kingship. Illness and murder had removed three of Clovis's heirs, and the last surviving son, Chlothar I, now ruled, like his father, as king of all the Franks.

This second unification of all the Franks under one crown lasted exactly three years. In 561, Chlothar came down with a high fever in the middle of a hunt. He died not long after, after a half-century reign, and left the crown to all four of his surviving sons.

His struggle against his own brothers had not convinced him to name a single heir. The old ideals of the Frankish warrior-chiefs survived: the king should earn his spurs, not merely inherit them. Chlothar had won his crown by outlasting, outwitting, and outfighting his brothers, and none of his four sons would get a free pass into the high kingship of the Franks.

The four brothers realized that they were in competition, and from the day of their father's death they behaved, not as joint rulers, but as separate kings of neighboring and sometimes hostile states.

When the second oldest brother, Charibert, died in 567, the three remaining kings seized his territory, and the Frankish kingdom assumed a three-way division that would dictate its politics for the next century. The northern territory, ruled by Sigebert, was known as Austrasia; its capital was originally the city of Reims, but Sigebert moved his seat to Metz, closer to the border, to guard against the invasions of wandering Avars. Guntram ruled over Burgundy, which had been folded into the Frankish territory some years before; Chilperic controlled the central and southern Frankish lands, a territory known as Neustria, which contained the cities of Soissons and Paris.

Burgundy was the minor of the three kingdoms; Neustria and Austrasia were almost equal in land and in strength. Both Chilperic of Neustria and

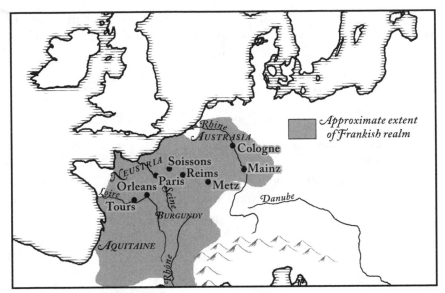

34.1: Territories of the Franks

Sigebert of Austrasia had an eye on the high king's seat; Sigebert decided to up his chances by making a match with the Visigothic princess Brunhilda, daughter of King Athanagild.

Athanagild agreed to the marriage and sent Brunhilda from her home in Hispania, along with a large dowry. When he heard of the match, Chilperic of Neustria realized that his brother had pulled ahead of him in the power race. "Although he already had a number of wives," Gregory of Tours writes, "he sent to ask for the hand of Galswintha, the sister of Brunhilda." He also promised that he would put all his other wives away if King Athanagild would agree to the match.[1]

The king of the Visigoths must have thought he had hit the jackpot. He sent Galswintha off after her sister, and when she arrived at the court of Chilperic, he kept his promise and honored her as his only wife: "He loved her very dearly," Gregory writes, deadpan, "for she had brought a large dowry with her."

But Galswintha soon discovered that her husband was actually still very much in love with one of his previous wives, a woman named Fredegund, who in spite of having been formally put away still showed up in the royal bedchamber on a regular basis. She complained; he insisted; she asked to go home; he refused; and finally, one morning, she was found strangled in bed. The court poet Venantius Fortunatus, who wrote the lament over her death, had to choose his words with great care. He describes the marriage and then goes straight from life to death without pausing to describe the hows and whys.

"Enjoying for so short a time the binding relationship with her husband," he explains, with tact, "she was snatched away by death at the start of her life."[2]

Both her husband Chilperic and her rival Fredegund were suspected of doing the snatching, or at least of arranging it. There was no proof (even though Chilperic now brought Fredegund back to court as his queen), and both escaped without penalty. But Brunhilda, now queen of Austrasia, never forgave or forgot the murder of her sister.

Seven years of inconclusive war followed, with none of the brothers managing to make significant gains on the others. Chilperic and Sigebert were always enemies, but Guntram, with his smaller territory, changed allegiances back and forth, depending on who seemed less likely to try and kill him. Finally, in 575, Fredegund (now queen of Neustria) sent two assassins to kill Sigebert in his palace. They pretended to be traitors from Chilperic's court, willing to change sides and recognize Sigebert as king, but when they got into Sigebert's presence they attacked him with poisoned scramasaxes—long Scandinavian knives normally used not as weapons but as eating tools.[3]

Sigebert died in agony when the poison did its work, leaving his five-year-old son Childebert II as his heir and his wife Brunhilda as regent. Brunhilda now had double reason to hate her sister-in-law: Fredegund, she believed, was responsible for the deaths of both her sister and her husband.

She took good care of her son's realm; she convinced his uncle Guntram, who was childless, to adopt the boy as his own. This made young Childebert II both the king of Austrasia and the heir of Burgundy, and would allow him to combine the two realms after Guntram's death.

She also supervised the day-to-day administration of Austrasia. Brunhilda turned out to be a thoroughly competent ruler—so much so that the Frankish nobles were annoyed by her. Her force of personality and the Frankish hostility to her survive in the later Germanic epic called the Song of the Nibelungs, in which she is brought from afar (Iceland, in the case of the story) to become the wife of the German king. His friends advise against it: "This queen," his friend Sigfrid tells him, "is a thing of terror."[4] But despite the Frankish hostility to his mother, Childebert II refused to send her away even when he reached his majority; he kept her at court as his advisor.

Fredegund, over in Neustria, intended to be just as powerful as her sister-in-law. Chilperic was murdered in 584 by a man with a personal grudge; he had no son, but right after the funeral, Fredegund announced that she was pregnant with her husband's heir.

This announcement was greeted with skepticism. In fact, once the baby was born, Guntram (who was normally mild-mannered; his chronicler Fredegar calls him "full of goodness") suggested publicly that the child's father was a Frankish courtier, rather than his dead brother. At this, Fredegund rounded up three bishops and "three hundred of the more important leaders. They all swore an oath that King Chilperic of Neustria was the boy's father."[5]

Guntram was forced to back off. He was too good a man to go against the word of a bishop, and so he went to Paris for the child's baptism. Fredegund named the little boy "Chlothar II," after his powerful (putative) grandfather, and ruled over Neustria as his regent.

In 592, Guntram of Burgundy died and left his part of the Frankish rule to Childebert II of Austrasia, his nephew and adopted son. This meant that Brunhilda was now helping her son to rule over both Austrasia and Burgundy, while Fredegund was acting as regent over Neustria. The Frankish rule had devolved to these two powerful women, the Frankish Fredegund and the Visigothic Brunhilda, who loathed each other with a deep, personal hatred—and who had the power to determine the actions of their kingdoms.

Neither woman would allow that power to slip from her hands. Brunhilda's son, Childebert II, died in 595; he was only in his mid-twenties, and Brunhilda at once accused Fredegund of poisoning him from a distance. His death, though, put her squarely back in control of the double realm of Austrasia and Burgundy. She became regent for his two young sons, aged nine and eight, who divided Austrasia and Burgundy between them.

Fredegund and her son, Chlothar II, immediately tried to seize Paris. The battle, says the Frankish chronicler Fredegar, created "great carnage" but didn't accomplish much of anything. The hatred between the queens might have swelled into a full-fledged war that would have destroyed the kingdoms of the Franks, but the following year, Fredegund died, and her son began to rule alone.[6]

Two years later, the dead Childebert's older son, Theudebert II of Austrasia, reached the age of thirteen. He could legally rule alone, and so he kicked his grandmother Brunhilda out, to the loud cheers of the Austrasian nobles. The old woman made her way south into Burgundy, hoping to join her younger grandson Theuderic II there, but apparently got lost on the way: "A poor man found her wandering alone," Fredegar says, "and took her, at her request, to Theuderic who made his grandmother welcome and treated her with ceremony."[7]

The Frankish kingdom had once again become three independent, essentially hostile realms. In 599, Chlothar II of Austrasia, now a precocious fifteen, tried to attack his cousins and get their land; but the two brothers decided to form a united front. They combined the armies of Burgundy and Neustria, defeated Chlothar II, and took much of his territory away, dividing it among themselves.

Burgundy, Brunhilda's new home, was growing in size and strength, and Brunhilda went back to her high-handed ways; the chronicler Fredegar says that she had at least one nobleman accused of treachery and put to death so that she could claim his land for the throne, and also accuses her of plotting the assassinations of various other powerful officials. Theuderic himself, once he turned thirteen in 600, was unable to get rid of his grandmother and rule Burgundy on his own. He had welcomed her in; in return she had attached herself to the power of the throne like a limpet. By the time Theuderic had turned twenty, well past the age when a king might be expected to marry and sire an heir, he was still single and still under his grandmother's thumb.

Unable to throw her out, reluctant to ask his brother in Austrasia or his cousin in Neustria for aid (he was the youngest of the three, and perhaps was afraid that opening the door to either might end with his losing the throne), he sought a new ally. In 607, he sent an ambassador to Hispania and asked the Visigothic king Witteric for the hand of his daughter Ermenberga.

The Visigothic kingdom was at its height, and a Visigothic-Burgundian alliance would have made Burgundy the strongest of the three Frankish kingdoms. But apparently Brunhilda could not bear the thought of losing her position as queen of the court. According to the historian Fredegar, she "poisoned him against his bride" with her words. Brunhilda was a crafty and resourceful woman, and by the time Ermenberga arrived, Theuderic had lost his taste for the whole project. He never even consummated the marriage and a year later sent his wife back to her father.[8]

Instead, he made an alliance with his cousin Chlothar II of Neustria against his brother, Theudebert II of Austrasia, and in 612, the joint force attacked Theudebert's army on the edge of the Forest of Ardennes. "The carnage on both sides was such that in the fighting line there was no room for the slain to fall down," Fredegar's account tells us. "They stood upright in their ranks, corpse supporting corpse, as if they still lived. . . . The whole countryside was strewn with their bodies." Theuderic and Chlothar marched to Cologne, took Theudebert's treasure, and captured Theudebert. A soldier, Fredegar adds, took Theudebert's young son and heir "by the heels and dashed out his brains on a stone."[9]

Brunhilda had not forgotten her older grandson's decision to throw her out of his court. She ordered Theuderic to imprison his brother and then had the young king murdered in prison. Theuderic claimed Austrasia as his own, making him joint king of Austrasia and Burgundy, but he died of dysentery less than a year later—still without a legitimate heir.

To keep the kingdom from falling into Brunhilda's hands, the two mayors of the palace—Warnachar, mayor for Austrasia, and Rado, mayor for Burgundy—took action.

"Mayor of the palace" was the Frankish title for the king's right-hand man, the official who took care of the royal estates, supervised the other government offices, and generally acted as prime minister and household steward combined. When the king was a child, or weak, or dead, his mayor ran the realm.

Neither Warnachar nor Rado wanted to see their domains taken over by Brunhilda, so together they invited Chlothar II to invade. In 613, he accepted the invitation and marched in, largely unopposed. He captured his aunt Brunhilda and put her to death in a particularly prolonged fashion: "He was boiling with fury against her," writes Fredegar in his chronicle. "She was tormented for three days with a diversity of tortures, and then on his orders was led through the ranks on a camel. Finally she was tied by her hair, one arm, and one leg to the tail of an unbroken horse, and she was cut to shreds by its hoofs at the pace it went."[10]

Once again, the Franks were under a single rule: that of Chlothar II, the only one of the kings who probably had no actual relationship to the royal family.

Chlothar II began to try to bring some sort of order to the chaotic landscape. In 615 he issued the Edict of Paris, which among other provisions promised that the king of the Franks would not try to overrule the authority of the local palaces of Austrasia, Neustria, and Burgundy. The three Frankish kingdoms would be united under Chlothar, but there would be no single centralized government, and the offices of mayor would not be combined into one. Instead, each mayor of the palace would continue to administer his own realm.[11]

Probably this had been part of the deal made by the mayors Warnachar and Rado: they wanted him in, but not at the expense of their own power. Chlothar's invasion got rid of Brunhilda and confirmed the authority of the mayors of the palace: each now had more authority than under the previous rulers. This authority grew even more entrenched when Chlothar agreed, two years later, to make the mayor of the palace a lifetime appointment.

Now the mayors not only were relatively independent but also could not be removed from office. Chlothar had made a devil's deal. He had the crown of the Franks, but two-thirds of his country was ruled by the mayors—whom he could not get rid of by legal means, who had the authority to legislate for their own realms, and who were now able to act independently of the pesky royal children and aunts who had once controlled them.

THE 617 DECREE that gave the mayors power for life began a slow transformation of the mayors into rulers—a transformation that would leave the Merovingian kings of the Franks without much of importance to do.

For several decades, the kingdom of the Franks had had three mayors: one each in the palaces at Austrasia, Neustria, and Burgundy. Chlothar's confirmation of this arrangement had been an attempt to combine the fiercely local nature of Frankish politics with the existence of a high king.

But it was not entirely successful. Even with an independent mayor of the palace, the nobles of Austrasia agitated for more independence—particularly from Neustria. Perhaps ancient tribal differences, or obscure clan hostilities, lay behind the division, but the eastern and western halves of the Frankish kingdom were increasingly likely to insist on the separation of their interests. The western Franks called their land *Francia*, and referred to the eastern half as the "East Land," or *Austrasia*. In return, the Austrasians refused to yield the title *Francia* to the west; they insisted on using *Neustria*, or "New West Land," for their counterparts on the other side of the Frankish kingdom.

Shortly after 617, Chlothar agreed to make his twenty-year-old son, Dagobert, ruler of Austrasia, thus giving the Austrasians not only an independent mayor but an independent king. This provided the Austrasians with their desired separation from Neustria and Burgundy, although the independence of Dagobert's rule was doubly illusory—he was firmly under his father's thumb, and in any case the real authority in his court was held by his mayor of the palace, one Pippin the Elder.

When Chlothar died in 629, after a forty-five-year reign, Dagobert got the chance to exercise some real power. His younger half-brother Charibert tried to claim the throne of Neustria, but Dagobert first threatened him into withdrawing to the small territory known as Aquitaine, and then supervised his assassination and claimed the whole kingdom for himself.[12]

Now the entire Frankish realm was under one king again, and again the nobles of Austrasia objected. Dagobert, who had once helped to preserve their independence, had become their problem.

Dagobert was forced to follow his father's strategy; he made his own three-year-old son, Sigebert III, king of Austrasia, and once again the mayor of the palace held the real power in the Austrasian realm. The Franks were trying to balance, awkwardly, the power of the king, the rights of a royal family, and the intense desire of the Frankish noblemen (the previous clan chiefs) to rule themselves, and the rule of an infant king under the power of a local mayor of the palace was a workable if unstable solution.

Dagobert died in 639 and the kingdom remained divided: Sigebert III and his mayor of the palace kept control of Austrasia, and Dagobert's younger son, Clovis II, was crowned king of Neustria and Burgundy, which he ruled with the substantial help of two mayors of the palace, one for each realm.

During all of these deaths and coronations, what really mattered was the power of the local mayor in each realm, not which royal son occupied the throne. But even though the post had been designed to preserve independent government in the three realms of the Franks, the mayors were not opposed to consolidating their own power. By 643, when Pippin the Elder died in Austrasia, he had also seized the mayoralties of Burgundy and Neustria.[13]

Not only that: he passed them on to his son Grimoald. The mayors of the palace had not previously been able to inherit their power; they were appointed by the king. But now the mayors were adopting the royal custom of blood succession.

Grimoald now convinced the young king of Austrasia, Sigebert III, to adopt Grimoald's own son as his heir. This would have catapulted the mayoralty into the throne room—but unfortunately for Grimoald's ambitions, Sigebert III soon fathered a son of his own.

Grimoald refused to be defeated. In 656, after Sigebert III died at an unexpectedly early age, Grimoald mounted a coup and took the throne. He ordered Sigebert's six-year-old heir, Dagobert II, to be tonsured (the top of his head shaved to indicate his intentions to become a priest—a sacred version of mutilation, rendering the user unfit for rule by dedicating him to the service of God) and sent him off to a monastery in England. Then he placed his own son, Childebert the Adopted, on the throne of Austrasia.

At this, Clovis II, king of Neustria and Burgundy, authorized an invasion. Clovis's army captured both Grimoald and his son Childebert the Adopted. Both were put to death, and the throne of Austrasia was empty.

Rather than bringing the tonsured rightful king (his nephew) back from England, Clovis II allowed his official Erchinoald to declare him king of the entire realm; Erchinoald also became mayor of the palace for all three palaces simultaneously. The mayors of the Franks, intended to preserve local authority, were themselves becoming a threat to it.[14]

Clovis II ruled as king of all of the Franks for barely a year before he died. He left three very small sons behind; two of them were duly coronated as kings of Austrasia and Neustria, while the third was raised in a monastery. But for the next fifteen years, the two young kings did almost nothing, while various mayors of the palaces battled for power. Later chroniclers would call these rulers the first of the *rois faineants*, the "do-nothing kings," and the name clung to the last generations of Merovingian rule.[15]

TIMELINE 34

VISIGOTHS BYZANTIUM LOMBARDS	FRANKS
	Chlothar / Childebert / Theuderic / Chlodomer
Timothy III of Alexandria (517–535)	(511–561) (511–558) (511–534) (511–524)
Justin (518–527)	
	Chlothar / Childebert / Theuderic
Justinian (527–565)	(511–561) (511–558) (511–534)
Justinian Code, first volume (529)	
Theudis (531–548)	**Chlothar / Childebert**
	(511–561) (511–558)
Athanagild (554–567)	
	Chlothar
	(511–561)
	Guntram / Chilperic / Sigebert / Charibert
Justin II (565–578) **Alboin**	(561–592) (561–584) (561–575) (561–567)
(565–572)	
	Guntram / Chilperic / Sigebert
	(561–592) (561–584) (561–575)
Leovigild (569–586)	
	Guntram / Chilperic / Childebert II (Brunhilda)
	(561–592) (561–584) (575–595)
Tiberius (578–582)	
	Guntram / Chlothar II / Childebert II
	(Fredegund) (Brunhilda)
	(561–592) (584–629) (575–595)
	Chlothar II (Fredegund) / **Childebert II** (Brunhilda)
	(584–629) (575–595)
	Chlothar II / Theudebert II / Theuderic II
	(Fredegund) (Brunhilda)
Witteric (603–610)	(584–629) (595–612) (595–613)
	Chlothar II / Theuderic II (Brunhilda)
	(584–629) (595–613)
	Chlothar II (584–629)
	Edict of Paris (615)
	Chlothar II / Dagobert / Pippin the Elder
	(584–629) (623–639) (623–640)
	Dagobert (623–639)
	Dagobert (623–639) / **Sigebert III** (634–c. 655)
	Sigebert III (634–c. 655) / **Clovis II** (639–655)
	Grimoald (643–656)
	Clovis II (639–655) / **Erchinoald** (656–658)

Chapter Thirty-Five

Gregory the Great

Between 572 and 604,
the pope negotiates with the Lombards
and sends Christian missionaries to Britain

I N ITALY, CURRENTS OF personal hatred were also shaping the Lombard kingship.

The Lombard king Alboin had folded the Gepids into his realm by force, killing their king and marrying the king's daughter Rosemund. At a drunken banquet in 572, Alboin handed her the goblet made from her father's skull and, in the words of Paul the Deacon, "invited her to drink merrily with her father." Rosemund's simmering hatred boiled over. She blackmailed a court official into assassinating Alboin while the Lombard king slept, first taking the precaution of binding his sword "tightly to the head of the bed"; Alboin apparently slept with his weapon.

Alboin woke up when the assassin entered his room and tried to defend himself with the only furniture in the room, a wooden footstool, but he was killed. Rosemund and her accomplice fled to Ravenna, where the exarch welcomed them, hoping to use them against the Lombards. But the two fugitives poisoned each other, not long after arriving in Byzantine territory, and both died on the same day.[1]

The essentially Germanic nature of the Lombards now reasserted itself. Alboin had been less a king than a warrior-chief; for almost his entire reign, the Lombards had been at war and on the move. After his death, they did without a king for a time. Warleaders took control of the army and conquered a series of cities, each warlord establishing his own little kingdom in the Lombard-controlled land. More than thirty of these little kingdoms, later known as duchies, stood side by side, in a period known as the Rule of the Dukes.

In 584, the Lombard dukes decided that their separate kingdoms would benefit from a shared defense. They elected one of their own, the duke Authari, to oversee Lombard resistance to any invasion. After Authari's death in 590, they chose another man for the same purpose: Agilulf, who was "raised to the sovereignty by all" at Milan, hoisted up on a shield in the ancient ceremony that gave him a power he was not born to.[2]

Two of the dukes declined to recognize Agilulf's overlordship. Both were in the south of Italy, cut off from the main Lombard kingdom by the narrow strip of land still claimed by the emperor of Constantinople. After a few clashes of arms, as Lombard armies trooped back and forth across the Byzantine land, Agilulf forced both to acknowledge him. After this, the two Lombard kingdoms in the south were known as the Duchy of Spoleto and the Duchy of Benevento; they would continue to act as small independent kingdoms, despite their allegiance to the Lombard overlord.

In the same year as Agilulf's election, Pope Pelagius II died, and the churchmen of Rome chose a successor. They offered the seat of St. Peter to a monk named Gregory, who did not particularly want it. Gregory had been sent to Constantinople twelve years earlier, on a diplomatic mission for the pope, and had returned from the city to his monastery with great relief. He preferred the abbey to the throne room.[3]

But by the time Pelagius died, Rome was in sore straits. The Lombards had cut the city off from Ravenna and from Constantinople, the plague made a sweep through the city, and the Tiber flooded so severely that "its waters flowed in over the walls of the city and filled great regions in it." The priests of Rome were unanimous: Gregory, who had now risen to be the abbot of his monastery, was competent, experienced, and knew how to handle relations with Constantinople. They wanted him to be the next pope.[4]

Gregory, dismayed, sent a letter begging the emperor at Constantinople not to confirm the appointment, but the chief official of Rome stole the letter and instead forged another, begging the emperor to make the appointment official as soon as possible. The emperor did so, and Gregory found himself, against his will, raised on the spiritual shield of his fellow churchmen.[5]

He took control of the church in Rome, shouldering his burden against his own inclinations. As pope he was supposed to be the spiritual

35.1: The Lombard Duchies

authority in the city, but since the civil authority of Rome was cut off from easy consultation with its superiors (and since Gregory theoretically had continual communication with God, who was unrestricted by Lombard armies), he found that not only the priests, but also the prefects and officials of Rome, turned to him for guidance. "I am now detained in the city of Rome," he wrote to a colleague, "tied by the chains of this dignity."[6]

Gregory was a problem-solver, a coper. It was not in his nature to turn away appeals for help, but rather to figure out a way to deal with them. The most pressing problems were earthly, not spiritual; the Lombard leader Agilulf was moving south towards Rome, anxious to take it from Byzantine control, and the dukes of Spoleto and Benevento were moving west to complete the pincer move. By 593, the Lombard armies were at the walls of Rome.

Gregory sent messages to Constantinople, warning the emperor of his peril and begging for help. Tiberius had died in 582, leaving the crown to his hand-chosen successor, his son-in-law Maurice; but the emperor Maurice was dealing with Avar invasions in the northwest and Persian complications to the east.

No imperial troops arrived. Neither did any pay for the soldiers remaining in the city; Gregory was on his own.

He took matters into his own hands. He paid the troops at Rome out of church funds ("As at Ravenna, the emperor has a paymaster for the First Army of Italy," he wrote to Constantinople, bitterly, "so at Rome for such purposes am I paymaster") and went out to negotiate with Agilulf on his own authority. He agreed to pay the Lombard king five hundred pounds of gold, also from the church treasury, and Agilulf withdrew.[7]

Gregory had saved Rome, a feat that even more than his spiritual accomplishments earned him the nickname "Gregory the Great." But the exarch at Ravenna—who was, theoretically, in charge of Byzantine lands in Italy—complained to the emperor Maurice that Gregory had overstepped his authority. Gregory defended his actions: he had no other choice. Furthermore, he wrote, Agilulf was not unreasonable. He would be willing to come to a general peace with all Byzantine territories, if only the exarch would agree: "For he complains that many acts of violence were committed in his regions," he wrote to Ravenna, "and if reasonable grounds for arbitration should be found, he also himself promises to make satisfaction in all ways, if any wrong was committed on his side. . . . It is no doubt reasonable to agree to what he asks."[8]

But the exarch refused. His pride had been injured, and a standoff with the Lombards lasted until he died in 596 and was replaced by a more reasonable man. The new exarch, Callinicus, agreed to sign a treaty with Agilulf. For a time, peace between the Lombards and the Byzantine territories resulted.[9]

Pope Gregory was finally able to turn away from political matters and spend time on his spiritual responsibilities. His commentary on Ezekiel had been interrupted by the Lombard crisis; now he could go back to writing. And he could also attend to another duty: sending a priest over the water to Britain, to take orthodox Christianity to the peoples there.

There had been Christians in Britain before. The Romans of the late empire had been Christian at least in name, and a few churches had been built. But since the collapse of Roman rule, there had been no organized Christian presence on the island. Churches in the south and east had crumbled as the unconverted Saxons had pushed in; the British churches that remained, mostly in the north and west, had been separated from the mother church at Rome for over a century.[10]

Gregory took it upon himself to bring the island back into the kingdom of God, which meant evangelizing the Saxons. At the end of the sixth century, Saxons ruled along the eastern coast and in much of the southeast. The descendents of the general Aelle still ruled in Sussex, the kingdom of the South Saxons; another royal line had established itself in the kingdom for the West Saxons; the descendents of Hengest, leader of one of the original Saxon strike forces, ruled the southern kingdom of Kent; and small kingdoms ruled by Saxons and Angles bracketed the remaining British kingdoms, which still held the west and north of the island.

To bring all of these Saxons into the Christian fold, Gregory chose a monk named Augustine who had served at Gregory's former monastery. Augustine started out with a large band of companions and plenty of supplies, got as far as the coast of the Frankish kingdom, and wilted ("seized with craven terror," Bede says). In August of 596, he returned to Rome and asked for permission to abandon the trip. Gregory refused to relinquish the mission. He sent Augustine back to his stalled party with a letter of exhortation: "Let neither the toil of the journey nor the tongues of evil-speaking men deter you," he wrote to them. "May Almighty God grant to me to see the fruit of your labour in the eternal country; that so, even though I cannot labour with you, I may be found together with you in the joy of the reward; for in truth I desire to labour." Still trapped in Rome, carrying out

35.2: Saxon Kingdoms

his administrative duties with dogged faithfulness, Gregory longed for the heady fulfillment of the mission field.[11]

Augustine's party took heart, crossed the channel, and in early 597 landed on Thanet Island, a tiny isle just off the coast of Kent that fell under the rule of Kent's king, Ethelbert.[12] Probably Augustine had targeted Ethelbert from the beginning; his wife, Bertha, granddaughter of the Frankish king Chlothar I, was already a Christian.[13]

When Ethelbert heard of the party's arrival, he sent a message telling the missionaries to stay put on the island until he could decide what to do with them. Finally he decided to go and see them, rather than inviting them into his kingdom: he was suspicious, not knowing whether this was a political or spiritual mission. Talking to them, he was reassured and decided that they were harmless. Even Bede, anxious as he is to show the triumph of Christianity, can't make Ethelbert's reaction a dramatic one: after listening to Augustine, the king said, "I cannot forsake the beliefs I have observed, along with the whole English nation, but I will not harm you; and I do not forbid you to preach and convert as many as you can."[14]

Eventually Ethelbert did agree to be baptized, and in Christmas of 597, Gregory wrote to the bishop of Alexandria of the mission's success. "For while the nation of the Angli, placed in a corner of the world, remained up to this time misbelieving in the worship of stocks and stones," he exults, "a monk of my monastery . . . proceeded . . . to the end of the world to the aforesaid nation; and already letters having reached us telling us of his safety and his work. . . . [M]ore than ten thousand Angli are reported to have been baptized." More priests were sent in 601. Ethelbert turned over a wrecked sanctuary in Canterbury to Augustine, to act as his headquarters, and Gregory consecrated Augustine as the bishop of the Angles at Canterbury.[15]

Gregory's epistles preserve the questions that Augustine sent back to him. Should the monks from Rome, trained and longtime Christians, actually *live* with the converts? The question suggests that the Roman mission had a low opinion of the Saxon people, an attitude Gregory at once condemned. He wrote back, "You ought not to live apart from your [new] clergy in the church of the Angli, which by the guidance of God has lately been brought to the faith. . . . Institute that manner of life which in the beginning of the infant Church was that of our Fathers, among whom none said that any of the things which he possessed was his own, but they had all things common." The Saxons were converts, which meant that in Gregory's eyes they had become one with the believers in Rome, part of the common Christian cause.[16]

The common cause spread slowly. Ethelbert was not Clovis; he did not require his subjects to convert or sponsor any mass baptisms. However, Bede says that he showed "greater favor" and "affection" to those who did—so that, inevitably, the politically ambitious in the higher classes of society tended to convert. Ethelbert's nephew, king of the East Saxons, accepted Christianity in 604, and the faith began to ripple out into Saxon society. The crimson tide of the cross had begun its slow advance across the island.[17]

TIMELINE 35			
FRANKS	ENGLAND	VISIGOTHS BYZANTIUM	LOMBARDS
Chlothar / Childebert / Theuderic (511–561) (511–558) (511–534)		Justin (518–527)	
Chlothar / Childebert (511–561) (511–558)		Justinian (527–565) Justinian Code, first volume (529) Theudis (531–548)	
Chlothar (511–561)		Athanagild (554–567)	
Guntram / Chilperic / Sigebert / Charibert (561–592) (561–584) (561–575) (561–567)			
Guntram / Chilperic / Sigebert (561–592) (561–584) (561–575)		Justin II (565–578) Leovigild (569–586)	Alboin (565–572)
Guntram / Chilperic / Childebert II (Brunhilda) (561–592) (561–584) (575–595)		Tiberius (578–582) Pope Pelagius II (579–590)	
Guntram / Chlothar II / Childebert II (Fredegund) (Brunhilda) (561–592) (584–629) (575–595)		Maurice (582–602)	Authori (584–590)
	Ethelbert of Kent (590–616)	Pope Gregory (590–604)	Agilulf (590–616)
Chlothar II (Fredegund) / Childebert II (Brunhilda) (584–629) (575–595)			
Chlothar II / Theudebert II / Theuderic II (Fredegund) (Brunhilda) (584–629) (595–612) (595–613)			
	Augustine's mission to England (597)	Witteric (603–610)	
Chlothar II / Theuderic II (Brunhilda) (584–629) (595–613)			
Chlothar II (584–629) Edict of Paris (615)			
Chlothar II / Dagobert / Pippin the Elder (584–629) (623–639) (623–640)			
Dagobert (623–639)			
Dagobert (623–639) / Sigebert III (634–c. 655)			
Sigebert III (634–c. 655) / Clovis II (639–655)			
Grimoald (643–656) Clovis II (639–655) / Erchinoald (656–658)			

—•—

Chapter Thirty-Six

The Persian Crusade

Between 589 and 632,
a North African becomes emperor,
the Persians besiege Constantinople,
and new kingdoms of Slavs and Bulgars appear

WHILE GREGORY THE GREAT was coping with the Lombards, the Byzantine emperor Maurice was dealing with the Persians—an ever-present challenge that continually distracted him from the plight of his remaining lands in the west.

The first part of his reign had been complicated by Khosru's son and successor Hurmuz, an ambitious and aggressive young man who spent over a decade battering the Byzantine frontier. The war had been long, dirty, painful, and expensive, and Maurice was tired of it. Nor had the war been popular with the Persians; the Persian army had not made any real or permanent gains, and the nobles at the court in Ctesiphon were embarrassed by the stalemate. Hurmuz had alienated them even further by trying to woo the Christians in Persia ("Just as our royal throne cannot stand on its two front legs without the two back ones," he had told the Zoroastrians at court, "our kingdom cannot stand or endure firmly if we cause the Christians to become hostile to us").[1]

Finally one of Hurmuz's generals revolted against his king. His name was Bahram Chobin, and he had earned a great reputation for himself by beating off a Turkish invasion on the far eastern border. Hurmuz, hoping for victory, had then dispatched him to the Byzantine frontier to press the war against Maurice, but in 589 Bahram lost a battle on the banks of the Araxes river to Byzantine forces. Hurmuz was furious. He sent his general a dress to wear, along with an insulting letter dismissing him from command.[2]

Bahram refused to give up his post, so Hurmuz sent troops to remove him by force. The troops promptly defected to Bahram's side, and the general marched on Ctesiphon. By the time he got there, the nobles at court had already seized Hurmuz, blinded him (he was killed in prison not much later), and put his son Khosru II on the throne.

This was not quite what Bahram had in mind, and he threatened to kill Khosru II unless the young man relinquished the throne. He had most of the army on his side, so Khosru II fled from the city—into Byzantine territory. Maurice was the only other king strong enough to fight Bahram, and as soon as Khosru got across the border, he sent a letter to Constantinople begging Maurice for help.

Maurice saw the chance to bring the war with Persia to an end. He sent a Byzantine army back to Ctesiphon with Khosru II, and after a protracted battle Bahram was forced out of the city. He fled eastward to the Turks (who first welcomed him and then helped Khosru II by assassinating him), and Khosru II took back his throne.[3]

In exchange for the help, Khosru II now agreed to a truce with Maurice and gave him back some of the frontier cities that had been captured decades earlier by the Persians. The two kings sealed the treaty with a marriage: Maurice sent one of his daughters to Ctesiphon to become Khosru II's wife. As Khosru II was an inveterate collector of women (one Persian writer insists that he had a harem of ten thousand), this was not as meaningful as it might seem; nevertheless, peace descended over the frontier for the first time in almost twenty years.

Finally Maurice could pay some attention to the west. He still had territories in Italy and North Africa, both under the supervision of the military governors known as exarchs; the exarch in Ravenna had a counterpart in Carthage, both men holding command of such soldiers as Maurice had been able to spare, along with the civil authority to make and enforce laws. He also had a trouble spot on the Danube border. The exarchs were not facing any immediate crises, so Maurice decided to deal with the Danube problem first.[4]

The Slavs were now crossing over the river in boats to raid the Byzantine lands on the other side. Maurice began to lead his soldiers to the new battlefield, but halfway to the Danube he changed his mind and went back to Constantinople. This did not endear him to the men who were being sent far away from home to fight a fierce enemy. The Slavs had begun to take on a frightening, Hun-like reputation: "refusing to be enslaved or governed," in Maurice's own words, "bearing readily heat, cold, rain, nakedness, and scarcity of provisions."[5]

Despite his retreat from the front, Maurice had done his research. He wrote a handbook for his men, the *Strategikon*, describing everything that contemporary generals knew about the Slavs. He warns them to attack in winter, if possible, when the trees are bare, since the Slavs are expert at guerilla tactics and prefer to fight in the deep woods; he tells them to look out for clusters of reeds in the river, since the Slavs might be lying on the bottom, breathing through the hollow stems; he suggests that since the Slavs have multiple chiefs instead of one king, it might be worthwhile trying to bribe some of them to turn against the others.

It isn't clear how useful these tips were, since the Slavs continued to push across the Danube. These invasions were joined by regular assaults from the Avars, who had come up behind them. Fighting on the northwest border of the empire continued for a full ten years, until the troops were exhausted and battered. Maurice grew more and more unpopular. In 599, the leader of the Avars offered to return twelve thousand Byzantine prisoners of war in return for a generous payment; Maurice refused, and the Avars executed all twelve thousand, which darkened the mood of the army even more.

Then in 602, Maurice—whose treasury must have been all but empty—sent orders to the front: The troops would not be returning home over the winter, as was usual. Rather, to save travel costs and supplies, they would camp across the Danube, foraging in enemy territory for enough food to sustain them.[6]

The army refused. Instead, they picked one of their own officers, a man named Phocas, and declared him to be their new general. As his first act, Phocas announced that the army was going home, and began to lead the soldiers towards Constantinople.

Maurice, who had no friends left in the army, rounded up the Blues and Greens, armed them, and told them to defend the city against the approaching troops. Apparently he thought that Phocas intended to take the throne; in fact, the army had sent a letter to Maurice's son and heir, Theodosius, asking him to take the reins of power away from his father. Theodosius had declined, and it is not clear just how much trouble Maurice was in. But he had created a brand new crisis by arming the Blues and the Greens, who, although reduced in number since Justinian's day, were still thugs. They stayed on the walls of the city, behaving like a garrison, for a day and a half and then started fighting each other. A mob set fire to the house of one of the senators. Rioting spread throughout the city.[7]

That night, Maurice decided to flee. He had gout, which made his journey to the harbor slow and painful. With his wife and sons he finally made it to a ship, and the royal family fled across the strait to the city of Chalcedon. There, Maurice stopped. But he sent his son Theodosius on towards Persia with a letter to Khosru II, asking him to shelter the Byzantine crown prince in return for the favor Maurice had done for him, ten years earlier.

Meanwhile Phocas had arrived at the city, and the army and the Greens had proclaimed him emperor. The Blues, who were the weaker party, retorted that Maurice was still alive, so another emperor could not be crowned. Phocas decided to remedy this problem. He sent a trusted officer across the water to

Chalcedon, where the soldier found Maurice and four of his sons and murdered all five of them. Another assassin followed young Theodosius on his path towards Ctesiphon, caught up with him in Nicaea, and killed him.[8]

The heads of all six men were brought back to Constantinople and staked out for the people to see, remaining on public view until, as the contemporary *Chronicle of Theophanes* tells us, "they began to stink." There was a good and practical reason for this: Phocas wanted to make sure that everyone knew Maurice and his heirs were dead. But despite the display, the rumor persisted that Theodosius had made it into Persia and was at the court of Khosru II; the head of the heir to the throne had been too disfigured for easy identification.[9]

At first Phocas was popular simply because he was not Maurice. The army was relieved to have a military man in charge; the people of Constantinople hoped for change; and Gregory the Great, in Rome, wrote a fulsome letter welcoming the new emperor to the throne. "Glory to God in the highest," he began, "who changes times and transfers kingdoms. . . . We rejoice that the benignity of your piety has arrived at imperial supremacy. Let the heavens rejoice, and let the earth be glad, and let the whole people of the republic, hitherto afflicted exceedingly, grow cheerful." Maurice had abandoned Rome, and although Phocas had in turn abandoned the Danube frontier (the land was now in the hands of the Slavs), Gregory hoped for better things from the new emperor.[10]

But Phocas immediately fell into another war, this one with Persia. Khosru II, who had spent the last few years strengthening his control over his empire, saw his chance to expand. He declared war on Phocas, claiming that Theodosius, the son of Maurice, had indeed survived and was with the Persian army.

Skirmishes began along the border, and the Persian army crossed the frontier in 605; Khosru stationed forces in Armenia, invaded Syria, and stormed through Asia Minor. Meanwhile Phocas, worried about the security of his crown, had been executing possible challengers to the throne left and right. He burned alive the general Narses, who had opposed his reign but who had also been responsible, in the past, for defeating the Persians; Theophanes says that Persian children "shivered when they heard his name" and that "the Romans were greatly distressed at his death, but the Persians joyfully exulted." He executed all of Maurice's male relatives, killed the commander of his bodyguard for plotting against him, and then sanctioned the deaths of Maurice's widow and her three daughters. The Greens turned against him, and he reacted by forbidding anyone with Green affiliations to take part in politics.[11]

At that point, North Africa rebelled.

The leader of the rebellion was none other than the exarch of Carthage, an old man and a lifelong civil servant who saw the empire crumbling before

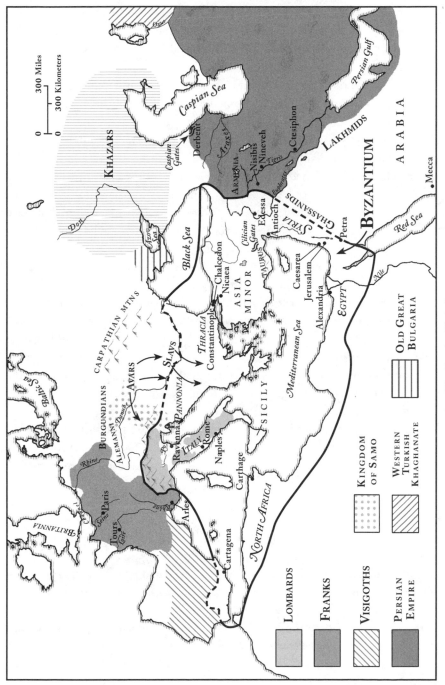

36.1: The Empire Shrinks

his eyes. Thracia and Pannonia were gone, and the Persian army was pressing across Asia Minor almost all the way to Chalcedon. In 610, the exarch assembled a fleet under the command of his son, Heraclius, and sent it towards Constantinople.

When the Byzantine commander at Alexandria in Egypt heard of the expedition, he too joined. The combined force sailed into the harbor at Constantinople on October 4 and found the gates open, the people waiting for them, and Phocas already under citizen's arrest. As Heraclius entered the city, Phocas was burned alive in the Forum.[12]

Heraclius was crowned emperor and found himself at the helm of a mess. "He found," Theophanes tells us, "that the Roman state had become exhausted. The Avars were devastating Europe, and the Persians had destroyed the Roman army in their battles." There were few veterans left alive among the troops.[13]

The Persians, almost unopposed, conquered Edessa and took the city's precious relic, the Mandylion, off to some archive in Ctesiphon. The following year, Caesarea fell into Persian hands as well. Simultaneously, the last remnants of the western kingdom crumbled. The Visigothic noble Sisebut seized the crown of the Visigothic kingdom by force in 612 and began to drive the Byzantines out of the lands they held along the coast of Hispania. He captured the imperial cities along the seaboard and, in the words of the Frankish chronicler Fredegar, "razed them to the ground. The slaughter of the Romans by his men caused the pious Sisebut to exclaim, 'Woe is me, that my reign should witness so great a shedding of human blood!'" His crisis of conscience didn't stretch to giving the land back, though. He had recaptured the peninsula, and the Visigothic kingdom had reached its height of power.[14]

Heraclius decided to sue for peace, even if it came on poor terms. He sent envoys to Khosru II, offering to pay tribute to bring an end to the war. But Khosru II was winning, and he refused. He had already consolidated his power in the northeast of the Arabian peninsula by executing the Lakhmid king and annexing his kingdom; in 614, he marched across to the northwest of Arabia and destroyed the power of the Arab Ghassanids, who had helped protect Syria on behalf of Constantinople.

He then besieged Jerusalem. The city fell. The Persians, who were irate over the length of the siege, stormed in and massacred the population. "Who can relate the horrors that were seen there?" wrote Antiochus Strategos, who pieced together the story from eyewitness accounts. "They destroyed persons of every age, massacred them like animals, cut them in pieces, mowed them down." Families were herded into the dry moat around the city and put under guard until thirst and heat killed them. In all, nearly sixty-seven thousand men, women, and children died under Persian swords. The most precious relic of Jerusalem, a fragment of the True Cross, joined the Mandylion in the Persian archives.[15]

Once again, Heraclius sued for peace. Once again, Khosru refused. "I will have no mercy on you," he is reported to have said, "until you renounce him who was crucified and worship the sun." The capture of the True Cross had already struck the Byzantines to the heart; it seemed as though divine favor had been entirely lifted from the country. Now, the Persians were advancing on Constantinople from the east, while the Avars and Slavs approached from the northwest. The army was exhausted; grain supplies from North Africa and Egypt had ceased.[16]

Heraclius saw no way to save the empire. He loaded all of Constantinople's treasures onto ships, sent them to North Africa for safekeeping, and began to make plans to abandon the city. He would go back to Carthage, the city of his youth, and from there would rule whatever Byzantine territories remained.

These plans stayed secret until the ships containing the Byzantine treasure sank in a storm, not too long after leaving the Golden Horn in 618. News of the disaster spread back to the people of the city and caused enormous angst. It had not occurred to them that the situation was so dire, or that Heraclius would ever consider leaving the city to destruction. Their horror was voiced to the emperor by the bishop of Constantinople, the patriarch Sergius, who convinced Heraclius that the defense of New Rome was his sacred duty. At the altar of the Hagia Sophia, Heraclius took a vow before God to stay in the city.[17]

Now he was forced to search for a way to dig himself out of an impossible situation. Fortunately for Heraclius, Khosru II sent him an extremely tactless letter demanding his surrender:

> The noblest of the gods, the king and master of the whole earth, to Heraclius his vile and insensate slave, . . . You say you have trust in God: why then has he not delivered out of my hand Caesarea, Jerusalem, Alexandria? Are you then ignorant that I have subdued land and sea to my laws? And could I not also destroy Constantinople? But not so. I will pardon all your faults if you will come hither with your wife and children. I will give you lands, vines, and olive groves, which will supply you with the necessaries of life; I will look upon you with a kindly glance. Do not deceive yourself with a vain hope in that Christ who was not able to save himself from the Jews, that killed him by nailing him to a cross.[18]

This letter was a misstep on Khosru's part. Zoroastrianism was the religion of the aristocrats of Persia, and casting the war as a religious conflict did not make Khosru's soldiers any more determined. But when Heraclius told the people of Constantinople that the Persians were blaspheming Christ, they were fired with indignation. Men began to join the army in increasing numbers. Sergius, the bishop of Constantinople, melted the treasures of Constantinople's churches, turned them into coins, and presented the money to Heraclius.[19]

The war had become a crusade.

Heraclius used the church's money to pay and provision new troops, outfit the army with new weapons, and build ships. He also bought a temporary peace with the Avars, protecting his western flank from attack and preventing the necessity of carrying on a two-front war. The Persians, meanwhile, were stalled at Chalcedon; Heraclius had sent his ships to guard the Bosphorus Strait, and the Persians were not quite ready to launch a full naval assault across the water.

On Easter Sunday, 622, Heraclius celebrated a solemn Easter mass at the Cathedral of St. Sophia, taking the Eucharist at the hands of Sergius. The mass was also a sendoff; the next morning, Easter Monday, he departed at the head of his troops, the first Byzantine emperor to ride personally into battle since Theodosius I. He left the bishop Sergius and the city official Bonus in charge of Constantinople, acting as regents for his ten-year-old son Constantine.

He did not try to sail straight across to Chalcedon, where the Persians waited. Instead, he ordered the army to be conveyed by ship southward, around the curve of Asia Minor, and landed at the Cilician Gates, the pass through the Taurus Mountains. The mountains protected the troops from immediate attack, and refugees from Syria could land on the shore to join the fight.

He spent the summer in Asia Minor, training this army. Apparently he had scores of men who had never fought before: "He found that the army was lazy, cowardly, disorderly, and disciplined," Theophanes tells us, and so he organized them and taught them how to fight by setting them against each other with wooden swords: "It was like seeing the horrible fearful spectacle without its danger, men converging for murder without bloodshed. Thus each man got a start from this dangerless slaughter and was more secure thereafter."[20]

It was unlikely that this army of baby soldiers would be able to defeat the hardened Persian troops, but Heraclius decided to try. In the fall, he began to march towards Armenia. The Persians were forced to draw away from Chalcedon to meet the challenge. The two armies met somewhere just south of the Armenian border; the exact battlefield is unknown, but Heraclius's men broke the Persian line and drove the Persian army into frantic retreat.[21] Heraclius himself led the attack, "leaping forward everywhere and fighting daringly," and his men followed him: "Who could have expected the invincible Persian race ever to show its back to the Romans?" Theophanes marvels.[22]

The tide of the war had turned. For the next three years, the Persian advances were slowly wiped out, one at a time, as Heraclius and his men drove the Persians backwards towards Nineveh. The Byzantine army reclaimed Asia Minor and parts of Armenia and Syria; Jerusalem, farther south, remained in Persian hands, but the soldiers were nevertheless fired by the idea that God was with them as they avenged the insult to his Son.

By 626, Khosru had decided that it would be necessary to make a drastic move to bring the war to an end. He was ready to besiege Constantinople.

He prepared for the assault by doing a little behind-the-scenes diplomacy; he sent an embassy to the Avars, offering friendship on better terms than Heraclius had been able to give, and the Avars agreed to switch sides. They were prized allies ("large of stature and proud of spirit," the *Russian Primary Chronicle* tells us), and Khosru arranged for them to launch an attack on Constantinople's western walls, while the Persians crossed the water and besieged the east.[23]

He reinforced the land attack on the west by buying the loyalty of the Slavs. The Slavs and Avars were not natural allies. In fact, the Avars had started to dominate the Slavs, forcing them to pay tribute and, according to Fredegar, "sleeping with their wives and daughters." In 623, a number of unhappy Slavic tribes had united under the leadership of a Frankish merchant named Samo, who had come into the Slavic land north of the Danube to trade. He was apparently a better general than merchant, and he had abandoned his goods in order to lead the Slavs into battle against their Avar overlords. "His prudence and courage always brought them victory," Fredegar tells us, and there were more concrete rewards for Samo as well: he had twelve Slavic wives.[24]

Samo's kingdom remained hostile to the Avars, but Khosru II's money convinced at least some of the Slavs to join with their Avar neighbors in the attack on Constantinople. In the last week of July 626, Slavs and Avars marched on the city, while the Persians prepared to sail from the opposite shore. Heraclius and the bulk of the army were far away on the northern Persia border, and defense of the city fell to the remaining soldiers under the command of Bonus and the patriarch Sergius.[25]

The details of the siege are preserved in a sermon preached afterwards by the clergyman Theodore the Syncellus. On the first day of the attack, the city was completely surrounded, and all of the buildings outside the walls were set on fire, ringing Constantinople with flame. Siege engines and catapults were moved into place, while archers kept up a hail of arrows over the city wall. The Avar and Slav troops, numbering at least eighty thousand, stretched as far as the eye could see: "The firm ground and the sea were both full of wild people," Theodore says.[26]

While the official Bonus organized the city's garrison for defense, the patriarch Sergius began holding regular sermons, vigils, services, and sacred processions. He was determined to remind the people that they were suffering through a war of religion. Liturgy was said almost without pause in the Hagia Sophia, and the entire city was seized with a fervor that would have carried the people through a much longer siege.[27]

On the tenth day of the siege, the general in charge of the Persian attack sent his entire fleet into the strait. His plan was for the Avars and Slavs to occupy the garrison so that his ships could approach by water without meeting much opposition. But the Byzantine navy proved much stronger than he expected. The ships from Constantinople drove back the Persian fleet, sinking ships and drowning their crews: "One could have said that all the bay could have been passed with dry feet, because of all the corpses lying there," says Theodore.[28]

With the attack from the east over, the garrison could concentrate on beating off the Avar and Slav assault from the west. Thousands of Avars and Slavs fell, until the allies began to retreat in disorder and chaos. The siege had failed. The Persians withdrew in disgrace; the Persian commander was forced to evacuate Constantinople and retreat back into Syria.

Heraclius, still far away, took immediate steps to strengthen the Byzantine position. Since he had lost the Avars and the Slavs as allies, he sent ambassadors north to yet another nomadic tribe.

Like the Avars, these nomads had been driven west to the Byzantine borders by the Turks, and they had made a home for themselves in the mountains north of the Black Sea. Heraclius knew them as the Khazars; his embassy to them is their first appearance in recorded history.

The Khazars agreed to join the fight. Together, the Khazar warriors and Heraclius's army began to fight their way south into Persian territory, pushing down between the Black Sea and the Caspian Sea into land that Khosru II had laid claim to. The Khazars sacked the city of Derbent, while Heraclius continued on towards Nineveh. By 628, the Byzantine army (without the Khazars, who had remained closer to their homes in the north) had reached the walls of Ctesiphon itself.[29]

The defenders of Ctesiphon did not have a patriarch to unify them in religious fervor. Instead, they turned on Khosru II. He tried to flee, but his own son and his courtiers caught him and crucified him—an end of agony and humiliation for a king who had lost all standing in the eyes of his people.

His son took the throne in 628 as Kavadh II and immediately sent to Heraclius, offering to make peace. The treaty that followed gave back to Heraclius all of the land that Khosru II had conquered; it also returned to Heraclius the fragment of the True Cross the Persians had taken from Jerusalem. Heraclius proceeded from Ctesiphon to Jerusalem in triumph, and on March 21 of 630, he returned the True Cross to the city with his own hands.[30]

The war was over, and the landscape had changed. Byzantium had regained its old shape again, but the Persian empire had been reduced to a weak and uncertain kingdom under shifting leadership. Kavadh II ruled for a matter of weeks before dying of unknown causes, and for the next four years a whole series of "transient rulers, pretenders and usurpers" passed through the Persian palace, none of them reigning for more than a few months at a time.[31]

North of the Black Sea, the Khazars had expanded into a political force to be reckoned with. The Avars, weakened by the defeat at Constantinople, lost more land to the Slavic kingdom of Samo, and their threat began to fade. The Bulgars, north of the Azov Sea, had been under the Avar thumb; but now their chief, a young man named Kubrat, sent a message directly to Heraclius, asking to negotiate with the emperor as an independent sovereign. Heraclius agreed to recognize Kubrat's kingship, and from 632 on the Bulgarian chief reigned as king of the first Bulgarian kingdom: Old Great Bulgaria.

Heraclius, returning to Constantinople in victory, had saved the empire. He had broken the Persian threat, he had almost single-handedly created two new nations, he had restored the Cross: Khosru II had died in shame, but Heraclius was exalted to the skies as almost divine. "In six years the Emperor had overthrown Persia," writes Theophanes, "and in the seventh he returned to Constantinople with great joy. God, Who had made every created thing in six days, named the seventh day that of rest. And so Heraclius, who had completed many labors in six years, returned with peace and joy in the seventh year and rested."[32]

Heraclius had accomplished everything he could have dreamed of. And in doing so, he had destroyed every barrier that lay between his empire and the Arabs to the south.

TIMELINE 36

VISIGOTHS LOMBARDS BULGARS BYZANTIUM	PERSIAN EMPIRE TURKS
Justin (518–527)	
Justinian (527–565)	
Justinian Code, first volume (529)	
Theudis (531–548)	Khosru (531–579)
	Bumin Khan of the
	Gokturk Khaghanate (552)
	Mukhan Khan (552–572)
Athanagild (554–567)	
Alboin (565–572) Justin II (565–578)	
Leovigild (569–586)	
Tiberius (578–582)	
Pope Pelagius II Hurmuz (579–590)	
(579–590) Maurice (582–602)	
Authori (584–590)	
Agilulf Pope Gregory Khosru II (590-628)	
(590–616) (590–604) Annexation of Lakhmids	
Phocas (602–610)	
Witteric (603–610)	
Heraclius (610–641) Destruction of Ghassanids	
Sisebut (612–621) Patriarch Sergius (610–638)	
Siege of Constantinople (626) Kavadh II (628)	
Kubrat of Old	
Great Bulgaria (632–669)	

The Prophet

*Between 590 and 622,
the prophet Muhammad forms a community
and rules over the city where it gathers*

Below the desert that separated them from the titanic struggles to the north, the tribes of south Arabia carried on the daily battle of surviving in a dry and hostile land. Himyar, on the southwest corner of the peninsula, was technically under Persian rule, but for most of Arabia, Persian ambitions and Byzantine crusades were irrelevant. They fought with each other, and with the elements.

In 590, a disaster far to the south shifted and broke the existing patterns of alliance and hostility.

In the center of Himyar, near the city of Marib, a man-made dam had been built back in the days of the Sabean kingdom. The dam closed off the Wadi Dhana,* the valley that collected rainwater and runoff from nearby mountains during wet seasons (usually only April and a thirty-day period in July and August). The dam allowed the residents of Marib to save water and channel it, through an irrigation system connected to the valley, into cultivated fields. Thanks to the Marib dam, the population of the city had been able to grow to around fifty thousand. Large cities were rare in Arabia; there was simply not enough food and water to support big and permanent gatherings of population in one place. Marib was the exception.[1]

Unpredictable shifts in weather patterns during the 530s and 540s had twice caused such severe and sudden rainstorms that the dam, unable to hold the runoff, had broken. Both times, the flood caused enormous damage. "The mass of water gushed out and came down, and there was great terror," wrote Simeon of Beth Arsham, who chronicled the history of Himyar under Persian government. "Many villages, people and cattle were flooded as well as every-

---

* A *wadi* is a valley whose floor becomes a river or stream during times of rain.

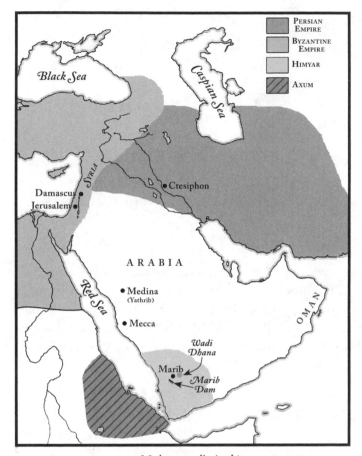

37.1: Muhammad's Arabia

thing which was standing in the way of the sudden mass of water. It destroyed many communities."[2]

The dam had been repaired twice. But the entire system had been badly weakened, and in 590 the dam gave way for a third time. This time, the flood was catastrophic. Villages downstream from the dam were wiped out for good; Marib, already shrunken from its former size after the previous breaches, was almost deserted. Tribes from the south who had relied on the water migrated towards the more welcoming oases along the northeast of the peninsula.

The moment of the dam's collapse remained in their memory, and the years before the flood became mythically glorious, the height of southern Arabian civilization. The final breach of the dam was remembered as the moment when the glory ended. Just as the great flood of the ancient Near East echoed into the book of Genesis, so did the breach of the Marib dam echo into the Qur'an:

There was for Sabea, aforetime, a sign in their homeland—
two Gardens to the right and the left.
"Eat of the sustenance provided by your Lord, and be grateful to Him:
a territory fair and happy, and a Lord Oft-Forgiving!"
But they turned away from Allah,
and We* sent against them the Flood released from the Dams,
and We converted their two garden rows into gardens producing bitter fruit. . . .
We made them as a tale that is told,
and We dispersed them all in scattered fragments.[3]

The dispersal northwards meant that Mecca, the home of the sacred Ka'aba, was no longer the only largish city where tribes gathered. Mecca did benefit from the migration; it sat on a trade route, and now it had little competition farther south. But tradition holds that many of the southern refugees ended up in the city of Medina, a sprawling settlement with fertile ground to the north. Medina was less prosperous than Mecca, but it had its own importance: it was a mixed town, made up of Jews who had migrated into Arabia long before and native Arabs, and intermarriage had tended to blunt the racial distinction between the two groups.[4]

The influx of peoples northward intensified the stresses in these towns. The Arabs of Mecca, like those in other Arab towns, were first and foremost members of clans (*banu*) linked together by blood and marriage, and the clans themselves were loosely associated into larger groups, or tribes. Mecca was governed by a council made up of the patriarchs of the most powerful clans. Among these were the clans of the Banu Hashim, the Banu Taim, and the Banu Makhzum, all of them belonging to the Quraysh tribe; the Quraysh tribe was dominant in Mecca, and its clan members controlled the Mecca council.

But all was not well. Quraysh dominance was resented by other tribes. In fact, the Quraysh had been forced to fight a bloody war with the Qays tribe, just four years before the Marib dam broke, to keep their power in the city. It was called the Sacrilegious War because it was fought during a sacred month;[†] control of Mecca and its resources had been deemed more important than worship.[5]

---

*The Qur'an uses both first-person singular and first-person plural pronouns for Allah. This does not imply plurality; the Arabic form, like the archaic "royal we" in English, conveys authority and command and is sometimes called the "plural of majesty." Some Arabic dialects also mix the first-person singular and first-person plural in colloquial conversation. See Abd Allah ibn Umar Baydawi et al., *Nature, Man and God in Medieval Islam* (Brill, 2001), p. 894; William C. Chittick, *The Sufi Path of Knowledge* (SUNY Press, 1989), p. 385; Abd Allah b. Buluggin, *The Tibyan* (Brill, 1997), p. 11.

†The Arabic tribes were supposed to observe four sacred months per year: the eleventh (Dhu al-Qi'dah), twelfth (Dhu al-Hijjah), and first (Muharram) in succession, providing a three-month break from fighting; and the seventh (Rajab). Since the old Arabic calendar was lunar, these months moved from year to year, and the tribal chiefs were fairly casual about delaying the beginning of the

And hostility between the clans of the Quraysh itself was growing more severe. The style of government that had served the Arabs for centuries had been developed in nomadic times, when the cooperation of the clans was necessary for the survival of the tribe. In the old dry desert days, war between clans could mean extinction for everyone; they all shared the common goal of finding food, finding water, and staying alive. Now, in a Mecca growing ever more wealthy, the clans were no longer forced into cooperation. Instead they were competing for the riches of Mecca, and some clans were doing much better than others. Personal fortunes were on the rise. Widows and orphans, deprived of their family support, were pushed aside.[6]

A strong king might have solved some of the knotty problems caused by this government of equals, but the Arabs were constitutionally anti-king; they had spent too many centuries relying on each other to put all of their trust in any single man.[7]

The clan of Banu Hashim was one of the poorer and more resentful clans, and it was into the Banu Hashim that the child Muhammad was born.[*] His father died six months before his birth; when he was six years old, his mother too died, leaving him a full orphan. His grandfather died two years later, and Muhammad was raised by his uncle Abu Talib, an ambitious man who had fought for the Quraysh in the Sacrilegious War, and who did not rate his nephew's comfort among his personal priorities. Muhammad grew up on the edge of survival, earning his keep by accompanying his uncle's merchant caravans on their journeys to other cities.[8]

At twenty-five, he agreed to a profit-sharing venture: leading a caravan for another Quraysh merchant, a widow named Khadija who could not take on the task herself. The first caravan he supervised went all the way to Syria, and Muhammad's management was so expert that he doubled the widow's investment. According to Muhammad's eighth-century biographer Ishaq, when he came back to Mecca with the money, Khadija saw an opportunity: she proposed marriage, and he accepted. Khadija was forty years old, fifteen years Muhammad's senior, but she would bear him three children, and Muhammad (somewhat against custom) did not take any other wives during her lifetime.[†]

The wealth from Khadija's caravans put Muhammad and his new family in the upper crust of Meccan society, but he seems to have been continually disturbed by the growing distance between rich and poor in his city, and the rampant materialism of his tribesmen. Ten years after his marriage, he took

---

sacred times if they weren't quite finished with an ongoing war.

[*]For simplicity I will refer to the prophet Muhammad as "Muhammad" throughout, although this was not his birth name.

[†]Ishaq lists seven children, but it is likely (given Khadija's age) that four of these were either orphans raised by Khadija or children from one of her two previous marriages.

part in the rebuilding of the wall around the sacred Ka'aba—necessary, because "men had stolen part of the treasure." Even the shrine was not exempt from greed.[9]

Muhammad, devout by nature, took it upon himself to spend one sacred month of each year providing for the poor: his biographer Ishaq tells us that he would pray, give food to all the poverty-stricken residents of Mecca who came to him, and then walk around the Ka'aba seven times. In 610, while observing his month of service, Muhammad was given a vision of the angel Gabriel. His own account of it was preserved in oral tradition and passed down to Ishaq, who set it down exactly as he heard it.

> He came to me while I was asleep, with a coverlet of brocade whereon there was some writing, and said, "Read!" I said, "What shall I read?" He pressed me with it so tightly that I thought it was death; then he let me go and said, "Read!" I said, "What shall I read?" He pressed me with it again so that I thought it was death; then he let me go and said, "Read!" I said, "What shall I read?" He pressed me with it the third time so that I thought it was death and said "Read!" I said, "What then shall I read?" and this I said only to deliver myself from him lest he should do the same to me again. . . . So I read it, and he departed from me. And I awoke from my sleep, and it was as though these words were written on my heart.[10]

The next day, he again saw the angel and received the rest of the vision: he was the prophet of God, appointed to take the messages of the angel to the rest of his people.

It is no mistake that the account does not say exactly what the words are. For the rest of his life, Muhammad would struggle to receive, and interpret, and then to pass on the revelations of God. In 610, when his first vision took place, he was given only the seeds of the religion that he would ultimately found, and those seeds were simple: he was to worship the one God, the creator Allah (a deity already known to Arabs), and he was to pursue personal purity, piety, and morality, all of which were already prescribed by Arab sacred practice. The word that he would use for righteous behavior, *al-mar'ruf*, means "that which is known." The problem with Meccan society was not a lack of revelation. It was a lack of *goodness*: the unwillingness to follow what the tribesmen must already have known (as Muhammad did) to be right.[11]

For three years after the vision, Muhammad told only his family and immediate friends of his call. His first followers were his wife, Khadija; a servant named Zaid, taken captive in a tribal battle, who had married and stayed with the clan and fathered four daughters, all of whom also became followers; his cousin Ali, son of the uncle who had raised him; and his close friend Abu Bakr. Not until 613 did he begin to preach his message to the rest of Mecca. By this point, it had taken a more distinct shape. After an agonizing silence during which he doubted the reality of his vision, the revelations had returned, and the most basic divine truths had become clear.

> The Guardian-Lord has not forsaken you, nor is He displeased.
> The hereafter will be better for you than the present. . . .
> Did He not find you an orphan and give you shelter?
> And he found you wandering and He gave you guidance.
> And He found you in need and made you independent.
> Therefore, treat not the orphan with harshness,
> Nor turn back the beggar unheard:
> But the Bounty of the Lord: rehearse and proclaim![12]

The core of the message was simple: worship Allah, care for the orphan, give to the poor, and share the wealth that had been divinely granted. At the root of Muhammad's teachings lay always the memory of the orphan he had been.

When he began to proclaim this in public, Muhammad collected more and more followers—primarily the weak, the poor, and the disinherited. The message did not go over as well with the newly prosperous upper classes of Mecca. The clan leaders of the Quraysh complained that Muhammad was insulting them and mocking their way of life: "Either you must stop him," they warned his uncle Abu Talib, "or you must let us get at him, for you yourself are in the same position as we are in opposition to him and we will rid you of him."[13]

To his credit, Abu Talib refused to turn against his own family, even to protect his wealth. The other clan leaders, seeing the spectre of a revolt of the underclass behind the charismatic and popular Muhammad, began a campaign of terror against any clan member who accepted Muhammad's message. His followers were attacked in the alleyways of Mecca, imprisoned on false charges, refused food and drink, pushed outside the city walls. Some of the new converts, afraid for their lives, fled across the Red Sea into the Christian kingdom of Axum, where they were welcomed by the Axumite king Armah as worshippers of one God. Others went farther north to Medina. The members of Muhammad's clan (the Banu Hashim) who remained in Mecca were forced into a ghetto, and a ban was declared on them: no one could trade with them, which cut off their food and water.

In these wretched conditions, both Muhammad's wife Khadija and his uncle Abu Talib grew ill and died. And it was in these wretched conditions that Muhammad was given a new revelation: God permitted those who were wronged and driven from their homes to fight back.[14]

Outside of Mecca, it was slightly easier to be known as a follower of

Muhammad. The tribes of Medina were looking for a solution to the unrest and intertribal warfare in their own city; having heard Muhammad's message from refugees who had fled Mecca for the more welcoming streets of Medina, a delegation came to visit the prophet and listen to what he had to say. Some were converted; Muhammad called these converts *Ansar,* "Helpers," a name that was often given afterwards to the followers of Allah who were not from the city of Mecca and not part of Muhammad's own tribe.

Muhammad, who believed that he had not yet been given divine permission to leave the city of his birth, remained in Mecca long after almost all of his followers had fled. Their departure put him in a much more dangerous position; he had little support left in the city, and the revelation allowing his followers to fight back against their oppressors had made the clan leaders of the Quraysh more suspicious of him than before. "When the Quraysh saw that the prophet had a party and companions not of their tribe and outside their territory," Ishaq writes, "they feared that the prophet might join them, since they knew he had decided to fight them."[15]

So the Quraysh planned that one representative of each clan would join in a group assassination of Muhammad. That way, no single family would bear responsibility for his death. "It was then," Ishaq concludes, "that God gave permission to his prophet to migrate."

Only Muhammad's cousin Ali and his old friend Abu Bakr were left with him in Mecca. Under cover of dark, Abu Bakr and Muhammad climbed out of the back window of Abu Bakr's house (which was being watched) and made for Medina, while Ali stayed behind to make sure that all the prophet's debts were settled. The day of his flight, the Hijra, was September 24, 622. Afterwards, all dates for the followers of Muhammad—now known as Muslims—were counted as "after the Hijra."*

The Hijra was the first day of the first year of a new way of reckoning. This, not the date of Muhammad's first vision, was the point at which Muslims reckoned that their identity began. It was only when Muhammad came to Medina that he was able to begin to shape his followers into something new. Like Constantine, he had discovered a bond that could hold together a group of Arabs who did not naturally count themselves as members of one clan, or one city, or one nation. This bond of belief—belief in the one Creator, commitment to a life of justice and purity in His name—had created a new kind of tribe. All those who followed the words of Muhammad were *umma,* "one community to the exclusion of all men."[16]

The *umma* were by far the most powerful group in Medina, and as their

---

*In English, the initials AH stand for the Latin phrase *anno Hegirae,* coined by western writers centuries later.

leader, Muhammad was the de facto ruler of the city. But not all of the residents of Medina were members of the *umma*; some of the Arabs and all of the Jews held themselves apart. One of Muhammad's first concerns was to protect their rights. He did not want to re-create the stratified system of his home city, with members of one tribe dominating the interests of others. He began to speak revelations to this problem: all men and women in Medina had equal rights, whether or not they worshipped Allah.

Almost from the point of his arrival in Medina, Muhammad took on the role not just of prophet to the believers, but as civil authority over the unbelievers. Medina, like Mecca, was torn by conflict between clans and tribes; unlike Mecca, it was not controlled by a powerful cabal able to unite itself, when necessary, against a threat to its interests. Muhammad offered the city a path towards peace, and it was accepted. He began to achieve political power, not through conquest, but through his reputation for wisdom.

From its very beginnings, Islam was unlike Christianity in this way. The followers of Jesus, not to mention the disciples of Paul and the early bishops, had no cities of their own; they had no kingdom. Christianity became a religion of empires only when Constantine brought it into Rome with him, across the Milvian Bridge; and between Jesus and Constantine lay several centuries of belief and practice, theology and tradition, war and conquest.

But Muhammad had a city. From the day of the Hijra onward, his revelations governing the purity of worship and the morality of the believer were mixed with his need to make civil legislation for Medina. From the very beginning, his teachings were affected by his need to establish a political order. The man who had lost his father and mother, his family, his wife, and finally his home, had found a new family among the community of his followers. His greatest concern was to keep those followers together in one body, united with each other and with him in loyalty and oneness of purpose—and for that, he needed not just the judge's balance scale, but also the sword of justice.

TIMELINE 37			
PERSIAN EMPIRE	**BYZANTIUM**	**ARABIA**	**NORTH AFRICA**
			Caleb of Axum (c. 510–540)
	Justin (518–527)		**Abraha** of Axum (525–c. 553)
	Justinian (527–565)		
	Justinian Code, first volume (529)		
Khosru (531–579)			
	Justin II (565–578)		
		Birth of Muhammad (c. 570)	
	Tiberius (578–582)		
Hurmuz (579–590)			
	Maurice (582–602)		
		Sacrilegious War (c. 585)	
Khosru II (590–628)		Breach of the Marib dam (590)	
			Armah of Axum (c. 600–640)
	Phocas (602–610)	Annexation of Lakhmids	
	Heraclius (610–641)	Destruction of Ghassanids	
	Patriarch Sergius (610–638)	Vision of Muhammad (610)	
		The Hijra (AD 622/1 AH)	
	Siege of Constantinople (626)		
Kavadh II (628)			

Chapter Thirty-Eight

—■—

Tang Dominance

Between 622 and 676,
the Tang empire of China battles with Tibet and the Turks
and tries to take over the kingdom of Silla,
while the Yamato dynasty of Japan joins in the resistance

B Y 622, THE NEW EMPEROR of China, Tang Gaozu, had signed a peace with Goguryeo (bringing an end to the long bloody conflict started by the Sui) and had begun the task of refilling the imperial treasury (emptied by war and canal-building). Despite the frequent outbreaks of minor rebellion in the unsettled country, the Tang dynasty was finding its way carefully forward into stability.

The dynasty's biggest problem came from the Turks to the north. After the death of the Turkish khan Bumin Khan, founder of the Turkish kingdom, Turkish unity had fractured from the inside and the kingdom had fallen apart into separate realms, the Eastern Khaghanate and the Western Khaghanate.

The Eastern Khaghanate was closest to the Tang border, and for a time Tang Gaozu managed to stay on reasonably good terms with the khagan. Gaozu's own family was not so very different, in custom and language, from the Turks. He had grown up in the northern reaches of China, where the Turks and Chinese mingled along the border. Gaozu's mother and grand-mother had been of nomadic blood, and Gaozu himself had raised his sons as hunters and warriors, more interested in horses and hunting dogs than in Confucian classics.[1]

But then the aggressive khan Hsieh-li took control of the Eastern Khaghan-ate. In the decades before Hsieh-li, the Eastern Turks had attacked the border, on average, about once every three years; under Hsieh-li's rule, the Turks began to raid the northern Chinese lands once every two or three *months*. In 624, the army of the Eastern Khaghanate marched all the way down to the Yellow river and then crossed it. The Tang troops panicked; only the intervention of Li Shimin, the emperor's second son, kept them from bolt-ing. Li Shimin rode out and offered to challenge Hsieh-li to single combat—

something no southern Chinese prince would ever have done—which struck the Turkish khan as the act of a man confident of victory. The khan began to suspect that his own men were in league with Li Shimin and that the duel was a trap. He refused to fight and instead accepted another huge payment and withdrew.[2]

Tang Gaozu, the dynasty's patriarch and founder, did not reign for much longer. He had served as the bringer of judgment on the previous dynasty's excesses, but this role was not naturally compatible with a long and virtuous rule as holder of the Mandate of Heaven. Instead, his son Li Shimin would take on this job, ruling for over twenty years and bringing the Tang dynasty into full legitimacy.

Li Shimin had fought for his father in the wars that brought Tang Gaozu to the throne, and had earned a loyal following of his own through his bravery against the Turks. In 626, he murdered (possibly in self-defense) his older brother, the crown prince of the new dynasty, and asked his father to appoint him heir instead. Tang Gaozu agreed. A few months later he abdicated and gave his son the throne. Li Shimin became Tang Taizong, the second emperor of the dynasty: like his father, he had come to power through violence, but the force was partly veiled by his father's decision to pass him the crown without struggle.[3]

As soon as he was acclaimed emperor, the Eastern Turks invaded again. Again Li Shimin, now Tang Taizong, put his own body on the line. "The Turks think that because we have had internal troubles, we cannot muster an army," he told his advisors. "If I were to close the city [the capital Chang'an], they would loot our territory. I will go out alone to show them that there is nothing to fear, and make a show of force to make them know I mean fighting."[4]

In fact, the Tang troops at Chang'an were too few to defeat the Turks, but Tang Taizong rode out with six men to the Wei river (just north of the city) anyway and reproached Hsieh-li for breaking their earlier peace. Meanwhile, his army assembled far enough away to make them difficult to count, but close enough for Hsieh-li to see them. Tang Taizong, exercising his knowledge of northern customs, then offered to go through a brotherhood ceremony with the Turkish khan, and Hsieh-li accepted.[5]

The Turks went home, but Tang Taizong exercised his new brotherhood by doing his best to encourage Hsieh-li's subjects to revolt against him; this was not so different from his relationship to his own brothers, two of whom he had killed on his way to the throne. He also encouraged Hsieh-li's nephew to lead a coup d'etat. Civil war between uncle and nephew began in 629; the Tang armies marched up to "help," and by 630, Tang Taizong had driven Hsieh-li into exile, accepted his nephew's surrender, and named himself "Heavenly Khan of the Eastern Turks" as well as Tang emperor. The Tang

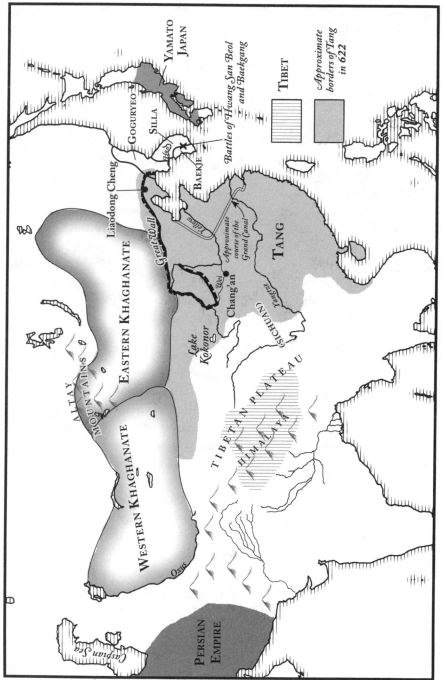

38.1: The East in the Seventh Century

empire had suddenly expanded—and Tang Taizong, once again showing his familiarity with northern affairs, managed to make himself popular with his new subjects by making tribal leaders into Tang court officials.[6]

For the next two decades, Tang Taizong led his kingdom into internal stability and outward conquest. Rather than making any great new innovations, he turned out to be expert at developing the network of government already traced out by the Sui; and he led his armies in expanding his control over the north, the northwest (where he conquered the eastern reaches of the Western Turkish Khaghanate with the help of his new Eastern Turkish subjects), and the southwest. His trust was placed not in scholars, but in men who, like himself, knew the northern methods of fighting: "Throughout his life," wrote the poet Li Bai of the Tang soldiers, "the man of the marches never so much as opens a book, but he can hunt, he is skillful, strong, and bold."[7]

In the southwest, the Tang generals encountered another empire-builder; but unlike Tang Taizong, who was building an empire on someone else's foundation, this king had laid his own groundwork. His name was Songtsen Gampo, and he lived on the high central Asian land known as the Tibetan plateau. The Tibetan tribes had come, thousands of years before, from the same area as the Chinese, but continued in a nomadic lifestyle long after the Chinese had started on the road to farming and town-building. Songtsen Gampo's father, Namri Songtsen, was the leader of one of the Tibetan tribes. He had taken the first tentative steps towards dominating the neighboring tribes when he died, sometime between 618 and 620, and his son—perhaps fourteen at the time—inherited his title.

Like Clovis of the Franks far to the west or Bumin Khan of the Turks up in the Altay mountains, Songtsen Gampo began to work at the task of turning a collection of tribes into a kingdom. And like most tribal leaders turned king, he chose outward conquest as a way to make his new territory cohere. After 620, he brought the nearby tribes under his authority and then launched campaigns against the Tuyu-hun nomads, around Lake Kokonor to the northeast, possibly as a way to distract the other tribal chiefs from the unpleasant fact that they were now under his domination. He sent armies west toward India and east toward the Tang border, but his mind was not only on conquest: he also worked at making alliances with his neighbors, establishing for the first time a Tibetan foreign policy.[8]

In 640, he sent an ambassador to the Tang court with a message: he wanted to make a marriage alliance with the ruling family.

Tang Taizong was unimpressed. In Tibet, Songtsen Gampo was a prodigy, a superstar statesman able to take his people from disorganized tribal structure to empire in less than a generation. In the universe of the Tang, he was merely a barbarian king with pretensions.

The Tang emperor refused to send a princess to the west, and Songtsen Gampo immediately invaded the southwestern territory of the Tang, the area now known as Sichuan. The Tang defensive garrisons managed to drive him back out, but Tang Taizong was surprised by the strength of the attack and decided that it would be prudent to rethink. He sent one of his nieces, Wen-ch'eng, westward to the court of Songtsen Gampo, and in 641 the two were married.

Wen-ch'eng seems to have brought with her Buddhist monks, Buddhist scriptures, and the Chinese habits of eating butter and cheese, drinking tea and wine, and consulting the stars. She was followed westward, in time, by experts she asked the Tang court to send: Chinese craftsmen who could teach the Tibetans how to make wine and paper, how to cultivate silkworms and build mills to grind grain, how to treat patients according to Chinese medical principles. Chinese culture—*northern* Chinese culture—infiltrated Songtsen Gampo's empire. So did Indian ways; Wen-ch'eng also suggested that her husband send one of his officials into northern India to bring back principles of written Sanskrit. The Tibetans had had no written language, but by the end of Songtsen Gampo's reign, a Tibetan script based on Sanskrit was in use.[9]

Songtsen Gampo died in 650, after building an entire nation in a single lifetime. Like so many empires built on personal charisma, the Tibetan kingdom began to waver. His heir was his infant grandson Mangson Mangtsen, and the real power at the palace was the baby's regent, the prime minister Gar Tongtsen. For a time, the empire halted its expansion and its foreign embassies, absorbed instead with an internal struggle for power and familiar conflicts between Buddhist worshippers and followers of the old nomadic religions.

Within months of Songtsen Gampo's death, Tang Taizong also died. His throne went to a grown heir: his favorite son, Gaozong, who had been at his deathbed fasting and weeping and was rewarded with the crown.

In the year he was acclaimed emperor, Tang Gaozong also added a new wife to the consorts he already had. He rescued one of his own father's concubines, Wu Zetian, from the Buddhist monastery where she had been sent after Taizong's death. Apparently the two had been sleeping together for some time. In 656, over the protests of his courtiers, the emperor demoted his first wife and made Wu Zetian empress, naming her three-year-old son crown prince.[10]

In the first years of his rule, Tang conquests continued. The Western Turkish Khaghanate had suffered a civil war between rival leaders, and in 657 the Tang armies marched through it, surprising the battling khans. The general in charge of the western front, Su Dingfang, rounded up his troops in a blizzard and sent them in for attack through two feet of snow: "The fog sheds darkness everywhere," he told them. "The wind is icy. The barbarians do not believe that we can campaign at this season. Let us hasten to surprise them!" The unprepared soldiers of the Western Turks were defeated, the land of the Khaghanate reduced to a Tang protectorate.[11]

Now the Tang empire stretched all the way to the borders of Persia. But on the cusp of a domination unlike any before, the emperor Tang Gaozong fell ill. Contemporary accounts tell us that he suffered from devastating headaches and dizziness, and lost his eyesight for a time. He had probably suffered a stroke, and in his weakness he relied on the intelligent and well-educated Wu Zetian, asking her to read him his state papers and authorizing her to make decisions in his name.[12]

She was in this position of power when ambassadors came to the Tang court from the Korean kingdom of Silla, asking for aid. The king of Silla, Muyeol the Great, still ruled the strongest kingdom on the peninsula, but he had watched his neighbors, Goguryeo and Baekje, forge friendships with the Wa of Japan, and the triple alliance alarmed him.

Wu Zetian agreed to send a Tang army of 130,000 to help Silla fight against Baekje, and in a great battle at Hwang San Beol, on the border between the two kingdoms, the Baekje army was devastated. The Baekje king, Uija, surrendered and was taken off as a prisoner—not to Silla, but to China. Wu Zetian had her eye on the Korean peninsula, and the Tang reinforcements had been a gentle probe into Korean territory.

Muyeol the Great declared himself king of Silla and Baekje, but Baekje rebels were already organizing a resistance. Survivors of the Battle of Hwang San Beol fled to Japan, where one of the captive king's sons already lived; he had gone to Japan some years before as a hostage and guarantor of the alliance between Japan and Baekje.

There, they appealed to Prince Naka no Oe, the crown prince of the Yamato dynasty, to help them get their country back.

The heavenly sovereign of Japan, the empress Saimei, had taken the throne in 642 after her husband's death. Her son Naka no Oe, sixteen years old, was perhaps a more natural choice—but the powerful Soga clan had thrown its weight behind Saimei, who was less independent-minded than her energetic son. In 593, the Soga had managed to put a dead emperor's wife on the throne and then control it from behind the dais. Now they repeated the feat, making Saimei the second woman to occupy the throne of Japan and the second to depend on the Soga for her power.

Naka no Oe was both old enough to rule and ambitious enough to resent this. He did not blame his mother; he blamed the Soga, and he began to lay plans to break their power. He found a willing ally in a senior member of the rival Nakatomi clan, Nakatomi no Kamatari. Together with a resentful younger member of the Soga clan itself, they plotted to get rid of the Soga influence by assassinating the most powerful members of its most senior family. Their primary target was Soga no Iruka, who together with his father Soga no Emishi had stood behind the empress's accession, and who together with his father stood to gain the most power by controlling the heavenly sovereign.

The plot took some time to lay. In 645, the year Isshi, on the twelfth day of the sixth month, it came to fruition. Soga no Iruka had come to court wearing his sword, as usual (he was, says the Japanese chronicle *Nihongi*, "of a very suspicious nature"), but Nakatomi no Kamatari had hired actors to put on an elaborate performance that would convince him to disarm. Soga no Iruka's suspicious nature deserted him when he most needed it; he laughed at the actors, took off the sword, and went into the empress's presence. The nineteen-year-old Naka no Oe quietly ordered the Guards of the Gates to lock all twelve entrances to the palace. He had given the task of carrying out the assassination of Soga no Iruka to three other members of the conspiracy, but as they stood in the throne room listening to the business of the day being read out, it became increasingly clear that the three swordsmen had lost their nerve.[13]

When none of them made a move towards their victim, Naka no Oe leaped forward and struck the first blow against Soga no Iruka. Wounded, the statesman staggered to the empress and begged for mercy; but Saimei stood and left the throne room, going farther into the palace so that she could not longer hear or see what was happening. The prince's three allies, spurred into action, finished the injured man off. When his father Emishi heard the news, he took his own life.[14]

The conspiracy, the "Isshi Incident," broke the back of the Soga clan. In the resulting power vacuum, a puzzling shuffle took place. Saimei, who had turned her back, stepped down from the throne, but Naka no Oe did not rise to replace her. Instead his uncle, the empress's younger brother, took the throne as Heavenly Sovereign Kotoku and ruled for nine years. When he died, Saimei returned from her retirement and again governed as heavenly sovereign from 655 until 661.

Even at her death, Naka no Oe did not rise to be heavenly sovereign. During the reigns of both his uncle and his mother, he exercised plenty of power at the Yamato court; in fact, when the Baekje survivors first appealed for help, Saimei was still on the throne, but Naka no Oe was the one who answered the call, the man who agreed to send Japanese ships to join the fight against the Sillan occupiers.

Before war could begin, Saimei died. Naka no Oe was now the ruler of Japan, but once again he did not take the title of heavenly sovereign. He governed, but he did not reign. It finally became clear that he believed himself to be defiled by the murder in the throne room. The blood shed in front of the heavenly sovereign had polluted the man who spilled it; Naka no Oe had gathered his three accomplices for just this purpose, so that his hand would not be the one stained with the curse. Their failure of nerve had forced him to draw it upon himself.[15]

But even without the sacred title, Naka no Oe acted as commander in chief of Japan's force. The Japanese fleet sailed towards Baekje, proclaiming that the Baekje prince Buyeo Pung, now brought from his exile as hostage and promoted to figurehead, was the rightful king of Baekje.

Just before the Japanese fleet arrived on Baekje's shores, King Muyeol of Silla died. His heir, King Munmu, took the throne and found himself facing invasion. He was particularly well fitted to fight back, though; in the war against Baekje, he had commanded a naval force for his father.

In 663, the combined Baekje-Japan alliance, led by Prince Naka no Oe of Japan and Buyeo Pung of Baekje, met the combined Tang-Silla forces in the Battle of Baekgang, fought in the same place as the Battle of Hwang San Beol three years before. The Tang-Silla alliance was triumphant; Prince Naka no Oe returned to Japan to shore up the defenses against invasion. Buyeo Pung escaped into Goguryeo. And Baekje was, effectively, no more.

Still reinforced by the Tang, the Silla armies now invaded Goguryeo, which fell under the assault in 668. Buyeo Pung was captured and, like Uija before him, was taken off to Tang China, where he disappeared from the historical record.

King Munmu now ruled over the entire peninsula. With Tang help, Silla had triumphed. The Three Kingdoms period had given way to the Unified Silla period, which would last until 935.

But almost at once, the alliance with the Chinese dragon turned against the Sillan king. Wu Zetian had intended to extend Tang rule all the way into the peninsula, not hand it over to one of the three kings. Now, she and her husband Tang Gaozong, who had made a partial recovery (although he would suffer attacks for the rest of his life), organized the peninsula into a set of administrative districts under Tang control. They declared King Munmu of Silla the governor-general of the Tang rulership, euphoniously named the "Protectorate General to Pacify the East."[16]

This did not please Munmu, who suddenly found himself subordinate to the force that had made his victory possible. Searching for a solution to his dilemma, he settled on an appeal to Goguryeo's freedom fighters—the same men who had fought against him, just months earlier, and who now were the last surviving resistance against Tang domination. Together, Munmu's army and the Goguryeo rebels formed a new alliance, this one against the Tang.

For five years, the rebels fought against Tang troops in all three of the former Three Kingdoms. In 676, after a series of losses in the Han river basin, Wu Zetian and Tang Gaozong decided to yield a good chunk of the Tang-controlled land to Munmu's rule, and moved the Office of the Protectorate General northwest to the city of Liaodung Cheng, outside the peninsula.[17]

The ways of the Tang had spread into the lands of the Turks and into the high plains of Tibet, but the Yamato remained outside of Tang power. And Munmu's resistance meant that, for a time, the Unified Silla kingdom would shake itself loose from the Tang and live in freedom.

TIMELINE 38							
NORTH AFRICA	ARABIA	TURKS	CHINA	TIBET	SILLA	BAEKJE	JAPAN
		Mukhan Khan (552–572)					
						Wideok (554–598)	
			Zhou Wu (561–578)				
Birth of Muhammad (c. 570)							
							Bidatsu (572–585)
			Fall of Northern Qi (577)				
			Zhou Xuan (578–579)				
			Zhou Jing (579–581)				
			Fall of Northern Zhou/Rise of Sui (581)				
			Sui Wendi (581–604)				
Sacrilegious War (c. 585)							Yomei (585–587)
							Sushun (587–592)
Breach of the Marib dam (590)			Reunion of China under Sui (589)				
							Suiko (593–628)/ Shotoku (593–621)
Armah of Axum (c. 600–640)				Namri Songtsen (c. 600–620)			
Annexation of Lakhmids			Sui Yangdi (605–618)				Seventeen-Article Constitution (602)
Destruction of Ghassanids Vision of Muhammad (610)							
			Fall of Sui/Rise of Tang (618)				
			Tang Gaozu (618–626)				
		Hsieh-li Khan (c. 620–630)	Songtsen Gampo (c. 620–650)				
The Hijra (AD 622/1 AH)							
		Defeat of Eastern Khaghanate (626)	Tang Taizong (626–649)				
					Uija (641–660)		
							Saimei (642–645)
							Kotoku (645–654)
			Tang Gaozong (650–683)	Mangson Mangtsen (650–676)			
					Muyeol the Great (654–661)		Saimei (655–661)
Defeat of Western Khaghanate (657)					Munmu (661–681)		Naka no Oe (661–668)
					Unified Silla (668–935)		

Chapter Thirty-Nine

—

The Tribe of Faith

Between 622 and 642,
Muhammad turns his followers into a tribe,
Abu Bakr leads the tribe in the conquest of Arabia,
and Umar takes them beyond the peninsula's borders

IN MEDINA, MUHAMMAD, leader of the *umma*, took on the job of judging the disputes of those outside the faith. Although he never claimed the titles, he found himself acting as both prophet and king in his adopted city; and soon he was forced to deal with the multiple practical difficulties pressing in upon the ideal community he had created.

For one thing, unity based on belief was not easy to maintain among people who were accustomed to thinking of themselves, first and foremost, as members of particular clans and tribes. Muhammad himself had recognized distinctions among his followers: he had given the name *Ansar,* "Helpers," to the Arabs of Medina, while the Arabs who had followed him from Mecca were known as the *Muhajirun,* the "Emigrants." He had taken steps toward creating traditional bonds of kinship between himself and his close supporters; after Khadija's death, he had become betrothed to the six-year-old daughter of Abu Bakr (although the marriage was not celebrated until the little girl grew older). His "new tribe," the one based on faith, was still central to his plans for the future, but ties of blood and family were still woven through his thinking.[1]

And in other ways, the new tribe was not quite what he had expected. Muhammad's vision for Medina had been to enfold the whole city into the *umma.* His careful protection of the rights of non-Muslims had been sincere and good-hearted, but it was always meant to be temporary, lasting only until they inevitably saw the light and became followers of Allah. However, it was becoming increasingly clear that the Jews of Medina were always going to hold themselves apart.

Muhammad, frustrated, was given the revelation that appears as Surah 2 in the Qu'ran. Allah, the Surah repeats again and again, is the same God that

Abraham worshipped, the same God that the Christians worship: it was Allah who "gave Moses the Book and followed him up with a succession of Messengers; [who] gave Jesus the son of Mary clear signs and strengthened him with the Holy Spirit." Jews and Christians were wrong to insist that "[n]one shall enter Paradise unless he be a Jew or a Christian; *both* shall enter Paradise, along with the *umma*, if they submit to Allah and do good." For Muhammad, Jews and Christians were practically already inside the *umma*, and he could not understand why they continued to hold themselves apart.[2]

Nor was he pleased with all of the Arabs who were converting. The *umma* was now the most powerful "tribe" in Medina; the city's schedule had been reorganized around the five daily prayers that Muhammad prescribed for faithful believers, fasting and the giving of alms to the poor had been written into city law, the place of worship (the mosque) Muhammad had built was the city's center. It was now politically advantageous to be Muslim, and some of the Arabs were joining the faith to get ahead.[3]

But the biggest difficulty of all was posed by Mecca. "Then the apostle prepared for war," his biographer Ishaq says, matter-of-factly, "in pursuance of God's command to fight his enemies . . . whom God commanded him to fight." The revelation given in Mecca, allowing the Muslims to fight against those who had expelled them from their homes, was still in force even though the Meccan enemies were now distant; and beginning in 623, the year after the Hijra, Muhammad began to send both Helpers and Emigrants out from Medina on exploratory, prefighting missions. His first target was not Mecca itself, but rather the caravans that went between Mecca and destinations to the north, passing Medina on the way.[4]

Raiding caravans was not exactly an act of war. For centuries, Arabs had considered the caravans of other tribes to be fair game. Getting valuable food and water from passing caravans would certainly make life in Medina easier, but in preparing to raid the caravans from Mecca, which were almost all Quraysh, Muhammad was also sending a message. Loyalty to the *umma* had replaced the old tribal loyalties, and the ties of birth had been broken and supplanted with ties of faith.[5]

For several months, the exploratory missions from Medina simply involved spying, reporting, and occasionally negotiating with the caravan leaders. No one was injured until a party from Medina, spying on an enormous and rich Quraysh caravan, decided to attack and take its goods. In the scuffle, one of the Quraysh merchants was killed by an arrow shot from a Medina bow.

When the expedition returned to Medina with its booty, Muhammad was furious—not because of the killing, but because it had happened during the sacred month in which fighting was forbidden. It was just this sort of disregard for ancient religious traditions that had led to the corruption and decadence of Meccan society, and he did not intend for Medina to go the same way.[6]

His anger threatened to pull the new community apart. The other members of the *umma* began to whisper that the raiding party was damned; outside of Medina, the Quraysh spread the word that Muhammad himself had committed sacrilege. Peace was not restored until Muhammad received another revelation: breaking the sacred month was bad, but the sins of the Meccans were much worse. "Fighting in the Prohibited Month is a grave offence," says Surah 2, "but it is graver in the sight of Allah to deny him and to drive out his followers. Tumult and oppression are worse than slaughter. Nor will they cease fighting you until they turn you back from your faith, if they can."[7]

This relieved the tension in Medina, and the raiding party went back to their homes in relief. But the ripple effect of this revelation was much wider. The scope of the original permission—to fight back when wronged—had, almost invisibly, expanded. It was now permissible to fight back against those who would *continue* to wrong you, given a chance.

The revelation gave Muhammad and his followers the justification they needed to launch a full-scale attack on a Meccan caravan. In 624, a large caravan loaded with goods from Syria passed Medina. It was led by an old enemy of Muhammad's, a man named Abu Sufian. The path he was on led past the Wells of Badr, an oasis and watering-place south of Medina; Muhammad assembled three hundred men (a huge force to overwhelm a single caravan) and set out for the wells, to intercept the caravan there.

Abu Sufian had been expecting trouble. His scouts went out ahead of him, asking for news of any large parties on the move, and brought back intelligence of the planned Medina raid. Abu Sufian sent a message to Mecca asking for reinforcements, and a huge army turned out: a thousand men, with representatives from every Quraysh clan. The conflict between Muhammad's religious revolution and the old order had finally come to a head.[8]

The Quraysh army from Mecca met the smaller force from Medina at the Wells of Badr on March 17, 624. Rallying his outnumbered forces, Muhammad called out that any man who was killed fighting with steadfast courage would certainly enter Paradise. Driven by loyalty to Muhammad, by religious fervor, by hatred for their enemies, and by the fear of losing everything they had gained, the men from Medina turned away the larger army. Only fifty or so of the Quraysh died, but the rest were driven back. Muhammad and his men took the goods recovered from the caravan (Abu Sufian had escaped and taken part of it back to Mecca with him) and returned to Medina in triumph.

It was the first battle of Islam, a turning point in the life of the *umma*. Between 624 and 630, the fighting escalated. The *umma* in Medina drove out, by force, two of the Jewish tribes that refused to recognize Muhammad's authority. Major battles between the armies of Mecca and Medina took place in 625 and 627; after this second battle, the Battle of the Trench (named because the people at Medina dug a moat in front of their city to protect it from invasion), the final tribe of Jews was also exiled from the city. They had refused to take part in the battle, which was a violation of Muhammad's declaration that Jews and Arabs support each other both in peace and in war. The Battle of the Trench had itself been a draw—cold weather had forced the attackers from Mecca to withdraw—and the Jews' nonparticipation probably did not alter the outcome. But the Muslims in the city were indignant over this breach of trust.

The Jews were besieged in their homes and finally forced to surrender. They were given a choice—conversion to Islam, or death and slavery—and chose the latter: "We will never abandon the laws of the Torah and never change it for another," Ishaq records them as saying. Muhammad appointed a judge to pronounce the sentence, a man named S'ad who was himself a Jewish convert to Islam. S'ad decreed that the men be executed and the women and children made slaves. Ishaq's account is stark:

> Then the apostle went out to the market of Medina (which is still its market today) and dug trenches in it. Then he sent for them and struck off their heads in those trenches as they were brought out to him in batches. . . . There were 600 or 700 in all, although some put the figure as high or 800 or 900.[9]

The new community was under attack from the outside, and the conditions of its existence had altered. There was no longer any place in Medina for neutrals.

By 630, the *umma* at Medina had grown so large and powerful that Muhammad was able to assemble an army of ten thousand: Helpers, Emigrants, and numerous soldiers from outlying tribes who either had accepted Islam or were willing to make common cause with it. At the head of this army, he marched against Mecca for the final time. Once again he was able to offer a justification for the attack. Nomadic allies of the Quraysh had attacked nomadic allies of the Muslims: this was a hostile act against the people of the faith, and the Muslims were simply fighting back.[10]

As Muslim power had grown, the people of Mecca had begun to lean more and more towards making peace with the powerful neighbor to the north (in fact, two treaties in the previous decade had allowed Muslims to enter the city on occasion and worship at the Ka'aba). Even Abu Sufian, owner of the caravan that had been attacked at the Wells of Badr, now favored a truce. When Muhammad arrived on the horizon with his army, it became perfectly clear that the truce would involve surrender.

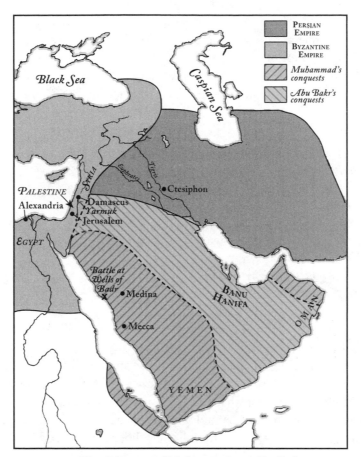

39.1: The Conquests of Muhammad and Abu Bakr

Abu Sufian, standing on the walls, extracted a promise that the Muslims would enter the city without bloodshed. Muhammad agreed, and the gates were opened. The promise was kept. The only violence done was to the idols of various deities around the city, which were smashed and thrown down. Muhammad himself worshipped Allah at the Ka'aba. He was joined by Abu Sufian, who had agreed to convert to Islam.

From this point on, Mecca was the core of Islam, the place of greatest devotion for any Muslim. Muhammad centered himself in the city, and for the next two years he directed various campaigns from his Meccan headquarters. More Arab tribes began to convert. His conquests reached so far down into the south that Himyar fell under his sway. The *umma* was becoming a kingdom.

But Muhammad was not a king. He had given the Arabs a collective identity; what he had done for them was not unlike what Alaric had given to the Goths, or what Clovis had done for the Franks. He had taken an assortment of competing tribes and provided them with a way to think of themselves as a group. The Arab hatred for kingship meant that Alaric's role as warrior-king and Clovis's role as Christian king were closed to him; instead, he was the Prophet, the creator of a new people.

In 632, just before his death, he preached a farewell sermon that laid out the mixture of religious and civil regulations that shaped this new people.

> *Allah has forbidden you to charge interest.*
> *Your women have the right to be fed and clothed in kindness.*
> *Worship Allah.*
> *Say your five daily prayers.*
> *Fast during the month of Ramadan.*
> *Give your wealth in charity.*
> *Perform Hajj [pilgrimage to Mecca] if you can afford to.*
> *An Arab has no superiority over a non-Arab.*
> *A white has no superiority over black.*
> *No prophet or apostle will come after me and no new faith will be born.*[11]

Not long after delivering the sermon, Muhammad grew ill and within a few days died.

He left no guide to his succession—no one appointed to receive his spiritual authority, no one to act in his role as ruler of the *umma*, no one to lead further campaigns. Perhaps he had no thought that a kingdom of Muslims would exist after his death. Certainly he had no intentions of leaving a hereditary kingship of some sort over his followers. His enormous achievement had a dark side: the identity of his followers was so closely bound up with his own person that the new Islamic community immediately began to spin apart. Old tribal loyalties, freed from the almost hypnotic effect of his personality, reasserted themselves.

Abu Bakr, his old friend and father of his young wife Aishah, was chosen as his successor by a gathering of Muslims in Medina. But the election was not uncontested; other Muslims, primarily in Mecca, wanted to appoint Ali ibn Abu Talib, Muhammad's son-in-law, who was busy washing Muhammad's body and mourning his death while the gathering was electing Abu Bakr.

It is not entirely clear what Ali himself thought of the situation. According to one version of events, Ali did not seriously argue with the selection of Abu Bakr as the next leader of the Muslim people; he retreated from the controversy, considered his position, and eventually offered his support to Muhammad's friend. But other accounts suggest that he believed he should succeed his father-in-law, and disputed Abu Bakr's election.*

---

*What remains unclear is whether Ali himself accepted Abu Bakr's legitimacy—or whether he simply ceased to press his claims, out of a desire to maintain unity among the Islamic tribes. Muslim oral

Either way, a number of Arabs resisted Abu Bakr's leadership, with or without Ali's support. Abu Bakr reacted not as a prophet, but as a general. He divided his own followers into eleven armed groups under eleven competent commanders, and assigned each one the task of subduing, by force, the areas where resistance to his leadership was making itself known.[12]

The subjugation was successful; Abu Bakr became the sole heir of Muhammad's power, the *Khalifat ar-rasul Allah*: the caliph, representative of the message of the prophet of God. (His original title, in fact, was "Caliph of the Messenger of God," acknowledging his second-place status in the line of revelation.)[13]

But the strike forces did much more than subdue rebellion. Later accounts called the resistance to Abu Bakr's rule the *ridda*, the "apostasy," and credited Abu Bakr with holding Muhammad's conquests together. In fact, the eleven columns, under the leadership of Abu Bakr's general and right-hand man, Khalid, fanned out and expanded the Islamic kingdom by conquering nearby tribes that had not yet fallen under Muslim domination. The conquest spread. Under Abu Bakr's supervision, the rest of the peninsula fell, tribe by tribe and oasis by oasis, under the rule of the caliph. Within a year, Arabia was united behind him.[14]

This left Abu Bakr at the head of an enormous armed camp that was not, as Medina and Mecca had been, necessarily convinced of the truth of Islam. It was, in the words of historian John Saunders, a kingdom filled with "recent, tepid, and unstable converts," a powder keg with Abu Bakr sitting on the lid.[15]

Abu Bakr decided to turn its energies outwards. Medina had prospered while grappling with outside enemies; nothing welded a people together like a war.

In 633, he sent his general Khalid against the first enemy outside of the peninsula: the Persian empire. After the long bloody war with Byzantium, Persia had been further weakened by ongoing quarrels over the crown. Finally the grandson of the crucified Khosru II, Yazdegerd III ("a curly-haired man with joined eyebrows and fine teeth," al-Tabari writes), had managed to take the throne by appealing to none other than Heraclius for help.[16]

He had been king over the remains of Persia for only a year when Khalid and his Arab armies appeared on the other side of the Euphrates. At the same time, other Arab troops were making their way towards the Byzantine provinces of Palestine and Syria, under the command of four other generals.

---

traditions preserve both points of view. The former tradition is accepted by those who call themselves Sunni Muslims; they believe that the passing of the caliphate to Abu Bakr was legitimate, and that the line of caliphs who follow him is thus also legitimate. Those who disagree and support Ali as the divinely chosen successor of Muhammad were known as Shi'at Ali, "The Party of Ali"—today, Shi'ite Muslims. The division did not occur in Islam until considerably later, but it is rooted in the events of 632.

The Byzantine troops put up a stronger resistance than Abu Bakr had expected, and just as Khalid was getting ready to attack the Persians, Abu Bakr recalled him and sent him westward to help out on the Palestinian front. Yazdegerd III had gotten a very brief reprieve, but at the expense of Heraclius. Byzantium, like Persia, had suffered from the long war; its soldiers were tired and depleted. The combined Arab troops defeated them in two large battles, capturing Damascus and moving through Palestine into Syria.[17]

Just as the conquests were gathering momentum, Abu Bakr died. He had been caliph for two years and was an elderly sixty-one. He had been careful to leave strict instructions as to the succession; he wanted his son-in-law Umar to inherit his power, and the transition occurred in Mecca without chaos. On the battlefront, the armies pressed forward without halting.

Umar knew that his first task was to keep fighting. Al-Tabari tells us that when he was first acclaimed, he was addressed as "Caliph of the Caliph of the Messenger of God." "Too long-winded," Umar said. "When another caliph comes along, what will you call him? Caliph of the Caliph of the Caliph of the Messenger of God? You are the faithful, and I am your commander." It was a moment of transition. As Commander of the Faithful, Umar was no longer merely Muhammad's successor; he was the commander in chief of a new and expanding empire.[18]

At this point, Heraclius realized that he had misjudged his enemy. This was not a bothersome raid—it was a serious and terrifying challenge to his power. To meet it, he put together a great coalition force: his own men, Armenian soldiers, Slavs from up north of the Black Sea, Ghassanid Arabs, and anyone else he could find. In this way, he managed to field an army of 150,000.

His coalition met the invading Arabic forces at the Yarmuk river in Syria. Fighting went on for six entire days. The narratives of the battle are confused and contradictory, but they all end in the same way: the Byzantine army was routed, and Heraclius was forced to give up the provinces of Syria and Palestine, which he had just gotten back from the Persians. Jerusalem held out until the end of 637; Heraclius's only victory was in managing to get the fragment of the True Cross out of the city and back to Constantinople before Jerusalem was forced to surrender to occupying Arab forces.[19]

Meanwhile, Khalid turned back eastward and marched against Persia. He stormed all the way to Ctesiphon, which surrendered in the same year as Jerusalem. Yazdegerd survived the conquest of the capital and fled eastward, still alive, but without his capital city.[20]

The conquests continued. In 639, Arab armies invaded the Byzantine holdings in Egypt, and by 640 all of Heraclius's Egyptian land except for the city of Alexandria was under Arab rule. Heraclius himself was in increasingly poor health. He had brought the empire back from the brink of destruction, only to see it fall away again in the face of an unexpected and unstoppable eruption of force from the south. He was unable to put together a counteroffensive, and in 641 he had a stroke and died.[21]

This left Constantinople in a bad position at a dreadful time. Heraclius had left the rule of the city to his son Constantine III, who was in perpetually poor health (he suffered from epileptic seizures); as insurance against Constantine III's sudden death, he had also made his younger son co-emperor. This younger son, Heraklonas, was Constantine III's half-brother—child of Heraclius's second marriage to his own niece Martina.

This marriage had been very unpopular in Constantinople, which widely regarded it as a breach of biblical law. When Constantine III died a few months after his coronation (just as his father had feared), Heraklonas became sole emperor—and because he was only fifteen, his mother, Martina, became his regent. The army revolted, under the leadership of the general Valentinus, and took Heraklonas and Martina captive. Both were ritually mutilated before being sent into exile: Heraklonas's nose was slit and Martina's tongue cut out.[22]

Mutilating a claimant to royal power was a ritual method of making him ineligible for rule. It had never been carried out in Constantinople before, and it wasn't actually foolproof; Heraklonas was perfectly capable of ruling with a slit nose. But it seems to have played on the Old Testament regulation which stipulated that deformed priests could not minister in the temple.* The sudden appearance of ritual mutilation in Constantinople suggests that the emperor had become much, much more than a king: he was also some sort of guarantor of God's favor, the channel of God's grace. The people of Constantinople saw Heraclius's incestuous marriage as a sin that was bringing judgment on them. As the unknown religion spread towards them from the south, they were desperate for a king who would bring salvation.

The options were limited, and the Senate chose Constans II, son of the dead epileptic Constantine III. He was only eleven, and on his accession he read to the Senate a statement that concluded, "I invite you to assist me by your advice and judgment in providing for the general safety of my subjects."[23]

The words had undoubtedly been provided for him. The Senate wanted Constans as the symbol of God's continuing presence in the palace at Constantinople, but they intended to keep power for themselves.

Neither the symbol nor their power seemed to work. The empire continued to shrink both to the west and to the east. In 642, the year after Constans II was crowned, the Lombard king Rothari carried out a quick and savage

*Leviticus 21:16–23.

conquest of the remaining Byzantine lands in Italy, leaving only the Ravenna marshes under the control of Constantinople. Of the few Byzantine troops left in Italy, eight thousand died in the fighting and the rest fled.[24]

At the same time, Alexandria fell to the Arabs. Egypt was completely gone; Hispania had disappeared years ago; Italy was almost out of reach; North Africa was cut off from the rest of the empire. Only Asia Minor and the land around Constantinople itself remained in Byzantine hands.

The new caliph of the Arabs, Umar, had his eye on even wider conquests. He sent an army through the conquered lands of Persia, far to the east: all the way to the Makran, the bare land that lay past the far eastern Persian border. Almost a thousand years earlier, the Makran had killed off three-quarters of Alexander the Great's army as they marched home from India. Apart from straggling settlements along the coast of the Arabian Sea where the sparse population subsisted on fish, there was no food or water in the Makran—just trackless sand and rock.

But the desert that had almost destroyed Alexander's legendary army was familiar to the Arabs. They knew how to survive in the dry sands; and they pressed on through the Makran until, as al-Tabari tells us, they reached "the river." They had come to the Indus, the edge of India itself.[25]

TIMELINE 39

CHINA	TIBET	SILLA	BAEKJE	JAPAN	ARABIA	PERSIAN EMPIRE	BYZANTIUM
					Birth of Muhammad (c. 570)		
				Bidatsu (572–585)			
Fall of Northern Qi (577)							**Tiberius** (578–582)
Zhou Xuan (578–579)						**Hurmuz** (579–590)	
Zhou Jing (579–581)							
Fall of Northern Zhou/Rise of Sui (581)							
Sui Wendi (581–604)							**Maurice** (582–602)
				Yomei (585–587)	Sacrilegious War (c. 585)		
				Sushun (587–592)			
Reunion of China under Sui (589)					Breach of the Marib dam (590)	**Khosru II** (590–628)	
				Suiko (593–628)/ Shotoku (593–621)			
	Namri Songtsen (c. 600–620)						
				Seventeen-Article Constitution (602)	Annexation of Lakhmids		**Phocas** (602–610)
Sui Yangdi (605–618)							
					Destruction of Ghassanids		
					Vision of Muhammad (610)		**Heraclius** (610–641)
							Patriarch Sergius (610–638)
Fall of Sui/Rise of Tang (618)							
Tang Gaozu (618–626)							
	Songtsen Gampo (c. 620–650)				The Hijra (AD 622/1 AH)		
					Battle at the Wells of Badr (624)		
Tang Taizong (626–649)							Siege of Constantinople (626)
					Battle of the Trench (627)		
						Kavadh II (628)	
					Death of Muhammad/	**Yazdegerd III** (632–636/651)	
					Election of Abu Bakr (632–634)		
					Umar (634–644)		
					Capture of Jerusalem (637)		
			Uija (641–660)				**Constantine III** (641)
				Saimei (642–645)			**Constans II** (641–668)
				Kotoku (645–654)			
Tang Gaozong (650–683)	**Mangson Mangtsen** (650–676)						
		Muyeol the Great (654–661)		**Saimei** (655–661)			
		Munmu (661–681)		**Naka no Oe** (661–668)			
		Unified Silla (668–935)					

Chapter Forty

Intersection

*Between 640 and 684,
the Arabs turn back from the north of India,
and the fractured south draws together*

A T THE INDUS, the Arab armies found a gathered Indian army waiting for them. The "Makran army" and the king Rasil had assembled on the bank of the river, says al-Tabari, apparently in an effort to keep the Arabs from attempting to cross the water, and the "ruler of Sindh" had crossed over to join with him.[1]

These were local Hindu kingdoms, independent of the huge realm ruled by Harsha a little farther to the east. The kingdom in the Makran and the kingdom in the Sindh had remained free from Harsha's grasp, as had the kingdom of the Shahi, farther up to the north. The Shahi was a Buddhist kingdom that had existed in the northern mountains for a hundred years, in control of the Khyber Pass, its capital city at Kabul. They had adopted the Persian title "king of kings" (*shahi-in-shahi*) from their great neighbors, but Persian rule had never stretched all the way to the Indus. The Arabs had already come farther east than any army since Alexander's.[2]

The Shahi, not yet threatened by conquest, did not come south to assist the kings from the Makran and the Sindh, and the combined army was defeated. The Arabs pursued them back to the Indus river and drove them across it. Then, before crossing, the commander al-Hakam camped in the Makran and sent a messenger back to the caliph Umar, bearing a fifth of the spoils from the battle and asking what to do next.

According to al-Tabari, when the messenger arrived, Umar asked what kind of land the Makran was. He got a less-than-enthusiastic report: "It is a land whose plains are mountains," the messenger told him, "whose only fruit is poor quality dates, whose enemies are heroes, whose prosperity is little, whose evil is long-lasting; what is much there is little; what is little there is nothing; as for what lies beyond, it is even worse."[3]

Umar decided that neither the Makran nor the Sindh were worth expend-

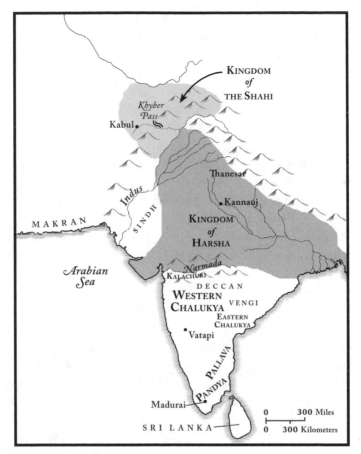

40.1: Indian Kingdoms in the Seventh Century

ing any more energy on. He wrote back to al-Hakam, forbidding him to pass over the river. The Arab armies turned back, and the eastern border of the growing Islamic realm remained, for the time being, in the Makran. In frustration, al-Hakam composed a verse in his own defense: "The army can place no blame on what I did, nor can my sword be blamed. . . . Were it not for my Commander's veto, we would have passed over!"[4]

Had Umar known that another great empire existed farther to the east, perhaps the Arabs would have pressed on. Harsha's northern Indian kingdom was, by this time, richer and more powerful than the Persians. His defeat by the Chalukya, some years earlier, had halted his southern expansion at the Narmada river, but he had continued his wars of conquest until the entire north and northeast were under his control. Probably the king of the Sindh and the ruler of the Shahi were his tributaries, at least for a time; the two independent kingdoms lay as a useful buffer between his realm and invasion from the west.

Now in his late thirties, Harsha had reached his full strength and maturity. His capital, Kannauj, had grown into the premier city of northern India. He sent at least one diplomat to establish friendly relations with the Chinese court to his east. His taxes, reports the Chinese pilgrim Xuan Zang, were reasonable, and if he forced his people to work on roads or canals, he paid them for their time. This particularly struck Xuan Zang, who had grown up during the last years of the Sui and had seen the brutal completion of the Grand Canal.[5]

Harsha's sister still reigned beside him, and it is probably no coincidence that at this time a particular form of Hinduism that highlighted female power, or *shakti*, became more prominent. The worshippers who pursued this stream of Hinduism (which was one among many) were called Shaivas, followers of the god Shiva and of his consort, the Goddess. For them, wisdom flowed from Shiva through the Goddess, and then from the Goddess to the human world. Harsha himself wrote a play, *Nagananda*, in which Shiva's goddess consort takes a leading role, resurrecting the dead son and heir of a grief-struck king to life and bestowing him with royal powers. In his youth, he had rescued his sister from a funeral pyre; in the play, the goddess lifts the dead young man from a funeral pyre and restores him to life.[6]

Yet Harsha also honored Buddhism. In 644, the year after the Arab army turned back from the Indus, he held an enormous assembly in the capital city so that thousands would have the opportunity to hear Xuan Zang's teaching; he had been much impressed by the monk and brought together (according to contemporary accounts) four thousand Indian monks to hear him. Towards the end of his life, he turned more and more towards Mahayana Buddhism and channelled more of the royal funds towards Buddhist monasteries. After a lifetime of war, he decreed that no living thing should be killed in his domain and that no one could eat meat for food.[7]

Harsha died in 647. It is not clear that he ever married. Certainly he left no sons; his prime minister seized the throne but held it only for a matter of weeks. His empire fell back apart into minor battling kingdoms, and over the next decades the historical records disintegrate into chaos. He was the last Indian king who would be able to build an empire in the north; the next ruler to dominate northern India would come from the outside.[8]

MEANWHILE, THE CHALUKYA DOMAIN to the south had fallen on hard times.

Pulakesi II's death in 642 had started a thirteen-year civil war between his sons, which weakened the kingdom and allowed the Pallava enemy to invade. Pulakesi had driven the Pallava out of the northern part of their homeland, the Vengi, and had claimed it for himself; by the time his third son, Vikramaditya, managed to triumph over his brothers and claim the throne in 655, the Pallava armies had taken Vengi back. Vikramaditya had the throne, but he had lost his father's conquests.

He had also lost the eastern part of the kingdom. Pulakesi had handed it over to his brother, Vikramaditya's uncle, to govern as his viceroy. When Pulakesi died, the viceroy proclaimed himself king over the eastern territories. The Chalukyas had divided; from now on, the Western Chalukya king would govern at Vatapi, while the Eastern Chalukya king would reign over the coastal area.

At the same time, a shrunken ancient kingdom in the far southwest was experiencing a revival. The Pandya dynasty had ruled the coast of the south in distant times; the Greek and Roman geographers had known of them, vaguely, as traders and fishermen. Their power had dwindled, although the clan itself had survived. But in the last decades, the Pandya had again begun to establish themselves, first as governors of the city of Madurai, then as rulers of the surrounding countryside.

An account from a century later tells us that Madurai at this time was the headquarters of the Sangam, an academy where poets and their patrons gathered to write and read. Poems and epics written in Tamil, the language of the south Indians, were joined by a translation of the Mahabharata into Tamil. The academy met at Madurai for a century and a half, from around 600 until 750.[9]

Vikramaditya of the Western Chalukya attacked the Pallava again in 670, fifteen years after coming to the throne. The Pandya, who had been forced to pay tribute to the Pallava king, were now drafted into the conflict as reluctant Pallava allies. Despite the reinforcements, the Chalukya army inflicted a painful defeat on the Pallava king, Paramesvaravarman I. The rivalry continued; four years later, the Pallava king retaliated by invading and sparking another giant confrontation. This time the fortunes were reversed; the Chalukya soldiers were defeated and driven back.[10]

The Western Chalukya king Vikramaditya died in 680. His son Vinayaditya inherited his rule; although hostility with the Pallava kingdom continued, Vinayaditya managed to avoid major confrontations during his sixteen-year reign. Chalukya power now stretched across the center of the subcontinent, covering the former patchwork.

The Pallava, meanwhile, extended *their* power to the south. The island that lay off India's southeastern coast, Sri Lanka, had at various times been claimed by south Indian rulers, but more often than not it played host to several different tiny, independent kingdoms at a time. In 684, a warrior named Manavamma asked the Pallava to lend him the soldiers he needed to make himself king of the entire island. Manavamma succeeded—but as payment for the soldiers, he was forced to pay tribute to the Pallava. Like the Chalukya kings, the Pallava dynasty had pushed its rule over the surrounding lands— and farther, down past the water, into the southern island.

TIMELINE 40

ARABIA	PERSIAN EMPIRE	BYZANTIUM	INDIA
			Eruption of Krakatoa (535)
			Pulakesi of the Chalukya (543–566)
			Rise of the Shahi
			Kirtivarman of the Chalukya (566–597)
Birth of Muhammad (c. 570)			
		Tiberius (578–582)	
	Hurmuz (579–590)		
		Maurice (582–602)	
Sacrilegious War (c. 585)			
Breach of the Marib dam (590)	**Khosru II** (590–628)		**Pulakesi II** of the Chalukya (597/610–642)
			Mahendravarman of the Pallava (600–630)
Annexation of Lakhmids		**Phocas** (602–610)	Meetings of the academy at
		Harsha (606–647)	Madurai (c. 600–750)
Destruction of Ghassanids			
Vision of Muhammad (610)		**Heraclius** (610–641) Patriarch Sergius (610–638)	
The Hijra (AD 622/1 AH)			
Battle at the Wells of Badr (624)			
		Siege of Constantinople (626)	
Battle of the Trench (627)			
	Kavadh II (628)		
Death of Muhammad/ Election of Abu Bakr (632–634)	**Yazdegerd III** (632–636/651)		
Umar (634–644)			
Capture of Jerusalem (637)			
		Constantine III (641) **Constans II** (641–668)	
			Arab invasion driven back
			Emancipation of the Eastern Chalukya
			Vikramaditya of the Western Chalukya (655–680)
			Paramesvaravarman of the Pallava (672–700)
			Vinayaditya of the Western Chalukya (680–696)
			Manavamma of Sri Lanka (c. 684)

Chapter Forty-One

———

The Troubles of Empire

Between 643 and 661,
the followers of Islam establish an empire
and suffer from power struggles, assassination,
and unrest

B Y 643, THE ARMIES OF ISLAM under their commander Umar had conquered more territory, in less time, than any army since Alexander the Great's. But Umar's enormous gains ended in 644, when he was stabbed six times by a Persian captive slave as he led morning prayers in Medina. The slave killed himself directly afterwards; Umar died slowly, over several days, which made it possible for him to arrange for a successor. Rather than electing one himself, he appointed a council of six Muslims from Mecca to pick the next caliph.[1]

Once again the supporters of Muhammad's son-in-law Ali suggested that he be given the title; once again, Ali was passed over. The council selected another of Muhammad's old companions, Uthman, who was (like them) Meccan and who was (like them) of the Quraysh tribe. In the years since Muhammad's death, Ali had spent most of his time with non-Quraysh Muslims, and the council wanted to ensure that the Quraysh stayed in control. Tribal loyalties were not yet dead in the *umma*.

As caliph, Uthman began the job of turning the extended conquests into something like a centralized empire. Umar had laid the foundation for an Arabic empire that, like Rome's, would draw a multiplicity of lands and languages under its banner. But the Arabic empire had sprung up in a matter of years, not over the course of centuries, and there had been no careful assimilation, no granting of citizenship to outsiders who had craved it—there had barely even been time for the Arabs under the banner of Islam to commit themselves to the new idea of empire.

Abu Bakr had provided a shaky cohesion by sending his new converts against the outside enemy. Umar, at the time of his death, had been putting into place an empire-wide hierarchy based on length of service—*saqiba*, "priority in Islam," giving the highest positions to those who had become Muslim the earliest.[2]

Had this continued, converts who persisted would have had the hope of rising to power; faithfulness to Islam over a long period might have provided glue to bind the new conquests to the old. But Uthman was old-school. He planned to keep the entire conquered realm under the tight control of the Quraysh clan—to turn it, in fact, into a fantastically distended mirror of Mecca. This required top-down control. He centered his government in Medina and appointed governors to supervise the outer reaches of the empire; he kept tight hold of the chief governors and military officials, appointing and removing them himself, and they were responsible only to him.

Under his guidance, conquests continued. Arab armies had occupied Alexandria. Now they could use the Alexandrian navy to reinforce their own ground forces. They had gained a grand new power: the use of the sea.[3]

The desert hardiness that had allowed them to push through the Makran was matched by a complete ignorance of the water. Umar had been terrified of the sea and had forbidden his armies to use it: "By Him who sent Muhammad with the truth, I shall never send any Muslim upon it," he had written, at the height of his power. The Arab governor of Syria, Muawiyah, had pleaded with him to change his mind, but he had refused.[4]

Uthman, on the other hand, granted Muawiyah permission to create a naval force, on condition that he use only volunteers for his sailors. But shaping a sea army from scratch was a slow process. The capture of the Alexandrian fleet catapulted the Arab ability to use the water forward by decades. Muawiyah, now admiral of the Arab navy, began to train his new force to sail across the Mediterranean towards even more distant targets.

Meanwhile, the new Arab governor appointed to run Egypt ordered his men to sack Alexandria and raze its walls. They chose a new city, Fostat (modern Cairo), to be a new capital: a new power in Egypt, a new beginning. A ground force marched from Egypt westward, through the old Roman lands of Libya. They stopped short of Carthage, but the North African towns, both the Romanized ones nearer the coast and the native African ones farther inland, fell under Arab control. The conquered towns paid tribute to the conquerors in slaves; the Arabs called all the natives of northern Africa west of Egypt "Berbers" (a name the Africans did not use for themselves), and the Berber slaves became involuntary recruits to the army—which grew and grew.[5]

By 649, Muawiyah's navy was ready to sail. He launched a fleet of seventeen hundred ships and landed on the island of Cyprus, a short trip to the west. Cyprus, which was still in Byzantine hands, fell almost at once.[6]

The new sea force began to launch raids on Byzantine cities along the coast of Asia Minor. At the same time, a powerful ground force marched through Armenia into the Caucasus Mountains, in a bid to move around the Black

Sea and take Constantinople from the north. Constantinople remained the jewel at the end of the quest. Even the North African conquests were ultimately intended to bring the Arab armies to the walls of New Rome: "Only through Spain can Constantinople be conquered," Uthman had told his commanders.[7]

But the attempt to circle the Black Sea failed; the Khazars fought back and prevented the Arab armies from passing through.

During all this time, the Persian king Yazdegerd III had been on the run, moving farther east with Arab soldiers behind him and still claiming to rule what remained of Persia. Throughout the 640s he seems to have been in Fars, leading a tiny persistent resistance movement. Towards the end of the decade, Uthman spared a detachment to go in and put the resistance movement down. The soldiers chased Yazdegerd north into the province of Kirman, but the Arab army was caught in a blizzard and froze. "The snow reached the height of a lance," al-Tabari says. Only the commander, one soldier, and a slave girl survived, the latter because her owner slit open the stomach of a camel and packed her inside it to keep her warm.[8]

Yazdegerd apparently intended to keep up his resistance, but he hadn't reckoned with the changed economics of his country. Putting a little more distance between himself and the Arab border, he went down into Sistan, where he ordered the governor to pay the taxes that had not been collected over the past year. The governor indignantly refused, so Yazdegerd travelled north into Khorasan, the last place where he might be able to mount that defense, and demanded shelter for the winter.

But he was still hauling along with him the remnants of his royal court—four thousand or so secretaries, displaced officials, palace staff, and their women and children. There was no way to support that many idle people during winter, in the mountains, in a province cut off from its former trade partners. Instead of turning the king away, the Khorasan governor hired a couple of assassins to solve the problem. The hired killers arrived in the middle of the night and did away with Yazdegerd's bodyguard. The king himself fled eastward and took shelter with a stonecutter on the banks of the Murghab river. As he slept, exhausted, the stonecutter murdered him and threw his body into the water.[9]

He had outlived his state and died trying to assert his authority over the corpse. With him, the entire medieval Persian state perished. The Persian empire was no more.

UTHMAN'S ATTEMPTS to turn his own conquered realm into a state now took a downturn.

The first six years of his tenure as caliph—the years from 644 to 650, which were spent in conquest—had gone well, but the last six years were increas-

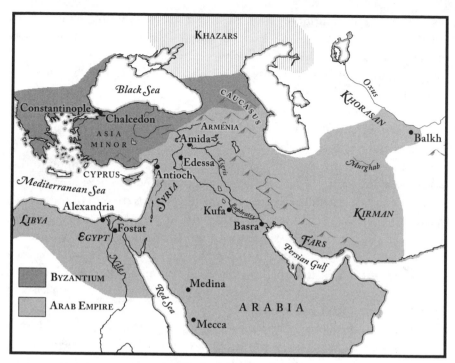

41.1: The Arab Empire Expands

ingly difficult. The Arab historians who chronicle his rule say that the turn in his fortunes came when he lost the signet ring of the Prophet. It was made of silver, with "Muhammad, the Messenger of God" engraved on it; Muhammad had used it to seal his correspondence with non-Arabs. It was passed, according to al-Tabari, from Muhammad to Abu Bakr to Umar to Uthman. Uthman was sitting on the edge of a well in Medina when he

> began fiddling with the ring and twisting it around his finger. The ring slipped off and fell into the well. They searched for it and even drained the well of its water, but without success. . . . When he despaired of finding the signet ring, he ordered another one like it in form and appearance and made of silver to be fashioned for him. On it was engraved "Muhammad, the Messenger of God." Then Uthman placed it on his finger until he perished.[10]

The story suggests not only that Uthman's legitimacy as the proper successor of the Prophet was called into question, but also that it was ultimately shown to be an illusion.

The difficulties were multiple. He had been unable to halt the continual rebellions of the conquered cities in Persia, and the desert-trained Arab armies did not fight well in the mountains of the provinces. There, the Persian aristocracy continued to survive, and Persian religion, language, and practice were carried out almost without interference. To the west, the conquests had not formed any sort of coherent empire: rather, Arab power existed in separated, highly reinforced areas along the North African coast, and communication between those enclaves required that Arab troops keep on conquering and reconquering the connecting areas.[11]

Uthman *had* made some steps towards developing an identity for his empire not based solely on swords. He had begun the project of assembling a definitive version of all Muhammad's teachings. The Prophet did not write; his revelations, or *surahs*, were conveyed orally and recorded by his followers, sometimes in several different forms. With the expansion of the empire, Muslims widely separated in geography were beginning to compile their own collections. There were differences among these local anthologies, and Uthman knew that without a unified sacred book, the extension of the empire had the potential to destroy the Islamic identity of those within it.

But this was a strategy that took time and a certain amount of peace to accomplish. Even once a definitive Qur'an was assembled, it had to be copied and then taken to the outskirts of the empire—and half of the time, those were inaccessible because of war.

Discontent with Uthman's rule grew. Revolt in the outlying conquered areas broke out on a regular basis. Uthman sent his governors the message that they should "maintain stringent control of those under their authority" and "keep the people tied up on campaigns" in order to keep them out of trouble. This made things even worse. Strong authority would not have been resented in Byzantium, or Persia, or even the kingdoms of the Franks. But Uthman was supposed to be one Muslim among brothers; he was not supposed to be a king. By 654, al-Tabari says, Uthman's enemies were writing to each other, planning to meet together and confront him with his inadequacies.[12]

Actual revolt began in the city of Kufa, on the western bank of the Euphrates. It had been founded by Arabs as military headquarters for the conquest of Persia and had since grown into a large and bustling Muslim city. Its Arab population had emigrated to the city from all over Arabia. But under Uthman's policies, only Quraysh were promoted into positions of power (and Uthman showed a particular preference for members of his own clan, the Banu Umayya). Resentment deepened when Uthman ordered the city to send all of its surplus revenue to Medina, for use by the Arabs there.

At this point, Ali ibn Abu Talib, son-in-law of Muhammad, reappeared on the scene, commissioned by a group of discontent Muslims to speak to Uthman on their behalf. He, like Uthman, was in Medina, the seat of the highly centralized government that Uthman relied on; the point of conflict was the appointment of one Abn 'Amir, a relative of Uthman but a man unpopular with many, to a high position in city government in Kufa. "If I have favored kinsmen," snapped Uthman, "what have I done wrong?" Ali answered, "You have been weak and easygoing with your relatives." "They are your relatives as well," Uthman said, and Ali retorted, "They are closely related to me, but merit is found in others."[13]

Ali remained the spokesman for the disenfranchised. The year after, in 655, the people of Kufa deposed the unpopular governor. Arab rebels from Kufa marched on Medina and besieged Uthman in his house. They were joined by men from Medina who were bitter over Uthman's partiality to his own Banu Umayya clan.

Uthman appealed to Ali ibn Abu Talib to intercede with the people on his behalf. Ali, after talking with Uthman, agreed to tell the people that in three days, Uthman would meet all of their complaints by doing "justice, whether it be against himself or anyone else, and that he will abandon everything that you detest":

> He wrote out a document . . . that gave Uthman a three-day grace period to do away with every injustice and remove every governor whom they disliked. . . . Ali had the document witnessed by a body of the leading Emigrants and Helpers. Thus, the people turned back . . . and withdrew until he should fulfill the promises that he had freely given them. But Uthman began preparing for war and gathering arms. . . . When the three days had passed and he had done nothing to alter anything which was hateful to the people or to remove any governor, they revolted against him.[14]

Uthman's enemies surrounded his house, intending to kill him. He had ruled not as a prophet of God, but as Commander of the Faithful, and although he claimed divine sanction for his authority, the support of the faithful was his ultimate legitimization. He had lost it.

Standing on the walls of his house, he warned his assassins, "If you kill me, you will never pray together again, nor will God ever remove dissension from among you." They answered, "You *were* worthy of authority, but since then you have changed."[15] Then they broke into his house and stabbed him to death with iron-headed arrows, grasped like spears in their hands.

Rather than being buried at once, as Muslim custom dictated, Uthman's body was thrown into a courtyard and left for three days. His family had to appeal to Ali (who had become the de facto leader of the city) to get permission to take the body. He was buried in a Jewish cemetery; no Muslim cemetery would allow him to be interred.

NOT LONG AFTER, a gathering of Ali's supporters—rebels and many of the Quraysh who were not from the Banu Umayya clan—declared him to be the next caliph. He must have seen this coming. Nevertheless, he hesitated. Another voice was protesting, and it was a strong one: the voice of Aishah, widow of the Prophet and daughter of the first caliph Abu Bakr. She insisted that Ali had no right to rule, that the leadership of the Muslim community (widely dispersed as it was) should stay within the clan of the Umayyad, with its blood tie to Muhammad himself.

Ali found himself in an odd position. He did not particularly want to come up against the wife of the Prophet in conflict. On the other hand, her argument was a difficult one. The Banu Umayya clan was related to Muhammad, but distantly: the Banu Umayya and the Banu Hashim, Muhammad's actual clan, had a common ancestor. Ali, by contrast, *was* Banu Hashim. He was not only Muhammad's son-in-law but also his cousin; and his son Hasan was the grandson of the Prophet, child of Muhammad's daughter Fatima.

Yet it was already known that Ali did not intend for the Quraysh tribe, to which both clans belonged, to continue to hold all the power for itself. In arguing that *Uthman's* clan, rather than Muhammad's own, become the "royal family" of the Islamic empire, Aishah was working to keep the tribe in power.

Ultimately Ali decided to accept the title of caliph. Later, he wrote to the Muslim governor of Egypt about his decision: "It could not even be imagined that the Arabs would snatch the seat of the caliphate from the family and descendents of the Holy Prophet, and that they would be swearing the oath of allegiance for the caliphate to a different person. At every stage I kept myself aloof from that struggle of supremacy and power-politics till I found the heretics had openly taken to heresy and schism and were trying to undermine and ruin the religion preached by our Holy Prophet." He believed that establishing the caliphate in the Banu Umayya clan would make it unambiguously into a political position, destroying its close connection to Muhammad and his mission.[16]

Yet to prevent this from happening, he would be forced to fight. Aishah and her supporters had already left Medina, heading for the city of Basra at the head of the Persian Gulf, where they hoped to gather more supporters for their cause. Ali gathered soldiers and followed them. In December of 656, six months after he had accepted the title, he met his enemies outside Basra's walls in the Battle of the Camel. More Arabs had come down from Kufa to support him, and he won a quick victory. Aishah's supporters were killed, and she was forced to return to private life.[17]

But this first fight over the caliphate began a civil war: the *Fitna*, the "Trials." Ali moved the seat of his caliphate from Medina to Kufa; Kufa was much more central to the newly conquered empire and was solidly behind him. He sent new governors, friendly to his cause, to take over the administration of the rebellious provinces. But one of the old governors refused. Muawiyah, founder of the navy, was still serving as governor of Syria, and Uthman had been his cousin. Instead of relinquishing his post, he threatened to fight back unless Uthman's murderers were put to death.[18]

Although Ali had not been directly involved in the bloodshed, the culprits were some of his strongest supporters; executing them was not an option. He wrote back to Muawiyah in defiance, accusing him of seeking justice (and even adopting Islam) for personal gain:

> When you saw that all the big people of Arabia had embraced Islam and had gathered under the banner of the Holy Prophet, you also walked in. . . . By Allah, I know you too well to argue with you or to advise you. Apostasy and avariciousness have taken a firm hold of your mind, your intelligence is of an inferior order and you cannot differentiate what in the end is good for you and what is not. . . . You have also written so much about the murderers of Caliph Uthman. The correct thing for you to do is to take the oath of allegiance to me as others have done and present the case in my court of justice and then I shall pass my judgment according to the tenets of the Holy Qur'an.[19]

Muawiyah had no intention of taking any oath. The two men traded increasingly testy messages ("I received your letter," Ali wrote, "and to me it appears to be an idiotic confusion of irrelevant ideas") until it became clear that only armed confrontation would sort out their difficulties.[20]

They met in July of 657 on the upper Euphrates, each at the head of an army. Neither commander seems to have been comfortable with the idea of battle between two groups of Muslims: "Do not take the initiative in fighting," Ali told his men, "let them begin it, and do not attack those who have surrendered." When the battle did begin, the fighting dragged on inconclusively for three days. Finally Muawiyah's men pulled back, impaled leaves of the Qur'an on the tips of their spears, and insisted that the two leaders work out their differences according to the laws of Islam. Ali's soldiers joined in the demand, and the rivals gave in to the inevitable.[21]

Negotiations, carried on through various intermediaries, were long-drawn-out and unsatisfactory for both sides. Eventually, Ali ended up with the title of caliph, ruling from Kufa; Muawiyah remained in Syria, without a title but ruling independently. Practically, the empire had been divided; its existence under one caliphate was a convenient myth.

Ali's tenure as caliph remained troubled. The undercurrent of guilt over

Uthman's murder continued to run through his camp. In 658, a segment of his army broke away, accusing Ali of injustice because he had not avenged Uthman's death. Injustice invalidated his charter; the unrighted wrong meant that he could not rule as true caliph.

Ali first tried to arbitrate with these rebels, whom his other troops called *Kharijis*, "Seceders." Then he attacked them. He was unable to get rid of them, and the soldiers who were still loyal to him had little stomach for continually warring against their own kin. His power was dwindling.[22]

In 661, a Khariji assassin murdered Ali in his camp. His remaining supporters tried to arrange the election of his son Hasan, the Prophet's grandson, as caliph. But far more Arabs were arrayed behind Muawiyah. Hasan, a mature man in his forties who was not suicidal, agreed to come to a settlement with Muawiyah (and his sixty thousand soldiers). He would retire peacefully to Medina as a private person; in return Muawiyah promised that the caliphate would pass back to Hasan should Muawiyah die before him.

The Fitna had ended, and the Banu Umayya had risen to power: Muawiyah, the fifth caliph after the Prophet, was Umayyad. But like his predecessor, he was forced to fight constantly against rebels who resented his power.

The Islamic empire, which had once been centered around the community of the faithful, was beginning to look more and more like any other medieval empire: a conquered mass of peoples, some in constant rebellion, with ongoing struggles for power at the top and an ever-present tendency for the whole thing to fly apart. In turning those first Arab warriors outward, Abu Bakr had preserved the unity of the *umma*. But victory and conquest were already tearing at it from the inside.

INDIA	ARABIA	PERSIAN EMPIRE	BYZANTIUM
Pulakesi II of the Chalukya (597/610–642)			
Mahendravarman of the Pallava (600–630)	Annexation of Lakhmids		**Phocas** (602–610)
Meetings of the academy at Madurai (c. 600–750)			
Harsha (606–647)			
	Destruction of Ghassanids		
	Vision of Muhammad (610)		**Heraclius** (610–641)
			Patriarch Sergius (610–638)
	The Hijra (AD 622/1 AH)		
	Battle at the Wells of Badr (624)		
			Siege of Constantinople (626)
	Battle of the Trench (627)		
		Kavadh II (628)	
	Death of Muhammad/	**Yazdegerd III** (632–636/651)	
	Election of Abu Bakr (632–634)		
	Umar (634–644)		
	Capture of Jerusalem (637)		
			Constantine III (641)
			Constans II (641–668)
Arab invasion driven back	**Uthman** (644–656)		
Emancipation of the Eastern Chalukya			
Vikramaditya of the Western Chalukya (655–680)			
	Ali (656–661)		
	The First Fitna (656–661)		
	Muawiyah (661–680)		
Paramesvaravarman of the Pallava (672–700)			
Vinayaditya of the Western Chalukya (680–696)			
Manavamma of Sri Lanka (c. 684)			

Part Four

STATES
AND
KINGDOMS

Chapter Forty-Two

Law and Language

*Between 643 and 702,
the emperor tries to leave Constantinople,
the Lombards and the Bulgarians move towards nationhood,
and North Africa falls to the armies of Islam*

THE LOMBARDS OF ITALY suffered no inconveniences from the Arab invasions to the east. In fact, the eastern wars made it possible for the Lombard king Rothari, elected in 636, to throw off almost all remaining tendrils of Byzantine control. While the emperor was occupied fighting with the armies of Islam, Rothari busied himself with systematically wiping out the emperor's claim on all Italian lands—except for the enclave at Ravenna and the walled city of Rome itself.

These gains meant that it was time for the Lombards to mature away from their beginnings as conquering invaders, toward existence as a nation.

The Lombards were partly worshippers of the old Germanic gods, partly Arian Christians, partly Catholic Christians. A shared religion could have provided them with cohesion, but Rothari, a man of vision, wanted to give them more than cohesion. He wanted to give them statehood; so in 643 he created a written law, something they had never had. "This king Rothari," writes Paul the Deacon, "collected, in a series of writings, the laws of the Langobards [Lombards] which they were keeping in memory only and custom, and he directed this code to be called the Edict."

The Edict of Rothari, all 388 chapters of it, was written in Latin, but the laws were Lombard: Germanic spirit inhabiting Roman flesh. Pulling a man's beard, an insult among Germanic warriors, drew a steep fine; those who deserted a comrade in battle were sentenced to death; a man who wished to transfer property to another had to do so in the presence of the *thing*, the assembly of freemen.[1]

The laws helped to establish the borders of the Lombard kingdom, which to this point had been rather amorphous. "All *waregang* who come from outside our frontiers into the boundaries of our kingdom," Rothari decreed,

referring to foreign warriors settling in Lombard land, "ought to live according to the Lombard laws." The Lombard lands in Italy were becoming Lombardy, a country for the wandering Lombards to call home.[2]

As part of its transition into statehood, Lombardy was leaning towards
orthodox Catholicism. The Arian Christianity of its leaders had been a marker
of their Germanic blood, a leftover of the days when they were outsiders both
to orthodoxy and to political power. Rothari's successor, Aripert, became the
first Catholic king of Lombardy, moving the Italian kingdom closer to the
political mainstream.

In 661, when Aripert died, a brief war erupted between his sons. It ended
with one son dead, the other in flight, and the crown in the hands of Duke
Grimoald of Benevento, one of the semi-independent Lombard chiefs who
was supposed to be loyal to the Lombard king.

All the way over in Constantinople, Constans II decided to intervene. Constans, fourteen when he came to the throne, had watched Egypt and North
Africa fall to the Arabs at the same time that Italy was breaking away. Now,
in 661, he was thirty years old, father of three sons, and nicknamed "Constans
the Bearded" because of his remarkably heavy beard. He had assumed control
of the empire, and the civil war in Lombardy gave him a plan. The Arab
assault may have seemed unstoppable, but Italy was vulnerable; Constans II
decided to leave Constantinople, set up his campaign headquarters in Tarentum, on the instep of the Italian boot, and reconquer the peninsula.[3]

Constans II was not popular in Constantinople, which no doubt made
the idea of re-establishing the throne in Rome even more attractive. But the
plan reveals the extent to which the Byzantines still thought of themselves
as Roman. Few of them had ever been to the Eternal City; no emperor had
visited Rome in generations; Italy itself had long been out of Byzantine hands.
Yet somehow Rome still occupied a place in the imagination. Constans II,
heading for Rome, was out to recapture the glorious past.

By 663, Constans II was established in Tarentum and carrying on a reasonably successful war against the Lombard holdings in the south. A number of
southern cities surrendered to him, and soon he was approaching the walls
of Benevento, Grimoald's hometown. King Grimoald, now at the Lombard
capital Pavia, far to the north, had left one of his sons in charge of the city.
The son sent to him for help, and Grimoald began the journey south with his
royal army.

It must have been a large army, because Constans II was "greatly alarmed"
at the news of Grimoald's approach. He retreated, first to the coastal city of
Naples (which had agreed to receive him; it had been loyal to Constantinople
since Belisarius had taken it away from the Ostrogoths in 536) and then to
Rome (the first visit of an emperor to the old city since Romulus Augustus

had been dethroned). He stayed in Rome only twelve days, attended divine services conducted by the pope, raided the city for any remaining gold or copper ornaments he could melt down and use to fund his war, and then departed for Sicily. He landed on the island, went to Syracuse, and declared it to be his new capital. His intention to reclaim Rome hadn't survived his first sight of the city. He had been imagining glories, but the real city—shabby, depopulated, demoralized—seemed beyond repair.[4]

From Syracuse, he again began to launch attacks on the south of Italy. He ruled the island like an emperor of old: despotic, demanding, and imperious. He also sent for his wife and sons, a clear indication that he intended to stay in the west, away from Constantinople.[5]

Thanks to his efforts, Byzantium kept control of the southern Italian coast. But his tyrannical behavior made him unpopular; his apparent desertion of New Rome, even more so. In 668, one of his house servants (undoubtedly part of a larger conspiracy) battered him on the head with a soap box until he died. His son Constantine IV was acclaimed in Constantinople and, profiting from his father's poor example, remained there.[6]

IN 670, TWO YEARS AFTER Constantine IV's accession, the Arab advance along the North African coast began again. At the same time, the Arab spread continued to the east. In the mountains north of India, Arab armies drove the king of the Shahi out of Kabul, his capital;* the Shahi kingdom kept control of the Khyber Pass but was forced to move its capital city east to Udabhandapura.[7]

The multipronged expansion reached Constantinople in 674, when Arab armies laid siege to the city itself. The siege lasted four years, but Constantinople was able to continually refresh its supplies by sea, and conditions never became desperate. The Arab navy launched a final sea attack in 678, but the Byzantine ships made use of their famous "Greek fire," a chemical concoction launched through tubes that kept burning even when it met the water, and finally the Arab ships withdrew—followed shortly after by the land forces.[8]

While the emperor and his men were occupied with the defense of Constantinople, the Bulgarian tribes were given the space and time to expand.

Thirty years earlier, the emperor Heraclius had recognized the kingship of the Bulgarian chief Kubrat, north of the Azov Sea. Kubrat had died in 669, after a long reign during which he pushed the boundaries of Old Great Bulgaria up to the Donets and down to the Danube. Like a Frankish chief, he left the kingdom to his five sons jointly.

In his history, the *Chronographikon syntomon*, the ninth-century patriarch

*See map 40.1.

Nicephorus says that while on his deathbed Kubrat brought his sons around him and challenged each to break a bundle of sticks with his bare hands. When they all failed, he undid the bundle and broke the sticks easily, one by one. "Stay united," he told them, "for a bundle is not easily broken."⁹

Instead, the five sons split apart almost at once. The second son, Kotrag, went north to the Volga and settled with his followers, where they became known as the Silver Bulgars. The third son, Asparukh, settled between the Dniester and the Prut river with over thirty thousand followers of his own. The fourth, Kouber, led a little band of Bulgarians first into Pannonia and then back toward Macedonia; the fifth son, Alcek, took his crowd all the way to Italy and formed a little Bulgarian enclave there. The oldest son, Bayan, remained in his homeland, ruling over the diminished population that remained once his brothers had left. The wisdom of Kubrat's warning became clear: almost at once, the Khazars attacked Bayan, reduced his kingdom to rubble, and swallowed his territory, bringing an end to the original Old Great Bulgarian kingdom.

Constantine IV tried to emulate the Khazar khan; in 679, once he had recovered somewhat from the siege of Constantinople, he marched against Asparukh's thirty thousand Bulgarians, who lay just on Byzantium's western border. He was at first successful. But Theophanes says that he was forced to withdraw from the lines because he was suffering from gout, and that his troops became disheartened and fled.¹⁰

The Bulgarian warleader Asparukh then made an alliance with the Slavic tribes nearby, fought his way down into Thracia, and generally caused a headache for the Byzantine armies on the northwestern border. By 681, Constantine IV had decided that he'd better make peace. He swore out a treaty with Asparukh, even agreeing to pay the Bulgars yearly tribute.

The Byzantine tribute payments and the conquests gave Asparukh more than a temporary settlement: his group of refugees, funded by Constantinople's tribute payments, became the First Bulgarian Empire.

THE PEACE WITH THE First Bulgarian Empire was followed, somewhat unexpectedly, by peace with the Arabs.

Muawiyah, the fifth caliph after the Prophet, died late in 680. He was followed by a string of short-lived caliphs: four within five years. Finally in 685, a caliph with the ability to both direct campaigns and administer the increasingly chaotic empire came to the throne: Abd al-Malik ibn Marwan, who began his rule by ruthlessly squelching the Arabs who supported other candidates to the caliphate. It would take him six years to wipe out the opposition—six years of spending more energy fighting other Arabs, rather than the rest of the world—at a time when he was also dealing with famine

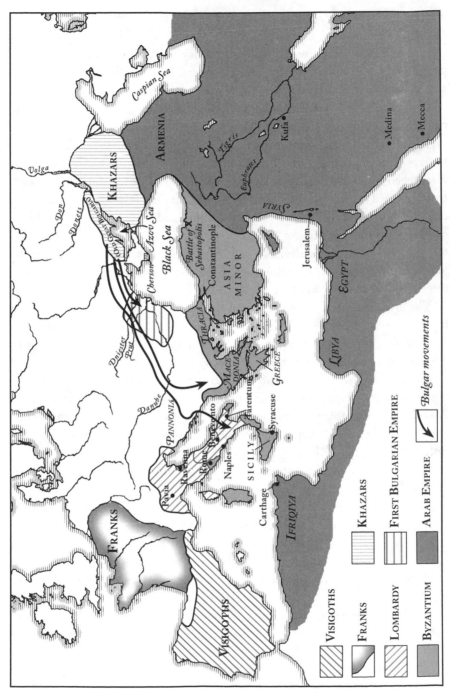

42.1: *Byzantium, the Arabs, and the Bulgars*

and an outbreak of sickness, possibly a minor visitation of the plague, in Syria.[11]

He sent to Constantine IV, offering to pay tribute in order to confirm a peace, and Constantine IV agreed to the terms. Shortly afterwards, Constantine IV died and left the throne of Constantinople to his son Justinian II.[12]

Justinian II, only sixteen, inherited an empire that had slowly been reorganized over the previous decades into more efficient, more easily defensible divisions. Rather than the unwieldy provinces of the earlier empire, Byzantium was now divided into "themes." Instead of being defended by troops dispatched from the capital, under the command of officers unfamiliar with their assigned territories, themes were defended by native soldiers: since Heraclius, the emperors had slowly been awarding land in the themes to soldiers in return for lifelong military service, and the tax system had been gradually reorganized so that the citizens in each theme paid their taxes directly to the local troops, rather than sending the money to the capital, where it might or might not get back to where it was meant to be.

The armies in each theme thus had strong motivation to protect it. Local loyalties, which always had the potential to rip an empire apart, had been directed into defending it. There were four themes in Asia Minor, another in Thracia, and two more in Greece and Sicily.[13]

Justinian II also inherited the peace treaty with Abd al-Malik, which he agreed to renew. This gave Justinian time to get his bearings as emperor, while Abd al-Malik was able to finish putting down the rebellions against his caliphate. By 692, he had mastered his enemies and was, without competition, the only caliph of the Muslims.

Both men now wanted to break the treaty: al-Malik was ready to go back to conquering, and Justinian wanted to prove his worth as emperor. In late 692, al-Malik provided a useful excuse for both of them when he paid his tribute with Arab coins rather than Byzantine currency.

He had been working for some time to stabilize the financial affairs in the Islamic empire by creating a standard Arabic coinage. Justinian II at once announced the coins counterfeit and unacceptable, and declared war. He had hired, to reinforce his own army, thirty thousand or so Bulgarian troops as mercenaries: "He levied 30,000 men, armed them, and named them the 'special army,'" Theophanes writes. He was "confident in them," certain he could meet al-Malik in battle with success.[14]

He was wrong. The Arab forces pushed into Byzantine land; when the armies met in 694 at the Battle of Sebastopolis, on the southern shore of the Black Sea, the Bulgarians cut and ran. Al-Malik had sent them money behind the scenes and promised them more if they would retreat once the battle began. The Byzantine troops were unable to hold the front without their allies and retreated. Al-Malik, flushed with victory, began a series of raids on the Byzantine coast.

Justinian II, still only twenty-four, took vengeance on the traitorous Bulgarians by massacring their wives and children. But his army was inclined to blame him, not the mercenaries. In 695, the officers rebelled against him, took him captive, and mutilated him by cutting off his nose, slitting his tongue, and sending him in chains to Cherson, the fortress where military prisoners languished. They acclaimed one of their own generals, Leontios, as emperor in his place.

With Leontios at the helm the empire suffered the final loss of Carthage, its complete occupation by Arab forces, and the end of eight hundred years of Roman settlement in North Africa. The caliph al-Malik appointed an Arabic governor named Musa bin Nusair to rule the new Muslim province, Ifriqiya. And back in Constantinople, the general Leontios suffered the wages of defeat and was in turn overthrown. In 698, he was taken prisoner, mutilated, and sent to a monastery, and the army chose another soldier as emperor.[15]

By 702, the Islamic conquest of North Africa was nearly complete. The Berbers, the native North Africans, converted in remarkable numbers. Their tribal structure made conversion a mass event rather than an individual decision; when the leaders of a tribe converted, the rest of the tribe followed.

The Arabic realm itself was beginning to cohere a little more tightly under al-Malik's expert administration. He had already introduced standard currency; he put his brothers, whom he trusted, into the most vital governors' offices; and he began to construct a new mosque in Jerusalem that would provide a place of worship and pilgrimage even more central than the Ka'aba in Mecca (although Mecca retained its importance). This mosque, the Dome of the Rock, was built on the site of the destroyed Second Temple of the Jews;* it protected the rock from which Muhammad was said to have ascended into heaven.

Al-Malik also decreed that the Arabic language would be the official language of the empire, something no previous caliph had done. This provided a desperately needed glue for the widely scattered realm. Islam and the Arabic language were the two constants throughout the lands of the Arab conquests; Christianity and Latin had parted ways somewhat, as the Franks and Visigoths and Lombards and Greeks translated the texts of their religion into their own tongue, but Islam and Arabic (and Islam and Arabic culture) would remain tied closely together.

*The "Second Temple" was built in the sixth century BC to replace Solomon's Temple, which had been destroyed by the Babylonians. See Susan Wise Bauer, *The History of the Ancient World* (W. W. Norton, 2007), pp. 453–454, 466–467.

TIMELINE 42

PERSIAN EMPIRE	ARAB EMPIRE	BYZANTIUM	LOMBARDS	BULGARS
		Phocas (602–610)		
	Annexation of Lakhmids	Witteric (603–610)		
	Destruction of Ghassanids			
	Vision of Muhammad (610)	Heraclius (610–641)		
		Patriarch Sergius (610–638)		
	The Hijra (AD 622/1 AH)			
	Battle at the Wells of Badr (624)			
	Battle of the Trench (627)	Siege of Constantinople (626)		
Kavadh II (628)				
Yazdegerd III (632–636/651)	Death of Muhammad/Election of Abu Bakr (632–634)			Kubrat of Old Great Bulgaria (632–669)
	Umar (634–644)		Rothari (636–652)	
	Capture of Jerusalem (637)	Constantine III (641)		
		Constans II (641–668)		
			Edict of Rothari (643)	
	Uthman (644–656)			
			Aripert (653–661)	
	Ali (656–661)			
	The First Fitna (656–661)			
	Muawiyah (661–680)		Grimoald (662–671)	
		Constantine IV (668–685)		
				Division of Bulgarian rule/Destruction of Old Great Bulgaria (669)
	Siege of Constantinople (674–678)			Rise of First Bulgarian Empire
		Justinian II (685–695/705–711)		
	Abd al-Malik (685–705)			
		Leontios (695–698)		

Chapter Forty-Three

Creating the Past

*Between 661 and 714,
the heavenly sovereigns of Japan decree a Great Reform,
issue a code of law, and write a legendary history*

THE TIDAL WASH and ebb of attacking and retreating armies had shaped the internal politics of almost every medieval nation but Japan. On their jagged islands, protected on the west by sea and on the east by a vast expanse of ocean, the heavenly sovereigns ruled: the borders of their power nebulous, making little attempt to conquer themselves an empire by force, their attention fixed firmly on home ground.

But although Tang warships did not dock at the harbors of the Yamato rulers, the Tang were nevertheless invading, by a slow and insidious infiltration of ideas.

After her second spell on the throne, Heavenly Sovereign Saimei died in 661, leaving the Yamato crown to her son. Naka no Oe finally stood at the top of the pyramid of power, with his long-time ally Nakatomi no Kamatari as his right-hand man. But for nearly seven years after his mother's death, Naka no Oe continued to govern as crown prince and regent. Not until 668 did he finally claim the rightful title of heavenly sovereign and the imperial name Tenji. He was forty-two years old; he had spent twenty-three years waiting for the stain of Soga blood to fade from his hands before reaching for the sceptre.

Not long after his formal accession, he rewarded Nakatomi no Kamatari's lifelong loyalty by giving him a new name: Fujiwara. By this act, he made his friend the patriarch of a new clan, founder of a new family. The Fujiwara clan would rise steadily in power, eventually reaching a height of influence greater than that of the broken-backed Soga.

Tenji's disastrous plunge into foreign politics—his attempt to help Baekje's king regain the throne had ended with a shattering defeat of the Japanese army by the Tang-Silla alliance—had merely reinforced the natural Yamato tendency to focus on the home front. As crown prince, and with the help of

Nakatomi no Kamatari, he had already written and tried to put into place a whole series of reforms intended to transform the Yamato domain—still a linked series of clans, dominated by clan leaders who jealously guarded their own authority—into a single royal realm, governed without dispute by a single monarch. The new sweeping decrees were called the Great Reform, or the "Taika reforms." By legal fiat, all of the Yamato domain was declared to be a single public realm, held by the crown on behalf of the people. Private estates and hereditary clan rights over them were abolished. So was the old system of titles. "Let the following be abolished," the first Reform Edict declared: "private titles to lands and workers held by ministers and functionaries of the court, by local nobles, and by village chiefs."[1] Instead of owning their land and claiming the titles of nobility, the former clan leaders and village chiefs would be *granted* the right to govern the land, which now essentially belonged to the Yamato ruler. And instead of claiming their noble titles, they would be awarded ranks that positioned them in a newly formed bureaucracy.

The Great Reform was not invented by the Yamato; it came over the water from China. Naka no Oe had sent scores of scholars and priests over to the Tang, to learn the long history of the Chinese emperorship, to study the structures of Tang government, and to bring back what they learned. The world that the Great Reform attempted to create is modelled after the ancient Chinese map of the world, a set of concentric rings with the emperor's power all-encompassing at the center and executed by proxy at the distant edges; in places, the edicts of the Great Reform quote, word for word, from the Chinese histories that Naka no Oe's emissaries brought back from their travels. The centuries of disorder in Luoyang and Nanjing made little difference. The Chinese emperors could claim—fairly or not—to belong to a tradition of royal authority that flowed down from the beginnings of time, and the Yamato aspired to join the ancient stream.[2]

As Heavenly Sovereign Tenji, the former Naka no Oe now set himself to create a court in which he would stand—like the emperors of China—not merely as warleader and chief general (a position vulnerable to the fortunes of war), but as representative of an entire culture, leader of civilization, guarantor of cosmic order. Historian Joan Piggott, borrowing the term from Confucius, calls this "polestar monarchy"; the sovereign, says the *Analects*, "exercises government by means of his virtue and thus may be compared to the north polar star, which keeps its place and all the stars turn towards it." In his effort to become the orienting point of Japanese culture, Heavenly Sovereign Tenji brought historians and poets to his court and founded a university. He and his court read the Chinese classics, which had arrived in the hands of a travelling Buddhist monk in 660. He led his court in celebrating Chinese rites that linked heavenly order to earthly tranquillity.[3]

According to his biographers, Heavenly Sovereign Tenji also ordered his ministers to collect the laws of Japan into a written legal code, distinct from the Great Reforms. Japan, filled with discrete communities, with a heavenly sovereign whose rule was largely theoretical rather than hands-on in many of its parts, had existed without a legal code for a long time. But partly due to the contact with Tang China and United Silla, partly due to Tenji's sense that a heavenly sovereign should have a little more power on earth, it was time for written laws.

This code does not seem to have ever been completed. Whatever work was done on it stalled when Heavenly Sovereign Tenji became ill after a mere four years of official rule. The illness caused him severe unrelieved pain in his last days and hours. Finally, the atonement for Soga no Iruka's death was complete.[4]

Tenji's grandson Mommu became heavenly sovereign in 697; the fourteen-year-old boy continued the task that Tenji had begun, and in 701 issued the first surviving set of laws from Japan. The *Taiho ritsu-ryo*, or Great Treasure, enfolded the legal work Tenji had begun within it. It outlined a thoroughly well-controlled country, one where authority was laid out in an elaborate series of branching bureaucracies, each with its own set of ranks and offices.[5]

It was a beautifully structured set of laws, and the world it envisioned was just as orderly as the concentric rings of authority laid out in the edicts of the Great Reform. But despite several royal generations of intense borrowing, the Tang-inspired decrees had a stronger existence on paper than in reality. The Tang template had been laid over the Japanese islands, but beneath the template vast swathes of the country ran along just as they had before. The clan leaders might hold bureaucratic ranks instead of noble titles, but they exercised the same authority; the land might belong to the crown in name, but it was still farmed and divided, plowed and shaped, by the same men who had owned it before the reforms.

Not long after issuing his legal code, Mommu died at the age of twenty-five and was succeeded on the throne by his mother. Gemmei, daughter of the heavenly sovereign Tenji, was the fifth woman to sit on the throne within a matter of decades—a preponderance of female rulers almost unknown elsewhere in the medieval world. Like the tip of an ancient pyramid, the heavenly sovereign touched the divine and connected it to the people at the base. Whether a man or woman occupied that position at the pyramid's tip was relatively unimportant. In the culture of the Tang Chinese, where trade routes and food supplies lay under the emperor's purview, only a woman unusually talented at administration and people management could convince her court that she was worthy of their loyalty. But Gemmei was not a Tang monarch, despite her court's adoption of all those Tang customs; and she could act as the polestar of her people, regardless of her gender.

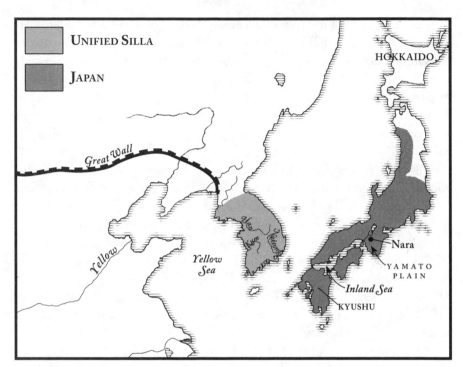

43.1: The Nara Period

In the third month of her reign, Gemmei announced that her capital would be at Nara, a city to which Heavenly Sovereign Mommu had intended to move, before his plans were cut short by death. Until this point, the capital city of the Yamato rulers had been moveable; each ruler declared his or her residence to be the new center of government. But Gemmei's new capital was an innovation. The city, which was known to her as Heijo, the City of Peace, would remain the capital for the next eighty years (the "Nara period" of Japan). She also had new plans drawn up for its enlargement and glorification, plans modelled (naturally) on the layout of the Tang capital of Chang'an. The glories of Chang'an had deeply impressed the Japanese visitors to the capital city.[6]

In the past, the dwelling place of the heavenly sovereign had been a minor matter because the sovereign was a locus of heavenly power, not earthly power. There was no need for earthly power to accrue in a physical place, no sense that a stone Senate building, a royal court, or even a throne was necessary to connect the heavenly sovereign's rule to the earth. But over the next decades, as the ruler remained at Nara, she would gain a slightly less tenuous connection with the political establishment. The polestar would not merely shine; it would reach meddlesome hands into earthly matters.

At the same time, the polestar would claim greater and greater divinity.

Gemmei abdicated in 714 in favor of her daughter, Heavenly Sovereign Gensho, and in the middle of her nine-year reign, Gensho presided over the publication of the Yoro Code. The Code put into words an idea that had been growing in popularity: that the heavenly sovereign not only touched the divine but was herself godlike. The polestar did not relay heavenly illumination. It was the source.[7]

During the rule of the next heavenly sovereign, Gensho's younger brother Shomu, a new foundation was carefully built underneath the shaky, already erected structure of Japanese royal privilege. For a Yamato king, Shomu ruled in "unprecedented grandeur," with an elaborate court, a rabbit-warren of bureaucrats, and all the trappings of full kingship. And he commissioned something that was, so far, missing: an ancient past for the Yamato kings. During his reign, the first mythical histories of Japanese kingship, the *Kojiki* and the *Nihon shoki*, were written.[8]

According to these accounts, the first Yamato king had been the grandson of the sea god and the great-great-grandson of the sun goddess. With the blood of both sea and sky running in his veins, the boy Jimmu rose to rule his people. As a grown man, he gathered his sons together and gave them a charter. Long ago, he told them, the world had been "given over to widespread desolation," to darkness, disorder, and gloom. But then the gods had given man a gift—the leadership of the imperial house. Under the heavenly sovereign, darkness and chaos had given way to beauty and order, and the land had become a place of fertility and light, good crops and peaceful days and nights. "But the remote regions do not yet enjoy the blessings of Imperial rule," he told them. "Every town has always been allowed to have its lord, and every village its chief, who, each one for himself, makes division of territory and practices mutual aggression and conflict. . . . [Those lands] will undoubtedly be suitable for the extension of the heavenly task, so that its glory should fill the universe. Why should we not proceed there?" And so they did, marching behind the god-king on their way to drive out chaos and darkness.[9]

It had become vital to lay a myth-foundation for Japanese kingship, even if that myth-foundation had to be partially constructed out of nothing. The histories of Japanese kingship created a past full of righteous warfare and divine approval, and that past was carefully thrust underneath the present. It re-created Yamato Japan as a country founded on heroism, legendary feats of strength, and the favor of the gods.

TIMELINE 43

BYZANTIUM LOMBARDS BULGARS	JAPAN	CHINA	TIBET
Phocas (602–610)	Seventeen-Article Constitution (602)		
Witteric (603–610)			
		Sui Yangdi (605–618)	
Heraclius (610–641)			
Patriarch Sergius (610–638)		Fall of Sui/Rise of Tang (618)	
		Tang Gaozu (618–626)	
			Songtsen Gampo
Siege of Constantinople (626)		**Tang Taizong** (620–650)	
		(626–649)	
		Kubrat of Old	
	Great Bulgaria (632–669)		
	Rothari (636–652)		
Constantine III (641)			
Constans II (641–668)	**Uija** (641–660)		
	Saimei (642–645)		
Edict of Rothari (643)	**Kotoku** (645–654)		
	Start of Taika reforms		
		Tang Gaozong	**Mangson**
		(650–683)	**Mangtsen**
			(650–676)
Aripert (653–661)	**Saimei** (655–661)		
	Naka no Oe (661/668–672)		
Grimoald (662–671)			
Constantine IV (668–685)	Foundation of Fujiwara clan		
Division of Bulgarian rule/Destruction of Old Great Bulgaria (669)			
Rise of First Bulgarian Empire			
Justinian II (685–695/705–711)			
Leontios (695–698)	**Mommu** (697–707)		
	Gemmei (707–714)/ Start of Nara period (710–794)		
	Gensho (715–724) Yoro Code		
	Shomu (724–749)		

Chapter Forty-Four

The Days of the Empress

Between 683 and 712,
the Empress Wu Zetian becomes the Son of Heaven

IN 683, THE CRIPPLED EMPEROR Tang Gaozong hovered at the edge of death, with his devoted empress Wu Zetian at his side. Despite a series of strokes, his mind was still clear. He called his chief minister to the Hall of Audience in the royal palace so that he could make his final choice of an heir known, and give his last instructions for the transfer of power. Later that same night, he died in the Hall, too weak to move to his bedchamber.[1]

He had chosen his twenty-seven-year-old son Zhongzong to be the next emperor, and had designated Zhongzong's two-year-old son Li Chongzhao as "Heir Apparent Grandson"—a highly unusual move, reflecting his own fears that the relatively young Tang dynasty had not yet established itself firmly on the throne. He had also issued a last order: that the new emperor consult Empress Wu whenever "important matters of defense and administration cannot be decided."[2]

He had intended this triple pronouncement to protect Tang power, and it did, although not quite in the way he had intended. With the power to make final decisions enshrined in her husband's last words, the empress removed her son after barely two months of rule. His offense was simple: he had made his wife's father his chief minister, which was a clear hint to his mother that it was time for her to retire to decent seclusion and give over the empress's throne to her daughter-in-law.

The empress, who had no intention of doing so, sent palace guards to surround Tang Zhongzong as he gave a public audience. They arrested the startled emperor and led him off to house arrest, along with his pregnant wife. Instead of elevating the Heir Apparent Grandson, Empress Wu then appointed her own younger son, Zhongzong's brother Ruizong, to be the new Tang emperor.

Tang Ruizong, in his early twenties, was intelligent but shy, and afflicted with a crippling stutter. He had no choice but to let his mother rule on his behalf. "Political affairs were decided by the empress dowager," one court historian records. "She installed Ruizong in a detached palace, and he had no chance to participate."[3]

None of this was exactly legal, but nor was it entirely illegal. The empress had not, after all, claimed the throne—although a decree six months after Ruizong's "accession" deepened suspicions that she intended to do so. The decree, the "Act of Grace," changed the colors of imperial banners, the styles of dress at court, and the insignia of court officials. This was the act of a ruler founding a new dynasty: the symbolism of change.

People muttered, but Tang China was temporarily prosperous and peaceful, the farmers and peasants were well fed and well supplied, and the general agitation needed for mass revolt was missing. An armed revolt against her de facto usurpation did break out, led by a nobleman whose family had been exiled not long before, but within three months the empress's soldiers had quelled it.

Over the next five years, the empress moved from strength to strength. As the power behind her husband's throne, she had already proved herself to be a competent administrator, military strategist, and lawmaker. Yet despite her obvious abilities, the aristocrats of the court continued to resent the fact that the former concubine had risen to a power they could only dream of.

So the empress turned to her own people, choosing her officials from the lower classes: men of ability whose birth had previously cut them off from advancement. The aristocrats would never be her friends, but they grudgingly had to admit her strengths as a ruler. Now the common people became her loyal supporters as well, grateful for the chance to rise through talent alone.

But that was not the only brick in the base of her power. She also created a secret police, headed by the two notorious officials Zhou Xing and Lai Junchen (author of the interrogators' handbook called *Classic of Entrapment*), who

> earned the same sombre notoriety as Himmler and his aides have gained in modern times. They formed a school where they taught their trade to disciples, composed a book of instructions and elaborated many new and frightful tortures to extract confessions. These contrivances they decorated with poetic names, and displayed the terrifying battery to a newly arrested victim, who would often confess anything to avoid these tortures.[4]

The empress's power was supported not only by the men who were grateful for their elevation to high office, but also by all the others who were too frightened to object.

In 690, the empress took the final step. One of her officials asked her to assume the title "Emperor, Son of Heaven." Like the first Sui emperor and the usurpers who had come before him, she refused—a customary act that meant nothing. A second petition signed by sixty thousand of her subjects was presented; again she refused. From his secluded palace, Tang Ruizong realized that he stood at the edge of a precipice.

He presented the third and final petition himself, asking that his mother do him the favor of removing him from the throne. The empress Wu agreed, graciously. She was coronated on September 24, 690, and Ruizong was demoted to the position of heir apparent, in which he lived, peacefully, in the safety created by his willingness to lay down power.[5]

With this formal recognition of her authority, the empress Wu became emperor. Yet there was no clear path in any of the ancient rituals through which a woman could claim the true Mandate of Heaven. In order to have any hope of bolstering her real political power with sacred sanction, the empress had to assume a new persona: she had to become, like all of the emperors before her, a Son of Heaven.

And so, for purposes of court ceremonies she put on a very particular illusion of masculinity: she did not change her dress or appearance, she did not try to *appear* male, but she stepped into a created male persona with which the entire country—having no way to place a female ruler into the complex patterns of the past—agreed to interact. She named herself the first emperor of a new dynasty, the Zhou, which put her in an appropriately patriarchal role; she moved the court back to Luoyang, creating a space between her rule as emperor and her previous tenure as empress.

It was a fiction unlike any that had been practised in China before. The new emperor's administration, which now boasted scores of talented, well-trained, competent, low-born men, was one of the strongest in recent history. Despite the black thread of terror woven through her power, the emperor was clearly capable of keeping Tang China strong and prosperous. Yet there seems to have been *no way* for the empress Wu to claim the throne without taking on this new identity. The willingness of the population to accept her as the Son of Heaven reveals not only the strength of the construct but also the extent to which it was now detached from reality.

FOR THE FIRST FIVE YEARS of the emperor Wu's new dynasty, Tang China flourished—although not without a constant current of resentment and complaint from the aristocrats who had been nudged out of power by Wu's new appointees. But the loyalty of the elevated commoners continued strong, and the emperor knew how to find sympathetic allies for her causes, be they political or personal.

She took a lover, a salesman of medical herbs named Xue Huaiyi, who became troublesome. Since there was certainly no space in the old rituals for the emperor to have a male concubine, she appointed him to be the abbot of one of the Buddhist monasteries she had endowed, a position that gave him the right to enter and leave the palace freely. He took advantage of his position to become jealous and possessive, finally burning down one of the great Buddhist temples in the city in a fit of rage. The emperor picked the strongest ladies-in-waiting at court and sent them to surround Huaiyi and strangle him. The women of the Tang court had suffered a long time from the whims of royal men; she had no difficulty finding volunteers.[6]

In 695, she faced a triple uprising in the north. The northern nomadic tribes known as the Khitan, who had originally lived somewhere around the Liao river, had moved south towards the Tang border and now were in the vicinity of the northern city of Beijing, headquarters of the northern military governor. At the same time, the Eastern Turkish Khaghanate, which had been under Tang rule since Tang Taizong's conquest in 630, rebelled. The Turks of the Eastern Khaghanate had grown increasingly unhappy with their place in Tang society; they had given up their empire and fought in the Tang armies, and in return they had gotten nothing but scorn and dismissive treatment. "For whose benefit are we conquering realms?" they complained. Descendents of the old royal family still lived, and one of them, a man named Mo-ch'o, led the Eastern Turks in a rebellion. While the Khitan were invading Beijing, the Turks under Mo-Ch'o were raiding the northwestern frontier.[7]

At the same time, the Tibetans began to launch attacks against the Tang land in the Tarim Basin. The Tibetan king Mangson Mangtsen, guarded by the regent Gar Tongtsen, had survived his infancy (against all odds) but then died in his twenties; by that point Gar Tongtsen was also dead, and Tibet was now controlled by Gar Tongtsen's son Khri-'bring, acting as regent for Mangson Mangtsen's young son Tridu Songtsen. The double passing on of power—regent to regent, emperor to emperor—provided the Tibetan empire with enough stability so that the conquests begun by Tridu Songtsen's great-grandfather Songtsen Gampo could resume.[8]

The timing of the attacks suggests that the three enemy armies were in some kind of communication. The driving force behind all three was probably the Eastern Turkish leader Mo-ch'o, who now began to work the situation to his advantage. He suggested to the Khitan that they attack; once their invasion was underway, he sent messages to Emperor Wu offering to fight the Khitan on behalf of the Tang, in return for very large payments. The former empress agreed to this plan. Mo-ch'o attacked and defeated the Khitan in 696. Then, after collecting his fee he went right back to attacking the Tang

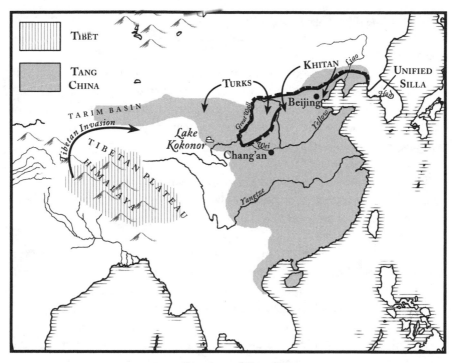

44.1: Invasions of Tang China

again. Within a few years, he had managed to rebuild the power of the Eastern Khaghanate. The Tibetans, meanwhile, conquered the southern part of the Tarim Basin, and Tibetan armies marched into China, getting as far as two hundred miles west of Chang'an itself. This was as far as they could extend themselves without danger of collapse, so they accepted the emperor's offer of a buyout, took the money, and retreated.⁹

The defeat of the Tang armies in battle made it harder for the former empress to maintain the illusion that she was the Son of Heaven. As so many aging emperors had done before her, the emperor Wu (now in her seventies) reassured herself of her potency and her power through the pleasures of the flesh. She began a dual affair with two brothers, both with the family name of Zhang. She granted them so many favors that they became the two most hated men at court, and her officials began to worry that the brothers might be able to talk her into making them her successors. An increasing number of court officials began to suggest that the retired Zhongzong should be brought back out of obscurity and restored to the throne. To silence them, the emperor brought Zhongzong out of his fourteen years of house arrest and declared him to be her successor, the Heir Apparent (despite the fact that he had already been emperor once). He was nearly fifty and had led a quiet life in semi-seclusion with his wife and children. With the amiability that had kept him alive up until this point, he accepted the title and did not press for more.[10]

Emperor Wu had held on to her health and strength for an extraordinarily long time, but now she began to weaken. She suffered the first major illness of her life in 699, and despite doses from court alchemists, further spells of sickness followed. By 705, the empress was eighty years old and ready for retirement. She abdicated, handing the crown over to her son Zhongzong, and took to her bed.

There she remained for the next year, apparently still popular with her people, holding audiences in bed like the grandmother of the entire nation, until she died filled with years and glory.[11]

WITH THE EMPEROR DEAD, the court records almost unanimously ignored her attempts to found a new dynasty, and went right back to chronicling the years of the Tang. Zhongzong ascended as the fifth Tang ruler (or as the sixth, depending on whether or not his two months in power, back in 683, was counted as a separate reign).

The pliancy that had saved him did not make him a good ruler. For the five years of his reign, from 705 until 710, the Tang court was run by his wife, the empress Wei, and her lover, the emperor's cousin Wu Sansi.[12]

Empress Wei had ambitions to be like her mother-in-law, but she lacked Emperor Wu's intelligence and competence. Within five years, the court was a disastrous, corrupt mess. The empress capped the disaster by poisoning her husband Zhongzong in 710. After surviving decades of court intrigue, the unfortunate man was finally brought down by a plate of cakes.

Empress Wei, who was not an original thinker, then tried to install her husband's young son (by a concubine) as emperor so that she could be regent—just as the empress Wu had done three decades before. But the court was now familiar with this routine, and a palace rebellion led by the dead emperor's sister and nephew ended with the young ruler imprisoned and the empress Wei, along with a score of her relatives and supporters, dead in the palace hallways.

The rebels then declared Ruizong, Zhongzong's younger brother, to be the next emperor. Ruizong, now forty-eight, had (like his brother) already been emperor once; he had been coronated at the age of twenty-two, back in 684, and had ruled for six years under his mother's thumb, until she had deposed him and declared herself emperor.

Ruizong had gone back to private life after his removal from the throne. He liked obscurity, and he did not want to re-enter the palace fray. But he finally allowed himself to be talked into returning to imperial life. In 710, he was recoronated; but by 712 he was fed up with court intrigue. When a comet appeared in the sky, he hailed it as an omen and abdicated.

He handed the crown over to his son, who became the emperor Tang Xuanzong. Tang Xuanzong, energetic and mature, began to reform the mess left in his father's wake. He cut the government tax breaks for Buddhist monasteries, which forced a number of monks and nuns to return to civilian, tax-paying life; he reinstituted the Confucian system of choosing officials through a series of examinations, which weakened the power of the aristocratic families that tended to monopolize court positions through claiming the privilege of blood; he drove back the Tibetans and forced them to sue for peace; he stabilized the frontiers by setting up a series of command zones along the trouble spots and giving a military governor vast powers to deal with any difficulties; and he moved the capital back to Chang'an, which (thanks to his new tax policies and the relative peace of the frontiers) began once again to attract trade caravans from as far away as Constantinople.[13]

Unlike the emperor Wu, he was able to pour his entire energies into ruling; none of it went towards transforming his power into legitimacy. He would rule for nearly half a century, bringing the Tang dynasty back from the edge of disintegration to the height of its glory, and earning himself the name "Brilliant Emperor."

TIMELINE 44

BYZANTIUM	LOMBARDS	BULGARS	JAPAN	CHINA	TIBET
				Fall of Sui/Rise of Tang (618)	
				Tang Gaozu (618–626)	
					Songtsen Gampo
Siege of Constantinople (626)				Tang Taizong	(620–650)
				(626–649)	
		Kubrat of Old			
		Great Bulgaria (632–669)			
	Rothari (636–652)				
Constantine III (641)					
Constans II (641–668)			Uija (641–660)		
	Edict of Rothari (643)		Saimei (642–645)		
			Kotoku (645–654)		
			Start of Taika reforms		
				Tang Gaozong	Mangson
				(650–683)	Mangtsen
					(650–676)
	Aripert (653–661)				
			Saimei (655–661)		
	Grimoald (662–671)		Naka no Oe (661/668–672)		
Constantine IV (668–685)			Foundation of Fujiwara clan		
		Division of Bulgarian rule/			
	Destruction of Old Great Bulgaria (669)				
					Tridu Songtsen
					(676–704)
	Rise of First Bulgarian Empire			Tang Zhongzong (683)	
Justinian II				Tang Ruizong (684–690)	
(685–695/705–711)					
				Tang Wu (second reign) (690–705)	
Leontios (695–698)				Rebuilding of Eastern Khaghanate	
			Mommu (697–707)		
				Tang Zhongzong (705–710)	
			Gemmei (707–714)/		
			Nara period	Tang Ruizong	
			(710–794)	(second reign) (710–712)	
				Tang Xuanzong (712–756)	
			Gensho (715–724)		
			Yoro Code		
			Shomu (724–749)		

Chapter Forty-Five

Paths into Europe

Between 705 and 732,
Arab armies destroy the Visigoths,
fail to capture Constantinople,
and are turned back from Frankish land
by Odo of Aquitaine (and Charles Martel)

THE LATEST GENERAL-TURNED-EMPEROR of Constantinople, Tiberios III, sat uneasily on the throne. He had received bad news: the young emperor who had been dethroned and mutilated, Justinian the Noseless, had escaped from his prison in Cherson. He was at the court of the Khazars, plotting to get his throne back.

The Khazar khans had driven back the Arabs and conquered Old Great Bulgaria, which made the current khan, Busir Glavan, the strongest ally around. But the Khazars had also been allies of the legitimate Byzantine emperors since the days of Heraclius. In order to convince Busir Glavan to help him overthrow the man who currently wore the crown, Justinian the Noseless promised him something he didn't yet have and couldn't get by fighting: the chance to be kin to the Byzantine throne. He offered to marry Busir Glavan's sister in exchange for help getting his throne back.

Busir Glavan agreed. Shortly afterwards, a secret message came from Tiberios of Constantinople: he would pay the khan handsomely to assassinate Justinian. Busir Glavan was a realist. Justinian would have to fight to get the throne back, and political alliance now was worth more than blood alliance with a man who might be emperor sometime in the uncertain future. He accepted Tiberios's money and told off two Khazar soldiers to murder his new brother-in-law.

But he had underestimated Justinian. Warned by his wife that something was afoot, Justinian summoned the two soldiers to his house, probably under the pretense that he wanted to hire them as bodyguards. He welcomed them in and, when they were relaxed, strangled both of them with a cord. He then fled again, this time in a fishing boat, and escaped from the Khazar territory.

He managed to pilot the boat north into the Dniester river, crossing as he did so into the First Bulgarian Empire. Asparukh's son Tervel now ruled over the Bulgarians, and he was an enemy of the Khazars, who had ravaged the original Bulgarian homeland farther east. Justinian convinced Tervel to support him with promises of alliance, cash, and the eventual marriage of his own daughter to Tervel; and in 705 Justinian was able to lead a Bulgarian army to the walls of Constantinople.[1]

They spent three days trying to negotiate their way into the city before the ex-emperor lost patience. Familiar with Constantinople's drainage system, he led his army in through a water main. They stormed the palace and seized Tiberios. Justinian reclaimed the throne and ordered Tiberios put to death. He also returned the favor of his mutilation by blinding the patriarch, who had supported Tiberios's rule.

Justinian II's second rule lasted six years, from 705 to 711. He was the only emperor who reigned after mutilation; he wore a silver nose to cover the hole where his own nose had been, and the people of Constantinople found it useful to pretend that the nose was real.[2]

But his second reign proved to be nothing more than a single-minded hunt for those who had betrayed him the first time around. The six years became a reign of terror, as he ordered enemies and suspected enemies to be hung on the walls, trampled by horses in the arena, thrown in the sea in sacks, poisoned, and beheaded. In 711 the army rose up and murdered him.[3] No natural successor or strong general was able to pick up the reins of power. Between 711 and 717, three ephemeral emperors claimed and lost the throne of Constantinople.

But the armies of Islam, occupied elsewhere, did not immediately take advantage of this weakness. The caliph Abd al-Malik had died in 705, and his son Walid I was acclaimed as his successor. With Walid I in power, the Arab armies began to move off the North African beach.

The governor, Musa ibn Nusair, had been appointed to the Islamic province of North Africa, Ifriqiya. He in turn appointed as his military commander a Berber soldier named Tariq bin Ziyad, who had once been a slave but had earned his freedom through military service. Together, the governor and the new commander led an assault on the coastal city of Tangiers. They hoped that Tangiers could serve as a staging point for the Arab armies to cross the mouth of the Mediterranean Sea and move into the Visigothic kingdom of Hispania.[4]

The realm of the Visigoths was ready to fall.

For nearly a century, the Visigoths had been struggling to keep their kingdom whole. An early hint of their difficulties had already appeared in 636, when the Fifth Council of Toledo—the gathering of priests, scholars, and officials that made the country's laws—decreed that only a Gothic noble, of Gothic blood, could ever be king. In 653, the Eighth Council of Toledo added another stipulation: the king not only would be a Goth but also would be chosen by the "great nobility": the Goths of the powerful families.[5]

This wrote into law the old Germanic custom of electing warriors to be kings—a practice that most of the other Germanic kingdoms had slowly abandoned. It was a dynamic practice that suited a wandering people well, but in a settled country with customs and laws, the combination of election and royal prerogative was a volatile one. An elected president knows his power to be limited and his time brief, and approaches his new task circumspectly; an elected king comes into an administration with which he has no continuity and begins to exercise autocratic power. The chances to make enemies were endless.

The Toledo decrees reveal a country in which the hope of stability—of some continuity between administrations, of the continued pursuing of shared goals—lay not in laws, in constitution, or in the existence of a royal family, but simply in the assurance that the king would be of Gothic blood. But as the Arab armies approached, this stability was showing itself to be an illusion.

In 694, the king of the Visigoths, Egica, had appointed as co-ruler his eight-year-old son, Wittiza, and had followed this up with a coronation ceremony around 700, when Wittiza reached adulthood (at the age of fourteen or so). Egica was already unpopular because he had claimed some of the land designated for the use of the king as his own personal property—an act that erased the line between the king's rights as a ruler and his rights as a private person. The coronation of Egica's young son was a clear attempt to introduce dynastic right to the throne into the Visigothic succession. It had been resented both by the nobles who prized their right to choose a king and by the nobles who thought they had a chance to be chosen. But the desire to revolt against Egica's presumption was temporarily quenched by an outbreak of plague, so severe that the capital city was deserted by anyone who could afford to get out. Egica and Wittiza left Toledo in 701, and Egica died shortly afterwards, possibly of the sickness.

Although we know little about Wittiza's solo reign, one contemporary chronicle mentions that he returned the land his father had claimed to the "royal fisc," transferring it from his personal ownership back into the service of the throne. He was young, but he must have seen the resistance to his father's innovations.[6]

The gesture did not save him. By 711, Wittiza had disappeared from the historic record; his fate remains a mystery, but another king, named Ruderic, sat on the throne with the support of the Gothic nobles. The events that follow are unclear, the accounts confused and contradictory. But mentions of two other kings in different parts of Hispania suggest that support for Ruderic was not unanimous among the Gothic nobles, and that civil war erupted. The system of election, meant to put competent kings on the throne while avoiding blood succession, broke down just at the moment that an attacking army was on its way.[7]

The army was a mix of Arabs and Berbers commanded by the Berber general Tariq bin Ziyad. Coastal raids on southern Visigoth towns had already begun. Ruderic assembled what defense he could muster, but some sources hint that his competitors for the throne had already allied themselves with the invaders, possibly even assisting Tariq's entrance into Hispania. If so, they had overestimated the goodwill of the newcomers. On July 19, 711, Tariq bin Ziyad and his troops met Ruderic at the Battle of Guadalete, and in a shattering defeat, Ruderic, his noblemen, and his officers were wiped out. "God killed Ruderic and his companions, and gave the Muslims the victory," writes the Arab chronicler Ibn Abd al-Hakam, "and there was never in the West a more bloody battle than this."[8]

This brought an abrupt end to the Visigothic kingdom in Spain: not because the king was dead, but because almost the entire stratum of aristocrats, the men who held the right to elect the monarch, was wiped out. There was no more king—and, more damaging, no one who could claim the right to appoint one. No one had the authority to organize a resistance or to negotiate a treaty with the invaders.

For the next seven years, the Arab and Berber army fought its way across the country, conquering and negotiating with local officials. Tariq himself was recalled from Hispania after a single year, and the newly conquered territory—now known as the Islamic province of al-Andalus—was placed under the command of the governor of North Africa.

In 715, the caliph Walid I died, leaving as his legacy the Arab entrance into Europe. His younger brother Suleiman took up the caliph's mantle and immediately refocused the energies of the Islamic armies on the Byzantine borders.

Byzantium was still suffering from turnover at the top of the chain of command. The third of three temporary and passing emperors, Theodosius III, sat on the throne.* He was a harmless tax official who had been elevated much against his will (in fact, Theophanes the Confessor says that he hid in the woods when he discovered that his soldiers were planning to acclaim him), and he had

---

*The city administrator Philippikos (711–713) had been replaced first by his secretary Anastasios II (713–715) and then by the tax official Theodosius III (715–717).

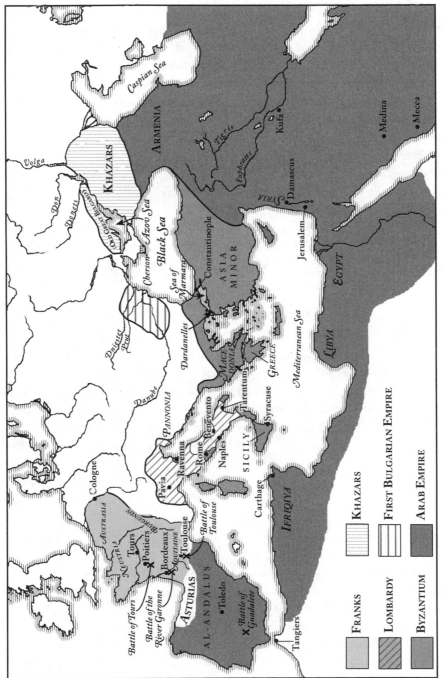

45.1: *The Arab Advance*

no stomach for facing the gathering Arab attack. When the armies at Nicaea proclaimed one of their generals, the Syrian Leo, as emperor, Theodosius abdicated with relief and went to a monastery, where he trained for the priesthood and eventually became bishop of Ephesus, a job much more to his liking.⁹

The soldier Leo, now Emperor Leo III, brought an end to the chaos in Constantinople. He prepared at once for an expected Arab assault, and within a matter of months the Arab ships, a fleet eighteen hundred strong, were sighted passing through the Dardanelles—the strait at the far end of the Sea of Marmara. They were under the command of the new caliph Suleiman. At the same time, Suleiman had sent a ground force of eighty thousand around through Asia Minor. The ships drew close to the city from the south just as the troops were arriving from the east.¹⁰

The entrance into the Golden Horn, the harbor at Constantinople, was protected by a giant chain; the ground forces would have had to fight their way forward and lift the chain to allow the ships into the harbor. Before they could do so, Leo III launched an attack force of burning ships, set alight with unquenchable Greek fire, into the approaching fleet. The wind was with him. Hundreds of the Arab ships were set on fire and either sank or went aground.

Suleiman regrouped his remaining ships, at which point Leo III himself unhooked the chain closing off the Golden Horn and opened the harbor. "The enemy thought he wanted to entice them and would stretch [the chain] out again," writes Theophanes, "and they did not dare to come in to anchor." Instead they retreated, anchoring at a nearby inlet. Before they could reorganize their attack, two disasters struck them: a sharp and unusually severe winter suddenly descended ("For a hundred days crystalline snow covered the earth," says Theophanes), and Suleiman grew ill and died.¹¹

His cousin Umar was proclaimed caliph in Damascus, the current capital of the Abbasid empire, as Caliph Umar II. A new admiral was sent from Egypt; when he arrived in the spring, the attack resumed. But Leo III had arranged a new treaty with the Bulgarians, and a Bulgarian army arrived in midsummer to help lift the siege.

Theophanes claims that twenty-two thousand Arabs died in the battle before the walls. Umar II sent word that the siege should be abandoned, and the Arabs "pulled out in great disgrace" on August 15, 718, and started home. Once again, Constantinople had resisted the Arab flood; it still lay inaccessible to the Islamic conquest, blocking the eastern path into Europe.¹²

But the western path had proved much easier for the Arab armies. Almost no roadblocks had been flung into their way by the Visigoths. In 718, a flicker of resistance appeared; a Visigoth noble named Pelayo retreated into the northern mountains with his followers and declared himself king of a Christian kingdom. The kingdom of Asturias, tiny and poverty-stricken, survived repeated Arab attacks, thanks to its mountain defenses; but it did nothing to halt the Arab advance. Under al-Samh, the new governor of al-Andalus, the Islamic army reached the edge of the old Visigothic land and came within hailing distance of the Frankish land known as Aquitaine.

THE FRANKS, LIKE THE VISIGOTHS, like the Byzantines, had been suffering a slight crisis in leadership.

The do-nothing Merovingian kings had been dominated for forty years by a succession of ambitious mayors of the palaces. In 680, the Austrasian nobles had chosen a Frankish official named Pippin the Fat to occupy their palace; he was the grandson of Pippin the Elder, the mayor who had first tried to make the office hereditary back in 643. At his election, the throne of Austrasia was empty; its last do-nothing king had just died. Pippin the Fat (later known as Pippin the Middle, since his grandson would also be named Pippin) refused to support a new candidate for the Austrasian crown. None of the Frankish nobles insisted, and Pippin the Fat ruled as de facto king of Austrasia.

This did not please the Merovingian king who sat on the throne of Neustria, Theuderic III (he happened to be the youngest son of Clovis II and had been retrieved from his monastery to ascend the throne after both of his brothers died). In 687, Theuderic III attacked Austrasia, but Pippin the Fat's army defeated the king so thoroughly that Theuderic had to agree to make Pippin the Fat the joint mayor of all three palaces: Austrasia, Neustria, and Burgundy.

After this, Pippin the Fat had begun to call himself *dux et princeps Francorum*, "Duke and Prince of the Franks." He was neither a king nor a servant of the king; he had returned to an older Germanic description of his power, calling himself the principal leader (*princeps*) among many leaders (*duces*, dukes). He ruled in Austrasia as *dux et princeps* for nearly thirty years, outliving various puppet-kings of the Merovingian family,* and died in 714, at age eighty, just as the Arab armies were storming towards the Frankish border.

This was bad timing. The various royal cousins who wore the Frankish crowns were not powerful enough to spearhead any effective defense, and Pippin's death left the mayoral offices empty as well. Both of his legitimate sons, born to his wife Plectrude, had died before him. He did have two illegitimate sons, the children of his mistress Alpaida; but Plectrude hated both Alpaida and her sons and did not want them inheriting Pippin's power.

Instead, she insisted that the real heirs to the office of mayor of the palace

---

*These were Theuderic III of Neustria, then Theuderic's two sons, Clovis IV (691–695) and Childebert III (695–711), and then Childebert's son Dagobert II (711–715).

should be her grandsons, the children of her dead sons. To make sure that Alpaida's sons wouldn't get power, she nabbed the older and most ambitious son, Charles Martel, and imprisoned him in Cologne.

Charles escaped from prison almost at once and returned to Neustria, where he had to fight Plectrude (acting as regent for her young grandsons) and various claimants to the office of mayor of the palace. The civil war lasted for two years, but by 717, Charles Martel had made himself mayor of the palace of Austrasia and had put a royal cousin on the throne as a do-nothing king.

He had control, although it was shaky, over most of the Frankish lands. But to the south, a local nobleman named Odo, who had the hereditary right to govern the region known as Aquitaine, had taken the opportunity of the civil war to make himself more or less independent. He was supposed to be loyal to the Franks, but he reserved his loyalty for the do-nothing king; he was suspicious of Charles Martel's ambitions and kept himself aloof from any alliance with the mayor of the palace.

As a result, when the Arab armies appeared on his southern border, Odo of Aquitaine had no powerful friends to come and help him. On June 9, 721, the tiny army of Aquitaine—reinforced by only a few resistance fighters from the mountains of Asturias—met the Arab armies at the Battle of Toulouse, under Odo's command.

With staggering self-absorption, the Frankish chronicles make almost no mention of this battle. They are preoccupied with Charles Martel's rise to power; Odo of Aquitaine appears in them only as Charles Martel's enemy, not as the savior of the Franks. But Odo defeated the Arabs at the Battle of Toulouse, killing the governor of al-Andalus in the fighting, and halted the Arab advance into Europe. It was one of the worst (and most unexpected) defeats suffered by an advancing Islamic army. "He threw the Saracens out of Aquitaine," the chronicles remark, laconically, and in doing so he preserved the culture of the Franks.[13]

The dead governor of al-Andalus was replaced by a new appointee, the military man al-Ghafiqi, and for a time the Arabs retreated from the Frankish border. Al-Ghafiqi spent eight or so years governing al-Andalus before leading an army back towards the northeast in 732.

Once again Odo of Aquitaine came out to meet the Arab attack. This time, Odo was horribly defeated at the Battle of the River Garonne. He was forced back into Aquitaine, and the Arab armies crossed the river, coming first to Bordeaux, then to Poitiers. According to the chronicle of Fredegar, they burned churches and slaughtered the population as they went.[14]

Odo, in desperation, sent to Charles Martel, offering to swear his loyalty if Charles would come and help. Up until this point, it seems, the Franks had not fully appreciated the danger of the Arab advance. But the previous decade had opened their eyes, and Charles Martel marched south at once, making Odo one of his commanders and giving him authority over the Aquitaine wing of the army.

The Arabs under al-Ghafiqi and the Franks under Charles Martel met near Poitiers in October. The battles that followed went on for more than a week, with no clear advantage emerging.

Days into the fighting, al-Ghafiqi was killed. At his fall, the Arab forces began to retreat, and Charles Martel followed them. The chronicle of Fredegar, which is relentlessly pro-Charles (and anti-Odo), announces that Martel pursued the Arabs in retreat to grind them small, utterly destroy them, and scatter them like stubble. This is not exactly true. They had lost the battle, but they were not entirely defeated; they burned and looted their way back into al-Andalus, more or less unhindered, while Martel came along behind.[15]

The battle at Poitiers in 732, immortalized by Frankish historians as the Battle of Tours, did turn the Arab advance back; the Muslim empire halted at the border of Aquitaine and did not again press forward. Charles Martel's victory had been competent and well planned. But his nickname "The Hammer"—given to him because he hammered away at his enemies and ground them to dust—was not completely deserved. Odo of Aquitaine, now reduced to paying homage to the mayor of the palace, had orchestrated the triumph. But Charles Martel had better court historians.

		BYZANTIUM KHAZARS ARAB EMPIRE	
CHINA	TIBET	BULGARS VISIGOTHS FRANKS	

TIMELINE 45

CHINA	TIBET	BYZANTIUM KHAZARS ARAB EMPIRE BULGARS VISIGOTHS FRANKS
		Kubrat of Old Great Bulgaria (632–669) **Umar** (634–644) Fifth Council of Toledo
		Clovis II (639–655)
		Constantine III (641)
	Mangson	**Constans II** (641–668
Tang Gaozong (650–683)	Mangtsen (650–676)	**Grimoald** (643–656) **Uthman** (644–656) Eighth Council of Toledo **Erchinoald** (656–658) **Ali** (656–661) The First Fitna (656–661)
		Muawiyah (661–680)
		Constantine IV (668–685) Division of Bulgarian rule/ Destruction of Old Great Bulgaria (669)
	Tridu Songtsen (676–704)	Siege of Constantinople (674–678) **Theuderic III** (675–691)
Tang Zhongzong (683) Tang Ruizong (684–690)		**Asparukh** (c. 680–c. 701) **Pippin the Fat** Rise of First Bulgarian Empire (680–714) **Justinian II** (685–695) **Abd al-Malik** (685–705)
		Egica (687–702)
Tang Wu (second reign) (690–705) Rebuilding of Eastern Khaghanate		**Busir Glavan** (c. 690–715) **Leontios** (695–698)
		Tiberios III (698–705)
Tang Zhongzong (705–710)		**Tervel** **Wittiza** (c. 701–715) (700–c. 711) **Justinian II** (second reign) **Walid** (705–715) (705–711)
Tang Ruizong (second reign) (710–712) Tang Xuanzong (712–756)		**Ruderic** (c. 711) Battle of Guadalete (711)
		Theodosius III (715–717) **Suleiman** (715–717) **Leo III** (717–741) **Umar II** (717–720) Charles Martel (717–741)
		Battle of Toulouse (721) Battle of Tours (732)

Chapter Forty-Six

——

The Kailasa of the South

Between 712 and 780,
the Arab armies establish a province in the Sindh,
and the southern Rashtrakuta
build a reflection of the sacred north

T HE ARAB ARMIES, blocked at Constantinople and at Poitiers, had better fortune at the Indus.

The conquest of the Sindh, begun back in 643, had halted when the caliph Umar realized how desolate the area was. Now al-Hajjaj, the governor of the eastern reaches of the Islamic empire, recalled his son-in-law Muhammad bin Qasim from his military post in Fars and sent him back towards the Indus to finish the job. Bin Qasim's first target was the port city of Debal, right on the eastern edge of the Makran desert.

At this time, the port seems to have been under the control of a tribal leader named Dahir, who probably ruled not only his own tribe but a few surrounding tribes as well. We know of him from the Arabic history *Tarikh-i Hind wa Sindh*, written sometime after the eighth century and translated from Arabic into Persian in the early thirteenth century. According to the anonymous author, when bin Qasim marched towards Debal in 712, Dahir had just inherited control of the port from his father. He was not a very important ruler, but he stood as a barrier between the Arabs in Makran and the lands farther east.[1]

Rather than simply attacking him, al-Hajjaj and bin Qasim manufactured an excuse for their aggression. Pirates had attacked Arab ships setting off from the coast of the Makran, and al-Hajjaj insisted that Dahir punish the sea raiders. Dahir, receiving this message, retorted that he had no authority over the pirates, which was undoubtedly true; he was not nearly as powerful as the Arabs seemed to think. But al-Hajjaj took Dahir's response as hostile and authorized his son-in-law's attack. The two men were searching for reasons to invade—which suggests that the invasion of India may have been undertaken without the complete sanction of the caliph in Damascus.

Muhammad bin Qasim approached Debal by land, while further reinforcements and siege engines arrived by sea. Al-Hajjaj supervised the offensive
by letter; *Tarikh-i Hind* says that he wrote every three days with instructions,
which is as close to micromanaging as he could get, given the difficulties of
eighth-century travel.

After an extensive siege, Debal was taken. Dahir, seeing that the city was
lost, withdrew with most of his men, and bin Qasim slaughtered the remaining defenders. He ordered a mosque to be built in Debal, left a garrison at the
port, and kept marching eastward.

Dahir fled to the other side of the Indus, abandoning the lands between the
port and the river (all the villages surrendered to bin Qasim as he approached).
He did not believe, the Arab historian tells us, that bin Qasim would attempt
to cross the river, but bin Qasim ordered a pontoon bridge (boats roped
together to form a wavering wooden path) laid across the Indus, stationing a
boat full of archers at the head of the bridge and thrusting it forward a little
farther as each boat was added behind. The archers kept Dahir's men at bay
until the line of boats reached the far shore.[2]

Bin Qasim then marched his men across the fragile bridge. "A dreadful
conflict ensued," the historian writes, with Dahir and his soldiers mounted on
elephants, and the Arab soldiers shooting flaming arrows into the howdahs—
the reinforced carriages on the elephants' backs. Towards evening, Dahir was
knocked from his elephant by a well-placed arrow. An axman on the ground
beheaded him.[3]

His men retreated upriver and fortified themselves at the city of Brahmanabad, well to the northeast. But over the next three years, bin Qasim
conquered a swath of land across the Indus that included Brahmanabad,
which he made into his capital. The new Indian province proved to be a
treasure trove for the eastern part of the empire; the tribes in the conquered
land paid regular and expensive tribute to the occupiers. The ninth-century
Persian historian al-Baladhuri writes that when the governor al-Hajjaj reckoned up the tribute paid during the first year, his profit was double the cost
of the conquest.[4]

THE NORTHERN INDIAN LANDS were perpetually troubled by outsiders
coming east across the Indus or south across the mountains. But a kind of
cyclical, indigenous battling, almost completely unaffected by outside forces,
had characterized the south of India for centuries. The kingdoms of the south
breathed, their borders expanding and contracting, each dynasty hanging on
to power but seeing the extent of that power change almost yearly.

In the eighth century, the Western Chalukya expanded again, dominating the south central plain under its king Vikramaditya II. This was nothing

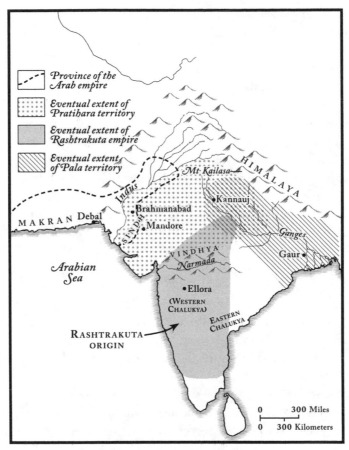

46.1: Indian Kingdoms of the Eighth Century

new; Vikramaditya's conquests simply pushed the kingdom back to the same borders ruled by Pulakesi II a century earlier.

But in 745, a new southern kingdom did arise; and its king not only travelled far enough north to encounter the outside invaders, but also tried to reproduce the northern geography in the south.

His name was Dantidurga, and in 745 he inherited the rule of his southern tribe. His father had kidnapped his mother, a noblewoman of Chalukya birth, and married her by force; so Dantidurga had Chalukya blood in his veins, however unwillingly. With it had apparently come the compulsion for conquest. He started out by fighting his neighbors, with growing success. Sometime around 753, he decided that he was strong enough to take on Kirtivarman II, son and heir of the Western Chalukya king Vikramaditya. A poem records the outcome of the battle during which Dantidurga apparently triumphed despite his much smaller forces:

Assisted by only a few
As if by a bend of his eyebrow
He did subdue
That tireless emperor [Kirtivarman II]
Whose weapons were of undimmed edge.[5]

Kirtivarman II kept only a small remnant of his father's domain; Dantidurga claimed the rest and annexed it to his own territory.

Immediately afterwards, Dantidurga pushed his way north across the Narmada. Kirtivarman II had been his greatest enemy in the south; in the north, his natural target was the tribal chief of the Pratihara, who ruled a territory that surrounded the city of Mandore and stretched all the way up into the Sindh.

An outlying Arab force met Dantidurga as soon as he crossed over into the Sindh, but he drove them back and made his way straight for Mandore. In 754, he managed to reach the city and occupy it, forcing the Pratihari king Nagabhata to surrender.

But there was no conquest of the north. Dantidurga apparently did not have the men, or the bureaucracy, to rule a far-flung empire. He took tribute from Nagabhata and went back south. As soon as he got back on the southern side of the Narmada, Nagabhata came after him and recaptured all the northern territory.

What Dantidurga's next move might have been will never be known. He died, like Alexander the Great, at the age of thirty-two, only two years later. But he had pencilled in the borders of the next great Indian power: the kingdom of the Rashtrakuta.[6]

He had come to the head of his tribe young, and his ceaseless campaigning had apparently left him no time for wife or children; he was succeeded as tribal leader and king by his uncle Krishna I. Krishna I went to work filling in the outlines with nearly eighteen years of unceasing warfare. His greatest accomplishment was to bring down the Western Chalukya king and seize the remaining Western Chalukya lands for his own.

Krishna never ventured as far north as his nephew, but the northern landscape apparently occupied his thoughts. In celebration of his victories, he commissioned a new temple to join the caves at Ellora: this temple, the Kailasa (or Krishnesvara), was carved out of the rock without seams. It was, in the words of one of his inscriptions, "an astounding edifice" that amazed even "the best of the immortals."[7]

More than that, it was a mirror of the north. Kailasa was not just a name; it was the name of the peak in the northern Himalaya where the Ganges river, the source of life, originated. Kailasa was the highest and holiest place in the mountains, the sacred spot from which creation sprang. By building its reflection in the mountains that lined the Narmada river valley, Krishna was proclaiming himself to be the southern equivalent to the ancient, godlike rulers of old, the mythological sovereigns of northern India. He was making the sloping, low Vindhya mountains into "Himalaya-in-the-Deccan," a new sacred border.[8]

After Krishna's death, his son Dhruva once again invaded the north, something his father had never done. In 786, he seized Mandore, this time for good, and headed even farther north, towards Kannauj.

Kannauj did not fall to him right away. The city lay at a three-way intersection of kingdoms: his own Rashtrakuta realm, reaching up from the south; the Pratihara, whose realm had shifted somewhat north and east and now extended over into the Ganges valley; and the Pala, whose capital was the city of Gaur, closer to the Ganges delta, but who had advanced westward as far as Kannauj.

For the next century, Kannauj would remain at the battlefront between the three crowns. But even without possession of the northern city, Dhruva had managed to bring northern and southern land together under one throne. When he crossed the Ganges, he had made his father's boast good: the borders of the Rashtrakuta had finally intersected the sacred river.

TIMELINE 46

BYZANTIUM KHAZARS ARAB EMPIRE BULGARS VISIGOTHS FRANKS	INDIA
	Pulakesi II of the Chalukya (610–642)
Umar (634–644) Fifth Council of Toledo Clovis II (639–655)	
Constantine III (641) Constans II (641–668 Grimoald (643–656) Uthman (644–656) Eighth Council of Toledo Erchinoald (656–658) Ali (656–661) The First Fitna (656–661) Muawiyah (661–680)	Arab invasion driven back Emancipation of the Eastern Chalukya Vikramaditya of the Western Chalukya (655–680)
Constantine IV (668–685) Division of Bulgarian rule/ Destruction of Old Great Bulgaria (669)	
	Paramesvaravarman of the Pallava (672–700)
Siege of Constantinople (674–678) Theuderic III (675–691)	
Asparukh (c. 680–c. 701) Pippin the Fat Rise of First Bulgarian Empire (680–714)	Vinayaditya of the Western Chalukya (680–696)
	Manavamma of Sri Lanka (c. 684)
Justinian II (685–695) Abd al-Malik (685–705) Egica (687–702) Busir Glavan (c. 690–715) Leontios (695–698)	
Tiberios III (698–705) Tervel (c. 701–715) Wittiza (700–c. 711) Justinian II (second reign) Walid (705–715) (705–711)	
Ruderic (c. 711) Battle of Guadalete (711) Theodosius III (715–717) Suleiman (715–717) Leo III (717–741) Umar II (717–720) Charles Martel (717–741)	Dahir of Debal (c. 712) Arab invasion of northern India
Battle of Toulouse (721)	
Battle of Tours (732)	Nagabhata of the Pratihara (730–756) Vikramaditya II of the Western Chalukya (733–744)
	Kirtivarman II of the Western Chalukya Dantidurga of the (744–755) Rashtrakuta (745–756)
	Krishna of the Rashtrakuta (756–774)
	Dhruva of the Rashtrakuta (780–793)

Chapter Forty-Seven

—-—

Purifications

Between 718 and 741,
the caliph tries to follow Muhammad's teachings exactly,
while the emperor of Byzantium destroys icons
and the pope is given a kingdom of his own

AFTER THE FAILED SIEGE of Constantinople in 718, the caliph Umar II led the Umayyad empire into its first reform. The empire was less than a century old, but already the tensions that ribbed it were stretching to breaking point.

Around the same time as the siege of Constantinople, Umar II had noticed a troubling problem in the empire's administration. Muhammad, long before, had instituted a "head tax," ordering Christians and Jews within Muslim communities to pay a fee in return for accepting the protection of the Muslim state. Theoretically, converts to Islam were at once freed from the obligation to pay the head tax. But the caliphs after Muhammad, administering a burgeoning empire that Muhammad had probably never envisioned, were reluctant to give up such a lucrative tax. More and more often, local officials "forgot" to exempt new converts from the head tax, and they simply went on paying it.

As a result, almost all non-Arab Muslims in the empire were currently sending the head tax to Damascus. This struck Umar II, who was a back-to-the-exact-prescriptions-of-the-Prophet radical, as corrupt. He declared that all Muslims, no matter their race or length of commitment to Islam, should be exempt from the tax.

This made him immensely popular, but it ruined the empire's tax base—particularly since huge numbers of conquered peoples suddenly converted en masse to avoid the tax. However, Umar II didn't have to deal with the consequences of his reforms. He died a natural death in 720, and his successor Yazid II immediately reimposed the tax before the empire went broke.[1]

At this, Yazid II's popularity plummeted, and the biggest crowd of recent converts—the non-Arab tribes in Khorasan—rebelled. Not only did they

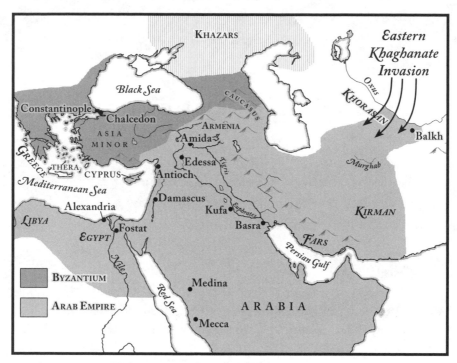

47.1: Struggle in Khorasan

rebel; they also sent a message to the khagan of the rebuilt Eastern Khaghanate, Mo-ch'o's nephew and successor, Mo-chi-lien, asking him for aid. Mo-
chi-lien had followed up on his uncle's conquests by pushing the Turkish
kingdom towards the Arab border, swallowing the land once belonging to the
Western Khaghanate and re-establishing a unified Turkish empire. Pleased
at an excuse to push farther southwest, he sent his troops towards the Oxus,
and a ten-year struggle between the Turkish and Islamic armies in Khorasan
began.[2]

With the Arab armies occupied elsewhere, the emperor Leo III took the
opportunity to do some doctrinal house-cleaning of his own. He issued a
command that all Jews in his empire be baptized as Christians; a few were,
but many more fled, some into Arabic lands, others up north into the lands
of the Khazars. And he began to campaign against a practice that had long
disturbed him: the use of icons in Christian devotion.

Constantinople was home to scores of icons—paintings of saints, or of
the Virgin Mary, or of Christ himself. An icon (the Greek word *eikon* meant
"image" or "likeness") was more than a symbol and less than an idol: an icon
was a window into the sacred, a threshold at which a worshipper could stand
and come that much closer to the divine.

Christians had been using icons as an aid to prayer and meditation for centuries, but a counter-thread of unease with these images had been stitched into Christianity from its beginnings. In the earliest years of apostolic teaching, Christians had been distinguished from followers of the old Roman religion primarily because they refused to worship images, and for the second- and third-century theologians the use of icons veered perilously close to idolatry.

Once the ancient Roman customs had died out, so did the risk that Christians would be drawn back into them, and the use of icons became much less fraught with danger. But a strong subset of Christian theologians continued to oppose the use of icons, not because of the danger of idolatry, but because painting an image of Christ suggested that the son of God was characterized by his human nature, not his divinity. God, Who was Spirit, could not be pictured; if Christ *could* be, didn't that imply that he was not truly God? Couldn't it be argued that an image of Christ "separates the flesh from the Godhead" and gives it a separate existence? Arguments over the use of icons became a subset of the arguments over the exact nature of Christ as God-man—arguments that had been going on for centuries, despite a whole series of church councils making declarations intended to settle the matter once and for all.[3]

Leo III had a less subtle concern: he was disturbed by the tendency of his subjects to treat icons as though they were magic. During the siege of Constantinople, the patriarch Germanos had taken the most venerated icon in Constantinople, a portrait of Mary that was rumored to have been painted by the gospel-writer Luke himself, and had paraded around the walls with it.[4] When the siege lifted, far too many of the citizens of Constantinople chalked the victory up to the icon (called the Hodegetria), as though it had been a sorcerer's wand waved over the enemy. This sort of thinking had no place in Christianity.

Perhaps Leo III also felt some justifiable indignation in seeing the praise for his hard-won triumph given to the icon. Still, his actions over the next years, which nearly lost him the throne, are those of a man acting against his own best interests, something explained only by deep conviction.[5]

In 726, Leo decided to begin to wean the people away from their magical thinking. According to Theophanes the Confessor he was finally moved to action by a serious eruption of the volcano on Thera: "The whole face of the sea was full of floating lumps of pumice," Theophanes writes, "[and] Leo deduced that God was angry at him." As a first tentative act against the icons, he sent a band of soldiers to take down the icon of Christ that hung over the Bronze Gate, one of the main entrances to the palace.[6]

His fears about the overreliance of the people on the icons were immediately justified. A mob gathered to find out what was happening, and when the icon began to come down they rioted and attacked the soldiers. At least one soldier was killed. Leo retaliated with arrests, floggings, and fines. With amazing rapidity, the conflict spread into the more distant regions of the empire. The army in the administrative theme of Hellas (Greece) rebelled and set up their own emperor, declaring that they could not follow a man who attacked the holy icons.

The rebellion was short-lived and the new emperor was captured and beheaded, but feelings continued to run high. In every great city across the empire, iconoclasts (icon-smashers) and iconodules ("icon-slaves," meaning icon-lovers) argued, while in Constantinople Leo III preached against "idol-worship." Iconoclastic bishops removed icons from their churches, while iconodules wrote long treatises defending their use: "The memory of Him who became visible in the flesh is burned into my soul," wrote the monk John of Damascus. "Either refuse to worship any matter, or stop your innovations."[7]

For an icon-lover, the philosophical problem underlying iconoclasm was its suspicion of matter, its willingness to relegate Christianity entirely to the spiritual realm and to separate off earthly existence as fundamentally flawed. And, like all theological debates, the use of icons had a political edge: iconodules also accused Leo III of having too much sympathy for Muslims, who refused to make images of living things. He was, sniped the icon-loving Theophanes, too much shaped by "his teachers the Arabs."[8]

To the west, Pope Gregory II waxed indignant. He was himself a supporter of icons, but more central than the issue of icons was Leo III's willingness to make theological pronouncements. The pope sent a sharp message rejecting Leo's pronouncements. "The whole West . . . relies on us and on St. Peter, the Prince of the Apostles, whose image you wish to destroy," he wrote. "You have no right to issue dogmatic constitutions, you have not the right mind for dogmas; your mind is too coarse and martial."[9]

More seriously for Leo, the pope ordered his own flock to ignore the imperial commands to destroy icons. By this time, only a handful of cities in Italy still maintained any loyalty to the Byzantine emperor: among them were the southern city of Naples, the port village of Venice on the northern Adriatic coast, Rome, and Ravenna, where the exarch still lived. Much of the rest of Italy was ruled by the Lombard king Liutprand. Pope Gregory II's condemnation meant that the peoples in these territories now had a theological justification for finally deserting Constantinople.[10]

The Italian cities had been feeling the pinch of higher and higher imperial taxes for some time, and their populations welcomed the justification. The duke of Naples actually tried to carry out the emperor's command to destroy the city's icons and was killed by an indignant mob. In Ravenna, the exarch was killed by his own subjects. And in Rome, the pope was acting with increasing disregard for the imperial stamp of approval.

King Liutprand of the Lombards saw the opportunity to extend his own power at the expense of the emperor's. He attacked Ravenna and took away the port, although the residents of the city put up resistance and Liutprand was unable to penetrate the marsh; Ravenna was now no-man's land, unable

to communicate with Constantinople, and no longer under an exarch.
The pope made no objection to this;
he had decided to see Liutprand and
the Lombards as co-belligerents in
the fight against the emperor's tyranny, and Liutprand was willing to
foster this opinion.

The growing alliance between the
two men was strengthened when a
new exarch appointed by Leo III came
from Constantinople. This exarch,
a man named Eutychius, landed at
Naples (the Ravenna port was now
inaccessible) and sent a series of gifts
and money bribes to Liutprand, promising more if the Lombard king would
help him to assassinate the pope.[11]

Liutprand refused. Instead, he went
south to Rome and took control of
Byzantine territory nearby: the city of

Map 47.2: The First Papal State

Sutri and the land surrounding it. In 728, he offered to turn the territory over to
the control of the church—a "gift" that became known as the Sutri Donation. It
was not, in fact, a donation; Pope Gregory II handed over an enormous payment
from the church treasury in exchange. But everyone benefitted. Liutprand got
back a good deal of the money he had spent attacking Ravenna, and the pope
now had, for the first time, a little kingdom of his own. It was the first extension
of papal rule outside the walls of Rome: the first of the Papal States.[12]

Undeterred by his critics or by his troubles in Italy, in January of 730 the
emperor Leo III issued a formal edict ordering the destruction of icons all
across the empire. When the patriarch Germanos refused to support the edict,
Leo deposed him and appointed a replacement.[13]

Pope Gregory II died not long afterwards, and his successor, Pope Gregory
III, called a church council, which met in 731 and excommunicated all the
icon-destroyers. Leo III, in return, announced that the handful of Byzantine
possessions left in Italy were no longer subject to the authority of the pope;
instead, they fell within the realm of the patriarch. The eastern and western
branches of the church had drawn that much farther apart.

Leo III died in 741, leaving behind a legacy of lost lands, shattered icons,
and displaced peoples. But the empire was no better off after his death; he was
succeeded by his son Constantine V, twenty-three and energetic, and even
more rabidly iconoclastic than his father.

T I M E L I N E 47

INDIA	BYZANTIUM ARAB EMPIRE FRANKS TURKS LOMBARDS
	Aripert (653–661)
Vikramaditya of the Western Chalukya (655–680)	**Ali** (656–661) Erchinoald The First Fitna (656–661) (656–658) Defeat of Western Khaghanate (657) **Muawiyah** (661–680) **Grimoald** (662–671)
Paramesvaravarman of the Pallava (672–700)	**Constantine IV** (668–685)
	Siege of Constantinople (674–678) **Theuderic III** (675–691)
Vinayaditya of the Western Chalukya (680–696)	Pippin the Fat (680–714)
Manavamma of Sri Lanka (c. 684)	**Justinian II** (685–695) **Abd al-Malik** (685–705) **Mo-ch'o** of the Eastern Khaghanate (692–716) **Leontios** (695–698) **Tiberios III** (698–705)
	Justinian II (second reign) (705–711)
Dahir of Debal (c. 712) Arab invasion of northern India	**Liutprand** (712–744) **Theodosius III** **Suleiman** Pope Gregory II (715–717) (715–717) (715–731) Patriarch **Mo-chi-lien** Germanos of the Eastern (715–730) Khaghanate (716–734) **Leo III** **Umar II** Charles Martel (717–741) (717–720) (717–741) Siege of Constantinople (718) **Yazid II** (720–724)
	Battle of Toulouse (721)
Nagabhata of the Pratihara (730–756)	Sutri Donation (728) Pope Gregory III (731–741)
Vikramaditya II of the Western Chalukya (733–744)	Battle of Tours (732)
Kirtivarman II of the Western Chalukya **Dantidurga** of the (744–755) Rashtrakuta (745–756)	**Constantine V** (741–775)
Krishna of the Rashtrakuta (756–774)	
Dhruva of the Rashtrakuta (780–793)	

Chapter Forty-Eight

—◆—

The Abbasids

Between 724 and 763,
the Khazars convert to Judaism,
the clan of the Umayyad loses the caliphate,
and the new Abbasid caliphs let go of the west

THE CALIPH YAZID II, who had kept the Umayyad empire from bankruptcy, died after four short years with the frontier lands in turmoil. His brother Hisham took over his post and began to bring iron-handed order to the turbulent empire: sending strike forces into Khorasan and Armenia to fight against the rebelling converts, and sending armies against the northern Khazars as well.

A triangle of power had emerged in the lands east of the Adriatic. The Byzantine emperor occupied one point of the triangle, the caliph another. At the triangle's tip stood the khan of the Khazars, Khan Bihar. He had been conquering his way steadily into the surrounding lands, and now his realm stretched from the Black Sea to the Caspian Sea and far up to the north: a massive empire, one of the largest in the world. The Khazars had taken the city of Ardabil out of Arab hands; the Arabs answered by invading Khazar land along the Volga river; the two armies struggled for control of Derbent, the port city that lay on the Caspian coast right between the two empires.[1]

Meanwhile Khan Bihar made a brilliant alliance. In 732, his daughter Tzitzak agreed to be baptized as a Christian, took the name Irene, and married Constantine V of Constantinople.

Despite the alliance, the Khazars treasured their independence—something that was made perfectly clear by the khan's decision, sometime around the middle of the century, that his people would convert to Judaism. There was no mystery about how the khan discovered Judaism; plenty of Jews had fled into Khazar land during Leo III's attempts to convert them by force, and Jewish travellers and traders had undoubtedly made their way to Khazar cities long before. But we have to read between the lines to discover his motivations. A tenth-century account remarks that both the Byzantine emperor and the Arab caliph were "incensed" at the khan's decision to convert, and a letter written slightly later by one of the Jewish kings of the Khazars elaborates:

> The king of the Byzantines and the Arabs who had heard of [the khan] sent their envoys and ambassadors with great riches and many great presents to the King as well as some of their wise men with the object of converting him to their own religion. But the King . . . searched, inquired, and investigated carefully and brought [a priest, a rabbi, and a *qadi* (specialist in Islamic law)] together that they might argue about their respective religions. . . . They began to dispute with one another without arriving at any results until the King said to the Christian priest: "What do you think? Of the religion of the Jews and the Muslims, which is to be preferred?" The priest answered: "The religion of the Israelites is better than that of the Muslims." The King then asked the *qadi*: "What do you say? Is the religion of the Israelites, or that of the Christians preferable?" The *qadi* answered: "The religion of the Israelites is preferable." Upon this the King said: "If this is so, you both have admitted with your own mouths that the religion of the Israelites is better. Wherefore, trusting in the mercies of God and the power of the Almighty, I choose the religion of Israel, that is, the religion of Abraham."[2]

Perhaps more to the point, he did not choose the religion of either of his powerful neighbors; like Dhu Nuwas of Arabia, 250 years earlier, he found a path between.

BY 743, HISHAM HAD TAMED the rebellions and invasions in the caliphate. But the victories came at great financial cost; and although Khorasan had been reduced back into order, the order was precarious at best.[3]

When Hisham died of diphtheria, the Umayyad caliphate too began to die. He was succeeded by his nephew Walid II, an alcoholic poet who was murdered by his cousin in less than a year; the cousin, Yazid III, lasted for six months and then grew ill. Just before his death, he named his brother Ibrahim to be his heir, but before Ibrahim could consolidate his power, the general Marwan swept down from Armenia with his army behind him, drove out the opposition (Ibrahim, prudently, surrendered and joined Marwan's men), and in 744 had himself declared caliph, as Marwan II, in the mosque at Damascus. He then moved the capital of the Umayyad caliphate to Harran, closer to his old Armenian territory.[4]

He almost succeeded in pulling the empire back together; it had not been under bad leadership for very long, and he had Hisham's twenty years of order to build on. But Constantine V now took the opportunity to attack. While Marwan was still struggling for internal control, Constantine V invaded Syria and inflicted a serious defeat on the Arab navy in a sea battle in 747.

The defeats fueled the internal opposition to Marwan's rule. Marwan, like his predecessors, was Umayyad. Since the death of Muhammad's son-in-law Ali back in 661, the caliphate had stayed within the Banu Umayya, the clan of Muhammad's old companion Uthman. The Umayyad caliphs had ruled as Arabs over an Arab empire. For nearly a century the strongest glue holding the Islamic conquests together had been Arabic culture: the Arabic language, Arab officials in high positions, a bureaucracy supported by the reimposed head tax on non-Arabs. The worship of Allah was, of course, inextricably entwined with Arabic language and Arabic culture. But the Umayyad caliphs were, in the last analysis, politicians more than prophets, soldiers more than worshippers.

So when political and military fortunes turned against them, their hold on power fragmented. "In the nine decades since the death of Ali," writes historian Hugh Kennedy, "it had become accepted by many discontented Muslims that the problems of the community would never be solved until the lead was taken by a member of the Holy Family"—a member of Muhammad's own clan.[5]

In the same year as the great naval defeat, Marwan faced both an uprising in Syria and another rebellion in Khorasan. Some of the rebels wanted a descendent of Ali to occupy the caliphate; since Ali's death, a strong subcurrent within Islam had insisted that only a man of Ali's blood could properly carry on as his successor (the followers of this current, who also believed that a successor of Ali would be spiritually and supernaturally fitted to rule, were known as Shi'at Ali, the "Party of Ali"). Others, willing to cast their net wider, argued that the caliphate should simply go to a member of Muhammad's clan, the Banu Hashim: they were known, generally, as Hashimites.[6]

The revolt in Khorasan soon spread through the entire province, taking it out of Marwan's control. In late 749, the Hashimites gathered in Kufa and elected a member of Muhammad's clan, Abu al-Abbas, as their caliph. Abu al-Abbas could trace his lineage back to Muhammad's uncle, but his election was not unanimous. The Shi'a rebels had still hoped for a descendent of Ali's and refused to support him. But even without Shi'a support, Abu al-Abbas was able to gather a sizable rebel army behind him.

Marwan II mustered over a hundred thousand men and marched from his capital of Harran towards Khorasan, meeting Abu al-Abbas and his supporters just east of the Tigris in early 750. The rebel army was fighting for a cause; Marwan's soldiers were largely unwilling recruits, and the Umayyad force was driven back and then scattered. Marwan himself was forced to flee. He went first into Syria and then south into Palestine, and then farther south into Egypt, attempting to raise another fighting force.

Meanwhile Abu al-Abbas sent out scores of men on horseback, their mission to find and kill the remaining Umayyads. Hisham's grandson and the heir apparent to the caliphate, the twenty-year-old Abd ar-Rahman, was living in Damascus with his family. When word of the defeat reached him, he fled eastward with his brother and a Greek servant, apparently hoping to hide in some small unremarkable village in the old Persian lands. Al-Abbas's men caught them on the banks of the Euphrates; Abd ar-Rahman flung himself into the water and began to swim, but his brother hesitated. The soldiers of al-Abbas beheaded him on the spot and left his body unburied on the shore.[7]

But Abd ar-Rahman made it to the opposite shore, as did his Greek servant. The two men kept on the move. Apparently they changed course, because they soon arrived in Egypt and then traveled on west through Ifriqiya; Egypt was not safe. Marwan, in Egypt trying to find an army, was caught sleeping in an Egyptian church in August. Deserted by most of his followers, he threw himself against the band of Abbasid soldiers and was murdered in front of the door. His head was sent back to al-Abbas, who by this time had earned the nickname *al-Saffah*, "The Slaughterer."[8]

Al-Abbas, ruling from Kufa as the new center of his caliphate, did his share to make the new Abbasid caliphate secure. He promised that all remaining members of the Umayyad family would be granted amnesty and given back their family property if they would come and swear allegiance to him. A contemporary chronicler tells us what happened: ninety unwary men and women showed up and were seated at a welcome banquet, but before they could eat, al-Abbas's guards surrounded the banquet hall and killed every single one.[9]

THE NEW ABBASID CALIPH had to deal with attacks on both the far east and far west of his land.

The first threat came from the east. For some years, the Tang general Gao Xianzhi, serving the Brilliant Emperor Tang Xuanzong, had been leading a slow progression across the Asian plateau, pushing his way almost all the way to the eastern reaches of the Islamic empire in Sogdiana, just east of the Oxus river. The Umayyad caliphs, increasingly weak and disorganized, had not been able to halt this advance. Now an Abbasid army of a hundred thousand men marched eastward to meet the threat.

Gao Xianzhi had travelled light and far, and his force of thirty thousand was no match for the opposition. At the Battle of Talas in 751, the Abbasids defeated the Tang force, ending the Tang attempt to take control of central Asia. Gao's forces were nearly wiped out, only a few thousand left alive. Without enough men to launch a counterattack, Gao Xianzhi turned for home.

"The Slaughterer" died in 754, and his brother al-Mansur succeeded him as caliph. Al-Abbas had ruled from Kufa, but al-Mansur moved the capital to the village of Baghdad. It was a strategic location to build the empire's wealth: "Here's the Tigris, with nothing between us and China, and on it arrives all that the sea can bring," he told his officers, "and there is the Euphrates on

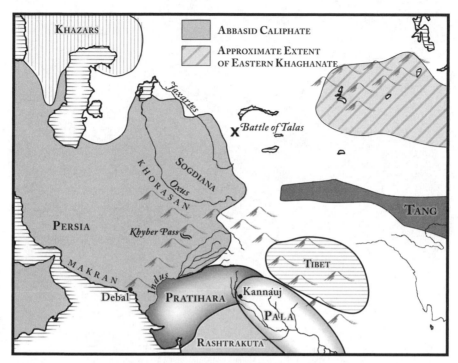

48.1: The Battle of Talas

which can arrive everything from Syria and the surrounding areas." He began to build, transforming the tiny town into an imperial capital.[10]

The move suggests a new eastward focus, and when another problem arose on the western edge of the caliphate, al-Mansur did not try very hard to solve it. In 756, the fugitive Umayyad heir Abd ar-Rahman had arrived in al-Andalus. He had made his way, over six long years, across North Africa to the edges of the last Umayyad province left in the Muslim world.

He sent a message to the Umayyad governor of al-Andalus, Yusuf al-Fihri, announcing that he had arrived to claim al-Andalus as his rightful territory. The message was not greeted with joy. After the Abbasids had seized power, Yusuf al-Fihri had gone right on governing as an independent Umayyad ruler. He was not pleased to discover that a man with a better claim to al-Andalus had appeared on the horizon, and he declined to hand the land over to Abd ar-Rahman.

The two men met in battle just outside Cordoba. Abd ar-Rahman was victorious; he defeated and beheaded Yusef al-Fihri and became the de facto caliph of al-Andalus. But he did not yet claim the title of caliph. Instead, he took the lesser title of "Emir of Cordoba": prince, not king, but still the ruler of the first Muslim kingdom to be entirely independent of the caliphate.

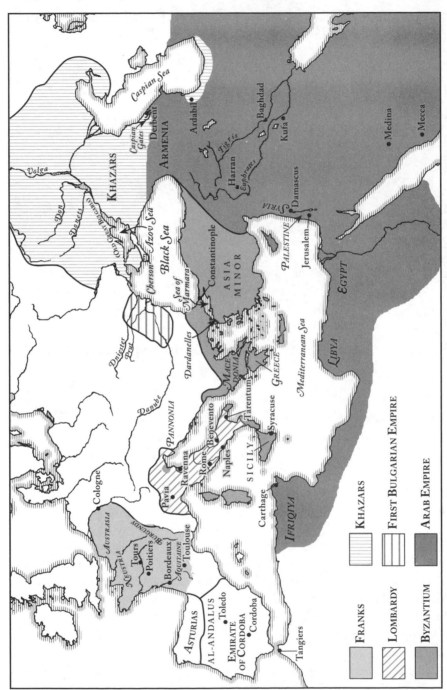

48.2: *The Early Abbasid Caliphate*

KHAZARS

FIRST BULGARIAN EMPIRE

ARAB EMPIRE

FRANKS

LOMBARDY

BYZANTIUM

In 763, al-Mansur sent an Abbasid army to al-Andalus, in an attempt to bring it back to the Abbasid empire. When Abd ar-Rahman fought back and defeated it, al-Mansur decided that it would be wisest to abandon al-Andalus to the Umayyads in order to keep manpower strong in the east.

The Umayyad caliphs had slowly shifted their base of power closer and closer to the Mediterranean Sea, ending up in Syria, closer to the center of the Islamic empire. But the Abbasids had recentered themselves in the lands that had once been Persia, putting distance between themselves and the western part of the empire.[11]

They also grew increasingly autocratic. Al-Mansur, like his brother, began his caliphate with murder; he arranged the assassinations of a number of prominent Shi'a leaders who had refused to support the Abbasid claim to power. He continued on as he had begun, ruthless and authoritarian, using his network of spies to root out dissent and ordering his enemies beaten, imprisoned, and executed. His intelligence was so frighteningly efficient that he was rumored to have a magic mirror that told him who was loyal and who was planning revolt.[12]

The center of Baghdad, which contained his elaborate royal residence, was home to more and more ornate buildings—a whole complex that housed the caliph and all of his family in royal luxury. In the hands of al-Mansur, the spiritual authority of the caliph took a definite second place to political ambitions, and the Abbasid caliph began to look more and more like an emperor.[13]

TIMELINE 48

BYZANTIUM LOMBARDS TURKS FRANKS	ARAB EMPIRE KHAZARS CHINA
	Muawiyah (661–680)
Grimoald (662–671)	
Constantine IV (668–685)	Siege of Constantinople (674–678)
Theuderic III (675–691) Pippin the Fat (680–714)	
	Tang Zhongzong (683) **Tang Ruizong** (684–690)
Justinian II (685–695)	**Abd al-Malik** (685–705)
	Busir Glavan Tang Wu
Mo-ch'o of the Eastern Khaghanate (692–716)	(c. 690–715) (690–705)
Leontios (695–698) **Tiberios III** (698–705)	
	Tang Zhongzong
Justinian II (second reign) (705–711)	(705–710) **Tang Ruizong** (710–712)
Liutprand (712–744)	**Tang Xuanzong** (712–756)
Theodosius III Pope Gregory II (715–717) (715–731) Patriarch Germanos (715–730)	**Suleiman** (715–717)
Mo-chi-lien of the Eastern Khaghanate (716–734)	
Leo III (717–741) Charles Martel (717–741)	**Umar II** (717–720) Siege of Constantinople (718)
	Yazid II (720–724)
Battle of Toulouse (721)	**Hisham** (724–743)
Sutri Donation (728)	**Bihar** (c. 730–c. 742)
Pope Gregory III (731–741) Battle of Tours (732)	
Constantine V (741–775)	**Walid II** (743–744) **Yazid III** (744) **Marwan II** (744–750)
	al-Abbas (750–754)
	Beginning of Abbasid Battle of Talas caliphate (750–1258) (751)
	al-Mansur (754–775)
	Abd ar-Rahman of Cordoba (emir, 756–788)

Chapter Forty-Nine

Charlemagne

Between 737 and 778,
the pope anoints the king of the Franks,
the king of the Franks protects the pope,
and the Iron Crown of the Lombards goes to Charles the Great

I N 737, THE DO-NOTHING KING of the Franks, Theuderic IV, died, and Charles Martel did not bother to appoint another ruler. He was mayor of the palaces of the Franks, *dux et princeps Francorum*, the most prominent Christian warrior in all of the old Roman lands, and he had more power than anyone else in the western landscape—with the possible exception of the Lombard king Liutprand.

So when Pope Gregory III fell out with Liutprand in 738, he appealed to Charles Martel for help. The argument began with the duke of Spoleto, who defied an order given by the Lombard king and then fled to Rome for sanctuary. When the pope refused to hand him over to the king, Liutprand expressed his displeasure by taking back bits of the brand-new Papal State and occupying them himself. Cut off from Constantinople, Gregory had no one else to help him, and so he sent a desperate message to Martel. "In our great affliction, we have thought it necessary to write to you," Gregory began. "We can now no longer endure the persecution of the Lombards. . . . You, oh son, will receive favor from the same prince of apostles here and in the future life in the presence of God, according as you render speedy aid to his church and to us, that all peoples may recognize the faith and love and singleness of purpose which you display in defending St. Peter and us and his chosen people. For by doing this you will attain lasting fame on earth and eternal life in heaven."[1]

The letter earns Gregory III partial credit for first articulating one of the goals that would motivate later crusaders: salvation, offered to those who fought in the name of the church. Unfortunately, it didn't work with Charles Martel. The *dux et princeps Francorum* sent a present back to Gregory but declined to get involved. He and Liutprand had fought side by side at least once, and making enemies of the Lombards would gain him absolutely nothing (apparently he wasn't convinced by Gregory's redemptive rhetoric).[2]

The standoff in Italy dragged on for several more years and was finally resolved by the death of everyone involved; Charles Martel and Pope Gregory III died in 741, and Liutprand died in 744 after an astounding thirty-two years as king of the Lombards. It had been a relatively minor political tangle, but Gregory's appeal to Charles Martel had revealed a shift in the landscape. In a universe where the protection of the Byzantine emperor had been whisked away, the bishops of Rome were on their own, forced to make alliances with whatever power might be willing to protect them.

In 751, even the nominal claim of the emperor to rule in Italy was destroyed. The Lombards captured Ravenna, under the guidance of the aggressive new Lombard king Aistulf, and took the last exarch captive. A few patches of Italian land remained loyal to the emperor—the city of Venice, notably, declared itself still Byzantine—but now there was no Byzantine government on the peninsula. Constantinople had no representative, Venice and the other Byzantine cities were forced to govern themselves, and the pope was entirely on his own.

Unlike Charles Martel, though, the new *dux et princeps Francorum* was willing to protect Rome from hostile Lombards—in return for a favor.

After Charles Martel's death, his two sons Carloman and Pippin the Younger had inherited his power, Carloman as mayor of the palace in Austrasia and Pippin the Younger in Neustria. The brothers had decided to put a figurehead king on the Frankish throne, which had been empty for seven years. Their choice was Childeric III; he was the son of the previous king, but his lineage was irrelevant since he took no part in governing.

Neither, after a few years, did Carloman. In 747, at the age of forty, he left his wife and children in the care of his younger brother and went to Rome to be consecrated as a monk. It was the culmination of a lifelong dream; despite his years in the mayor's palace at Austrasia, he had, as Fredegar tells us, a "burning for the contemplative life." According to Charlemagne's biographer Einhard, Carloman tried to live in a monastery near Rome but was continually disturbed by Frankish noblemen coming to visit him. So shortly after his consecration, he travelled to Monte Cassino, to the monastery established by Benedict himself, where the rules of silence and isolation were strictly observed. "There," Einhard writes, "he passed in the religious life what remained of his earthly existence."[3]

This left Pippin the Younger as sole mayor, and in 751 he decided to remove Childeric III and claim the throne himself. Yet that lingering regard for royal blood caused him to search for a greater sanction than himself for his usurpation of the throne.

And so he sent two men south to Rome with a brief message for the pope,

Gregory III's successor Zachary. The official chronicles of the Frankish kings, *Annales Regni Francorum*, give us a terse account:

[They] were sent to Pope Zachary to ask whether it was good that at that time there were kings in Francia who had no royal power. Pope Zachary informed Pippin that it was better for him who had the royal power to be called king, than the one who remained without royal power. By means of his apostolic authority, so that order might not be cast into confusion, he decreed that Pippin should be made king.[4]

Zachary, facing the hostile Aistulf, was willing to trade the church's approval for protection from the Lombards.

Pippin ordered Childeric III tonsured and sent to a monastery, where he died five years later, the last of the Merovingians. Pippin was crowned the first king of the Carolingian dynasty in the city of Soissons, in a brand-new sacred ceremony that involved anointing with holy oil in the manner of an Old Testament theocratic king.*

Zachary died in 752, but his successor, Pope Stephen II, was careful to put himself in a position to reap the benefits of that coronation. In 754, he travelled north into the lands of the Franks and re-anointed Pippin in an even more elaborate ceremony, which also included the anointing of his sons, seven-year-old Charles and three-year-old Carloman, as his heirs. "At the same time," according to an anonymous addition to Gregory of Tours's history of the Franks, "he bound all the Frankish princes, on pain of interdict and excommunication,† never to presume in future to elect a king begotten by any men except those confirmed and consecrated by the most blessed pontiff."[5]

He had tied the Frankish king's power to the authority of the pope, and King Pippin responded by marching across the Alps down into Italy, driving Aistulf out of the papal lands and the lands once governed by the exarch, and giving all of them to the pope. Aistulf's army was badly defeated, and he was forced to recognize Pippin as his overlord. After Aistulf was thrown from his horse while hunting, and died in 756, Pippin chose the Lombard nobleman Desiderius to be the next king of Italy. In half a decade, he had become not only king of the Franks but the de facto ruler of Italy as well.[6]

Pope Stephen II didn't do badly either. He now ruled over a much expanded papal kingdom, which included both Rome and the old impe-

---

*The Carolingian dynasty took its name from *Carolus,* the Latin form of Charles Martel's name.
†Excommunication blocked a single person from taking part in the sacraments of the church; interdict blocked an entire community. When the church declared an interdict over a country or province, no one within it could receive a sacrament and all public worship was halted.

rial center of Ravenna. To justify his possession of these lands, he presented Pippin with a document that (he claimed) had been written by Constantine and had been in the possession of the church ever since. In it, Constantine explained that the fourth-century pope Sylvester had healed him of a secret case of leprosy. In gratitude, he decreed that the papal seat "shall be more gloriously exalted than our empire and earthly throne," that the pope would henceforth be supreme over "the four chief seats [of the church]—Antioch, Alexandria, Constantinople, and Jerusalem—as also over all the churches of God in the whole world," and that Constantine himself was handing over to the pope "the city of Rome and all the provinces, districts and cities of Italy. . . . We are relinquishing them, by our inviolable gift, to the power and sway of himself and his successors."[7]

This document had been forged by some talented cleric, and the ink on it was barely dry. Pippin, who was not an idiot, undoubtedly knew this. But the popes had given him the authority he craved, and in return he was willing to award them power over Rome and the surrounding lands. The forgery, known as the "Donation of Constantine," gave the transfer of authority a spurious sort of legitimacy.

But as long as no one examined it closely, spurious legitimacy served the purposes of everyone involved perfectly well.

FIVE YEARS AFTER al-Andalus became entirely independent from Baghdad, King Pippin of the Franks died.

He left his crown jointly to his sons Charles, now twenty-one, and Carloman, eighteen.* Both young men had been anointed along with him in 754 and so could claim to rule with the approval of God. They divided the administration of the empire, although not along the traditional Neustrian-Austrasian lines; instead, Charles ruled the northern lands and the coast, and Carloman took control of the southern territories.

Two years after his accession, Charles married the daughter of Desiderius, the king of the Lombards whose accession Pippin had supervised. "Nobody knows why," writes Einhard, "but he dismissed this wife after one year." In her place, he married an Alemanni girl named Hildegard, who was only thirteen years old. This gave him a useful connection with the eastern region of his empire where the sometimes-troublesome Alemanni people lived. Naturally, it infuriated the Lombard king, who proposed to Carloman that they unite together to destroy Charles; but in 771, just as the plan was being formed, Carloman died.[8]

---

*The birth year of Charles (Charlemagne) is not known for certain; it has traditionally been listed as 742, but more likely was 747 or 748.

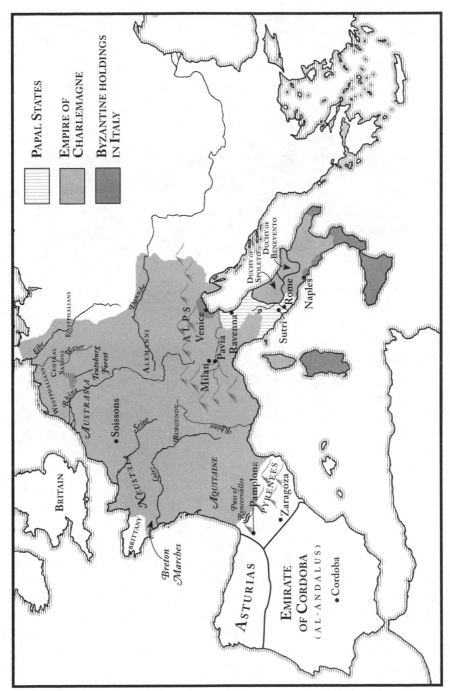

49.1: Charlemagne's Kingdom

49.1: The Iron Crown of the Lombards, made of gold and precious stones with the iron band (said to be a nail from Christ's cross) visible inside. Credit: Scala/Art Resource, NY

Charles now ruled as sole monarch of all of the Frankish lands. Almost at once, he began to enlarge them through conquest. In 772, he set off to fight against the Saxons, just across the Rhine river. He was not yet thinking about the south, where the Lombard king Desiderius was still planning an attack. First, Charles wanted to expand his empire to the north; the land around the Rhine was rich, and the Saxon tribes were not well united. They fell into three main divisions—the central Saxons on the Weser river, the Eastphalians on the Elbe, and the Westphalians closer to the coast—but rarely fought together.[9]

Charles pushed into the Saxon land in 772 and beat his way through the disorganized Saxon resistance into the Teutoburg Forest, where he ordered his men to destroy the most sacred shrine of the Saxons: the Irminsul, a great wooden pillar representing a tree trunk which symbolized the sacred tree that supported the vault of the heavens. He intended to show the Saxons that, as the God-appointed Christian king, he dominated both the Saxons *and* their gods. But the destruction of the Irminsul would haunt him. The Saxons were not politically united enough to mount a strong defense, but they held a single set of religious beliefs, and for decades to come the destruction of the Irminsul remained in their memories.[10]

Leaving the Saxons temporarily subdued, Charles returned home and prepared to march into Italy. The following year, he crossed the Alps, set on punishing Desiderius for his plots and aiming to claim Italy for his own.

Desiderius and the Lombard army met him in the north of Italy, but Charles pushed the Lombard king back into his capital city of Pavia and laid siege to it. The siege lasted nearly a year; Charles (in the words of his biographer) "did not stop until he had worn Desiderius down and had received his surrender."[11]

Rather than executing Desiderius, Charles imprisoned him in a monastery in northern Francia. Desiderius's son and heir fled to Constantinople, where he took refuge at the imperial court. Charles, at twenty-seven, was now the king of all the Franks and Lombard Italy as well. In 774, he claimed the traditional Iron Crown of the Lombards (so called because the Lombards believed that the iron band inside it was beaten from one of the nails from Christ's cross), and the Lombard kingdom ceased to exist. It was the first of the great, empire-expanding victories that would earn him the name Charles the Great or "Charlemagne."

Exalted by his victories in the northeast and southeast, Charlemagne then set his sights on the southwest.

Abd ar-Rahman's seizure of the Emirate of Cordoba had not sat well with all of the Muslims in al-Andalus. In 778 a group of dissidents in the northeastern part of al-Andalus, led by the chief administrator of the region, Sulayman al-Arabi, invited Charlemagne to help them get rid of the Umayyad rule. They promised him that the city of Zaragoza, well inside the borders of the emirate, would open its gates and welcome him in so that he could use it as his base of operations.

This must have seemed like a good idea, but it ended in disaster. Charlemagne marched to Zaragoza with his men, visions of conquering al-Andalus in his head. When he arrived at its walls, however, the governor of the city—who had up until this point been in alliance with Sulayman and the dissidents—changed his mind and refused to let him in. Charlemagne camped outside the walls for weeks, but the gates never swung open. Without a walled city to protect him, he was finally forced to withdraw back through the Pyrenees. He was furious, and on the way home he sacked the fortress of Pamplona as he passed it.

This, like his destruction of the Irminsul, was a miscalculation. Pamplona was not firmly in the control of the emir of Cordoba. It was instead the home of the Vascones, a tribe that had been in Hispania before the Romans arrived and had survived in the mountains through the Roman occupation, the Visigoth takeover, and the arrival of the Arabs.* They were tough, independent, and resourceful, and they took vengeance on Charlemagne as he went back through the mountains towards his own kingdom. At the Pass of Roncesvalles, the Vascones attacked the end of the Frankish column, wiping out the baggage train and killing the rear guard "to the last man." They were

---

*The Vascones were probably the ancestors of the present-day Basque people, who still live in the same mountain region.

lightly armed and experienced in the mountains, and after the slaughter they disappeared into the rough terrain. The Franks, weighed down by their own weapons and armor, were unable to pursue them.[12]

The ambush was disproportionately devastating to Charlemagne, because a number of his officers and personal friends were in the rear when the Vascones descended. Among them was a man whom Einhard calls "Roland, Lord of the Breton Marches"—the nobleman who governed the Frankish territory on the western coast, just above the mouth of the Loire. Stories were told about the minor ambush until it had been transformed into a pivotal battle; Roland became the hero of the first French epic, the twelfth-century *Song of Roland*, which turns the bloody incident into a major conspiracy between the Arabs of Zaragoza and a traitor within Charlemagne's own camp. In the epic, four hundred thousand Arabs descend on the rear of the Frankish army, and Roland refuses to blow his horn for help until he has fought to the end of his strength. When he finally does blow the horn, Charlemagne rides back from the front of the column to help, but the force of the horn's sound has shattered the bones of Roland's skull.

Charlemagne then takes vengeance on the Arabs, with the help of God:

For Charlemagne a great marvel God planned:
Making the sun still in his course to stand.
So pagans fled, and chased them well the Franks
Through the Valley of Shadows, close in hand;
Towards Sarraguce by force they chased them back
And as they went with killing blows attacked.[13]

But in reality, the Battle of Roncesvalles ended Charlemagne's ambitions in al-Andalus. He never pushed his way past the Pyrenees again.

	TIME	LINE	49		
ARAB EMPIRE	**CHINA**	**KHAZARS**	**FRANKS** **BYZANTIUM**	**TURKS**	**LOMBARDS**
			Theuderic III (675–691)		
			Pippin the Fat (680–714)		
	Tang Zhongzong (683)				
	Tang Ruizong (684–690)				
Abd al-Malik (685–705)			Justinian II (685–695)		
	Tang Wu	Busir Glavan	Mo-ch'o of the Eastern		
	(690–705)	(c. 690–715)	Khaghanate (692–716)		
			Leontios (695–698)		
			Tiberios III (698–705)		
	Tang Zhongzong		Justinian II (second reign)		
	(705–710)		(705–711)		
	Tang Ruizong (710–712)				
	Tang Xuanzong (712–756)			Liutprand (712–744)	
			Theodosius III	Pope Gregory II	
			(715–717)	(715–731)	
Suleiman (715–717)			Patriarch Germanos (715–730)		
			Mo-chi-lien of the Eastern		
			Khaghanate (716–734)		
Umar II (717–720)			Charles Martel Leo III		
Siege of Constantinople (718)			(717–741) (717–741)		
Yazid II (720–724)					
			Battle of Toulouse (721)		
Hisham (724–743)			Theuderic IV (721–737)		
				Sutri Donation (728)	
		Bihar (c. 730–c. 742)			
				Pope Gregory III (731–741)	
			Battle of Tours (732)		
			Carloman **Constantine V**	Pope Zachary	
			(741–747)/ (741–775)	(741–752)	
			Pippin the Younger (741–751)		
Walid II (743–744)			Childeric III (743–751)		
Yazid III (744)					
Marwan II (744–750)					
				Aistulf (749–756)	
al-Abbas (750–754)					
Beginning of Abbasid					
caliphate (750–1258)					
	Battle of Talas (751)		Pippin the Younger (751–768)		
al-Mansur (754–775)			Beginning of Carolingian	Pope Stephen II	
Abd ar-Rahman of			dynasty	(752–757)	
Cordoba (emir, 756–788)				Desiderius (756–774)	
			Charles (768–814)/		
			Carloman (768–771)		
				Charles (774–814)	

Chapter Fifty

—·—

The An Lushan Rebellion

Between 751 and 779,
the Brilliant Emperor falls in love with his son's wife,
and loses her, along with his throne

WHEN GAO XIANZHI arrived back home after the Battle of Talas, he discovered that his emperor was in trouble.

Tang Xuanzong had been on the throne for forty years, leading the Tang into the most brilliant era of its existence. The empire was at the very height of its power and size. The arts flourished. Tang porcelain, as clear and thin as glass, was prized by every country that bought goods from the trade route that stretched from China toward the west: the Silk Road. The Tang painter Wu Daozi created portraits and murals so breathtaking that he was rumored to have opened a painted door in one of his landscapes and stepped through. Tang poets composed verses that would endure for centuries. Li Bai, whose reputation had spread empire-wide, wrote in the new "regulated" style, orderly and metered:

> Cut water with a sword, the water flows on;
> Quench sorrow with wine, the sorrow increases,
> In our lifetime, our wishes are unfulfilled.[1]

Wang Wei, poet and painter, wrote *jueju*, "cut-short" quatrains that glanced at a truth and then away, leaving the reader to seek the deeper meaning.

> A morning shower in Weicheng has settled the light dust;
> The willows by the hostel are fresh and green;
> Come, drink one more cup of wine,
> West of the pass you will meet no more old friends.[2]

But the flowering of the arts at court could not disguise the rot at its roots. The Brilliant Emperor, now nearing seventy, had become obsessed with his son's young wife Yang Guifei. He had forced his son to divorce her and had taken her for his own consort. Her cousin, the official Yang Guozhong, had been given more and more power at court through her influence; she was fond (perhaps overly fond) of the army officer An Lushan, and the Brilliant Emperor pliantly awarded An Lushan greater and greater authority. He had dismissed his chancellor Zhang Jiuling, a man who had gained his position through examination (he was famous for his wisdom, his asceticism, and his stern moral compass; he once gave the emperor advice, rather than a present, for his birthday), and in his place had appointed the dictatorial, privileged aristocrat Li Linfu.[3]

And the expansion of the empire had not come without cost. Resentment was building over the extensive military campaigns that the Brilliant Emperor ordered. "White bones are the only crop in these yellow sands," wrote Li Bai, after one protracted war against the northern barbarians,

> There seems no end to the fighting.
> In the wilderness men hack one another to pieces,
> Riderless horses neigh madly to the sky. . . .
> The blood of soldiers smears grass and brambles;
> What use is a commander without his troops?
> War is a fearful thing—
> And the wise prince resorts to it only if he must.[4]

The emperor's growing preoccupation with his personal life meant that the generals on the frontiers took more and more authority themselves, even as wars multiplied. In 751, while Gao Xianzhi was struggling with the Arabs to the far west, the Khitan invaded the north once again and a year-long struggle to drive them out began. The peace with Tibet disintegrated, and Tibetan attacks and raids on the central Asian frontier intensified.

At the end of that same year, a southwestern tributary kingdom of the Tang rebelled. The Nanzhao kingdom had coalesced in the land around Lake Erhai, out of six tribes known to the Chinese as the Bai. As with so many other newborn nations, this one could trace its existence back to the conquering instincts of a single personality: the Bai chief Piluoge. Twenty years earlier, Piluoge had not only claimed the rulership of all six tribes, but also burnt the chiefs of the other tribes alive. His rise had been so meteoric that, barely a decade after seizing power, he had managed to make a match between his grandson and a princess of Tang descent.

The Brilliant Emperor had seen Piluoge's strengthening domain as a useful buffer between the Tang border and the hostile soldiers of Tibet, and had bestowed a title on Piluoge; he even invited the new king and his grandson to

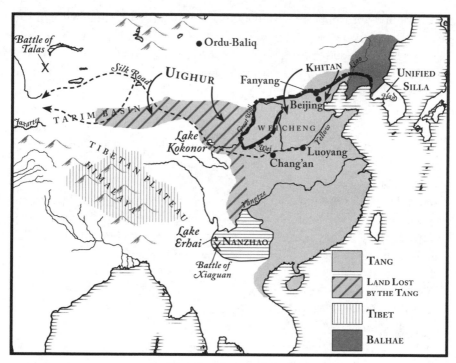

*50.1: New Kingdoms and the Tang**

come and celebrate the marriage in Chang'an itself. But Piluoge's successor Geluofeng now took advantage of the weakness he saw in the Tang and went on the attack. The Tang governor of the southwest territories sent an army to respond, but Geluofeng and the Bai army handed them an unexpected and embarrassing defeat.[5]

A few months later, the aristocratic minister Li Linfu died, and the consort Yang Guifei used her influence to have her cousin Yang Guozhong appointed as next chancellor of the Tang. This was not a bad thing; Yang Guozhong was ambitious and not averse to working his family connections for his own gain, but he was also loyal to his emperor. Once admitted to the inner workings of the government, he grew increasingly worried about his cousin's marked preference for the general An Lushan. In his opinion, An Lushan was not only ambitious, but unprincipled, and he feared that the general was plotting against the throne.[6]

In 754, a second victory by the Nanzhao gave the general An Lushan his chance. A large Tang force under another general had been sent south to

---

* From the eighth century on, the Great Wall of China plays a much less important role in the defense of the frontier; for clarity's sake, it does not appear on maps after 50.1.

punish Geluofeng for daring to defeat the southwest border force, but at the Battle of Xiaguan, the Tang army was massacred. Almost all of the survivors were killed by plague as they limped home. It was said that two hundred thousand soldiers died fighting the small southern kingdom, and this merely heightened the anger and discontent of an army that had already been embarrassed by the defeat at the Battle of Talas three years before.

In 755, An Lushan declared himself an open rival to the Brilliant Emperor, with a royal capital of his own at Fanyang, the northern military garrison where his command had been centered for some years. He commanded over a hundred thousand men, a mixture of well-trained soldiers and northern horsemen recruited from the Khitan. They followed him south along the Yellow river to the fortress at Luoyang, a center of administration for the east of the empire, which they captured without difficulty. Here, An Lushan lingered, resting his army and preparing for an attack on Chang'an itself.[7]

The Brilliant Emperor was furious. He gave Gao Xianzhi, commander at the Battle of Talas, the task of campaigning against An Lushan—and, when the veteran general did not meet with quick success, had him beheaded. In order to pacify the emperor, the loyal chancellor Yang Guozhong then planned an enormous frontal assault—against the advice of military advisors who recommended circling the rebel forces, cutting them off from the supplies and reinforcements coming from Fanyang, and waiting them out.

In the summer heat of July 756, six months after the fall of Luoyang, the Tang royal army marched to meet the rebels and was destroyed. One hundred and eighty thousand men fell, leaving no one to defend Chang'an itself. The Brilliant Emperor and the chancellor fled to the west. Ten days after the battle, An Lushan arrived at the walls of the capital and occupied it, almost unopposed.

On the road into exile, the Brilliant Emperor's royal guard turned on the chancellor. They blamed him for the disaster, and despite the emperor's objections, they surrounded and murdered both Yang Guozhong and his son. Then they demanded that the Brilliant Emperor hand over his consort, the beautiful Yang Guifei, for execution. She had helped Yang Guozhong rise to power; in their eyes, her partiality both for her cousin and for the rebellious An Lushan had helped bring Tang power down.

The emperor stalled, objected, refused, and then finally realized that he had no choice. Rather than handing her over to the angry soldiers, he ordered one of his loyal court eunuchs to kill her quickly. His grief was made famous, half a century later, by the poet Bai Juyi:

Covering his face with his hands,
He could not save her.

Turning back to look at her,
His tears mingled with her blood.
Yellow dust filled the sky;
The wind was cold and shrill. . . .
Heaven and earth may not last forever,
But this sorrow was eternal.[8]

The Brilliant Emperor retreated to the southern city of Chengdu, mourning all the way.

The An Lushan rebellion ended badly for both the Brilliant Emperor and for the rebel An Lushan. The emperor's son Suzong, the heir apparent, forced the old broken emperor to abdicate in 756 and claimed the throne (in exile) himself. Meanwhile, in Chang'an, An Lushan had declared himself the emperor Yan. But he had contracted some disease that caused him to suffer from large and excruciatingly painful boils on his face, and he was growing increasingly short-tempered and paranoid. After months of unpredictable and cruel behavior, he was murdered in the middle of the night in 757 by one of his house servants.[9]

An Lushan's son picked up his banner, but Tang Suzong managed to re-enter Chang'an with his own soldiers later in the same year and drive the remaining rebels out. This didn't end the fighting, though. Resistance continued for the next six years, in a long-drawn-out series of inconclusive battles. Tang Suzong died of a heart attack in 762, and his son Tang Daizong finally managed, in 763, to put down the last remnants of the An Lushan rebellion.[10]

But the internationally feared power of the Tang was broken. Almost all of the border guard had been recalled to fight on one side or the other of the civil war, and the frontiers of the empire had begun to crumble. In late 763, while the new emperor Tang Daizong and his general were in Luoyang mopping up the remnants of rebellion there, Tibetan troops whirled all the way into Chang'an and looted it before withdrawing. For the next decade, Tibetan attacks from the southwest would be an annual event.[11]

To the north and northwest, the Tang border suffered just as badly from the incursions of Uighur tribes. The Uighurs had been a vassal tribe of the Eastern Turkish Khaghanate, but they had broken away from their overlords and established their own kingdom, with its capital at Ordu-Baliq. Both Tang Suzong and his son Tang Daizong had hired Uighur mercenaries to help fight against the rebels, and the heavy payments that the emperors handed over had boosted Uighur wealth. The mercenaries had taken some knowledge of Chinese writing back home with them (along with loot stolen from both Chang'an and Luoyang), and this became the basis of a Uighur writing system; the imported culture sparked a transformation that gradually turned the tribes of warrior nomads into a more stable kingdom.[12]

To the northeast of the empire, the Korean kingdom of Unified Silla, which now dominated most of the peninsula under the rule of King Gyeongdeok, felt the sting of the Tang civil war. The kings of Silla had gained their unified empire with the help of Tang forces, and they needed Tang support because their power over the peninsula was not unchallenged. Survivors of the destroyed Korean kingdom of Goguryeo had gathered in the north, where they had settled and intermarried with the semi-nomadic tribes of the Malgal and formed a new kingdom called Balhae. In the aftermath of the An Lushan rebellion, the Balhae king Mun took advantage of the lessened Tang presence to conquer the surrounding territory, until Balhae had grown even larger than Unified Silla to its south.[13]

With so much fighting going on at the borders, the population of the Tang empire shifted away from the north and west, towards the central and southern lands. The ancient cities of the north fell into decline. By the time Tang Daizong died in 779, the Tang had lost all of its holdings in central Asia. The trade routes to the west had been disrupted and blocked. The generals who were tasked with protecting the shrunken outer reaches of the empire gained more and more power; neither the Tang emperor nor his ministers were able to check their growing independence. The surrounding peoples—Tibet, Nanzhao, the Uighurs, Balhae, Unified Silla—had shifted and changed. The An Lushan rebellion had reshaped not just Tang China, but the political landscape of the entire continent.[14]

TIMELINE 50

FRANKS BYZANTIUM	TURKS LOMBARDS	CENTRAL CHINA	UNIFIED ASIA SILLA	ARAB EMPIRE
Justinian II (second reign) (705–711)		**Tang Zhongzong** (705–710) **Tang Ruizong** (710–712) **Tang Xuanzong** (712–756)		
	Liutprand (712–744)			
Theodosius III (715–717)	Pope Gregory II (715–731)			Suleiman (715–717)
Patriarch Germanos (715–730)				
	Mo-chi-lien of the Eastern Khaghanate (716–734)			
Charles Martel **Leo III** (717–741) (717–741)				Umar II (717–720) Siege of Constantinople (718) Yazid II (720–724)
Battle of Toulouse (721)		Wu Daozi		
Theuderic IV (721–737)				Hisham (724–743)
	Sutri Donation (728)		**Piluoge** of the Nanzhao (728–748)	
	Pope Gregory III (731–741)			
Battle of Tours (732)		Li Bai		
			Mun of the Balhae	
Carloman **Constantine V** (741–747)/ (741–775)	Pope Zachary (741–752)	Wang Wei	(737–793)	
Pippin the Younger (741–751)				
Childeric III (743–751)			Gyeongdeok (742–765)	Walid II (743–744) Yazid III (744) Marwan II (744–750)
		Geluofeng of the Nanzhao (748–779)		
	Aistulf (749–756)			al-Abbas (750–754)
Pippin the Younger (751–768) Beginning of Carolingian dynasty		Battle of Talas (751)		Beginning of Abbasid caliphate (750–1258)
	Pope Stephen II (752–757)			
		Battle of Xiaguan (754) **al-Mansur** (754–775)		
		An Lushan rebellion (755–763)		
	Desiderius (756–774)	**Tang Suzong** (756–762)		Abd ar-Rahman of Cordoba (emir, 756–788)
		Tang Daizong (762–779)		
Charles (768–814)/ **Carloman** (768–771)				
	Charles (774–814)			

Chapter Fifty-One

Imperator et Augustus

Between 775 and 802,
the empress Irene seizes power in Constantinople,
while Charlemagne conquers his neighbors for Christ's kingdom
and allows himself to be crowned as emperor

IN THREE DECADES on the Byzantine throne, Constantine V had presided over the ongoing quarrels between icon-lovers and icon-haters; he had seen the end of the Umayyad caliphate and the beginning of the Abbasid rule; he had watched Byzantine rule in Italy fail, and Rome finally slip from the grasp of Constantinople; he had heard news of the crowning of Pippin the Younger as the first Carolingian king and the rise of Charlemagne's power. He had married a Khazar wife and been troubled by the raids of Avars and the invasions of Arab armies.

In 775, the thirty-fourth year of his reign, he began to plan a war against the First Bulgarian Empire.

The Bulgarians had been more or less allies of Byzantium since Tervel and his men had helped Leo III lift the siege of Constantinople, back in 718. But Constantine V's habit of settling captive peoples (mostly from his battles with the Arabs) in Thracia, crowding the Bulgarian borders, had annoyed the Bulgarian khans.

In retaliation, Bulgarian troops had begun to raid Byzantine land. Constantine V decided that the Bulgarians needed to be put in their place. But in September, as he was preparing to start out on his anti-Bulgarian campaign, he fell ill with what Theophanes describes as an "overpowering inflammation" in his legs that caused severe fever. He died on the fourteenth day of the month, screaming that he was burning alive.[1]

For a time, the plan to invade Bulgaria dropped into oblivion. Constantine V was succeeded by his half-Khazar son Leo IV, who abandoned the Bulgarian project in order to secure his throne. He had five half-brothers, the sons of his father's third marriage, who were threats to his power, and immediately after taking the throne he was forced to exile two of them when he discovered that they were at the center of a conspiracy to remove him from the throne. Then he began to plan an attack against the Arabs in Syria, which he saw as more urgent than the Bulgarian campaign.[2]

He never sent his troops into war, though; he died in 780 after only five years on the throne, and his nine-year-old son became the emperor Constantine VI. The little boy's mother served as his regent. Her name was Irene, like her Khazar mother-in-law, but she was from an old Athenian family.

The youth of the emperor and the regency of a woman in Constantinople struck the new Abbasid caliph al-Mahdi, son of al-Mansur, as a fatal weakness in the empire. He launched a new offensive into Asia Minor and drove the Byzantine defenders away in record time, sweeping all the way to the Bosphorus Strait and setting up a camp at the port city of Chrysopolis, right across the water from Constantinople.[3]

This was embarrassing for the regent Irene, who had to pay him an enormous ransom and agree to a yearly tribute in order to get him to withdraw. Perhaps feeling the need for a strong alliance to back her up, in 782 she sent two messengers all the way across to the kingdom of the Franks, and asked Charlemagne to betroth one of his daughters to the eleven-year-old emperor.

Charlemagne could easily think of himself, at this point, as equal in stature to the regent of Constantinople. He controlled the lands of the Franks and Italians, and he was creating a dynasty; he had crowned his third son Pippin* as king of Italy, his fourth son Louis the Pious as king of the Frankish territory Aquitaine, and he ruled over them as an emperor rules over vassal kings. His second son, Charles the Younger, had been designated to inherit the job of king of the Franks. Charlemagne had taken on the responsibility of protecting and defining the Papal States (the pope's land now stretched from Rome in a band across Italy, encompassing Rome, Sutri, and the old Byzantine lands once governed from Ravenna), which made him defender of the Christian faith.

He was the most powerful king in the west, and also the king with the strongest sense of Christian mission in his empire-building. An alliance between the Carolingians and the Byzantine emperors would create not only a united front against the Arabs, but an empire of the spirit: a western mirror for the eastern empire, a Christian counterpart to the ever-advancing Islamic kingdom.

Charlemagne also had plenty of daughters to make useful alliances with (and a lot of sons; in his long life, he had four wives, six additional consorts, and twenty children), and he agreed to marry his third-oldest daughter,

---

*Charlemagne's oldest son, Pippin the Hunchback, had quarrelled with his father and been disinherited, and Charlemagne then renamed his third son, Carloman, "Pippin" so that he would still have a Pippin in the family line.

Rotrude, to Constantine VI. The little girl was eight years old, so the betrothal took place in name only while both children remained with their parents.[4]

Theoretically, the marriage could have become reality when Rotrude reached adolescence—which, in the eighth century, was fairly loosely defined. Certainly when Constantine VI turned sixteen, in 787, he could have asked for the thirteen-year-old Rotrude to be sent to him. But instead, his mother Irene broke off the engagement. Her position was more secure now, and she no longer needed an alliance with the Frankish king. In fact, Charlemagne's growing power threatened the remaining enclaves of Byzantine-loyal land on the Italian peninsula.

The broken engagement was an insult to Charlemagne, who had been growing not just in power but also in his role as Christian king. The days of the mayor of the palace, reluctant to lay full hold of royal power, were long past. Charlemagne had gathered around him a royal circle of scholars and clerics who were filling in the gaps from his early education (he had received from his father much more military training than book-learning and had never learned to write); they not only discussed with him the finer points of theology, philosophy, and grammar, but also called him "King David," after the Old Testament monarch who was handpicked by God to lead the chosen people.* Under the guidance of his personal tutor Alcuin, a British churchman whom Charlemagne had recruited to teach his sons, the king of the Franks developed a stronger and stronger sense of mission. His conquests were, in his own eyes, forceful evangelism: bringing the Gospel to stubborn unbelievers who needed to be saved not just from their sins but from their own unwillingness to hear.[5]

Earlier in the decade, he had concluded a campaign against the Saxons with exactly this sort of persuasion. The Saxon resistance to his rule and the Saxon toll on his army had so angered him that, in 782, he had ordered forty-five hundred Saxon prisoners to be massacred. Their leader Widukind had escaped, but after three years on the run he had finally been forced to surrender. As part of his surrender, Widukind had to agree to Christian baptism; and afterward Charlemagne decreed that any "unbaptized Saxon who conceals himself among his people and refuses to seek baptism, but rather chooses to remain a pagan shall die." A Saxon who stole from a church, or did violence to a priest, or indulged himself in the old Saxon rites instead of Christian worship, would be put to death. And any Saxon who did not observe Lent properly would be executed.[6]

---

*Charlemagne's intellectual curiosity and his personal tutor's teaching combined to spark a revival of learning often called the "Carolingian renaissance": innovations in art, music, architecture, and calligraphy can be traced back to their beginnings under Charlemagne's sponsorship.

Alcuin objected. "Abate a little of your threatening," he told the king, "and do not force them by public compulsion until faith has thoroughly grown in their hearts."7 Charlemagne considered the argument and agreed, revoking the death penalty. This did not change his sense of duty. He was bringing not merely salvation, but right doctrine and practice, to the western world.

Irene of Byzantium did not see Charlemagne as the king of the Christian west. As far as she was concerned, *she* held the highest God-sanctioned authority in the known world. After she broke Constantine VI's engagement, she refused to yield the throne to her son even though he was old enough to rule in his own name. She named herself not just regent, but empress; and on that authority, she summoned a church council—the Second Council of Nicaea—to reverse all of the icon-condemning pronouncements made during the reigns of Leo III and his successors.8

Irene struggled for three years to reign as empress, but too many of the men in Constantinople resented her usurpation, and in 790 the army forced her to hand over authority to Constantine VI. Unfortunately, the rightful emperor turned out to be weak, sadistic, and incompetent. In 791, he set out on the Bulgarian campaign that his grandfather had planned, and was twice defeated by the Bulgarian khan Kardam: "He joined battle without calculation or order," Theophanes writes, "and was severely defeated. He fled back to the city after losing many men." The imperial guard, deciding that it had made a mistake, began to plan a revolt that would put Constantine VI's uncle Nikephorus—one of the half-brothers who had been involved in the conspiracy against Constantine's own father—on the throne instead.9

Like his father, Constantine VI discovered the plot. Unlike his father, he did not show mercy by exiling the conspirators. Instead he had all five of his uncles arrested and brought to court. He blinded Nikephorus (who probably had not even been centrally involved in the conspiracy) and, in an act of completely gratuitous cruelty, cut the tongues out of the other four brothers.

Then he blundered back into conflict with the Bulgarians. This time, the khan Kardam threatened to invade Thracia unless Constantine VI paid him tribute. "The Emperor put horse-turds into a towel," Theophanes writes, "and sent him this message, 'I have sent you such tribute as is appropriate for you.'" After insulting Kardam, he lost his nerve; when the Bulgarian khan approached at the head of his army, Constantine VI went out to meet him and agreed to send him tribute after all.10

This was too much for the army, and Irene was able to talk the officials and chief officers at court into a plot against her son. On a June morning in 797, Constantine VI was leaving the Hippodrome after watching a horse race when he saw palace guards approaching him. He knew at once that they were coming to overpower him; he ran through the streets of the city, down to the port, and escaped on board one of his warships. But his companions on board were in the pay of his mother. They brought him back to the city, led him into the palace, and shut him in the imperial chamber where he had been born: the Purple Room, reserved for the lying-in of empresses. "By the will of his mother and her advisors," Theophanes tells us, "at around the ninth hour he was terribly and incurably blinded with the intention of killing him. . . . In this way his mother Irene took power."[11]

As far as Charlemagne was concerned, the throne of Constantinople was now empty. Irene was a woman, and she had no legitimate claim to the Byzantine throne. Also Charlemagne, with his passion for correct doctrine, found Irene's support for icons unacceptable. Although the pope had assured him that icons were not "graven images," he was not convinced; he even put together a theological committee of his own to study the report of the Second Council of Nicaea and write a rebuttal. (The rebuttal, called the *Libri Carolini*, was sent to Rome, where the pope apparently ignored it.) In his eyes, Irene was not only female and a usurper, but also an idol-worshipper.[12]

At the same time, Charlemagne was receiving constant proofs of his own high status among the kingdoms of the west. In 798, the ruler of Asturias, the Christian kingdom in the mountains north of al-Andalus, sent him a formal embassy that requested his recognition for the legitimacy of the king. Since its beginnings in 718 as a tiny and poverty-stricken realm of resistance to Muslim rule, Asturias had grown; the Asturian king Alfonso II now ruled over a realm that included the neighboring city of Leon and the land along the coast all the way down to the city of Lisbon. Alfonso II wanted recognition from Charlemagne, the greatest Christian king of the west, for the legitimacy of his own throne. Charlemagne, never doubting that such an assurance was in his power, gave it.

The following year, he was asked to carry out an even more imperial duty. Pope Leo III, who had occupied the papal throne in Rome since 795, had run into trouble. He was not terribly popular in Rome, either because he was not an aristocrat or because he was immoral and dishonest; no proof for the latter accusations survives, so it is difficult to trace the roots of the enmity. For whatever reason, the hostility swelled in Rome until, in 799, a band of his enemies attacked him in the middle of a sacred procession and tried to cut out his eyes and tongue.[13]

Unlike the unfortunate Nikephorus, who had received the same treatment over in Constantinople, Leo III managed to escape with cuts on his face, but with his eyes and tongue intact. He fled to Charlemagne and asked the king to help him drive his enemies from the city.

At Leo's consecration as pope, Charlemagne had promised to defend him.

51.1: The Empire of Charlemagne

"My task, assisted by the divine piety, is everywhere to defend the Church of Christ," he had written to Leo, "abroad, by arms, against pagan incursions and the devastations of such as break faith; at home, by protecting the Church in the spreading of the Catholic faith." He had not envisioned defending the church at home with arms, which was what Leo needed; and the situation was complicated by the fact that most of his Frankish officials believed that the charges were true.[14]

But whether or not Leo was guilty was almost a side issue. The *position* of the bishop of Rome had to be unassailable. If the pope spoke for God, he could not be removed by the same sorts of earthly machinations that had brought Constantine VI to a wretched end. Yet in order to protect the office of the papacy from becoming another throne to be contested and won by force, Constantine would have to exercise force on its behalf.

He delayed taking action, thinking the problem through. Ultimately, it seems, his advisor Alcuin swayed his mind, pointing out that Charlemagne was now the only remaining representative of God in the known world who still had any power to right wrongs.

> There have hitherto been three persons of great eminence in the world, namely the Pope, who rules the see of Peter . . . and you have kindly informed me what has happened to him. The second is the Emperor who holds sway over the second Rome—and common report has now made known how wickedly the governor of such an empire has been deposed. . . . The third is the throne on which our Lord Jesus Christ has placed you to rule over our Christian people, with greater power, clearer insight and more exalted royalty than the aforementioned dignitaries. On you alone the whole safety of the churches of Christ depends.[15]

As the last protector of the church, Charlemagne's duty was clear.

So, in 800, Charlemagne sent the pope home to Rome with an armed bodyguard. He followed, marching "in full martial array," with his army into the city. When he arrived, Leo put his hand on the copy of the Gospels in St. Peter's Cathedral and swore, in the presence of onlookers, that he was guiltless of any wrongdoing. With Charlemagne and his soldiers standing by, the oath was effective.[16]

Charlemagne lingered in the city until Christmas Day. He went to morning mass, knelt for the prayers, and as he began to get to his feet, Leo III came forward and put a gold crown on his head. The crowd, which had been coached, cheered: "Long life and victory to Charles, the most pious Augustus, the great, peace-loving Emperor, crowned by God!" He had been crowned *imperator et augustus*, two titles that belonged to the emperor of Rome—titles that, in the eyes of the Byzantine court, had long ago been transferred to Constantinople.[17]

But in the eyes of Charlemagne, the title of emperor had been unclaimed until his coronation. The official description of the event, written afterwards by a Frankish cleric, explains, "When, in the land of the Greeks, there was no longer an emperor and when the imperial power was being exercised by a woman, it seemed to Pope Leo himself and . . . to the whole Christian people, that it would be fitting to give the title of emperor to the king of the Franks, Charles."[18]

Charles's biographer Einhard claims that Charlemagne knew nothing about the plan to crown him and denied ever wanting the imperial title. But he is the only writer who assumes such massive ignorance on the part of the sharp-minded and wary king. The crowning on Christmas Day was simply a formal recognition of an authority that Charlemagne had been claiming for some time: the authority to stand as the protector of faith, guarantor of civilization, and highest civil power in the Christian world.

In Constantinople, the coronation was scorned as meaningless. But Irene was not in a good position to defend herself as the true protector of the faith and guarantor of civilization. Her rule had been chaotic, murderous, and ineffective. In 802, her finance minister led a coup against her and removed her from the throne. He forced her to go into exile within the walls of a monastery she had built herself, and was crowned emperor in her place as Nikephoros I.[19]

The following year, Nikephoros I approached Charlemagne by way of ambassadors and suggested a treaty that would protect the city of Venice, still Byzantine-loyal, from Frankish occupation. Eventually the two men came to an agreement, the *Pax Nicephori*. Nikephoros I and Byzantium would keep control of Venice and its important port. In return, Charlemagne would receive a generous annual payment.

The terms made it very clear that this was a treaty between equals. But in signing it, Nikephoros I gave himself the imperial title, yet refused to call Charlemagne "Emperor."

TIMELINE 51

CENTRAL UNIFIED ARAB CHINA ASIA SILLA EMPIRE	FRANKS BULGARS LOMBARDS BYZANTIUM ASTURIAS

Tang Xuanzong (712–756)

Suleiman (715–717)

Tervel (700–721)

Liutprand (712–744)

Theodosius III
(715–717)

Pope Gregory II
(715–731)

Patriarch Germanos
(715–730)

Umar II (717–720)   Charles Martel   Leo III
Siege of Constantinople (718)   (717–741)   (717–741)

Yazid II (720–724)   Pelayo (718–737)

Wu Daozi   Battle of Toulouse (721)

Hisham (724–743)   Theuderic IV (721–737)

Piluoge of the
Nanzhao (728–748)   Sutri Donation (728)

Pope Gregory III (731–741)

Li Bai   Battle of Tours (732)

Mun of the Balhae   Carloman   Constantine V   Pope Zachary
Wang Wei   (737–793)   (741–747)/   (741–775)   (741–752)

Gyeongdeok (742–765)   Pippin the Younger (741–751)

Walid II (743–744)   Childeric III (743–751)

Yazid III (744)

Marwan II (744–750)

Geluofeng of the
Nanzhao (748–779)

al-Abbas (750–754)   Aistulf (749–756)

Beginning of Abbasid

Battle of Talas (751)   caliphate (750–1258)   Pippin the Younger (751–768)

Beginning of Carolingian   Pope Stephen II
Battle of Xiaguan (754)   al-Mansur (754–775)   dynasty   (752–757)

An Lushan rebellion (755–763)

Tang Suzong   Abd ar-Rahman of   Desiderius (756–774)
(756–762)   Cordoba (emir, 756–788)

Tang Daizong (762–779)

Charles (768–814)/Carloman (768–771)

Charles (774–814)

al-Mahdi (775–785)   Leo IV (775–780)

Kardam (777–c. 803)

Constantine VI/Irene (780–797)

Louis the Pious (781–813)   Pippin (781–810)
as subject king   as subject king

Second Council of Nicaea (787)

Alfonso II (791–842)

Pope Leo III
(795–816)

Irene (797–802)

Coronation of Charlemagne (800)

Nikephoros I (802–811)

The New Sennacherib

Between 786 and 814,
Abbasid merchants spread across the west,
Charlemagne becomes Protector of the Faith in Jerusalem,
and the Bulgarian khan Krum nearly brings Constantinople down

THE ABBASID CALIPH Harun al-Rashid was more willing than Nike-phoros I to court Charlemagne's goodwill. As an Abbasid ally, Charlemagne could not only halt Byzantine expansion to the west but also help guard Abbasid interests against the breakaway Umayyad realm in al-Andalus, the Emirate of Cordoba.

Those interests had more to do with trade routes than with conquest. Harun al-Rashid had been elevated to the caliphate in 786, after the death of his father, al-Mahdi, and very soon had earned himself the nickname "The Righteous." One of his first acts as caliph was to lead the annual pilgrimage to Mecca in person, and when he arrived in Arabia he gave enormous money gifts to the leaders of both Mecca and Medina. "Through Harun, the light has shone forth in every region," declared one of his court poets, "and the straight path has become established by the justness of his conduct. He is a leader whose greatest concern is with raiding the infidels and the Pilgrimage."[1]

In actuality, al-Rashid was more interested in trading than raiding. He did not completely neglect the ongoing war with Byzantium, but during the first fifteen years of his caliphate he was more concerned with security and prosperity than with conquest; most of his energies went into establishing and guarding trade routes. Ten years after his accession, he moved his court from Baghdad to Ar Raqqah, which was closer to the northern trade routes into Khazar territory. Thanks to a semi-peace with the Khazar khan, Arab merchants were now able to travel up north through the Caspian Gates (the pass through the mountains just west of the Caspian Sea) to the Volga river, where they could trade not only with the Khazars but also with Scandinavian merchants. By the eighth century, adventurers from the northern Scandinavian kingdoms had crossed the Baltic Sea and built little trading posts southward along the rivers that reached down into Europe; they offered furs, exotic and luxurious to the Arab buyers, and they wanted gold and silver coins, which were scarce in their own lands.[2]

Al-Rashid's care for the trade routes meant that the Arab hand reached into far distant lands that had remained untouched by conquest. Embassies between Charlemagne's court and al-Rashid's imperial palace at Ar Raqqah travelled back and forth; the Arab ambassadors took the sea route from the Mediterranean coast, south around Italy and up to the port city of Genoa, and then travelling north to Charlemagne's court at Aachen (his newly chosen capital city). With the ambassadors, al-Rashid sent gifts: a water-driven clock, a chess set, spices, and an albino elephant named Abu'l-Abbas, which had been captured from an Indian king. Charlemagne liked the idea of a war elephant. He took it on campaign with him when he had to fight against invading Scandinavians to the north, which undoubtedly startled them.[3]

Al-Rashid's coins ended up even farther away than his elephant. Sometime around the turn of the century, one of his merchants paid a gold dinar into the hands of a Scandinavian trader, who took it north and used it to buy goods from an Anglo-Saxon merchant, who sailed home with the coin and landed at a port in the English kingdom of Mercia. Mercia, which by this point had expanded to cover a good bit of the southeast of England, was under the rule of King Offa, a Christian monarch who considered himself almost equal to Charlemagne in dignity.* Offa even suggested, by way of diplomatic correspondence, that his son and heir should marry one of Charlemagne's daughters—which Charlemagne found so presumptuous that he closed Frankish ports for a while to Mercian ships.[4]

Once in Mercia, the merchant used the coin to buy a night's lodging from an innkeeper, who later that year used it to pay the king's tax-collector. And so it came into the hands of Offa's silversmith, who was mulling over the designs for the next year's English coinage. He liked the pretty patterns on al-Rashid's gold dinar and decided to copy them. The following year, the coins of the English monarch were minted with "OFFA REX" written on one side and, the Arabic words for "There is no God but Allah, and Muhammad is his prophet" on the other. The silversmith, of course, had no idea what the words said; "OFFA REX" is written right side up, but the Arabic letters are all upside down.[5]

Back in Ar Raqqah, enriched by trade with such far-flung lands (and also by his practice of confiscating the goods of his wealthy subjects when they died), al-Rashid grew richer and richer. His splendor was so great that it

*Christianity had spread through southern England after Augustine's mission to the court of Ethelbert in 596; in 664, the Synod of Whitby declared England to be a Christian country, subject to the authority of the pope.

*52.1: Coin of Offa of Mercia, showing inverted Arabic inscription copied from an
Abbasid dinar.* Credit: © The Trustees of the British Museum/Art Resource, NY

became legendary. Less than two generations after his death, tales were already
weaving themselves around him. Within a century, these tales would begin
to take shape as the sprawling *Arabian Nights*: a thousand and one nights'
worth of stories about thieves and heroes, courtesans and queens, with Harun
al-Rashid and his jester at the center of the adventures.[6]

Al-Rashid was also careful with the empire's defenses. He fortified the eastern borders of the empire by making an alliance with the Tang emperor, Tang
Shunzong, in order to check the power of the Tibetans, who threatened to
push into Arabic land near the Oxus river. He defended the western borders
by authorizing ongoing raids into Byzantine land, finally forcing Nikephoros
I to hand over a sizable annual tribute in order to keep the peace: three hundred thousand dinars, which worked out to around a ton and a quarter of gold
added to the caliph's treasury each year.*

In 807, al-Rashid granted Charlemagne yet another proof of the Frankish king's high place in the Christian hierarchy. He agreed to make a decree
that protected the Christian holy sites in Jerusalem, which was under Arab
governance: Christian pilgrims would be allowed, without restriction, to visit
the Church of the Holy Sepulchre (said to stand on Golgotha, the hill of the
Crucifixion), the Via Dolorosa ("way of suffering," the path taken by Christ
on the way to his death), and the other landmarks of their faith. It was a
decree that would naturally have been sent to the pope, the spiritual father of

---

*The dinar was a gold coin with a standard weight of 4.25 grams; the dirham was a silver coin of 3
grams. Typically, twenty dirhams equalled one dinar. See Jere L. Bacharach, "The Dinar versus the
Ducat," *International Journal of Middle East Studies* 4:1 (Jan. 1973), pp. 82–84.

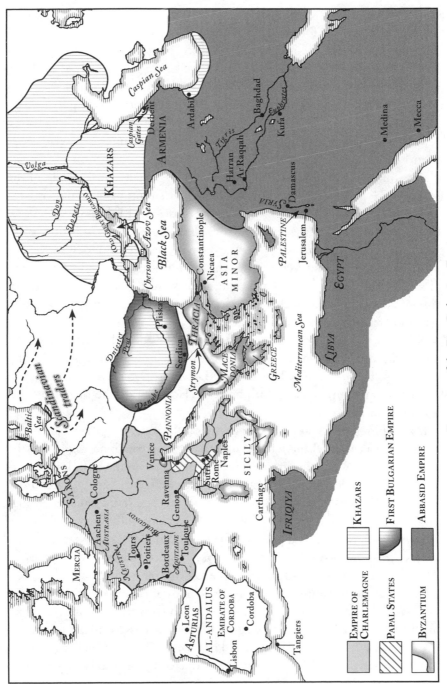

52.1: Expansion of the First Bulgarian Empire

all Christians. But al-Rashid directed his pledge to Charlemagne and promised special treatment for Frankish pilgrims in particular.

At the same time, the bishop of Jerusalem sent two monks to Aachen so
that they could present Charlemagne with the key to the Church of the Holy
Sepulchre itself. Even though the pope himself had crowned Charlemagne as
Protector of the Faith, these must have been sharp-edged little pills for Leo
III to swallow.[7]

Meanwhile the emperor of Constantinople, Nikephoros I, had been
given little leisure to complain about Charlemagne's usurpation of his role
as emperor of the Romans. He was too busy worrying about the khan of the
Bulgarians, who had rocketed (without much attention paid to him by contemporary historians) into a position as one of the great rulers of the west.

The Bulgarian khan was named Krum, and under his rule—which began
sometime between 796 and 803—Bulgaria swelled into a major power. Krum's
southern territories lay directly against the Byzantine border, and Constantine
VI's disastrous attempt to defy the Bulgarian khan Kardam, Krum's predecessor (and possibly his uncle), had clearly revealed just how vulnerable the
Byzantine territory now was.[8]

Nikephoros knew this. Around 805, Krum invaded the territory of the
once-great Avars and folded it into his own, which brought his empire directly
to the eastern border of Charlemagne. Deciding not to wait until Krum
became even more powerful, Nikephoros declared war on the Bulgarians and
began to arm his troops.

It took him over a year to get the troops on the road, partly because he had
to put down a palace rebellion in the middle of his preparations. But by 808, he
was moving troops into the Strymon river valley, on the southern Bulgarian border. Krum's men descended on them before they were at full strength and drove
them back, killing a number of soldiers and officers and (even more damaging)
capturing all of the money Nikephoros had sent along with his generals to use
for payroll—eleven hundred pounds of gold, according to Theophanes.[9]

Hostilities now began in earnest. In 809, Krum led his army against the city
of Serdica, a frontier city within Byzantine territory, and captured it, slaughtering six thousand Byzantine soldiers and hundreds of civilians. Nikephoros did
not handle the defeat well. The officers who had escaped the massacre, afraid
that they would be blamed and executed, sent him a message asking for immunity. When he refused, they all deserted and joined the Bulgarian army.[10]

It took Nikephoros I (who was again distracted by yet another rebellion at
home, this one brought about by his decision to raise everyone's taxes) more
than a year to prepare his army for a return attack. He had decided that the
only appropriate response was to wipe Krum out entirely, and to that end
he imported soldiers from Thracia and Asia Minor to beef up the depleted

forces at Constantinople. In 811, the Byzantine army marched towards Krum's headquarters at Pliska, just west of the Black Sea.[11]

At first, Krum's defenders were defeated and pushed backwards as the Byzantine army advanced. Alarmed by the ferocity of the approaching troops, Krum decided to abandon Pliska. Nikephoros arrived at the Bulgarian capital on July 20, at the head of his army, and ordered his men to slaughter the population, take the goods, and burn the place down: "He ordered that senseless animals, infants, and persons of all ages should be slain without mercy," Theophanes writes. He finally had the upper hand, and he refused to listen to a message from Krum suggesting a treaty.[12]

But Krum was not finished. He had retreated, along with every man he could recruit, into the mountains through which the Byzantine army would have to march on their way home, and had built a wooden wall across the pass. On July 25, heading for Constantinople in triumph, Nikephoros and his men ran directly into the wooden wall. The Bulgarians attacked the trapped army as it piled up in front of the barrier. Nikephoros, fighting at the front, was killed almost at once. Soldiers who tried to climb the wall and escape fell into an enormous ditch that the Bulgarians had dug on the other side and filled with burning logs.[13]

The Byzantine troops were slaughtered. Krum turned out to be no more gracious in victory than his opponent. He beheaded the emperor's corpse, stuck the head on a pole, and—once the flesh had rotted off—had the skull coated in silver so that he could use it as a drinking goblet.

Meanwhile, Nikephoros's son and second-in-command, Staurakios, had escaped, badly wounded by a blow to his spine. His companions hauled him back to Constantinople, where he was crowned emperor in his father's place while lying on a litter. But Staurakios's wound proved incurable. He sank into paralysis, and by October was forced to give power over to his brother-in-law Michael Rangabe. Early the next year, Staurakios died. For months, he had suffered from pressure ulcers on his back, and the wounds turned gangrenous: "No one could bear to approach him because of the foul stench," Theophanes writes.[14]

Krum suggested to Michael Rangabe that it was time for a truce, but even when the Bulgarian king began to approach Constantinople—by early 812, most of Thracia was in Bulgarian hands—the new emperor refused to come to terms. Krum was the second (or perhaps third) most powerful sovereign in Europe for a time, but his skull-goblet represented a world of savage barbarity. In Michael Rangabe's eyes, Krum was a khan, not a king; a wild man, not an equal; a barbarian, not the ruler of a western kingdom. In such a strait, Michael Rangabe decided that it would be more palatable to make his treaty with Charlemagne. The Frankish king might be presumptuous, but he was Christian, and the Franks were at least two centuries past dismembering enemies and using their body parts for tableware.

As Krum drew near to the city walls, Michael Rangabe agreed to acknowledge Charlemagne's claim to be emperor. But the language of the agreement reveals its grudging nature. Michael Rangabe hailed Charlemagne as emperor of the Franks and praised him for the establishment of his Roman empire; but nowhere, at any time, did he call him emperor of the Romans. In exchange for this unwilling admission, Charlemagne agreed to stop contesting Byzantine possession of the Italian city of Venice and its port.[15]

Reassured that Krum would now find an enemy at his back, Michael Rangabe resumed the battle against the Bulgarians. By 813, he had recaptured some of the Thracian territory and had set his army up for a massive, war-ending confrontation near Adrianople.

The two armies met on June 22. "The Christians were grievously worsted in battle," writes Theophanes, "and the enemy won, so much so that most of the Christians had not even waited for the first clash before they took to headlong flight." Clearly, Michael's army had serious doubts about the wisdom of the assault.[16]

Michael Rangabe was forced to flee back to Constantinople; Krum chased him to its walls and then laid siege to the city. Once back inside the walls, Michael Rangabe offered to abdicate, in the face of almost certain assassination should he remain on the throne. The army and the officers had "despaired of being ruled by him any longer" and had decided that Leo the Armenian, military governor of the Byzantine lands in Asia Minor, should be acclaimed as the new emperor.

After a token protest, Leo the Armenian accepted and marched from Asia Minor to Constantinople. He fought his way into the city and was crowned Emperor Leo V by the patriarch on July 12, while Michael and his sons took refuge in a church and put on monks' clothes to demonstrate their willingness to give up power. This saved their lives but not their manhood; Leo V's first act was to castrate Michael's sons before sending them off into monastic exile, wiping out any chance that they might later claim the legitimate rule of Byzantium.[17]

In the meantime Krum was terrifying the city, not least by carrying out a demon-summoning sacrifice right in front of the Golden Gate. He was, in the words of Theophanes, "the new Sennacherib": the Assyrian king of ancient times had tried to wipe out the people of God when he attacked Jerusalem,* and Krum was doing the same.[18]

Leo V offered to meet with Krum under a flag of truce. But he had no

*II Kings 18–19.

intention of honoring the conventions of such a meeting. Conventions governed Christian monarchs, but they did not constrain emperors to treat barbarians like real kings. When Krum approached the meeting place, just outside the city walls, Leo's men tried to assassinate him. "Through their incompetence," Theophanes writes, "they merely wounded him and did not inflict a fatal blow."[19]

Krum escaped, but he was too weakened by his injuries to continue the siege. In fury, he ordered his army to sack the land around Constantinople before he was forced to retreat back towards his homeland to recover. On the way, he burned a good part of Thracia and took scores of captives, whom he settled in Bulgaria as exiles and constant reminders of the Byzantine treachery.

Once recovered, Krum began to plan a final assault on Constantinople. But he was still preparing for the attack when, in 814, he died. Without Krum's fury behind it, the Bulgarian juggernaut lost some of its momentum. Leo V, sending his army against the Bulgarians in an attempt to drive them back out of Thracia, began to have some success. Before long, Krum's successor, his son Omurtag, agreed to a thirty-year peace.

The crisis had ended, but the wild man had almost brought the empire of the Greeks down. More than that, Krum's reign began a Bulgarian dynasty that would control the country without interruption for a century. With the help of the Christianity that was already spreading from the Byzantine captives through the Bulgarian population, the descendents of Krum would begin to shape the Bulgarian horde into a state that could take its place among the kingdoms of the west.[20]

TIMELINE 52

CHINA BYZANTIUM ARAB EMPIRE	FRANKS BULGARS LOMBARDS BRITAIN ASTURIAS
Tang Xuanzong (712–756)	
Suleiman (715–717)	
Leo III (717–741) Umar II (717–720)	Charles Martel
Siege of Constantinople (718)	(717–741) Pelayo (718–737)
Yazid II (720–724)	Battle of Toulouse (721)
Wu Daozi	Theuderic IV (721–737)
Hisham (724–743)	Sutri Donation (728)
Li Bai	Pope Gregory III (731–741)
	Battle of Tours (732)
Wang Wei	Carloman/Pippin the Younger Pope Zachary
	(741–747) (741–751) (741–752)
Constantine V (741–775)	Childeric III (743–751)
Walid II (743–744)	
Yazid III (744)	
Marwan II (744–750)	Aistulf (749–756)
al-Abbas (750–754)	Pippin the Younger (751–768)
Beginning of Abbasid	Beginning of Carolingian Pope Stephen II
Battle of Talas (751) caliphate (750–1258)	dynasty (752–757)
Battle of Xiaguan (754) al-Mansur (754–775)	
An Lushan rebellion (755–763)	Desiderius (756–774)
Tang Suzong Abd ar-Rahman of	Offa of Mercia
(756–762) Cordoba (emir, 756–788)	(757–796)
Tang Daizong (762–779)	Charles (768–814)/Carloman (768–771)
	Charles (774–814)
Leo IV al-Mahdi	Kardam (777–c. 803)
(775–780) · (775–785)	Louis the Pious (781–813) Pippin (781–810)
Constantine VI/Irene (780–797)	as subject king as subject king
Harun al-Rashid (786–809)	
Second Council of Nicaea (787)	Alfonso II (791–842)
	Pope Leo III
Irene (797–802)	(795–816)
	Coronation of Charlemagne (800)
Nikephoros I (802–811)	Krum (c. 803–814)
Tang Shunzong (805–806)	
Staurakios (811)	
Michael Rangabe (811–813)	
Leo V (813–820)	Omurtag (815–831)

Chapter Fifty-Three

Castle Lords and Regents

Between 790 and 872,
the aristocratic clans take control of Silla,
and the Fujiwara take control of Japan

THE KINGS OF Unified Silla and Balhae, east of the crumbling Tang, were adjusting to the new landscape. In the absence of the Tang soldiers who had kept hostilities alive between them, they had worked out a treaty. For the first time in decades, the Sillans were not fighting an unending war; they could put some thought instead into Silla's internal workings.

These were not in the best of shape. By the eighth century, power in Silla was based almost entirely on bloodline, known as "bone rank." An aristocrat whose parents were both of royal descent could boast "Hallowed Bone" status; if only one parent was royal, the child was "True Bone." Until the middle of the seventh century, only Hallowed Bone aristocrats had ruled in Silla, but after the time of King Muyeol the Great (who had begun the unification of the peninsula by conquering Baekje in 660) True Bone aristocrats had held the Sillan throne.[1]

Below the privilege level of those who could claim royal parentage were layers and layers of nobles who held various "head ranks" in decreasing importance, according to the purity of their family descent. There were seventeen bone ranks in all, and those not born to rank could count on a life without privilege. "In Silla, the bone rank is the key to employment," an official named Seol Kyedu had written, in disgust. "If one is not of the nobility, no matter what his talents, he cannot achieve a high rank. I wish to travel west to China."[2]

Seol Kyedu did eventually go to China, where he hoped to earn rank by performing his duties well; the Confucian academies of eighth-century China allowed diligent students to work their way up through the ranks by demonstrating virtue and mastery of the orderly rituals that gave Confucian society its framework. But back in Silla, the bone rank system continued to congeal Sillan society into elaborate and unmoving stratifications, concentrating power only in the hands of the aristocrats and barring capable commoners from ever rising higher.

Around 790, King Wonseong of Silla began to work out a way to bypass these stiff, unyielding categories. Wonseong was True Bone by birth, but he was not in the direct royal line; he had been crowned five years before as the successor to his cousin Seondeok, who had died without sons. Wonseong owed his power to the very True Bone noblemen whose insistence on hereditary privilege was weakening the country.

Nevertheless, he was determined to get capable administrators back into power; so three years after his coronation, he installed a new state examination system. Rather than claiming official positions because of bone rank, candidates would have to show understanding of the Chinese texts and principles taught in the National Confucian Academy, which had been founded in Goguryeo in the fourth century and had managed to survive during the following chaotic centuries. King Wonseong built his new examination system around its teachings: virtue and intelligence, not mere social connections, were the qualities Silla needed in its leaders.[3]

This return to an emphasis on learning, rather than mere heritage, was supported by Confucian monks such as Seol Chong, who grew famous for his ability to take Chinese classics and transcribe them into the language spoken by the people: "He interpreted the Nine Classics in the vernacular, and taught the young," his biographer tells us in the *Samguk sagi*.[4]

This was no easy task. Since writing had come to the Korean peninsula from China, Chinese characters were used by the learned, but they were used primarily to write in Chinese, and the language of Silla still remained without a writing system of its own. To finish his translations, Seol Chong was forced to invent a new system that used Chinese characters to represent Sillan words. The match between characters and words was awkward and imperfect, with tens of thousands of Sillan words left unwritten, but Seol Chong's method survived for almost seven hundred years. The peninsula, very slowly, was inching out from beneath the vast umbrella of Chinese culture.[5]

Like Seol Chong's writing system, Wonseong's reforms were imperfect. His attempts to open the government up to those of lower (or no) bone ranks were unpopular with the True Bone aristocrats who saw their hold on power loosening. The most powerful official in the Sillan government, the vice minister of state (*chipsabu sirang*), led the resistance to Wonseong's efforts, and the king's position was further weakened when his son died before him, leaving a grandson in poor health as his only heir. When King Wonseong died in 798, the grandson, King Soseong, ruled for less than two years before his own death; Soseong's young son Aejang was then crowned, but he was not yet thirteen and power was held by his uncle, who served as his regent.[6]

This brought Unified Silla into a time of slow decline, known to historians

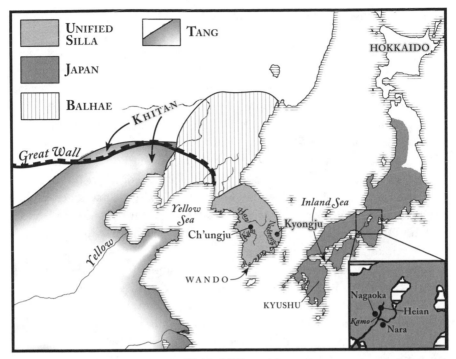

53.1: Unified Silla and Japan

as the Late Period. The turnover of rulers was frequent and violent. In 809, young King Aejang was murdered by his uncle, who ascended the throne as King Heondeok. Immediately Heondeok had to put down a rebellion, led by a descendent of King Muyol who used the excuse of the usurpation to declare himself king in the central city of Ch'ungju. The revolt was quashed, rose up again under the rebel leader's son, and was quashed a second time.[7]

Wonseong's descendents remained on the throne, but the monarch was losing his mandate. And although the aristocracy of Silla had joined in resisting the king's reforms, the nobles didn't stay united for long. Instead, men of high bone rank collected private armies and began to fight amongst themselves for the chunks of power they had pried from the king's hands. In struggling to keep the power to which they had been born, they inadvertently began to change the basis of that very power: increasingly, the size and skill of a man's private army, not his bone rank, became the source of his influence.[8]

The usurping king Heondeok died in 826. His successor, his brother Heungdeok, faced a struggling, armed countryside. The king's forces had withdrawn inwards, towards the capital. Pirates from China roamed the coast, blocking the trade routes, kidnapping unwary Sillans and selling them into slavery. When Heungdeok's young commander Chang Pogo asked for permission to establish a coastal garrison on the southwestern island of Wando,

Heungdeok agreed at once: "The king gave Chang an army of ten thousand men," the *Samguk sagi* tells us, "and bade him pitch camp on the island." Chang's patrol of the Yellow Sea drove most of the pirates out of Silla's waters, but it also made him increasingly powerful; in his offshore base, out of sight of the king, he built himself a little private kingdom of his own.[9]

When Heungdeok died without sons, open war broke out. His cousin and nephew fought over the throne; one was killed, the other committed suicide after less than a year on the throne, and a third relative claimed the crown. He too was removed in a matter of months by Chang Pogo, now master of the Yellow Sea, and Chang Pogo's ally Kim Ujing. Together, the two men marched into the capital of Kyongju; Kim Ujing had himself crowned as King Sinmu, and Chang Pogo took up the position of power behind the throne.

Sinmu lasted for all of four months before an illness struck him down. His son Munseong was crowned in his place. But unlike his predecessors, Munseong managed to hang on to the throne for almost two decades—in large part because the Sillan nobility and their private armies were beginning to work out a satisfactory division of power. Rather than fighting for control of the capital city and the crown, they turned outwards; like Chang Pogo, they built themselves little private enclaves in outlying areas, where they reigned supreme. From their personal kingdoms, they traded—as Chang Pogo had— with the merchants of Tang China and with Japan, building their wealth as well as their power. King Munseong survived so long, in part, because he had become increasingly irrelevant.[10]

In 846, Chang Pogo—who had provided the blueprint for these private kingdoms—proposed to marry his daughter to King Munseong, which would have given him a royal connection to add to his private army and his control of the sea. This was too much power for the True Bone aristocrats to take, and several of them joined together to mastermind Chang Pogo's assassination.[11]

This left Munseong on the throne but not in control. In less than a century, Unified Silla had become a country unified only in name. The most powerful aristocrats with the largest private armies erected fortresses at the center of their domains, ruling them almost as independent petty kings; they were called "castle lords" and exercised the right to collect taxes for themselves, without passing any of the money on to the putative center of government in Kyongju. The Buddhist monasteries that dotted the countryside took advantage of the king's weakness to do the same, collecting land and tax revenues on their own account. Farmers and tradesmen, with no armies and no protection from the king, increasingly began to turn outlaw, and robber bands roamed through the hills.[12]

Silla was tottering, and about to fall.

JUST ACROSS THE WATER to the east, a few clouds had begun to drift across the light cast by the heavenly sovereign of Japan, the polestar of his people.

Heavenly Sovereign Kammu sat on the throne, but he no longer ruled from Nara, the capital where the Yoro Code had been published. Instead, he had decided to break with the past. Now he ruled from a brand new court, thirty miles northwest, in the city of Nagaoka.*

Kammu was the polestar of Japan, the country's connection with the divine, the guarantor of order and law—but these resounding responsibilities were rapidly becoming symbolic. Power in Japan was scattered through the countryside, where clan leaders continued to claim their own authority. The chronicles from Kammu's reign suggest that the monasteries and aristocrats of Nara had been actively gathering more and more wealth and power to themselves; in the year of the move to the new court, one account tells us, the "Buddhist temples in the capital were forbidden to accumulate wealth in an unreasonable manner," while "the wealthy were forbidden to make loans to the poor in exchange for mortgages on their homesteads." Like the monasteries, the aristocrats had been lending money at usurious rates, and claiming the farms of those who could not pay.[13]

One particular aristocratic clan, the Fujiwara—descendents of Nakatomi no Kamatari, lifelong friend of the heavenly sovereign Tenji—had become more powerful in Nara than all the rest. The Fujiwara clan had inherited from Nakatomi no Kamatari the privilege of overseeing court rites and rituals, a responsibility that gave Fujiwara officials control over the center of the palace. By the beginning of Kammu's rule, there were no fewer than four major branches of the family living in and around the capital city.

Kammu moved to Nagaoka, in large part, to get away from the Fujiwara courtiers who surrounded him at every moment of the day. The move was made in a frenzy, almost desperate in its haste; three hundred thousand men, working around the clock, built an entire royal complex in less than six months. But although he could leave Nara behind, he could not escape the tentacles of Fujiwara power. His chief consort was the daughter of a Fujiwara nobleman; the posts of "Great Minister of the Right" and "Great Minister of the East" were held by Fujiwaras; and he was forced by necessity to appoint a Fujiwara official as overseer of his new capital city.[14]

For ten years, Heavenly Sovereign Kammu lived in his expensive palace in Nagaoka. He was battered by bad luck, illness, death in his family, and bloody infighting among his court officials, and by 794 he had decided that a curse hung over the city. He would not go back to Nara, which had been equally troublesome for him. Instead he moved the capital again, this time to the city of Yamashiro-no-kuni. Rather wistfully, he ordered it renamed Heian-kyo, "Capital of Peace."[15]

*Not the same as the modern city of Nagaoka; see inset of Map 53.1.

This time the move stuck. Nagaoka slowly crumbled away, while Heian—modern Kyoto—remained the capital of Japan for nearly a thousand years.*

Kammu died in 806, after ruling for over two decades and fathering thirty-two children. Between 806 and 833, he was succeeded by three of his sons in turn. These sons shared a single characteristic: each one abdicated, handing the throne over to the next. The oldest, Heizei, was on the throne for only three years, when he became seriously ill and abdicated in favor of his younger brother Saga.† After fourteen years, Heavenly Sovereign Saga abdicated as well, and the throne went to the third brother, Junna. Junna reigned for ten years before handing the crown to his nephew Ninmyo, Saga's twenty-three-year-old son, in 833.[16]

All of these abdications made one thing very clear: the heavenly sovereign was no emperor, not in the sense of a Chinese or Byzantine or Persian emperor. He did not rule, as they did, controlling armies and laws. He shone, and in his light, power was dispersed to others. Fujiwara officials controlled the day-to-day running of the court and its rituals. The provinces farther away from the city were controlled by their governors, who were responsible for collecting their own taxes—and who quite often used those taxes for their own purposes, rather than passing them on to the capital.[17]

They were not above padding the tax bills either, and both inside and outside of the capital, the farmers and small tradesmen of Japan found themselves under continual pressure to hand over more of their meagre profits. This extortion, unchecked by the heavenly sovereign, fell on a countryside already strained by Kammu's two successive moves. Each change of the capital city had required a raise in taxes to pay for the new construction and the drafting of able-bodied farmers into a temporary workforce to build the emperor's new residences. A note in the royal chronicles for 842, during the reign of the heavenly sovereign Ninmyo, gives us a glimpse of grotesque poverty just outside Heian's own walls: "The Office of the Capital was ordered to gather up and burn some five thousand, five hundred skulls lying around," the chronicler tells us. The peasants who lived along the Kamo river, which flowed past Heian, were so poor that they could not afford tombs or deep graves for their dead; instead they scratched holes in the sand for the bodies, and as the river wore the sand away, the bones were flung up onto the shore.[18]

The heavenly sovereign Ninmyo abdicated in 850; he had married a Fujiwara noblewoman, and his half-Fujiwara son Montoku became the heavenly

---

*The move to Heian marked the end of the "Nara period" (710–794) and the beginning of the "Heian period" (794–1185) in Japanese history.

†Heizei recovered, unexpectedly, and mounted an attempt to get the throne back, which ended badly; Saga resisted, Heizei's accomplices were arrested or committed suicide, and the ex–heavenly sovereign was forced to enter a Buddhist monastery, where he remained until his death fourteen years later.

sovereign. Montoku, twenty-three when he inherited his crown, had little to do during his royal days. The Fujiwara officials were ruling the country on his behalf, and he seems to have spent most of his time in the women's quarters of the palace. By the time he was in his early thirties, he had fathered twenty-seven children.[19]

But his primary consort was Akira Keiko, daughter of the ambitious Fujiwara nobleman Fujiwara no Yoshifusa. Yoshifusa engineered the marriage, watched with satisfaction as Akira Keiko gave birth to a son and heir, and then leveraged his connection with the throne to be appointed Chief Minister, *daijo daijin*, in 857. The heavenly sovereign Montoku died just one year later, at the age of thirty-two. His son Seiwa, eight years old, was crowned his heir; and Yoshifusa, the child's Fujiwara grandfather, had himself appointed as *Sessho*, or regent, for the underage king.

It was the first time that an "outsider," someone not from the royal line, had been given the job of regent. But by this time, the royal line and the Fujiwara clan had become so intertwined that the whole concept of a separate royal line was merely symbolic—as symbolic as the power of the young heavenly sovereign. Seiwa sat on the throne as the polestar, beautiful, honored, and powerless; the Sessho ruled on his behalf.

Even when Seiwa reached the age of the maturity, the Sessho remained on. He was an official outside of the law, beyond the royal sphere, with his power derived from the heavenly sovereign but eclipsing its source. Yoshifusa even arranged Seiwa's marriage for him, wedding him to Yoshifusa's own niece (the young ruler's first cousin once removed). This made him, simultaneously, the emperor's grandfather, regent, and uncle-in-law; the marriage created once more tie between the royal line and the Fujiwara clan, one more point of reflected power. The young woman herself, Takaiko, was given no choice in the matter. She had a lover of her own, but later poems tell of his unpleasant fate: he was exiled from court, forced to enter a monastery, and did not see his beloved again until he had grown old and feeble.[20]

In 872, Yoshifusa died, but he passed the power of his office on to his adopted son, Fujiwara no Mototsune. Heavenly Sovereign Seiwa was at this time twenty-two and in no real need of a regent. But Mototsune was anxious to exercise the full power of his office. Four years later, he convinced Seiwa to abdicate, at the age of twenty-six, and hand the crown over to the heir apparent, Seiwa's five-year-old son Yozie.

To die and leave the throne to a child was often unavoidable. But to *abdicate* in favor of a child shows one thing clearly: the heavenly sovereign no longer needed to rule. The Sessho, refracting his glory, would rule for him. The sovereign himself needed merely to exist: a necessary, but passive, node of connection with the divine order.

TIMELINE 53

FRANKS   BULGARS   LOMBARDS
BRITAIN   ASTURIAS

CHINA JAPAN   UNIFIED   ARAB
SILLA   EMPIRE

Mun of the Balhae

Wang Wei   (737–793)

Carloman/Pippin the Younger   Pope Zachary   **Gyeongdeok** (742–765)
(741–747) (741–751)   (741–752)   **Walid II** (743–744)
Childeric III (743–751)   **Yazid III** (744)
                                   Marwan II (744–750)

Aistulf (749–756)   **al-Abbas** (750–754)

Pippin the Younger (751–768)   Battle of Talas (751)   Beginning of Abbasid
Beginning of Carolingian   Pope Stephen II   caliphate (750–1258)
dynasty   (752–757)
                          Battle of Xiaguan (754)   **al-Mansur** (754–775)
              Desiderius (756–774)   An Lushan rebellion (755–763)
Offa of Mercia   **Tang Suzong**   **Abd ar-Rahman** of
(757–796)   (756–762)   Cordoba (emir, 756–788)
                          Tang Daizong (762–779
Charles (768–814)/**Carloman** (768–771)
              Charles (774–814)   **al-Mahdi** (775–785)
      Kardam (777–c. 803)

                                Seondeok (780–785)
Louis the Pious (781–813)   Pippin (781–810)   **Kammu** (781–806)
as subject king   as subject king   Move to Nagaoka
                          Wonseong (785–798)
         Alfonso II (791–842)
              Pope Leo III   Seol Chong
               (795–816)   Move to Heian

                                Soseong (798–800)
Coronation of **Charlemagne** (800)   **Aejung** (800–809)

      Krum (c. 803–814)   **Tang Shunzong** (805–806)
                             Heizei (806–809)
                              Saga (809–823)**Heondeok** (809–826)
      Omurtag (815–831)

                              Junna (823–833)
                                Heungdeok (826–836)
                                 Chang Pogo
                          Ninmyo (833–850)
                                 Sinmu (839)
                           Munseong (839–857)

                            Montoku (850–858)

                              Seiwa (858–876)
                            Yoshifusa as Sessho
                             (858–872)

                              Mototsune as
                           Sessho (872–891)
                              Yozie (876–884)

Chapter Fifty-Four

The Triumph of the Outsiders

Between 806 and 918,
military governors, rebels, and Turks destroy the Tang
and the period of the Five Dynasties and Ten Kingdoms begins,
while rebel commanders and exiled princes
divide Unified Silla into the Later Three Kingdoms

THE TANG EMPIRE was shrunken and struggling, but all was not lost. In the aftermath of the An Lushan rebellion, the Tang emperors had managed to restore a reasonably effective system of tax collection. The sale of salt was now a royal monopoly, pouring yet more cash into the royal coffers. The crown was weakened, but not poverty-stricken.

Taxes and salt may have been under royal control, but the outlying provinces that had once been firmly under Tang rule definitely were not. Far too many of the *fanzhen*, the military governors appointed by earlier emperors, had turned into mini-monarchs controlling their own lands. Some of these military commanders were of Chinese ancestry; many others were of "barbarian" descent, warrior chiefs who had been allowed to settle their people within Tang borders and had, in exchange, agreed to defend the Tang land against outside invaders.

The loyalty of the *fanzhen* to the Tang varied widely. Some of the border peoples, like the Turkish tribe of the Shatuo, were transforming themselves into Chinese, while others ignored the emperor at Chang'an. The borders of the Tang empire had gotten not just permeable, but indistinct. The farther from Chang'an a traveller got, the harder it was to figure out whether or not he had left Tang land.[1]

In 806, the emperor Tang Xianzong began an attempt to restore his power in these outlying lands. In a series of wars fought between 806 and 817, he slowly whipped the *fanzhen* back into the fold. When he captured the recalcitrant governors, he brought them to the capital city and had them executed. By 820, he had almost managed to restore the palace's control over the old Tang land.[2]

And then, just as he reached for the final prize of a unified empire, the vigorous young emperor died. He was only forty-two, and it was whispered that two court eunuchs who resented the emperor's power had poisoned him; it was more than whispered that his son and heir Muzong had a hand in the unexpected death. Whether or not this was true, Muzong ascended the throne and let his father's conquests slip away. Both Tang Muzong and his successor, his son Tang Jingzong, were known for their devotion to banqueting and ball games; they allowed the court eunuchs to run the day-to-day operations of the palace, and one chronicler laments that "the business of the state was almost entirely given up."[3]

By 827, the *fanzhen* were once again entrenched in their independent fortresses, and the palace eunuchs were thoroughly in control of the doings at court. They murdered Tang Jingzong, who was eighteen and had ruled less than three years, and instead supported the coronation of Jingzong's younger brother Tang Wenzong.

Tang Wenzong remained alive and on the throne for fourteen years, but only because he was willing to relinquish the real power of the throne to the *fanzhen* on the edges of his empire and the officials in his palace, most of whom were eunuchs (thus less likely to seize the throne in hopes of establishing a dynasty). This state of affairs could have led to chaos and disorganization, as in fact it had in Unified Silla. But the eunuchs did a perfectly adequate job of running the country. In 838, twelve years into Wenzong's puppet reign, the Japanese monk Ennin travelled to Tang China. His travel diary chronicled a well-organized, efficient state that appeared to be prospering: he remarks, impressed, that there were over four thousand shops in one central district in the capital city Chang'an, that the canals were "lined on both sides with rich and noble houses quite without a break," that the river was filled with merchant ships and boats carrying the royal salt.[4]

Efficient administrators though they were, the eunuchs would have been helpless in any military crisis; they were bureaucrats, given no training in the art of warfare. But by pure good luck, no invasion threatened. No ambitious *fanzhen* tried to take over the center of the Tang empire. The kingdoms of Balhae and Unified Silla and Yamato Japan were preoccupied with their own affairs. During the rule of Tang Wenzong's successor, the Uighur empire to the north was divided by civil war and disintegrated; nomads from the north took advantage of its weakness to invade and sack the Uighur capital, Ordu-Baliq, and its people fled to the south and west. And the Tibetan empire, which had for so long troubled the southwestern border of the Tang, was ripped apart by a religious war.[5]

The tentative stability of the Tang meant that the emperors and their eunuchs could concentrate on trade, on that useful salt monopoly, on careful tax collection, and on literary pursuits. In 869, during the reign of the emperor Tang Yizong, the king of Unified Silla even sent his son, the Sillan crown prince, to study in the Chinese capital.

All continued well—until the dreaded military crisis erupted. It came not from outside, but from inside. And although it was not led by one of the *fanzhen*, it was precipitated by the same tension that many of them felt: that of an outsider who wished to become an insider.

In 874, a young man named Huang Chao took the civil service examination and failed it. He was furious. Since childhood Huang Chao had been known for his intelligence and his literary abilities and he could not believe that the exam had judged him unworthy. The examination system had been criticized before; a few decades earlier, the public official and poet Han Yu had complained bitterly that the training that prepared students to do well on the exams merely taught "literary tricks" and pat answers, and had nothing to do with real learning. Now Huang Chao, smarting from his failure, proclaimed that the exam system was nothing more than a tool of exclusion, used by the government to block the unwanted from official positions.[6]

Huang Chao turned outlaw. Stationing himself in the northeast of China, near the coast and just south of the Yellow river, he began to sell salt illegally, breaking the government monopoly—which he believed to be unjust. He was soon joined by other malcontents. Several bad growing seasons in the north of China meant that too many farmers were hungry and desperate. The band of smugglers grew larger and began to indulge in Robin Hood escapades, robbing rich merchants on the nearby roads, raiding wealthy towns, and then attacking and killing foreign traders along the coast.[7]

Tang troops were finally dispatched from Chang'an to arrest the trouble-makers, but Huang Chao and his confederates fought back. More and more farmers and peasants joined their cause. Before long, the robber band had swelled into a full-fledged rebellion with over half a million followers.

Four years of fighting followed. The rebels captured Luoyang and fought their way far south, crossing the Yangtze and capturing Tang land all the way down to the city of Guangzhou. From this base Huang Chao turned back north and began to make his way towards Chang'an itself. In 880, he arrived at the walls of the capital city and captured it in what he later called a "blood bath."[8]

The emperor Tang Xizong, Tang Yizong's successor, fled with his court from the city and fortified himself instead at the western city of Chengdu. In control of the capital city and the palace, Huang Chao ascended the throne and announced himself king of a new dynasty.[9]

Tang Xizong, determined to fight back, hired Turkish mercenaries from the northern border tribes of the Shatuo to reinforce his damaged army. Like the *fanzhen*, they were a more or less independent military power on the outer edge of Tang power; unlike the *fanzhen*, who hoped to escape Tang control altogether, the Shatuo were outsiders who desperately wished to be insiders.

The Shatuo commander Li Keyong, a Turk who had already adopted a Chinese name and Chinese customs, led forty thousand horsemen south and helped Tang Xizong lay siege to Chang'an. In 882, outside Chang'an's walls, the Tang army and the Turkish mercenaries together met an enormous rebel army commanded by Huang Chao. The Battle of Liangtianpo was a defeat for Huang Chao. He was driven northwards, away from Chang'an and the land he had already conquered, back towards the home territory of the Shatuo. Li Keyong followed him, harassing him all the way.

In this he was aided by one of Huang Chao's former allies, Zhu Wen, who had deserted Huang Chao and gone over to the side of the Tang. He was given charge of part of the royal army, and together the two men worked to put the rebellion down.

The rebels met the government forces again in 884 on the banks of the Yellow river. This time, Huang Chao and his men were decisively defeated. Huang Chao, fleeing from the carnage, was cornered and committed suicide so that Li Keyong would not get the credit for his capture.

The emperor Tang Xizong rewarded Li Keyong by making him the military governor of most of the north. He then returned to Chang'an, but his re-entry was far from triumphant. The empire was in tatters. The cities of Luoyang and Yangzhou had been put to the torch; the city of Chang'an was destroyed and demoralized. "Chang'an lies in mournful stillness: what does it now contain?" mourned the poet Wei Zhuang:

> Ruined markets and desolate streets, in which ears of wheat are sprouting.
> Fuel-gatherers have hacked down every flowering plant in the Apricot
>   Gardens,
> Builders of barricades have destroyed the willows along the Imperial
>   Canal. . . .
> All the pomp and magnificence of the olden days are buried and passed
>   away;
> Only a dreary waste meets the eye. . . .
> All along the Street of Heaven one treads on the bones of State officials.[10]

Tang Xizong had kept his title, but his power was gone and the days of his dynasty were drawing to an end.

He was succeeded in 888 by his son Tang Zhaozong, who presided over a dying world. For two more decades, the empire lingered on, while the turncoat Zhu Wen and the Turkish general Li Keyong continued to grow in power. Li Keyong had extended his military governorship of the north into a minor kingship—just as *fanzhen*, given the chance, had always done. He had

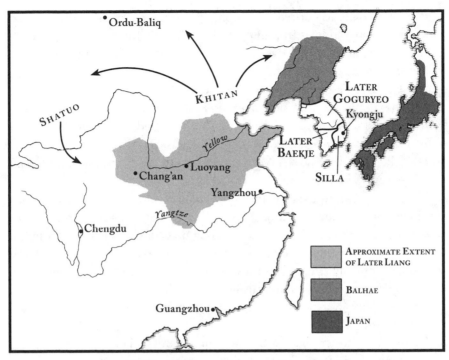

54.1: The Later Liang and the Later Three Kingdoms

installed his own Shatuo allies in official positions throughout his realm and no longer acknowledged the rule of the Tang emperor.[11]

He had also fallen out with his co-commander Zhu Wen. After the end of the rebellion, Zhu Wen had begun to resent the greater rewards given to Li Keyong. He had been slowly taking for himself more and more land between Chang'an and the borders of Li Keyong's province. In 901 and 902, he tried to invade Li Keyong's land, and both times was driven back.

But Zhu Wen had more luck in Chang'an itself. Fearing the power of the general Li Keyong, and hoping to keep Zhu Wen loyal, the emperor gave him a royal title. Zhu Wen accepted the title and then began a slow, careful campaign to isolate the emperor from his supporters: killing or exiling them as traitors, surrounding the unfortunate emperor with his own men, and finally ordering, in the emperor's name, that the whole royal court be moved to the city of Luoyang.[12]

This raised alarm all over the remnants of the empire, and from various cities, loyal officials and soldiers set out for Luoyang, determined to rescue the emperor. When Zhu Wen heard of their approach, he sent his own men to murder the emperor and then—loudly proclaiming his own loyalty to the crown—executed the assassins. The would-be rescuers, either deceived or giving up hope, withdrew.

Zhu Wen then authorized the coronation of the emperor's thirteen-year-old son as Tang Aidi: a true puppet-king, thoroughly under the general's control. The outsider had arrived almost at the center of the Tang empire. He was king in all but name.

The name came next. The following year, Zhu Wen forced Tang Aidi to decree the murder of his nine remaining brothers and all the ministers who were still loyal to the royal family. They were strangled, and their bodies were thrown into a nearby river. Now, Zhu Wen was ready to claim the title for himself. He forced the sixteen-year-old emperor to abdicate and founded his own dynasty, the Later Liang.[13]

It was a short-lived dynasty: the Later Liang would only survive from 907 until 923. But the abdication of the last Tang emperor (and his murder the following year) plunged China into a roiling mass of struggle between minor kingdoms. This period, known as the Five Dynasties and Ten Kingdoms, would last until 960. In a span of just over fifty years, the *fanzhen* would create and then lose a slew of minor realms. Five ruling dynasties would rise and fall in the north; more than ten separate kingdoms would appear and disappear in the south.*

In the far northern lands, a new empire arose. The northern Khitan warchief Abaoji made an alliance with the Shatuo and began a series of conquests that would eventually create an enormous Khitan realm. With the death of the last Tang emperor, the inside of China had disappeared and only the outside remained.[14]

As the *fanzhen* divided China among themselves, the castle lords of Unified Silla were carving lines into their own homeland, and the cracks were deepening to the point of fracture.

The king Gyeongmun, who had sent his son to study in Tang China before its fall, had unwittingly driven a wedge into the fissures. He had married a well-born noblewoman, but she had not borne him an heir, so he had married her sister as well. The second bride was equally barren. While the two royal sisters existed in unhappy tension at the palace, one of King Gyeongmun's concubines bore him a son and heir.

The two queens, resentful and afraid, arranged for the concubine and her baby to be murdered. But as her mistress was dying, the child's wet-nurse snatched her charge away from the assassins and fled with him, finally taking refuge at a monastery. The little boy, Kungye, grew up there, nurtured by the monks and aware of his royal heritage. He could never forget the murder of

---

*The Five Dynasties were the Later Liang (907–923), Later Tang (923–936), Later Jin (936–947), Later Han (947–951), and Later Zhou (951–960); the Ten Kingdoms were the Wu (907–937), Wuyue (907–978), Min (909–945), Chu (907–951), Southern Han (917–971), Former Shu (907–925), Later Shu (934–965), Jingnan (924–963), Southern Tang (937–975), and Northern Han (951–979).

his mother and his own displacement; he had lost an eye in the assassination attempt.[15]

Some years later, another of the king's concubines gave birth to a second son. Gyeongmun protected this child, named him crown prince, and dispatched him to China to learn the principles of Confucian government. Returning to his homeland, the boy became King Heonggang after his father's death. He must have discovered the truth about the older half-brother exiled in a monastery; we know nothing about his reaction.

During the eleven years of his reign, Heonggang did his best to pretend that all was well, in part by spending money like water and burnishing the capital city to a high gloss. Every house had a tile roof; every fireplace burned charcoal, rather than cheaper firewood, so that the skies remained clear of woodsmoke. Meanwhile, a hundred miles out from Kyongju, the countryside seethed with thieves and bandits, private armies and ambitious warlords.[16]

Most of Heonggang's courtiers seem to have encouraged his delusion that all was well with his country, but the poet and scholar Ch'oe Chi'won was an exception. The son of a Sillan aristocrat, Ch'oe Chi'won had also spent his school years in Tang China. Unlike Heonggang, he had actually absorbed the principles of Confucian government; the *Samguk sagi* tells us that he passed the civil service exam in China on his first try and was appointed "Chief of Personnel" for a Tang province. But as his adopted country began to spin into chaos, Ch'oe Chi'won returned home.[17]

In 885, Ch'oe Chi'won applied for a post in Heonggang's government. He wanted to reform Silla before it too collapsed, but Heonggang and his hangers-on weren't enthusiastic. "Upon returning to Korea," the *Samguk sagi* says, "[Ch'oe Chi'won] wished to realize his ideas, but these were decadent times, and, an object of suspicion and envy, he was not accepted."[18]

The following year, King Heonggang died without an heir. First his brother and then his sister Jinseong inherited the throne and its problems; Jinseong ruled for ten years, from 887 to 897, while Silla crumpled around her.

Queen Jinseong comes off badly in the contemporary accounts; she was "of manly build," one chronicle tells us, and then reverses itself and accuses her of bringing "pretty young men" to court and installing them in paper positions. To be female and on the throne during the collapse of a medieval kingdom generally elicited accusations of lust, corruption, and general viciousness: the queen's sex life becomes a convenient explanation for the end of an era. But the real culprits in Silla's ongoing crisis were the castle lords, who continued to shake down the peasants and farmers who lived under their power, building luxurious lives on the backs of Silla's laborers.[19]

Queen Jinseong tried to keep her government funded by cracking down on taxpayers. Taxes from rural areas hadn't reached the capital for years, so she ordered armed men to perform a forced tax collection. This was a desperate and short-sighted solution. The farmers and craftsmen had been paying tax all along; the payments had just gone into the coffers of their local castle lords. Now they were paying double taxes. Poverty and desperation drove more men into careers as bandits ("grass brigands," the contemporary chronicles call them), and before long the bandits were organizing themselves into small and powerful anti-government armies under capable rebel leaders. The lands just below Kyongju were dominated by the Red Trousered Bandits; a farmer turned soldier named Kyonhwon led a rebel army in the southwest; and a robber leader named Yanggil organized the resistance to the northeast. His second-in-command was none other than Kungye, the one-eyed prince, now grown and hoping to reclaim some of the power that could have been his.[20]

For the moment, though, the farmer Kyonhwon had emerged as the strongest of the rebel leaders. In 892, Queen Jinseong tried to stave him off by giving him a title; she awarded him the rule of the lands south of the capital, along with the honorary appellation "Duke of the Southwest." With this semi-official authority behind him, Kyonhwon negotiated an agreement with Yanggil and his right-hand man Kungye: he would rule in the southwest, and they would govern an area farther to the north.

Over the next few years, Kyonhwon firmed up his hold on the southwest lands while the one-eyed prince Kungye built his power to the north. In name, Kungye remained second-in-command to the bandit leader Yanggil. In reality, he was collecting personal support for himself, sleeping on the ground with his men, dividing his spoils evenly with them, and suffering their hardships.[21]

Meanwhile, Queen Jinseong remained on her throne, but she was rapidly becoming a monarch in name only. Once again, the Confucian scholar-poet Ch'oe Chi'won tried to help out, this time by submitting a ten-point proposal for reform that would, in his estimation, have begun to lift the remains of the Sillan kingdom out of its current mudhole. Once again, his reforms were rejected by the Sillan court.

Ch'oe Chi'won left the doomed palace and retreated to a distant mountain monastery, where he devoted himself instead to the pursuits of the spirit and the composition of mournful lyrics in Chinese.

> The frenzied rush through the rocks roars at the peaks,
> and drowns out the human voices close by.
> Because I always fear disputes between right and wrong
> I have arranged the waters to cage in these mountains.[22]

Back at court, Queen Jinseong was forced to give up her throne. The courtiers brought forward a boy whom they claimed to be yet another son of Heonggang, this one the child of a girl from an outlying village where the king had spent the night during a hunting trip. In 897, Queen Jinseong abdicated in his favor, and the fourteen-year-old boy became King Hyogong.

Kungye, the one-eyed prince, is said to have responded to the exaltation of his supposed half-brother by finding his portrait and slashing it to bits with his sword. His own ambitions were becoming clearer; later that same year, Kungye murdered his chief Yanggil and made himself leader of the rebels in the north.[23]

By 900, the Duke of the Southwest, the ex-farmer Kyonhwon, felt secure enough to proclaim himself king. Kyonhwon had actually been born in the old territory of ancient Silla, but the land where he was most powerful had once belonged to old Baekje, so he named his new state Later Baekje. The following year, Kungye followed suit. He too was a native Sillan, but he centered his new state at Kaesong, in the old lands of Goguryeo, and named his kingdom Later Goguryeo.

The days of Unified Silla had ended. Once again, three nations occupied the peninsula. All peace had ended; Ch'oe Chi'won lamented that the bodies of those who had starved to death or fallen in action were "scattered about the plain like stars." The observation is repeated by Wang Kon, a competent naval officer who fought in the forces of Kungye: "People scattered in all directions," he wrote, "leaving skeletons exposed on the ground." The period of the Later Three Kingdoms had begun with war and famine.[24]

The one-eyed Kungye, driven by anger as well as ambition, intended to completely destroy the remnants of Silla; he spent the first years as king of Later Goguryeo pushing deeper and deeper into Sillan territory, while the young Sillan king Hyogong took refuge from a hopeless future in alcohol. Slowly, Kungye's resentment and fury unbalanced his mind. When he was not fighting, he was parading through his new kingdom on a white horse, clad in a purple robe and a gold crown, with a choir of two hundred monks following behind to sing his praises. He grew paranoid, ordering first his wife and then both of his sons put to death for treachery. "Kungye," wrote his general Wang Kon, "became tyrannical and cruel. He considered treacherous means to be the best, and intimidation and insults to be necessary devices. Frequent corvée labor and heavy taxes exhausted the people, forcing them to abandon the land. Yet the palace was grand and imposing, and he ignored the established conventions."[25]

Wang Kon is hardly an objective observer. By 918, Kungye had become so unbearably tyrannical that his own officers murdered him and elevated Wang Kon to the kingship instead. Kungye had claimed ties both to the royal house of the present and to the old Goguryeon kingdom of the past, but his rule was supported by military might, not by aristocratic lineage. He had claimed his crown by conquest, not by right of blood, and in doing so set himself up to die by the same sword with which he had lived.

TIMELINE 54

FRANKS ASTURIAS BULGARS LOMBARDS	CHINA JAPAN TURKS/KHITAN UNIFIED SILLA

Louis the Pious (781–813) Pippin (781–810)
as subject king   as subject king
    Alfonso II (791–842)
         Pope Leo III (795–816)

Coronation of **Charlemagne** (800)
    Krum (c. 803–814)

    Omurtag (815–831)

Kammu (781–806)
Move to Nagaoka   **Wonseong** (785–798)
                 Seol Chong
Move to Heian
             Soseong (798–800)
             Aejung (800–809)
Tang Shunzong (805–806)
Tang Xianzong (806–820)
Heizei (806–809)
    Saga (809–823)   **Heondeok** (809–826)

Tang Muzong (821–824)
    Junna (823–833)
Tang Jingzong (824–826)
Tang Wenzong (826–840)   **Heungdeok** (826–836)
                   Chang Pogo
    Ninmyo (833–850)
                   Sinmu (839)
            Munseong (839–857)
    Montoku (850–858)

    Seiwa (858–876)
Yoshifusa as Sessho (858–872)
Tang Yizong (859–873)
         Gyeongmun (861–875)

    Mototsune as Sessho
        (872–891)
Tang Xizong (873–888)
        Heonggang (875–886)
    Yozie (876–884)
Rebellion of   Li Keyong
Huang Chao   of the Shatuo
Battle of Liangtianpo (882)
            Ch'oe Chi'won
           Jinseong (887–897)
Tang Zhaozong (888–904)
         Hyogong (897–912)

        Kyonhwon of Later Baekje
            (900–935)
       Kungye of Later Goguryeo
            (901–918)
Tang Aidi (904–907)
Fall of Tang/   **Abaoji** of the Khitan
Rise of Later Liang   (907–926)
Period of Five Dynasties and
Ten Kingdoms (907–960)

      Wang Kon of Later Goguryeo (918–943)

Chapter Fifty-Five

———

The Third Dynasty

———

Between 809 and 833,
the Abbasid caliphate is challenged
by the independent Tahirids to the east

IN 809, THE RIGHTEOUS CALIPH Harun al-Rashid was on his way to Khorasan with an army. The people of the province were making rebellious noises, and al-Rashid had decided to tend to the matter in person. But he grew ill on the journey and was forced to halt at the little town of Tus, where he died. He left a fortune behind. "It has been said," al-Tabari writes, "that there were nine hundred million odd dirhams in the state treasury," which, if true, means that al-Rashid died with three thousand tons of silver in his possession.[1]

Al-Rashid had wavered over the choice of an heir. His oldest son, al-Amin, was the obvious choice, but he was also fond of his slightly younger son al-Mamun, the son of a concubine, and he thought that al-Mamun had a greater talent for governing. In the end, he made a strange, almost Frankish arrangement. He decreed that while al-Amin would succeed him as caliph, al-Mamun would become governor of Khorasan and his brother's heir.[2]

As al-Amin had children of his own, this was not to his liking. He insisted that al-Mamun come to Baghdad and recognize al-Amin's oldest son as the heir. But for two years, al-Mamun refused to come. If he left Khorasan, the chances were that he would never return. At the same time, he stopped sending any reports to Baghdad and removed al-Amin's name from its place in the official mottoes embroidered on the robes of state used at Khorasan—all acts that declared his independence.[3]

Al-Amin retaliated by ordering that no one was to pray for al-Mamun any more during the Friday sermons. When al-Mamun received word of this, he realized that his brother was preparing to depose him as governor of Khorasan. He began to prepare for war, and al-Amin did the same. In the early days of 811, the armies of the two brothers met in battle. The army of al-Mamun, although smaller, outfought and defeated the caliph's forces. Al-

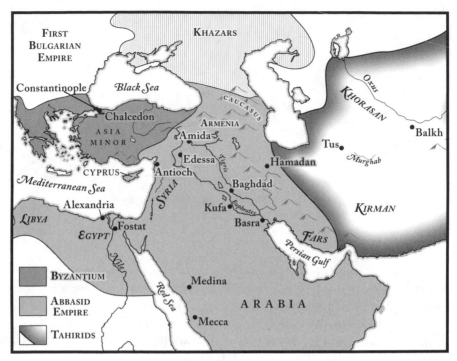

55.1: The Tahirids

Mamun's victory was in no small part due to the brilliant leadership of his chief general, a man named Tahir.[4]

Once hostilities were in the open, fighting went on, and for over a year the Abbasid empire was divided by civil war. Al-Mamun's rebel army captured Hamadan, Basra, and Kufa; Mecca and Medina both declared themselves against the Abbasid caliph and placed their loyalty with al-Mamun instead. In a little over a year, al-Mamun had arrived at Baghdad—not as a loyal subject and brother, but as an invading conqueror.

Al-Amin and his men barricaded the city's gates, and for another year the siege dragged on. The walls, pounded by siege engines, began to crumble. Merchants sailing into the city were forced to duck a fusillade of rocks hurled by al-Mamun's catapults. The surrounding villages were forced to surrender; those that refused were burned to the ground. Inside Baghdad, the people grew desperate, hungry, and lawless. On the outside, al-Mamun's general, Tahir, promised that anyone who left the city and came over to the attackers' side would be treated well and given gifts.

At the end of the summer of 813, the defenders finally gave up. Tahir led his master's army into the city. In the fighting and chaos that followed, al-Amin tried to swim across the Tigris to safety. A band of soldiers captured him, beheaded him, and brought the head to Tahir, who presented it to his master. Al-Mamun, who had conveniently not been in on the decision to execute his brother, prostrated himself in grief; but this did not prevent al-Amin's head from being stuck up on the city walls—the fate of usurpers and rebels, not of duly appointed caliphs.[5]

Al-Mamun was proclaimed rightful caliph, and by September most of the empire had dutifully agreed to obey him. But the authority he had seized by force never sat easily in his hands. He was forced to put down a serious rebellion in 815, and another in 817 led by his own uncle. Troubles down in Egypt, where the people were unhappy with their tax burden and their governor, were continuous. He was losing his grip on the east: he had given the governorship of Khorasan over to his general Tahir, out of gratitude for the man's service, and Tahir had begun to pay less and less attention to commands from his caliph. One Friday evening, Tahir did not pray for the caliph during his Friday sermon—a clear declaration of his own independence.[6]

Al-Mamun's intelligence agents in Khorasan immediately sent word of this defiance to Baghdad, but on that same night Tahir died. A certain amount of confusion surrounded his death. One of his younger sons claimed that he died of a sudden high fever that struck him while he slept. An official reported that he was actually talking to Tahir when the governor's face convulsed and he fell down in the middle of a speech. However it happened, his death seemed like good news to al-Mamun, who clapped his hands when news of Tahir's end reached him, right after the report of his old friend's defiance. "Praise be to God," he announced, "who has sent Tahir on to the next life and kept us back."[7]

His celebration was premature; Tahir's oldest son Talhah picked up his father's defiance and declared himself ruler of Khorasan. A new dynasty had joined the already divided Muslim empire: the Tahirids, who would rule in the east, paying empty respect to the authority of the caliph but acting in independence.

Al-Mamun had won his position by conquest, and he held on to it for his entire life; he ruled as caliph until his death from typhoid in 833 and was succeeded by the heir he had designated, his half-brother al-Mutasim. But Talhah also passed on *his* authority to his brother, and the Tahirids grew in power in the east, just as the Umayyads had in al-Andalus. Now, three Islamic dynasties ruled in the once-unified Muslim lands, and the fractures would continue to spread.

TIMELINE 55

CHINA	JAPAN	TURKS/ KHITAN	UNIFIED SILLA	ABBASID EMPIRE	BYZANTIUM
	Kammu (781–806)				Constantine VI/Irene (780–797)
	Move to Nagaoka		Wonseong (785–798)		
			Seol Chong	Harun al-Rashid (786–809)	
	Move to Heian				Second Council of Nicaea (787)
			Soseong (798–800)		Irene (797–802)
			Aejung (800–809)		
Tang Shunzong (805–806)					Nikephoros I (802–811)
Tang Xianzong (806–820)					
	Heizei (806–809)				
	Saga (809–823)		Heondeok (809–826)	al-Amin (809–813)	
					Staurakios (811)
					Michael Rangabe (811–813)
				al-Mamun (813–833)	Leo V (813–820)
Tang Muzong (821–824)				Rise of Tahirid dynasty	
	Junna (823–833)			Talhah ibn Tahir (822–828)	
Tang Jingzong (824–826)					
Tang Wenzong (826–840)			Heungdeok (826–836)		
			Chang Pogo		
	Ninmyo (833–850)				
			Sinmu (839)		
			Munseong (839–857)		
	Montoku (850–858)				
	Seiwa (858–876)				
Yoshifusa as Sessho (858–872)					
Tang Yizong (859–873)					
			Gyeongmun (861–875)		
Mototsune as Sessho (872–891)					
Tang Xizong (873–888)					
	Yozie (876–884)		Heonggang (875–886)		
Rebellion of	Li Keyong				
Huang Chao	of the Shatuo				
Battle of Liangtianpo (882)					
			Ch'oe Chi'won		
			Jinseong (887–897)		
Tang Zhaozong (888–904)					
			Hyogong (897–912)		
			Kyonhwon of Later Baekje (900–935)		
			Kungye of Later Goguryeo (901–918)		
Tang Aidi (904–907)					
Fall of Tang/		Abaoji of the Khitan			
Rise of Later Liang		(907–926)			
Period of Five Dynasties and					
Ten Kingdoms (907–960)					
			Wang Kon of Later Goguryeo (918–943)		

Chapter Fifty-Six

—■—

The Vikings

*Between 813 and 862,
the empire of Charlemagne divides into four pieces,
Viking longships sail down the Seine,
and the Rus make their first appearance at Constantinople*

B Y 813, CHARLEMAGNE'S IMPERIAL POWER had been recognized, however grudgingly, by both Byzantium and Baghdad. He claimed to rule lands as far north as Scandinavia, where he had campaigned against the little tribal kingdoms of the Suetidi, known to us as the Swedes; the Dani, or the Danes; and the Hordaland and Rogaland peoples, in the lands that are now Norway. He had extended his empire down into the Spanish Marches, the mountainous land between the Emirate of Cordoba and the Frankish border (*march* comes from the Frankish word for "borderland"). He controlled the northern part of Italy, the old Lombard kingdom, and acted as the protector of the Papal States in the middle of the peninsula; he was the master of the dukes who ruled the Italian territories of Spoleto and Benevento.[1]

He was nearing seventy years old and intended to leave his kingdom divided among his three sons in the traditional Frankish manner. The will he had drawn up in 806 split the kingdom into thirds, giving each son complete independence. His heirs were expected to cooperate only in "the defense of the Church of St. Peter." He was the emperor of the Romans, but this did not, in his mind, mean that he now ruled a Roman empire that should be passed on whole to his successor. It meant that he had an obligation to defend the pope and to establish God's kingdom on earth.[2]

His plans to divide his lands came to nothing. By 813, only one son was still alive. His third son Pippin, subject king in Italy, died in 810; Charles the Younger, his heir apparent, suffered a fatal stroke the following year. His only remaining heir was his youngest son Louis the Pious, who was thirty-five years old and currently ruling as a sub-king to his father in the Frankish territory of Aquitaine.*

---

*Pippin the Hunchback, his oldest son, had been disinherited and sent to a monastery, where he

Charlemagne called the court nobles together and, in their presence, crowned Louis as joint king and co-emperor; the old Germanic tradition of electing a king meant that although he had no intention of giving the noblemen a voice in the succession, they needed to be included in the ritual. The following year, Charlemagne died. "Above all," writes his chronicler Nithard, "I believe he will be admired for the tempered severity with which he subdued the fierce and iron hearts of Franks and barbarians. Not even Roman might had been able to tame these people, but they dared to do nothing in Charles's empire except what was in harmony with the public welfare." As emperor, Charles had done what the ancient rulers had failed to do: he had instilled *civilization* into those who lacked it.[3]

Guardian of civilization, defender of the bishop of Rome: these were fine descriptions of the function of the emperor of the Romans, but Louis was not on the throne long before it became clear that the definition of emperor was already changing.

Louis—who earned the nickname "the Pious" for his love of morality and good order—had expected to end up with one share of the Frankish land, not the whole vast thing. Now, as the second emperor of the Romans, he had unexpectedly inherited not a ceremonial title, but a huge and undivided kingdom. He at once adjusted his thinking. Charlemagne had, until the end of his life, referred to himself with the unwieldy formula "Charles, serene Augustus governing the Roman Empire, at the same time king of the Franks and of the Lombards," which neatly separated out all of the parts of his power. But the year after his accession, Louis began to call himself, simply, "Emperor Augustus." In his mind, the different realms under his control were already merging together.[4]

Like his father, Louis crowned his sons. His oldest son Lothair was crowned king of Italy and co-emperor; his second son Louis was coronated in Bavaria, a little Germanic territory to the east that had coalesced out of the remnants of several tribes; the youngest, Pippin, became king of Aquitaine. But they ruled less as kings than as governors, under their father's hand. Louis had bound all the disparate Frankish lands under him, using the title "emperor" in order to tighten his grasp over the imperial realm.

His sons—who, like their father, had grown up watching their grandfather treat the domains as separate—did not take well to this heavy oversight. Louis the Pious may have thought of his sons as his subjects, and his empire as a single realm, but the kings themselves viewed their kingdoms as peculiarly their own. In 829, the two different points of view clashed and threw the empire into civil war.

---

died in 811. (Pippin of Italy had originally been named Carloman, but when Pippin the Hunchback was disinherited, Charlemagne renamed his third son Pippin.)

The immediate cause of the war was Louis's clear preference for his newest son. After the death of his first wife, Louis had remarried, and his bride had given birth to another son: Charles, born in 823. Louis had a soft spot for Charles. In 829, he decided that the six-year-old should have a kingdom of his own. He chose Alemannia, the old territory of the Germanic Alemanni, now under Frankish rule.

Unfortunately, Alemannia was part of Lothair's territory, so when Louis the Pious gave it to little Charles he reduced Lothair's land. This seemed reasonable to him. He was, after all, the emperor; it was his realm to do with as he pleased. But Lothair was furious over the hostile takeover of part of *his* kingdom.

He suggested to his two younger brothers that their kingdoms would be the next ones impoverished for the sake of the little half-brother. By 830, he had convinced Pippin of Aquitaine and Louis of Bavaria (more commonly known as "Louis the German," owing to the Germanic flavor of his little patch of land) to declare war on their father.

Vicious infighting between the three kings and their father raged on for three years. Finally, in 833, the brothers gained the upper hand. They trapped Louis the Pious and put both him and young Charles under guard. Lothair claimed the throne as emperor. "He held his father and Charles in free custody," Nithard tells us, "and ordered monks to keep Charles company; they were to get him used to the monastic life, and urge him to take it up himself."[5]

Charles did not take the hint, however. At the same time, the deposed Louis sent a proposal to his two remaining sons, Pippin and Louis the German. He promised that he would make both of their realms larger if they would join together against Lothair and help him get his throne back.

Both sons agreed: "The promise of more land," Nithard remarks, "made them only too eager to comply." Louis appeared unexpectedly at a public assembly, and Lothair found himself standing alone against his father and all of his brothers. He was forced to return to Italy and to swear an oath to be content with his own kingdom for the rest of his life.[6]

Relations between father and sons remained cool. In 838, Pippin died unexpectedly in Aquitaine; Louis the Pious announced that Aquitaine would now go to the half-brother Charles, whose rule over Alemannia had lasted less than a year. But the people of Aquitaine rebelled and instead crowned a king of their own: Pippin's own son, Pippin II. Louis the Pious had lost his control over Aquitaine, and a chunk of his empire had disappeared.

By now, the Franks had nicknamed young Charles "Charles the Landless" (sometimes translated "Charles the Bald"). Louis the Pious decided to give to his youngest son part of his own central domain, the land of Neustria. When he died in 840, Charles became king of the Franks.

Lothair was still co-emperor and king of Italy; Louis the German still sat on the Bavarian throne; Aquitaine belonged to their nephew Pippin II. Charles the Landless held his father's throne, but neither of his two older half-brothers was in the mood to see the upstart keep power over their homeland. War began again and went on for another three years, largely driven by Lothair's resentment over the loss of his land. "Puffed up by the imperial title," the *Annals of St. Bertin* tell us, "he took up arms against both of his brothers, Louis and Charles, and attacked first one, then the other, engaging them in battle, but with very little success in either case."[7]

In 841, an engagement between the brothers and their armies at Fontenoy left forty thousand Franks dead and shocked the Frankish world. "I, Engelbert, fighting alongside the others, saw this crime unfold," wrote an eyewitness who described the carnage in verse.

> On the sides of both Charles and Louis,
> The fields are white with the shrouds of the dead,
> Just as the fields become white with birds in autumn.
> This battle is not worthy of praise, not fit to be sung.
> Let not that accursed day be counted in the calendar of the year.[8]

While the civil war killed off Frankish warriors and destroyed crops, pirates from Scandinavia and al-Andalus sailed down the Seine and burned Rouen, destroyed trading posts, raided the coast, and generally produced terror across the countryside. Finally the brothers decided that they'd better make peace before the entire country went up in flames: the chronicler Regino of Prum writes that the Frankish kings, "conquerors of the world," had lost so many men that they were having difficulty protecting their own frontiers.[9]

They met together in 843 and agreed to divide the empire (including Aquitaine, which had now fallen back into dependence on the larger kingdom) into three parts, more or less along the lines that Charlemagne had indicated in his will almost forty years earlier. The division was laid out in a document known as the Treaty of Verdun, which all three of them signed. Charles the Landless got Neustria and the rest of the old western Frankish kingdom; Louis the German took Bavaria and the eastern Frankish lands, roughly the old territory of Austrasia; and Lothair added the lands between the Rhine and Rhône rivers to his holdings in Italy. Burgundy, where the third mayor of the palace had once ruled, was divided into two; Lothair claimed the larger part of it, the southeastern portion, and Charles the Landless got the dog's portion to the north.*

---

*Charles the Landless got Neustria, Britanny, Aquitaine, Gascony, the Spanish Marches, Septimania, and the northwestern third of Burgundy; Louis the German got East Saxony, Alemannia, Austria, Bavaria, and Carinthia; Lothair, already ruling in Italy (along with his son Louis II the Younger), got Lorraine, Alsace, Provence, the southeastern two-thirds of Burgundy, and also the northern Low Countries around the area of Frisia.

The treaty had permanently divided the lands of the Franks back into separate realms. Once again, the empire was more of an idea than a reality; Lothair, theoretically emperor of the Romans, held no more land than the other two. Separated from the western Frankish kingdom, Louis the German's eastern lands began to take on a slightly different character than Charles the Landless's territory in the west. The two halves of the Frankish land, Eastern Francia and Western Francia, would never be reunited.

And Charles the Landless shortly found himself facing a threat that was harder to deal with than his land-hungry brothers: invaders from the north who found the broad Loire river an ideal path into his kingdom.

THE INVADERS WERE VIKINGS: young adventurers from the Scandinavian lands, sailing out from the cold towns that could barely support their fathers' families. They had been venturing out onto the seas for centuries, but a strange shift in the weather had suddenly set them free to sail to lands where they had never been before.

This shift was a phenomenon known as the Medieval Warm Period, or the Medieval Climactic Anomaly. Beginning around 800, temperatures in Europe had begun to rise—just a few degrees, but enough to melt ice away from northern sea routes that previously had been impassable. Sailing on the cold North Sea had always been a risky proposition, possible only during certain months, but by the middle of the ninth century the restless young men looking for wealth and adventure could sail out in search of both year-round.

Vikings had been responsible for burning Rouen and wrecking the towns along the Seine during the civil war, and they had already invaded the kingdoms to Charles's southwest. A few years earlier, a band of Vikings had targeted Pamplona, a small independent state that had grown up around the fortress Charlemagne had incautiously sacked sixty years before. Pamplona was a Christian kingdom, but it was independent from both the emir of Cordoba and the Franks. The Vikings had kidnapped the son of Pamplona's king, Inigo I, and had demanded a sizable ransom for his release.

In 844, the year after the Treaty of Verdun, Vikings also descended on the emir of Cordoba, Abd ar-Rahman II. He managed to drive them away (the Vikings were still more inclined to raid than to settle in for a long war) but realized that he might not be able to hold off further raids. So he began to build himself a fleet of ships.

The year after, Viking pirates launched a serious invasion of Charles the Landless's kingdom. The Franks proved less able to cope with the invaders than either Inigo I or the emir. Within a matter of weeks, Viking ships had pushed almost all the way into Paris, while their crews sacked the surrounding lands. The ships arrived outside the city on Easter Day; Charles the Landless managed to buy off their leader, the pirate Ragnar Lodbrok, with seven thou-

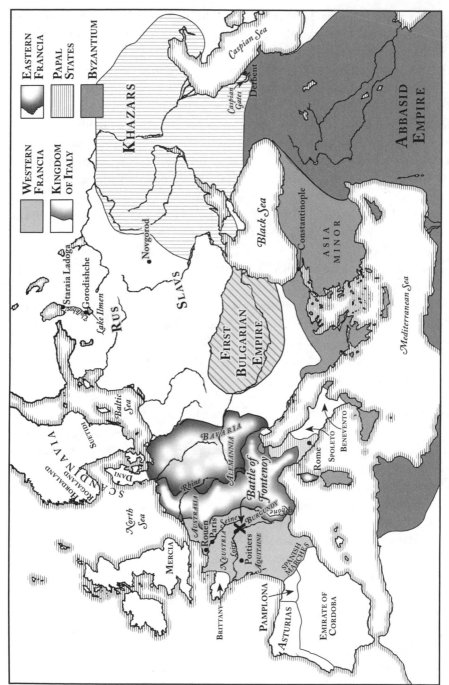

§6.1: The Treaty of Verdun

sand pounds of gold, but even after the ships retreated back down the river the raids continued.

Between 858 and 860, Viking fleets made continual raids on the southern and eastern coasts of Hispania. Other Viking ships sailed into the Mediterranean and harassed the Italian coast; some even made it all the way across the Mediterranean and tried to raid Alexandria. In 859, Viking invaders tried again to take over Pamplona. By this time, Inigo I was dead (an ill-planned rebellion against the emir of Cordoba had left him badly wounded and paralyzed for some time before his death), and his son Garcia I, the former Viking hostage, was ruling Pamplona. Together with Ordono I of Asturias, the northwest Christian kingdom once recognized by Charlemagne, Garcia of Pamplona turned back the bulk of the Viking invaders.[10]

Charles the Landless was less successful. Vikings kidnapped his chaplain and forced him to pay a ransom to get the man back. They burned the great church at Poitiers and roamed through his northern land. Every time he paid them off, they would leave; but they always came back, and this made Charles less and less popular with the people who paid taxes into the Frankish treasury. "I do not think," fumed the cleric Paschasius Radbertus, "that even a few years ago any ruler on earth would have imagined . . . that a foreigner would enter Paris. . . . Who would have thought that such a glorious kingdom, so strong, so vast, so populous, and so vigorous would be humiliated and smeared with the filth of such people?"[11]

In 860, Charles began to build fortified bridges at the rivers to block Viking invaders. The first bridges on the Seine proved so useful in slowing down the Viking longboats that flimsy barriers were soon going up all around the country, and Charles had to issue an edict forbidding such "unauthorized strongholds" to be built. His own fortifications turned out to be a very long-term project; it would be years before the bridges were completed. Meanwhile the farms on the lowland near the mouths of the rivers remained completely vulnerable to the unexpected Viking attacks that broke out of the morning mist without warning.[12]

FARTHER EAST, THE VIKING INFLUX caused a ripple that washed up and broke against the walls of Constantinople.

Even before the ice had begun to melt, Scandinavian merchants had struck out from their homes, sailed across the Baltic Sea, and built settlements along the opposite coast. The settlements had remained small, the lands around them largely unconquered, but for three hundred years traders had used them as stopping places on their journeys farther east. During the caliphate of al-Rashid, this trade had grown even busier; more and more silver dirhams had moved westward, as luxurious northern furs moved east. Bands of Scandinavian merchants made their way towards the port of Derbent, on the Caspian Sea, where they traded with Khazar and Muslim merchants.[13]

The lands through which they travelled were populated by tribes who spoke a set of related languages known to linguists as Finno-Ugrian. The Finno-Ugrian villagers didn't trade far away, nor did they use the rivers as roads as the Scandinavians did. They called the travellers who came through their villages *Rhos*, or Rus—the word may mean "red," referring to the foreigners' ruddy coloring.[14]

Apparently some of the travellers adopted this word for themselves. A Frankish chronicle tells us that back in 839, the Byzantine emperor had sent a friendly embassy to Louis the Pious to reaffirm the treaty sworn out in the days of Michael Rangabe and Charlemagne. The Byzantine ambassadors were accompanied by strangers: "men who said that their people were called Rus, and had been sent to him by their king, whose name was the Khagan, for the sake of friendship." To Louis the Pious, they looked like Swedes. He knew who Swedes were, and he suspected that the men were spies.[15]

But they were neither spies nor Swedes. They were traders who had settled down and intermarried with the Finno-Ugrian natives, and who now lived in a newly coalesced state ruled by a *khagan*, a borrowed word for "king." Their little nation was probably centered around the village of Gorodishche, on Lake Ilmen, at the southern end of the Volkhov river.[16]

Whoever the khagan of the Rus was, he exercised only loose and informal control over the mix of Scandinavian newcomers and Finno-Ugrian natives who lived around him. But sometime around 860, as the Vikings spilled out of their native lands into the surrounding waters, a sizable party of them appear to have made their way across the northern waterways, down into the land of the Rus, where they found their distant cousins settled and prospering in trade.

This was a setup for disaster, but the khagan of the Rus knew more about Scandinavian ways than Charles the Landless. Rather than trying to drive the Vikings out and starting a minor war, he suggested that they head downriver towards Constantinople, where they would find richer targets to raid. In all likelihood, he sent a few of his own men to accompany them.[17]

Constantinople was by now under the rule of Michael III, grandson of the ambitious and capable general Michael II, who had seized the throne for himself in 820 by assassinating Leo V during Christmas mass. Michael III had inherited the Byzantine crown in 842, at the age of two, but his mother and uncles held the real power in Constantinople.*

Like Charles the Landless, the regents were helpless in the face of the

---

*Michael II ruled from 820 to 829 and was succeeded by his son Theophilus (829 to 842). Together, Michael II, Theophilus, and Michael III (842 to 867) make up the "Phrygian dynasty" of Byzantine emperors.

onslaught. Two hundred ships sailed down into the Black Sea, filled with thousands of raiders who came ashore, burned and plundered everything outside the walls of Constantinople, and shook their swords at the terrified people lining the walls. They came, said the patriarch Photius afterwards, "like a thunderbolt from heaven," unlike any other attack in history in its sudden, harsh savagery:

> A nation dwelling somewhere far from our country, barbarous, nomadic, armed with arrogance, unwatched, unchallenged, leaderless, has so suddenly, in the twinkling of an eye, like a wave of the sea, poured over our frontiers, and as a wild boar has devoured the inhabitants of the land like grass, or straw, or a crop (O, the God-sent punishment that befell us!), sparing nothing from man to beast, not respecting female weakness, not pitying tender infants, not reverencing the hoary hairs of old men, softened by nothing that is wont to move human nature to pity . . . but boldly thrusting their sword through persons of every age and sex.[18]

The raids went on for a little over a week before the raiders sailed away from Constantinople's locked gates. Michael's regents immediately claimed that fear of the Byzantine reprisals had driven the enemy away. But raiding and retreating was what the Vikings did best; it was their natural pattern to arrive, plunder, and leave.[19]

Ruins along the Volkhov river hint that the Viking visitors may have fallen out with their Rus hosts, before returning home. Just a year or two after the attack on Constantinople, fires destroyed part of Gorodishche and all of the nearby village of Staraia Ladoga.

The *Russian Primary Chronicle*, written 250 years later, says that in 862, the Viking warrior Rurik settled in Europe and built himself a kingdom among the native Slavs, with his capital at Novgorod. The *Chronicle* adds that he had to fight other Vikings for control of the subject Slavs. Rurik is probably legendary, but his tale gives us a glimpse of what may have been a real struggle between the Viking newcomers and the Rus who had already settled down along the Volkhov.[20]

It seems that the resident Rus eventually came out on top; but their numbers seem to have swelled suddenly, suggesting that at least a few of the Viking newcomers also settled down and stayed. The wooden buildings of Gorodishche were repaired; Staraia Ladoga was rebuilt, this time in stone. The Rus, resisting and adapting at the same time, had absorbed the Viking wave. It was a flexibility that neither the emperor of Constantinople nor the kings of the Frankish empire possessed.

TIMELINE 56						
ABBASID EMPIRE	BYZANTIUM	EMIRATE OF CORDOBA	RUS	FRANKS Roman Emperor	ITALY	PAMPLONA ASTURIAS
	Constantine VI/Irene (780–797)			*Louis the Pious (781–840)*	*Pippin (781–810)*	
Harun al-Rashid (786-809) Second Council of Nicaea (787)						
					Pope Leo III (795–816)	
	Irene (797–802)			**Charlemagne (800–814)**		
	Nikephoros I (802–811)					
al-Amin (809–813)	Staurakios (811) Michael Rangabe (811–813)					
al-Mamun (813–833)	Leo V (813–820)			Louis the Pious (813–840)		
				Pippin of Aquitaine (817–838)/Louis the German (817–876)	*Lothair (818-855)* **(Emperor 817–855)**	
	Michael II (820–829)					
Rise of Tahirid dynasty Talhah ibn Tahir (822–828)		Abd ar-Rahman II (822–852)				
					Charles of Alemannia (829)	**Inigo I** (824–852)
						Viking attack on Pamplona
				Pippin II of Aquitaine (838–852)		
				Charles the Landless (840–877)		
	Michael III (842–867)			Treaty of Verdun (843)		
		Viking attack on Cordoba		Viking attack on the Franks		
					Ordono I (850–866)	**Garcia I** (852–882)
	Viking/Rus attack on Constantinople					
			Rurik (?) (862–?)			

Note: Primary rulers are in bold type; subject kings, in italics.

Chapter Fifty-Seven

—·—

Long-Lived Kings

Between 814 and 900,
three Indian kingdoms battle for Kannauj in the north,
while a new king in the south gains power by fighting
and wealth by trading with the eastern islands

IN THE NORTH OF INDIA, three kingdoms touched edges at the city of Kannauj. Three strong and long-lived kings, each the son of a strong and long-lived king, ruled over the intersecting realms. The Pala were ruled by Devapala, who had inherited from his father Dharmapala a realm swelled by captured territory; the Pratihara, by Nagabhata II, whose father Vatsaraja had, in a thirty-year reign, managed to strengthen and establish the Pratihara as a power to be reckoned with. And in 814, the thirteen-year-old king Amoghavarsha received from his father, Govinda III, the enormous Rashtrakuta empire.*

Kannauj, filled with Hindu temples and Buddhist monasteries, had been the capital city of the great king Harsha two centuries earlier. It had grown into a metropolis, and all three kings coveted it. Already the city had passed back and forth between the Pala and Pratihara kings, much to the dismay of the citizens, who had to flee for cover whenever a new army stormed through the gates. It was extremely uncomfortable to live in a symbol of dominance.

In 814, the city was in the hands of the Pala king, Devapala. But the Pratihara king, Nagabhata II, planned to take it away. Nagabhata II was in his ninth year of reign. He had already campaigned successfully against the Pala king, annexing some of the northern Pala lands (the old territory of Magadha) for his own. He had also driven off a Muslim attempt to storm across the Sindh into his land and capture his capital city of Ujjain. "He crushed the large armies of the powerful Mleccha king, the destroyer of virtue," his

---

*The Pratihara are also known as the Gurjara Pratihara; the word "Gurjara" probably refers to their ancestry, as descendents of the central Asian Gurjaras who came down through the northern mountains just after the fall of the Guptas. See Rama Shankar Tripathi, *History of Kanauj* (Motilal Banarsidass, 1964), pp. 221–222.

inscription at the city of Gwalior tells us, using the traditional Indian name for these Arabic-speaking invaders.[1]

By 820—perhaps earlier—Nagabhata II had driven the Pala forces out of the city of Kannauj and was holding court there himself. "Nagabhata . . . alone gladdens the heart of the three worlds," his inscriptions boast. "He revealed himself, even as the rising sun, the sole source of manifestation of the three worlds, reveals himself by vanquishing dense and terrible darkness. . . . The kings of Andrah, Sindhhu, Vidarbha, and Kalinga succumbed to his youthful energy, as moths do to fire." The inscriptions are undoubtedly political spin, but if there is any truth in them at all, then the Pratihara empire of Nagabhata II had not only pushed into Pala territory but also taken land away from the Rashtrakuta empire.[2]

The Rashtrakuta domain had shrunk since Govinda's death. The teenaged Amoghavarsha, barely old enough to inherit, had been forced to spend the first decade of his reign putting down rebellions against his power. In fact, revolt had grown so pervasive that in 818, Amoghavarsha fled from his own country and left his elderly cousin Karka to deal with the problems on his own.[3]

Karka not only did so, but—once the king had returned and the Rashtrakuta empire was back under control—retired to his family lands on the western coast instead of seizing the throne for himself. Unfortunately for Amoghavarsha, Karka's son Dhruva was not as loyal; as soon as the old man died, Dhruva declared his own independence, and Amoghavarsha spent the next twenty years fighting him into submission. Thanks to all these domestic troubles, Amoghavarsha had been in no position to resist the Pratihara attacks.[4]

Given the essential likeness of the Indian kingdoms across the subcontinent (they had, more or less, the same governments, armies, and military playbooks), their fates were decided by two interlocking qualities: the spark of ambition in each king, and that king's ability to stay on the throne long enough to fan the spark into fire. Amoghavarsha, king of the shrinking Rashtrakuta realm, was not essentially a warlike ruler. He built a beautiful new cave-temple in the city of Ellora, wrote poetry, dabbled in art, and left defense of the realm to his generals. But he sat on the throne long enough to give his kingdom a stability that resisted complete conquest. The Pratihara were temporarily dominant, but the Pala were still strong, and the Rashtrakuta did not dwindle completely away.[5]

The triumphant Nagabhata II died in 833, and the Pratihara fortunes wavered a bit; his short-lived son and successor spent only three years on the throne before dying, and his grandson Mihirbhoj had to beat off a Pala attempt to invade. Mihirbhoj's first forays against the Pala king Devapala

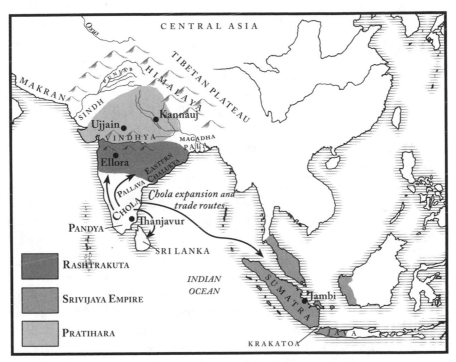

57.1: The Rise of the Chola

were triumphant, but then the tide began to turn against him. Devapala was in the third decade of a forty-year reign, and his experience allowed him to resist the attacks of the younger Pratihara king with increasing success. His own inscriptions claim that he reconquered land from the Himalaya down to the Vindhya range, poetically described as "piles of rock [which are] moist with the rutting juice of elephants." "Devapala," another inscription boasts, "brought low the arrogance of the lord of the Pratihara."[6]

But the coincidence of long life, which had led first the Pratihara and then the Pala into victory, abruptly abandoned the Pala. Devapala died in 850 and was succeeded by short-lived rulers incapable of following up on his conquests. Mihirbhoj of the Pratihara, who would remain on the throne for another thirty-six years, pushed back into the lost territory: "He wished to conquer the three worlds," an inscription notes. Slowly the pendulum swung back to the west. In Mihirbhoj's final years, the Pratihara kingdom grew to enormous size; the Pala were reduced to a minor tributary in the east.

Mihirbhoj was still on the Pratihara throne when Amoghavarsha of the Rashtrakuta finally died in 878. He had reigned for an astounding sixty-four years, and although he had none of the aggressive campaigning skills of his neighbor, his longevity had lent the Rashtrakuta kingdom a tenacious coherence. But Amoghavarsha's son and successor Krishna II, no more war-like than his father, lacked his father's tough resilience. Almost at once, the Eastern Chalukya, who had been weak and fragmented for decades, showed new strength and declared their opposition to Krishna II; and the Pratihara launched new attacks against his borders.[7]

Krishna II, troubled in the north, was equally unsuccessful in the south. He had the misfortune to lie between two energetic ambitious kings; Mihirbhoj in the north, and a newly crowned southern ruler named Aditya.

The far south of India had been in the hands of two competing powers, the Pallava and the Pandya, for centuries. Aditya belonged to a clan that had been subject to the Pallava, the Chola clan. His father, the Chola warlord Vijayala, had been permitted by the Pallava king to attack the city of Thanjavur and take it as his headquarters. In Thanjavur, the Chola chief then took advantage of the ongoing preoccupation of the Pallava and Pandya kings with each other and conquered a kingdom.

Aditya, coming to his father's throne in 871, would rule for nearly forty years: another long-lived king with ambitions. His tenure allowed his Chola domain to grow stronger and richer. Chola merchants carried on active sea trade to the east, sending ships across the Indian Ocean to the island of Sumatra. After the disastrous eruption of Krakatoa in 535, the people of Sumatra had slowly returned to rebuild their villages and replow their fields; the Sumatran village of Jambi had grown into a city and spread its authority across the water to the eastern parts of Java, and by the ninth century, Java, Sumatra, and the peninsula that jutted down from the Asian mainland were all under the rule of a single king. The Chola knew this as the Srivijayan empire, a wealthy and powerful trading partner that could help the Chola rise to dominance in the south.

By the end of the ninth century, Aditya had killed the Pallava king and claimed his land, and had begun to chip away at the southern border of the Rashtrakuta.[8] Like the Pratihara kings far to the north, his long life had allowed him to realize his ambitions: the foundation of a new dynasty. What-ever legitimacy a king claimed for himself—whether he announced that his right to rule came from blood or bone, from the anointing of priests or the possession of a Divine Mandate—that legitimacy only mattered as long as the king lived. And in India, over the course of the ninth century, the life spans of the rulers had determined the advance and retreat of power.

At the beginning of the century, the struggle in India had been centered in the north, with armies fighting for dominance from east to west and back again. But by the century's end, the axis of conflict had shifted; the struggle was a vertical one now, with the Pratihara on the north, the Rashtrakuta in the center, and the Chola in the far south all positioned for conquest. The king of the Rashtrakuta sat in the most precarious place: sandwiched between two tenacious neighbors who could reach each other only by going through him.

TIMELINE 57

FRANKS · ITALY · PAMPLONA Roman Emperor · ASTURIAS	INDIA
Charles (768–814)/ **Carloman** (768–771)	**Dharmapala** of the Pala (770–781) **Vatsaraja** of the Pratihara (775–805)
Charles (774–814)	**Dhruva** of the Rashtrakuta (780–793)
Louis the　*Pippin (781–810)* *Pious (781–840)*	**Govinda III** of the Rashtrakuta (793–814)
Pope Leo III (795–816)	
Charlemagne (800–814)	**Nagabhata II** of the Pratihara (805–833) **Devapala** of the Pala (810–850)
Louis the Pious (813–840)	**Amoghavarsha** of the Rashtrakuta (814–878)
Pippin of Aquitaine *(817–838)/Louis*　*Lothair* *the German*　　*(818-855)* *(817–876)*　　**(Emperor** 　　　　　　**817–855)**	Rebellion of Dhruva
Charles of　**Inigo I** 　　　*Alemannia (829)*　(824–852)	
Viking attack 　　　　　　on Pamplona	**Mihirbhoj** of the Pratihara (836–886)
Pippin II of Aquitaine (838–852)	
Charles the Landless (840–877)	
Treaty of Verdun (843)	**Vijayala** of the Chola (848–871)
Viking attack on the Franks　**Ordono I** 　　　　　(850–866)　**Garcia I** 　　　　　　　　(852–882)	
	Aditya of the Chola (871–907)
	Krishna II of the Rashtrakuta (878–914)

Note: Primary rulers are in bold type; subject kings, in italics.

Chapter Fifty-Eight

—•—

Foreign and Domestic
Relations

Between 856 and 886,
Byzantine missionaries invent a new Slavic alphabet,
Louis the German and Michael III joust over Moravia and Bulgaria,
and Michael III's complicated domestic arrangements catch up with him

I N 856, MICHAEL III of Byzantium turned sixteen years old and
assumed power with a careful ruthlessness. He declared his most trustworthy
uncle his heir, ordered the other regents exiled or assassinated, and shipped
his mother and sisters off to a nunnery.

Constantinople was relatively stable, thanks in large part to Michael's
mother and uncle; they had presided over a council that restored icon-use to
Byzantium and brought a final end to over a century of theological struggle.
But the empire's encounters with outside powers had been disastrous. The
Rus had raided its land at will, Abbasid armies had beaten its troops in battle,
and the Khazars had refused offers of closer alliance.

In 862, Michael was given a chance to reverse the empire's bad luck at
foreign relations. A letter from a king named Rastislav arrived at his court,
asking for help. "We have no one to teach us the truth and to explain to us the
meaning of Scripture," Rastislav wrote. "Send us then, Lord, a man capable of
teaching us the whole truth."[1]

This was more than a chance to send missionaries. It was an opportunity
to change the political landscape.

Rastislav's kingdom, Moravia, was less than forty years old. His uncle
Mojmir, the leader of a Slavic tribe north of Bulgaria, had conquered the
tribe next door and united the two territories. Mojmir had ruled this kingdom
from 833 until 846, and when he died Louis the German, now king of Eastern
Francia, had sent his own soldiers into Moravia to make sure that Rastislav
would inherit his uncle's throne. This was not a kindness on Louis's part. He
wanted Moravia's king to be dependent on him, and the kingdom itself under

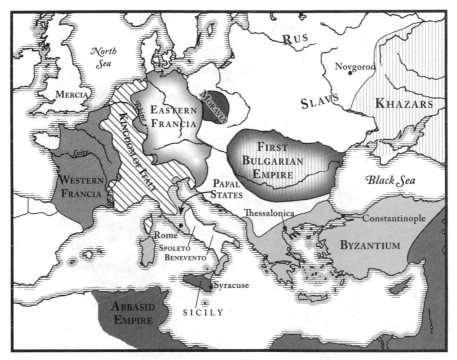

58.1: Moravia

Frankish supervision. Louis had dispatched his own Frankish missionaries to evangelize the Moravians, hoping to convert them into the Roman church, which would have given him another layer of control over Moravia's people.

Rastislav could see that Louis the German intended to swallow his kingdom whole. He cast his eye eastward and decided that his people would be better off submitting themselves to the patriarch of Constantinople, who owed no political favors to the Franks.[2]

Michael III saw the request for what it was: a chance to whip Moravia out of Frankish hands. He immediately sent two missionaries to the Moravian court. They were brothers named Cyril and Methodius who had already travelled together as missionaries to the Khazars (it was an unsuccessful mission, as the Khazars declined to convert from Judaism). They were natives of Thessalonica, which had a large Slavic population, and they had spoken Slavic languages from birth.*

Cyril and Methodius arrived at Rastislav's court in 863, bearing gifts from Michael III and copies of the sacred liturgy used in the churches of Constantinople. But before the Moravians could be folded into the traditions of the

---

*Cyril is also widely known as Constantine, the name he used before becoming a monk.

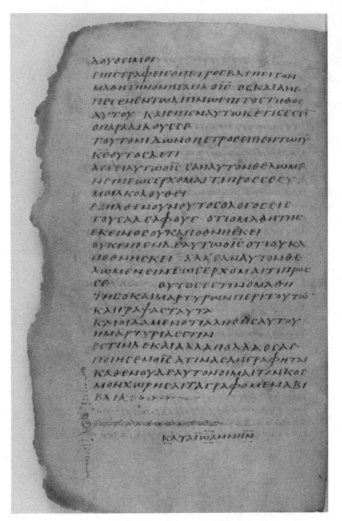

58.1: Greek uncial script in the fifth-century Codex Washingtonianus.
Credit: Freer Gallery of Art

eastern church, the liturgies would have to be translated into Slavonic—and Slavonic had no written form.

Cyril, undaunted, invented a new alphabet called Glagolitic (from the Slavic word for "speak"), basing it on the Greek letters known as uncials. He and his brother spent the next three years translating the liturgy and the Gospels into Moravian. The first passage written down in this newborn language was from the Gospel of John: *In the beginning was the Word.*[3]

Moravian was still considered a barbaric language; certainly it ranked far, far below Hebrew, Greek, and Latin (the three languages written, by tradi-

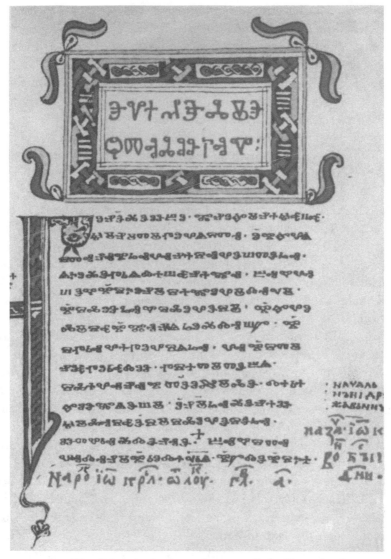

58.2: Glagolitic script in the tenth-century Codex Zographensis.
Credit: Quattuor Evangeliorum Codex Glagoliticus

tion, above the cross of Christ) as an acceptable tongue for worship. This made no difference to Michael III or to his missionaries. Giving the Slavs their own language, a language tied to the Greek of the east rather than the Latin of the west, did that much more to weaken Frankish control.[4]

While the brothers were still in Moravia, Michael III discovered that Louis the German was hedging his bets. He was also sending Frankish missionaries into Bulgaria in an attempt to do exactly what Michael III was doing in Moravia. Bulgaria was too big, too close, and too well armed to risk a Frankish-Bulgarian alliance, and Michael III decided not to play around with competing monks this time; he assembled his army and prepared to invade. Bulgaria was too important to leave to the missionaries.

The king of Bulgaria, Boris, had been considering conversion for some time. He had gone so far as to send a message to Louis the German, announcing that he was ready to join the Roman church. But the Bulgarian aristocracy was appalled by the possibility: "His leading men were very angry," the *Annals of St. Bertin* tells us, "and stirred up his people against him, aiming to kill him. All the warriors there were in all the ten counties of that realm came and surrounded the king's palace."[5]

Boris backtracked and stalled on a final decision, sending messages to Louis the German that he had more questions and needed more priests to come and answer them. But when Michael III's army appeared on his frontiers and the Byzantine navy drew up to the shores of the Black Sea, Boris changed tactics. He made a deal with Michael: he would convert and be baptized in Constantinople, taking the baptismal name "Michael" in honor of the emperor, and in return, the Byzantine forces would withdraw.[6]

Michael III, impressed with his success so far, now sent a missionary upriver to the Rus, but no conversions resulted; the Rus were not interested. And the missions in Moravia and Bulgaria, like all of Michael III's foreign maneuvers, did not do him much good in the end. Boris, now Michael I of Bulgaria, remained Christian, but in 866 he announced that he would submit himself to the pope; then in 870 he reversed himself again and resubmitted Bulgaria to the patriarch of Constantinople. This too would be temporary. He had already decided that what Bulgaria really needed was its *own* state church, neither Roman nor Byzantine, in order to preserve Bulgarian independence.

Over in Moravia, Cyril and Methodius were trying to complete their work. Cyril died of illness in 869, begging his brother to continue the mission; so Methodius went on, faithfully translating the Scriptures into Slavonic. But a little more than a year after Cyril's death, Louis the German managed to reassert himself in Moravia. He promised to help King Rastislav's nephew, Svatopluk, usurp the throne. In 870, Frankish armies accompanied Svatopluk to the royal palace, arrested Rastislav, and handed him over to Louis. Louis took revenge for Rastislav's turn to the east by blinding and jailing him; Rastislav died in prison not long after.

Svatopluk now ruled Moravia, and Louis the German controlled him. Frankish bishops, coming into Moravia to reorient its Christianity back towards Rome, managed to have Methodius arrested and thrown into jail. No one paid much attention to him there, and it was almost three years before the pope learned of his fate and ordered Louis the German to release him.

Methodius tried to pick his work back up, but the theological tide had turned against him; the Moravian Christians who had welcomed his efforts were now fleeing into Bulgaria to avoid any trouble with the Frankish bishops. When Methodius died in 885, his work in Moravia was in tatters.

But the Moravians who had chosen exile in Bulgaria passed their liturgy and Scriptures on to the Bulgarian clerics. The Bulgarian churches began to use Methodius's works in preference to the Greek rituals, distancing themselves bit by bit from the eastern church hierarchy. Methodius's disciples, attempting to follow the example of their master, began to create a new script, again based on Greek uncials, meant especially for the Bulgarian tongue. They named this script "Cyrillic," after the missionary Cyril, and it took root and grew. A decade later, the Bulgarian church forbade its clerics to use any Greek in the liturgy. The Bulgarian church would now worship only in its own native language.[7]

Methodius and Cyril had set out to free Moravia from the Franks. Instead, they freed Bulgaria from both Rome and Constantinople; but neither lived to see this.

MEANWHILE, MICHAEL III was suffering from domestic troubles.

The troubles were almost entirely self-inflicted. Since the age of fifteen, he had been sleeping with the same woman, his mistress Eudokia Ingerina. However, his mother announced that Ingerina was not an acceptable wife, and instead ordered him to marry a woman she had handpicked for him, Eudokia Dekapolitissa. Michael had trouble defying his mother; he agreed to marry Dekapolitissa, and then after the wedding ignored her and went right on sleeping with Ingerina.

The patriarch disapproved of this crowded marriage, and to preserve appearances, Michael married off his mistress Ingerina to his best friend, a horse-trainer from Macedonia named Basil. Michael continued sleeping with her, however, and so that Basil would not be deprived, he brought one of his sisters out of her convent and installed her at court as Basil's mistress.[8]

What with climbing in and out of each other's beds, Michael III and Basil became closer, and Basil began to get a glimpse of what *real* power could be like. He began to suggest to Michael III that Michael's uncle and heir had too much influence around the court, and finally convinced Michael to give him permission to murder the unfortunate man. In his uncle's place, Michael made Basil his co-emperor and heir. In 867, he also legally adopted Basil as his son; he was twenty-seven, Basil was fifty-six.

This weird adoption made a twisted kind of sense. The year before, Ingerina had given birth to a son. Technically, the child was Basil's. In all likelihood, he was actually Michael's. So by adopting Basil, Michael became his illegitimate son's legitimate grandfather, and the little boy, Leo, had a legitimate path to claim the throne.

Unfortunately, the path led through Basil. Now that he was adopted, co-emperor, and heir, Basil had no more use for Michael. After a drunken banquet one night later in 867, Michael III staggered off to bed; Basil's men murdered the emperor in his sleep, and Basil claimed the crown for himself as Basil I, founder of the new Macedonian dynasty.

Basil maintained peace, more or less, with most of his neighbors except for the Abbasid empire; the two empires continued their pattern of inconclusive and damaging battles, with the high (or low) point the Arab capture in 878 of the city of Syracuse on Sicily, which until this point had been Byzantine. Basil's greatest project as emperor was an attempt to revise and update the laws of Justinian. He intended to publish the updated laws in an enormous collection that would be called "Purification of the Old Law." It was an odd project for a man who had come to the throne in such a sideways manner, and it was never finished.[9]

At some point, Basil also began sleeping with his wife, since she bore him two more sons after Michael's death. (Basil, understandably, displayed a marked preference for his younger sons over his oldest.)

In 886, Basil was hunting with his attendants when he rode out ahead of them to pursue a huge stag. The animal turned on him; Basil's horse bolted and threw him onto the stag's antlers, and the stag dragged him through the woods until one of his guards caught up with him and cut him loose. Basil, badly wounded, had just enough strength left to accuse the guard of trying to kill him with the drawn sword the man had used to free him; he ordered the guard put to death, and died not long afterwards. Only the introduction to his great Purification was ever published.[10]

When Basil's entourage returned to Constantinople with this story of his death, it was greeted with skepticism. More than one chronicler suggested that it was covering up some sort of assassination plot, perhaps directed by Basil's son Leo. Relations between the two had grown sourer as Leo grew, which merely fed the rumors that Leo was actually the son of the dead Michael.

But Leo was never publicly accused of Basil's death. He was crowned emperor. Shortly afterwards, he had Michael's body exhumed from its burial place in a monastery outside of Constantinople and reburied in Constantine the Great's own mausoleum.[11]

	BYZANTIUM FRANKS ITALY BULGARIA
INDIA	MORAVIA Roman
	Emperor
	Charlemagne (800–814)
	Nikephoros I (802–811)
Nagabhata II of the	Krum (c. 803–814)
Pratihara (805–833)	
Devapala of	Staurakios (811)
the Pala (810–850)	Michael Rangabe (811–813)
	Leo V (813–820) Louis the Pious (813–840)
Amoghavarsha of the	Omurtag (815–831)
Rashtrakuta (814–878)	
	Pippin of Aquitaine
Rebellion of Dhruva	*(817–838)/Louis Lothair*
	the German (818–855)
	(817–876) (**Emperor**
	817–855)
	Michael II (820–829)
	Charles of Alemannia (829)
Mihirbhoj of the	**Mojmir** of Moravia
Pratihara (836–886)	(833–846)
	Pippin II of Aquitaine (838–852)
	Charles the Landless (840–877)
	Michael III (842–867)
	Treaty of Verdun (843)
	Viking attack on the Franks
Vijayala of the	**Rastislav** of
Chola (848–871)	Moravia (846–870)
	Boris (852–889)
	(Michael I)
	Viking/Rus attack on Constantinople (860)
	Arrival of Cyril and Methodius
	Basil I (867–886)
Aditya of the	**Svatopluk** of
Chola (871–907)	Moravia (871–894)
Krishna II of the	
Rashtrakuta (878–914)	
	Leo VI (886–912)

Note: Primary rulers are in bold type; subject kings, in italics.

Chapter Fifty-Nine

The Second Caliphate

Between 861 and 909,
Turkish soldiers take control of the Abbasid caliphate,
new dynasties break away in the east,
and a new caliph proclaims himself in Egypt

I N EARLY DECEMBER OF 861, the Abbasid caliph was murdered.

The murder of a caliph was not anything new or startling. But by 861, the surface tension that held the Islamic world together was already strained by cross-currents of doctrine and practice, and this particular assassination strengthened those currents until the surface unity finally, and fatally, burst apart.

The chain of events that led to this particular murder had begun back in the early years of the century, with the caliph al-Mamun himself. Before his death in 834, al-Mamun had developed a particular interest in a form of doctrine known as Mu'tazilism, which suggested that he had the responsibility to purify the community—by force, if necessary.

The Mu'tazilites believed that God was perfect reason, which meant that his divine judgment of men, both sinners and righteous, was also completely rational. In Mu'tazilism there was no uncertainty about God's intentions. There was no need to appeal for mercy: mercy required the giver to change his mind about the severity of an offense, and God did not share in such human qualities as changing one's mind. God was so completely transcendent, so far beyond the limitations of man's existence, that he was almost an abstraction: Divine Logic.[1]

Like all medieval (and modern) arguments about the nature of God, this one had a political application. Mu'tazilite leaders argued that since men have the ability to reason, they can think their way to a clear understanding of right and wrong: they can predict, with certainty, what God's judgment on their acts will be. They may not always choose the righteous act, however; and so it is the leader's job to guide the community in right belief and right practice.*

---

*Mu'tazilism had five foundational principles: Seyyed Hossein Nasr defines them as unity (God's nature as a single transcendent being), justice (God's judgment governed by rational principle), the

It is also the leader's job to stamp out wrong belief and evil practice, and al-Mamun had taken this task quite seriously. He instituted an inquisition: the *mihna*, or ordeal. Teachers, scholars, and leaders were subjected to intense questioning, which sometimes involved quite forceful persuasion, until the interrogated were "convinced" that Mu'tazilite ideas were true.[2]

In many cases, the conviction was shallow; agreeing hastily to the doctrines that al-Mamun decreed improved the chances of quick release from his prisons. But al-Mamun, who died just as his inquisition was getting underway, did not quite grasp this truth. He left orders to his half-brother and heir al-Mutasim to continue the inquisition, convinced that it would not only make the Islamic community stronger but also bolster the power of the caliphate.

Unfortunately al-Mutasim, carrying out his brother's wishes, ran slap into another difficulty. Mu'tazilite doctrine assured him that as caliph, he had the authority to reward good and punish evil (and to define what good and evil *were*). But he ruled in a world where Muslims were increasingly divided over who could claim the right to be the true caliph, the rightful leader of the community.

The arguments about who should be caliph had been going on for two centuries. Many Muslims still believed that the Islamic world should be led by a direct descendent of the Prophet. They had hoped, since the death of Muhammad's son-in-law Ali back in 661, to see a descendent of Ali and his wife, the Prophet's daughter Fatima, become caliph. Instead, the caliphate had been taken over first by the Umayyads and then in 750 by the Abbasids, who traced their descent back to Muhammad's uncle but not to Muhammad himself. At both crises of leadership, the supporters of Ali—the Shi'a—had called for a caliph of Ali's blood.

Neither time had their voices been strong enough to triumph against the majority, known as the Sunni. So the party of Ali, rejecting the caliphs as illegitimate, had exalted its own series of leaders: not caliphs, but *imams*, religious leaders who refused to swear allegiance to the caliphate. The Shi'a (a relatively small group who lived within the Sunni majority, sometimes peacefully, sometimes in a state of minor war) were willing to obey their *imams* without question. They believed that the Prophet himself had *designated* his successor, and that each *imam* had the God-given, infallible knowledge that allowed him

---

"promise and the threat" (those who obey will be given rewards, while those who fail to repent will suffer eternal torment), the "in-between position" in relation to Muslims who commit sins (they are in the moment of sinning neither believers nor infidels, but something "in between"), and the leader's responsibility to exhort the community to do good and forbid them to do evil. See *Islamic Philosophy from Its Origin to the Present* (State University of New York Press, 2006), pp. 120–125; for additional clarification, see Fauzan Saleh, *Modern Trends in Islamic Theological Discourse in Modern Indonesia* (Brill, 2001).

to designate the *next* successor. The *imams* could not make mistakes, because they were filled with the wisdom of the Divine.[3]

But the Abbasid caliph could not boast the same kind of authority that the Shi'a granted to their *imams*. Sunni Muslims *chose* their caliphs; the pool of candidates was limited to the Abbasid line, but the caliph himself was elected by the community. Which was a problem for al-Mutasim, because while God and the Prophet were incapable of error, the community of Muslims might realize, after electing a caliph, that they had blundered.

And if a caliph started arresting and torturing members of the community who disagreed with him, it was very likely that the community might decide that he was a mistake sooner rather than later. During his caliphate, al-Mutasim had to put down three separate major revolts and a handful of minor ones. It became very clear that if the caliph were to hold on to his power, he needed an army that came from *outside* the community—an army that would fight for him but had no right to remove him from power in favor of another candidate.[4]

Al-Mutasim formed this army around the core of his own personal guard—captives who had been brought back to Baghdad after wars with the Western Turkish Khaghanate and the other Turkish tribes across the Oxus river. These Turkish captives had become slaves to the Abbasid caliphate, and many of the slaves were trained to be soldiers in the Abbasid army. Those who did well were often set free, and some were even given government offices to hold.

The influx of Turks into Baghdad had been constant, over the last century of warring, and al-Mutasim had a personal guard of four thousand Turkish slave-soldiers even before he became caliph. As caliph, he began to transform this guard into a real army. Within just a few years, he had expanded his force until he had seventy thousand men under his control—mostly Turks, but also a few Slavs and North Africans who had been captured in battle and brought to the capital as slaves.[5]

These men, chosen for the specific reason that they were outsiders, now surrounded and protected the caliph, pushing his Arab and Persian officials to the edge of the inner circle. Resentment grew in Baghdad. Continual scuffles—and worse—broke out on the streets between Turks and the men they had supplanted. Finally al-Mutasim decided to move his capital to another city: north along the Tigris to Samarra, where he constructed separate quarters for his Turks and kept them isolated from the population. This prevented street riots, but it also transformed the Turks into a highly cohesive, self-contained community that had no particular loyalty to Muslim doctrine. Al-Mutasim was succeeded first by his older son and then by his younger son al-Mutawakkil, both of them living in Samarra. During the caliphates of both, the Turkish community strengthened until the Turks were the single most powerful segment of Abbasid society.[6]

In 861, all of these tensions came to a head when the caliph al-Mutawakkil threatened to disinherit his oldest son al-Muntasir. The young man went to the Turks and persuaded them that they would prosper better under *his* rule than under the rule of any of his brothers. Before al-Mutawakkil could carry through on his threat, his Turkish guards murdered him in his own quarters and arrayed themselves behind al-Muntasir's election as the new caliph.

Al-Muntasir died of illness shortly after his ascension, and the Turkish army picked the next caliph as well. When he displeased them, they tried to depose him. He fled to Baghdad and barricaded himself inside the city; the Turks laid siege to the old capital and, after a year, forced the powerless caliph to abdicate and chose a new one. Baghdad, now under Turkish control, became once again the political center of the caliphate.

Brought from the outside to protect the power of the caliph, the Turks had become kingmakers. The newly chosen caliph, al-Mutazz, lasted only three years. In a massive miscalculation, he spent too much money on his court and ran out of cash to pay his army. Once again the Turks intervened. Al-Tabari preserves an eyewitness account of what happened when they dragged the twenty-four-year-old caliph from his palace:

> I thought that they had already beaten him with clubs, for he came out with his shirt torn in several places and traces of blood on his shoulders. They stood him in the sun in the palace at that time when the heat is oppressive. I saw him lift his foot time and again due to the heat of the place where he had been made to stand. I also saw some of them slap him, as he tried to protect himself with his hand. . . . After he had been deposed, he was reportedly given over to someone who tortured him, and he was forbidden food and water for three days. . . . Finally they plastered a small vault with heavy plaster, put him in it, and shut the door behind him.[7]

By the next morning, the young caliph was dead. The Turks were in power, and one thing had become perfectly clear: the Abbasid caliph might claim to be God's spokesman, but that claim would no longer protect him.

The loss of control over the palace at Baghdad was mirrored by the caliphate's loss of control over the eastern reaches that had once belonged to the Abbasid empire.

The Tahirids of Khorasan, descendents of the general Tahir, were still ruling over the territory that had been given them by al-Mamun half a century earlier. But their power was soon shaken. In 867, a coppersmith turned bandit named Ya'qub-i Laith Saffari began conquering a territory south of his home city of Zaranj, halfway between the Tigris and the Indus. The Tahirids tried to defend their realm, but by 873, Saffari had fought all the way to the Tahirid capital city Nishapur. He captured the young Tahirid ruler and took the city for himself. The Tahirid dynasty was shattered; it had lasted only seventy years.

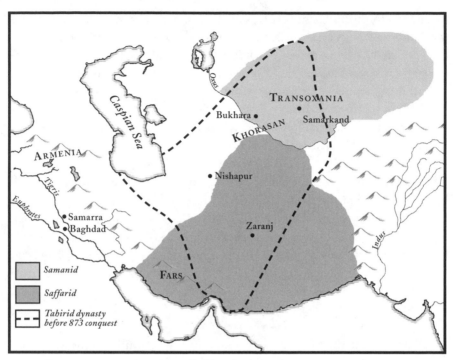

59.1: The Saffarid and Samanid Dynasties

Saffari then began to advance towards Baghdad, intending to storm the city and force the caliph to grant him official recognition as a legitimate Muslim ruler. The caliph, of course, was more or less powerless; the Turks had put another handpicked candidate, al-Mutamid, into the caliphate, and he would survive for twenty-two years by allowing his officials and army to control the palace. But although the illusion of a God-ordained caliph was flickering, it was still functioning. Even as he built his own separate empire, Saffari wanted the caliph's stamp of approval.[8]

The chaos of the last twenty years made the most straightforward solution—sending an army large enough to wipe out Saffari's rebellion—impractical. Instead, the caliph's officials set out to find an ally who could help by pressuring Saffari on the other side. A message was sent to the city of Samarkand on the far side of the Oxus river, offering the governor there the title "Ruler of Transoxania" if he would rally his forces against Saffari.

This governor was named Nasr, and he too was worried about Saffari's expanding power. His family, the Persian clan of the Samanids, had been governors of Samarkand since 819, and for some years they had been the strongest power east of the Tahirids. Now that the Tahirids were gone, Saffari would likely turn on the Samanids in the future.

Nasr agreed to the caliph's proposal, and the Samanid family became rulers of Transoxania. Led by Nasr's brother Ismail, the Samanids began to fight against Saffari from the northeast, while the Turkish army, in the name of the Abbasids, erected defenses in the west.

In 876, the Turks and Abbasids won a victory against Saffari's men, halting the advance towards Baghdad. They also recaptured the young Tahirid ruler Muhammad, who had been held prisoner by Saffari's army for the last three years. They sent him back to Khorasan so that he could try to take up the governorship again, but his power was shattered, his authority gone; he was unable, even with the help of Turkish forces, to recapture the land he had lost to Saffari.

His weakness offered the Samanids the chance to do some empire-building of their own. In 892, the Samanid ruler Nasr I died and his brother Ismail, who for some years had been the actual power behind the Samanid throne, took control. He established his own military headquarters in the city of Bukhara and began to expand his control across Khorasan. Now the far reaches of the Abbasid empire had been chiseled away to almost nothing. Instead, the emirs of two independent dynasties, the Saffarids and the Samanids, claimed the east.

Back in Baghdad, the parade of caliphs through the throne room continued. Al-Mutamid was succeeded in turn by his nephew, his nephew's half-Turkish son, and the son's son; the names of the caliphs are irrelevant, since power during that quarter century was held by the royal guard and the court officials. The post of senior *vizier*—literally, "helper" to the caliph—accumulated more and more power, until the vizier's authority was as great as any caliph's of the past.[9]

With the complete abdication of any real Abbasid authority at Baghdad, a gash opened across the fractured surface of the Islamic lands.

In the westward lands of northern Africa, known generally to Muslims as "the Maghreb," Shi'a Muslims had been gathering in greater and greater numbers. These Shi'a Muslims were a particularly militant community. For some decades, the Shi'a had been divided by arguments over the legitimacy of the *imam*; all of them agreed that there should be a designated *imam* leading the Prophet's people, but figuring out exactly *who* had been designated had proved unexpectedly difficult. All Shi'a agreed that the designated line of Shi'a *imams* began with Ali himself and continued on with his sons, his grandson, his great-grandson, and his great-great-grandson, Ja'far al-Sadiq.*

---

*In Shi'a doctrine, Ali was followed by his son Hasan ibn Ali, who lived from 625 to 670; his second son Husayn ibn Ali (626–680); Husayn's son Ali ibn Husayn (also known as Zayn al-Abidin, 654–713); Ali's son Muhammad ibn Ali (also known as Muhammad al-Baqir, 676–743); and Muhammad's son Ja'far ibn Muhammad (also known as Ja'far al-Sadiq, 702–765). After Ja'far, the Shi'a party split and two different lines of descent were traced from Ja'far. The Twelvers (the majority group) believed that the rightful *imams* were descended from Ja'far's younger son, Musa, and recognized twelve *imams* in total, ending with Musa's descendent Muhammad ibn Hassan, who

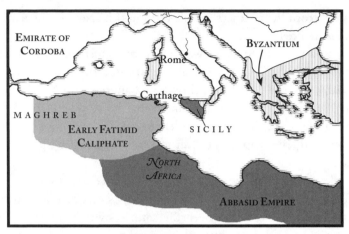

59.2: The Fatimid Caliphate

At that point, the Shi'a had an internal argument. The largest group of Shi'a Muslims insisted that the rightful *imams* were descended from Ja'far's younger son, Musa, and a smaller group claimed that Ja'far's older son Ismail had instead been the heir to his power. This smaller group, the Ismailis, were inclined to be more aggressive and warlike in pressing their claims than their Shi'a brothers. From North Africa, they had been watching the charade at Baghdad play itself out. And in 909, the Ismailis offered a candidate of their own for the caliphate: Ubaydallah al-Mahdi, who claimed to be a descendent not only of Ismail but also (tracing his ancestry back a few more generations) of Ismail's great-great-great-grandmother Fatima, the Prophet's daughter. Al-Mahdi did not simply make himself emir, like the leaders of the Saffarids and Samanids. Instead, he proclaimed himself caliph in the Maghreb.

This North African caliphate—the "Fatimid" caliphate—was a direct challenge to the authority of the Abbasids. Until this point, all of the fragments of the Islamic empire had been painted the same color; even the Umayyad emir in al-Andalus had declined to call himself a caliph; even the Saffarid and Samanid rebels had paid lip service to the Abbasid caliphate.

But now, three hundred years after Muhammad, the Islamic world had cracked irreparably into two. The "Islamic empire" had been a convenient myth for over a century. Now it was not even possible to speak of it. There was no empire based on religion in the east, any more than in the west: simply a collection of nations and states, each fighting for survival.

---

disappeared when he was ten and who, they believe, will one day return. The Ismailis insisted on descent from Ja'far's oldest son, Ismail. A third and smaller group of Shi'a, the Zayids, recognize Ali and his sons as true successors to the Prophet but hold that later *imams* can come from any descendent of those two sons. See Efraim Karsh, *Islamic Imperialism* (Yale University Press, 2006), p. 54; Paul E. Walker, *Fatimid History and Ismaili Doctrine* (Ashgate, 2008), 2.3.

TIMELINE 59

BYZANTIUM FRANKS ITALY BULGARIA MORAVIA — Roman Emperor	ABBASID EMPIRE EASTERN DYNASTIES CORDOBA EMIRATE NORTH AFRICA
Leo V (813–820) **Louis the Pious** (813–840) **Omurtag** (815–831)	**al-Mamun** (813–834)
Pippin of Aquitaine (817–838)/Louis Lothair the German (818-855) (817–876) **(Emperor 817–855)**	
Michael II (820–829)	Rise of Tahirid dynasty **Talhah ibn Tahir** (822–828) **Abd ar-Rahman II** (822–852)
Charles of Alemannia (829)	
Mojmir of Moravia (833–846)	**al-Mutasim** (833–842)
Pippin II of Aquitaine (838–852)	
Charles the Landless (840–877)	
Michael III (842–867) Treaty of Verdun (843) Viking attack on the Franks	Viking attack on Cordoba (844)
Rastislav of Moravia (846–870)	**al-Mutawakkil** (847–861)
Boris (852–889) (Michael I)	
Viking/Rus attack on Constantinople (860) Arrival of Cyril and Methodius	**al-Muntasir** (861–862)
Basil I (867–886)	**al-Mutazz** (866–869) Rise of the Saffarid dynasty **Ya'qub-i Laith Saffari** (867–878)
Svatopluk of Moravia (871–894)	Rise of the Samanid dynasty **Nasr** of the Samanids (875–892)
Leo VI (886–912)	**Ismail** of the Samanids (892–907)
	Rise of the Fatimid caliphate **al-Mahdi** of the Fatimids (909–934)

Note: Primary rulers are in bold type; subject kings, in italics.

Chapter Sixty

—

The Great Army of the Vikings

Between 865 and 878,
Alfred of Wessex makes peace with the Vikings
by dividing his island with them

I N 865, A DETACHMENT of the Vikings who had been pillaging the lands of the Franks sailed away from the fortified bridges of Charles the Landless and followed the sea to easier country.

Across the water from Western Francia lay the island of Britain, covered with an uneasy network of kings and warleaders. Since Roman times, Pictish tribes in the north had struggled with the Scoti—pirates from the western island of Ireland who had landed on the cold mountainous shores and rooted themselves in. Farther south, seven Anglo-Saxon kings divided up the English countryside.* The craggy southwestern coasts remained in the hands of the Welsh, descendents of the Romans and Irish and native Britons who had settled there since the days of the fourth-century Roman general Magnus Maximus. Between the central kingdom of Mercia and the kingdom of Wales lay a massive fortification built by the eighth-century Mercian king Offa, a great ditch in front of a twenty-foot wall of earth. "The Welsh devastated the territory of Offa," says the thirteenth-century *Chronicle of the Princes*, "and then Offa caused a dike to be made, as a boundary between him and Wales; it extends from one sea to another."[1]

The previous century had seen several attempts at unification. Some twenty years before the Viking invasion of Britain, Cinaed mac Ailpin, ruler of the Scoti kingdom Dal Riata on the northwestern coast, attacked the Picts to his east. He folded their land into his own, creating a kingdom that stretched across the north. Cinaed mac Ailpin was later known as Kenneth MacAlpin

---

*The seven English kingdoms that dominated in the ninth century were Northumbria, Mercia, East Anglia, Essex, Kent, Sussex, and Wessex.

60.1: Offa's Dike, photographed in the 1990s near Knighton in Wales
Credit: Homer Sykes/Corbis

or Kenneth I, the first king of Scotland; his dynasty, the House of Alpin, ruled over this united northern kingdom from the city of Scone.[2]

In the south, the Mercian kings who came after Offa had managed to dominate the eastern kingdoms of Kent and East Anglia for a time, but both soon broke away. By 860, Mercia had declined in power and Wessex had ascended: the king of Wessex had annexed both Kent and Sussex, and the southeast of England was more or less united under a single throne.[3]

But there was still no high king who could pull the divided Anglo-Saxon forces together in resistance to the Vikings.

The Vikings who arrived in 865 landed in Wessex. They were under the command of three brothers: Halfdan, Ivar, and Ubbe, sons of the Viking pirate Ragnar Lodbrok himself. The oldest brother, Ivar, was known as Ivar the Boneless. He may have been the victim of a bone disease that weakened his legs; all we know for certain is that he was often carried on a shield into battle, where he fought with a long spear. His arriving hordes flew the Raven Banner, the symbol of the god Odin.

Odin, king of battles, could blind and deafen his foes. He could still the sea and turn winds to give victory; he could awaken the dead, and his two ravens flew over the land and brought him intelligence of his enemies. "It is told," wrote the ninth-century Welsh monk John Asser, "that the three sisters of Ivar and Ubba wove that banner, and completed it entirely between dawn and dusk on a single day. Moreover they say that in every battle in which that banner goes before them, the raven in the midst of the design seems to flutter as though it were alive, if they were destined to gain the day; but if they were about to be conquered, it would droop down without moving. And this has often been proved to be true."[4]

The Raven Banner was more than a standard. It was a sign of the ancient religions whose power still lingered in the memories of the Christian Anglo-Saxons. England had been officially Christian since 664, when the Northumbrian king Oswiu called a council at the monastery of Whitby and announced that his kingdom would join the rest of the Christian world in "one rule of life . . . and the celebration of the holy sacraments." But the faith itself had spread unevenly. As long as the country remained a quilt of independent political allegiances, ninth-century Christians carried out their devotions separately, with the old British religions still practiced in the mountains and crags of Wales, in the deep patches of forest that lay between villages, in the darkness that surrounded the struggling churches of Wessex and Mercia and Northumbria.[5]

In the old English epic *Beowulf,* which reflects a ninth-century world, a Christian king and his warriors live on top of a well-lit hill, but a monster prowls through the tangled swamps below: a demon, a kinsman of Cain, an enemy of God. He haunts "the glittering hall," attacking at night to drag the warriors away into the heathen darkness. "These were hard times," the poet says; the threat of the monster's attack even drove the warriors back to pagan shrines, where they made offerings to the old gods in hopes of deliverance. "That was their way," the poet writes, "their heathenish hope; deep in their hearts they remembered hell."[6]

By the time *Beowulf* was written down, a century or so later, the Vikings were rooted deeply into the Anglo-Saxon countryside, and the Christian king was himself of Viking blood. But in 865, the Viking invaders—the Great Army of the Vikings—were part of a hellish attack: warriors from the old world, with the god's demons on their banners. Their victory would not merely deprive the Anglo-Saxons of land. It would pull them back into the dark waters of the ancient religions.

Ivar the Boneless and his men first landed in East Anglia, where their overwhelming might forced the East Anglian king into quick agreement: in exchange for keeping his throne, he would provide food and shelter over the winter and horses in the spring. The Great Army spent the winter of 865 in their East Anglian haven, and when the worst of the cold was over, began the march north into Northumbria.[7]

Northumbria had been divided by civil war between two men who claimed the throne, but at the Viking approach they gave up their struggle, united their forces, and turned together to face the new threat. Their cooperation was too little, too late. By the end of 867, the Great Army had overrun Northumbria, taken York, and laid waste to the monastery at Whitby. It would lie wrecked and ruined for the next two hundred years. "An immense slaughter was made of the Northumbrians," the *Anglo-Saxon Chronicle* tells us, "and the same raiding-army [then] went into Mercia."[8]

The king of Mercia sent to his neighbor, King Ethelred of Wessex, for help. Ethelred, who also controlled Sussex and Kent, answered the call. Together with his younger brother Alfred (now about twenty years old, serving as Ethelred's second-in-command), King Ethelred came to meet the Vikings at Nottingham, and there arranged a temporary peace: "No heavy fight occurred there," the *Chronicle* says, "and the Mercians made peace, and the raiding-army went back to York and stayed there one year." Probably Ethelred and Alfred paid the Vikings off; in exchange for saving Mercia, young Alfred got the daughter of the Mercian king as his wife, which essentially promised him the kingdom of Mercia at some point down the line.[9]

At the end of that year, having regathered their strength (and restocked their provisions), the Vikings went back into East Anglia, killed the king who had provided them with winter quarters, and took it for themselves. Now they were masters of the north and part of the east, and Wessex itself was in danger.

The Great Army marched into Wessex during the winter, in January of 871. Ethelred and Alfred braced themselves for the attack, but despite their resistance, the Vikings moved steadily westward into Ethelred's kingdom. On January 4, the Anglo-Saxon army was defeated at Reading in Sussex. The soldiers retreated and retrenched. Four days later, they met the Great Army again at Ashdown. This time they were able to push the Vikings back, but Ethelred's army was seriously weakened by the victory: "There were many thousands killed, and fighting went on until night," the *Chronicle* tells us.[10]

Two weeks later the tide turned back towards the Vikings, and in another enormous clash at the southern town of Basing, the Great Army was victorious. Halfdan took over the rule of London, and Viking reinforcements arrived to swell the Great Army's ranks.

Although Ethelred continued to resist, he died of illness in April, aged thirty. Alfred, now in his early twenties, inherited the kingship of Wessex, the command of the struggling Anglo-Saxon army, and the unenviable task of meeting the Great Army in battle. "He was a great warrior and victorious in virtually all battles," wrote his contemporary John Asser: this is clearly hindsight, since Alfred promptly lost another fight against the Great Army and was forced to make a temporary peace treaty.

Meanwhile, the Vikings firmed up their dominance in Northumbria, and then in 874 moved back into Mercia and took the kingdom for their own. At some point during these months of battle, Ivar the Boneless died; but the Vikings continued strong, led by Ivar's brother Ubbe (Halfdan had fallen out of favor with his followers, thanks to his ruthlessness) and by Ubbe's lieutenant, the warrior chief Guthrum.

It seemed to be only a matter of time before the entire island fell into Viking hands. So Alfred, in command of an exhausted and ravaged army, went into hiding. He had watched Ethelred fight battle after battle at the cost of thousands of lives, and could see no future in continuing a war of attrition. By 878, Anglo-Saxon refugees were sailing away from the island, looking in desperation for new homes; the Vikings were camped firmly on the Avon; and Alfred and his men were far out of sight, living in the swamps of Athelney in Alfred's Wessex kingdom. "He led a restless life in great distress amid the woody and marshy places," writes Asser, ". . . [with] nothing to live on except what he could forage by frequent raids . . . from the Vikings."[11]

All was not yet lost. He was not the only general leading attacks against the Vikings; in early 878, Ivar's brother Ubbe was killed in the Battle of Cynuit, possibly on his way to try to flush out Alfred's army. The Anglo-Saxon forces were led in this fight by the nobleman Odda, a Saxon ealdorman (or alderman, a *dux* who governed in the king's name), who not only triumphed over the Vikings but also captured the Raven Banner, the sign of Odin's power.

Perhaps this good omen heartened Alfred, but he didn't come out of hiding. Guthrum was still at the Great Army's head, and the Vikings were still in control of the countryside. Alfred had decided to take the long view: he was willing to risk the kingdom so that he could build up his fighting force. Stories would later multiply around this self-imposed exile, including the most famous tale of all: Alfred, hiding out incognito in the hut of an Athelney cowherd, was told by the housewife to watch the cakes baking on the hearth. Preoccupied with thoughts of his war against the Vikings, he ignored the cakes when they began to burn, and the housewife came storming back into the hut. "You're anxious enough to eat them when they're hot!" she scolded, "why can't you turn them when they're burning?"[12]

This story was inserted by the sixteenth-century clergyman Matthew Parker, who claims that it was found in a ninth-century source; it probably arose later, but its essence tells us something about the memory of Alfred, who humbly turns the cakes and doesn't reveal to the housewife that she has just told off the king of England. Even his contemporaries saw him as virtuous and holy, a God-provided deliverance from the pagan threat: which is why John Asser characterized him as victorious even when he was losing, and why the later chronicler Simeon of Durham insisted that his face shone like an angel's, and that his armor was faith, hope, and the love of God.[13]

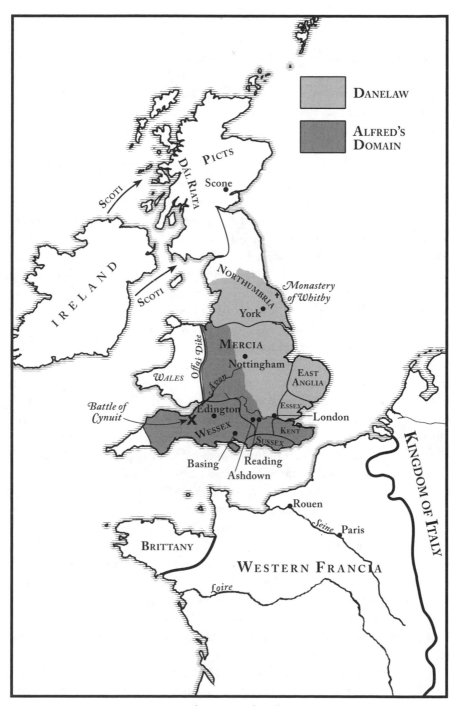

60.1: The Treaty of Wedmore

Theological conviction can founder in the face of defeat though, and Alfred kept his place in the pantheon of divinely appointed rulers by emerging from the Athelney marshes with a strong and desperate army behind him. In the late spring of 878, he met the Great Army of the Vikings at the Wessex town of Edington and triumphed. "Fighting fiercely, with a compact shield-wall," Asser writes, "he persevered resolutely for a long time; at length he gained the victory through God's will. He destroyed the Vikings with great slaughter, and pursued those who fled."[14]

After the battle at Edington, the Viking chief Guthrum agreed not only to sign a treaty with Alfred but also to convert to Christianity. He brought thirty of his strongest warriors with him, and all of them were baptized on the same day. Afterwards, they retreated to their own land. The agreement signed by Alfred and Guthrum, the Treaty of Wedmore, divided England in two. The south and southwest remained in Anglo-Saxon hands; Alfred ruled the southern lands, and placed the rule of the shrunken Mercian kingdom in the hands of his daughter and son-in-law, who governed it under his supervision. Guthrum and his Vikings were awarded independent control of Northumbria, the eastern coast, and the eastern half of Mercia.

Alfred's victory at Edington may have been decisive, but the Vikings had suffered greater defeats without surrender. The truth was that the Viking troops, once raiders and havoc-makers, had now been in England for almost fifteen years. They had rooted themselves into the English countryside, married Anglo-Saxon women, fathered children, planted farms, and lost a little of their piratical edge. They had begun to feel like natives, not invaders; they were ready to start new lives; and they were willing to accept the new faith if that would give them their farms and families. And Alfred's men were no less anxious to go back to their fields, their wives, and their lives.

In the years after Wedmore, Alfred was forced to put down several Viking attempts to seize more land for themselves. But the division of England into two kingdoms, the Anglo-Saxons and the Danelaw, would stand. The Treaty of Wedmore was a compromise, but it gave everyone what they wanted. Guthrum and the Viking warlords got a new home; Alfred was able to lay claim to the greatest Anglo-Saxon kingdom yet, a southern realm he could pass on to his son Edward; and Alfred's followers, the exhausted and war-beaten Anglo-Saxons of Wessex and Mercia, were finally permitted to return to their old, barely remembered lives.

It was for this that Alfred was remembered with gratitude: he was both conqueror and peacemaker. "Renowned, warlike, victorious, the zealous supporter of widows, orphans, and the poor," the twelfth-century historian John of Worcester concluded, "most dear to his people, gracious to all. . . . [H]e awaits the garment of blessed immortality and the glory of the resurrection with the just."[15]

T I M E L I N E   6 0

ABBASID EASTERN EMPIRE DYNASTIES	CORDOBA EMIRATE NORTH AFRICA	BRITAIN FRANKS ITALY	Roman Emperor
		Offa of Mercia (757–796)	
al-Mamun (813–833)			Louis the Pious (813–840)
		Pippin of Aquitaine (817–838)/Louis Lothair the German (818-855) (817–876) (Emperor 817–855)	
Rise of Tahirid dynasty Talhah ibn Tahir (822–828)	Abd ar-Rahman II (822–852)		
		Charles of Alemannia (829)	
al-Mutasim (833–842)			
		Pippin II of Aquitaine (838–852) Charles the Landless (840–877)	
	Viking attack on Cordoba (844)	Cinaed mac Treaty of Verdun (843) Alpin of Dal Riata (843–858) Viking attack on the Franks	
al-Mutawakkil (847–861)			
al-Muntasir (861–862)			
al-Mutazz (866–869) Rise of the Saffarid dynasty Ya'qub-i Laith Saffari (867–878)		Ethlelred of Wessex (865–871) Great Army of the Vikings arrives in Britain	
Rise of the Samanid dynasty Nasr of the Samanids (875–892)		Alfred of Wessex (871–899)	
		Treaty of Wedmore (878)	
Ismail of the Samanids (892–907)			
Rise of the Fatimid caliphate al-Mahdi of the Fatimids (909–934)			

Note: Primary rulers are in bold type; subject kings, in italics.

Chapter Sixty-One

—■—

Struggle for the Iron Crown

Between 875 and 899,
Charles the Landless buys the title "Emperor of the Romans,"
Charles the Fat inherits the entire empire by chance,
and the Magyars arrive in northern Italy

I N 875, CHARLES THE LANDLESS became emperor of the Romans by the most direct method possible. He offered Pope John VIII a huge bribe; the chroniclers agree that John crowned him, on Christmas Day, in exchange for *dona, pecunia, multa et pretiosa munera.*[1]

This infuriated Louis the German, who thought that the title should have come to him. Their older brother Lothair had died in 855, leaving his son Louis II the Younger as king of Italy and emperor of the Romans; Louis II had died earlier in 875, and Louis the German, the oldest Frankish king left, had expected to be the next emperor. He was now sixty-nine years old; he had seen the title passed to brother and nephew, and he wanted the *imperium* for himself.

Apparently it hadn't occurred to him to pay for it. But now that the coronation was over, all he could do was take revenge. While Charles the Landless was still in Rome, Louis the German stormed into his western Frankish lands, destroying and burning in fury. Charles hurried back home, but before the brothers could face off, Louis the German died. A lifetime of frustrated ambition had come to a sudden end.

Shortly afterward, Charles the Landless died of sudden illness; his son and heir, Louis the Stammerer, barely survived him by two years. The complicated mass of Frankish kingdoms devolved onto the surviving heirs: Louis the German's two sons Carloman and Louis the Younger (Louis III) divided the eastern Frankish realms between them, but when Carloman had a stroke, his lands passed on to his younger brother Charles the Fat, who was already ruling in Italy. The western Frankish kingdom was ruled jointly by Charles the Landless's two grandsons.

The Frankish kings negotiated and jousted for position. In 881, the pope decided to crown Charles the Fat of Italy as the emperor of the Romans. This had less to do with Charles (who was not much of a warrior) than with the fact that he was technically in control of Italy. The pope was worried that the Papal States might come under attack from one of his neighbors: Guy, the ambitious duke of Spoleto. If the pope were to invest any other Frankish king with the title of emperor, Charles might not allow him to come into Italy in defense of the pope—even though that was the purpose of the title.

Charles accepted the title of emperor, but after his coronation he never returned to southern Italy again, and certainly never bothered to help the Papal States against Guy of Spoleto's raids. But despite his disinterest, Charles the Fat—originally a younger brother with no chance of inheriting anything for himself—was soon not only emperor of the Romans, but the most powerful monarch in the west. In 882, two of the Frankish kings died of separate natural causes. In 884, the third was killed while hunting. All of these realms, one at a time, were added to the kingdom of the remaining legitimate heir: Charles the Fat. Chance and fate had managed to reunite the old empire and title of Charlemagne under a single king—with the sole exception of the territory of Provence, which had rebelled and declared itself independent.* What Louis the German had failed to do in a lifetime of fighting, negotiating, and sweating blood, Charles the Fat had gained without lifting a finger.[2]

But gaining and keeping were two different things, and Charles the Fat—weak and inept, with no legitimate son or heir and no plans for ruling his enormous new empire—almost immediately ran into trouble. In 885, the year after the entire empire had fallen under his rule, he began to have increased trouble with Vikings. They had been raiding his lands on a regular basis, but he had generally managed to buy them off with silver and (occasionally) hostages. Now the invasions grew more severe. Not all of the Great Army of the Vikings had settled in England; some of the warriors, not liking the idea of farming, had made their way back to the mainland to resume their life of raiding. They had also branched out from raiding by ship. Now, they were apt to land horses on the coasts and thunder across the countryside on horseback, raiding and killing in a much wider swath. "The Northmen do not cease capturing and killing the Christian people," lamented a Frankish monk,

> destroying churches, demolishing fortifications, and burning towns. Everywhere, there are only corpses of priests, laymen, whether noble or not, women, young people, suckling babes. There is no road, there is no place, where the ground is not strewn with corpses.[3]

Charles the Fat seemed entirely unable to stop the raids. He assembled an army that marched against the Vikings at the city of Louvain, where the

---

*Aquitaine had been reunited with the western Frankish lands and now fell under Charles the Fat's rule as well.

Franks were badly defeated. Victorious, the Vikings captured the city of Rouen, then organized a massive invasion up the Seine: seven hundred ships sailed up to the walls of Paris and laid siege to the city.[4]

Charles, who was far away from Paris at the time, sent an army, which failed to lift the siege. In desperation, he offered the Vikings seven hundred pounds of silver and winter quarters in Burgundy in exchange for their retreat.

The Vikings agreed to the bargain and lifted the siege of Paris. But Charles the Fat had lost whatever sympathy his people still had for him. They were furious: if he were going to hand over their tax money instead of driving the invaders away, why hadn't he done so at the beginning of the siege and spared them a great deal of trouble? The Burgundians, particularly annoyed by the cavalier offer of their homeland, revolted. Charles's nephew, Arnulf of Carinthia, raised an army, and in 887 he marched into the Frankish territory to remove his uncle by force.

In the face of all this hostility, Charles the Fat agreed to give up his titles as king and emperor. His willingness to surrender may have had something to do with his health; he had been suffering from a serious condition in his skull, even undergoing trepanning in an attempt to relieve his pain. In January of 888, just months after his abdication, Charles the Fat died.

The empire disintegrated into even smaller pieces than before, and a scramble for the title of emperor of the Romans began. Arnulf of Carinthia became the king of Eastern Francia; two Italian noblemen, Berengar of Friuli and Guy of Spoleto (the same duke of Spoleto who had been threatening to trouble the Papal States), began to quarrel over the right to become king of Italy; five different noblemen claimed other parts of the empire.* "As though bereft of a legitimate heir," writes the chronicler Regino of Prum, "the kingdoms that had obeyed him no longer waited for a ruler given by nature, but each chose to create for itself a king from its own innards. This situation sparked tremendous warring."[5]

In such chaos, the pope, Stephen V, protected his own interests. He declared Guy of Spoleto king of Italy and crowned him, in 891, as emperor. This bore the earmarks of a deal: the papal sanction and the title of emperor, in exchange for Guy's agreeing to leave the Papal States alone. It was, perhaps, not exactly what Charlemagne had meant when he declared that the emperor of the Romans had the responsibility of protecting the pope.

After only three years as emperor of the Romans, Guy of Spoleto died unexpectedly, intending his fourteen-year-old son Lambert to succeed him as king of Italy: "an elegant youth," writes the historian Liudprand of Cremona, "and, though still an adolescent, quite warlike." Berengar of Friuli, who had not

---

*Arnulf of Carinthia became king of Eastern Francia and Lotharingia; Odo was elected king of Western Francia; Guy of Spoleto and Berengar fought over Italy; Louis, son of the Provence nobleman Boso, was acclaimed in Provence; in Upper Burgundy, a nobleman man named Rudolph was made king; Ranulf II made himself king of Aquitaine and also announced that Charles the Simple, youngest son of Louis the Stammerer and now nine years old, was the rightful king of Western Francia.

given up hope of becoming king of Italy, was still causing trouble in the north; he at once advanced to the city of Pavia and declared himself rival king.[6]

In the midst of all this, the pope—Stephen V's successor, Formosus—sent a message to Arnulf of Carinthia, now king of Eastern Francia, and promised him the title of emperor if he would come down and restore peace. To Formosus's mind, his predecessor had overstepped himself by granting the honor to a random Italian warrior rather than to a king from the family of Charlemagne. Arnulf of Carinthia, Carolingian by birth, was the obvious candidate for the position.

Arnulf agreed and, in 896, finished the long journey to Rome at the head of his army. Lambert, hearing of the Frankish king's approach, had fled to his father's old homeland, Spoleto; Arnulf allowed Formosus to declare him not only king of Eastern Francia but also king of Italy and emperor of the Romans, and then began to march towards Spoleto to deal with Lambert.

But on the short journey between Rome and Spoleto, he suffered from a stroke, which partly paralyzed him. Abruptly, he gave up the plan to defeat Lambert and returned home.

Lambert emerged from Spoleto and reclaimed the title "King of Italy," but before he could get to Rome and punish Formosus, the pope died. Lambert barely allowed this to stop him. With adolescent outrage, he ordered Formosus's successor, Stephen VI, to open Formosus's casket. The dead pope was dressed in vestments and set behind a table, and Stephen VI convened a synod of churchmen to condemn and defrock the body. "Once these things were done," writes Liudprand of Cremona, "he ordered the corpse, stripped of its holy vestments and with three fingers cut off, to be tossed into the Tiber." The fingers were those with which Formosus had blessed the people of Rome. The synod itself was labelled, later, as the *Synodus Horrenda*, the "Trial of the Cadaver."[7]

With his feelings relieved, Lambert marched back up north and made a deal with Berengar: Lambert would rule the southern lands of Italy, Berengar could govern the north, and Lambert would seal the deal by marrying Berengar's daughter, Gisela. Berengar agreed. He probably had no intention of keeping to the terms of the deal, but he had no chance to violate it. Just months later, at the age of eighteen, Lambert broke his neck. Liudprand of Cremona wrote, in the first draft of his history, that Lambert was out hunting boars and fell off his horse; later, he revised his draft to add, "There is another account which seems to me more likely." In this second version of events, Lambert had been murdered by a young man from Milan whose father had been executed, and the assassin had then arranged the body so that a hunting accident would be suspected instead.[8]

However it happened, the death allowed Berengar to announce himself as king of all Italy. But although he had finally grasped his crown, an evil coincidence was about to remove it.

61.1: The Magyars

To his north, a storm was gathering. Once again a warrior had united separate tribes into a nascent nation: this time, the tribes were Finno-Ugrian, like the peoples among whom the Rus had settled. The warrior's name was Arpad, and he had created an alliance in which he was the first king. "Before this Arpad, they had never, at any time, had any other prince," wrote the Byzantine emperor Constantine Porphyrogenitus, in his history of the Magyars.[9]

Under Arpad, soldiers of the Magyar alliance began to move westward. Around 895, they had arrived at the edge of Moravia; in 898 they attacked Venice but then retreated. But in 899, just as Berengar claimed the Iron Crown of the Lombards, they advanced towards the north of Italy. They had been encouraged to do so; Arnulf of Carinthia, back in Eastern Francia, had offered them clothing and money if they would direct their energies towards northern Italy. Arnulf had been forced to give up the conquest of Italy, but he had not given up hope of removing his competitors.[10]

Berengar and his army fought back, but the Magyars were fresh, hungry, and hard to defeat. They were also experts at guerilla warfare, and for the next year, they sacked Italian towns and retreated before Berengar's men could catch up with them. Berengar began to lose the support of the Italian noblemen who had been willing to support his rule; if he couldn't get rid of the Magyars, what use was he?

Led by a northern Italian duke named Adalbert, whose lands had been hit hard by the Magyars, the noblemen invited a minor Carolingian prince, Louis of Provence (great-great-great-grandson of Charlemagne on his mother's side), to come into Italy and take up the Iron Crown. Berengar put up a token fight, but his army had shrunk, while Louis of Provence's supporters were increasing in number. Berengar was forced to flee from northern Italy, leaving the Iron Crown in the hands of his rival and the Magyars victorious in his wake.

T I M E L I N E 6 1					
BRITAIN FRANKS		ITALY	Roman Emperor	MAGYARS	MORAVIA
	Pippin II of Aquitaine (838–852)				
	Charles the Landless (840–877)				
Cinaed mac Alpin of Dal Riata (843–858)	Treaty of Verdun (843)				
	Viking attack on the Franks	**Louis II** (844–875)			**Rastislav** of Moravia (846–870)
			Louis II (855–875)		Arrival of Cyril and Methodius
Ethlelred of Wessex (865–871)					
	Louis the Stammerer (866–879)				
Great Army of the Vikings arrives in Britain					
Alfred of Wessex (871–899)		Pope John VIII (872–882)			**Svatopluk** of Moravia (871–894)
			Charles the Landless (875–877)		
Treaty of Wedmore (878)					
	Louis III (879–882)/ **Charles the Fat** (879–887)				
	Carloman II (879–884)				
			Charles the Fat (881–887)		
		Pope Stephen IV (885–891)			
	Arnulf of Carinthia (887–899)	**Guy of Spoleto** (889–894)			
		Pope Formosus (891–896)	Guy of Spoleto (891–894)		
		Lambert (896–898)	Arnulf of Carinthia (896–899)	Arpad (895–907)	
		Pope Stephen VI (896–898)			
		Berengar (898–900)			
		Louis of Provence (900–902)		Magyar entrance into Italy	

Chapter Sixty-Two

Kampaku

---

*Between 884 and 940,
the Fujiwara create a new position for themselves,
and the heavenly sovereign Uda tries and fails
to break Fujiwara power*

Bʏ 884, ᴛʜᴇ Fᴜᴊɪᴡᴀʀᴀ ᴏғғɪᴄɪᴀʟ Mototsune was the most power-ful man in Japan. He had been Sessho, regent for the child emperor Yozei, and in 881 he was appointed prime minister as well. Now, with Yozei well into his teens and capable of claiming rule for himself, Mototsune invented a new title for himself. He would be *Kampaku*, or "Civil Dictator"—a sort of super-advisor to the crown. It was a title that allowed him to have almost the same amount of power over a grown emperor as a Sessho had held over the underage ruler.[1]

Meanwhile, the fifteen-year-old Yozei, who had been a crowned and idle sovereign for ten years, was mutating from bored child into budding psy-chopath. He had developed a fondness for watching dogs kill monkeys and feeding frogs to snakes; he had also begun to suggest that he should carry out the execution of criminals with his own hands. Mototsune took advantage of this troubling behavior and called a council of palace officials, all of whom agreed with him that the young emperor should be dethroned. The Kampaku then lured his heavenly sovereign into a carriage, promising him a visit to the races, and whisked him out of the city. In his place, the court acclaimed his great-uncle, the fifty-four-year-old heavenly sovereign Koko.[2]

Yozei was never imprisoned; his psychopathy took an occasional downward turn (he was reputedly responsible for at least two murders), but he seems to have been allowed to roam through the mountains on horseback, hunting and sleeping out and sometimes appearing without warning at the gates of one or another great landowner, demanding to be let in. He fell in love at least once and wrote a poem to the woman he desired, its imagery drawn from the remote northeastern coast, where the Mina river plunged from the three-thousand-foot Mount Tsukuba into a boiling pool:

The Mina stream comes tumbling down
    From Mount Tsukuba's height;
Strong as my love, it leaps into
    A pool as black as night
    With overwhelming might.

There is no record that he ever married.[3]

Back in Heian, Heavenly Sovereign Koko paid no attention to politics. Mototsune remained as Kampaku, keeping the reins of the government completely in his own hands. For the first time, the Kampaku openly ruled for an emperor who was an adult at the time of his coronation. It was a turning point in the development of this office, which had never been officially created or sanctioned, and which owed its existence to the ambition and energy of a single family. And Mototsune's unquestioned dominance continued for another three years, until Koko died.[4]

He was succeeded by his twenty-one-year-old son, Heavenly Sovereign Uda, who immediately began a careful but determined campaign to get real power back from his prime minister. On the death of the emperor Koko, Mototsune had offered his ceremonial resignation as Kampaku, something that had become (like the resignation of all White House staff at the end of an American presidency) a standard gesture in Japanese politics. Uda was supposed to accept it and, in an equally standard gesture, reappoint Mototsune as his own Kampaku.

Uda accepted the resignation, but then rebelled against the custom. He did not dare infuriate the powerful Fujiwara clan by neglecting to reappoint Mototsune altogether. Instead he wrote a fulsome official letter to the older man, offering Mototsune the post not of Kampaku, but of *Ako*, or "Supreme Minister," in the new administration.

The title of Ako was old and respected, but largely ceremonial. Mototsune was so furious that he went on strike. He was still prime minister, after all, and as long as he refused to sign papers or answer petitions, the business of the court ground to a halt.

For nearly a year, Heavenly Sovereign Uda resisted the growing pressure from his other officials to pacify Mototsune by giving him back the title of Kampaku. Government business grew more and more snarled, and the scholars at court debated with increasing heat about whether or not the title Ako was an insult. "All affairs of government, great and small, have stagnated," Uda wrote in his diary. "All the provinces and all the ministries complain ceaselessly."[5]

Finally, in November of 888, Uda was forced to buckle. He blamed the offer of the post of Ako on his unfortunate secretary, the scholar Hiromi, saying that Hiromi had misunderstood his intentions and written the wrong title in the letter. This was about all the face-saving he could do; he was embarrassed, Hiromi's career was sharply curtailed, and Mototsune (with dignity) accepted the appointment as Kampaku and started signing papers again.[6]

He had proved that he, and not the heavenly sovereign, had the last word at court. But even Mototsune could not live forever. Some years before, the poet Ariwara no Narihira—a man of royal blood, a distant relative of the heavenly sovereign Kammu, who had run afoul of the Fujiwara and had seen his chances of advancement at court go up in flames—had voiced the hope of Mototsune's enemies: that old age and death would finally bring an end to Mototsune's lifelong grab for more power.

> Scatter and cover
> With clouds, cherry blossoms,
>   That you may hide the path
> By which old age
> Is said to approach.[7]

In 891, his hopes were realized. Mototsune, in the grip of worsening illness, resigned his position as Kampaku and died just a few weeks later.

Mototsune's oldest son, Tokihira, was barely twenty-one, and Uda refused to award him (or anyone else) the title of Kampaku. Instead he left the post empty and appointed members of other clans to as many official positions as possible. He could not ignore Tokihira, but he gave the young man a junior post and put no reliance in him. His most trusted advisor was Sugawara no Michizane, a poet with an unimportant family background and a talent for scholarship; Michizane, who was in his fifties, had experience serving as a governor in the provinces and had earned Uda's gratitude by coming out in support of the scapegoat secretary Hiromi during the earlier struggle with Mototsune.[8]

Uda's humiliation at Mototsune's hands made him wary of out-and-out defiance of Fujiwara expectations. Over the next ten years, he promoted Mototsune's son through the ranks at court at a reasonable rate, but he also promoted Michizane with equal diligence. By 896, the two men held the two highest positions in his government.

Meanwhile, the heavenly sovereign had been working hard to improve the relationship between the court at Heian and the outer provinces. Aware that the noblemen in the outer reaches of the kingdom were collecting taxes for the crown and then keeping them for themselves, he passed a series of reforms to prevent those noblemen from seizing the land of the peasants under their power. And then, when these reforms were well underway, he abdicated.[9]

He was only thirty-one, and the abdication was a risky and bold move. His oldest son Daigo had just turned thirteen and could rule without the supervision of a Sessho. By stepping down and allowing Daigo to be crowned as heavenly sovereign in his place, Uda could supervise the transfer of power. In any case, Uda had no intention of giving up his power. Although he went through the formal steps of putting off his royal robes, taking up the study of Buddhism, and applying for entrance to a monastery, he kept his hand in court politics so heavily that he became known as "the Cloistered Emperor." His fight against Fujiwara power had not exactly been intended to restore the real political power of the heavenly sovereign; that position remained relatively passive, a vital but highly ceremonial connection between the people of Japan and the divine order. Instead, it had been a struggle to resist the overwhelming ambitions of a single family, and he had placed Michizane in the front lines of that battle.

Michizane found the position uncomfortable. In 899, two years after Uda's abdication, he petitioned the young heavenly sovereign Daigo to be allowed to resign. He had got wind of a plot against him, led by Fujiwara no Tokihira, and he was frightened.[10]

Daigo, directed by his father, refused to accept the resignation. In 901, Tokihira struck. He convinced Daigo, who was (after all) not quite seventeen and suffering the usual teenage anxieties, that his father was plotting with Michizane to remove him and place one of his brothers on the throne instead. Daigo was persuaded to issue an imperial decree, without notifying his father, that would exile Michizane from the capital city for life.

As soon as the boy set his name to the decree, Tokihira ordered his rival and his family arrested and hauled off to the outer limits of the empire. As soon as the arrest was made, the cat was out of the bag; officials loyal to Uda ran to the monastery where he lived and told him what was happening. Uda rode to the palace at once, but Tokihira had locked the doors. He was unable to get in and spent the night standing in the street. By morning, Michizane and his sons were already well out of Heian, on their way to exile on the southern island of Kyushu.[11]

Uda's gamble had failed, and Sugawara no Michizane paid the price; he died in exile two years later, without ever returning to the capital. With young Daigo under his thumb, Tokihira began to make himself as powerful at court as his great father had been. He did not try to claim the title of Kampaku, but he once again filled the ranks of courtiers and officials with Fujiwara noblemen and their flunkies. Uda, in his monastery, was cut off from his son, from authority, and from the role he had hoped to play in the government of his country.[12]

Tokihira's rise was cut short by his premature death in 909, but his brother, Mototsune's younger son Fujiwara no Tadahira, took over as his succes-

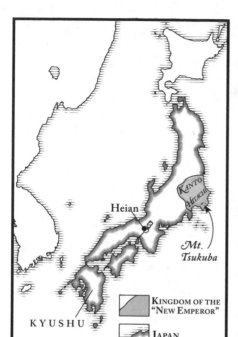

62.1: The Rebellion of Masakado

sor. When the heavenly sovereign Daigo died in 930, at age forty-six, the court elected Tadahira as Sessho to the emperor's seven-year-old son. A year later, Uda also died: still in his monastery, still excluded from the palace. When the new heavenly sovereign Suzaku reached the age of responsibility, Tadahira claimed the post of Kampaku. He had regained his father's position, and once again the Fujiwara clan held almost every important post in Heian.[13]

THE JOSTLING FOR POWER in Heian did not erupt into assassination and civil war, as it did in China, or in Byzantium, or in the kingdoms farther west. For one thing, the heavenly sovereign of Japan had no standing army. When the heavenly sovereign needed troops, they were drafted from the civilian population of free men older than twenty and younger than sixty. Even these draftees lived, when not actually fighting, as "on-call" civilians. For the most part they remained in their own homes, living in their own provinces, carrying on their regular lives as farmers and merchants, and generally giving no more than thirty-five or forty days per year to military service. And so the Fujiwara (or other ambitious noblemen) did not have the option, so popular to the west, of pursuing a career as a general, gaining the army's support, and using it to overthrow the sovereign.*

What they *could* do was gain legislative power at court, like the Fujiwara, or else use their own private armies to control an outlying region, away from the capital city.

In 939, a landowner named Taira no Masakado followed the second path. He lived in the fertile northeastern area known as the Kanto; he was skilled at fighting on horseback and ambitious for his family's honor, and he could boast descent from the emperor Kammu himself. The men of his clan, the

*The Japanese military structure was somewhat more complex than this brief summary allows me to describe; for a more detailed explanation, see Karl F. Friday, *Hired Swords* (Stanford University Press, 1992), pp. 1–32.

Taira, held various official positions in the Kanto, and Masakado himself had spent time at the court in Heian as a young man. There he had seen firsthand the power of the Fujiwara clan; the sight, perhaps, fired his ambition.[14]

His climb to power began as a local squabble. On his return home from the Heian court, Masakado quarrelled with several of his neighbors over land rights, and the quarrel escalated into a fight. The armed retainers of the battling landowners began a small local war, which tipped Masakado's way.

Encouraged by his success, Masakado directed his private army—now numbering over a thousand men—to follow him in attacking the nearest provincial governor, the royal official in charge of the province of Hitachi. The governor's office, not designed to hold off an army, surrendered quickly. Masakado, even more impressed by his own might, declared himself to be a monarch in his own right: the "New Emperor." He captured the surrounding royal outposts as well and started to appoint court officials of his own to help run them.[15]

But his rule lasted only three months. Tadahira ordered a price put on his head; the heavenly sovereign didn't have a standing army, but he had plenty of money. Two other great landowners, one of them a Fujiwara and the other a member of Masakado's own clan, banded together to fight against the New Emperor (and claim the reward). Three months after Masakado had crowned himself, his two opponents descended on the northern border of his captured territory with their own private troops.

Masakado's army, like all the other armies in Japan, was in flux; the men who served him were not full-time soldiers, and they tended to come and go so that they could take care of their private lives. At the moment of attack, it had temporarily shrunk to about four hundred men. The tiny force was wiped out, and Masakado was killed. "His horse forgot how to gallop as the wind in flight," says the *Shomonki*, the contemporary history of his revolt, "and the man lost his martial skills. Struck by an arrow from the gods, in the end the New Emperor perished alone."[16]

Masakado's armed revolt was the unruly provincial version of the Fujiwara grab for power in the center of the kingdom. It was less successful than the sophisticated political maneuvering in Heian, but it was a foretaste of things to come. For the next century, the Fujiwara would continue to dominate, in their hereditary semi-legal dictatorship; but their power would not go unchallenged. The heavenly sovereign had been slowly boxed into a smaller and smaller space, and outside that space the aristocratic families of Japan fought for power with increasing ferocity.

TIME LINE 62					

FRANKS	ITALY	Roman Emperor	MORAVIA	MAGYARS	JAPAN
Treaty of Verdun (843) Viking attack on the Franks		**Louis II** (844–875)			
			Rastislav of Moravia (846–870)		
					Montoku (850–858)
		Louis II (855–875)			**Seiwa** (858–876) Yoshifusa as Sessho (858–872)
			Arrival of Cyril and Methodius		
Louis the Stammerer (866–879)					
	Pope John VIII (872–882)		**Svatopluk** of Moravia (871–894)		Mototsune as Sessho (872–891)
	Charles the Landless (875–877)				**Yozei** (876–884)
Louis III (879–882)/ **Charles the Fat** (879–887) **Carloman II** (879-884)		Charles the Fat (881–887)			Mototsune as Kampaku (881–891)
	Pope Stephen IV (885–891)				**Koko** (884–887)
Arnulf of Carinthia (887–899)	**Guy of Spoleto** (889–894)				Uda (887–897)
	Pope Formosus (891–896)	**Guy of Spoleto** (891–894)			
				Arpad (895–907)	
	Lambert (896–898) Pope Stephen VI (896–898)	**Arnulf of Carinthia** (896–899)			**Daigo** (897–930)
				Magyar entrance into Italy	
	Berengar (898–900) **Louis of Provence** (900–902)				
					Suzaku (930–946) Tadahira as Sessho (930–941)
					Rebellion of Masakado (939) Tadahira as Kampaku (941–949)

Chapter Sixty-Three

Basileus

Between 886 and 927,
Leo the Wise defies the patriarch of Constantinople,
the Bulgarian king demands the title of emperor, and
Romanos Lecapenus explains that Christians should not fight wars

LEO VI, LEGAL SON OF BASIL I, was twenty when he became sole emperor of Constantinople. Almost at once, he began to earn himself the nickname "Leo Sophos," or "Leo the Wise." This title did not necessarily suggest enormous skill in government; it meant something more like "Leo the Bookish." Leo read widely, had a prodigious memory, and occupied his evenings by writing military manuals, revising legal codes, composing hymns and poems, and preparing sermons, which he delivered on feast days and special occasions.[1]

He was not the first emperor to preach sermons—his predecessor Leo III had given a whole series of anti-icon homilies—but Leo the Wise had his hands in church affairs up to the elbows. The theologian Arethas of Caesarea called him *theosophos*, "wise in the things of God," which may be a code phrase for "meddler in sacred things." He had barely come to the throne when he decided to replace the patriarch, the senior churchman in Constantinople, with his own nineteen-year-old brother, Stephen, and after Stephen's death he appointed the next two patriarchs on his own authority as well.[2]

The second of these patriarchs, the monk Nicholas Mystikos, proved less malleable than Leo the Wise intended. By 901, Leo had to face the unpleasant truth that the succession to the throne was in danger. At nearly forty, he had married three times, but he had not managed to father a son; in fact, he had been forced to crown his brother Alexander as co-emperor and heir.

He had not given up hope, though. When his third wife died in 901, Leo tried to marry again, this time choosing his mistress, Zoe Karbonopsina, "Zoe the Black-Eyed."

At this the patriarch Nicholas Mystikos balked. Even marrying three times was not exactly legal; an arcane bit of church doctrine said that while it was perfectly acceptable to marry again if your spouse died, you should only do it once. The patriarch had squinted at the third marriage, but he'd have had to close his eyes for the fourth, and this he was unwilling to do.

Leo put up with this through the birth of Zoe's first baby, a girl. She became pregnant again at the beginning of 905; when she went into labor, Leo moved her into the porphyry-walled palace chamber where, by tradition, empresses gave birth to royal heirs. To be born in the Purple Chamber meant that the court had admitted you into its center; and the court of Constantinople was much more powerful, as a whole, than any single emperor. "Emperors might and did come and go," writes the historian Arnold Toynbee, "able adventurers might and did oust an ephemeral dynasty, but the Court lived on." Venerated by the court, the emperors of Constantinople were also hostage to the court's goodwill, and an emperor's power was only as great as the loyalty of his ministers and officers.[3]

Leo's court was loyal enough to support his quest for an heir, so Zoe delivered in the purple room, surrounded by the traditional attendants. Much to Leo's relief, her baby was a boy. Reaching for every strategy that might help legitimize his new son, the emperor gave him the hallowed royal name "Constantine."[4]

Both the name and the birth in the Purple Chamber were props to the baby's legitimacy, but to ensure his position beyond challenge, Leo still needed to marry his son's mother. He suggested again to the patriarch that he should wed for a fourth time. Again the patriarch refused. Leo, *theosophos* that he was, decided that patriarchal permission was unnecessary, and married Zoe anyway, in a lavish public ceremony that infuriated the senior churchmen of Constantinople. "The mother was introduced into the palace, just like an emperor's wife," Nicholas Mystikos later wrote, in a letter to Rome, "and the very crown was set on the woman's head. . . . [T]he archpriestly and priestly body was in uproar, as though the whole faith had been subverted."[5]

Despite his objections to the marriage, Nicholas Mystikos was essentially the emperor's man. But the loud yells of outrage from the other churchmen in Constantinople forced him to uphold the church's authority. Since Leo had defied the church, Nicholas Mystikos barred him, reluctantly, from entering the churches of his own city.

This was unacceptable to Leo. In 907, he sent his soldiers to remove (by force) and exile not only Nicholas but also the whole tier of priests who had objected to Zoe's installation as empress. Then, when Constantine reached the age of six, Leo crowned him as co-emperor. He gave the little boy the royal name "Constantine VII Porphyrogenitus," meaning "purple-born," to remind everyone who approached the new emperor that the court had supported Constantine's right to inherit.

He intended to make the succession as secure as possible before he died, because Byzantium was under hard pressure from the outside. For at least two centuries, the Islamic armies had been the greatest threat to Constantinople's safety. Now, the Abbasids were preoccupied with their own troubles, and the main locus of the threat had shifted west.

The Bulgarian king Boris, who had presided over his country's formal conversion to Christianity, had been distant but cordial, and had even sent his son Simeon to be educated in Constantinople. But Simeon, once on the Bulgarian throne, turned into an enemy.* Like Leo the Wise, Simeon was a reader: Nicholas Mystikos described him as a man whose "love of knowledge led him to reread the books of the ancients," and his reading had fired his imagination. He wanted to turn Bulgaria into a great empire like the empires of old, and while Leo was absorbed by his marital troubles, Simeon was able to advance Bulgarian forces all the way to the walls of Constantinople. In 904, Leo had been forced to make a treaty giving the entire north of the Greek peninsula to Bulgaria—which made Simeon the emperor over almost all of the Slavic tribes in the lands now known as the Balkans.[6]

This had lifted one western threat, but another was approaching. In 906, the same year that Constantine Porphyrogenitus was confirmed as co-emperor, the Rus also pushed their way to the gates of Constantinople.

The Rus had been growing in strength since their conversion. Their own accounts tell us that Rurik, the legendary Viking warrior who settled at Novgorod, had steadily spread his power among the surrounding peoples, and that when he died in 879, he left both his kingdom and the guardianship of his young son to another Rus nobleman, Oleg of Novgorod. Oleg took power for himself and three years later moved the center of his power to Kiev.

Since this same Oleg apparently was still alive and active seventy years later, most historians suspect that "Oleg" is a title rather than a personal name. The story reflects a general spread of Rus power under their warrior leaders; by the end of the ninth century, the Rus had forced the neighboring Slavic tribes to pay them tribute. The *Russian Primary Chronicle* lists a multitude of subjected peoples, including the eastern Slavic tribe of the Drevlians, who were forced to supply troops for the 906 attack on Constantinople—a total of two thousand ships, stuffed with men from twelve different nations. According to the colorful but unreliable *Chronicle*, the Rus made "wheels which they attached to the ships, and when the wind was favorable, they spread the sails and bore

---

*Boris abdicated in 889 and entered a monastery, leaving the throne to his older son Vladimir. Vladimir tried to reverse his father's policy on Christianity and started to drive out priests; Boris came out of the monastery, removed and jailed Vladimir, and crowned his younger son Simeon as his heir instead.

63.1: Loss of the Balkans

down upon the city from the open country. When the Greeks beheld this, they were afraid."[7]

Whatever terrified them, the people of Constantinople agreed to pay a huge tribute so that the Rus would retreat. A second treaty in 911 established a fragile peace, but the future looked grim to Leo. He died in 912, predicting on his deathbed that the empire would totter in the hands of his heirs.[8]

With Leo's death, his brother became senior emperor. Alexander, now forty-two, had been a crowned emperor without power for thirty-three years. He had spent most of his adult life drinking, hunting, and waiting for his brother to die, and his new authority went to his head. He was no fool; he dismissed Leo's court officers and recalled instead old Nicholas Mystikos, who was not likely to support any effort of the improperly born Constantine VII to usurp his uncle's authority. But then Alexander immediately announced that Constantinople would not pay the Bulgarian king Simeon I the yearly tribute Leo had promised.[9]

This defiance simply begged Simeon to descend on Byzantium and prove that he was no paper king. Simeon I took up the dare and doubled it; the historian Leo the Deacon writes that he sent a message to Constantinople, demanding that the new emperor acknowledge that Simeon too was an emperor, *basileus* of the Bulgarian people and so equal in rank to Alexander himself.[10]

Alexander, of course, refused.

Leo the Deacon is no fan of non-Greeks—using the ancient and dismissive term for Bulgarians, he chalks Simeon's demand up to "customary Scythian madness"—but in fact Simeon now had been not only cheated of his money but also insulted, and so could justify to his own people the risk of besieging the great city itself. As he began to march towards Constantinople, Alexander, having started the fight, died; he had a stroke in the middle of a post-dinner game of ball on horseback (a sort of medieval polo), living only long enough to appoint Nicholas Mystikos as his young nephew's head regent. His death left the city in turmoil, ruled by a child and facing an approaching Bulgarian army led by a determined and insulted warrior king.

The decision of how to deal with Simeon I was thus left to Constantine VII's council of regents, now headed by old Nicholas Mystikos. The patriarch was still smarting over Leo's decision to overrule his judgment in favor of the pope's, back when Constantine was a baby. Should Nicholas Mystikos admit without reservation that Constantine VII was legitimate and therefore the rightful ruler of Constantinople, he would also be admitting that the bishop of Rome had been right and he had been wrong—not a likely scenario. When Simeon I appeared outside the walls of Constantinople, Nicholas Mystikos found himself in an awkward position: supporting the rule of an emperor he thoroughly believed to be illegitimate.

He agreed to admit Simeon to the city for a parley and proposed a peace treaty. Byzantium would pay tribute to the Bulgarians, Constantine VII would agree to take one of Simeon's daughters as his wife, and he himself, the patriarch of Constantinople, would crown Simeon as emperor of the Bulgarians: *basileus*, bearing the same authority (although only over his own people) as the emperor of Byzantium.

Undoubtedly Nicholas Mystikos would have been much more reluctant to take this route had he not firmly believed that Constantinople *had* no legitimate emperor. There was no harm in allowing Simeon I to take the title of emperor, since no one (in his view) actually *held* it at that particular moment.[11]

Constantine's mother, Zoe, was naturally appalled by the proposal, as were a good many of the soldiers and courtiers at Constantinople. Once Simeon was safely out of the gates, Zoe led a palace revolt, threw Nicholas Mystikos out of the palace (he remained regent, but she warned him to mind the business of the church and stay out of hers), and took control of the council. She then cancelled the entire peace treaty with Simeon.

In revenge, Simeon embarked on a series of raids and attacks. He began to capture cities on the border between the two countries with increasing and worrying frequency. By 917, it was clear that the Byzantine army would have to launch a major strike against the Bulgarians.

Constantine VII was still only eleven, so the planning of the strike lay in Zoe's hands. She had two commanders to make use of: Leo Phocas, general of the Byzantine ground forces, and Romanos Lecapenus, admiral of the Byzantine navy. Romanos Lecapenus was a skilled officer, but he was also the son of a peasant and did not cut much of a figure in Byzantine society; Phocas, who was generally thought by army men to be a commander of limited talent, was a handsome aristocrat. But Liudprand of Cremona tells that he "ardently desired to be made father of the emperor," and Zoe decided to entrust the attack to him.[12]

He marched his army north along the Black Sea coast to meet Simeon I and the Bulgarian army at Anchialus, on the shores of the Black Sea, while Romanos Lecapenus lay off the shore with his fleet. On August 20, the two armies clashed. Accounts of the battle contradict each other, perhaps because most of the eyewitnesses died; the Battle of Anchialus was the bloodiest day of fighting in centuries. Almost all of Leo Phocas's officers and tens of thousands of regular soldiers fell. The battleground was unusable for decades afterwards because of the corpses stacked on it; according to Leo the Deacon, piles of bones still cluttered the field nearly eighty years later.[13]

The Bulgarians won the day, chasing the remnants of the Byzantine army southwards. Leo Phocas barely escaped. As for the admiral Romanos Lecapenus, he ordered his ships to pull up anchor and retreated back into the safety of the Black Sea as soon as he realized the battle was lost.

Leo Phocas tried to make another stand right outside Constantinople, but the Bulgarians massacred his remaining men a second time. By the time he managed to struggle back inside the city walls, Romanos Lecapenus was already there. He had sailed straight for the city, and now his fleet was anchored in the water nearby.

Before Leo Phocas could explain his defeat, Romanos Lecapenus struck. He invited the city officials to board his flagship to discuss strategy and then locked them in the hold, after which he marched into the city and removed Zoe and all of her supporters. He was practically unopposed; he had managed to escape blame for the defeat, which had fallen squarely on Zoe and her lover Phocas.[14]

Romanos took charge of the council of regents, promising safety and deliverance. Leo Phocas, recognizing trouble, discreetly removed himself from Zoe's offers of marriage and retreated to Chrysopolis. No one tried to keep him from leaving.

By April of 919, Romanos had gained so much popular support that he decided to try for the crown itself. He sent Zoe to a convent and convinced the council of regents to name him Constantine's second-in-command. He then arranged for the marriage of his own daughter, nine-year-old Elena, to the thirteen-year-old Constantine VII Porphyrogenitus. As both father-in-law and vice emperor, he had only one more step to ascend to the throne itself.

It proved to be a short step. The patriarch, old Nicholas Mystikos, saw Romanos as a welcome replacement for Constantine VII, who remained illegitimate in the unbending old man's eyes. Mystikos agreed to crown Romanos as Romanos I, co-emperor of Byzantium, and young Constantine was again in the shadow of a senior emperor. He would stay there for the next quarter century. The court loyalty that had allowed him to assume the crown had shifted to the able older man, pushing Constantine to the side.

When Leo Phocas objected strenuously to all of this from his distant retreat, Romanos sent two men to arrest him. They overstepped their authority and blinded him. Romanos declared himself to be extremely distressed by this turn of events.[15]

Meanwhile Simeon I of Bulgaria had regrouped and was again fighting his way towards Constantinople. He had already been to its walls, more than once, and knew that the city was all but unconquerable with a ground force. His only hope of taking it was with ships, and Bulgaria had no navy. He would have to borrow one; so he sent an embassy to the Fatimid caliph al-Mahdi, who had now extended his control eastward to the old city of Carthage, and asked al-Mahdi to make a formal alliance with him.

Al-Mahdi agreed; the alliance undoubtedly struck him as a prudent preemptive strike. Unfortunately for Simeon, on the way back from North Africa his ambassadors were taken prisoner by Byzantine soldiers and sent to Constantinople. Romanos then sent an offer of his own to the Fatimid caliph: if al-Mahdi would become his ally, rather than Simeon's, he would pay tribute and guarantee a peace.

On consideration, Romanos decided that he'd better make sure that neither Islamic empire attacked him, and so also sent offers of peace to Baghdad.

Both caliphs accepted Romanos's terms. Deprived of his ally, Simeon asked for parley instead. Romanos agreed to meet with him, and careful preparations were made; both sides remembered the Byzantine attack on Simeon's predecessor Krum. The two kings sent hostages to each other, and a wooden platform with a wall across its center was built in the waters of the Golden Horn. On September 9, 924, Simeon rode up onto the platform from land, on horseback; Romanos sailed up to it on the royal ship; and the two men looked each other in the eye across the wall.[16]

Simeon's ambitions had been thwarted by canny politics and alliances, the same canny politics and alliances that had brought Romanos to the throne. But, face to face with his enemy, Romanos used the language of faith, not the language of war. His speech to Simeon, as historian Steven Runciman points out, is recorded word for word in various chronicles, suggesting that an official record was made of his words. He said,

I have heard that you are a religious man and a devoted Christian; but I do not see your acts harmonizing with your words. . . . If then you are a true Christian, as we believe, cease from your unjust slaughter and shedding the blood of the guiltless, and make peace with us Christians—since you claim to be a Christian—and do not desire to stain Christian hands with the blood of fellow-Christians. . . . Welcome peace, love concord, that you yourself may live a peaceful, bloodless and untroubled life, and that Christians may end their woes and cease destroying Christians. For it is a sin to take up arms against fellow-believers.[17]

Coming from a man who had just made peace with two different caliphs in order to thwart his fellow-believer, this was a bit thick. Nevertheless, Simeon was taken aback. He agreed to a peace in exchange for restoration of the annual tribute, and returned back home.

In 927, Simeon had a heart attack and died. He was succeeded by his son Peter, who made a lightning-quick destructive invasion of the Byzantine territory in Macedonia and then retreated and offered to make peace. Romanos, taking his cue from the destruction Peter had just wrought, agreed. As part of the treaty, Peter I married Romanos's granddaughter.

Even more important, Romanos, yielding the point that had begun the whole fight, recognized him as emperor. The Bulgarian king had risen to the same status as the ruler of Constantinople.

TIMELINE 63

JAPAN	BYZANTIUM ABBASID FATIMID RUS MORAVIA EMPIRE CALIPHATE BULGARIA
	Michael III (842–867)
	Rastislav of al-Mutawakkil Moravia (846–870) (847–861)
Montoku (850–858)	
	Boris (852–889)
Seiwa (858–876) Yoshifusa as Sessho (858–872)	Viking/Rus attack on Constantinople (860)
	al-Muntasir (861–862) Rurik (?) (862–c. 879)
	Arrival of Cyril and Methodius
	al-Mutazz (866–869) Basil I (867–886)
Mototsune as Sessho (872–891)	Svatopluk of Moravia (871–894)
Yozei (876–884)	Oleg (?) (c. 879–?)
Mototsune as Kampaku (881–891) Koko (884–887)	
	Leo VI (886–912) Patriarch Stephen I (886–893)
Uda (887–897)	
Daigo (897–930)	Simeon (893–927)
	Patriarch Nicholas Mystikos (901–907/912–925)
	Rus attack on Constantinople (906)
	al-Mahdi of the Fatimids (909–934)
	Alexander (912–913) Constantine Porphyrogenitus (913–959)
	Battle of Anchialus (917)
	Romanos Lecapenus as senior co-emperor (920–944)
Suzaku (930–946) Tadahira as Sessho (930–941)	Peter (927–969)
Rebellion of Masakado (939)	
Tadahira as Kampaku (941–949)	

Chapter Sixty-Four

The Creation of Normandy

Between 902 and 911,
Berengar blinds the emperor of the Romans and takes Italy for himself,
and Charles the Simple gives part of Western Francia to the Vikings

I N 902, THE ITALIAN NOBLEMAN Berengar finally won back the Iron Crown of the Lombards. He defeated Louis of Provence, who held the triple titles "King of Provence," "King of Italy," and "Emperor of the Romans," in battle. As part of his surrender, Louis promised Berengar that he would return to his homeland and would content himself with ruling Provence (as an independent king; he refused to swear allegiance to the king of the eastern Franks) and being emperor of the Romans; he would never enter Italy again.

This promise lasted only until 905, when Adalbert and the other Italian nobles invited Louis back again. Berengar, says Liudprand of Cremona, was "perceived to be tiresome," which probably means that he was behaving in a more royal manner than they liked. The Italian nobility was accustomed to having a fair amount of independence, and Louis of Provence had been a hands-off ruler.[1]

So Louis came back into Italy and set himself up with great ceremony in the city of Verona. He knew that Berengar would attack him again, but he had been guaranteed soldiers from the private armies of Adalbert and the others, and he was confident of victory.

He was a little taken aback, though, by the size of the private armies—and by the luxury in which Adalbert and the others lived. Tactlessly, he remarked to one of his generals that Adalbert seemed to aspire to royal splendor, and that only the lack of a royal title made Adalbert less than a king.

Adalbert's wife overheard the conversation. It struck her as a veiled threat and she warned her husband that Louis of Provence might not prove quite as willing to let them go their own way as he had once been. Behind the scenes, as Louis set himself up for battle, the noblemen consulted, argued, and then agreed to withdraw their support quietly from Louis's cause. Berengar, getting wind of the change, offered a substantial bribe if they would let him into Verona late at night while Louis was off guard.

They agreed, and while the unsuspecting emperor of the Romans slept, Berengar and his men crept into the city. Berengar's guards found Louis and dragged him in front of Berengar, who snapped, "I let you go out of pity, when I captured you before, and you promised that you would never re-enter Italy. This time I will spare your life, but I will take your eyesight."[2]

His men then gouged out Louis's eyes. Louis survived the operation, but now that he was mutilated and unable to function without help, he was forced to relinquish the title of emperor as well as the Iron Crown of Italy. He returned to Provence, where he lived almost twenty years. For the rest of his life, he was known as Louis the Blind.[3]

Berengar, once more on the Italian throne, hoped to become emperor of the Romans in Louis's place, but the pope made no motion to offer him the title. Berengar was not a Carolingian, and there was no guarantee that he would be king of the Italian territory for long.*

Back up to the north, the kings who *were* Carolingian were too preoccupied with their own difficulties to campaign for the title of emperor. The jumble of Frankish mini-kingdoms had begun to sort itself out as some of the minor players were conquered, or murdered, or simply fled. Arnulf of Carinthia had died right after hiring the Magyars to harass northern Italy and had been succeeded, as king of Eastern Francia, by his six-year-old son Louis the Child. The noblemen of Western Francia had elected Charles the Simple, grandson of Charles the Fat, to rule them. The upper part of Burgundy, which had rebelled when Charles the Fat offered it to the Vikings as a playground, remained independent under one of its own nobleman, Rudolf of Burgundy. Invading Magyars troubled the eastern Frankish lands, and Vikings harassed Charles the Simple in the west.

The Viking raids, brought temporarily under control by Charles the Landless's fortified bridges, had once again intensified. In 911, Charles the Simple settled on a drastic solution to the Viking raids. He decided to give part of his land in Western Francia to Viking invaders, in a treaty that would guarantee protection for the rest of his realm.

He chose to negotiate this deal with a Viking chief who was already known to him: a man named Rollo who had already spent a good part of his adult life fighting in Western Francia. He had been a junior commander of the fleet that besieged Paris in 885, and had returned on a regular basis ever since: raiding, fighting, accepting payment, withdrawing, and then raiding again.

Charles the Simple offered Rollo a homeland of his own on the western coast and promised to make him ruler of it. In exchange, Rollo would have

---

*Berengar would eventually serve as Roman emperor from 915 to 924; because of Louis's blinding, the title remained vacant from 906 to 915.

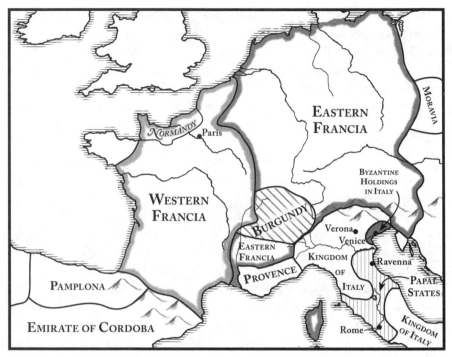

64.1: The Creation of Normandy

to agree to accept Christian baptism, to be loyal to the king of the Western Franks, and to fight against any other Viking invaders who might trouble Charles's kingdom.

Rollo agreed to the deal. He picked Robert as his baptismal name, and the Treaty of Saint-Clair-sur-Epte transformed the Viking warrior into the first duke of Normandy. It also transformed him into Charles's son-in-law; to seal the treaty, Robert of Normandy married Gisela, Charles the Simple's daughter.

But seeds of trouble were visible, even at the ceremony that awarded Rollo his new land. One of the nearby bishops ordered Rollo to kiss the king's foot, a common gesture of respect from a subordinate to the king. According to the contemporary *Gesta Normannorum Ducum*, Rollo at first refused. Then,

> pressed by their prayers he eventually ordered one of his soldiers to kiss the king's foot. This man promptly took it, lifted it to his lips, and pressed a kiss upon the foot while standing upright, so that the king fell over backwards. This resulted in a great roar of laughter and a mighty tumult among the people.[4]

Having demonstrated his intention to remain independent, Rollo then cheerfully took all of his oaths. He would rule in Normandy for the next two decades, theoretically in subjection to the king of the Franks, but in reality doing exactly as he pleased.

TIMELINE 64

ABBASID BYZANTIUM	RUS EMPIRE	MORAVIA BULGARIA	FRANKS WEST EAST	VIKINGS ITALY	Roman Emperor
					Louis II (855–875)
Viking/Rus attack on Constantinople (860)					
al-Muntasir (861–862)					
	Rurik (?) (862–c. 879)	Arrival of Cyril and Methodius			
al-Mutazz (866–869)			Louis the Stammerer (866–879)		
Basil I (867–886)					
		Svatopluk of Moravia (871–894)			
				Pope John VIII (872–882)	
					Charles the Landless (875–877)
	Oleg (?) (c. 879–?)		Louis III (879–882)/ Carloman II (879–884)	Charles the Fat (879–887)	
					Charles the Fat (881–887)
			Charles the Fat (882–887)		
			Charles the Fat (884–887)	Pope Stephen IV (885–891)	
Leo VI (886–912)			Louis of Provence (887–928)		
Patriarch Stephen I (886–893)			Arnulf of Carinthia (887–899)		
				Guy of Spoleto (889–894)	
				Pope Formosus (891–896)	Guy of Spoleto (891–894)
		Simeon (893–927)	Charles the Simple (893–923)		
				Lambert (896–898)	Arnulf of Carinthia (896–899)
				Pope Stephen VI (896–898)	
				Berengar (898–900)	
			Louis the Child (899–911)		
				Louis of Provence (900–902)	Louis of Provence (901–902)
Patriarch Nicholas Mystikos (901–907/912–925)				Berengar (902–924)	
Rus attack on Constantinople (906)			Rollo of Normandy (911–932)		
Alexander (912–913)					
Constantine Porphyrogenitus (913–959)					
Battle of Anchialus (917)					
Romanos Lecapenus as senior co-emperor (920–944)					
		Peter (927–969)			

Chapter Sixty-Five

———

The Kingdom of Germany

———

Between 907 and 935,
Henry the Fowler transforms Eastern Francia into Germany

Whᴇ ᴄʜᴀʀʟᴇꜱ ᴛʜᴇ ꜱɪᴍᴘʟᴇ was solving his Viking problem,
Louis the Child was desperately fending off Magyar invasions. As soon as their
employer Arnulf of Carinthia had died, the Magyars had romped through
Moravia and into Eastern Francia, burning, destroying, killing, and horrifying
the Franks with their ferocity: "Nothing pleases them except to fight," Liudprand of Cremona wrote. "Their mothers cut their boys' faces with very sharp
blades as soon as they come into the world, so that, before they may receive
the nourishment of milk, they may learn to endure wounds."[1]

By 907 the Moravian kingdom had disintegrated under their assaults, and
the Frankish noblemen had taken on the job of protecting their lands from
Magyar destruction.

Louis the Child was neither a hardened soldier nor a strong ruler. Crowned
at the age of six, he had given over rule to a council of regents and officials
and had never fully taken it back; his weak reign had allowed the tribal territories of Francia, the lands that had once belonged to the Germanic barbarian
tribes, to regain their character as semi-independent kingdoms, or "duchies."
Although the territories had once been defined by tribal loyalties, those bonds
were now in the past. The land of the Saxons had become the Duchy of
Saxony, the Bavarians had lent their name to Bavaria, and a handful of other
duchies (Lotharingia, Franconia, Swabia) lay around them.* Each of these
duchies was controlled by a powerful family, and the heads of these families—
the "dukes"—were now forced to defend themselves against the plunderers

---

*These duchies, which functioned as small individual realms within the larger kingdom of Eastern
Francia, are generally known as stem duchies. The phrase implies that the duchy's coherence came
from its distant past as a single tribal unit. The tribal identity, although long past, is the root from
which the duchy's identity stems. Elsewhere in Europe, "duchy" tends to refer to a geographical area
laid out for the sake of administration.

from the east. They raised their own armies, fought their own battles, ruled their own lands, and paid less and less attention to their supposed king.[2]

In 910, at the age of eighteen, Louis the Child tried to make one huge push against the Magyars, in a double bid to defeat the invaders and to assert his own power. He assembled the noblemen, their armies, and his own soldiers into a great army at Augsburg, ready to face the Magyar threat.

The Magyars approached more quickly than Louis expected and attacked before dawn, catching many of the soldiers still in their beds. Hours of fighting followed, with heavy casualties on both sides: "the meadow and the fields completely littered with corpses, and river and banks turned red by the blood that mixed in." Towards evening, the Magyars pretended to retreat; when the Frankish army broke rank and chased after them, the Magyars doubled back around and attacked from behind. The Frankish resistance was broken, the army scattered. Louis's bid had failed. The defense of the Frankish lands returned to the hands of the dukes. Louis retreated to a monastery and died there, less than a year later.[3]

When he died, Charles the Simple claimed, as an obvious truth, that Western Francia and Eastern Francia should be reunited under his rule. But the dukes of Eastern Francia refused, unwilling to give up their own power to a Carolingian king who would insist on his right to control them. Instead, they elected as king one of their own: Conrad, duke of Franconia.

Conrad was supposed to rule as a leader among equals, not as a king with unquestioned royal power, but the other dukes had mistaken their man. Once he had a crown on his head, Conrad began to act like a Carolingian monarch, with all of the accompanying pomp; the crown, Liudprand of Cremona dryly notes, "was not just decorated but *burdened* with most precious gems." He insisted that the dukes acknowledge his power and follow his bidding. When they refused, he spent the next seven years fighting against them, trying without success to force them into obedience.[4]

When Conrad died in 918, the dukes gathered together and decided to try again. This time, they elected the duke of Saxony to be their leader. Henry the Fowler (the nickname came from his love for bird-hunting) was in his early forties, had been duke of Saxony for seven years already, and had a keen appreciation for the independence of the duchies; he too had resented Conrad's attempts to rule as a monarch. In his first three years as king of Eastern Francia, Henry negotiated a series of oaths between himself and the dukes of Eastern Francia. The oaths of "vassalage" laid out an almost-equal relationship; they acknowledged that both kings and dukes had responsibilities towards each other, and recognized the dukes as "senior partners" in the job of governing, with authority to administer their own laws and lands as they pleased.[5]

When the noblemen in Western Francia rebelled against Charles the

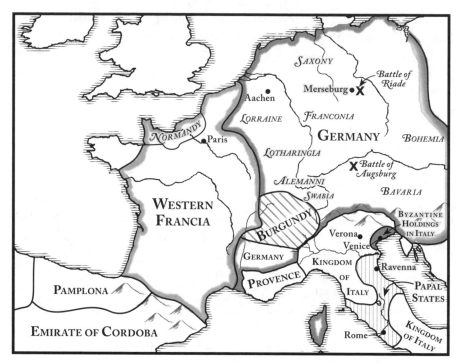

65.1: Germany

Simple in 922 (they were unhappy with his decision to give away Normandy), Henry the Fowler took the opportunity to claim a slice of the western kingdom as his own. By 925, five duchies—Franconia, Saxony, Bavaria, Swabia, and Lorraine—made up the core of Henry's kingdom, and Henry controlled Aachen itself, Charlemagne's old capital.[6]

But Henry still made no effort to become a "Carolingian" monarch. In Henry's hands, Eastern Francia was becoming something new. It was no longer a kingdom of Franks, but a kingdom in which the old Germanic tribal identities were playing a larger and larger role: a Germanic kingdom, a kingdom of Germany.

Henry's open-handed rule made it, paradoxically, easier for him to unite the dukes behind him when necessary; they no longer feared that answering a royal command might chip away at their own power. In 933, he summoned the duchies to join him in halting the Magyar advance.

The armies met at the Battle of Riade, near the eastern fortress of Merseburg. Perhaps mindful of Louis the Child's horrendous defeat twenty-three years earlier, when Henry himself had been in his mid-thirties and fighting with the Saxons, Henry gave his troops very specific directions:

Let no one try to advance beyond his comrades, though he has a faster
horse; instead, take the first strike of their arrows on your shields . . . then
rush on them with the fastest charge and with the most vehement attack,
in such a way that they cannot fire a second volley of arrows on you before
they feel the cuts of your weapons upon them.[7]

Liudprand of Cremona explains, "The Saxons, mindful of this most salutary
warning, charged with an orderly, even line, and there was no one who out-
ran the slower with a faster horse; and they took on their shields the harmless strikes of the [Magyars'] arrows. . . . [O]nly then did they surmount the
enemy with a vigorous charge."[8]

The Magyar advance had been broken; after the Battle of Riade, they
retreated back to the east, leaving the German borders in a temporary peace.

As part of his strategy to keep them permanently away, Henry planned to
turn the little dukedom on his eastern flank into a vassal state that would act
as a buffer between Germany and another Magyar advance. The dukedom
was called Bohemia, and like the duchies of Germany it had once been a
Germanic tribal territory. When the Magyars had begun to make raids into
Moravia, the Moravian nobleman Spytihnev—a Christian whose father had
been baptized in Moravia by the missionary Methodius—moved his family to
the west, away from the Magyar threat. With the help of Arnulf of Carinthia's
Eastern Frankish soldiers, he had established himself as ruler of the peoples
there: the first duke of Bohemia.[9]

The new duke of Bohemia was a young man named Wenceslaus, who was a
Christian and enthusiastic about an alliance with the powerful German king.
Wenceslaus was the grandson of Spytihnev, the first duke; he had inherited
his title when he was only fourteen, and his regents had been his Christian
grandmother Ludmila, Spytihnev's widow, and his mother, Drahomira, a
young woman who clung to the ancient religions of her Slavic ancestors and
refused to be baptized.

Ludmila, who was a forceful matriarch, had taken over the education of
the young Wenceslaus, instructing him in Christianity, and she now intended
to teach him how to rule as a Christian king. But Drahomira sent two of her
palace guards to strangle her mother-in-law and, with Ludmila dead, took
over the sole task of regent.[10]

Drahomira then began efforts to convert her son back to the ancient ways.
But Wenceslaus refused to give up his Christianity, and as soon as he turned
eighteen, in 925, he exiled Drahomira and took power in his own name. When
Henry the Fowler approached him for an alliance, Wenceslaus agreed.

This was not a universally popular decision. Some of the Bohemian officials
at his court thought that Henry was dangerous, that Bohemia's independence

was threatened, and that the Christian religion—which had originally come to them as a tool of domination—only made Bohemia more vulnerable to conquest. Led by Wenceslaus's younger brother Boleslav, this faction insisted that Wenceslaus break the alliance and give up Christianity as well, all in the name of a strong and autonomous Bohemia.

But Wenceslaus refused. In 935, he came to church in the predawn dark for an early mass; Boleslav and the dissident officials met him at the church's door and stabbed him to death.

Boleslav then declared himself prince of Bohemia, an act that explicitly rejected Henry's attempt to make Bohemia into yet another German dukedom. But despite the political nature of the assassination, Wenceslaus was hailed by the Christians in Bohemia as a martyr for Christ. Stories blossomed around him. The fourteenth-century emperor Charles IV made a personal collection of these tales; it is from his manuscript that we hear the story of Wenceslaus walking in the snow with one of his soldiers, in a storm so great that the soldier is afraid they will freeze:

Wenceslaus said to him, "Place your feet in the prints left by mine." The soldier did so, and his feet became so warm that he no longer felt the cold in the least. But stains of blood could clearly be seen in the prints the glorious martyr left.[11]

(This last detail did not make it into the Christmas carol.)

Henry I did not take revenge for his ally's death, because he had grown ill. In 936, the year after Wenceslaus's murder, he died. In a decisive break from Frankish tradition, he excluded all but one of his sons from the inheritance, and left the German kingdom whole to his son Otto.

TIMELINE 65

BYZANTIUM BULGARIA MORAVIA · RUS	FRANKS (WEST · EAST) BOHEMIA VIKINGS ITALY	Roman Emperor
	Pope John VIII (872–882)	
Svatopluk of Moravia (871–894)		Charles the Landless (875–877)
Oleg (?) (c. 879–?)	Louis III (879–882)/ Carloman II (879–884) Charles the Fat (879–887)	Charles the Fat (881–887)
	Charles the Fat (882–887)	
	Charles the Fat (884–887) Pope Stephen IV (885–891)	
Leo VI (886–912) Patriarch Stephen I (886–893)	Louis of Provence (887–928) Arnulf of Carinthia (887–899)	
	Guy of Spoleto (889–894)	
	Pope Formosus (891–896)	Guy of Spoleto (891–894)
Simeon (893–927)	Charles the Simple (893–923) Spytihnev of Bohemia (894–915)	
	Lambert (896–898) Pope Stephen VI (896–898)	Arnulf of Carinthia (896–899)
	Berengar (898-900)	
	Louis the Child (899–911) Louis of Provence (900–902)	
Patriarch Nicholas Mystikos (901–907/912–925)	Berengar (902–924)	Louis of Provence (901–902)
Rus attack on Constantinople (906)	Battle of Augsburg (910)	
Destruction of Moravia by Magyars	Conrad of Franconia (911–918) Rollo of Normandy (911–932)	
Alexander (912–913) Constantine Porphyrogenitus (913–959)		
Battle of Anchialus (917) Romanos Lecapenus as senior co-emperor (920–944)	Henry the Fowler (919–936) Wenceslaus of Bohemia (921–935)	
Peter (927–969)	Battle of Riade (933) Boleslav of Bohemia (935–972)	
	Otto (936–973)	

Chapter Sixty-Six

——

The Turn of the Wheel

Between 907 and 997,
the Chola kingdom rises and falls,
the Pandya kingdom falls and rises,
the Rashtrakuta kingdom falls,
the Western Chalukya kingdom rises

THE RASHTRAKUTA KING, situated uneasily between Pratihara ambitions in the north and Chola expansion in the south, realized that his days were numbered. The Pratihara had already reached its height and was fading, drained by the effort of fighting wars on its southern border and holding off the Arabs in the north. But the southern Chola realm was still in its ascendancy, its greatest years yet to come. Aditya, the ambitious Chola king who had defeated the Pallava, had just died after a thirty-six-year reign; his son Parantaka, inheriting his crown, would inevitably push north against the Rashtrakuta.

But first, Parantaka embarked on the conquest of the remaining Pandyan resistance in the south. The Pandyan king, Rajasimha II, knew that he could not resist the Chola armies all alone. Finding an ally was no easy task, though; after nearly four decades of Chola expansion, few kings were willing to defy the new Chola king.

Instead, Rajasimha II was forced to send a message across the southern strait, to the island of Sri Lanka.[1] The Sri Lankan king agreed to the alliance. In 909, Sri Lankan armies sailed across the water and joined with the Pandyan forces. Together, they fought against the Chola threat—and were completely defeated. Parantaka's commemorative inscription boasts that the Chola army not only crushed the two kings but also slew "an immense army dispatched by the lord of Lanka, which teemed with brave soldiers and was interspersed with troops of elephants and horses."[2]

Rajasimha II of Pandya survived the battle but fled with the Sri Lankan king back to the southern island, where he remained in hiding. He took with him his crown and his royal regalia, and for the next decade he planned and schemed in exile to get his throne back.

Meanwhile, the Chola steamroller made a turn to the north and met the Rashtrakuta armies. Krishna II, whose rule had been even more disastrous than that of his long-lived father, had just died in 914, and his grandson Indra III became king in his place. Right at the beginning of his reign, the inexperienced king was forced to defend himself against the Chola threat.

Sometime around 916, the two armies met at the Battle of Vallala. Once again, the Cholas triumphed.

The Chola king Parantaka had now defeated three kings in succession: the rulers of Sri Lanka, Pandya, and Rashtrakuta. His dominance seemed inevitable. Down in Sri Lanka, the exiled Pandyan king gave up all hope of ever recovering his throne. He left his crown and regalia in Sri Lanka and went home, back to his mother's ancestral lands on the southwestern coast of India, well away from the places where he had once held power. The Pandyan kingdom had disappeared, swallowed by the Chola aggression.[3]

The Rashtrakuta still clung to life, though, and after his defeat at the Battle of Vallala, Indra III of the Rashtrakuta tried to regain his power by turning north against the unstable Pratihara. He managed to fight his way all the way to the crown jewel of the Pratihara kingdom, the city of Kannauj itself, and conquer it. For a brief moment, the Chola and Rashtrakuta kingdoms dominated the subcontinent between them, while the Pratihara dwindled away almost to nonexistence.

But Indra III died prematurely in 929, and his successors fought over the throne. Four kings followed in quick succession, as the Rashtrakuta kingdom turned inwards. Parantaka of the Chola, relieved from the immediate threat of Rashtrakuta invasion, was able to firm up his hold on the south. Around 943, he sent an expedition down into Sri Lanka on a secret mission to find and bring back the regalia that the Pandyan king had left there, more than twenty years earlier. The effort failed, but even without the regalia, the Chola had now become the strongest kingdom in all of India.[4]

Parantaka's four decades on the southern Chola throne had been glorious, but it all fell down in a hurry. The Rashtrakuta chaos came to an end when Krishna III, great-nephew of Indra III, seized the throne. He would prove to be a talented administrator, a fierce warrior—and the last great Rashtrakuta king.[5]

Krishna III marshalled his forces to attack the dominant Chola, and in 949 the two kings met in battle at the city of Takkolam. Their forces were evenly matched, and a bow drawn at a venture decided the victory; a chance arrow killed Parantaka's son, the crown prince Rajaditya Chola. When he fell, the wing of the army under his command scattered, and the chain reaction infected

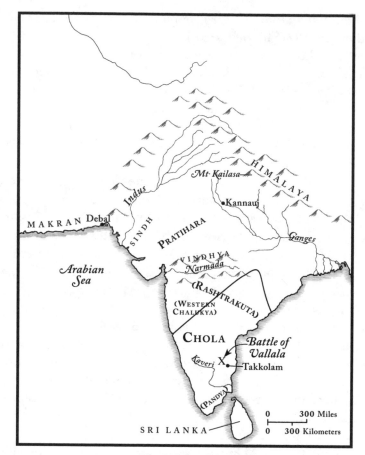

66.1: The Height of the Chola

the whole Chola army. Parantaka was forced to retreat and to hand over northern territory—and, as the lack of inscriptions over the next decades indicates,
was probably forced to pay homage to Krishna III as a subordinate ruler.[6]

It was a sudden and shattering reversal. Grief-struck, his power fractured,
Parantaka of the Chola died in 950. He had made his younger son Gandaraditya crown prince, after the death of his eldest and favorite child. And
Gandaraditya, who was a careful and pious man, dealt a death blow to the
empire.

The Chola, after all, had laid the foundation of their empire with their
swords. They claimed power by right of conquest. The great warrior-kings of
the previous century had forced cities and warlords to swear allegiance to the
Chola throne, and had then boasted of the extent of their kingdom based on
the vast amount of land under their sway. The development of any kind of
infrastructure had lagged far, far behind. A weak double web—the threat of

the king's armies, and the building of Hindu temples in the king's name—held the Chola expanse together.

Until Gandaraditya's coronation, the building of temples had been a valuable tool of Chola dominance. The kings who ruled after Vijayalaya, the founder of the empire, were Shaivite: like the northern empire-builder Harsha and his sister long before, they were devotees of the god Shiva and his divine consort. Later inscriptions tell us that the great Chola expander Aditya, most certainly a man of war, had built temples for Shiva to inhabit "all along the Kaveri River," a sacred watercourse. Like the Pandyan regalia, the temples were a symbol of power. The Chola kings did more than simply fight; they had invited the god to come and live in their empire, and the invitation was itself a boast of their dominance.[7]

But the temple-building, although important, had been a secondary tool of Chola dominance—until Gandaraditya. He and his queen, Sembiyan Mahadevi, were particularly devout followers of Shiva. Together they began to build new temples and repair old ones, all through the Chola realm. This stamped their names across the countryside; at the same time, though, Gandaraditya let the exercise of political power slide through his fingers. Piety was more to his taste than warfare. So far as we know, Gandaraditya fought no major battles. Instead he made his younger brother Arinjaya his heir and co-regent and handed the day-to-day administration over to him.

Arinjaya was not a talented ruler, and the Chola kingdom began to fade. Before long, the Chola authority was so weakened that a relative of the Pandyan king came out of obscurity and claimed the old Pandyan lands for himself. By 957, both brothers were dead, and the Chola kingdom had dwindled back down to a tiny state. Its northern territory was occupied by the Rashtrakuta, under the rule of Krishna III; in the south, the Pandyan pretender had reclaimed his land.[8]

The sudden Chola decline might have allowed the Rashtrakuta king to swing the balance of power back in his direction, but the Rashtrakuta empire too was troubled by rot at the top. In 967, Krishna III died. He had ruled for nearly thirty years and had managed to save the Rashtrakuta empire from disintegration. But now it too began to fall apart. Krishna III's successor, the weak Khottiga, faced a welter of revolt around the edges of his realm; and in 972, after less than five years on the throne, he was killed in a minor battle at the border.

Now revolt moved to the center of the empire. A Western Chalukya war-leader named Tailapa had been waiting, watching the empire disintegrate from the top down. He declared independence and crowned himself as Tailapa II, king of the Western Chalukya—the first Western Chalukya leader in two hundred years to claim sovereignty.

The unfortunate royal relative who held power in the Rashtrakuta palace, a young man named Indra IV, was forced to take up arms against this rebellion. But in 975, Tailapa inflicted such a horrendous defeat on the Rashtrakuta army that all hope of Rashtrakuta recovery was gone. Indra IV's chief ally, his uncle Marasimha, was so humiliated that he retreated from the war, set the struggle for power aside, and starved himself to death. The ritual suicide, called *sallekhana*, was an honorable way out: it earned merit for the one courageous enough to commit to it, and offered the possibility of a permanent end, the cessation of the cycle of birth and rebirth.[9] Centuries of war had done nothing but turn the wheel of fortune, bringing one empire and then another to the top. *Sallekhana* might not stop the wheel, but at least Marasimha could make a stab at getting off.

After another seven years of struggle, Indra IV too gave up. He followed his uncle in *sallekhana* and died of starvation in 982: the last Rashtrakuta king. Tailapa II of the Western Chalukya seized his territory, in one stroke becoming ruler of the center of India and soon, with aggressive campaigning, extending his empire all the way up to the Narmada. Kingdoms fell; kingdoms rose; the wheel turned on.

TIMELINE 66

FRANKS WEST	EAST	VIKINGS	ITALY	Roman Emperor	INDIA
					Aditya of the Chola (871–907)
Louis III (879–882)/ **Carloman II** (879–884)	**Charles the Fat** (879–887)			**Charles the Fat** (881–887)	**Krishna II** of the Rashtrakuta (878–914)
Arnulf of Carinthia (887–899)			**Guy of Spoleto** (889–894)	**Guy of Spoleto** (891–894)	
Charles the Simple (893–923)			**Lambert** (896–898) **Berengar** (898-900)	**Arnulf of Carinthia** (896–899)	
Louis the Child (899–911)			**Louis of Provence** (900–902) **Berengar** (902–924)	**Louis of Provence** (901–902)	**Rajasimha II** of the Pandya (900–920)
Battle of Augsburg (910) **Conrad** of Franconia (911–918)	**Rollo** of Normandy (911–932)				**Parantaka** of the Chola (907–950) Chola defeat of Pandyan and Sri Lankan kings (909)
Henry the Fowler (919-936)					**Indra III** of the Rashtrakuta (914–929) Battle of Vallala (916)
Battle of Riade (933) **Otto** (936–973)					**Krishna III** of the Rashtrakuta (939–967)
					Gandaraditya of the Chola (950–957)
					Khottiga of the Rashtrakuta (967–972)
					Tailapa II of the Western Chalukya (973–997) **Indra IV** of the Rashtrakuta (973–982)

Chapter Sixty-Seven

—▪—

The Capture of Baghdad

Between 912 and 945,
the Fatimid caliph fails to overthrow the Abbasids,
the emir of Cordoba becomes a caliph,
and the Buyids in the east take control of Baghdad

DOWN IN EGYPT, the Fatimid caliph al-Mahdi set his eyes on Baghdad. He did not claim to be *a* caliph; he claimed to be the *only* rightful caliph, bearer of holy authority over all Muslims worldwide.

But unless he could work this claim out in victory against the Abbasids, his pretensions would remain merely local. He had established a new capital city on the coast, Mahdia; he had the support of the North African Berbers, who had long resented Abbasid rule; but to lay hold of full authority, he needed to push his way eastward into the Abbasid holdings.[1]

In 912, he proclaimed his son to be his co-ruler and his successor, giving the nineteen-year-old boy the title *al-Qaim bi-amr Allah,* "The One Who Executes God's Command." He then put al-Qaim at the head of an army, which would proceed to the east in order to wipe out the Abbasid control of Egypt.[2]

But al-Qaim and his men had a long way to travel, through North African territory unfriendly to the Fatimid cause, before Egypt would even appear on the horizon. In 913 young al-Qaim (aided by two experienced generals lent to him by his father) forced Tripoli to surrender after a six-month siege. The following year, the Fatimid armies used Tripoli as a base to march even farther east along the coast into Cyrenaica, the far edge of Abbasid control. By August, Fatimid soldiers were streaming into Alexandria. In November, al-Qaim himself arrived in the city, and the mosques of Alexandria were ordered to honor the Shi'a rulers, not the Abbasids of Baghdad, in their prayers.[3]

The court at Baghdad was nominally ruled by the nineteen-year-old caliph al-Muqtadir, but unlike his young Fatimid rival, al-Muqtadir had no real power. His vizier and generals planned to respond to the Fatimid threat without his help. They knew that the Fatimid armies intended to march all the way to Baghdad (al-Qaim had sent to his father an exultant letter, promising that

67.1: The Fatimids and Cordoba

he would spread Fatimid power all the way to the Tigris and Euphrates), and so they put the skilled eunuch soldier Mu'nis at the head of the resistance.

Mu'nis marched towards Egypt at the head of the Abbasid forces in 915. The Fatimid expansion east collapsed as quickly as it had expanded. Al-Qaim's men had fought beyond their strength; faced with a determined Abbasid resistance (the treasury at Baghdad was opened, and Mu'nis was given two million dirhams, the equivalent of six and half tons of silver, to fund his counterattack), al-Qaim quickly retreated and gave up his Egyptian holdings. Al-Mahdi built himself a fleet of warships and launched a second attack in 920. This time, the return Abbasid assault all but destroyed his new navy.[4]

The Fatimid power was not yet a major threat to Baghdad, but al-Mahdi's rebellion had an unintended consequence. Over in Cordoba, the emir Abdullah had died in 912, to be succeeded by his grandson, twenty-one-year-old Abd ar-Rahman III; and ar-Rahman III saw in the Fatimid rebellion a possible solution for his own difficulties.

67.2: Competitors of the Samanids

The Spanish Marches, the mountainous lands between the Emirate of Cordoba and the Frankish border, had been occupied since the end of Charlemagne's reign by independent warlords who were propped up by the power of the Frankish kings. These warlords, who often bore the title of count, had grown increasingly independent and aggressive, and their power threatened the emirate's lands in the northeast; the count of Barcelona had proved to be particularly troublesome. To the south, an elusive rebel named Umar ibn-Hafsun had been leading guerilla attacks on Cordoban forces for almost thirty years; Abdullah had been unable to either catch or drive him out.[5]

Directly to the north, the Christian kingdoms of Pamplona and Asturias were thriving in an alarming fashion, doing their best to reconquer the Muslim-held land in al-Andalus. The king of Asturias, Alfonso III, had managed to draw together the territories of Asturias, Leon, and Galicia into a triple-sized Christian realm known as the Kingdom of Leon. He had also married a Pamplona princess, creating a solid wall of Christian alliance against Cordoban power.

And just across the mouth of the Mediterranean, on the southern side of the water, al-Mahdi had declared himself caliph, rightful ruler of all Muslims, including ar-Rahman III himself. Ar-Rahman had come to power at the eye of a hurricane.

Unsurprisingly, he spent the first fifteen years of his rule fighting. He launched yearly attacks against the southern rebel ibn-Hafsun until the revolt finally disintegrated; he fought against the soldiers of the Spanish Marches; he campaigned against the Kingdom of Leon.[6]

Against the caliphate of North Africa, he took an even more aggressive stance. He would not swear loyalty—but neither would he continue to swear loyalty to the distant caliph in Baghdad. The emir of Cordoba had no more reason to give even surface allegiance to any fictional leader of the Muslim world.

Instead, he aspired to become a leader himself. On January 16, 929, ar-Rahman declared himself to be caliph of Cordoba, Commander of the Believers, Defender of the Religion of God. Unlike the Fatimid caliph, ar-Rahman was not claiming to be the one true caliph, supplanter of the Abbasid rule. Instead, he was declaring his complete and total independence from both the Abbasid and Fatimid claims. Ar-Rahman would rule on his own account, claiming his authority from his Umayyad ancestors; he had placed himself outside of the Fatimid-Abbasid conflict.[7]

Now there were three caliphates in the Muslim world, with three caliphs claiming imperial power. And the Abbasid caliph at Baghdad was the weakest by far.[8]

To the east of Baghdad, the emir of the Samanids was acting with almost complete independence from Baghdad. Samanid merchants travelled all the way up the Volga river to trade with the Khazars and the Rus, and the Samanid realm had grown increasingly wealthy, increasingly strong. In 911, the Samanid emir, Ahmad, had captured the remaining strongholds of the rival eastern dynasty, the Saffarids. This had extended Samanid control across the east.[9]

Ahmad was now the ruler of a de facto Muslim kingdom, and he decided to make Arabic the official language of his Samanid court. This was quite in line with the myth that he was acting as a lieutenant for the caliph in Baghdad, but he had underestimated the national feeling of the Persian speakers in the old Saffarid lands. They didn't want to be folded into yet another Arab-dominated Muslim kingdom; they wanted their own Persian lands back again. Ahmad found himself putting down continual rebellions in the old Saffarid province of Sistan, centered around the city of Zaranj. He had just begun to triumph over the revolts when, in 914, he was assassinated in his own tent by his servants.

His son Nasr became the Samanid emir in his place. But Nasr was eight years old, and power lay in the hands of his regent, the vizier al-Jaihani. At this, Abbasid officers in Sistan rebelled and claimed Sistan, making it into their own little country and finding a Saffarid family member to install as their puppet-emir. This faux-Saffarid domain would last until 963.

Not too many years later, the Samanids also lost control of their territory near the Caspian Sea, when a soldier named Mardaviz al-Ziyar helped the local Samanid officials to seize power and then took it himself. His little emirate, the Ziyarid dynasty, expanded quickly to cover land south of the Caspian Sea, as far as the city of Isfahan. It also gave birth to yet another rival dynasty: in 932, one of al-Ziyar's own officials, Ali ibn Buya, seized the city of Karaj and used it as a base to battle south into Fars.

Now the Samanids had spawned three rival lines in the east: the neo-Saffarids in Sistan, the Ziyarids south of the Caspian Sea, and the Buyids battling the Ziyarids for territory. At the same time, the governors of Aleppo, all members of the Hamdanid family, were establishing their own independent domain.*

This patchwork rivalry did not remain all Muslim. Counting on local feeling to help keep him in power, Mardaviz al-Ziyar announced himself the restorer of the old Persian empire, a follower of Zoroastrianism, undoer of the Muslim conquest. He was probably insane (he claimed to be a reincarnation of Solomon, son of King David, although it is difficult to see how this made him Persian), but he was a powerful and charismatic personality, and the willingness of the natives to support him demonstrates just how shallow the conversion to Islam had been in many parts of the empire. He was so successful that the competing emir Ali ibn Buya, governing his own land farther south, followed his lead and began to call himself not "emir" but "shah" of his newly conquered territory, using the old Persian honorific.[10]

Over the next decades, the dynasties of the east would form confederacies, break apart, and rejoin, each clan hoping to check the power of the others, each governing family limited by the ambitions of its neighbors. And as the east disintegrated, the Abbasid caliphate slid further into irrelevance.

In 932, the figurehead caliph al-Muqtadir, who had remained alive because he had been content to be powerless, was deposed by his brother al-Qahir, who ruled as caliph for two years. Unlike al-Muqtadir, al-Qahir tried to exercise power, which ended badly. Only two years after becoming caliph, he was deposed and blinded by his Turkish courtiers and soldiers. He spent the last years of his life begging on the streets of Baghdad. His nephew al-Radi, son of al-Muqtadir, became puppet-caliph instead.

Like his father, al-Radi ruled with no authority. But until this point, the Abbasid caliphs had continued to carry out the ritual responsibilities of their office: they sat in council, led Friday prayers in Baghdad, appeared at assemblies, gave alms to the poor. Al-Radi too walked through these motions, but he would be the last to do so. By 936, al-Radi—twenty-nine years old, caliph for barely two years—realized there was no way for the caliph to continue on as head of the Abbasid state. The breaking away of the eastern territories

---

*The Buyids are often called Buwayhids; both names are accurate.

meant that the tax base of the empire had been ruined. He could not pay his soldiers; he could barely supply his own court; he certainly could not fight off any real challenges to his power.[11]

His most powerful general, Muhammad ibn Ra'iq, had taken control of the lands southeast of Baghdad and was refusing to send the taxes he collected there on to the capital. Now Muhammad ibn Ra'iq offered the caliph a solution. If al-Radi would agree to recognize ibn Ra'iq with the title *amir ul-umara*, "Commander of Commanders," the general would come into Baghdad with his handpicked band of Turkish soldiers, bring his collected tax revenues with him, and take over the administration of the empire—allowing al-Radi to remain caliph in name.

With no other options left to him, al-Radi finally agreed. He awarded ibn Ra'iq the title and gave him what little power the caliph still had. Ibn Ra'iq arrived in Baghdad with his loyal Turks, disbanded the existing Baghdad army, and put the current vizier to death.[12]

It was the end of the Abbasid caliphate in all but name. From now on the Commander of Commanders would control the remains of the empire, while the Abbasid caliph was left with little more than the title.

Far from bringing peace, ibn Ra'iq set off a struggle in Baghdad for control of the caliphate. His tenure as Commander of Commanders came close to destroying what was left of the empire. In his battles with his rivals, he even ordered the breaching of the Nahrawan Canal, the man-made water system that stretched two hundred miles across the salty dry plains just east of Baghdad; this temporarily blocked the advance of one of his challengers, but it also destroyed the irrigation that kept the plains populated. The farmers who had sent their produce to Baghdad began to move away; their farms withered.[13]

And then ibn Ra'iq was overthrown, two years later, by one of his lieutenants, and three other Commanders of Commanders claimed and lost the position in short succession. Al-Radi died of illness in 940, and the struggling factions agreed to elect his brother to his position, but the man held no power—and would never observe even the forms of the caliphate.

To the north, the Buyids were on the move. They were battling their way towards the chaos and division of Baghdad. As they approached, the Abbasid puppet-caliph fled; the Turkish soldiers in the capital chose a new caliph, but his time was brief. In 945, the Buyid general Ahmad ibn Buya (brother of Ali) marched into Baghdad and claimed the title "Commander of Commanders" for himself.

The figurehead caliph was deposed and blinded. Ahmad ibn Buya allowed a new caliph to be elected but barred him from any participation in the government of the city. The Buyids were in control of the empire, and Baghdad had fallen under the rule of an upstart family, one that no longer required even the meaningless approval of a powerless caliphate to claim rule.

TIMELINE 67

INDIA	ABBASID EMPIRE	EASTERN DYNASTIES	WESTERN DYNASTIES	ASTURIAS
	al-Muntasir (861–862)			
	al-Mutazz (866–869)			Alfonso III (866–910)
		Rise of the Saffarid dynasty Ya'qub-i Laith Saffari (867–878)		
Aditya of the Chola (871–907)				
		Rise of the Samanid dynasty Nasr of the Samanids (875–892)		
Krishna II of the Rashtrakuta (878–914)			Abdullah as emir of Cordoba (888–912)	
		Ismail of the Samanids (892–907)		
Rajasimha II of the Pandya (900–920)				
Parantaka of the Chola (907–950) Chola defeat of Pandyan and Sri Lankan kings (909)	al-Muqtadir (908–932)	Ahmad of the Samanids (907–914)	Rise of the Fatimid caliphate al-Mahdi of the Fatimids (909–934)	
		Destruction of the Saffarids (911)	Abd ar-Rahman III as emir of Cordoba (912–928)	
Indra III of the Rashtrakuta (914–929) Battle of Vallala (916)		Nasr II of the Samanids (914–943)		
		Rise of the Ziyarid dynasty Mardaviz al-Ziyar (928–935)	Abd ar-Rahman III as caliph of Cordoba (929–961)	
	al-Qahir (932–934) al-Radi (934–940)	Rise of the Buyid dynasty Ali ibn Buya (932–949)		
Krishna III of the Rashtrakuta (939–967)		Buyid capture of Baghdad (945)		
Gandaraditya of the Chola (950–957)				
Khottiga of the Rashtrakuta (967–972)				
Tailapa II of the Western Chalukya (973–997)	Indra IV of the Rashtrakuta (973–982)			

Chapter Sixty-Eight

Three Kingdoms

Between 918 and 979,
the kingdoms of Goryeo, Liao, and the Song
draw the shattered east back together

THREE KINGDOMS now lay on the peninsula east of China, two of them in the hands of rebels who had managed to transform themselves into monarchs. The southwest lands were ruled by the bandit king Kyonhwon, who had named his realm Later Baekje; the north, by the naval officer Wang Kon.*

Wang Kon, elevated to the throne of Later Goguryeo by court officials who had resented his predecessor's tyranny, was particularly aware that the crown was only tentatively his. He did his best to erase the traces of past revolt, renaming his kingdom Goryeo, moving the capital city to Kaesong, and announcing himself to be the founder of a new royal dynasty. "Owing to your hearty support, I became king," he told his people. "By joining together to correct laws, we can rejuvenate the country. Learning from past mistakes, we should look for solutions to problems in our immediate surroundings and recognize the mutual dependence of ruler and subject, realizing that our relations are like those of fish and water. The country will join in the celebration of the peace."[1]

This was a web of wishful thinking; there was no peace on the horizon. Kyonhwon of Later Baekje had not revolted in order to share the peninsula with other kings. Now that he had established his own kingdom, he aimed to wipe out his competitors.

However, Kyonhwon did not immediately invade Goryeo; he set his sights first on the tattered Sillan kingdom to his southeast. The alcoholic King Hyogong of Silla had died childless, and his successors—a series of short-lived royal relatives—were unable to mount a successful defense. The castle lords had no loyalty to the throne. Instead, they treated with Kyonhwon of Later

---

*Wang Kon is frequently referred to by his posthumous royal title, Taejo, and his kingdom is also known as Taebong.

Baekje or Wang Kon of Goryeo (depending on whose army was closest) as though they were independent rulers.[2]

Wang Kon did not immediately take advantage of the Sillan disintegration. His speech to his people had not been entirely untrue: he had glimpsed a truth that Kyonhwon was blind to. Silla, weary of war, was more likely to be won by friendship than by battle.

Kyonhwon, delighted by Wang Kon's absence from the struggle, fought his way into Sillan territory. By 927, his armies had reached the capital city of Kyongju. The Sillan king of the moment, Gyeongae, could not hold the gates against him; Later Baekje's soldiers flooded into the city, sacked and burned its buildings, killed civilians and defenders alike, and broke into the royal palace. King Gyeongae was murdered in his own banquet hall.

This gave Wang Kon the chance to play deliverer. "Kyonhwon, having an evil nature that nourished rebellion, killed the Silla king and oppressed the people," the Goryeon statesman Choe Seung-no wrote. "Hearing this, T'aejo [Wang Kon's royal title] wasted no time sending troops to punish the crime and finally restored order. Such was T'aejo; remembering his former king, restoring order, and halting a dangerous situation in this way."[3]

In fact, Wang Kon was now taking over by stealth. Once Kyonhwon had done the hard work of breaking down the capital city's walls, Wang Kon sent his own army in, drove the Later Baekje forces out, and elevated a royal cousin named Gyeongsun to the Sillan throne. He married one of his daughters to Gyeongsun, garrisoned the capital city with Goryeon troops, and announced that he had rescued Silla.[4]

Gyeongsun was, of course, a puppet-king. Wang Kon's strategy, which placed both the government of Silla and the loyalty of its castle lords firmly into his hands, won him the great prize: rule of the entire peninsula. Kyonhwon tried to retake the Sillan land, but over the next nine years Wang Kon drove him steadily backwards. In 932, a deciding battle between the Later Baekje and Goryeo armies ended with the surrender of most of Kyonhwon's troops. Kyonhwon himself kept on fighting, doggedly, with no more than a handful of soldiers still loyal to him. Finally, in 935, his sons turned against him and imprisoned him, taking the defense of the remaining Later Baekje territory into their own hands.

Once again, Wang Kon showed himself capable of playing a very deep game. First of all, he demanded the abdication of his Sillan son-in-law, the puppet-king Gyeongsun. The young man hurriedly obliged, and Wang Kon folded the remains of Silla into his own realm. He was now the only other king on the peninsula.

Then, some months later, Kyonhwon escaped from prison in Later Baekje. Most probably he had help from Wang Kon's agents, because within weeks he was up in Goryeo, a prosperous slave-owner, living in peace with his old enemy. The slaves were a present from Wang Kon, a bribe intended to turn his one-time opponent into a friend. "T'aejo honored Kyonhwon," the *Samguk sagi* records, "and gave him the South palace as an official residence. His position was made superior to those of the other officials. . . . [he was given] gold, silk, folding screens, bedding, forty male and female slaves each, and ten horses from the court stables."[5]

The bribe worked because Kyonhwon was furiously angry with his sons— and already ill with the cancer that would kill him. Not long after settling in Goryeo, he asked Wang Kon for an army: "It is my hope," he told the king, "that you will enlist your divine troops to destroy the traitorous rebels, and then I can die with no regrets."

Nothing could have pleased Wang Kon more. He dispatched his oldest son, the crown prince Mu, and his most trusted general to accompany Kyonhwon back into Later Baekje with ten thousand soldiers. He himself followed at the head of another strong division. The army of the rebellious sons was crushed; the three oldest brothers, the ringleaders, surrendered, and Wang Kon ordered them put to death. He ceremoniously gave the kingdom back to his old enemy. Just days later, Kyonhwon died of his illness, and Later Baekje fell into Wang Kon's hands. All three kingdoms were now under a single crown.[6]

"In the past," Wang Kon told his people, in a set of injunctions intended to shape the future of his newly unified country, "we have always had a deep attachment for the ways of China, and all of our institutions have been modeled upon those of the Tang. But our country occupies a different geographical location and our people's character is different from that of the Chinese. Hence there is no reason to strain ourselves unreasonably to copy the Chinese way." Under Wang Kon, the country of the Koreans would take its shape. Silla had only been a foretaste of unification; after Wang Kon, the peninsula would remain a single nation for the next thousand years.[7]

OVER ON THE MAINLAND, the northern nomads known as the Khitan still longed for Chinese ways.

The Khitan had now adopted a more settled existence under the warchief Abaoji, who had become their Great Khan in 907. Freed from the shadow of the Tang, the Khitan kingdom—like Goryeo—had the chance to mature according to its own lights.

But Wang Kon's Goryeo had hundreds of years of tradition to build on, and the Khitan had nothing but the very recent nomadic past. Abaoji, distancing himself from the uncertain and unsettled life of the nomads, grasped onto the customs of the extinct Tang. By 918, he had given himself the Chinese royal name "Celestial Emperor Taizu," built himself a new Tang-style capital city at Shangjing, and had named his oldest son to be crown prince and heir. Blood succession was not a Khitan tradition; the nomads had always chosen their leaders for their skill in battle. But a settled kingdom with a settled capital needed a settled royal line.[8]

Just before his death in 926, the new Celestial Emperor began to fight his way towards Balhae, the kingdom north of Goryeo. The Khitan armies invaded Balhae's land, sending its people flooding down into Goryeo for refuge. Just as the Balhae capital fell, Taizu died—leaving his people with a newly expanded territory, an inexperienced crown prince, and an unfamiliar set of royal traditions.

His redoubtable wife kept the Khitan empire from falling apart.

In the tenth-century chronicles she is called "Shu-lu shih," which merely means "of the Shu-lu clan." But her skills as a leader were as great as her husband's. The dead Celestial Emperor had appointed their oldest son as heir, but Shu-lu shih preferred her second son, Deguang. She assembled the tribal leaders, mounted both boys on their horses, and then told them that Deguang deserved to be the new emperor. Then she added, "I love these two sons of mine equally and cannot decide between them. Grasp the bridle of him who seems to you the worthier!"[9]

The tribal leaders, taking the unsubtle hint, chose Deguang, who from this point on ruled (along with his mother) as the emperor Taizong; Shu-lu shih had successfully reimposed on her husband's royal line the old Khitan succession of the worthiest. The erstwhile crown prince, the older son Bei, took Balhae as his own (renaming it Dongdan) and ruled it as an independent kingdom.

Meanwhile, Shu-lu shih developed a useful way of making sure that her wishes became law. Whenever a Khitan leader opposed her, she sent the leader to her husband's tomb in order to ask his advice—at which point the guards who watched over the dead emperor's final resting place did away with the visitor. Together with her prime minister, Han Yanhui, she continued the Celestial Emperor's mission of turning the Khitan horde into a Chinese kingdom.[10]

In 930, the displaced older Bei fell out with his brother, the Celestial Emperor Taizong. Taizong sent his own son to govern Dongdan; Bei fled into the chaos of China. By 936, Taizong had simply annexed Dongdan and had given his empire a new name to go along with its new customs: the old Khitan realm became the kingdom of the Liao. The northeast now lay under the rule of two strong and unified kingdoms, Goryeo on the peninsula and the Liao empire across the north.

Meanwhile a bewildering assortment of states and kingdoms rose and fell south of the Liao. Not until 960—with the Liao stable under the reign of Taizong's son Liao Muzong, and Goryeo prospering under the rule of Wang Kon's son Gwangjong—did one of the would-be royal dynasties of China manage to root itself firmly into the former Tang landscape.

This dynasty grew out of the Later Zhou state, which had occupied the land around Chang'an and the lower curve of the Yellow river from 951 until 960. Nine years was a fairly average survival time for a ruling dynasty during the Five Dynasties and Ten Kingdoms period; the Later Zhou ruler had overthrown the Later Han dynasty, which had ruled in the same area for all of three years, and the Later Han itself followed on the heels of the Later Jin (eleven years), the Later Tang (thirteen years), and the Later Liang (sixteen years), all occupying more or less the same territory.

In 960, the Later Zhou dynasty went the way of its predecessors. Its emperor (the second in nine years) died, leaving only a baby as heir and a young empress as regent. The officers of the Later Zhou army disliked the empress, who had no experience with war. Afraid that the army would lose its pre-eminent place in Northern Zhou society, they rebelled and declared their favorite general to be emperor, founder of yet another new dynasty: Emperor Taizu of the Song.

There was no particular reason why Taizu's dynasty should be more successful than any of the ones that had come before. Yet he seemed to have an unusually strong sense of what needed to be done to restore the China of the past. "From the moment that he grasped the reins of power," one of his chroniclers notes, "his mind seemed to be absorbed with one great thought: to restore the unity of the empire."[11]

Taizu, like the rulers before him, had taken his crown by force; but like the great Chinese rulers of the past, he managed to weave a story around himself that lent him the sheen of heavenly approval. "Immediately after he was born," the chronicler tells us, "the sky was filled with reddish clouds that overhung the house where the child was, and for three days the dwelling was pervaded by a most fragrant odour. People at the time remarked to each other that all this portended a great future for the boy."[12] After-the-fact prophecy had always worked well for Chinese emperors who could back up the prophecies with victories in battle, and Song Taizu was a good fighter.

He had also learned from the past. The army had made him emperor and could dethrone him just as easily. As soon as he was firmly on the throne, he summoned all of his officers to a banquet and made them an offer: if they would renounce their ranks, give up all military authority, and retire to the countryside, he would give them handsome severance pay and turn over to them "the best lands and most delightful dwelling-places," where they could pass their lives "in pleasure and peace."[13]

This unexpected act seems to have broken the cycle of revolt that had brought one dynasty after another into power. Song Taizu reformed his army from the ground up and then led them in a series of campaigns against the surrounding states. There were six states to his south and one to his north, but just beyond the northern state (the Northern Han) lay the enormous Liao.

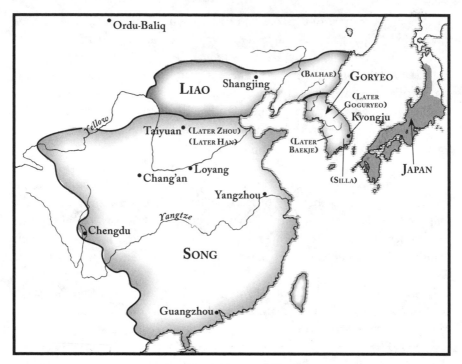

68.1: Song, Liao, and Goryeo

Song Taizu decided that he first would tend to the south, where no powerful enemy lurked behind the divided landscape.

Reunifying the south turned out to be a lifelong task. In the sixteen years of his reign, Song Taizu defeated three of the six southern states. Halfway through his time on the throne, he made a run at attacking the Northern Han; but he was forced to retreat and afterwards resigned himself to the Northern Han's existence.

Struck down by illness on campaign, Song Taizu died in 976. His younger brother, Song Taizong, took the throne. Within two years he had finished the conquest of the south and was ready to bring the Northern Han—the last remaining state—to heel. In 979, Song Taizong personally led his army against the Northern Han capital, the city of Taiyuan. A long savage siege followed. At last Song Taizong, showing the same canny political sense that had characterized his older brother, offered the Northern Han ruler a golden handshake: if he would step down and hand his kingdom over, Song Taizong would reward him with safety, an estate, and a lifetime of ease.[14]

Finally, the Northern Han was in Song hands. With the surrender, the Song had spread itself once again over the Chinese mainland. The fractured landscape of the east had drawn itself together: the Song, the Liao, and Goryeo now governed the once divided lands.

TIMELINE 68

ABBASID EMPIRE	EASTERN DYNASTIES	WESTERN DYNASTIES	CHINA	KOREAN PENINSULA	KHITAN/ LIAO
al-Mutazz (866–869) Rise of the Saffarid dynasty Ya'qub-i Laith Saffari (867–878)					
Rise of the Samanid dynasty Nasr of the Samanids (875–892)			Tang Xizong (873–888) Heongang of Unified Silla (875–886)		
			Rebellion of Huang Chao Battle of Liangtianpo (882)		
Ismail of the Samanids (892–907)		Abdullah as emir of Cordoba (888–912)	Tang Zhaozong (888-904) Hyogong of Unified Silla (897–912)		
			Kyonhwon of Later Baekje (900–935) Kungye of Later Goguryeo (901–918)		
		Ahmad of the Samanids (907–914)	Tang Aidi (904–907) Fall of Tang/Rise of Later Liang (907–923) Period of Five Dynasties and Ten Kingdoms (907–960)		Abaoji/Taizu (907–926)
al-Muqtadir (908–932) Rise of the Fatimid caliphate al-Mahdi of the Fatimids (909–934) Destruction of the Saffarids (911) Nasr II of the Samanids (914–943)		Abd ar-Rahman III as emir of Cordoba (912–928)			
	Rise of the Ziyarid dynasty Mardaviz al-Ziyar (928–935)	Abd ar-Rahman II as caliph of Cordoba (929–961)	Wang Kon of Later Goguryeo/ Goryeo (918–943) Fall of Later Liang/Rise of Later Tang (923–936) Gyeongae of Silla (924–927) Gyeongsun of Silla (927–935)		Deguange/Taizong (926–947)
Rise of the Buyid dynasty al-Qahir (932–934) al-Radi (934–940)	Ali ibn Buya (932–949)		Silla absorbed into Goryeo (935) Fall of Later Tang/ Rise of Later Jin (936–947)	Later Baekje absorbed into Goryeo (936)	
Buyid capture of Baghdad (945)			Fall of Later Jin/ Rise of Later Han (947–951) Fall of Later Jin/ Rise of Later Zhou (951–960) Muzong (951–979)	Gwangjong of Goryeo (949–975)	
			Fall of Later Zhou/Rise of Song (960–1279) Song Taizu (960–976)		
			Song Taizong (976–997) Song dynasty reunites China (979)		

Chapter Sixty-Nine

—▪—

Kings of England

Between 924 and 1002,
England and Norway are both united under single kings,
Norse colonists settle in Greenland,
and Sweyn Forkbeard adds England to his North Atlantic empire

IN 924, EDWARD THE ELDER—king of southern England, son and heir of Alfred the Great—capped a quarter century of fighting with his finest achievement yet: he forced the west and the north to submit to him. "All the race of the Welsh sought him as their lord," the *Anglo-Saxon Chronicle* tells us, ". . . the king of Scots and all the nation of Scots chose him as father and lord. [So also did] . . . all those who live in Northumbria, both English and Danish and Norwegians and others."[1]

Edward was not king of a united island. The far edges of Northumbria remained independent from him, and the submission of the Welsh and the Scots appears to have been a simple matter of tribute payment. But he could claim with justice to be the first king of all the Anglo-Saxons. He had inherited the kingdom of Wessex from his father Alfred and after the death of his sister had taken control of Mercia as well. With the exception of the Danish kingdom which remained in the far north, the country that we now think of as England was his.[2]

He had decreed, in a reversion to Germanic custom, that his realm be divided between his two elder sons. But one of these sons died "a few days after his father" (William of Malmesbury, who records the death, gives no details) and the other, Athelstan, became sole king.[3]

Like his father and grandfather, Athelstan spent his life in war. He fought rivals for the throne; he fought rebel Anglo-Saxon noblemen who disliked the idea of a single Anglo-Saxon king; he had to reconquer the Welsh and the Scots, who tried to slip from his control. And he mounted a stealth takeover of the Viking holdouts in the northern reaches of the Danelaw. "The most vigorous and glorious Athelstan, king of the English, gave his sister in marriage with great ceremony to King Sihtric of the Northumbrians," John of Worcester tells us. Sihtric, ruler of that persistent Danish kingdom in the north, was already elderly. When he died the following year, Athelstan invaded in his sister's name and claimed the holdout lands in Northumbria for his own.[4]

He had brought an end to the Danelaw, and he was well on his way to wiping out the last traces of the independent Anglo-Saxon kingdoms that had once carpeted the island. The task was finally finished in 936, when Athelstan fought a pitched battle in an unknown location (probably somewhere in the northeast of England) against an alliance of Northumbrian Vikings, Anglo-Saxon noblemen—five of whom claimed the title of king over their own patches of land—and Scots, led by their long-lived king of Scotland, sixty-year-old Constantine II. There, he crushed the resistance to his overlordship: "King Athelstan and his brother, the atheling Edmund . . . killed five underkings, and seven earls," writes John of Worcester, "and more blood was shed than hitherto had been shed in any war in England."* Constantine II of Scotland lost his son in the fight and was forced to flee. The Battle of Brunanburh was so fierce that it earned its own poem in the *Anglo-Saxon Chronicle*:

> Here King Athelstan, leader of warriors,
> ring-giver of men, and also his brother,
> the aetheling Edmund, struck life-long glory
> in strife round Brunanburh. . . . There the ruler of
> Northmen, compelled by necessity,
> was put to flight, to ship's prow,
> with a small troop. . . . Never yet in this island
> was there a greater slaughter.[5]

The victory brought all of England firmly under one king for the first time. Alfred the Great had been king of Wessex; Edward the Elder, king of the Anglo-Saxons; Athelstan was now king of England and had even forced the kings of Wales and Scotland to acknowledge his power. He had lived up to his father and grandfather and moved beyond them. "Intent on not disappointing the hopes of his countrymen and falling below their expectations," William of Malmesbury writes, "[he] brought the whole of England entirely under his rule."[6]

It had taken over three generations of fighting to pull the struggling English inside a single national border, and that border—straining under the tension—popped open again almost at once. Athelstan, king of all England,

---

*"Atheling," also spelled "aetheling," was the Anglo-Saxon word used to designate a man eligible to inherit the throne.

69.1: Athelstan's England

died in 939 and was succeeded by his seventeen-year-old half-brother, Edmund the Just. The Irish king Olaf I of Dublin invaded and took the midlands of England away, and Edmund was not able to reconquer them until 942, after Olaf died.

Edmund ruled his reunified country for barely four more years. In 946, he was killed in a freak encounter. He was presiding over a feast in honor of St. Augustine, founder of Christianity in England, when he noticed among the guests a thief whom Edmund, sitting in judgment (one of the king's regular duties), had ordered exiled. The sight infuriated him. He stood up and tackled the robber, who drew out a knife and stabbed Edmund in the chest.[7]

Edmund's guard came running and hacked the criminal to pieces, but Edmund died within hours. He was twenty-four years old; he left a five-year-old son, but during the child's minority the crown was taken by Edmund's brother, Edred Weak-Foot. The nickname came from Edred's generally poor state of health. Nevertheless, he held the country together, even in the face of a revolt in Northumbria: "He almost wiped them out," William of Malmesbury says, "and laid waste the whole province with famine and bloodshed." When he died of chronic illness in 955, he passed a unified nation on to his nephew.[8]

The new king, Edwy All-Fair, was fourteen: "a wanton youth," William tells us, "and one who misused his personal beauty in lascivious behaviour. . . . On the very day of his consecration as king, in a very full gathering of the nobles, while serious and immediate affairs of state were under discussion, he burst out of the meeting . . . and sank on a couch into the arms of his doxy." William adds that the English bishop Dunstan, who was at the meeting, followed his king into the bedchamber, dragged him back out, and together with the archbishop of Canterbury forced him to give up his mistress and attend to his business.[9]

This extraordinarily precocious behavior is probably a myth, but Edwy did soon make an enemy of both Dunstan and the archbishop. Raised without a father, he had become a puppet of court officials who hoped to gain control of the kingdom for themselves. Under their influence, he deprived the monasteries of their tax revenues, destroying the power of the abbots and monks to defy the throne. (William of Malmesbury adds, indignantly, "Even the convent of Malmesbury, where monks had dwelt for over two hundred and seventy years, he made into a bawdy-house for clerks"—which probably explains his dislike of Edwy.)

Once again, the ghosts of the old Anglo-Saxon kingdoms reared their heads. The Mercian and Northumbrian noblemen, seeing the opportunity to reassert their power against both king and church, decided to throw their weight behind Edwy's younger, easily controlled brother Edgar. They proclaimed him as rival king to Edwy. In 957, only two years after coming to the throne, Edwy lost a battle against his brother and his brother's supporters at Gloucester, and the two divided the kingdom: fourteen-year-old Edgar ruled north of the Thames, and Edwy, now sixteen, ruled in the south.

In 959, Edwy died at the age of nineteen, and his brother Edgar became king of all England. Edgar proved more strong-minded than his older sibling. Once on the throne, he took his own road. He restored the monasteries of England, giving the abbots and monks the power to govern their own lands: "They are to have in their court the same liberty and power that I have in my own court," he decreed, "both in pardoning and in punishing." This shrewd legislation at once made all of the abbots and priests in England into king's men, and gave Edgar the backing he needed to reduce the power of his would-be masters. By 973, Edgar was in full control of his country and had extracted oaths of loyalty from the king of the Scots and the king of the Welsh.[10]

He had now been on the throne of England for fourteen years but had never actually been crowned. In fact, up until this time none of the kings of England had gone through a coronation ceremony; Edgar was the fourth king to rule over the entire country, but all of Alfred's descendents, like their great forebear, had reigned as warriors, holding their power only as long as they could hold their swords.

But Edgar, in making the church his firm ally, had earned the right to be legitimized by a greater power than the god of war. Dunstan, now archbishop of Canterbury, created a formal ceremony that would recognize the king's sovereignty—a ceremony that is described in all of the chronicles of Edgar's reign. "He was blessed, crowned with the utmost honour and glory, and anointed king in his thirtieth year at Pentecost, 11 May," writes John of Worcester, highlighting the king's age; thirty, according to the Gospels, was when Jesus emerged into the public eye as the Son of God. The *Anglo-Saxon Chronicle* remembers the coronation in alliterative Anglo-Saxon verse:

> Here, Edgar, ruler of the English,
> was consecrated as king in a great Assembly
> in the ancient town. . . . There was great rejoicing
> come to all on that blessed day,
> which children of men name and call
> Pentecost Day. There was gathered,
> as I have heard, a pile of priests,
> a massed multitude of monks.[11]

With the church behind him, Edgar sat on the throne as crowned king of England, his country bound together both by battle and by ceremony.

Two years later, he was killed by a swift illness and his heirs found the crown slipping from their hands. The Northmen were coming, and this time they were under the command of a king.

THE EARLY HISTORY of the peoples north of the Baltic is preserved very imperfectly in heroic sagas; what glimpses we get show a familiar, slow progression from tribal patchwork to unified kingdom.

By the middle of the ninth century, the southeastern lands were ruled by Swedish kings from the area known as Uppland; the very southern tip of the Scandinavian peninsula, the islands in the Baltic itself, and the peninsula of Jutland were under the control of kings from the peoples known as the Dani.

The peninsula's western half, home of the Norse tribes, remained divided and chaotic for longer. Sometime around 870, the rule of the coastal lands known as Vestfold fell to a ten-year-old named Harald; Harald, first with the help of his uncle and regent, and then on his own, began a seventy-year campaign to unite the Norse under one crown.* "King Harald swore an oath not to cut or comb his hair, until he had become sole king of Norway," the epic *Egil's Saga* tells us, "and so he was called Harald Tangle-Hair."[12]

In a great sea victory around 900, the Battle of Havsfjord, Harald Tangle-Hair defeated the armies of his most dangerous enemies, the Norse princes Thorir Long-chin and Kjotvi the Wealthy. "This was the last battle King Harald fought in Norway," *Egil's Saga* concludes, "for he met no resistance afterwards and gained control of the whole country."[13]

It actually took Harald most of his long life to unify Norway under his rule, and even then his control over the country remained shaky and contested. The western Scandinavian lands were chaotic and blood-soaked, and the constant fighting sent more Vikings abroad looking for new homes: more to England, more to Normandy, and quite a few westward to the large island of Iceland, where they joined the small struggling colonies that had been established there in the ninth century.[14]

Harald Tangle-Hair's personal life did nothing to smooth the troubled waters; his appetite for conquest was matched by his libido, and he fathered between ten and twenty sons with a variety of wives and mistresses. When he died, probably in the early 940s, the loosely united country again fell apart into a mess of battling noblemen and princes: the noblemen vying for power over their own estates, the princes hoping to establish themselves as the next king of all Norway.

Harald's youngest son, Hakon the Good, eventually emerged as the victor, but he had to fight hard to keep the title: his older brother Erik Bloodaxe, who was married to the sister of the Danish king Harald Bluetooth, mounted a fifteen-year campaign to take the crown away. Erik Bloodaxe himself fell in battle against his brother around 955, but his "wolf-pack" of sons, in alliance with Harald Bluetooth of Denmark, carried on with the civil war.[15]

Erik Bloodaxe had earned his nickname from his exploits in battle; Hakon, although just as warlike, was labelled "the Good" because of his faith. Most Scandinavians still worshipped the old gods: Odin with his ravens, the warlike Thor with his deadly hammer, and a whole host of others. But Hakon had spent some time as a child at the court of Athelstan, in England, where he had learned Christianity. Harald Bluetooth had also become a Christian at some point, but the conversions didn't particularly inconvenience either man; being a nominal Christian simply made it easier to deal with both the English and the merchants on the continent. To "take the sign of the cross,"

---

*The exact dates of Harald's reign are unknown, but recent research suggests that he was born around 870 and carried out the bulk of his campaigning during the lifetimes of Alfred the Great and Athelstan of England. See, for example, Gwyn Jones, *A History of the Vikings* (Oxford University Press, 1984), pp. 88–90.

according to *Egil's Saga*, was "a common custom then among both merchants and mercenaries who dealt with Christians. Anyone who had taken the sign of the cross could mix freely with both Christians and heathens, while keeping the faith that they pleased."[16]

But when Hakon the Good finally died on the battlefield, fighting against his nephew Harald Greycloak, Christianity came strongly to the fore. With the help of Danish troops provided by his uncle Bluetooth, Harald Greycloak, son of Erik Bloodaxe but himself a convert to the new faith, seized the throne of Norway. He soon proved to be a Christian of a more zealous and driven kind. He could "do nothing to make the men of the land Christians," says the twelfth-century chronicler Snorri Sturluson, but "broke down temples and destroyed the sacrifice and from that . . . got many foes."[17]

Unfortunately, Harald Greycloak's sacking of the old places of worship was followed by hard winters, poor crops, and bad fishing: "There was great want in the land," chronicler Sturluson writes, "and folk lacked everywhere corn and fish." An unnatural cold snap caused snow in midsummer. Harald Greycloak grew more and more unpopular with his people; resentment grew against him; and this gave his uncle Bluetooth an opportunity.[18]

Harald Bluetooth had not supported his nephew's claim to the throne of Norway out of the goodness of his heart; he hoped to add Norway to his own Danish kingdom. As Harald Greycloak grew less popular, Bluetooth plotted with one of his noblemen, Hakon of Hladir, to assassinate the Norse king.

Around 976, the plot came to fruition. Greycloak was betrayed and murdered; Harald Bluetooth took the eastern Norse lands for his own and, for his trouble, awarded Hakon of Hladir control of the upper Norse coast. He did not allow Hakon to take the title of king, though; and so for a time, the Danish and Norse lands lay under the control of Harald Bluetooth. He kept firm hold on them with the help of his son and warleader Sweyn Forkbeard.

For the next decade, Harald Bluetooth's soldiers and explorers ranged south and west, pushing the sphere of his power ever outwards. Danish soldiers attacked the borders of Germany, which was now under the rule of Henry the Fowler's son Otto. More raiding parties went west again to England, where Edgar's ten-year-old son Ethelred had been crowned as king. And the Norseman Eric the Red sailed northwest, pushing Scandinavian power past the island of Iceland to more distant shores.

Eric the Red, a troublemaker by nature, had been forced to leave Norway and settle in the Icelandic colonies after a feud with another villager that ended in death (Eric's henchmen, according to the thirteenth-century *Saga of Eirik the Red*, "caused a landslide" to fall on the man's farm). In 982, he started a brawl with one of his Icelandic neighbors and killed two of the man's sons. The other colonists forced him to leave Iceland, and Eric the Red set sail, searching for a new place to live.[19]

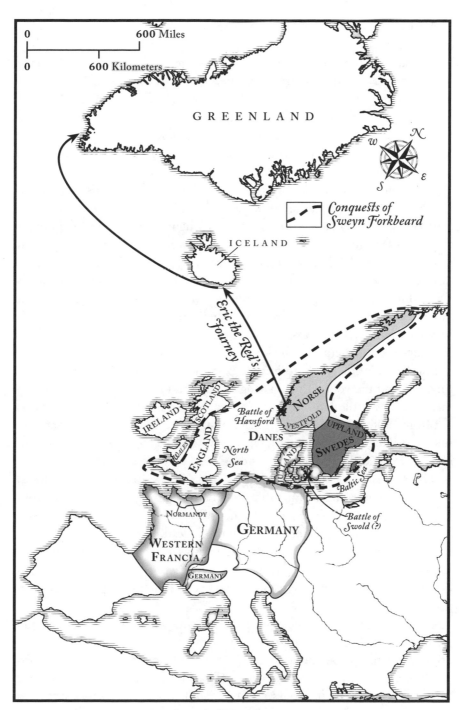

69.2: Spread of Norse Power

After three years of exploring, he settled on a massive island five hundred miles to the west. There were no people on it, which suited his personality, but he had ambitions to found a new colony there. Thanks to the unusually warm temperatures during Eric's lifetime, the island's shores were partly free from ice, but it was an inhospitable, bare, sandy place. Eric named it Greenland: as his epic notes, "people would be attracted there if it had a favorable name." The ruse was successful, to a point. Colonists came, although very slowly, building a tiny outpost of Scandinavian power halfway across the north Atlantic.[20]

Back home, old Harald Bluetooth died by the sword. His son Sweyn Forkbeard had hoped that his father would divide his realm and give part of it to Sweyn, but Harald Bluetooth had not fought for his whole life in order to yield his kingdom to his son. As his father's righthand man, Sweyn had ships of his own. He gathered them and challenged Harald Bluetooth for the throne. In a sea battle fought in 987, Harald Bluetooth turned back his son's ships. But in the fighting, he was badly wounded. He died just days later, and Sweyn Forkbeard's followers proclaimed him king.[21]

Sweyn inherited the throne of Denmark, the Danish-controlled lands in Norway, and (theoretically) the loyalty of Hakon of Hladir, ruling the upper coastal lands. With an eye to further expansion, he stepped up the raids on England, and the young English king Ethelred found himself unable to stop them. Scorn for the king who was incapable of protecting his people bursts out from William of Malmesbury's account: "Ethelred occupied (rather than ruled) the kingdom," he writes. "His life [was] cruel at the outset, pitiable in mid-course, and disgraceful in its ending."[22]

The Danes ravaged Wessex, burned the city of Exeter, pillaged Kent. The death of able-bodied Englishmen in battle and the destruction of crops plunged England into deepening famine and distress.

In 991, the East Saxon nobleman Brihtnoth, leading a massive force against the Danish enemy, was killed at Maldon and his army was routed. Ethelred's advisors suggested that the time had come to pay off the invaders; and, following their lead, Ethelred agreed to hand over ten thousand pounds of silver to the Danes.[23]

Sweyn Forkbeard accepted the payment, known as the Danegeld, and withdrew. But Ethelred's solution turned out to be self-defeating. Sweyn's original intention had been to conquer the island; the chronicler Snorri Sturluson claims that Sweyn made an oath, at his coronation feast, "that ere three years were gone he would go to England with his army and slay King Ethelred and drive him from his land." But he now realized England could be far more useful as a source of income. So Sweyn had extended his own deadline; it was better to allow Ethelred to pay his expenses than to try and conquer him. In 994, Sweyn himself returned and fought all the way to London. Once again Ethelred bought him off. But the English king's ability to raise ransom money from his noblemen was almost tapped out, and no one doubted that the Danes would return.[24]

In the meantime, Sweyn used the English cash to fund his conquest of the rest of Norway. Late in 994, Hakon of Hladir died, and control of upper Norway was claimed by a grandson of old Harald Tangle-Hair, Olaf Tryggvason. Sweyn Forkbeard was a formidable enemy, and Olaf's reign was short. In 1000, his warships clashed with Sweyn's in the western straits of the Baltic at the Battle of Swold. The Norse ships were sunk, one by one, and King Olaf found himself standing on the deck of his own flagship, the *Long Serpent*, surrounded by the dead. "So many men on the *Serpent* were fallen that the railings were empty of men," Sturluson says, "and [Sweyn Forkbeard's] men began to come aboard on all sides." Olaf leaped overboard and was never seen again. Triumphant, Sweyn Forkbeard claimed all of Norway for himself.

For years, it was rumored that Olaf would return from the depths and free Norway from its Danish overlords. "About King Olaf, there were afterwards many tales," Sturluson concludes, "but he never again came back to his kingdom in Norway."[25]

Now in control of both Norway and Denmark, Sweyn Forkbeard turned back to the English project.

Ethelred of England, now in his early thirties, had spent his entire reign so far fighting against Danish invasion. In an attempt to get the Normans on his side against the Danes, their distant relations, he had offered them a powerful alliance: he would marry Emma, sister of Duke Richard the Good of Normandy, if the Normans would provide him with soldiers to help fight off the Danes. "For Richard was a valiant prince, and all-powerful," writes the chronicler Henry of Huntingdon, "while the English king was deeply sensible of his own and his people's weakness, and was under no small alarm at the calamities which seemed impending."[26]

Ethelred had already been married once and had fathered four sons, so it wasn't likely that any of Emma's children would ascend to the English throne. Still, the duke of Normandy liked the idea of an English alliance; it would further prove his independence from the kings of Western Francia. In 1002, Emma travelled to England for the wedding and was crowned queen of England.

But even with Norman reinforcements, Ethelred could not muster a force large enough to turn the Danes away. Nor could he raise enough money to buy them off. He was staring defeat and death in the face. Right after the wedding, he flew into a panic and ordered a drastic step. All Danish settlers in England were to be murdered: man, woman, and child.

The massacre was carried out in a single day. On November 13, 1002, the king's men spread throughout the island, slaughtering the Danes in every village. In Oxford, Danish families fled to the church of St. Frideswide; the soldiers burned it down with them inside. "All the Danes who had sprung up in this island," Ethelred later wrote, defending his actions, "sprouting like weeds amongst the wheat, were . . . destroyed by a most just extermination."[27]

Sweyn Forkbeard had already determined to conquer England. The massacre lent him the justification of revenge. William of Malmesbury insists that Sweyn's own sister, who had married an Englishman, was killed on November 13. This may or may not be true, but without a doubt, relatives of Sweyn's own soldiers died in the purge, and anger as well as ambition now fueled the Danish attacks.[28]

Sweyn continued to fight a measured, planned war. Over the next ten years, he sent multiple armies to England. The invasions occupied all of Ethelred's time, killing his soldiers and draining his treasury. The Danes would attack, sack and burn, accept a payment, and then withdraw; each time, Ethelred seems to have hoped that the Danegeld would keep them away for good; each time, they returned.

In 1013, Sweyn Forkbeard himself arrived on the northern coast of England, ready for his final push against the English king. His forces swept southward across the countryside, and the English surrendered, one village at a time. As he approached London, where Ethelred had taken shelter, the Londoners shut their gates. "The inhabitants of the town would not submit," the *Anglo-Saxon Chronicle* tells us, "but held out against them with full battle because King Ethelred was inside."[29]

With the rest of the country in his hands, Sweyn turned aside from London and went to Bath, the city where the first coronation of an English king had taken place. In Bath, he announced himself "King of England," and demanded that all the English recognize his title.

The city of London, which was the only holdout, had been inspired by Ethelred's presence. But as soon as Sweyn Forkbeard left for Bath, Ethelred fled to the Isle of Wight, sending his wife Emma and her two sons to Normandy to stay with her brother, the duke Richard the Good. Without their king, the Londoners crumpled. They sent tribute and hostages to Bath, acknowledging the Dane as their ruler.[30]

Sweyn Forkbeard now ruled a North Atlantic empire that stretched across the Baltic and the North Sea. He celebrated Christmas in England as its king. A century and a half after the Great Army of the Vikings landed on English shores, the island had finally fallen under Scandinavian rule.

CHINA	KOREAN PENINSULA	BRITISH ISLES	SCANDINAVIA
		Alfred of Wessex	**Harald Tangle-Hair** of Norway (870–c. 940)
Tang Xizong (873–888)		(871–899)	
	Heongang of Unified Silla (875–886)		
		Treaty of Wedmore (878)	
Rebellion of Huang Chao			
Battle of Liangtianpo (882)			
Tang Zhaozong (888–904)			
	Hyogong of Unified Silla (897–912)	**Edward the Elder** (899–924)	
	Kyonhwon of Later Baekje (900–935)	**Constantine II**	Battle of
	Kungye of Later Goguryeo (901–918)	of Scotland (900–943)	Havsfjord
Tang Aidi (904–907)			
Period of Five Dynasties and			
Ten Kingdoms (907–960)			
	Wang Kon of Later Goguryeo/		
	Goryeo (918–943)	**Sihtric** of Northumbria (921–927)	
Fall of Later Liang/			
Rise of Later Tang (923–936)			
	Gyeongae of Silla (924–927)	**Athelstan** (924–939)	
	Gyeongsun of Silla (927–935)		
		Olaf I of Ireland (934–941)	
	Silla absorbed into Goryeo (935)		
Fall of Later Tang/	Later Baekje absorbed		
Rise of Later Jin	into Goryeo (936)		
(936–947)		**Edmund the Just**	**Hakon the Good**
		(939–946)	of Norway (c. 940–961)
		Edred Weak-Foot	
Fall of Later Jin/		(946–955)	
Rise of Later Han (947–951)			
	Gwangjong of Goryeo (949–975)		
Fall of Later Jin/			
Rise of Later Zhou (951–960)			
		Edwy All-Fair (955–959)/	
		Edgar (957–975)	
			Harald Bluetooth of
Fall of Later Zhou/			Denmark (958–987)
Rise of Song (960–1279)			**Harald Greycloak**
Song Taizu (960–976)			of Norway (961–976)
		Coronation of **Edgar** (973)	
Song Taizong (976–997)		**Ethelred** (978–1013)	
Song dynasty reunites China (979)			Arrival of Eric the Red
			on Greenland (985)
			Sweyn Forkbeard
			of Denmark (987–1014)
			Sweyn Forkbeard of
			Norway (1000–1014)
		Massacre of the Danes (1002)	
		Sweyn Forkbeard (1013–1014)	

Chapter Seventy

—•—

The Baptism of the Rus

Between 944 and 988,
the Rus fight against the enemies of Constantinople,
and then attack Constantinople,
and finally convert to Christianity

T HE SENIOR EMPEROR Romanos Lecapenus was balancing Constantinople carefully on a very narrow spit of political safe ground. The ambitious emirs of the former Abbasid caliphate were continually driven away from his borders by yearly campaigns, costly in men and money but crucial for Byzantium's survival. On the other side of the city, the triangle of western powers—the Rus, the Bulgarians, and the constantly invading Magyars from the north—were kept at bay through a combination of negotiation, threat, and tribute payment. Assuring Constantinople's safety was an exhausting and exacting job, but Romanos had managed it for over twenty years.

He was now seventy-four years old and ruled along with four co-emperors. Constantine Porphyrogenitus, son of Leo the Wise, still lived in Romanos's shadow; he was married to Romanos's daughter Elena, and was forced to share the title of emperor not only with Romanos but also with Romanos's two sons and his oldest grandson, all of whom had been crowned as co-emperors.[1]

Romanos had arranged the coronations to ensure the succession for his own family. But in 944 his two sons, Stephen and Constantine Lecapenus, grew weary of waiting. With the help of their own personal bodyguards, they pulled their elderly father from his throne and put him on a ship headed for a monastery on a desolate island in the Sea of Marmara.

This turned out to be only the first act in the drama. Apparently all four co-emperors were in on this plot, but Constantine Porphyrogenitus—now thirty-nine, diffident and unassertive by nature—had allowed the two younger men to carry it out. Stephen and Constantine Lecapenus assumed that this gave them the authority of senior emperors, and Constantine Porphyrogenitus wasn't inclined to argue with them.

But their sister, Constantine's wife Elena Lecapenus, did not intend to share imperial power with her brothers. She had been married to Constantine Porphyrogenitus for twenty-six years, ever since she was nine, and she had grown to adulthood along with her amiable, unambitious husband. She knew he would never grasp the crown for himself.

She arranged for her brothers to come to dinner, and convinced her husband to authorize their arrest during the meal. The royal guard seized them as they sat down to eat. Both men, along with Romanos's grandson (the other co-emperor), were put on ships and sent to distant monasteries, suffering the same fate as their father. Constantine Porphyrogenitus was, after nearly forty years of eclipse, the sole emperor of Constantinople.[2]

Romanos would die at his monastery of peaceful old age, three years later. He had failed to guarantee the crown for his sons, but his dynasty survived; the heir to the throne, Constantine's seven-year-old son, was Romanos's grandson.

CONSTANTINE PORPHYROGENITUS began his reign as senior emperor by negotiating a treaty with the Rus. For over two centuries, the empire of Byzantium had turned its battle face east: the armies of Islam had been the single most enduring, most persistent threat to Constantinople. But the Rus, barely civilized in the eyes of Byzantines, were just as anxious as the Arabs to take their turn at besieging the great city by the sea.

Less than thirty years earlier, the Arab geographer Ibn Fadlan had travelled up the Volga, through the lands of the Khazars into the domain of the Rus. His accounts raise the curtain on a people still half-wild: always armed, tattooed from neck to fingertip, living in temporary wooden shelters, copulating in public, and sacrificing to strange bloody gods. "They are the dirtiest creatures of God," Ibn Fadlan wrote, hardly able to believe the disgustingness of their habits:

> A slave girl brings each morning early a large vessel with water, and gives the vessel to her master, and he washes his hands and face and hair. Then he blows his nose and spits into the bucket. The girl takes the same vessel to the one who is nearest, and he does just as his neighbor had done. She carries the vessel from one to another, until each of them has blown his nose, spat into, and washed his face and hair in the vessel.[3]

Bands of Rus merchants travelled long distances, buying and selling but never bothering to build. To Ibn Fadlan's eye, they were completely transient, leaving nothing behind them: not even burial grounds, since they preferred to burn their dead.[4]

By 945, the Rus had grown some visible roots. They had a capital, a prince, and at least the semblance of a central government: Igor, prince of Kiev, had enough power to swear out a treaty on behalf of his people with Constantine Porphyrogenitus. The treaty bound both parties, once again, to observe the terms laid out in the 911 peace: Rus merchants could enter Constantinople, but they had to be unarmed and in groups of no more than fifty men; if they went back to Kiev peacefully, they would get a month of free food; and if Constantine Porphyrogenitus needed soldiers to keep the Bulgarians or Arabs at bay, the Rus would serve in the Byzantine army as paid mercenaries.[5]

The treaty catches the Rus in mid-transformation, partway through the complicated (and by now familiar) morph from tribal collection into kingdom. Igor's role in negotiating it was kinglike, and the terms of the treaty were Byzantine: "If a criminal takes refuge in Greece, the Rus shall make complaint to the Christian Empire, and such criminal shall be arrested and returned to Rus regardless of his protests," reads one article, laying out the sovereign right of each state to execute justice on its own people, "and the Rus shall perform the same service for the Greeks." But the Rus who put their names to it, underneath their princes, were fifty warleaders with a mixture of Viking and Slavic names, each boasting the limited authority of a tribal chief.[6]

Right after signing the treaty, Igor met the death of a tribal chief. The Rus had conquered the Slavic tribes on the western side of their lands, the Drevlians, fifty years earlier; but the Drevlians had continued to resist their rulers. On his way back from signing the treaty, Igor made a detour through Drevlian territory to collect overdue tribute. "He was captured by them," writes Leo the Deacon, "tied to tree trunks, and torn in two."[7]

His wife Olga took over as regent for their son Svyatoslav. Her first act was to burn the Drevlian city of Korosten to the ground and slaughter hundreds of Drevlians in revolting ways, burning and transfixing and burying them alive. But Olga too was changing. Once her warrior-queen revenge was finished, she picked up the task of turning the Rus into a state; she divided her realm into administrative districts, *pogosts*, each one responsible for a set tax payment. The Drevlians became their own *pogost*, with regular payments due to the government at Kiev.[8]

In 957, Olga made a state visit to Constantinople, where Constantine received her as a fellow sovereign. The floors of the imperial palace were strewn with roses, ivy, myrtle, and rosemary; the walls and ceilings were hung with silken drapes; a choir from the Hagia Sophia sang as she was ushered into the emperor's presence; and mechanical toy lions in the throne room roared in her honor. She was banqueted and entertained for over a week. At the end of her visit, she agreed to be baptized. Constantine's wife Elena stood as her godmother, and Olga of the Kievan Rus was welcomed into the spiritual family of Byzantium.[9]

In less than half a century, the Rus had progressed from their wooden shelters by the Volga to the royal reception halls of Constantinople. It was an extraordinarily fast metamorphosis—and it proved to be partly temporary.

In 963, Igor's son Svyatoslav took power in his own name, at the age of twenty-one. His mother Olga retired from public life and spent her time trying to talk her fellow Rus into accepting Christianity. Her conversion had not brought the entire country within the fold, and Svyatoslav was a throwback. He was an aggressive, war-minded man who rejected his mother's faith: "My retinue would laugh at me," he told Olga, when she suggested that he consider baptism.[10] Instead he "followed heathen usages" and generally behaved like a tribal chief from earlier times:

> When Prince Svyatoslav had grown up and matured, he began to collect a numerous and valiant army. Stepping light as a leopard, he undertook many campaigns. Upon his expeditions he carried with him neither wagons nor kettles, and boiled no meat, but cut off small strips of horseflesh, game, or beef, and ate it after roasting it on the coals. Nor did he have a tent, but he spread out a horse-blanket under him, and set his saddle under his head; and all his retinue did likewise. He set messengers to the other lands announcing his intention to attack them.[11]

He spent the first years of his solo rule fighting against the Khazars, the Slavic tribes, and the Turkish nomads called Pechenegs on his east, as Olga's dream of a Christian people receded.

Meanwhile, in Constantinople, Constantine Porphyrogenitus had died in his mid-fifties, after a reign of indifference to affairs of state.[12]

He was succeeded, briefly, by his twenty-one-year-old son, Romanos II, grandson of the usurper Romanos Lecapenus. Like his father, Romanos II was amiable and pleasant and easily manipulated. "He was distracted by youthful indulgences," Leo the Deacon explains, "and introduced into the palace people who encouraged him in this behavior. . . . [T]hey destroyed the young man's noble character by exposing him to luxury and licentious pleasures, and whetting his appetite for unusual passions." The "people" in question probably refers to his wife Theophano, the beautiful daughter of an innkeeper who had caught his eye when he was eighteen.[13]

For the four years of Romanos II's reign, Theophano and the general Nikephoros Phocas (a career officer who had sworn an oath of chastity after his first wife's death, and now channelled his energies into conquest) ran the empire. It was a good four years for Byzantium. With his nephew John Tzimiskes at his side as second-in-command, Nikephoros Phocas first led the Byzantine navy in recapturing Crete, and then led the Byzantine army in the conquest of Aleppo, retaking territory that had been lost to the Arabs for decades.[14]

In March of 963, the same year that Svyatoslav took control of the Rus,

70.1: The Rus and Byzantium

young Romanos II died of a fever. He left his two sons, Basil II (five) and Constantine VIII (three), as co-emperors, with the empress Theophano as regent.

Theophano was still in her twenties; she was not enormously popular (she was suspected by Leo the Deacon, among others, of poisoning her husband with hemlock), and she was afraid for herself and her babies. The general Nikephoros Phocas was on his way back to Constantinople after fighting at the eastern front, and Theophano sent messengers to him, making private offers of alliance and support.[15]

It isn't clear exactly what these offers promised him; Nikephoros Phocas was more than thirty years her senior and had sworn that awkward oath of chastity. But the empress's letters inspired Nikephoros Phocas to claim the crown. His army proclaimed him emperor in July, while still on the march, and he arrived at Constantinople in August. The patriarch agreed to coronate him in the Hagia Sophia in exchange for Nikephoros Phocas's promise that he would never harm either of his toddler co-emperors, and on August 16 he became Nikephoros II, emperor of Byzantium.[16]

In a matter of weeks, he had also married Theophano, which kept her on as empress and made him the stepfather of the heirs to the throne. But although contemporary historians claim that he was bewitched by her beauty, the marriage was likely a business arrangement. Nikephoros Phocas may well have kept his vow of chastity. Certainly he spent more time on the battlefield, over the next few years, than in the bedroom; he returned to the eastern front and went on fighting the Arabs, while Theophano began a hot and heavy affair with his nephew and chief lieutenant John Tzimiskes, a dashing officer in his late thirties.

Nikephoros Phocas was a lifelong soldier, and now that he was emperor he saw himself not as Defender of the Faith or Chief Administrator of the Empire, but as Supreme Commander. He was a man who could not bear to simply maintain his borders; he was compelled to expand them. In 968, he hired Svyatoslav of Kiev and fifty thousand Rus mercenaries to fight for him and declared war on Bulgaria.

Svyatoslav had just finished reducing the Khazar empire to rubble, and Bulgaria was the next and nearest big target. Like Nikephoros Phocas, the leader of the Rus was a man who had to fight in order to rule. He marched down to the Danube and launched a shattering attack on the Bulgarians—so shattering that he was able to seize the entire north of the country for himself. Peter I of Bulgaria had a stroke and died, leaving his son Boris II in charge of the remains of the country.

Svyatoslav now turned against his employer; he sent a message to Nikephoros Phocas, "announcing his intention to march against them and capture their city." He was a talented fighter, but a poor ally.[17]

Before Nikephoros Phocas could deal with the threat, he was murdered.

He had the soldier's habit of sleeping on the floor instead of his bed when he was in Constantinople (although he tempered this asceticism by spreading a leopard skin and a scarlet felt cloth on the hard stone). On the evening of December 10, he was sleeping on his leopard skin when his wife Theophano and his nephew John Tzimiskes broke into the room, accompanied by hand-picked members of the royal guard. Leo the Deacon writes,

> They surrounded him and leapt at him and kicked him with their feet. When Nikephoros was awakened and propped his head on his elbow, [one of the palace guards] struck him violently with his sword. And the emperor, in severe pain from the wound (for the sword struck his brow and eyelid, crushing the bone, but not injuring the brain), cried out in a very loud voice, "Help me, O Mother of God!" . . . John, sitting on the imperial bed, ordered them to drag the emperor over to him. When he was dragged over, prostrate and collapsing on the floor, John . . . grabbed hold of his beard and pulled it

mercilessly, while his fellow conspirators cruelly and inhumanly smashed his jaws with their sword handles so as to shake loose his teeth and knock them out of the jawbone. When they had their fill of tormenting him, John kicked him in the chest, raised up his sword, and drove it right through the middle of his brain, ordering the others to strike the man, too.[18]

Nikephoros Phocas had grown unpopular with his people, since his expensive campaigning had forced them into higher and higher tax payments. Within seven days, John was able to convince the entire city and the patriarch to crown him as emperor in his uncle's place. "At times of great changes in government, usually a lot of unrest and tumult flares up," Leo the Deacon marvels, "but good order and deep quiet prevailed over the people, and only the emperor Nikephoros and one of his bodyguards were killed, no one else receiving so much as a slap in the face."[19]

The only other casualty of the coup was Theophano, who had counted on remaining empress. John immediately exiled her to an island in the Sea of Marmara (although he allowed the two boys to remain at court) and instead married one of Constantine Porphyrogenitus's daughters. This allowed him to claim, with some truth, that he (unlike his uncle) was a member of the rightful imperial dynasty.

Meanwhile Svyatoslav of the Rus had threatened Boris II of Bulgaria into an alliance with him, and their combined armies had crossed the Danube and were approaching Constantinople. John Tzimiskes organized a defensive force and marched towards them. The two armies met at Arcadiopolis, sixty miles west of the Byzantine capital, and the Rus were pushed backwards. The Bulgarians, who had not been completely committed to the operation anyway, retreated home. John followed them. He captured Boris II, along with his brother and heir Romanus, and sent the two men back to Constantinople as prisoners. And then he annexed Bulgaria.

Svyatoslav fared even worse. On his way back to Kiev, he was ambushed and assassinated by the nomadic Turkish tribe of the Pechenegs, who had been his enemies for his entire twenty-eight-year rule. The Pecheneg chief made a gold-overlaid cup out of his skull and passed it around for all of his warriors to drink from.[20]

With Svyatoslav dead, his sons fought over the throne of the Rus. The youngest, Vladimir, eventually triumphed, and in 980 he became king of the Rus. Eight years later, after John Tzimiskes died from dysentery and Theophano's sons Basil II and Constantine VIII had been crowned co-rulers in Constantinople, Vladimir negotiated a treaty with the two young emperors. The Rus would remain at peace with Constantinople and would supply soldiers for the Byzantine army when needed; in return, he would marry the emperors' sister Anna and convert to Christianity.

Anna was not overly pleased with this arrangement: Vladimir was rumored to have over eight hundred wives and concubines scattered around in various Rus villages, so that he would always have at least one on hand no matter where he went. But Basil II, as senior emperor, convinced her that she would be doing God's work, since Vladimir would only agree to be baptized if the marriage went through.[21]

Anna went to Kherson to meet her new husband, taking her own priests with her, and Vladimir submitted to baptism: "Now you will have her as your wife, inherit the kingdom of God, and be our companion in the faith," Basil II wrote to his new brother-in-law.[22]

Vladimir was more interested in the kingdoms of the earth, though, and he saw a monotheistic religion with a strong internal network of priests and scholars as an important part of his country's stability. (He had investigated Islam, the *Russian Primary Chronicle* reports, and rejected it when he learned that he would have to swear off alcohol; he also hadn't been too pleased with the Jewish requirement of circumcision.) As soon as he arrived back home, he ordered all his people to follow him into the new faith:

> When the Prince arrived at his capital, he directed that the idols should be overthrown . . . cut to pieces and others burned with fire. Thereafter Vladimir sent heralds throughout the whole city to proclaim that if any inhabitant, rich or poor, did not betake himself to the river, he would risk the Prince's displeasure. . . . On the morrow, the Prince went forth to the Dnieper with the priests of the Princess and those from Kherson, and a countless multitude assembled. They all went into the water: some stood up to their necks, others to their breasts, and the younger near the bank, some of them holding children in their arms, while the adults waded farther out. The priests stood by and offered prayers. When the people were baptized, they returned each to his own abode.

The conversion was a state decision, not an act of faith, and thus too important to leave to individual conviction.[23]

Vladimir ordered churches built, created a parish system with priests in charge of different districts throughout the country, and instituted a system of Christian education: "He took the children of the best families," the *Primary Chronicle* says, "and sent them for instruction in book-learning. The mothers of these children wept bitterly over them, for they were not yet strong in faith, but mourned as for the dead."[24]

The old ways were past. Vladimir had wiped out the past and transformed the warrior alliance of the Rus into a state. He had created a new Christian Russia, one that could stand as full ally to Byzantium and take its place as equal to the kingdoms of the west.

TIMELINE 70

BRITISH ISLES	SCANDINAVIA	BYZANTIUM	BULGARIA	RUS
			Simeon (893–927) of Bulgaria	
Edward the Elder (899–924) Constantine II of Scotland (900–943)				
		Rus attack on Constantinople (906)		
		Alexander (912–913) Constantine Porphyrogenitus (913–959)		Igor of the Rus (912–945)
Sihtric of Northumbria (921–927) Athelstan (924–939)		Romanos Lecapenus as senior co-emperor (920–944)		
Olaf I of Ireland (934–941)			Peter (927–969) of Bulgaria	
Edmund the Just (939–946)	Hakon the Good of Norway (c. 940–961)	Constantine Porphyrogenitus as sole emperor (945–959)		Olga of the Rus as regent (945–963)
Edred Weak-Foot (946–955)				
Edwy All-Fair (955–959)/ Edgar (957–975)				
	Harald Bluetooth of Denmark (958–987) Harald Greycloak of Norway (961–976)	Romanos II (959–963) Nikephoros II as senior co-emperor (963–969)		Svyatoslav of the Rus (963–972)
Coronation of Edgar (973)		John Tzimiskes (969–976)	Boris II of Bulgaria (969–971)	
Ethelred (978–1013)		Basil II as senior co-emperor (976–1025)		
				Vladimir of the Rus (980–1015)
	Arrival of Eric the Red on Greenland (985) Sweyn Forkbeard of Denmark (987–1014)			
Massacre of the Danes (1002)	Sweyn Forkbeard of Norway (1000–1014)			
Sweyn Forkbeard (1013–1014) of England				

Part Five

CRUSADES

Chapter Seventy-One

The Holy Roman Emperor

Between 950 and 996,
the king of Germany fights for God and chooses a new pope,
the family of the Capetians rules in Western Francia,
and the Peace of God is declared in Christian lands

IN 950, AN OLD ENEMY RETURNED. The Magyars had left the German kingdom alone for over two decades, but now Magyar raids on the south of Germany began again. In 955, a sizable band of Magyars under the command of two warlords named Lél and Bulcsu set up camp on the Lechfeld flood plain, just across the river from the city of Augsburg. The *Gesta Hungarorum*, the national history written three hundred years later by the Hungarian cleric Simon of Kéza, tells us that they "mounted attacks upon the city day and night," raiding the lands around the walls with their light quick-moving cavalry. Desperate, the people of Augsburg "sent messengers to the emperor urging him to come to the aid of the city."[1]

Otto I had already taken note of the increasing Magyar threat. He assembled a heavily armed German cavalry force and marched as swiftly as he could from his court at Ulm to Augsburg. "There he fell on them at the third hour during a rainstorm," writes Simon of Kéza, "swiftly overwhelming the army which was nearer the city."

Later stories about the Battle of Lechfeld insisted that only seven Magyar warriors survived; this is unlikely, but the German attack was absolutely devastating, slaughtering an entire skilled class of Magyar warriors and officers. Lél and Bulcsu tried to flee down the Danube in a boat, but German naval forces intercepted the boat, arrested the two men, and brought them before Otto. He sentenced them to be hanged like common felons.[2]

This broke the back of the Magyar attack. The Magyar alliance stopped in its tracks. Between 955 and the turn of the century, the Magyars settled ever more firmly into the Carpathian Basin, the flat lands surrounded by the ring of the Carpathian mountain range. Although they couldn't quite break the habit of raiding their neighbors, they spent more time farming and less time

71.1: The Magyars and the West

fighting. Christian practices and Christian baptism began to spread into the Magyar community from the outside.

The Battle of Lechfeld convinced Otto's subjects—not to mention the historians who chronicled his reign—that he had God on his side. While still on the battlefield, his soldiers hailed him as the God-appointed head of the Christian world. His victory over the heathen Magyars had convinced them that divine favor rested on Otto above all other men; the bloody defeat of the enemy had proved, beyond all doubt, the righteousness of Otto's rule.[3]

Otto was already both king of Germany and king of the Italian lands, the first man to hold that particular combination of titles; four years earlier, after a nasty fight over the rule of northern Italy, the dukes had invited Otto to take the Iron Crown. Now he was also the savior of Germany, conqueror of the Magyars. In 962, Pope John XII yielded to the inevitable and crowned him emperor of the Romans, after the title had lain vacant for nearly forty years.

The title of emperor did not come free. In exchange, the pope demanded that Otto take an oath: "I will never make laws or rules in regard to the things which are under your jurisdiction, or the jurisdiction of the Romans without your consent," the oath ran, "and I will restore to you all of the lands of St. Peter that shall come into my hands." Those lands were enumerated with careful accuracy: Rome and the land around, Ravenna and its port, the island of Corsica, and dozens of other towns, fortresses, and cities, each one listed by name. The pope not only governed these lands but also collected taxes from them: "We confirm your possession of all these things," the oath concluded, "they shall remain in your right and ownership and control, and no one of our successors shall on any pretext take from you any part of the aforesaid provinces, cities, towns, fortresses, villages, dependencies, territories, patrimonies, or taxes, or lessen your authority over them." John XII did not intend to give Otto the sacred *imperium* unless he could be quite sure that it would not be wielded against him.[4]

Otto took the oath, in a way: he sent an ambassador to take it on his behalf, which was legally binding but displayed a certain lack of enthusiasm. The circumlocution worried John XII. Despite having just crowned the new emperor, he had serious doubts about Otto's growing power. He decided to take prudent pre-emptive action; he sent ambassadors to the Magyars, encouraging them to distract Otto from empire-building by attacking the Germans once more.

Word of this behind-the-scenes negotiation reached Otto. Furious, he marched south towards Rome in 963. When John XII heard that the angry emperor was approaching, he packed up and fled the city—taking much of the treasury with him.[5]

This was not calculated to make Otto any happier, and when the emperor arrived in the city, he announced that John had been deposed. On his own authority, he appointed a new pope: Leo VIII.

In the past, popes had been given their titles by an undefined and shifting process: the senior priests of Rome would gather together and argue until they came to some agreement about who should be the next leader of the church, and as long as the people of Rome didn't riot, the candidate was publicly proclaimed as the next pope. Although previous "emperors of the Romans" had also jumped into the fray, offering imperial approval if disagreement over the election threatened to cause trouble, the selection of St. Peter's successors had generally rested firmly within the Christian church itself.

But Otto had now taken this task on his royal and secular shoulders.

For him, this was not such a huge departure from ordinary practice. In the kingdoms of Germany and Western Francia, it wasn't unusual for a lay man to appoint a priest, a practice called "lay investiture." Over the previous centuries, landowners had been accustomed to build private churches on their own estates; it was the Christian version of the old Roman "home altar," a reasonable-enough action for a Christian Goth or Frank to take, in a world where they were too distant from great cities to make regular visits to the bigger churches or cathedrals built there.

These churches were used by villagers and vassals nearby, but the building belonged to the landowner—and he generally chose, and installed, his own priest to run the services that happened inside. It wasn't uncommon for a father to install a younger son as priest, and for the priesthood itself to become hereditary, passed down for several generations.[6]

In the centuries before Otto, bishops and landowners tussled over the control of these churches. By and large, though, they remained under the control of the families who had built them, which meant that the right to appoint a priest could be sold, or given as a gift in exchange for goodwill. A clergyman with money might pay a landowner to make him a priest—a practice that church authorities frowned on (it became known as *simony*, after a New Testament magician named Simon who tried to buy the divine gift of healing from the disciples of Jesus).[7] Kings built not only churches but also monasteries on their own royal holdings and, like noble landowners, appointed priests and abbots to run them—a practice that tended to bleed over into other parts of the country, not just the land specifically held by the king's family. The king, after all, could claim (in a way) to own all of his country, not just his royal estate.*

Otto had done his share of building monasteries, appointing abbots, and choosing priests; the difference was that he had done it mostly in Germany, where he was king (although even there, he and Pope John XII had argued about who had the right to appoint a bishop in several of the German cities). Although Otto was king of Italy as well, Rome was a Papal State and not under his jurisdiction, which meant he had no right to appoint a pope.[8]

He dealt with the problem by ordering his newly chosen pope, Leo VIII, to make a new proclamation: "We, Leo, bishop, servant of the servants of God," Leo decreed, obediently, "with all the clergy and people of Rome, by our apostolic authority bestow upon lord Otto I, king of the Germans, and upon his successors in the kingdom of Italy forever, the right of choosing the successor of the pope, and of ordaining the pope and the archbishops and bishops. . . . They shall receive their investiture and consecration from him." The pope, chosen by the emperor, had completed the circle of power: he had given the emperor the right to choose all future popes.[9]

Otto I had now claimed for himself the sole, the only, the *inalienable* right of the emperor to choose the leader of the Christian church. And in doing so, he had become more than emperor of the Romans. He had extended his scepter into the realm of the ineffable. He was no longer content simply to

---

*This is a simplified recounting of the development of a very complicated situation. Under Charlemagne and Louis the Pious, decrees were passed that gave bishops the right to approve any appointments made by laymen; however, this right was exercised very inadequately during the reign of later kings. For useful overviews of this situation, which led to the Investiture Controversy of the late eleventh century, see Uta-Renate Blumenthal, *The Investiture Controversy* (University of Pennsylvania Press, 1988).

surround the church with his soldiers and shield it from harm; he had opened the doors, walked up the aisle, and taken his place in front of the altar.

He had become the first *holy* emperor.

Folding sacred duties into the secular job was a two-steps-forward, one-step-back sort of process. Otto remained in the city for three months; as soon as he left, John XII returned and (with the support of most of Rome) announced that Leo was not the pope and that the decree had been invalid. Otto, who hadn't gotten too far away, reversed his direction and headed back towards Rome, and once again John fled from the city.

This time he never returned. He had a stroke in the village where he had taken refuge (he was rumored to have been in bed with a married woman at the time) and died, not yet thirty years old. Otto's man, Leo, was reinstalled with the help of the German army, and when Leo died, Otto exercised his authority as pope-maker once more and appointed another hand-chosen pope, John XIII.[10]

Once again, power pulsed neatly around the closed circle. John XIII, appointed by Otto, agreed to crown Otto's son and heir Otto II as co-emperor, guaranteeing a smooth transition of the emperorship. The right to claim the *imperium* had never been hereditary before. But Otto was establishing a dynastic claim not just over Germany but over the less tangible realm of the "Holy" Roman Empire as well. Both would now be ruled by the Ottonian or Saxon dynasty, which was German and imperial in its claims.

The strength of both claims was put to the test over the next decades. When Otto I died in 973, his titles passed at once to his eighteen-year-old son. Otto II was now king of Germany without election and emperor of the Romans without coronation.[11]

Not all of the German nobles were content to see their ancient power of election decaying before their eyes. At once Otto II faced numerous rebellions, particularly in the southern duchies of Germany. The most troublesome of the rebels was his own cousin Henry, duke of Bavaria, four years his senior. Henry's abrasively aggressive personality had earned him the nickname "Henry the Quarrelsome," and he saw no reason why he should not lobby to be elected king in Otto II's place.

Otto II spent the first seven years of his reign fighting against these revolts. By 980, he had confirmed (by force) his right to be king of Germany, driving Henry the Quarrelsome into exile and seizing part of Bavaria as a royal possession. He then decided to firm up his claim of emperor of the Romans in the same way. He planned a military campaign into Italy that would drive all remaining Byzantine control off the peninsula, putting it firmly and singly under the Ottonian crown. He would fight for Italy, he declared, under the banner of the Roman emperor. No longer content to be "Emperor of the Romans" as his predecessors had been—an emperor whose subjects were heirs of the remnants of old Roman civilization—he aspired to be *Roman emperor*: fully imperial, fully Christian, and fully in control of the old Roman lands.

Otto II, says the contemporary chronicler Thietmar of Merseburg, was "noted for his outstanding physical strength and, as such . . . tended towards recklessness." His energy and ambition plunged him into enormous trouble; the attempted conquest was a horrendous failure. Otto II fought in Italy for three years, repeatedly losing his battles with the Byzantine garrisons still on the peninsula. Southern Italy slipped from his hands, as the duchies detached themselves from any allegiance to the northern Italian kingdom. In 983, still claiming to be Roman emperor, still fighting, he grew ill. He died in the city of Rome, not yet thirty years old.[12]

He had already declared his three-year-old son Otto III to be co-emperor. But Otto II himself had barely managed to hold onto the titles transferred to him by *his* father, and the baby Otto was in no position to insist on his hereditary rights. The pope declined to recognize him as Roman emperor. And the rebel nobleman Henry the Quarrelsome, skulking around on the northern coast of Germany, laid a plan to get the throne of Germany away from the baby.

He insisted that, as the young king's nearest male relative, he should be awarded the care and control of Otto III. This was in fact legal. Otto III's mother was in Italy, where her husband had died, so the little boy's temporary guardian, the unsuspicious archbishop of Cologne, handed the toddler over.[13]

At once Henry took the child south into Saxony, where his supporters were gathered. While little Otto was kept in safe seclusion, Henry's cronies began to address him as king and lord; when Easter came, they serenaded him with *laudes*, the formal songs of praise sung to a monarch.[14]

The other noblemen of Germany, unimpressed, insisted that Otto would have to give consent before Henry could call himself king. As Otto was not yet speaking, consent was not exactly easy to determine. Henry suggested that, as guardian, he could speak for Otto and give himself permission to become king, but this proposal was rejected as well.

It soon became clear to Henry that if he wanted to become king, he would have to fight for it—and he doubted that he had the strength to resist not just the opposing noblemen in Germany, but also the king of Western Francia, Lothair IV, who had declared himself on Otto's side in the debate. Instead, he agreed to negotiate a compromise. He would again be given the duchy of Bavaria, which Otto II had taken away; and in exchange he would hand little Otto back to his mother, who became his regent.[15] With the transfer, Otto III again became king of Germany. The hereditary transfer of power had not been clean, but it had partially succeeded.

To the west, though, the hereditary movement of power from one generation to the next suddenly failed. Lothair IV of Western Francia, who had been prepared to fight in defense of Otto III's claim to kingship, died in 986. He left his own crown to his son Louis the Sluggard. The name, like Henry's, points to a difficult personality. Louis the Sluggard kept the throne for a single year before he died—in all likelihood, poisoned by his own exasperated mother.

The dukes of Western Francia, like the dukes of Germany, now insisted on taking their traditional role in the election of a ruler. The king's family had not done an impressive job of ruling in generations, and the dukes rejected the idea of finding a distant blood relation to elevate. Instead, they crowned a king from a new family: Hugh Capet, son of the count of Paris, one of their own. The Carolingian dynasty had finally ended in the west; Charles the Great's blood kin no longer sat on the throne.

As the first king of a new dynasty—the Capetians—Hugh Capet ruled an old Frankish kingdom that had lost its eastern expanse to Germany, and the southeastern and northwestern territories of Burgundy and Normandy to independence. The lands that remained under the crown were engulfed by multiple currencies, a slew of languages, and a mass of independent-minded Frankish nobles. Hugh Capet had to rule carefully: he had been elected by those noblemen with the tacit understanding that he would not act as a despot. He made Paris his home city, the center of his government, and began in a very gingerly manner to try to pull Western Francia together into a slightly more coherent country.

But his shaky authority was unable to bring peace to his country. Private warfare between French dukes, private oppression of farmers by aristocrats, armed spats between men of different loyalties and languages, dishonest trade, altered weights: Francia was a sea of chaos from border to border. The nightmarish conditions forced the rich to hire personal armies to keep their possessions safe. The poor had no such luxury; instead, they offered to serve their wealthier neighbors in exchange for protection. This became the root of the later practice of feudalism: the exchange of service, on the part of the poor, for protection and provision from the rich.[16]

In 989, Christian priests gathered at the Benedictine abbey of Charroux, in the center of the Frankish land, and took the problem into their own hands. For Francia to survive, someone had to quench the flames of private war that had followed the disintegration of Frankish royal power. The priests had no army, no money, and no political power, but they had the authority to declare the gates of heaven shut.

Now they began to wield it. Noncombatants—peasants and clergy, families and farmers—should be immune from ravages of battle, they announced. No matter whose army he fought for, private or royal, Frankish or foreign, any soldier who robbed a church would be excommunicated. Any soldier who stole livestock from the poor would be excommunicated. Anyone who attacked a priest would be excommunicated, as long as the priest wasn't carrying a sword or wearing armor; the decrees at Charroux recognized the potential overlap between priest and soldier, and were careful to avoid giving armed clergymen a free pass.[17]

The synod at Charroux—the first step in a gathering movement known as the Peace and Truce of God—was the first organized attempt by the Christian church to lay out an official policy on the difference between combatants and noncombatants in war. It took another tentative step forward in 994, when the pope announced that the Abbey of Cluny, in the eastern Frankish lands, would become a place of refuge. When the abbey had been established around 930 as a private monastery, its founder, William the Pious of Aquitaine, had written into its charter a remarkable degree of independence. Cluny, unlike other private monasteries, was placed directly under the supervision of the pope. No secular nobleman—not even the founder or his family—had the right to interfere in its government. Cluny (theoretically) answered to no political sovereign. Nor was it under the authority of any local bishop. So, as a place of refuge, it could offer safety to anyone who made it to the abbey's walls, no matter how unpopular the refugee was. Cluny itself was protected, by threat of excommunication, from being invaded, sacked, or burned.[18]

The Peace of God movement was more than an attempt to sort out the ethics of war. It was a desperate response to a world in which the possibility of salvation and the mission of the Christian church were increasingly tied to the territorial ambitions of particular kings. The setting of Cluny as a place of refuge gave the pope—the man who was supposed to have inherited St. Peter's power to open and close the gates of heaven—ultimate authority to grant safety during time of war.

But it was an imperfect solution.

Just how imperfect became clear in 996, when Otto III of Germany reached the age of sixteen. The nobles of Italy agreed to recognize him as king of the land that had once been northern Lombard Italy, and now was simply the Italian Kingdom, part of the peninsula but not all of it, an appendage of the German realm. With the kingship of Italy in his hands, Otto III immediately appointed his twenty-four-year-old cousin to be Pope Gregory V, the first German pope. At once the new pope returned the compliment by crowning him "Holy Roman Emperor," Protector of the Church and ruler of the old Roman lands.

The symbiotic relationship between pope and emperor strengthened both; it was a return to the days of Otto's grandfather, when the circle of power had first been created. But the return dealt a serious blow to the idealism of the Peace of God. The church could only offer peace and refuge during time of war as long as it remained free from the state; refuge could only be found in a place whose leaders had nothing to gain, or lose, from the king.

TIMELINE 71

BYZANTIUM BULGARIA	MAGYARS RUS	WESTERN FRANCIA GERMANY	ITALY	Roman Emperor
				Louis of Provence (901–902)
				Berengar (902–924)
Rus attack on Constantinople (906)	Destruction of Moravia by Magyars	Battle of Augsburg (910)		
Alexander (912–913)	**Igor** of the Rus (912–945)	**Conrad** of Franconia (911–918)		
Constantine Porphyrogenitus (913–959)				
Romanos Lecapenus as senior co-emperor (920–944)	**Lél** (c. 920–955) **Bulcsu** (?–955)	**Henry the Fowler** (919–936)		
	Peter (927–969) of Bulgaria			
Constantine Porphyrogenitus as sole emperor (945–959)	**Olga** of the Rus as regent (945–963)	Battle of Riade (933) **Otto** (936–973)		
		Otto (951–973)		
		Lothair IV (954–986) Battle of Lechfeld (955)	Pope John XII (955–963/964)	
Romanos II (959–963)				
Nikephoros II as senior co-emperor (963–969)	**Svyatoslav** of the Rus (963–972)		Pope Leo VIII (963/964–965) Pope John XIII (965–972)	**Otto** (962–973)
John Tzimiskes (969–976)	**Boris II** of Bulgaria (969–971)			
Basil II as senior co-emperor (976–1025)				**Otto II** (973–983) as king of Germany and Italy and Roman emperor
	Vladimir of the Rus (980–1015)	**Otto III** (983–1002) **Louis the Sluggard** (986–987) **Hugh Capet** (987–996)		
		Birth of "Peace of God" movement		
			Pope Gregory V (996–999)	**Otto III** (996–1002)

—■—

The Hardship of Sacred War

Between 963 and 1044,
Alp Tigin establishes the Ghaznavid empire
by conquering the enemies of Islam,
the Turks establish a kingdom by conquering the Ghaznavids,
and the Chola dominate the south of India in the name of Shiva

THE ISLAMIC LANDS had fractured again and again. One caliph ruled in Cordoba, another in North Africa; the third caliph, of Abbasid blood, sat in Baghdad under the complete control of the Buyid clan. The Samanids ruled in the east, the neo-Saffarids in the south, and the Hamdanids near the coast of the Mediterranean. South of the Caspian Sea, the Ziyarid dynasty ruled over a little kingdom that had turned away from Islam and back to the old Zoroastrianism of the disappeared Persian empire.

And then there were the Turks: men descended from the once nomadic tribes of the northeast who had come down into the Islamic kingdoms as slaves and soldiers, and who had risen slowly to claim greater and greater influence there. They had no titles, but they had strength.

In 963, one of these Turks took the final step towards kingship. Alp Tigin had once been a stalwart general for the Samanid emir, chief commander of the Samanid armies. However, he had fallen out of favor the year before, when the Samanid emir died. Instead of supporting the emir's closest blood relation (his brother Mansur), Alp Tigin tried to force the election of his own son to the Samanid throne.[1]

This indirect bid for power failed, and Alp Tigin left the Samanid capital just ahead of Mansur's hit men, heading east. He arrived at the city of Ghazni, southwest from the Khyber Pass, and conquered it. There he ruled as king, over a much tinier empire: the breadth of one city.

In 975, Alp Tigin died. His son-in-law Sebuk Tigin and his son Abu-Ishaq took control of the town together. Of the two, Sebuk Tigin proved the cannier politician. Alp Tigin had been content to rule as an outlaw king, but Sebuk Tigin had ambitions to build a real, legitimate empire. He convinced Abu-Ishaq to travel west with him to the court of Mansur, king of the Samanids, Alp Tigin's old enemy. There, they negotiated a tricky peace. They swore loyalty to Mansur, in return for recognition: Mansur agreed to make Abu-Ishaq the legitimate governor of Ghazni and to appoint Sebuk Tigin to the position should Abu-Ishaq die.

It is not entirely surprising that Abu-Ishaq promptly died, leaving Sebuk Tigin as the Samanid-approved governor of Ghazni. Almost at once, Sebuk Tigin attacked and captured Kandahar, which for a short time had been in the hands of the neo-Saffarid dynasty of the south. He was still swearing loyalty to the Samanids, but now he was more than just a city governor; he ruled a territory that would slowly develop into a kingdom in its own right. This development worried the Samanids, but they had troubles of their own. Northern Turkish nomads known as the Karakhanids had begun to cross the Oxus river south into Samanid land, raiding the silver mines on which the Samanids relied. The Samanid army, busy fighting for its silver, didn't have energy to spare for Sebuk Tigin.

But his expansion did not go unnoticed. At the capture of Kandahar, the nearest Indian king, Jayapala of the Shahi, began to prepare an attack.

The Shahi kingdom, which controlled the Khyber Pass, had once been a Buddhist kingdom with Kabul as its capital; but Kabul had fallen into Muslim hands three hundred years earlier, and the Buddhist kings had been driven from the throne a century before by a Hindu ruling line. The Hindu king Jayapala, who now ruled from the city of Udabhandapura, launched several unsuccessful assaults against Ghazni. In retaliation, Sebuk Tigin attacked the western border of the Shahi and took some of Jayapala's territory away. Jayapala was forced to move his capital once more, this time to the city of Lahore. But although he shifted the center of his government to Lahore, he remained in Udabhandapura, now the dangerous frontier of his country.[2]

The Samanids continued to be distracted, both by the raids from the north and by the increasing power of the Buyids to their west. Sebuk Tigin fought on. He captured Kabul; he battled his way steadily east into Shahi land; and by 986 it had become clear to Jayapala that an all-out war was on his hands. "Observing the immeasurable fractures and losses every moment caused in his states," says the sixteenth-century Arab history *Tabaqat-i-Akbari*, "and becoming disturbed and inconsolable, he saw no remedy except . . . to take up arms."[3]

He assembled an enormous army—perhaps as many as a hundred thousand men—and marched northeast to confront Sebuk Tigin near Kabul. "They came together on the frontiers of each state," the *Tabaqat-i-Akbari* tells us. "Each army mutually attacked the other, and they fought and resisted in every way until the face of the earth was stained red with the blood of the slain, and the lions and warriors of both armies were worn out and reduced to despair."[4]

The battle was not a clear victory for either side, but Jayapala was the first to draw back. Sebuk Tigin's men were motivated not merely by the joys of conquest but also by religious fervor in a way foreign to the Hindu soldiers who opposed them. Sebuk Tigin's battles against his Muslim counterparts had been motivated by sheer ambition, but in northern India he could exhort his men with a more worthy battle cry. "He made war upon the country of Hindustan," writes the contemporary Arab chronicler al-Utbi, "whose inhabitants are universally enemies of Islam, and worshippers of images and idols. He extinguished, by the water of his sword-wounds, the sparks of idolatry. . . . He undertook the hardship of that sacred war and displayed unshaken resolution in patiently prosecuting it."[5]

In the face of this holy enthusiasm, Jayapala sued for peace, paid his enemy tribute, and withdrew. But he was really regathering his forces. "Unless he set his face to resist," al-Utbi writes, "his hereditary kingdom would go to the winds." As soon as he had managed to collect another army from among his tributaries and allies, Jayapala reneged on the deal and marched on his enemy again.

72.1: The Khyber Pass. Credit: Roger Wood/CORBIS

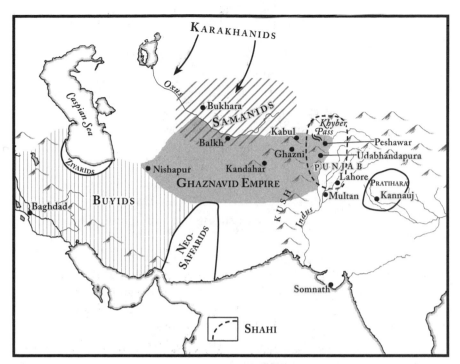

72.1: Expansion of the Ghaznavids

Again he was defeated, this time just west of the Khyber Pass. Sebuk Tigin, vexed by Jayapala's breaking of his oath, seized the Khyber Pass for his own. He now owned the highway into northern India, and he "proceeded to the country of the infidel traitor, plundered and sacked the country, dug up and burnt down its buildings, carrying away their children and cattle as booty." In the face of the sacking and burning, Jayapala retreated to the east, his kingdom contracting still further.[6]

Sebuk Tigin died in 997, ruler of a realm that had expanded well into the Kush mountains: the Ghaznavid empire. After a sharp and very brief civil war, his oldest son Mahmud claimed the throne.

Mahmud's first great conquest was not in the north of India, but over on the western flank of his realm. The Turkish Karakhanids had now been harassing the Samanids for more than twenty years. In 992, they had rushed so far into Samanid territory that they were able to capture the capital, Bukhara; but when their chief died unexpectedly, they withdrew and gave the city up. Now, led by their new chief Nasr Khan, they again pushed all the way to Bukhara and sacked it. This time they kept the city. The young Samanid emir withdrew to the south of the Oxus river. The Karakhanids seized the territory around Bukhara for their own, while Mahmud—now the strongest ruler in those parts—claimed the rest of the Samanid land north of the Oxus for the Ghaznavids.

The strongest opponent of Ghaznavid power was now Jayapala, and Mahmud made an oath: he would invade India every year until the northern lands were his. On November 27, 1001, Mahmud Ghazni met Jayapala and his army just on the other side of the Khyber Pass, near Peshawar. Once again, the hard-fought battle damaged both armies: "Swords flashed like lightning amid the blackness of clouds," writes al-Utbi, "and fountains of blood flowed like the fall of setting stars."[7]

Jayapala lost heart. He had been defeated again and again, each time backing slowly away from his enemy, and he was humiliated and sinking into despair. Not long after the battle at Peshawar, he built himself a funeral pyre, entered it, and set it on fire.[8]

His son Anandapala took up the resistance. Like his father, he fought hard against the persistent invaders, and Mahmud's advance into the Indus delta was a slow progression of two steps forward and one step back. But mile by laborious mile, he moved deeper and deeper into lands that had once been Shahi. By 1006, after five years of bloody fighting, he had made his way into the upper lands of the delta. By 1009, he controlled most of the Punjab. Around 1015, Jayapala's son Anandapala, the last Shahi king, was driven completely from his lands and disappeared into exile.

The list of conquests dragged on. In 1018, Mahmud even made an advance to the walls of Kannauj itself, where he slaughtered the remnants of the Pratihara army and drove the Pratihara king out of his capital. As he moved farther east, his fast, mobile cavalry proved impossible for the slower armies of foot-soldiers and elephants to resist.[9]

His devastation had now enveloped most of India's northwestern quarter. He circled around the outside of the territory he had laid waste, and in 1025 reached the height of his conquests in India: he arrived at the harbor town of Somnath, on the western coast, where one of the most sacred images of Shiva stood, and where hundreds of thousands of pilgrims travelled to pay devotion to the god.

The Ghaznavid armies slaughtered thousands of pilgrims and sacked the temple of Shiva. Mahmud himself toppled the image, pulverized the head and shoulders, and ordered the rest taken back to Ghazni. There, he placed it at the foot of the steps into the mosque, so that Muslim worshippers could wipe their feet on it as they entered. His entire life had been spent in victorious empire-building; now, at the end, he could boast that those victories were the triumph of his God over the gods of his enemies.[10]

Five years later, Mahmud died of a malarial fever, at age sixty-three. His empire had already reached its high point. The fracturing of the Muslim east into separate kingdoms allowed for the sudden mushroom-like growth of any realm that was lucky enough to be led by an energetic and long-lived general, but the kingdoms that grew so suddenly into empires were equally likely to shrink. Mahmud had spent thirty-three years conquering his way into India, but another kingdom was already beginning to swell on the western border of the Ghaznavids, led by a warrior named Togrul.

The unruly Karakhanid attacks had gained the Turkish nomads a little land of their own, and in 1016 the young chief Togrul had inherited the command of his own particular tribe. This did not give him much authority with the others. The Turks had absolutely no respect for an overlord, something that had shocked the Muslim traveller Ibn Fadlan; journeying through Turkish lands some decades before, Ibn Fadlan had earned the friendship of one powerful Turkish chief and had assumed that the alliance would protect him. Running into another Turkish chieftain on the plains, Ibn Fadlan demanded passage in the name of the Turkish khan. The nomad laughed at him: "Who is the khan?" he said. "I shit on his beard."[11]

But the tribes near the Oxus had land of their own, and they were surrounded by the rule of Muslim empires; they had begun to absorb the new standards of a settled people. Togrul, as driven as the great Ghaznavid ruler Mahmud, took command of his tribe and began to conquer. While Mahmud was building his empire in northern India, Togrul was building a realm of his own around the Oxus. And after Mahmud's death, Togrul began to fight his way through the western Ghaznavid land. By 1038, he had reached the Ghaznavid capital of Nishapur and claimed it as his own. He had himself crowned there as sultan of the Turks, overlord of his tribes.

Which was not entirely true. Other Turkish chiefs were also on the move, and they did not yet recognize the overlordship of Togrul's dynasty. But Togrul was certainly the most victorious of the Turkish chiefs so far, and his conquest of the Ghaznavid lands to the west had given him the largest Turkish realm. By 1044, Togrul's Turks controlled most of the lands west of the mountains; and the Ghaznavid empire, which had begun as a Muslim dynasty in the Muslim lands, now existed only as a northern Indian kingdom.

THE IMAGE OF SHIVA had fallen in the north; but in the south, the god's devotees were gaining power.

The Chola kings, devoted to the worship of Shiva and his goddess consort, had allowed most of their realm to slip through their fingers. Now, like the northern Ghaznavids, the Chola inherited an ambitious leader. Rajaraja I, who came to the throne in 985, began to lead his armies in the reconquest of the south. He wiped out the southern kingdom of the Pandya, which had

revived itself under a line of pretender kings; he defeated the Eastern Chalukya and made them his vassals; he fought against the powerful Western
Chalukya, forcing them to halt their own spread to defend their borders; he
sent his men over the strait to the island of Sri Lanka.

Western Chalukya inscriptions accuse the Chola army of atrocities: the
slaughter of women and children, the massacre of priests, rape and pillage and
plunder. But the ruthlessness of Rajaraja's conquests sent the Chola back up the
rotating wheel of royal fortunes. "Having subdued in battle the Ganga, Kalinga,
Vanga, Magadha, Aratta, Odda, Saurashtra, Chalukya and other kings, and
having received homage from them," the royal inscriptions boast, "the glorious
Rajaraja, a rising sun . . . ruled the earth whose girdle is the water."[12]

He didn't quite rule the earth, but after thirty years of fighting, he dominated the south. To commemorate the extent of his triumphs, he built a huge
temple in his capital city Thanjavur: a temple devoted to Shiva, with three
hundred priests dedicated to the service and worship of the god and fifty
musicians who were salaried to sing the sacred liturgies. A mighty lingam—
a seamless pillar with no features, a representation of the all-encompassing,
transcendent essence of Shiva, more powerful and more sacred than the image
that had fallen in the north—stood at its center. On the walls were painted
scenes of Shiva as conqueror, Shiva as destroyer of cities.[13]

Rajaraja's son and commander Rajendra succeeded him in 1014 and ruled,
like his father, for three full decades. This second long reign, following on
the first, achieved what the Ghaznavids up north had failed to do: establish a
hold on the conquered land that outlasted the death of its founder. Like his
father, Rajendra was a vicious and skilled fighter. He "reduced to ashes all
the kings who stood aloof from him," his inscriptions tell us, "wrought ruin,
annihilated the country."[14]

Rajendra's great achievement was to set sail. He sent trade ships east to the
court of the Song, carrying elephant tusks, frankincense, aromatic woods, and
over a thousand pounds of pearls. He also sent warships across the southern
strait, carrying naval forces to the island of Sri Lanka. There, he claimed to
have captured "the lustrous pure pearls . . . the spotless fame of the Pandya
king"—the crown and regalia of the legitimate Pandya line, which had rested
on the island since the Pandya flight there a century before, and which the
Rashtrakuta kings had sought but failed to find.[15]

He then began a two-year march up the coast of the Indian subcontinent,
towards the lands of the Pala and towards the sacred mountain of Kailasa,
where, as his own records tell us, "Shiva is residing." He had captured the
symbol of southern rule; now he was heading towards the residence of the
god, the symbol of northern dominance. "His army crossed the rivers by way
of bridges formed by herds of elephants," his chronicles tell us. "The rest of

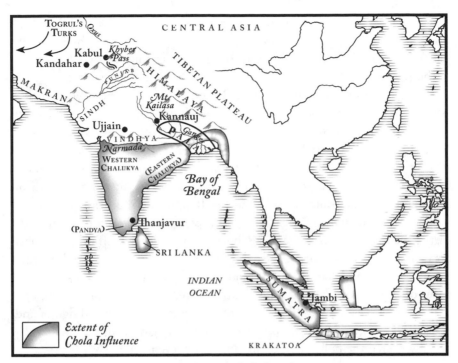

72.2: *The Spread of Chola Influence*

the army crossed on foot, because the waters in the meantime had dried up, being used by elephants, horses, and men."[16]

When he arrived at the Ganges, he was faced by the armies of the Pala king. The once great Pala kingdom had shrunk from its former heights, but under its long-lived king Mahipala had begun to grow again. Mahipala had been on a conquering spree of his own, taking advantage of the preoccupation in the northwest with invading Ghaznavids to rebuild Pala power in the northeast.

Rajendra met Mahipala on the banks of the Ganges and won a great victory against him. But so far from home, he did not have the resources to follow up with an attempt at conquering the entire kingdom. Instead he pushed past it, across the Ganges delta, and forced the people along the coast to pay tribute.

Continuing on by land would have taken his army even farther away from the resources of the Chola heartland; it would have been simple for the Pala army (or another hostile force) to come from behind, breaching the thin strip of conquests along the coastline and cutting them off. Instead, Rajendra led his army back home and began to plan a naval expedition. It launched in 1025, sailing all the way across the Bay of Bengal to land on the coast of the kingdom of Srivijaya. Srivijaya, dominating the islands of Java and Sumatra, controlled the shipping routes into southeast Asia; the Chola armies, invading the island, collected tribute from the Srivijayan king and seized control of the routes.

By the time of his death in 1044, Rajendra left a southern empire that boasted tributaries all the way up to the north and far to the east. His son Rajadhiraja, grandson of the great Rajaraja, inherited his crown without chaos or struggle. Never before had a southern Indian kingdom ruled so much for so long. The traditional division of the south into separate realms had ended; Chola language, Chola power, Chola customs now blanketed the south of India and were spreading across the Bay of Bengal into southeast Asia.[17]

The wealth of the court, gathered from conquered cities and from trade with the southeast, meant that the Chola kings could now afford to support poets and scholars at court. Under the patronage of Rajadhiraja and his successors, southern Indian literature bloomed. The poet Tiruttakadevar, composer of one of the most enduring southern epics, was from the same blood as the Chola royal house. His tale told of the prince Jivaka, skilled fighter and general, who earned a kingdom and then willingly gave it up; in victory, he had discovered the hollowness of all human achievement.[18]

WESTERN FRANCIA	ITALY GERMANY	Roman Emperor	EASTERN DYNASTIES	INDIA
			Nasr II of the Samanids (914–943)	**Indra III** of the Rashtrakuta (914–929)
	Henry the Fowler (919–936)			
	Battle of Riade (933) **Otto** (936–973)			**Krishna III** of the Rashtrakuta (939–967)
				Gandaraditya of the Chola (950–957)
	Otto (951–973)			
Lothair IV (954–986)	Battle of Lechfeld (955)	Pope John XII (955–963/964)		
			Mansur of the Samanids (961–976)	
	Otto (962–973) Pope Leo VIII (963/964–965) Pope John XIII (965–972)		**Alp Tigin** of the Ghaznavids (963–975)	**Jayapala** of the Shahi (964–1001)
			Khottiga of the Rashtrakuta (967–972)	
	Otto II (973–983) as king of Germany and Italy and Roman emperor			**Indra IV** of the Rashtrakuta (973–982)
			Abu-Ishaq of the Ghaznavids (975–977) **Sebuk Tigin** of the Ghaznavids (977–997)	
	Otto III (983–1002)			**Rajaraja** of the Chola (985–1014)
Louis the Sluggard (986–987) **Hugh Capet** (987–996)				
Birth of "Peace of God" movement				**Mahipala** of the Pala (995–1043)
	Otto III (996–1002) Pope Gregory V (996–999)		**Mahmud** of the Ghaznavids (997–1030)	
			Nasr Khan of the Karakhanids (c. 998-1017)	
				Anandapala of the Shahi (1001–1015)
				Rajendra of the Chola (1014–1044)
			Togrul (as Sultan) (1038–1063)	
				Rajadhiraja of the Chola (1044–1054)

Chapter Seventy-Three

—■—

Basil the Bulgar-Slayer

Between 976 and 1025,
a steel-hard emperor rules in Constantinople,
the Church of the Holy Sepulchre is razed in Jerusalem,
and the Abbasid caliphate denounces the Fatimids as heretics

THE DEATH OF JOHN TZIMISKES from dysentery left young Basil II, at seventeen, as senior emperor in Constantinople. His sixteen-year-old brother Constantine VIII ruled as co-emperor, but the government belonged to Basil; Constantine spent most of his time hunting, with an occasional diplomatic mission interrupting his free time. "Basil," the medieval biographer Michael Psellus tells us, "always gave an impression of alertness, intelligence, and thoughtfulness; Constantine appeared to be apathetic, lazy, and devoted to a life of luxury. It was natural that they should abandon the idea of joint rule."[1]

Basil II had been a crowned emperor since toddlerhood. Now for the first time he had actual power, and the first trouble spot he had to deal with was Bulgaria. John Tzimiskes had annexed Bulgaria, but he had been able to control only the east of the country. Freedom fighters in the west, led by four brothers with the biblical names of David, Moses, Aaron, and Samuel, were agitating for independence.

They claimed that they wanted the release of their imprisoned king Boris II, who along with his brother and heir Romanus had been tossed into jail by John Tzimiskes. Basil II suspected that the oldest brother, the freedom-fighter Samuel, was more interested in Bulgaria than in Boris. He decided to appeal to everyone's worst instincts. In 981, he set Boris II and Romanus free. By this point, at least two of the Bulgarian brothers had died in battle, and Samuel was in sole charge of the resistance. Basil hoped that if the royal family actually returned to Bulgaria, Samuel would be forced to admit that he was only using them as a useful rallying point. Then, a civil war might break out and bring the independence movement to a messy end.

Romanus and Boris II made their way back to the west of Bulgaria, as planned; after that, things went to seed quickly. They were challenged by a border guard, and before they could identify themselves, the guard killed Boris II. Romanus managed to convince the guard of his identity and survived.[2]

This turned out as well as possible for Samuel. Boris II would have claimed the throne and ruled on his own, but Romanus proved more amenable. Even more conveniently, he had been castrated during his imprisonment, so there would be no royal offspring. Samuel declared Romanus to be king of Bulgaria and simply kept power in his own hands, a turn of events that makes one wonder about the "accident" at the border.[3]

Basil had been right about Samuel's motivations, but this was not exactly the outcome he had hoped for. Now Samuel began to fight his way into Thracia, capturing Byzantine towns for his own. He also put his only remaining brother to death. Clearly he was positioning himself to claim the title "Emperor of Bulgaria."

Unfortunately, Basil's ability to strike back was hampered by ongoing domestic troubles. His general Bardas Phocas—a man of royal blood, the nephew of Nikephoros Phocas—convinced the troops in Asia Minor to declare him emperor. Bardas Phocas was a formidable opponent; Michael Psellus describes him as a man who believed life had wronged him, "always wrapped in gloom, and watchful, capable of foreseeing all eventualities . . . thoroughly versed in every type of siege warfare, every trick of ambush, every tactic of pitched battle. . . . Any man who received a blow from his hand was dead straightaway." In comparison, Basil II was less impressive: "He had just grown a beard," Psellus writes, "and was learning the art of war from experience in actual combat."[4]

While Samuel was systematically ripping away chunks of land from the western border, Basil was forced to mount an attempt to remove Bardas Phocas in the east. His overextended army was too thin to face Phocas's loyal Asia Minor troops, so he asked his brother-in-law Vladimir of Kiev, prince of the newly Christian Rus, to supply reinforcements. Vladimir sent him six thousand Rus soldiers: "These men," says Psellus, "fine fighters, he had trained in a separate corps." The Rus didn't mix well with the Byzantine army, but on their own were a fierce and powerful company.[5]

In April 989, Basil led his combined Byzantine and Russian forces into battle against Bardas Phocas at Chrysopolis. The general prediction seems to have been that Bardas Phocas would mop him up, despite the Rus reinforcements. But as Bardas Phocas led his supporters towards the imperial line, he fell dead from his saddle, victim of either stroke or poison. His army disintegrated at once and fled; Basil's men chopped up the body with their swords and brought the head to Basil.

The young emperor's throne was temporarily safe, but Michael Psellus tells us that his personality changed drastically after this time: "He became suspicious of everyone, a haughty and secretive man." He had discovered that to be emperor was to be always on guard, always alert, and never trusting.

He decided not to send his Rus tribute fighters home. With Vladimir's consent, he kept them close to him: like the Abbasid caliphs, he now felt the need for a personal guard from outside the empire, a guard that would be less vulnerable to recruitment by would-be conspirators. These Russian bodyguards became known as the Varangian Guard. They would remain in the emperor's confidence, and in his personal service, his most trusted companions in a world filled with traitors.

His opinion of his own people was not improved when another general, Skleros, picked up the banner of Phocas's rebellion. Unlike Phocas, Skleros decided not to risk an out-and-out battle for supremacy. "His idea was rather to . . . harass the enemy by guerilla tactics without committing himself to open warfare," Psellus writes. Basil's transports were halted on the roads, shipments to and from Constantinople were seized, royal couriers waylaid and their orders stolen. The emperor was unable to quell the guerilla revolt, which dragged on into the next year and then the year after, constantly distracting him from his plans to launch a full-scale invasion of Bulgaria.*

Finally Basil took the pragmatic path and offered Skleros a deal. If the general would call off his forces, give up his claim to the crown, and retire to the countryside, Basil would grant him the rank of second in the empire and give all of his supporters immunity. Skleros was growing old; by now he was walking with difficulty, relying on bodyguards to help him move, and he accepted the emperor's bargain.

Michael Psellus says that Basil then asked Skleros, as an experienced general and the leader of a successful rebellion, for advice: how could he preserve the empire from dissension in the future? Skleros answered with searing honesty. "Cut down the governors who become overproud," he said. "Let no generals on campaign have too many resources. Exhaust them with unjust exactions, to keep them busied with their own affairs. . . . Be accessible to no one. Share with few your most intimate plans."[6]

The counsel matched Basil's own inclinations: to be private, withdrawn, and thoroughly in control. As he turned to face the external threats to his rule, he extended an autocratic control over the internal affairs of the empire, standing entirely alone at the top. "He alone introduced new measures, he alone disposed his military forces," Psellus writes. "As for civil administration, he governed, not in accordance with the written laws, but following the

---

*Skleros had already led one revolt against the throne and had been driven out of the empire; the opposition against him had been led by none other than Bardas Phocas, in the days when Phocas had been loyal to the throne (before Phocas had laid claim to it for himself).

unwritten dictates of his own intuition. . . . All his natural desires were kept under stern control, and the man was as hard as steel." He campaigned year-round, fighting throughout the cold of winter and the heat of summer: "His ambition," Michael Psellus concludes, "was to purge the Empire completely of all the barbarians who encircle us and lay siege to our borders, both in the east and in the west." Any anger, any disappointed desire for loyalty, came out in his campaigns against his enemies on the outside.[7]

Those enemies lay on both the eastern and western horizons. Battling on in Bulgaria, Basil's army managed to capture Romanus and haul him back to Constantinople. This had almost no effect on the Bulgarian war, which just went to show how irrelevant Romanus was (and had always been). Samuel, who had been in control for decades, simply remained at the head of the Bulgarian army. Nevertheless, he waited until Romanus died in captivity to claim the title of king for himself. With Samuel's coronation, the dynasty of Krum came to an end.

But Basil was now forced to leave the Bulgarian front in the hands of his generals (something that went against his inclination to stay in complete control). His presence was desperately needed in the east, where the Muslim threat had once again grown worrisome.

It came not from any of the smaller kingdoms that had fragmented the east, but from the Fatimids of North Africa. In the decades since al-Mahdi's declaration that he, and only he, was the legitimate leader of the Muslim people, the Fatimid domain had spread eastward from its North African birthplace. By 969, the Fatimids had finally managed to seize control of Egypt; there, the Fatimid caliph al-Muizz directed that the foundations of a new Fatimid city be laid in his new territory. He moved his palace to this new city, which was named Cairo. By 973, the balance of Fatimid power had shifted so far to the east that Cairo had become the functioning capital of the empire, and the Fatimid caliph had lost control of the North African tribes in the Maghreb.

Under the command of al-Muizz's son, al-Aziz, Fatimid armies spread across the Red Sea into Arabia and took control of the holy cities Medina and Mecca. Fatimid soldiers marched up into the Abbasid-held provinces of Palestine and Syria and, in a year of savage campaigning, conquered both.

Basil's counterattack began in 995. He led a massive push into Syria and managed to recapture much of the land that had fallen to the Fatimid armies. His year-long campaign fell short of Jerusalem, which remained in Fatimid hands, a failure that would throw a very long shadow indeed; but Basil was not unhappy with the outcome. When al-Aziz died in 996, his eleven-year-old son, al-Hakim, was appointed caliph in his place. Basil sent to him, suggesting that they negotiate a peace. He had retaken most of his Syrian lands, and he wanted to return to the fight on the western border.

73.1: The Fatimid Caliphate and Byzantium

Al-Hakim and his advisors agreed to a treaty. The terms were finally concluded in 1001, and the war on the eastern frontier halted for ten years. Basil rode back to the west to fight against Samuel.

But after four years of slow, painful advance and retreat, the Byzantine front had progressed only halfway across Samuel's territory. Basil decided that it was time for a breather. In 1005, he returned to Constantinople to take care of domestic business; his generals held the frontier in place while Samuel remained pinned in the west. For some years the Bulgarian war was suspended.[8]

Meanwhile, the young Fatimid caliph al-Hakim was tightening his hold over his empire in his own way. He was a deeply pious man who wished to establish himself as the perfect Muslim ruler: just and lawful, austere in his personal life and generous in public. But his piety led him into a series of decrees that, although reasonable enough from his own perspective, sounded harsh and meaningless to the many non-Muslims who lived inside his borders. He ordered vineyards destroyed, so that wine (forbidden to Muslims) could not be made anywhere in his realm; he decreed that women in Cairo remain in their homes, to protect their virtue; he commanded that the marketplace in Cairo be lit and open all night, demonstrating the complete peace and safety of his realm even in the dark (and forcing merchants to grab sleep throughout the day whenever possible).[9]

Like Basil, al-Hakim was a man who closed his hand tightly over the internal workings of his kingdom; and over the ten years of the treaty, he grew increasingly worried about the non-Muslims within the Fatimid kingdom. In 1003, he ordered the church of St. Mark just south of Cairo razed, flattened the Jewish and Christian cemeteries around it, and built a mosque where the complex had stood. Throughout Egypt, Christian land was confiscated, crosses destroyed, and churches closed. And then, to discourage pilgrimage to Jerusalem, al-Hakim ordered the great Christian complex built by Constantine destroyed: the Church of the Holy Sepulchre, which protected the tomb of Jesus, commemorated as the site of the resurrection, and Golgotha, the hill of crucifixion. The enormous stones were hacked to bits with axes, and the rock itself was removed from the city.[10]

From the patriarch of Constantinople and the pope in Rome down to the man on the street, Christians were aghast. But Basil, the nearest Christian ruler, refused to take immediate revenge for this act, since the treaty bound him to peace. He was getting ready to reignite the war against the Bulgarians, and a full-scale invasion of the Fatimid realm would have occupied all of his attention.

Matters grew worse when al-Hakim ordered the Jerusalem synagogue destroyed, early in 1011. Basil still declined to intervene, but the Muslims to the east used al-Hakim's actions to denounce the entire Fatimid regime. The Abbasid court at Baghdad put out a decree under the name of the current Abbasid caliph, al-Qadir, officially (and vehemently) denying the legitimacy of the Fatimid caliphate. This "Baghdad Manifesto" was read out loud in mosques all throughout the Muslim world; it wrote into law the breach between the Fatimid and Abbasid caliphates.[11]

While the east boiled, Basil led the Byzantine army in a final enormous assault on the Bulgarian border. The two forces met near Kleidion, just north of the Aegean Sea in the old Macedonian lands, on July 29, 1014.

Basil's break from the war, his refusal to take revenge on the Fatimid regime, had allowed him to rebuild his army into shattering strength. The Bulgarians were laid waste. A contemporary historian claims that fifteen thousand Bulgarian troops were taken captive and arrayed before the victorious Basil.

Basil had absolutely no tolerance for treachery—even treachery carried out in the open by nationalistic freedom-fighters. He ordered ninety-nine out of every hundred captives blinded. The hundredth man was left with only one eye so that he could lead his comrades back to Samuel, who had remained back in the capital city of Ohrid. At the sight of his mutilated troops, Samuel—now an old man, veteran of nearly forty years of war—had a heart attack and died.[12]

Without their chief, the Bulgarian resistance faltered. Over the next four years, Bulgarian nobles began to surrender to Basil II, one at a time. By 1018, Bulgaria was again enfolded into Byzantium—this time, all the way to the Danube river.

Meanwhile, al-Hakim of the Fatimids had quietly gone mad. In 1016, he declared himself divine and ordered his name inserted into Friday prayers in place of Allah's. At this his Muslim subjects joined the Christians and Jews in revolt. Al-Hakim ordered vicious reprisals, but in 1021, with his realm in total chaos, he rode off into the desert alone and disappeared from view. He was thirty-six years old; his successor, his young son, was guided by al-Hakim's sister, and the Fatimid realm slipped further into disarray.[13]

Basil made no attempt to take control of the east. He was an old man by the time al-Hakim disappeared; his life-long war against the Bulgarians had earned him the nickname "Basil the Bulgar-Slayer." He died in 1025, at the age of seventy-two, and his crown passed on to his younger brother Constantine.

Constantine was now seventy years old and totally incapable of coping with either revolt at home or trouble abroad. Basil, who had spent his entire life stamping out rebellion, had never taken the time to marry; he left behind him an empire built on blood, but no heir.

EASTERN DYNASTIES	INDIA	BYZANTIUM BULGARIA	CALIPHATES RUS
	Krishna III of the Rashtrakuta (939–967)	Constantine Porphyrogenitus as sole emperor (945–959)	Olga of the Rus as regent (945–963)
	Gandaraditya of the Chola (950–957)		al-Muizz of the Fatimids (953–975)
		Romanos II (959–963)	
Mansur of the Samanids (961–976) Alp Tigin of the Ghaznavids (963–975)		Nikephoros II as senior co-emperor (963–969)	Svyatoslav of the Rus (963–972)
	Jayapala of the Shahi (964–1001) Khottiga of the Rashtrakuta (967–972)		
	Indra IV of the Rashtrakuta (973–982)	John Tzimiskes Boris II of (969–976) Bulgaria (969–971)	al-Aziz of the Fatimids (975–996)
Abu-Ishaq of the Ghaznavids (975–977) Sebuk Tigin of the Ghaznavids (977–997)		Basil II as senior co-emperor Romanus of (976–1025) Bulgaria (977–991)	
	Rajaraja of the Chola (985–1014)		Vladimir of the Rus (980–1015)
		Establishment of Varangian Guard (989)	
	Mahipala of the Pala (995–1043)		al-Qadir of the Abbasids (991–1031) al-Hakim of the Fatimids (996–1021)
Mahmud of the Ghaznavids (997–1030) Nasr Khan of the Karakhanids (c. 998-1017)		Samuel of Bulgaria (997–1014)	
	Anandapala of the Shahi (1001–1015)		
	Rajendra of the Chola (1014–1044)		Baghdad Manifesto (1011)
		Constantine VIII (1025–1028)	
Togrul (as Sultan) (1038–1063)			
	Rajadhiraja of the Chola (1044–1054)		

Chapter Seventy-Four

——

Defending the Mandate

Between 979 and 1033,
the Song emperors fight to prove that divine favor is theirs

THREE EMPIRES had spread themselves across the fractured east: the Song, drawing together the bits and pieces of China; the northern Khitan, transforming themselves from nomads into the Chinese-style kingdom of the Liao; and the single realm of Goryeo. All three had united their lands by force, and the impulse to conquest did not stop just because the worst of the divisions were overcome.

Song Taizong, now in his third year of rule, had done what his brother could not: he had conquered the last holdout state in the old Chinese territory, the Northern Han. Rather than halting, he decided to go on and attack the Liao borders.

Unfortunately, his army was massively beaten just west of Beijing, in a defeat so shattering that it put Song Taizong's crown in jeopardy. He was already under a cloud of suspicion—more than a few army officers had muttered that his brother's death was too convenient to be anything but poison, and others objected that Song Taizong had usurped the throne of the dead man's son, Taizong's own nephew—but his victories against the Northern Han had temporarily silenced his critics.[1]

Now, in defeat, the complaints became audible again. The Song emperors had aligned themselves with the great Chinese emperors of the past, claiming the Mandate of Heaven to bring the divided country back to its former unity. The Mandate of Heaven always had a sting in its gilded tail, though; the Mandate was conditional, held by the ruler only as long as he could prove himself worthy, and it made the removal of unworthy rulers a positive moral duty.

Even more tricky was the *proof* that an emperor held the Mandate. The Mandate descended from the divine realm upon those who were morally upright, and gave the emperor victory against his enemies. So in practice, the strongest proof of the Mandate was success in battle. The victorious emperor could claim, by definition, to be morally worthy, no matter what his private life looked like; the defeated emperor could protest about his upright nature all he liked, but the Mandate had obviously been removed.[2]

Song Taizong's defeat at the border—he was so badly injured in the fighting that his men had to toss him into a donkey cart to get him away from the front line—tarnished the shine of the Mandate. He had listened to army gossip; he knew that his officers might lead a revolt against him at any time, and that his brother's two sons could be installed on the imperial throne in his place. Back in his capital city of Kaifeng, he called the older of the young princes into his presence. By the time the audience was over, the boy had been made perfectly aware that his uncle intended to kill him. He forestalled the assassination by going to his room and cutting his own throat.

In the next few years, the younger nephew and Taizong's own brother also died suddenly, and Taizong himself refused to name an heir; his crown was too unsteady. Instead he tried to redeem himself by once again attacking the Liao—against the advice of at least two high-ranking generals who told him that the Song were not strong enough to wipe the northern enemy out.[3]

At first, this second campaign met with greater success. In 986, three separate divisions of Song soldiers marched across the Liao border, each headed for a different pass through the mountains. The Liao king, the teenaged Liao Shengzong, and his regent, the empress dowager Xiao, were taken by surprise. Bad intelligence led Liao Shengzong to believe that the Song would also attack by water, so he divided his army and sent half of it to the coast. The Song armies pushed quickly forward against the weakened Liao forces, taking cities in the west as they moved into Liao land. "The Liao," writes a contemporary chronicler, "was in very, very grave danger."[4]

But the empress dowager Xiao, a formidable old lady with a good head for war, was not ready to retreat. Under her direction, the Liao generals retreated from the Song forces, and then surrounded and attacked them from behind. All three Song armies were defeated; the Liao forced them to surrender and then took their weapons and food as booty.[5]

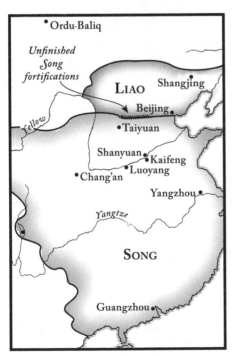

74.1: The Song and Liao

Song Taizong held onto his throne, after this second embarrassing defeat, only because he had killed off all of his possible rivals. But he was forced to give up any thought of recapturing the north of China.

Instead, he turned his attentions back to the rule of his own realm—a place where he expected, daily, to be assassinated or betrayed. His fear of usurpation made him unusually suspicious of any official with royal, or even noble, blood; he also systematically pushed military officers into lower and lower posts with less and less authority. He preferred to rely on bureaucrats of undistinguished families who had passed the civil service exams with flying colors. Belonging to an old noble clan no longer opened a path into government service. The wars of the previous century had already fractured the great families, and Song Taizong's reliance on the examination system to appoint and promote his officials made noble ancestry even less important.[6]

His suspicious nature played midwife to a newly emerging Chinese class: professional bureaucrats who entered political office after years of studying to the test. The old scholar-officials had pursued learning for its own sake; these new officials were more concerned with figuring out what answers the emperor wanted to hear. They became government officials because they had mastered a certain amount of knowledge and were able to parrot it back on the test to the emperor's satisfaction. They were well educated within very specific parameters, and they were loyal to the emperor. When each candidate passed, the emperor met with him personally, hoping to dazzle the new recruit with imperial favor and persuade him into personal loyalty. The bureaucrats were generally dazzled. They had, after all, no other kind of power—no military accomplishment, wealth, or old family name. They were able, quick-minded, and completely dependent on the emperor.

And they quickly filled the ranks of Chinese government. Song Taizong's willingness to appoint and promote anyone who had passed the exam attracted hordes of seekers to the capital. In 977, five thousand men had sat for the civil service exams; in 992, over seventeen thousand tried their hand at it.[7]

Song Taizong finally named an heir to his crown in 997, when he felt his final illness taking over. His eldest son had gone mad, and his second had died. His choice fell on his third son, who shortly after his father's death was crowned as Song Zhenzong. The new emperor was twenty-nine; he had always been Song Taizong's favorite child, possibly because he was passive, agreeable, uninterested in fighting, and unlikely to grab his father's throne prematurely.[8]

Unfortunately, these were not useful qualities for an emperor who had inherited a kingdom with an enormous and growing bureaucracy and a hostile, ambitious northern neighbor. Yearly raids from the Liao were causing increasing angst in the northern reaches of the Song empire, and Song Zhenzong's

first big project was to build a series of canals and dikes along the Song-Liao
border, dotted with well-garrisoned fortresses, to keep the Liao troops out. It
promised to be a formidable barrier, and as it neared completion, the Liao—
still ruled by Liao Shengzong, no longer a teenager and hardened by twenty
years of rule—launched a last major attack against their southern neighbor,
bursting through the unfinished fortifications and sweeping southwards.[9]

Song Zhenzong folded. The raids of the previous years had seen Song
soldiers killed, Song villages burned, Song farmlands destroyed; and although
he had sent armies north again and again, the Liao threat had never wavered.
The empires were deadlocked.

In 1005, Song Zhenzong agreed to peace terms that were unequivocally
humiliating to the Song. The Liao would give up their attempts to seize
Song land; both kings would respect the border and build no more fortifications along it; the Song emperor would address the Liao ruler properly, as
an emperor in his own right; and the Song would hand over two hundred
thousand bolts of silk and a massive payment in silver—equivalent to about
one and a half tons—to the Liao every single year. Song Zhenzong told his
people that the payment was a "gift of an economic nature"; Liao Shengzong
told *his* people that the payment was tribute from a subject people.[10]

The Liao wording was probably closer to the truth. The Song were not subjects, but when Song Zhenzong signed the Treaty of Chanyuan, he brought
an end to the first era of the empire's existence. Conquest had brought the
Song into existence; now the time of conquest was ending. Zhenzong had
turned the empire's gaze from the outside to the inside, giving up the uncertain glories of conquest in favor of predictable and peaceful co-existence.

For the next fifteen years, Song Zhenzong devoted himself to domestic
matters. His first order of business was to make sure that his people knew the
Mandate of Heaven had not deserted him. He had not exactly been defeated
by the Liao, but he certainly hadn't triumphed over them, and the jury was
still out on whether or not the Mandate was firmly his.

In 1008, the emperor made a startling discovery: a sacred text, buried in
the palace grounds, explaining that the Song dynasty reigned with heaven's
favor. Then Song Zhenzong had a supernatural vision, which he described
in great detail to his people: the mythical and sacred first emperor of China
had appeared and explained that he, the Yellow Emperor, had been reincar-
nated as Zhenzong's ancestor. Not only did Zhenzong have the Mandate of
Heaven, but his clan was literally (more or less) descended from China's greatest ruler.[11]

It is impossible to know how much of this dog-and-pony show the people
of Song China actually believed. But despite his weaknesses as a ruler, Zhenzong apparently had a flair for stage management; he put on a whole series

of sacrificial pilgrimages and built memorial structures to commemorate each discovery and vision. Even more to the point, the Song people were growing wealthier and more comfortable in the absence of war. The population doubled in just a few decades, in part because Zhenzong had introduced a new kind of rice into his country: he had bought thousands of bushels of a quick-maturing, drought-resistant seed from rice-growers in the far south and imported them into the north for use by the Song farmers. The new rice grew so quickly that two crops per year could be planted and harvested, and its tolerance for dry land meant that fields farther north and higher up could now yield a crop.[12]

Song Zhenzong died in 1022, leaving his empress as regent for his young son. The new emperor, Song Renzong, embarked on his own solo reign when his mother died, eleven years later. He was twenty-four, and over the next thirty years he would preside over a richer and richer country.

Without major wars to fight, tax money went not to the army but to roads, buildings, schools, and books. Books were in higher demand than ever; like his grandfather, Song Renzong relied on the results of the civil examinations when he chose his officials, which meant that young men all over the empire were buying the standard texts and studying up, hoping to ascend the first rank of the professional ladder. The technique of printing books with carved wooden blocks, rather than writing them by hand, made it possible to produce multiple copies of the most popular books and to sell them for prices that wouldn't break a student budget. Song Renzong himself was a collector; a catalogue of his personal library lists eighty thousand volumes.[13]

Woodblock printing proved useful in another way as well. Up until this point, the Chinese economy had been fed with heavy coins, which were awkward to carry even in small amounts, let alone large stacks. A system for dealing with these massive piles of metal had evolved: merchants would leave their coins in special, privately run "deposit houses," receive stamped receipts, and then use the receipts to buy and sell. Song Renzong, anxious to encourage trade, helped this sensible practice along: sometime early in his reign, a royal office was established in the city of Chengdu to print these receipts in set amounts. The woodblock receipts, circulated through the markets of Song China, served as the world's first paper money.[14]

Giving up war had been an act of surrender, but the temporary peace that followed the Treaty of Chanyuan allowed Song China to grow rich. And prosperous and well-fed people, it turned out, were not inclined to be skeptical of the Mandate—even in defeat.

T I M E L I N E 7 4			
BYZANTIUM CALIPHATES BULGARIA RUS	CHINA	KHITAN LIAO	KOREAN PENINSULA
			Silla absorbed into Goryeo (935)
	Fall of Later Tang/		Later Baekje absorbed
	Rise of Later Jin		into Goryeo (936)
Constantine Olga of the Rus	(936–947)		
Porphyrogenitus as regent (945–963)			
as sole emperor (945–959)			
	Fall of Later Jin/Rise of Later Han (947–951)		
			Gwangjong
			of Goryeo
			(949–975)
	Fall of Later Jin/	Liao Muzong	
al-Muizz of the	Rise of Later Zhou	(951–979)	
Fatimids (953–975)	(951–960)		
Romanos II (959–963)	Fall of Later Zhou/		
	Rise of Song (960–1279)		
	Song Taizu		
Nikephoros II as senior Svyatoslav of the	(960–976)		
co-emperor (963–969) Rus (963–972)			
John Tzimiskes Boris II of			
(969–976) Bulgaria (969–971)			
al-Aziz of the			
Fatimids (975–996)	Song Taizong (976–997)		
	Song dynasty reunites China (979)		
Vladimir of the		Liao Shengzong	
Rus (980–1015)		(982–1031)	
Establishment of			
Varangian Guard (989)			
al-Qadir of the			
Abbasids (991–1031)			
al-Hakim of the			
Fatimids (996–1021)			
Samuel of			
Bulgaria (997–1014)			
	Treaty of Chanyuan (1005)		
Baghdad Manifesto			
(1011)			
	Song Renzong (1022–1063)		
Constantine VIII			
(1025–1028)			

Chapter Seventy-Five

——

The New Found Land

Between 985 and 1050,
Leif Ericsson leads an expedition to North America,
the biggest Mayan cities collapse,
and the Toltecs leave paradise on earth

FAR TO THE WEST, the tiny Norse colony of Greenland was preparing to send colonists of its own to an unknown land.

Eric the Red's son, Leif Ericsson, had long wanted to follow up on a fifteen-year-old rumor: that there were rich hospitable lands farther west. In 985, the Norse merchant Bjarni Herjolfsson had arrived home to discover that his parents had emigrated to Greenland while he was off trading, so he left his homeland to go and visit them. He had never sailed the Greenland sea before. When fog and north winds descended on his ship he was unable to find his way. "For many days," says the thirteenth-century *Saga of the Greenlanders*, "they did not know where they were sailing." When the sun finally came out, they found themselves off an unfamiliar forested coast. Bjarni's crew wanted to go ashore, but their captain refused; instead he set course back to the east and finally sighted the coast of Greenland. When he told the settlers there of his journey, the saga adds, "many people thought him short on curiosity, since he had nothing to tell of these lands."[1]

Leif Ericsson had no shortage of curiosity. He bought Bjarni's ship, stocked it, and in 1003 convinced Eric the Red, now in his fifties, to head up one more expedition to the west. The legendary explorer was reluctant to leave his home ("he was getting on in years," the saga says, "and not as good at bearing the cold and wet as before") but unable to turn down the challenge.

As the father and son rode towards the harbor where their ship lay anchored, Eric's horse stumbled and threw him, injuring his foot. Eric took this as a bad omen and went back home, leaving his son in command.

Leif and his men sailed northwest until they reached the southern end of Baffin Island, and then down along the coasts of the North American islands and peninsulas. He named the lands as he passed them: inhospitable Baffin

Island earned the name "Helluland," or "Stone-slab land"; forest-covered Labrador became "Markland," or "Forest land"; Nova Scotia was named "Vinland," or "Wineland," since the explorers found grapes there and immediately put them to use.[2]

Leif decreed that the crew would build a winter camp on this new found land and remain there through the cold months.* But these were less severe than he expected. The unusual warmth of the Medieval Climatic Anomaly still blanketed the northern lands: "There was no lack of salmon both in the lake and in the river," the *Saga of the Greenlanders* tells us, "and this salmon was larger than they had ever seen before. It seemed to them the land was so good that livestock would need no fodder during the winter. The temperature never dropped below freezing, and the grass only withered very slightly." When spring came, Leif returned home with a ship filled with virgin timber, grapes, and wine. Eric the Red was able to see the long-delayed fruit of that original journey west just before his death in 1004.[3]

The shores of the new country, apparently unclaimed, seemed like the ideal place for a permanent colony, and the following year Leif's brother Thorvald launched an expedition to find the perfect settlement spot. He and his men settled in at Leif's winter camp and began to mark out the borders of farms and claims. For over a year, they saw no "signs of men or animals" except for a single wooden grain cover, left on a small island by unknown inhabitants.

Then, during the second summer, they spotted inhabitants: nine men and three hide-covered boats drawn up in a sheltered cove. It doesn't seem to have occured to the Norsemen to make any sort of peaceful approach; they went directly into conquest mode. "They managed to capture all of them except one, who escaped with their boat," says the *Saga of the Greenlanders*, "[and] killed the other eight."

This brought an immediate counterattack. That same night, a "vast number" of hide-covered boats swept down the nearest inlet, with the inhabitants raining arrows upon the Norsemen, and then almost as quickly whisked themselves away. The retaliatory raid left the Norsemen unhurt—except for Thorvald, who had been fatally struck by an arrow in the armpit. His men buried him on the farm site he had chosen for himself and went back home.[4]

Three years later, a wealthy and experienced Norse explorer named Thorfinn Karlsefni arrived on Greenland's shores from the homeland. Within weeks he had professed his love for Leif Ericsson's sister Gudrid; when Leif (now head of the family) gave permission, Thorfinn married her.

---

*Explorer Helge Ingstad and archaeologist Anne Ingstad found the remains of this camp in 1960 at L'Anse aux Meadows. See Helge Ingstad and Anne Stine Ingstad, *The Viking Discovery of America* (Checkmark Books, 2001).

75.1: The Hopewell Serpent Mound from the air, surrounded by modern pathways
Credit: Ohio Historical Society

That same spring, the couple decided to make another expedition to the west. Thorfinn hired a crew of sixty men—along with five women and plenty of livestock. This time, the Norsemen intended to stay in the new land if they could.

They arrived in Vinland without difficulty and began to build a settlement. The new land was just as fertile as previous expeditioners had told them, and their timber homes were soon stocked with grapes, fish, game, and (thanks to a chance beaching) whale meat. Less than a year after their arrival, Gudrid "gave birth to a boy, who was named Snorri"—the first European baby born in North America.[5]

But the natives of their new homeland were now on the alert, and the settlers were soon building palisades and arming themselves for battle. Skirmishes broke out, and there was at least one large-scale fight with fatalities. The *Saga of the Greenlanders* gives few other details, but the attacks must have been seriously worrying, because the following year Thorfinn "declared that he wished to remain no longer, and wanted to return to Greenland." Another saga adds that the natives had catapults and were well armed, and attacked while "shrieking loudly." For this reason the Greenlanders called them *Skrael-ings*, the "Shriekers."[6]

The Norse sagas give us a rare glimpse into the world of people who have left only physical remains behind—in the words of anthropologist Alice Beck Kehoe, a "history without documents." The Greenlander settlement sat on the northeastern corner of the North American continent, a land mass that was probably populated millennia earlier, when the Bering Strait was still a land bridge connecting North America with Asia. Some of the travellers who came into the northern reaches settled on the icy shores. One town, just east of the strait, was built at least five hundred years before the Greenlanders arrived on the opposite coast, over three thousand miles away. Archaeologists have given its culture the name "Ipiutak"; the Ipiutak settlement boasted more than six hundred houses and a huge cemetery, and the remains of the town are scattered with elaborate ivory carvings, knife handles, and harpoons.[7]

By AD 1000, another culture had grown up from the Ipiutak ruins, and was rapidly spreading eastward to the coast; archaeologists call the people of this culture the "Thule," distinguished from their ancestors by their use of iron tools instead of stone. The Thule managed to displace the culture that had already grown up on the northeastern American coast: the Dorset, a seal-hunting people who gave way, in the face of the invaders, and scattered into oblivion. The Skraelings who fought against Thorfinn's men were either Dorset or Thule, possibly bands of both.[8]

We know what these tribes built, what weapons they used, what animals they hunted, and roughly how they lived; we know nothing of their stories, their histories, or their ambitions. The same is true of the tribes farther south. By Leif Ericsson's day, the Hopewell culture had spread across what is now Ohio and Illinois, reached its height, and dwindled away. The Hopewell builders left behind enormous tomb mounds, each a geometric set of circles and squares, and a winding mysterious earthwork, five feet tall and over a thousand feet long, in the shape of a serpent devouring an egg.

In their place, and slightly more to the south, the Mississippian peoples built cities. The largest of these was Cahokia, spreading across almost five square miles, with perhaps thirty thousand people living in it. They have left behind them tremendous earthen mounds, the remains of foundations and well-planned streets, tools and figurines, burial grounds and sacrificial pits— one containing fifty young women, all apparently executed at the same time to accompany a great nobleman into death.[9]

Farther west, the Anasazi people built complexes from adobe bricks of baked clay and sand: rows of linked dwellings, some with as many as seven hundred rooms, housing thousands. The Anasazi were hunters, farmers, and turquoise-miners; their civilization reached its height just before AD 1100.[10]

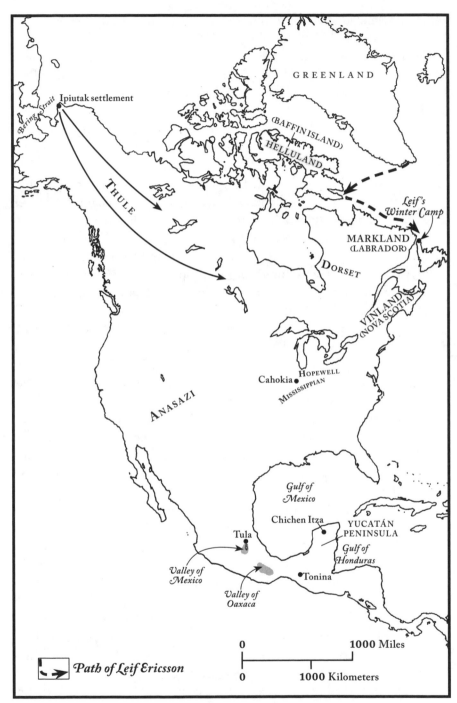

75.1: Settlements of the Americas

The history of these North Americans, and the dozens of smaller tribes and states that spread across the continent, remains unknown. Archaeologists have pieced fragments together into kaleidoscopes that give us glimpses of daily life, but the large story of each civilization has been lost to the historian's view. Cahokia was as large as the Mesoamerican city of Teotihuacan, as populous as the Zapotec city of Monte Alban; its rulers were as powerful as the Mayan sovereigns. But without written history we know nothing of the names of their kings and queens, the nature of their gods and goddesses, the struggles of their noblemen and peasants.*

FAR TO THE SOUTH, the Mayan and Zapotec chronicles emerged from the long silence of drought, famine, and disorder. Bits and pieces of those chronicles have come down to us through translations made by Spanish conquerors, centuries later. Broken apart and distorted by their interpreters, they provide us names of kings and queens and a few cryptic details: a tiny, fogged peephole into the distant Mesoamerican past.†

Put together, the chronicles and the ruins of cities tell us that the Maya never regained their former grip on the land bridge between the continents. The southern cities began to collapse, brought down in part by their own prosperity; a population boom filled the streets, the surrounding fields, and the more distant villages with hungry mouths. Mayan farmers were forced to make use of every single bit of fertile land. Swamps were converted to gardens, flood plains were cultivated, forested areas slashed and burned to create new fields. Food production kept up with demand, but just barely. There was no extra grain left at the end of the growing season.[11]

This was fine as long as the weather remained good, but when drought hit in the middle of the ninth century, the Maya began to starve. Excavations in Mayan cemeteries show the slow but escalating signs of malnutrition. Adult skeletons grow shorter and shorter, signs of scurvy and anemia abound, striations in the teeth of young children testify to long periods of fasting.[12]

The aristocracy tried to cope by seizing food for themselves, but in the end both aristocrats and commoners were forced to leave the overcrowded cities in search of fresh lands. Buildings were left half-finished as the population of the great urban centers drained away. The last Mayan monument in the

*The history of North America in the Middle Ages is largely unwritten "prehistory," well beyond the scope of this book. For a survey of the major cultures and movements, see Stuart J. Fiedel, *Prehistory of the Americas* (Cambridge University Press, 1987); a useful and slightly more technical guide to the archaeological evidence can be found in Guy E. Gibbon and Kenneth M. Ames, *Archaeology of Prehistoric Native America: An Encyclopedia* (Garland, 1998).

†The Mesoamerican cultures that flourished between c. 900 and the Spanish conquest are known to archaeologists as "Post-Classic."

75.2: *The Wall of Skulls (Tzompantli) at Chichen Itza.*
Credit: Steve Winter/National Geographic/Getty Images

south was erected on January 15, 909, in the city of Tonina, which sat on a ridge south of the Gulf of Mexico. After that, silence. The Maya who were still strong enough to travel moved elsewhere. Some journeyed far to the southeast and settled on the high ground south of the Gulf of Honduras. Others went north; excavations show a sudden surge in northern population as the refugees arrived, along with newly terraced hill-fields, necessary to feed the newcomers.[13]

They left behind a fragmented landscape in which a melange of tribes and peoples mingled, blended, and fought. The Mixtec, hill-dwellers who had lived in scattered villages in the Oaxaca Valley, began to press in on the land vacated by the Maya. They also began to stake a claim to fields and valleys that had once been Zapotec; the bleedout of the great Zapotec city of Monte Alban had not destroyed Zapotec civilization, but the Zapotec territory had become a series of smaller settlements, each centered around the estate of an aristocrat or wealthy farmer who served as the de facto ruler of his community. The settlements were prosperous and stable, but vulnerable to Mixtec takeover and occupation.[14]

With the collapse of the old cities, energy shifted to new sites. Northwest of ancient Teotihuacan, where squatters still lived in the ruins, the city of Tula began to grow.

The new peoples flooding into Tula, which sat on high ground some 150 miles from the Gulf coast, probably came from the southern valley now known as the Valley of Mexico. The newcomers were led by a prince named Topiltzin, and their entry into Tula set off a chain of events which became the Arthurian legend of Mesoamerica: a foundational myth shaping the memories and histories of the surrounding peoples for centuries.*

The multiple stories of Topiltzin and the city of Tula are embroidered with conflicting details, and many of them have come down to us broken and incomplete. But they agree that Topiltzin became the king of Tula, and that he was worshipped as the son of a god during his lifetime. His father was said to be a divine conqueror, his mother a goddess, and Topiltzin himself was given the title "Topiltzin Quetzalcoatl," high priest and earthly incarnation of the great god of wind and sky.[15]

Tula was filled with craftsmen and merchants who specialized in the trade of obsidian. Its buildings lay over five square miles, and thirty-five thousand people lived within its walls. Its beauty, its security, and its wealth earned it an honorary title: the people of central Mesoamerica called it "Tollan," a mythical name suggesting paradise, a place where every material need was met, where the gods had come down to teach the citizens craft and skill. The walls of its temples were carved with jaguars and eagles, clasping human hearts in their claws and talons; it was a paradise where human blood, the holy liquid that glued the seams of the cosmos together, was regularly shed in celebration.[16]

Topiltzin ruled in Tula for over a decade, but trouble boiled under the surface. He had enemies within the city. One early story tells us that Topiltzin wanted to bring peace to Tula, and so insisted that winged creatures and reptiles—quail and butterflies, large grasshoppers and snakes—be sacrificed in the place of human captives. He was opposed by a demon in human form named Tezcatlipoca, who refused to allow the practice of human sacrifice to stop. This struggle over whether or not to shed human blood grew more savage, until Topiltzin decided to leave the city for good. He went into voluntary exile, travelling across the countryside until he reached the ocean.[17]

There, on the shores of the Gulf of Mexico, something happened. In some versions of the tale Topiltzin dies, beaten down by grief and exile, and is cremated by his followers. But in many others, he builds a raft and sails into the light; from the distant land of the sun, he will one day return and deliver Tula from its enemies.

Through the mesh of tales, we can see the sharp clash between the natives of Tula and the newcomers; Tezcatlipoca's resistance is the act of a nobleman who has seen his own kinsmen supplanted, at the highest ranks, by outsiders. But we also see something more: an attempt to reconcile a real city with a

---

*A comprehensive and fascinating comparison of the myths can be found in H. B. Nicholson, *Topiltzin Quetzalcoatl* (University Press of Colorado, 2001).

mythical paradise. Tula/Tollan has a double existence in the Mesoamerican chronicles. It is a place of real walls and living people, but it is also a numinous city where the gods come to earth. Its inhabitants called themselves not Tulans, but "Toltecs": inhabitants of blessed Tollan, beneficiaries of the gods. They were fortunate enough, they told themselves, to live in an earthly paradise, a physical city whose stones and walls somehow incorporated the beauty of the divine.

But as a physical city, Tula flourished for less than a century. Around 1050, large swathes of the city burned; the pyramids were pried apart by human hands, columns of ceremonial buildings toppled. The Toltecs, no longer residents of the sacred city but still clinging to their name, left the ruins and settled in various places, some joining the populations of nearby cities, others travelling farther south, where they mingled with the Mixtec.

At least one band of ambitious Toltecs went north, up into the Yucatán peninsula. Topiltzin and his people had come into Tula as outsiders; now these refugees from the fallen city of Tula broke into the largest Yucatán city, the flourishing metropolis of Chichen Itza, and seized control of its throne. It was not an easy transition. The conquest is depicted on reliefs and paintings throughout the city's ruins, showing houses on fire, Toltec siege towers assaulting the walls, Toltec warriors rampaging through the streets, captives from the defeated population sacrificed to the gods.[18]

Chichen Itza was already a sacred city. Pilgrims came from all over Mesoamerica to visit its sacred well, an enormous sinkhole nearly two hundred feet across and over a hundred feet deep. They threw offerings into it—carvings, jewels, keepsakes—and hoped for divine guidance from the gods. Once the city was under Toltec control, human sacrifices were also hurled into the sacred well. A new temple to the god Quetzalcoatl was built near the sinkhole, and its walls were adorned with the same images of heart-devouring eagles and jaguars that had decorated the sacred surfaces of Tula. The conquerors also built a *tzompantli*, a platform adorned with carved skulls, which held on it a display rack for the real skulls of sacrificial victims.[19]

Topiltzin's exile had allowed the old ways to flourish in Tula. The human blood spilled in the city's temples had not kept the earthly paradise safe; the warriors and noblemen who had driven the peacemaker out had themselves been driven into exile. But in their new home, they once again began to shed blood, hoping that this time the sacred rites would keep disaster at bay.

TIMELINE 75

CHINA	KHITAN LIAO	KOREAN PENINSULA	SCANDINAVIA	NORTH AMERICA	MESO AMERICA
		Silla absorbed into Goryeo (935)			Collapse of Mayan cities
Fall of Later Tang/ Rise of Later Jin (936–947)		Later Baekje absorbed into Goryeo (936)	Hakon the Good of Norway (c. 940–961)		
Fall of Later Jin/Rise of Later Han (947–951)		Gwangjong of Goryeo (949–975)			Migration of the Mixtec
Fall of Later Jin/ Rise of Later Zhou (951–960)	Liao Muzong (951–979)		Harald Bluetooth of Denmark (958–987)		Topiltzin of Tula (?)
Fall of Later Zhou/ Rise of Song (960–1279) Song Taizu (960–976)			Harald Greycloak of Norway (961–976)		
Song Taizong (976–997)					
Song dynasty reunites China (979)					
	Liao Shengzong (982–1031)		Arrival of Eric the Red on Greenland (985) Sweyn Forkbeard of Denmark (987–1014)		
Song Zhenzong (997–1022)			Sweyn Forkbeard of Norway (1000-1014)	Development of Thule culture Arrival of Leif Ericsson on North America (1003)	
Treaty of Chanyuan (1005)					
				Mississippian culture flourishes	
Song Renzong (1022–1063)					Sacking of Tula
					Invasion of Chichen Itza
				Height of Anasazi culture	

Chapter Seventy-Six

—▪—

Schism

Between 1002 and 1059,
the emperors insist on their right to run church affairs,
the Normans invade Italy,
and the western and eastern churches split permanently apart

OTTO III, KING OF GERMANY and Holy Roman Emperor, was having unexpected difficulties with his imperial plans. The words *Renovatio imperii Romanorum* appeared on Otto's seal, along with a portrait of Charlemagne and Otto's own name: the young emperor intended to restore the Roman empire, in the footsteps of his legendary predecessor and as a *Christian* empire.

Yet Rome itself was at the far edge of Otto's proposed renewal. Despite the *Romanorum* on his seal, the empire he had in mind drew its identity from Christianity, not from its old relationship with the empire of the Caesars. It was centered in Germany, not in Italy; and as far as he was concerned, the pope was no more than his chaplain, meekly carrying out his orders.[1]

This was exactly why he had appointed a pope who was both German and a blood relation. The choice of Gregory V (the papal name of his cousin Bruno) seemed eminently wise to the clergy in the Germanic kingdoms: "The news that a scion of the imperial house, a man of holiness and virtue, is placed upon the chair of Peter is news more precious than gold and costly stones," wrote the Frankish monk Abbo of Fleury. But the Romans were indignant—not merely because the emperor had set a foreigner at the head of their city (although that was bad enough), but because Otto was so clearly dismissive of Rome's importance. He returned to Germany in June of 996, just a few months after his coronation, turning his back on the Eternal City and leaving it in the hands of his flunky.[2]

He was still only sixteen, after all, and his grandiose plans were accompanied by a complete lack of imagination. He had made his decrees, appointed his pope, and wrapped up his business, and he did not see why the Romans might be irate. But as soon as he was safely over the Alps, the Roman senator Crescentius rounded up a mob of indignant citizens. They vented their resentment over Otto's high-handedness by chasing Gregory V right out of the city.

Gregory took refuge in Spoleto and sent a messenger to Germany, begging the emperor for help. Otto III did not hurry back to help his cousin; he had other important tasks to deal with. He did not start south until the middle of December 997, and even then he took his time, holding courts and audiences and pausing to celebrate Christmas on his way. By the time Otto III arrived in Rome, in mid-February of 998, Gregory V had been in exile for fourteen months, and Crescentius and the Roman churchmen had chosen a new pope of their own.[3]

Angry though the Romans were, a glance over the wall told them that they had little chance of beating the German army. The ringleader, Crescentius, shut himself in a fortress that had been built long ago by the emperor Hadrian on the banks of the Tiber; the new pope, Johannes Philagathos, fled from the city; and the people of Rome opened the gates.

Otto III marched in and stayed for two months, which gave Gregory V enough time to return to the city and settle back in. He starved Crescentius out of the fortress, and his soldiers captured Johannes Philagathos on the run. Crescentius and twelve of his allies were beheaded and their bodies were hung upside down on the highest hill in Rome. Johannes Philagathos's life was spared, but he was treated with even greater cruelty: his eyes were gouged out, his nose and ears were cut off, and he was ridden through the streets of Rome backwards on a donkey.[4]

This sort of savagery was more Germanic than Christian, but to Otto's mind the penalties made sense. Crescentius was punished as a traitor, Philagathos as a heretic. To defy the emperor's right to direct church matters was to rebel against the very essence of his rule, the great mission of his life: to be *the* Christian monarch of the west.

He soon had a new ally to help him with this task. Gregory V did not live long after returning to Rome; he died suddenly and mysteriously, from causes that were never determined. Otto had already left the city, but when he heard of Gregory's death he came back hastily to appoint a new pope. He chose his old tutor Gerbert, currently the archbishop of Ravenna, a priest who had already shown himself willing to cooperate with the emperor's ambitions.

As pope, Gerbert took the name "Sylvester II." This was not a casual choice of name; the first Sylvester had been bishop of Rome in the days of Constantine the Great. Although that Sylvester had done nothing of importance during his twenty-one-year bishopric (he hadn't even attended the Council of Nicaea, sending two priests in his place), legends of great deeds had grown up around him. The *Acts of Saint Sylvester*, written well after his death, claimed that he had personally converted Constantine to Christianity, baptized him, and received the Donation of Constantine (itself a myth) from the emperor's own hands.[5]

Sylvester I, in other words, had shaped the emperor's faith, helped him to create the Papal States, and worked with him to make the Roman empire Christian. The fact that he probably hadn't done any of these things was irrelevant. As Sylvester II, the new pope intended to cooperate just as closely with the emperor in building a holy kingdom of their own.

Together, the two men started on their project of making the Roman empire into the Holy Roman Empire. Their method was to wind political and theological aims together into one binding cord, a strategy they first followed in dealing with the Magyars.

The Battle of Lechfeld was now half a century in the past. Under their prince Geza, the Magyars settled in the Carpathian Basin had travelled three-quarters of the way down the long road from warrior-state into a nation: the principality of Hungary. Geza had helped the process along by agreeing to be baptized. He may or may not have believed the creed he swore allegiance to, but his lip service to Christianity allowed Hungary to stake out its place as a Western nation, complete with parish system and archbishop.

Hungary was now ruled by Geza's son Stephen, who, like his father, was known not as king of Hungary, but as grand prince of the Magyars. Otto and Sylvester planned to incorporate him into the Holy Roman Empire as a Christian king (and useful ally to the east). So Sylvester wrote him a papal letter. "Sylvester, bishop, to Stephen, king of the Hungarians," the letter began, "greeting and apostolic benediction. . . . By the authority of omnipotent God and of St. Peter, the prince of the apostles, we freely grant the royal crown and name and receive under the protection of the holy church the kingdom which you have surrendered to St. Peter; and we now give it back to you and your heirs and successor to be held, possessed, ruled, and governed."

The pope, not the emperor, had awarded Stephen the title of king. Normally, an emperor would extend recognition to a newly minted ruler, but this letter allowed Otto and Sylvester to clearly assert authority over the Hungarians, without the secular threat of swords behind it. "Your heirs and successors," the letter concludes, "shall duly offer obedience and reference to us, and shall confess themselves the subjects of the Roman church."[6]

Stephen took this in a slightly different way than it was offered. To him, it seemed an acknowledgment of his independence as a sovereign Christian king. He accepted the letter and the jeweled cross that came with it, and ignored the implication that he would be subject not just to the pope, but to the pope's patron, the emperor Otto.

The tendency of newly converted peoples to ignore the pope's authority was only one of the difficulties facing the two men. Sylvester was not Roman, any more than the unpopular Gregory had been; he was Frankish, and with the emperor in the city, the Romans found themselves dominated by the active rule of a Frank and a German. In 1001, the people rioted.

Otto decided, on advice of his counselors, to leave the city; he did not have his entire army with him and was worried that the riots might escalate into out-and-out revolt. He and Sylvester set off north to Ravenna, where Otto III planned to gather troops and then return to Rome to straighten out its citizens. But while he was waiting for soldiers to arrive from Germany, he began to suffer from attacks of fever. These grew suddenly more intense. He was infected, his companions muttered, with "the Italian death"—some epidemic disease, described by his biographer Thietmar as "internal sores which gradually burst." In January 1002, Otto III died. His soldiers took him back to Aachen and buried him next to Charlemagne. Otto was unmarried and left no heirs; he was twenty-two years old and had barely begun his adult life.[7]

THE MAN WHO WON Otto's empire was Henry of Bavaria, son of old Henry the Quarrelsome. The German nobles elected him as King Henry II almost at once; the Italian cities refused to recognize his rulership at first, but after two years of fighting, Henry II had quelled the resistance in Italy and had himself crowned king of Italy in Pavia. Ten years later, when Henry II had proved himself a competent ruler of his two realms, he was crowned Holy Roman Emperor by Pope Benedict VIII.*

Otto's seal had read *Renovatio imperii Romanorum*; Henry II's proclaimed *Renovatio regni Francorum*. With Henry, the scrim covering the Germanness of the Holy Roman Empire became completely transparent. This was no kingdom of the past: it was a German empire, centered not on the holy city of Rome but on Henry's own land.[8]

Like the emperors who came before him, Henry II used lay investiture (the right of the king, as a layman, to award church positions) to keep the power of his empire centered on his own German circle. Like Otto, he gave offices and control over churches and monasteries to men who would be loyal to him. Like Otto, he treated the church like a faithful junior lieutenant of the emperor, rather than as an independent power; his particular method of keeping churchmen in line was to take a strong stand on clerical celibacy. Priests who married and had children were apt to pass land and responsibility down to them, creating lines of hereditary authority and wealth that became less and less dependent on the emperor. A childless priest, on the other hand, died and returned his post to the hands of those who had given it away in the first place.

Henry II was willing to give away posts, as long as the positions were going

---

*Sylvester II died in 1003, the year after his king, and three short-lived popes (John XVII, John XVIII, and Sergius IV) followed him before Benedict's election in 1012.

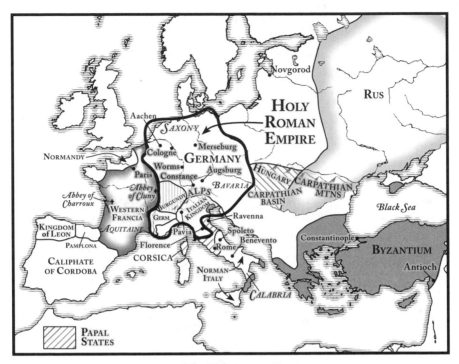

76.1: The Holy Roman Empire

to return to his control in the future, and as long as the parishes in his domain accepted the priests he appointed without argument or question. Some churches were able to brandish charters at him that promised free elections, the right for the churches to choose their *own* bishop; Henry simply insisted that the phrase *salvo tamen regis sive imperatoris consensu* be added. Certainly these churches could choose their own bishops—as long as the imperial consent was granted to the results of the free election.[9]

In his ten years as Holy Roman Emperor, Henry II settled quarrels between monasteries, insisted that his own candidates benefit from the "free elections" of German bishops, and even tinkered with the liturgy; attending a service in Rome, he objected that the clergy did not always repeat the Creed during Mass, and insisted that it be inserted.[10]

During his reign, the German priest Burchard, bishop of Worms, put together a twenty-volume collection of canon law. Anyone who resists the power of the emperor, reads one canon, is liable to excommunication, since the emperor's power comes from God himself. No secular law, reads another canon, can be contrary to the law of God, which is above all royal laws. The innate contradiction stands without commentary—as do multiple contradictory canons that demand respect for the authority of the king and the primacy of the church, simultaneously, without resolution. The longer the Holy Roman Emperors ruled, the more glaring these unresolved contradictions became.[11]

In 1024, Henry II died unexpectedly. He had been married for years, but he and his wife (a distant descendent of Charlemagne) had no children, and it was rumored that they had decided to be celibate, making their marriage into a spiritual union only. Whether or not this was true, it ended Henry's dynasty, the Saxon dynasty of emperors, and left Germany, the Italian kingdom, and the Holy Roman Empire headless.

The German noblemen elected another of their own, Conrad II, the first emperor of a new dynasty: the Salians. Like Henry, Conrad II became king of Germany and then had to fight to assert himself in Italy. By 1027, he had control of both realms and was crowned Holy Roman Emperor on Easter of that same year; not long after, he had incorporated both Burgundy and Provence into the empire under his rule.

This rapid coronation as emperor was sheer boot-licking on the part of the pope, John XIX. John XIX was the brother of Benedict VIII, the pope who had crowned Henry II; the tenth-century Frankish monk Rodulfus Glaber tells us that when Benedict died, John used his considerable personal wealth to convince the Romans that he should ascend the papal throne next. The payments were substantial enough, apparently, to make up for the fact that John was actually a layman. With Henry II's blessing, he had been run up through the ranks of the church in a single day and made pope before nightfall.[12]

He hoped that the new king of Germany and Italy would be his friend and ally, so he invited Conrad to Rome to receive the title right away. Unfortunately Conrad was not particularly impressed by John's cooperation; he took the coronation in stride, as his right. Conrad II was an intelligent man and a good soldier, but he was also illiterate, uninterested in theology, and not overly concerned about the delicacies of church-state relationships. As far as he was concerned, the pope was there to do his bidding, and the church was there to help him carry out his own goals. He demanded that bishops and archbishops obey without question, and if they resisted he treated them as he would treat a rebellious soldier or courtier: with exile or imprisonment.[13]

He ruled in this way until 1039, when convulsions carried him off before his fiftieth birthday. He had already crowned his son Henry the Black as co-ruler of Germany and Italy, and the young man, twenty-one at the time of his father's death, assumed the thrones of both countries as Henry III.

Unlike Conrad, Henry was a literate ruler with an ear for church politics. Conrad, tone deaf to theological niceties, had nevertheless recognized his own shortcomings; he had given his son the education he had never had, hiring priests to tutor the boy in literature, music, and the affairs of the church. Henry lived in a landscape his father could not have imagined: one where the earthly and heavenly realms were both visible to him, each real and powerful and compelling him to action.[14]

One of his earliest actions was to add the weight of royal authority to the Peace and Truce of God. In the last forty years, two church councils had extended the conditions of the Peace and Truce. Merchants and their goods had now joined peasants, clergymen, and farmers as official noncombatants, immune from attack. Certain days were now completely off limits for fighting: under threat of excommunication, no one could wage war on Fridays, Sundays, church holidays, or any of the forty days of Lent. In 1041, Henry III decreed that the Peace would be observed in Germany from Wednesday evening through Monday morning of every week of the year. In 1043, he attended a synod held in the Germany city of Constance and himself preached from the pulpit, imploring his people to keep a peace "unknown in previous centuries." As an example to them, he forgave—on the spot—all of his own enemies, including several noblemen in Swabia who had been attempting rebellion.[15]

Conrad had shoved the church roughly in whatever direction suited him; Henry III followed its decrees, studied its theology, worked for its purity. Yet in doing so, he managed to make it even more subordinate to the crown. His theological sensibilities were highly offended by the goings-on in Rome. The worldly John XIX, who had bought his way into the papacy, had handed the papal throne to his teenaged nephew Benedict IX, who ruled in Rome as pope for a decade and a half while carrying on the life of a wealthy young Italian nobleman: drinking, fornicating, and generally indulging himself. Conrad II had found the young pope acceptable, as Benedict IX was willing to excommunicate the emperor's enemies when necessary, but the people of Rome got fed up. In 1045, an armed mob drove Benedict IX from the city and anointed a new pope of their own, a bishop who became Sylvester III.

Benedict IX had a powerful family, and they supplied him with armed men so that he could re-enter Rome. Within two months he had broken back into the city and reclaimed his title, while Sylvester III fled to a village on the edge of the Papal States, where he remained, still claiming to be pope.

Now there were two popes, and Benedict was about to complicate the situation further. He hadn't enjoyed his brush with rebellion, and he offered to sell the papal throne to his godfather, the priest John Gratian, for a thousand pounds of silver. John Gratian handed over the money and was acclaimed as Pope Gregory VI.

Benedict then changed his mind. Apparently he had hoped to marry once he was no longer pope, but his lady love had rejected him; possibly he also missed the pomp and power more than he had expected. He declared that he was taking the seat of St. Peter back again.[16]

So by 1046 there were three popes in Italy, none of them clearly legitimate. Someone needed to step in, but Henry III was not yet Holy Roman Emperor;

he was merely king of Germany and the Italian kingdom. Yet his earthly power allowed him to become master of the church, even without the title of Protector and Defender. Henry III marched into Rome—"with a great force and an immense army," the medieval *Pontificum Romanorum Vitae* tells us—and declared the papal throne empty and all three candidates unfit. "He tried the case canonically and justly," the *Pontificum* continues, "and made the rights of the matter plain to the holy and religious bishops, and condemned [the three popes] with perpetual anathema."[17]

He then chose a new pope—Clement II, an "excellent, holy, and benign churchman"—who took up his new job on Christmas Day and before night-fall had crowned Henry III as Holy Roman Emperor. All together, the people and clergy of Rome repeated the grant made by Pope Leo VIII to Henry's predecessor Otto, the first "holy" emperor, eighty years earlier: that as emperor, Henry had "the right to create popes and bishops. . . . [A]nd it was further agreed that no bishop should be consecrated until he had received his investiture from the hand of the king."[18]

Concerned for the purity of the church, Henry III had now taken control of it. As the impromptu hearing in Rome makes clear, he could also appropriate, when necessary, the power of anathema: the power of excommunication, of opening and closing the gates of heaven. Since the days of Pope Sylvester II, just a few decades earlier, the balance of power between church and emperor had swung far, far back towards the crown.

Now that he had dealt with the sacred troubles in Italy, Henry turned to deal with the political problems.

The south of Italy, long under the control of a patchwork of local counts and dukes who swore a loose loyalty to the emperor, had been infested by Normans. Over the last twenty years, chaos in their homeland (an extended struggle over the right to claim the title "Duke of Normandy") had sent more and more Norman adventurers wandering east. Norman mercenaries had settled in the south of Italy, hiring themselves out to Italian noblemen as useful private swords—while carving out little independent domains of their own.

Looking south from Rome, Henry III could see a welter of competing powers, ready to erupt into full-scale war. Rather than going down and attempting to conquer them all, one at a time, he made a peaceful imperial trip south, circled through the battling states, and summoned the jostling dukes, counts, and mercenaries to reaffirm their pledges to the imperial crown, one at a time. The most powerful Norman warrior, Drogo of Hauteville, agreed to become the emperor's man in return for an official title: Duke and Master of Italy, Count of the Normans of all Apulia and Calabria.*

---

*Drogo inherited control of Apulia from his brother William Ironarm, who had first conquered the territory and put it under Norman rule.

This established an actual Norman state in the south of Italy, and kept Henry III out of a long and damaging war. But his solution proved to be temporary. He went back to Germany; and almost at once, a new Norman adventurer arrived on the shores of southern Italy. His name was Robert Guiscard; he was Drogo's half-brother, and his crafty ambition had earned him the nickname "Robert the Fox."

Drogo was not about to divide his newly acquired realm with his half-sibling. The family was large—Drogo's father, Tancred, had married twice and sired twelve sons—and Drogo already had awarded a minor command and the right to inherit his title to another younger brother, Humphrey. But he gave Robert the Fox a castle on the western edge of his kingdom, and Robert began to use this as a base to fight his way into the toe of the Italian boot in a vicious series of campaigns: "The start of his career was marked by bloodshed and many murders," writes the twelfth-century historian Anna Comnena.[19]

All of this Norman aggression aroused a great deal of hatred for Robert and his brothers among the non-Normans in the south. But Henry III was far to the north in Germany, and so the people of southern Italy made their complaints about the savagery of their Norman overlords to the pope in Rome.

Clement had died after less than a year, and the throne of St. Peter was now occupied by Leo IX, the cousin of Henry III.* Even though he had been appointed by his own blood relative, Leo IX was a reform-minded man; he had refused to accept the papacy until the people of Rome gave their approval. He was, in the words of the Norman chronicler William of Apulia, "an admirable man," well liked and powerful, and he coaxed Drogo into taking an oath to halt the pillage and conquest in the south.[20]

But Drogo's oath came too late. A conspiracy was already afoot among the people of the south, and in 1051 it erupted. Drogo was assassinated on his way to church, and a desperate message was dispatched to Rome: "The Apulians sent secret envoys to Pope Leo IX," writes the Benedictine monk Malaterra, "inviting him to come to Apulia with an army, claiming . . . that they themselves would help him and the Normans were cowardly, their forces diminished and few in number. . . . The emperor sent an army of Germans to help him and he entered Apulia, trusting in the assistance of the Lombards."[21]

In his concern for the purity of the church, the emperor had become master of the pope; now the reform-minded pope had become the head of the emperor's army. Leo IX rode at the head of the imperial forces to the Fortore river. There, his army was met by the Normans of the south, under the command of Drogo's brothers, Robert the Fox and Humphrey.

---

*Two short papacies came between Clement and Leo IX. Benedict IX had briefly grabbed the papal throne for the third time just after Clement's death (1047–1048); in July of 1048 he was driven out by Henry III's next appointee, Damasus II, but Damasus died of malaria after two months and Henry nominated Leo IX in his place.

In the battle that followed, the anti-Norman forces were driven back and shattered. Robert Guiscard fought with particular savagery: "He speared [the enemy] with his lance, beheaded them with his sword," writes William of Apulia. ". . . He was unhorsed three times, thrice he recovered his strength and returned more fiercely to the fray. . . . He cut off feet and hands, sliced heads from bodies, ripped into breasts and chests, and transfixed those whose heads he had cut off."[22]

Leo IX fled into a nearby fortress, where he shut himself up while the Normans laid siege. Finally, he had to surrender. But the Norman brothers Humphrey and Robert the Fox were too wily to kill the pope; that would have turned even some of their own followers against them. Instead they kept him in respectful captivity at Benevento; there, surrounded by Norman guards, he was forced to give them official papal recognition as rulers of the south.

The ripples were far-reaching. Furious at Leo's assumption that he could bind and loose the duchies of the south, the patriarch of Constantinople—who still claimed to have spiritual authority over the remnants of the old Byzantine lands in lower Italy—resurrected a series of ongoing theological arguments between the eastern and western Christian churches and announced that the western faith had become so corrupt that it was now heretical.*

From his comfortable prison, Leo ordered a clerical delegation to go east and try to work out the difficulties between east and west. Unfortunately, the two men in charge of the negotiations were equally short-tempered: the patriarch of Constantinople, Michael Cerularius, was autocratic, ambitious, and jealous of his authority; the senior priest of the delegation from Rome was Cardinal Humbert, suspicious of all things eastern and anxious to take offense. After weeks of fruitless argument and growing indignation on both sides, Cardinal Humbert wrote an official excommunication of Michael Cerularius and his supporters and threw it onto the altar at the Hagia Sophia. Michael Cerularius burned the excommunication and, in turn, excommunicated the entire papal delegation. Humbert led the priests out of Constantinople, shaking the dust of the east from his feet.[23]

---

*At the head of the list were two issues: the western church used unleavened bread for the celebration of communion, while the east did not; and the western church spoke of the Holy Spirit as proceeding from both the Father and the Son, while the east refused to use this formulation (known as the "Filioque clause"). Neither issue was theologically insignificant. The eastern patriarch believed that the use of unleavened bread was too close to Jewish practice, meaning that the western church had not fully accepted the transition from Old Testament law to New Testament grace; the eastern priests were also widely convinced that to speak of the procession of the Holy Spirit "from the Father and the Son" suggested that God the Father and Jesus Christ were separate beings in a way that violated the unity of the Trinity. However, the real quarrel between east and west was one of authority: whether pope or patriarch ultimately had the last word on which Christian beliefs were and were not orthodox. For more on the specific theological problems involved, see Jaroslav Pelikan, *The Growth of Medieval Theology* (600–1300) (University of Chicago Press, 1978), particularly chapter 5, "The One True Faith."

By the time Humbert arrived back in Italy, Leo IX was dead. He had grown ill in March, and his captors had set him free so that he could draw his last breath in Rome. Only a few weeks after returning to his home, he died.

Leo IX had never been able to respond to Cerularius's excommunication, and both condemnations stood. From 1054 on, the two churches—already separated by theology, language, and politics—remained separated by official decree. The year 1054 became known as the date of the Great Schism, the division of the once-unified Christian church into two separate bodies that would never be reunited.

In the next three years, all of the major players changed. Henry III died in 1056 without launching another expedition against the south of Italy; he left his six-year-old son, Henry IV, as king of Germany, which meant that the German noblemen were temporarily in charge of the country. Humphrey, the Norman count of Apulia, died in 1057, and Robert Guiscard, Robert the Fox, seized his title and his land. And in 1059, the bishop of Florence was elected pope as Nicholas II.*

There was no emperor now to protect Rome, and the king of Germany was a child. Nicholas II decided (prudently) to make an alliance with the Normans, who were right on his doorstep. In 1059, he negotiated the Treaty of Melfi with Robert the Fox. Nicholas II would now acknowledge the Norman count as ruler of the southern Italian territories of Apulia and Calabria, in return for Robert's willingness to accept the pope's spiritual authority. (The treaty also recognized Guiscard as ruler of Sicily, although the island was currently under the control of the Fatimids; Guiscard would have to conquer it for himself.)

But the Treaty of Melfi did much more. It renounced the special right of the "Roman Emperor" to protect the heirs of St. Peter. In signing it, Nicholas II took away the central duty that made the office of the emperor holy. That duty had now been handed over to the Normans, who—as part of the treaty—even promised that they would fight *for* the pope, and *against* any future Holy Roman Emperor, if necessary.[24]

In the same year, a church council declared that the pope should be elected by a gathering of high-ranking bishops: the College of Cardinals. For the first time in decades, the papacy was freed from its dependency on the goodwill of the Holy Roman Emperor. Should young Henry IV ever rise to the ranks of emperorship, he would find the title stripped of its two most precious rights: the emperor's sacred role as Defender of the Church, and his authority to name the successor to Peter's power.

*Henry III chose Victor II (1055–1057) as pope just before his death; when Victor died of fever, he was succeeded by Stephen IX (1057–1058) and then by the Italian Benedict X (1058–1059), who was never properly consecrated and tried to oppose Nicholas II's ordination before he was forced to leave Rome by Nicholas II's supporters.

TIMELINE 76

SCANDI-NAVIA	NORTH AMERICA	MESO-AMERICA	WESTERN FRANCIA	ITALY GERMANY	MAGYARS	Roman Emperor
Harald Bluetooth of Denmark (958–987)		Topiltzin of Tula (?)				
Harald Greycloak of Norway (961–976)						Otto (962–973)
				Pope Leo VIII (963/964–965)		
				Pope John XIII (965–972)		
					Geza of Hungary (970–997)	
				Otto II (973–983) as king of Germany and Italy and Roman emperor		
			Otto III (983–1002)			
Arrival of Eric the Red on Greenland (985)			Louis the Sluggard (986–987)			
			Hugh Capet (987–996)			
Sweyn Forkbeard of Denmark (987–1014)			Birth of "Peace of God" movement			
						Otto III (996–1002)
				Pope Gregory V (996–999)		
					Stephen of Hungary (997–1038)	
				Pope Sylvester II (999–1003)		
Sweyn Forkbeard of Norway (1000–1014)	Development of Thule culture		Henry II (1002–1024)			
	Arrival of Leif Ericsson on North America (1003)					
				Pope Benedict VIII (1012–1024)		
						Henry II (1014–1024)
	Mississippian culture flourishes		Conrad II (1024–1039)	Pope John XIX (1024–1032)		
						Conrad II (1027–1039)
				Pope Benedict IX (1032–1045/1048)		
		Sacking of Tula	Henry III (1039–1056)			
				Pope Sylvester III (1045–1046)/ Pope Gregory VI (1045–1046)		
		Invasion of Chichen Itza		Pope Clement II (1046–1047)		Henry III (1046–1056)
				Robert Guiscard's arrival in Italy		
				Pope Leo IX (1049–1054)		
				"Great Schism" of eastern and western churches (1054)		
	Height of Anasazi culture		Henry IV (1056–1106) as king of Germany and Italy			
				Pope Nicholas II (1059–1061)		

Chapter Seventy-Seven

Danish Domination

Between 1014 and 1042,
Danish kings rule in England,
and Macbeth overthrows the high king of Scotland

F OR TWO CENTURIES, the English had resisted Viking invasion. Now the Viking grip on the island had tightened; the Danish king Sweyn Forkbeard had just been crowned king of England, while the defeated Anglo-Saxon king Ethelred the Unready cowered on the Isle of Wight and his wife and children took refuge in Normandy.

Five weeks after his coronation, Sweyn Forkbeard died suddenly at night, in his bed. The North Atlantic empire wavered a little on its foundations; the conquered land of Norway slipped from the grasp of the Danes and was reclaimed by a Norse nobleman, Olaf the Saint. But Sweyn's heir, his son Canute the Great, claimed the crowns of Denmark and England.[1]

He soon discovered that the crown won by force could also be lost by force. Without the imposing figure of Sweyn at the head of the Danish forces, the people of London took courage. They sent a message to Ethelred, asking him to return and fight against the new foreign king. Ethelred agreed and arrived back on the shores of England, ships filled with Normans in tow. His son Edmund, child of his first marriage, led troops on the ground; together, the two men launched a pincer attack against the Danes.

Canute, who had been crowned in January, held out until Easter. Then, abruptly, he left England and headed for Denmark. The Danish chronicles are cagey about the reasons, but it seems likely that his brother, who had been serving as regent in Denmark while Canute was in London, was making a play for the Danish throne. England was a prize for the Danes, but it was newly conquered and insecure, and Canute first intended to secure his home-land. As a parting gesture, he cut the ears and noses off his English prisoners of war and dumped them on the shores right before he sailed away.[2]

The hostile gesture was clear: as far as Canute was concerned, the fight was not over. Ethelred claimed the crown again and brought his wife Emma and

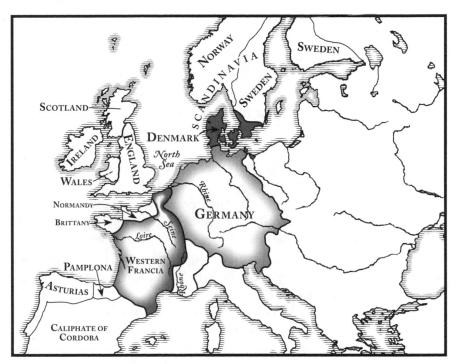

77.1: England and Scandinavia

his two younger sons back from Normandy, but his triumph was temporary; Canute returned the following year with 160 ships and launched his attempt to reconquer England.

Ethelred the Unready was still fighting off Danes when he died in April of 1016. His son Edmund was elected king by the witan, the gathering of the English nobility who still claimed the right to choose their king. England had been under a single monarch for less than a century, its aristocracy still remembered the days when their ancestors had been petty kings in their own right, and Ethelred's rule had not been such a shattering success that his son could automatically claim the succession. But Edmund had outfought his father in the war against the Danes; he had earned the nickname "Ironside" "on account of his prodigious strength and his extraordinary resoluteness in war," and he was duly crowned king and given the job of driving off Canute.[3]

In the next few months, the two armies fought at least seven major engagements. The slaughter on both sides was vicious and devastating. The land where they battled was laid waste, farmland trampled and nearby villages burned. In the seventh battle, at Ashingdon, the ranks of the witan itself were laid waste as the nobility of England fell—"all the chief men of the nation of the English race," mourns the *Anglo-Saxon Chronicle*. "On that field Canute destroyed a kingdom," writes William of Malmesbury, in language that would be echoed by English chroniclers nine hundred years later, "there England's glory fell, there the whole flower of our country withered."[4]

Neither Edmund nor Canute was willing to stop the fight, but the remains of the witan insisted. It was time for a truce. In November 1016, less than a month after the Battle of Ashingdon, the two kings met, warily, on a small muddy island in the middle of the River Severn, each arriving on a small fishing boat that couldn't carry an armed retinue. They agreed to divide the country: Canute would rule from Mercia to the north, and Edmund would keep London and remain king of the south. Edmund was also forced to disinherit his own sons (one a toddler, the other not much more than a newborn) and agree to make Canute his heir.[5]

A little more than a month after the treaty was signed, Edmund Ironside was dead. Henry of Huntingdon is the only chronicler to claim that he was murdered by order of Canute; the other records simply note that he died, leaving the whole country to the Danish king. Canute's guilt remains uncertain, but the chronicles are unanimous concerning his next actions: he marched into London, claimed the crown, and then put to death the members of the witan who had been Edmund's most trusted counselors.

He also ordered Edmund Ironside's two young sons put on a ship and taken back to Scandinavia. This was to create deniability: "It would seem a great disgrace if they perished in England," says John of Worcester, ". . . [so] he sent them to the king of Sweden to be killed." The king of Sweden, who was Canute's ally, met the ship but refused to comply when he found that he was expected to put two babies to death. Instead, he sent them as far away as he could arrange—to King Stephen of Hungary, with whom he had a passing acquaintance. The journey was too much for the younger baby, who died of illness and hunger; but the toddler survived and grew up under the care of a Hungarian foster-mother.[6]

Canute then sent for Emma of Normandy, Ethelred's widow, and married her. He already had a long-term mistress (or common-law wife), a woman named Aelfgifu who had given him one son the year before and another the same year he married Emma. What Emma thought of this arrangement, we are not told; we do know that she sent her two sons, Alfred and Edward, back to Normandy to stay with their uncle. Undoubtedly she feared that they too would succumb to the mysterious illness that killed healthy sons of kings. Edward, the older, was ten years old; Alfred was still a baby.

Two years later Emma gave birth to a son, Canute's third; he was named Harthacanute, after his father, and became heir to the crown of England.

77.2: The Earldoms of England

England remained under Canute's rule for the next two decades. The demoralized witan resisted him no longer, and Canute put most of the administration of his new kingdom into the hands of his own trusted men. He divided England into four earldoms, known as Wessex, Mercia, East Anglia, and Northumbria, and he appointed Danish earls to rule over three of the realms: Thorkell the Tall over East Anglia, Siward over Northumbria, Leofric over Mercia. With some hesitation, he awarded Wessex to an Anglo-Saxon: Godwin, a native of Sussex who had supported Canute in his battle for the English throne. Godwin was outnumbered by Danes, but he was canny. He courted and married Canute's sister, not long afterwards, linking himself by blood to the foreign king.

In 1028, Canute forced Olaf the Saint of Norway to abdicate and crowned himself "King of Norway" as well. Now he held his father's old empire in reality: England, Denmark, and Norway.* His ambitions were not yet satisfied, though. In 1031, he invaded Scotland and fought against Malcolm II, high king of the Scots, until the Scottish armies agreed to a truce.†

As high king, Malcolm II was first among equals. When he decided to surrender, he did not do so alone. "Malcolm, the king of Scots, submitted to Canute," the *Anglo-Saxon Chronicle* records, "and two other kings, Maelbeth and Iehmarc." Not just the high king, but the other kings of Scotland were recognizing Canute's authority.⁷

By the time Canute died in 1035, the Danish grip on England seemed almost unbreakable. The most that the witan could now hope for was the ascension of Emma's son Harthacanute to the throne; he was half-Danish and half-Norman, but at least he had some vague connection with the English royal line of the past.

Even this hope, however, was soon dashed. Harthacanute, barely twenty, had been dispatched to Denmark, where he was supposed to be watching over the double realm of Norway and Denmark for his father. But as soon as Canute died, the illegitimate son of the deposed Olaf the Saint mounted an armed challenge for the throne. His name was Magnus the Good, and he had the support of much of Norway. Harthacanute, trapped by this Scandinavian war, was unable to return to England.

Instead, the Danish army in England, along with the earls of the four territories, made Canute's oldest son, the fully Danish Harold Harefoot, "regent" in England. Ostensibly this was for Harthacanute's benefit, but in reality it was a play for the throne, and the witan disapproved: "Earl Godwin and all of the foremost men in Wessex opposed it," the *Anglo-Saxon Chronicle* tells us.⁸

Into this tiny gap of opportunity, Ethelred's two younger sons attempted to step. Backed by a small group of unhappy Anglo-Saxons, reinforced by a small force of Norman soldiers, Edward and his younger brother Alfred Atheling tried to return to their homeland. The effort was cut short by the treachery of Godwin. After opposing Harold Harefoot's regency, Godwin—who was more interested in power than anything else—had backtracked and embarked on the project of making himself Harold's closest friend. He sent word to Edward and Alfred that he was behind their return, all the time reporting to Harold about the whereabouts of the regent's younger half-brothers. When Edward and Alfred landed, their party was ambushed. Edward escaped, but most of his supporters were captured: "Some of them were sold for money, some cruelly destroyed," the

---

*He also called himself "King of Sweden"; the Swedes already had a king, but since Canute by this time had managed to battle his way into some Swedish land, he gave himself the right to call himself king of England, Denmark, Norway and Sweden. The Swedish king ignored this.

†The *Anglo-Saxon Chronicle* puts the year of surrender at 1031, but other sources suggest 1027 as a more likely date.

Chronicle says, "some of them were fettered, some of them were blinded, some maimed, some scalped." Alfred, taken prisoner, was hauled in chains towards the abbey of Ely. On the way, he was blinded so ineptly that his brain was pierced. He died in agony, aged twenty-four.[9]

Edward returned to Normandy, nursing a hatred for Godwin and a boiling rage at Harold Harefoot. His mother Emma fled from her stepson and his cruelty as well—but she had no wish to return to Normandy. Emma was now fifty years old. She had been queen of England twice and given birth to three sons and two daughters; she had been forced to send her first family away and had lost a son. She wanted peace and security, and Normandy was in chaos. Her brother Richard the Good, twenty years her senior, had died in 1027; his two sons had followed each other in rapid success, both dying young, and by 1035 the bastard William, son of her younger nephew, had been acclaimed as duke. He was only eight, and the duchy was torn between the ambitions of powerful Norman nobles who wanted to control him.

The *Encomium Emmae Reginae*, written in Emma's praise, tells us that she found refuge and quiet in Western Francia; the Frankish nobleman Baldwin of Flanders "received her well there, and maintained her as long as she had need."[10]

Meanwhile, Harold Harefoot celebrated by abandoning the title of regent and having himself crowned as king of England: "Harold was everywhere chosen as king," the *Chronicle* says, "and Harthacanute forsaken because he was too long in Denmark."[11]

All was not going Harold's way, though. For one thing, Scotland was slipping from his control. The submission of Malcolm seems to have been less than unanimous among the lesser kings of Scotland. He had died in 1034 and had been succeeded as high king of Scotland by his young son Duncan. With the old honored king out of the way, one of the subject rulers rebelled.

The rebel was Mac Bethad mac Findlaich, king of the small northern kingdom called Moray. English chroniclers rendered his name, simply, as Macbeth.* Five hundred years later, Shakespeare would make Macbeth infamous as a traitorous host who killed his king in his·sleep, but the historical revolt was a perfectly routine declaration of independence, the rejection of a high king whose clan had been willing to bow to a foreign invader. Mac Bethad was a powerful man in his own right; the twelfth-century Irish poem *The Prophecy of Berchan* calls him "the red king who is generous," and adds

---

*Mac Bethad of Moray has sometimes been identified as the "Maelbeth" who accompanied Malcolm II at his surrender to Canute; however, the two names are distinctly different, and it is unlikely that Mac Bethad was in power in Moray as early as 1031. See Charles Plummer and John Earle, *Two of the Saxon Chronicles Parallel*, vol. 2 (Clarendon Press, 1899), pp. 207ff.

that Duncan was a weak and ineffective ruler with nothing but his bloodline to recommend him.[12]

The Scots, like the English, retained the right to accept or reject their kings. In 1040, Mac Bethad declined to pay the taxes that subject kingdoms yielded to the high king. Duncan marched into Moray to collect the payment by force. In the battle that followed, Duncan was killed. His widow fled from Scotland with her two children; Mac Bethad claimed the high kingship of Scotland and refused to yield to the Danish king in the south.

Before he could march to the north and fight against the Scots, Harold Harefoot—halting for a night in Oxford, during a royal progression south—grew ill and died. At once, Harthacanute made for England's shores. He arrived with sixty ships, was welcomed as the new king of England and Denmark, and immediately made himself unpopular. "He started a very severe tax that was endured with difficulty," the Chronicle says, "and all who hankered for him before were then disloyal to him." He didn't improve his position by ordering Harold Harefoot's body dug up and flung into a swamp, or by sending his soldiers to collect the severe tax by force when the people of western Mercia were unable to pay it.[13]

Fortunately, the English did not have to suffer under his reign for long. Less than two years later, Harthacanute was giving the toast at a wedding when he had a convulsion and fell down dead. It is impossible to know whether he had a stroke or whether the wine in his cup was less than wholesome; in any case, his death left the throne of Denmark open (it was claimed almost at once by Magnus the Good, who united Norway and Denmark under his rule), and it opened the way to the English throne for the last living son of Ethelred the Unready.

TIMELINE 77

WESTERN FRANCIA	ITALY GERMANY MAGYARS	Roman Emperor	BRITISH ISLES SCANDINAVIA NORMANDY
			Ethelred (978–1013)
			Sweyn Forkbeard of Denmark (987–1014)
Birth of "Peace of God" movement			
	Pope Gregory V (996–999)	Otto III (996–1002)	
			Richard the Good (996–1027)
	Stephen of Hungary (997–1038)		
	Pope Sylvester II (999–1003)		
	Henry II (1002–1024)		Massacre of the Danes (1002)
			Malcolm II of Scotland (1005–1034)
	Pope Benedict VIII (1012–1024)		
		Henry II (1014–1024)	Sweyn Forkbeard (1013–1014)
			Ethelred Canute the Great (1014–1016) (1014/1018–1035)
			Olaf the Saint of Norway (1015–1028)
			Edmund II (1016)
			Canute the Great (1016–1035)
	Conrad II Pope John XIX (1024–1039) (1024–1032)		
		Conrad II (1027–1039)	Submission of Malcolm II to Canute the Great (1031)
	Pope Benedict IX (1032–1045/1048)		**Duncan** of Scotland (1034–1040)
			Harold Magnus Harthacanute William Harefoot the Good of Denmark the Bastard (1035–1040) of Norway (1035–1042) (1035–1087) (1035–1047)
Henry III (1039–1056)			Harthacanute (1040–1042)
			Macbeth of Scotland (1040–1057)
			Magnus the Good of Denmark (1042–1047)
	Pope Sylvester III (1045–1046)/ Pope Gregory VI (1045–1046)		
	Pope Clement II (1046–1047)	**Henry III** (1046–1056)	
	Robert Guiscard's arrival in Italy		
	Pope Leo IX (1049–1054)		
	"Great Schism" of eastern and western churches (1054)		
Henry IV (1056–1106)			
	Pope Nicholas II (1059–1061)		

—■—

Chapter Seventy-Eight

The Norman Conquest

Between 1042 and 1066,
Earl Godwin fails to put his sons on the throne,
Halley's Comet passes overhead,
and William of Normandy conquers England

E DWARD WAS NOW thirty-eight, his personality permanently stamped by his early life. Before his twelfth birthday, his father had died, his mother had married a man who wanted to kill him, and he had been sent away to live in a country whose language he did not know. He was a withdrawn and silent man, known for piety (his devotion earned him the nickname "Edward the Confessor") but nevertheless hard and unforgiving. The witan acclaimed him as king, and as soon as he was in possession of the throne he ordered that all of his mother's worldly goods be confiscated: "He took from his mother whatever gold, silver, gems, stones, or other precious objects she had," writes the chronicler John of Worcester, "because . . . she had given him less than he wanted." Hatred had been nursed within him for so many years that he could not let it go, even when the crown was his.[1]

Edward soon discovered that the throne was shaky beneath him. By this time, the earls who ruled the four earldoms of England practically controlled the decisions of the witan; they had gained so much power that no king could stay in power without their assistance, and Godwin, the Anglo-Saxon weathercock, was the strongest of them all. In fact, William of Malmesbury says that Godwin told the king as much: "My authority carries very great weight in England," Godwin says, in Malmesbury's *Gesta Regum Anglorum,* "and on the side which I incline to, fortune smiles. If you have my support no one will dare oppose you, and conversely."[2]

Godwin probably never said anything quite so explicitly threatening, but Edward certainly understood the old earl's power. In 1045, the king ensured himself of Godwin's goodwill by marrying Godwin's daughter Edith and giving Godwin's son Harold the title of "Earl of East Anglia." The Godwin family now controlled two of the four earldoms as well as occupying the king's

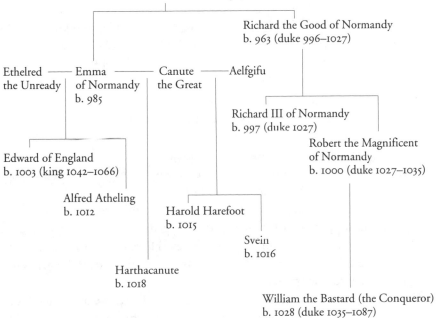

78.1: The English and Danish royal families.

bedchamber; and old Godwin himself undoubtedly hoped that his daughter would give birth to the next king of England.

But it seems likely that the marriage was never consummated. Edward was irretrievably celibate: the iron self-possession that had walled him off and protected him during his horrible childhood never allowed him to share his body with another, male or female. Nor was he particularly fond of Edith, who was a political pawn in the game he was playing with Godwin. He married her, says Henry of Huntingdon, "under obligation for his kingdom to the powerful Earl Godwin," and he never forgot it. (Another chronicler says that those who saw the new queen were struck, simultaneously, by her learning and her "lack of intellectual humility and of personal beauty.")[3]

And he had still not resigned himself to Godwin's control. Over the next seven years, Edward worked unceasingly to gain the loyalty of the other two earls, Leofric of Mercia and Siward of Northumbria. Both saw advantage for themselves in getting rid of the leechlike Godwins. By 1051, Edward felt secure enough to exile Godwin, Harold, and all the rest of the family. He sent Edith to a nunnery, reclaimed Wessex as a royal possession, and gave young Harold Godwin's earldom of East Anglia to Leofric's son; Siward was rewarded for his support with treasure and a bishopric.[4]

Old Godwin went to Western Francia, but he refused to accept his exile. He was, says John of Worcester, "a man of assumed charm and natural eloquence in his mother tongue, with remarkable skill in speaking and in persuading the public to accept his decisions." Now he collected his supporters, sailed up the Thames before Edward could assemble a fleet to keep him out, and made his case directly to the people. "He met the London citizens," says John of Worcester, "some through mediators, some in person . . . and succeeded in bringing almost everybody into agreement with his desires." By this time, Edward's armed forces had gathered, but they were reluctant to go against public opinion: "Almost all were most loath to fight their kinsmen and fellow countrymen," John says. "For this reason, the wiser on both sides restored peace between the king and the earl."[5]

Edward had been outmaneuvered. He backed down, in the face of the overwhelming support that Godwin had managed to whip up, and restored the old man to the position of Earl of Wessex. He was also forced to bring Edith back from her nunnery, and to take East Anglia away from Leofric's son and give it back to young Harold Godwinson.

Old Godwin did not last much longer; he died of a stroke on Easter Monday of 1053 and was buried with great honors. But by then, young Harold had displayed his father's talent for engaging popular support. He was well liked, charming, and a good administrator; and Edward, once again giving way to public sentiment, awarded Godwin's old position of earl of Wessex to his son.

The other earls clung to their power in the face of Godwin's maneuvering. In 1054, Siward of Northumbria won particular renown by marching north, confronting the Scots, and killing the high king Mac Bethad in battle; the Scots were once again forced to swear loyalty to the king of England. But Harold Godwinson matched old Siward's accomplishment by marching west and fighting against the rebellious Welsh, forcing *them* to swear submission just as the Scots had.

By 1057, Harold and his Godwin brothers held three of the four earldoms of England.* Harold, the oldest and most powerful brother, soon proved that he had as much power as the king. When his brother Tostig, earl of Northumbria, began to persecute the taxpayers of Northumbria by raising the rates and then sending soldiers to collect the money, Harold took charge

---

*When Harold became earl of Wessex, Edward restored Leofric's son to the position of earl of East Anglia. Siward of Northumbria died in 1055, and Harold Godwinson's brother Tostig was awarded his earldom. Leofric of Mercia died in 1057; at that point his son was transferred from East Anglia over to Mercia, and East Anglia was awarded to a third Godwin brother, Gyrth. This put East Anglia, Northumbria, and Wessex all under the control of Godwins, and left only Mercia in non-Godwin hands.

of disciplining him—normally the prerogative of the monarch. He marched against Tostig's soldiers with his own forces, defeated his brother, and forced him to leave England. Tostig fled to Norway and took refuge at the court of Harald Hardrada, king of Norway, who had followed Magnus the Good to the throne. There, Tostig simmered in fury, waiting for revenge.

A series of unexpected events soon gave him the chance to wreak it.

The first happened sometime in 1064, when Harold Godwinson ran into fairly routine trouble at sea. He was sailing in the English Channel when a storm caught him and drove him eastward until his ship came up onto the shores of Normandy. Without ship, men, or money, he was forced to appeal to William the Bastard, duke of Normandy, to provide all three so that he could get home again.

By this time, the chaos in Normandy had resolved itself. Emma's bastard great-nephew William, who had become duke at the age of eight, had grown into a man and had put down the rebellion in his dukedom with a firm hand. By 1064 he was thirty-six years old with the military experience of a soldier twice his age.

We have no way of knowing exactly what passed between the two men. There are, as historian David Howarth points out, nine different versions of the encounter, with English, Norman, and Danish chroniclers telling different stories about what Harold promised to William in order to get home again. All we can say for certain is that by the time Harold left Normandy, William the Bastard was determined to become the next king of England. Edward the Confessor was just past sixty and clearly uninterested in fathering an heir; William, his first cousin once removed, was his closest adult male relative. Harold's father Godwin had been a kingmaker; Harold Godwinson could help William gain the favor of the English nobility.

But he could not promise much more. The crown was not his (or anyone else's) to give away. It lay in the gift of the witan.[6]

In any case, William gave Harold Godwinson men and ships and sent him back to England. A little more than a year later, during the Christmas festivities of 1065, Edward the Confessor fell ill. He died on January 5, 1066, and was buried the next day in Westminster Abbey, which had just been finished. On the very same day, just as soon as the coffin was out of sight, the witan met and chose Harold Godwinson to be the next king of England.

He was not the only choice. Edward the Confessor had, some years before, retrieved Edmund Ironside's grandson from Hungary; the toddler son of the king, who had been saved from death by the king of Sweden and fostered by strangers in Hungary, had married a Hungarian wife and fathered a son named Edgar. Edward the Confessor had brought Edgar back to England and was raising him as an adoptive son.

78.2: Detail from the Bayeux Tapestry, showing bystanders pointing at Halley's Comet as it passes overhead, with Harold and attendant on the right
Credit: Erich Lessing/Art Resource, NY

But Edgar was only fourteen years old and essentially a foreigner. The witan preferred a grown-up, one who had already proved himself in battle; the *Anglo-Saxon Chronicle* suggests that Edward himself, on his deathbed, had recommended that Harold follow him to the throne. So Harold Godwinson was declared Harold II of England in Westminster Abbey, the first monarch to be crowned there.

At once William the Bastard began to prepare an invasion. Winds and tides held him off for the time being, but Harold knew that the Norman duke was on his way. Sure that the Normans would attack in the spring, when the weather allowed, he assembled a standing army and kept them encamped, on high alert. A dreadful sign in the heavens, during the last week of April, confirmed that a great threat was approaching. It was, the *Anglo-Saxon Chronicle* says, "a sign such as men never saw before . . . a haired star." The elliptical orbit of Halley's Comet had brought it into sight of England, where it burned in the skies for a full week.[7]

But by the end of August, Harold had begun to relax his guard. The English army and navy had been waiting for months: "all the summer and the autumn; and a land-army was kept everywhere by the sea. . . . When it was the Nativity of St. Mary, the men's provisions were gone, and no one could

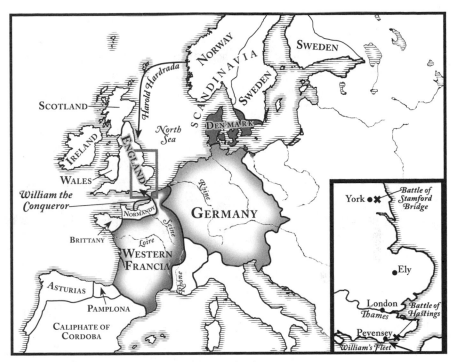

78.1: The Battle of Hastings

hold them there any longer. Then the men were allowed to go home, and the king rode inland, and the ships were sent to London."[8]

The feast of the Nativity of St. Mary was on September 8, and it was perfectly reasonable for Harold to conclude that no one was coming. Sailors stayed off the sea during the fall and winter, fearing the same high winds that had driven Harold onto the shores of Normandy two years earlier. But just as Harold was returning to London, ready to take up the task of governing his country, two things happened. His brother Tostig, whose anger had tipped over into obsession, had finally convinced Harald Hardrada of Norway that England would reject Harold Godwinson and rally to his banner as soon as he landed on England's shores. The two men had recruited men and ships from the unhappy Scots. They were keeping a close eye on the troop movements in the south, and when the English camps began to break up for the winter, the joint Norwegian and Scottish expedition began to move towards invasion.[9]

At the same time, and apparently by sheer chance, William the Bastard lost patience. He was tired of waiting for good winds. Late in the second week of September, he launched his attack fleet into the English Channel, where they were promptly battered by an enormous storm that sank some of his ships, blew others off course, and drowned part of his invasion force.

Harold of England knew nothing of the struggle offshore. He was in London when he heard horrible news from the north: Harald Hardrada and Tostig had landed near York, with Harald's black-raven banner flying above them. A hastily assembled English army had marched out to meet them and had been slaughtered. York had agreed to a formal surrender, complete with hostages, to be carried out on September 25.[10]

In a superhuman effort, Harold rounded up the dispersing soldiers and left London. They reached York on the morning of the planned surrender. Harald and Tostig rode to the agreed-upon meeting place, Stamford Bridge, to find the king of England and his army waiting in place of the cowed citizens of York and their chosen hostages.

Both armies drew their swords at once. Henry of Huntingdon gives us a vivid picture of the battle: "It was desperately fought," he says,

> the armies being engaged from daybreak to noonday, when, after fierce attacks on both sides, the Norwegians were forced to give way. . . . Being driven across the river, the living trampling on the corpses of the slain, they resolutely made a fresh stand. Here a single Norwegian, whose name ought to have been preserved, took post on a bridge, and hewing down more than forty of the English with a battle-axe, his country's weapon, stayed the advance of the whole English army till the ninth hour. At last some one came under the bridge in a boat and thrust a spear into him through the chinks of the flooring.[11]

The English army advanced across the bridge and slaughtered the remnants of the Norwegian force. Both Harald Hardrada and Tostig were killed in the fighting; Harold II received the Norwegian surrender from Harald's son and allowed the young man to go home. He took with him the remnants of the Norwegian force: twenty-four ships, out of an invasion force of more than three hundred.

Harold's hard-won victory had just lost him his kingdom. He went into York with his men, to provision and rest them for the journey home. They were still in York when another messenger arrived with even worse tidings. A few days earlier, William the Bastard had landed at Pevensey, on the southern coast, and there were at least eight thousand men with him, even after the battering from the channel storms.

Harold hurried his damaged, weary, footsore army on yet another forced march. They arrived in the south of England on October 5, and Harold at once sent ambassadors to William to attempt to resolve the situation without further fighting. William was unyielding. He insisted that Edward the Confessor had intended *him* to receive the crown of England, and he further accused Harold of swearing a sacred oath, after that shipwreck in Normandy, to hand over the throne to William.

A week of fruitless negotiations made it very clear that William would not leave without a fight. On October 14, the English army—mostly foot-soldiers—met the Norman force of cavalry, infantry, and archers near the town of Hastings. They were killed in droves. Later stories embroider the Battle of Hastings with multiple details, but the oldest account, in the *Anglo-Saxon Chronicle*, is brief and stark. "King Harold gathered a great army, and came against him at the grey apple-tree," it reads, "and there was a great slaughter on either side. There were killed King Harold, and Earl Leofwine his brother, and Earl Gyrth his brother, and many good men. And the French had possession of the place of slaughter." By day's end, every Godwin man was dead, and William the Bastard had become William the Conqueror.

There was one heir left in the English line—fourteen-year-old Edgar, still in London. In a last act of defiance, the witan met and crowned him as king. Edgar was young but not stupid. He escaped from his honor guard, got to William, and surrendered as quickly as possible. William sent the boy back to Normandy and ordered him to be treated well. "And then William came to Westminster," says the *Chronicle*, "and the Archbishop consecrated him as king."[12]

He was now William I, properly crowned in Westminster Abbey. The English struggle against the Vikings had ended; by way of France, a Viking king finally had full possession of the English throne.

TIMELINE 78

GERMANY	ITALY MAGYARS	Roman Emperor	BRITISH ISLES	SCANDINAVIA	NORMANDY
					Richard the Good (996–1027)
	Stephen of Hungary (997–1038) Pope Sylvester II (999–1003)				
Henry II (1002–1024)			Massacre of the Danes (1002) **Malcolm II** of Scotland (1005–1034)		
	Pope Benedict VIII (1012–1024)		**Sweyn Forkbeard** (1013–1014)		
		Henry II (1014–1024)	Ethelred (1014–1016)	**Canute the Great** (1014/1018–1035) **Olaf the Saint** of Norway (1015–1028)	
			Edmund II (1016) **Canute the Great** (1016–1035)		
Conrad II (1024–1039)	Pope John XIX (1024–1032)				
		Conrad II (1027–1039)	Submission of Malcolm II to Canute the Great (1031)		
	Pope Benedict IX (1032–1045/1048)		**Duncan** of Scotland (1034–1040)		
			Harold Harefoot (1035–1040)	Magnus the Good of Norway (1035–1047)	Harthacanute of Denmark (1035–1042)	William the Bastard (1035–1087)
Henry III (1039–1056)			Harthacanute (1040–1042) **Macbeth** of Scotland (1040–1057)		
			Edward the Confessor (1042–1066)		
	Pope Sylvester III (1045–1046) Pope Gregory VI (1045–1046) Pope Clement II (1046–1047) Robert Guiscard's arrival in Italy Pope Leo IX (1049–1054) "Great Schism" of eastern and western churches (1054)	Henry III (1046–1056)		**Harold Hardrada** of Norway (1047–1066)	
Henry IV (1056–1106)	Pope Nicholas II (1059–1061)		Death of Macbeth in battle (1054)		
			Harold Godwinson shipwrecked in Normandy (1064)		
			Harold II (Godwinson) (1066) Battle of Hastings (October 14, 1066) **William the Conqueror** (1066–1087)		

Chapter Seventy-Nine

The Kings of Spain

Between 1016 and 1108,
the Caliphate of Cordoba disintegrates,
the northern Christian kingdoms battle with each other,
the Muslim Almoravids cross over into Spain,
and El Cid accidentally creates an oasis of tolerance

I N 1016, THE CALIPHATE OF CORDOBA—which had risen to a sudden and dizzy height of magnificence—paused at the edge of the crest and then plummeted downwards. The caliph Sulayman II was captured and put to death by his rivals for power, and the caliphate itself began to split apart.

The catastrophe of 1016 can be traced back forty years, to the same man who led the caliphate into magnificence: Muhammad ibn Abi Amir, known more widely as al-Mansur, "The Victorious." In 976, the young caliph Hisham II had inherited the rule of Cordoba on the death of his father. Hisham II was only ten years old, which opened the caliphate up to control by his ministers; and of these, al-Mansur was the most ambitious. He had arrived in Cordoba some years earlier, travelling from his home on the southern coast, and had devoted himself to the study of law—and the task of rising up through the ranks of civil service. "Despite his humble antecedents," wrote the eleventh-century chronicler Abd Allah, "he achieved great things, thanks to his shrewd-ness, his duplicity, and his good fortune."[1]

Al-Mansur, who was around forty when Hisham II became caliph, saw the child's rule as his chance to grasp power. In 978, through a combination of persuasion and threat, he had himself appointed vizier to the little boy—prime minister and household administrator rolled into one.

At once he ordered construction of a new palace. When it was finished, in 981, he moved himself and the entire bureaucracy of Cordoba into it. Hisham II, now fifteen, was left in the caliph's palace alone, without daily contact from any of his ministers or courtiers. Al-Mansur announced that the boy had decided to devote himself to good works, and kept him isolated. At the same time, the vizier accused of heresy and disloyalty other high officials who might also aspire to power, and had them exiled or put to death. "His pretext," Abd Allah says, "was that their survival would have led to much discord and dissension and culminated in the ruin of the Muslims." His name was now spoken, along with the caliph's, in Friday prayers—proof that he had risen to the top of the palace hierarchy.[2]

Al-Mansur may have been ruthless, but he was also an excellent strategist and administrator. He reinforced the Cordoban army with crowds of Berber soldiers, brought over from North Africa, and during his rule as vizier, the Caliphate of Cordoba triumphed in battle after battle against the Christian kingdoms to the north. Barcelona, which had been governed by independent Christian dukes for over a century, was sacked in 985. The king of Pamplona, Sancho II, suffered a series of humiliating defeats and finally came to Cordoba to make peace—which al-Mansur accepted, along with Sancho's daughter as his wife. In 999, the caliph's armies flooded over the border of the Kingdom of Leon and destroyed much of the city of Santiago de Compostela, which was doubly embarrassing because it was not only Christian territory but also a site of pilgrimage for Christians from all over the world; the bones of the apostle James, the disciple of Jesus, were said to rest in its cathedral.[3]

In all, al-Mansur was said to have won fifty-seven battles over the northern resistance: "He gained decisive victories over the enemy," Abd Allah concluded, "and during his time, Islam enjoyed a glory which al-Andalus had never witnessed before, while the Christians suffered their greatest humiliation." Under his capable and unforgiving rule, al-Andalus prospered, even with the rightful caliph under house arrest.[4]

But the rapid expansion had driven the Muslim kingdom on the peninsula past the place where its underpinnings could support it. Beneath the surface triumphs, the foundations were beginning to disintegrate.

When al-Mansur died in 1002, his son Abd al-Malik was forced to fight continuously to keep the borders of the caliphate out to where al-Mansur had pushed them. He claimed the post of vizier, as though it had become hereditary; and he too kept Hisham away from any involvement in government. But he spent the six years of his caliphate at war and did little governing himself. During the dank cool October of 1008, he was campaigning in the north against the Christian region of Castile when he caught a chest cold. He had always had weak lungs, and the cold turned into a cough that killed him.[5]

Now the decay that al-Mansur's glorious victories had whitewashed began to show through. Al-Malik's brother, al-Mansur's younger son Abd al-Rahman, saw no reason to keep on hiding his power beneath the umbrella of a legitimate caliph. To be ruler in all but name didn't suit him; he wanted the name as well. He forced Hisham II (now in his forties) to name him heir to the caliphate.

This would have brought a final end to the Umayyad hold on the caliphate in Cordoba, and the other members of the Umayyad family—who already resented the privileges claimed by al-Mansur and his family, and who particularly disliked the high position held by so many Berbers in the army, to the exclusion of Arab officers—revolted.

Unfortunately, they didn't unify behind a single Umayyad candidate—some supported Hisham II, others wanted another Umayyad caliph to replace him—and a civil war broke out. Abd al-Rahman and his Berbers fought against the various Umayyad factions who wanted the caliphate back, and the Umayyads fought against each other. In the years of struggle that followed, both Abd al-Rahman and Hisham II were killed. Eventually, the Umayyad claimant Sulayman managed to beat back the opposition and become caliph, but he held the throne for only a handful of years.

The civil war had so fractured the kingdom that it was vulnerable to outside attack, but the attack didn't come from the Christian kingdoms in the north. Instead, it came from a Berber soldier named al-Nasir, who in 1016 marched into Cordoba at the head of his own North African forces, took Sulayman II captive, and beheaded him in public with his own hands. He then proclaimed himself caliph in Cordoba. Sulayman's head and the heads of the Berber chiefs who had fought against al-Nasir instead of joining him were then cleaned up, perfumed and preserved, and carried around al-Andalus by al-Nasir's men, so that all could see the fate of those who opposed him.[6]

Despite the show and tell, al-Nasir survived only two years before he was assassinated in his bath. The rot had set in to stay. After 1018, no caliph managed to rule in Cordoba for more than a few years, and few of the claimants died a natural death. In 1031, the last man to try to claim the title died, and al-Andalus fell apart into a fragmentation of little city-states. Their kings were called *reyes de taifas*, the "party kings," each the head of his own tiny political movement. Some were Arab, others were Berber. Over the next half-century, over thirty of these *taifa* kingdoms would blanket the former territory of the caliphate.[7]

THE NORTHERN CHRISTIAN KINGDOMS had spent their entire existence defending themselves against the threat of the caliphate. Now, as the caliphate disintegrated, the Christians of al-Andalus were able to draw their eyes away from the Muslim south. They began, instead, to look at each other: no longer allies, but competitors.

The first aggressor in the north was the king of Pamplona, Sancho III ("the Great"), grandson of the king who had given his daughter in marriage to the vizier al-Mansur. His ambitions had begun to grow back in 1016. His territory already enfolded not only the fortress city of Pamplona (built by the tribe of the Vascones centuries earlier, and sacked by Charlemagne during his retreat from al-Andalus), but also the northern region known as Navarre and the rich upper valley of the Ebro river. As the caliphate to the south turned inwards and started to fracture, Sancho the Great cast a covetous eye on the neighboring Christian territory to his west: Castile, ruled by noblemen who called themselves counts, rather than kings. Sancho the Great began his take-over peacefully, by marrying the count's daughter. The next year, when the count of Castile died, Sancho the Great offered to "protect" Castile on behalf of its new count: his young brother-in-law Garcia II, a child of three.

Becoming Castile's regent gave Sancho the Great the opportunity to fold Castile into his territory, making Pamplona the largest northern kingdom. Alfonso V ("the Noble"), king of Leon, took notice. He made secret arrangements of his own to pull Castile back into his own orbit; when Garcia II reached the age of thirteen, Alfonso offered to betroth the young count to his own sister.

Sancho the Great, preserving appearances, agreed enthusiastically to the match—and announced that in order to do his brother-in-law honor, he and his entire army would accompany the boy to Leon for the formal celebration of the betrothal. No sooner had they arrived in Leon than three assassins, brothers from the Castilian family of Vela, attacked the boy and stabbed him to death in front of his sister, his brother-in-law, and their retinue. They then fled—into the kingdom of Pamplona.[8]

This was enough to confirm that they were in the pay of Sancho the Great, but he was no fool; he had hired Castilians to preserve deniability, and when they took refuge in his own territory he sent armed men after them, arrested them, and burned them to death for murdering the count. If his young wife had suspicions about her husband's role in her brother's death, she never expressed them in public; she became countess of Castile, which meant that the kingdom had effectively been united with Pamplona.

The joint realm, increasingly known as the Kingdom of Navarre, now went to war with Leon. For the next six years, Leonese soldiers resisted the invasion of Sancho the Great's armies; but the war ended in 1034, when Sancho drove the king of Leon out of his capital city and entered it in triumph. The exiled ruler retreated into the small territory of Galicia, where he was killed three years later.

Sancho the Great now controlled all three Christian kingdoms of the north, plus a few of the smaller regions. The conquered lands "submitted to his rule," the official court history tells us, "because of his conspicuous integrity and virtue." In fact Sancho had gained his kingdoms through ruthless war and manipulation, and ruled them without apology: the history concludes, "Because of the extent of the lands he possessed and ruled, he had himself called 'emperor.' "9

But the imperial title was merely that. Sancho still thought like a local ruler; instead of passing the entire realm on to his heir, he decreed that the lands would be divided among his four sons. He died in 1035 at the age of sixty-five, barely a year after adding *imperator* to his titles.

The Christian empire fell apart. His four legitimate heirs, along with a fifth illegitimate son, spent the next twenty years ravaging each other's territory and fighting for dominance. Not until 1056 did peace descend over the north, and then only because all of the heirs but one were dead. The second-born son, Ferdinand, was the last man

79.1: Sancho the Great and the Taifa *Kingdoms*

standing. He claimed his father's lands for himself, along with the imperial title: Emperor Ferdinand I. Once again, the northern kingdoms were one. The fragmentation in the south had allowed for the unification of the north: the Christian kingdoms of the peninsula, of *Spain,* had begun to take on a single identity, as the Muslim kingdoms of Spain had fallen apart.

But it was not a peaceful identity. Two decades of interfamily war had prevented Christian Spain from taking full advantage of the collapse to the south, and Ferdinand himself had built his empire on blood. He tried to wash away the stain with devotion: "King Fernando always used to see to it with special care," says the twelfth-century *Historia Silense,* "that the better part of the spoils of his victories should be distributed among the churches and Christ's poor, to the praise of that highest Creator who gave him victory. . . . [But] Fernando was still enmeshed in corruptible flesh and knew that he was not close to divine grace."10 When, in 1065, he felt himself fatally weakening and realized that his last illness was upon him, he took off his royal robes and crown and put on a hair shirt instead. He spent his last days in penance and died wearing the garments of a sinner.

He passed on both his empire and the tradition of civil war to his three sons. The oldest, Sancho II ("the Strong"), became king of Castile; his middle son Alfonso inherited Leon; and his youngest, the little territory of Galicia. But Sancho the Strong was unwilling to leave his brothers in peace. Accompanied by his right-hand man, the general Rodrigo Diaz, he began a war of reunification.

Rodrigo Diaz, better known by his nickname "El Cid" (Arabic for "The Lord"), was only in his early twenties at the time. But he had been a soldier since his early teens and was already experienced in battle. "King Sancho valued Rodrigo Diaz so highly," writes El Cid's biographer, "that he made him commander of his whole military following. So Rodrigo throve and became a most mighty man of war."[11]

After seven years of fighting, Sancho the Strong managed to drive his brother Alfonso out of Leon. He reunited Castile and Leon into one kingdom, while Alfonso took refuge in the *taifa* kingdom centered around Toledo. But like his grandfather, Alfonso was crafty and willing to shed family blood; he paid off one of Sancho the Strong's own soldiers to kill the king during the siege of an outlying city. "By treachery," says the *Historia Silense*, "the king was transfixed with a spear by him, unexpectedly, from behind, and shed his life together with his blood."[12]

Alfonso denied until his death that he was involved in Sancho's murder, but the benefit came to him; with his brother dead, Alfonso returned from his exile in the Muslim lands and reclaimed both kingdoms as Alfonso VI of Castile and Leon. He also inherited Sancho the Strong's army, along with its general, El Cid.

Alfonso did his best to buy El Cid's loyalty, giving him a position at court and a royal cousin as his wife. But he never fully trusted his dead brother's general, and over the next few years El Cid was sent on numerous foreign trips, acting as Alfonso's ambassador to the *taifa* kingdoms in the south and east. This kept him out of Castile and Leon and away from Alfonso, but it also gave him a chance to demonstrate his brilliance as a warrior. Some time around 1080, he was dispatched for a friendly visit to the *taifa* kingdom at Seville, which was under the rule of the Arab king al-Mu'tamid. While he was there, Seville was attacked by the neighboring *taifa* kingdom at Granada. El Cid and his men marched out with al-Mu'tamid to assist him in his fight against the army of Granada. El Cid fought so ferociously that he won all credit for the victory. He wrapped up this performance by attacking Toledo, taking seven thousand captives and wagons of treasure back to Castile and Leon with him.

"In return for this success and victory granted to him by God," his biographer laments, "many men both acquaintances and strangers became jealous and accused him before the king of many false and untrue things." Alfonso was jealous of El Cid's reputation and popularity, and he took the attack on Toledo as an excuse to exile El Cid from his kingdom. The anonymous twelfth-century poem that praises El Cid's heroic exploits adds that Alfonso also sent his men to sack El Cid's home:

> rifled coffers, burst gates, all open to the wind,
> nor mantle left, nor robe of fur, stripped bare his castle hall.[13]

Deprived of his home, his lands, and his profession, El Cid exercised his professional skill in the only way he could: he became a mercenary. His reputation ensured him of employment, and he was snapped up at once by the Arab king of Zaragoza, a *taifa* state with its capital not far from Alfonso's border.

This put him on the wrong side of his previous employer. Although the two men did not come face to face in battle, El Cid was fighting for the Arabs, and Alfonso VI was planning a serious attempt to reconquer large parts of Muslim Spain. In 1079, he captured the city of Coria, well south of his own kingdom, and by 1085 he had pushed eastward all the way to Toledo, center of one of the stronger *taifa* states. When he conquered it, ripples of fear went through the surviving *taifa* kingdoms: if Alfonso VI managed to fight his way through the *taifa* kingdoms all the way to the coast, he could divide the northern and southern *taifa* kingdoms from each other and pick them off, one at a time. They could not fight the determined Christian advance without reinforcements.[14] Led by the king of Seville, the *taifa* rulers sent an appeal across the Strait of Gibraltar to the North African Muslims known as the Almoravids.

Until this point, the Almoravids had been confined to North Africa. Originally an unruly collection of North African tribes, they had been shaped into a nation by a North African chief named Yahya ibn Ibrahim, who had come to power some fifty years earlier. The tribes had been vaguely Muslim for two centuries, but since they were spread across the western desert with no central city or mosque for them to gather around, their practice of Islam had become more and more idiosyncratic. In 1035, ibn Ibrahim, at that time merely the chief of one of the tribes, had made his way to Mecca for the sacred pilgrimage, the *hajj*. There he discovered just how odd the western African version of Islam was.[15]

A reformer by nature, ibn Ibrahim spent years studying the faith practiced by the Arabs in Islam's homeland, and when he returned to west Africa he brought with him a missionary, an *imam* named ibn Yasin. Ibn Yasin spent the next twenty years among the tribes, teaching them his brand of Islam. It was a militant and ascetic interpretation that ordered the heterodox believers to straighten up, shun alcohol, devote their time to prayer and fasting, study the Qur'an—and then to spread these practices, by force if necessary. "God has reformed you and led you to his straight path," he told them. "Warn your people. Make them fearful of God's punishments. . . . If they repent, return to the truth, and abandon their ways, let them be. But if they refuse, continue in their error, and persist in their wrongheadedness, then we shall ask for God's help against them and wage Holy War on them."[16]

By 1085, the Almoravids' dedication to holy war had roused them to conquer most of the northwestern African coast. Led by ibn Ibrahim's brother Abu-Bakr, they built a capital city and central mosque at Marrakesh; they proclaimed their loyalty to the Abbasid caliphate in Baghdad and took for their own the existing Abbasid laws and customs. In bringing his message to northwest Africa, ibn Yasin had also brought with him a template for life as an empire, giving these nomads a fast track to nationhood.

When the panicked message arrived from Seville, Abu-Bakr sent his cousin, the general Yusuf ibn Tashfin, to answer it. Ibn Tashfin transported an Almoravid army across the strait and marched north to fight against Alfonso VI. On October 23, 1087, the combined armies of the *taifa* kingdoms and Almoravids defeated the soldiers of Leon and Castile in pitched battle at Sagrajas, southwest of Toledo. The slaughter covered the ground with the dead: "There was no place for a foot but a corpse or blood," wrote one chronicler.

Alfonso survived but was forced to flee the battlefield in agony, badly wounded in the leg. The defeat frightened him so badly that he recalled El Cid from exile to fight the Almoravid threat; El Cid agreed to come home in exchange for two castles, a small territory of his own, and a written pardon from Alfonso, which stipulated that "all lands and castles which [El Cid] might acquire" by conquering *taifa* territory would belong solely to him.[17]

El Cid helped Alfonso's armies hold the border of Leon-Castile in place. Meanwhile, ibn Tashfin was soon frightening the Muslims of the south as much as he had terrified the Christians. The *taifa* rulers who had invited him in knew their history; they remembered the conquests of Tariq in 711, which had first brought Islam to Spain, and they were aware that asking a North African army for help was not unlike asking a fox to guard the henhouse. But they had been desperate. As a shaky defense against Tashfin's ambitions, they had managed to get him to promise that he would return to Africa as soon as the Christians were defeated.[18]

By 1091, the promise was ancient history. Abu-Bakr had died in 1087, leaving ibn Tashfin as ruler of the Almoravid lands. Tashfin had conquered Granada, Cordoba, and Seville; southern Spain had become merely a province of the Almoravid empire, which now stretched from Marrakesh across the water. But the extent of the empire made it difficult for Almoravid armies to advance much farther north. Alfonso's kingdom remained intact in the north. The peninsula was divided between the two empires; the *taifa* kingdoms, falling one at a time, were a thing of the past.

But with the peninsula divided into Christian and Muslim segments, El Cid resisted belonging to either. Instead, in 1094 he laid siege to the city of Valencia, on the eastern coast, between the borders of the northern Christians and the southern Muslims. Once the city was in his hands, he claimed it as his own under the terms of Alfonso's pardon and moved into it. Around Valencia, he conquered himself a kingdom.

El Cid was now in his fifties, and he had spent his entire life fighting for Muslim kings against other Muslims, for Muslim kings against Christians, for Christian kings against Muslims, for Christian kings against their own brothers. He was tired of war and fed up with changing sides. And for a brief time, his kingdom was home to both Christians and Muslims, a brief mingling of faiths in a polarized land.

79.2: The Almoravid Empire

El Cid was no peacemaker; he killed the inhabitants of Valencia who opposed him, sacked villages that refused to surrender, and stole treasure from the conquered for his own personal use. But neither was he a zealot. He served neither Christianity nor Islam, but simply himself. Any Spaniard who behaved himself and obeyed El Cid could live in the kingdom of Valencia. In a world divided by religion, the great general's self-interest had accidentally built an oasis of tolerance.

BY 1097, THE ALMORAVID commander Yusuf ibn Tashfin had conquered almost all of the land that had once belonged to the Caliphate of Cordoba; his Muslim empire stretched from northwestern Africa up into the south of Spain. The Christian realm of Leon-Castile, ruled by the long-lived Alfonso VI, dominated most of the north. The little kingdom of Aragon-Navarre was the junior power on the Iberian Peninsula; the only realm smaller than Aragon-Navarre was Valencia, the independent realm of El Cid, which lay on the eastern coast.

Valencia existed entirely through the strength and resolution of El Cid; when he died, Valencia fell. He drew his last breath peacefully in his bed in

1099, at age sixty. As soon as the news of his death reached the Almoravids, they marched against Valencia, invaded its territory, and besieged the city for seven months.

His wife finally sent an appeal to Alfonso of Castile, begging for deliverance. She knew that this would be the end of her independence as queen of Valencia, and so it was. Alfonso arrived with his army and fought his way into the city to rescue her, but he refused to commit himself to lifting the siege. "It was far removed from his kingdom," the *Historia Roderici* tells us, "so he returned to Castile, taking with him Rodrigo's wife with the body of her husband. . . . When they had all left Valencia the king ordered the whole city to be burnt." The Almoravids, who had backed away, returned and claimed the burned city. They "resettled it and all its territories," the *Historia* concludes, "and they have never lost it since that day."[19]

The fall of Valencia was the beginning of a series of changes in the Spanish landscape. In 1104, Alfonso VI's first cousin (once removed) inherited the throne of Aragon-Navarre and began a double quest: to reconquer the Muslim south and to reverse the relationship between Leon-Castile and his own kingdom so that the larger realm paid homage to the smaller. Like his elder cousin, he was named Alfonso; while Alfonso VI of Castile eventually earned himself the nickname "Alfonso the Brave," the thirty-year reign of Alfonso of Aragon-Navarre earned the younger cousin the nickname "Alfonso the Battler."

The Battler's rise to power was assisted by the deaths, in rapid succession, of Tashfin, Alfonso the Brave's only son, and Alfonso himself.

Tashfin died in 1106 at nearly a hundred years old. Preoccupied with age and infirmity, he had allowed the armies of Leon-Castile to push deep into Muslim territory in the years before his death. He left the Almoravid empire to his son Ali ibn Yusuf, who recognized the need to drive back the Christian invaders.

In 1108, an Almoravid army commanded by ibn Yusuf's two younger brothers laid siege to the border city of Ucles. Alfonso the Brave of Castile sent his fifteen-year-old son Sancho at the head of ten thousand troops to lift the siege. He had given the boy two experienced generals to help him, and he expected a quick victory. But with the elderly Tashfin dead, the Almoravids had regrouped. In vicious fighting around the city, young Sancho and both of his generals were killed. The Almoravids occupied Ucles, creating a new frontier.

Alfonso the Brave, devastated by his son's death and in failing health, had one surviving legitimate child: his daughter Urraca, who had been married and widowed several years before. Since she would inherit the crown of Castile and Leon, her father arranged for her to marry the king of Aragon; Alfonso the Battler, now an experienced soldier in his early thirties, could then defend the realm from the Almoravids.[20]

The old man died not long after, and Alfonso the Battler became king of

Aragon and Navarre, Leon and Castile, *rex Hispania*. But he held Leon and Castile only through his wife, and their marriage was a disaster. Urraca was a grown woman in her late twenties, not a naive young girl. She had a four-year-old son from her previous marriage, and this child, not Alfonso the Battler, had the right to become the next ruler of Leon and Castile. She insisted on ruling her own part of the empire without her new husband's help, going so far as to banish her old tutor because he referred to Alfonso the Battler as "king of Castile." On top of the political problems, she simply didn't like Alfonso; there was a "want of affection between the wedded pair," says one chronicler. They quarrelled, and separated within a matter of months.[1]

But Alfonso the Battler still claimed the title of king over the whole realm. During the next eight years, he fought a constant war with the Almoravid armies along the frontier. Urraca also sent the armies of Leon-Castile against the Almoravids.

Periodically, the estranged husband and wife also fought against each other; once Alfonso the Battler even captured his spouse and kept her for a while as a prisoner of war. The hostility between the Christian king and queen thwarted their attempts to fight the North African enemy; thanks to their decaying marriage, the Almoravids kept power a little longer.

TIMELINE 79

ENGLAND	NORMANDY	EASTERN MUSLIM DYNASTIES	WESTERN MUSLIM DYNASTIES	CHRISTIAN SPAIN
Coronation of **Edgar** (973)				**Sancho II** of Pamplona (970–994)
			al-Aziz of the Fatimids (975–996)	
			Hisham II of Cordoba (976–1008)	
Ethelred (978–1013)			**al-Mansur** as vizier of Cordoba (978–1002)	
		al-Qadir of the Abbasids (991–1031)		
	Richard the Good (996–1027)		**al-Hakim** of the Fatimids (996–1021)	
				Alfonso V of Leon (999–1028)
Massacre of the Danes (1002)			**al-Malik** as vizier of Cordoba (1002–1008)	
			Sulayman II of Cordoba (1009/1012–1016)	
			Baghdad Manifesto (1011)	
Sweyn Forkbeard (1013–1014)				
Canute the Great (1014)				
Ethelred (1014–1016)				
Edmund II (1016)			**al-Nasir** of Cordoba (1016–1018)	
Canute the Great (1016–1035)				**Sancho III (the Great)** of Pamplona (1017–1035)
			az-Zahir of the Fatimids (1021–1036)	
			Rise of the *taifa* kingdoms (1031)	
Harold Harefoot (1035–1040)	**William the Bastard** (1035–1087)			**Ferdinand I** of Leon and Castile (1037–1065)
Harthacanute (1040–1042)				
Edward the Confessor (1042–1066)			**al-Mu'tamid** of Seville (1042–1069)	
			Abu-Bakr of the Almoravids (1061–1087)	
Harold II (Godwinson) (1066)				**Sancho II (the Strong)** of Castile (1065–1072)
William the Conqueror (1066–1087)				**Alfonso VI (the Brave)** of Castile and Leon (1072–1109)
			Tashfin of the Almoravids (1087–1106)	
				Establishment of El Cid's kingdom at Valencia (1094–1102)
				Alfonso the Battler of Aragon-Navarre (1104–1134)
			ibn Yusuf of the Almoravids (1106–1142)	

Chapter Eighty

The Arrival of the Turks

Between 1025 and 1071,
the empress Zoe crowns three husbands,
and the Seljuq Turks make themselves an empire

BACK TO THE EAST, eleventh-century Constantinople emerged from its self-absorption just in time to see a brand new enemy appear on the eastern horizon.

Basil the Bulgar-Slayer died in 1025; Constantine VIII, his young brother and heir, wore the sole crown of Byzantium for only three years. He was in his sixties and had spent his entire life hunting, horseback riding, and eating. He had no skill at governing and no experience as a soldier: "a man of sluggish temperament, with no great ambition for power," Michael Psellus writes, "physically strong, but a craven at heart." As a ruler, his greatest expertise was in "the art of preparing rich savoury sauces." He had no sons and no heir; he had three daughters but had refused to let any of them marry, afraid that their husbands might try to unseat him. His reign was one of staggering irresponsibility.[1]

When his last illness struck him in 1028, he was finally forced to arrange for a successor. The city governor of Constantinople, Romanos Argyros, was an experienced official in his sixties and also happened to be the great-grandson of Emperor Romanos I; Constantine suggested that Romanos Argyros marry his middle daughter, Zoe, and be crowned along with her.

Romanos Argyros was already married, and Zoe was forty-eight years old, but he didn't turn down the chance to become emperor. He sent his wife to a monastery and proposed to the middle-aged princess. The two were married on November 12, 1028; three days later, Constantine VIII died, and Romanos Argyros and his new wife were crowned as Romanos III and Empress Zoe, rulers of Byzantium.

Romanos turned out to be a man with grand dreams and no talent for carrying them out. He gathered a huge army and marched against the Muslim border to the east; he raised taxes, hoping to make himself famous through enormous building projects; and he worked hard at siring an heir so that his dynasty would last forever. All of these projects backfired. The assault on the Muslim border ended with an embarrassing defeat; the new taxes made him hugely unpopular; and Zoe, nearly fifty, was well past childbearing years. Michael Psellus remarks that Romanos found it easier to ignore this unpleasant truth: "Even in the face of natural incapacity, he clung ever more firmly to his ambitions, led on by his own faith in the future," the chronicler says. He hired specialists, doctors who claimed that they could cure sterility; he "submitted himself to treatment with ointments and massage, and he enjoined his wife to do likewise." The specialists suggested to Zoe that she bejewel herself with magic charms whenever her husband visited her, which he did, often.[2]

Ultimately, though, Romanos was forced to give up hope. He was too old to continue the sexual marathon he had instituted, and Zoe showed no signs of recovering from menopause. Discouraged, he abandoned her bedchamber altogether.

This was fine with Zoe. She had begun a torrid affair with the palace chamberlain, Michael the Paphlagonian, a handsome and pliable young man whose brother was a powerful palace eunuch. As Romanos's popularity plummeted, Zoe decided that the elderly husband her father had lumbered her with had to go. She probably began to dose his food with poison; his courtiers noticed that he grew weak and short of breath, his face swollen and discolored. His hair began to fall out. One morning he was bathing alone when he slipped beneath the water and drowned. Apparently Zoe had expected the accidental drowning, because she married Michael the Paphlagonian on the evening of the same day and ordered the patriarch to crown him as emperor.[3]

Although charming and clever, Michael was frequently ill (he was probably epileptic), and his short reign was a disaster on both political and personal fronts. It soon became clear that a puppet-master held his strings: not the empress, but Michael's brother John, the powerful palace eunuch.

Many of the castrated men who served in Constantinople were slaves or prisoners, but Byzantium had its share of native-born eunuchs. Young boys with royal blood were often castrated to keep them from claiming the throne; even more commonly, rural parents with numerous sons would castrate two or three and send them off to the capital city to make their fortunes. They couldn't all stay on the farm, and since eunuchs had no sons of their own and no ambitions to build dynasties, they had a distinct advantage at court.[4]

John and Michael came from a farming family in Paphlagonia with five sons; John had been castrated, Michael spared. John's competence and Michael's beauty had secured both a place at court, and John, the more intelligent and driven of the two, had masterminded his brother's affair with the empress. Now Michael was emperor, and John, nicknamed "Orphanotrophus" because he had charge of the official state orphanage in Constantinople, was the power behind the throne. Psellus, who as a boy met the eunuch in person, says that John Orphanotrophus was shrewd, meticulous, and devoted to his brother's success: "He never forgot his zeal for duty, even at the times which he devoted to pleasure," Psellus says. "[N]othing ever escaped his notice. . . . [E]veryone feared him and trembled at his superintendence."[5]

Under John's guidance, Michael began to hem Zoe in, reducing her influence at court. He confined her to her chambers and ordered that anyone visiting her had to be cleared by her honor guard. Meanwhile, he had also stopped sleeping with her; his epilepsy had grown worse, and he had become impotent. Zoe fought back in the only way she could; now well into her fifties, she began an affair with another younger man, a bureaucrat named Constantine Monomachos who had just entered his thirties.

Michael IV was annoyed enough by this to exile Constantine Monomachos to the island of Lesbos, the traditional exile-spot for malfeasants. But Constantine Monomachos was hardly Michael's greatest problem. The epileptic attacks were coming more frequently, often in full view of Michael's subjects; he could no longer go out in public without a band of attendants, who would circle him, if he fell into a seizure, so that no one could see his convulsions.

John Orphanotrophus took steps to preserve the family's power; he suggested that Michael adopt as his son and heir their twenty-five-year-old nephew (their older sister's son), also named Michael. The adoption was completed in 1040. By the middle of 1041, Michael IV was barely able to walk: "The power of nature could not be mastered," Psellus writes, "nor could the emperor vanquish and overwhelm this disease for ever. Secretly and step by step it advanced to the final dissolution." He died in December, aged thirty-one, and his nephew was crowned as Michael V in his place.[6]

Michael V was anxious to shake off the control of his powerful uncle. Once he was on the throne, he ordered both his uncle and his adoptive mother Zoe banished. He had overestimated his authority, though. John Orphanotrophus was respected, if not particularly popular, but Zoe, still beautiful, charismatic, and badly treated, was loved: "The indignation was universal, and all were ready to lay down their lives for Zoe," Psellus says. He was actually in Constantinople at the time of the riot, and describes mobs in the streets armed with axes, broadswords, spears, and stones, ready to kill Michael V as soon as he showed his face.[7]

In disguise, Michael sneaked down to the port and set sail for a nearby monastery. He took refuge in the church there, clinging to the altar. The mob followed him, dragged him away, and blinded him with a sharp iron. They left him there and returned to the city, where Zoe and her sister Theodora were acclaimed as co-empresses. "So the Empire passed into the hands of the two sisters," Psellus says, "and for the first time in our lives, we saw the transformation of the women's quarters into an emperor's council chamber."[8]

Zoe, now sixty-three, recalled from exile and married her young bureaucratic lover, Constantine Monomachos, and had him crowned as emperor—the third man to gain his power through marriage to her. It was an impressive career for an eleventh-century woman. Even in her sixties, she remained attractive. "She had golden hair, and her whole body was radiant with the whiteness of her skin," writes Michael Psellus, who saw her himself. "There were few signs of age in her; in fact . . . you would have said that here was a young woman, for no part of her skin was wrinkled, but all smooth and taut, and no furrows anywhere." The golden hair undoubtedly owed something to art—Psellus adds that she kept an entire chamber stocked with lotions, creams, and other beauty aids—but Zoe was apparently gifted with amazingly good genes.[9]

The men who ascended to power with her help were not as lucky. Constantine Monomachos now found himself at the head of an empire threatened on almost every side by outside powers. The personal had taken center stage at court for too long; Byzantium had begun to slip, little by little, from the heights that Basil II had attained. Constantine Monomachos was forced to deal with a rebellion by one of his generals, an attack from the Rus, a migration of Pecheneg refugees across the frozen Danube, and hostile Muslim forces to the east. He coped with these problems one by one, but in 1048, six years after his coronation, he came face to face with an enemy he could not conquer.[10]

THE ENEMY WAS TOGRUL, the Turkish chief who had led his coalition in the conquest of the Ghaznavid lands west of the Indus mountains. Togrul had now been at the head of his tribe, the Seljuq Turks, for twenty years. They were, in the words of historian René Grousset, "a horde without tradition, and the least civilized of all the nomad clans," but Togrul had provided them with a path into nationhood. He had himself crowned sultan of the Turks in 1038 and had established his capital at Nishapur. His Turks were now strong enough to challenge Byzantium.[11]

The first Turkish raid into Byzantine territory came in 1046; it was only a tentative prod at the Byzantine borders, and the Turks who came into Armenia withdrew without causing any real damage. But in 1048, a much larger Turkish army breached the eastern border and captured the rich border city of Erzen. Constantine Monomachos sent an army of fifty thousand to drive the invaders back; in a sharp nasty battle on the city's plain, the Byzantine soldiers were badly defeated. The Seljuq Turks took thousands of prisoners, with the

Byzantine commanding general among them, and captured the army supplies as well: thousands of wagons filled with food, dry goods, and money.[12]

Constantine Monomachos decided to make a treaty with the Seljuq Turks instead of continuing to fight. In exchange for peace and the return of the captives, he agreed to give up some of the land on the eastern frontier. He also sent expensive gifts to Togrul and promised that he would allow Muslims to worship freely in Constantinople; the Turks had converted to Islam, and this was a gesture of friendship. Togrul accepted the terms and sent Constantine's commander back to Constantinople unharmed.

For the moment, fighting was over. But the treaty was a devil's deal. Like every emperor since Basil II, Constantine Monomachos's biggest concern was surviving as emperor; fighting to keep the throne he had married, rather than inherited, absorbed him. As he held onto the empire, it shrank in his hands like a treasured and much-guarded balloon.

He was also ill. He had suffered for some time from a disease that racked him with painful muscle convulsions and slowly paralyzed him. "His fingers . . . completely altered from their natural shape, warped and twisted with hollows here and projections there," Psellus writes. "His feet were bent and his knees, crooked like the point of a man's elbow." He was forced to give up first riding and then walking. Breathing became difficult; talking caused him pain; beating off the Turks must have seemed entirely impossible.[13]

Soon the problem of the Turks passed to the next generation. Zoe died in 1050 at seventy-two, still wearing thin dresses and presiding as the great beauty of Constantinople. The much younger Constantine Monomachos followed her in 1055; the elderly Theodora, left alone on the throne, died in 1056. Before her death she declared that the throne should pass to her trusted minister Michael Bringas, a man who was not much younger than she, and who instantly was nicknamed "Michael Gerontas," or "Michael the Aged."

Meanwhile Togrul was closing his grip tightly around the Muslim lands to the south. The Buyid dynasty, much weaker than it had once been, still controlled Baghdad; in 1056, as Michael the Aged was ascending to the throne in Constantinople, Togrul marched into Baghdad and removed it firmly from Buyid control, driving the last Buyid rulers into exile. The Abbasid caliph still lived in Baghdad. He still retained some spiritual authority, although not a shred of political power, and Togrul made a deal with him. The caliph could remain peacefully in Baghdad as long as he agreed to recognize Togrul as supreme sultan, highest authority in the Muslim world, in the Friday prayers. Once, the mention of anyone other than the caliph or his heir in the Friday prayers had been tantamount to treachery. Now the caliph himself would pray for the sultan. In the Abbasid realm, the divorce between political and spiritual power was complete.

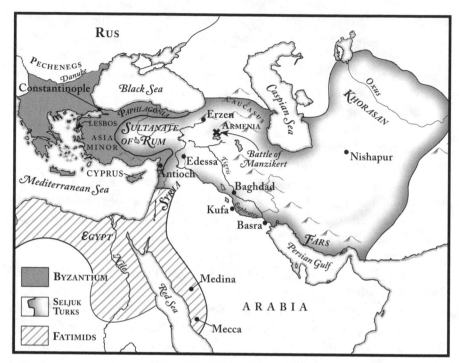

80.1: The Battle of Manzikert

Togrul's triumphs in the south made the Byzantine army nervous; Michael the Aged did not inspire confidence in them. In 1057, the soldiers in Constantinople proclaimed their own commander, Isaac Comnenus, as emperor in the old man's place. Michael the Aged offered to make him heir to the throne instead, but the people of Constantinople rioted, clamoring for Isaac. Michael VI had neither the energy nor the ambition to fight popular opinion. He abdicated peacefully and became a monk, dying two years later in his bed.

Constantinople celebrated the coronation of the new emperor. At last a soldier sat on the throne, a man who could drive back the Turkish advance. "All the populace of the city poured out to honour him," Psellus writes. "Some brought lighted torches, as though he were God Himself, while others sprinkled sweet perfumes over him. . . . There was dancing and rejoicing everywhere."[14]

Unfortunately their hopes were dashed. Isaac Comnenus had a short and unimpressive tenure as emperor. He almost immediately made himself unpopular at court by proposing massive government reforms, and then—before he could carry most of them out—he grew ill, probably with pneumonia, and died. In his place, the bureaucrat Constantine Doukas was crowned, and although Constantine Doukas managed to stay in power for eight years, he paid little attention to the Turkish advances in the east. Not until 1068 did Constantinople get another soldier on the throne: the general Romanos Diogenes, who was crowned as Romanos IV, senior co-emperor along with Constantine Doukas's sons.

Togrul, sultan of the Turks, had died of old age in 1063, leaving no sons. His nephew Alp Arslan (the name means "valiant lion") had inherited his power and now led the Turks. He had his eye on the Byzantine land in Asia Minor and Romanos, recognizing the danger of Turkish growth, finally organized a campaign against the eastern border. Driving forward against the Turks, he pushed into the land they had already taken. In 1070, in a series of hard-fought battles, he managed to drive them back across the Euphrates. His years of campaigning had taught him the best way to deal with the lightly armed, fast-moving Turkish cavalry: keep the army bunched together, not spread out into a line, with bowmen protecting the slow, heavily armed cavalry on all sides.[15]

Alp Arslan's retreat had been a strategic one, allowing him to regather his forces. In 1071, he advanced again into Byzantine territory, and Romanos marched out to meet him at the head of sixty thousand soldiers.

But this time Romanos IV suffered from a severe attack of overconfidence. He didn't know exactly where Alp Arslan and the bulk of his army had camped, and rather than holding his men together until he could get firm intelligence, he divided his army in half and sent thirty thousand men off to attack a nearby fortress. He marched with his remaining men to the city of Manzikert, right on the frontier between Byzantine and Turkish territory, and captured it.

All this time, Alp Arslan was just beyond Manzikert, keeping tabs on the emperor's movements. Three days after the capture of Manzikert, as Romanos IV advanced cautiously into Turkish territory, he met what appeared to be a band of Turkish raiders. He drew up his army in a single line to drive them back. They retreated in front of him; delighted with his victory, he led the Byzantine troops after them, pursuing them on into the late afternoon.

But the raiders were merely the front edge of Alp Arslan's massive force. As soon as the sun set, the Turks surrounded the strung-out army and massacred them in the twilight. "It was like an earthquake with howling, sweat, a swift rush of fear, clouds of dust," one of the survivors later wrote. "Each man sought safety in flight." Most of the Byzantine troops were caught and killed as they tried to escape; Romanos IV was captured and taken back to Alp Arslan's camp as a prisoner. The other thirty thousand soldiers disappeared from history; in all likelihood they too were ambushed and slaughtered.[16]

Alp Arslan, rubbing salt in the emperor's wounds, treated him with honor, fed him from the sultan's own table, and set him free—after extracting from him solemn vows of friendship and peace. Romanos, in a state of high embarrassment, began the journey back to Constantinople; just as the Battle of Manzikert had destroyed most of the Byzantine army, so the captivity and the oath had destroyed his reputation. Michael Psellus himself declared that Romanos's young co-emperors, the sons of Constantine Doukas, had no obligation to let the humiliated ruler back into the city. A handful of trusted men, including members of the Doukas family, set off to intercept Romanos on his way home. They captured him, blinded him, and left him in a monastery to die.[17]

Now the oldest son of Constantine Doukas, Michael VII, became senior emperor, an event marked by a second coronation in October 1071. But he ruled over a changed map. The sultan of the Seljuq Turks had established a new Turkish outpost in Asia Minor, in lands that had once been Byzantine: a vassal ruler, the sultan of Rum, presided over this new Turkish state. The Turks had rooted themselves into Asia Minor and intended to remain; the massacre of the army at Manzikert had made it impossible for the Byzantines to muster a force large enough to drive them out.

TIMELINE 80

EASTERN MUSLIM DYNASTIES	WESTERN MUSLIM DYNASTIES	CHRISTIAN SPAIN	BYZANTIUM BULGARIA	RUS TURKS
	Hisham II of Cordoba (976–1008) al-Mansur as vizier of Cordoba (978–1002)		**Basil II** (976–1025) **Romanus** of Bulgaria (977–991)	
				Vladimir of the Rus (980–1015)
al-Qadir of the Abbasids (991–1031)			Establishment of Varangian Guard (989)	
al-Hakim of the Fatimids (996–1021)		**Alfonso V** of Leon (999–1028)	**Samuel** of Bulgaria (997–1014)	
	al-Malik as vizier of Cordoba (1002–1008)			**Nasir Khan** of the Karakhanids (c. 998–1017)
	Sulayman II of Cordoba (1009/1012–1016) Baghdad Manifesto (1011) **al-Nasir** of Cordoba (1016–1018)			
		Sancho III (the Great) of Pamplona (1017–1035)		
az-Zahir of the Fatimids (1021–1036)				
			Constantine VIII (1025–1028) **Zoe** (1028–1050) **Romanos III** (1028–1034)	
	Rise of the *taifa* kingdoms (1031)			
		Ferdinand I of Leon and Castile (1037–1065)	**Michael the Paphlagonian** (1034–1041)	
				Togrul (1038–1063)
	al-Mu'tamid of Seville (1042–1069)		**Michael V** (1041–1042) **Constantine Monomachos** (1042–1055)	
			Theodora (1055–1056) **Michael Gerontas** (1056–1057) **Isaac Comnenus** (1057–1059) **Constantine X Doukas** (1059–1067)	Capture of Baghdad
	Abu-Bakr of the Almoravids (1061–1087)			**Alp Arslan** (1064–1072)
		Sancho II (the Strong) of Castile (1065–1072)		
			Romanos Diogenes (1068–1071) **Michael VII** (1071–1078)	Battle of Manzikert (1071)
		Alfonso VI (the Brave) of Castile and Leon (1072–1109)		
	Tashfin of the Almoravids (1087–1106)			
		Establishment of El Cid's kingdom at Valencia (1094–1102)		
	ibn Yusuf of the Almoravids (1106–1142)	**Alfonso the Battler** of Aragon-Navarre (1104–1134)		

Chapter Eighty-One

The Loss of the Song

Between 1032 and 1172,
the Jurchen sweep down from the north,
and the Song are driven from the Yellow river valley

THE SONG DYNASTY had not lost its fascination for those on the outside. In 1032, the strongest outsiders lived in the kingdom of the Western Xia, and they had their eyes fixed on the wealth and culture of the Song.

The Western Xia had been nomads who wandered up from the south. Between 982 and 1032, their great chief Li Deming had managed to organize the tribal confederation into a state. He had ambitions to educate his son, Li Yuanhao, into a true monarch. Just before his death in 1032, Li Deming sent seventy horses as a gift to Song Renzong, asking for a copy of the Buddhist scriptures so that he could complete Li Yuanhao's training.[1]

Apparently the Song emperor ignored the request, because in 1035 Li Yuanhao, now ruler of the Western Xia state, asked for the scriptures again. This time, his envoy returned with the books. The volumes of Buddhist teachings helped to support Li Yuanhao's efforts to become the emperor of a civilized nation rather than the warleader of a tribal confederation: to be a monarch as great as the ancient Chinese monarchs meant accepting the religion of the Chinese throne (even though the Buddhism held by the Song court did not stretch back nearly to the times of the semidivine Sage Emperors).

At Li Yuanhao's public enthronement, carried out once the Buddhist scriptures were in hand, his ministers declared him to be Sage of Culture and Hero of War, like the emperors of the distant Chinese past. The title has survived because Li Yuanhao had thrown his energies behind the creation of a script for his native Tangut language, a complicated system based on Chinese principles; using the new lines and strokes, his chronicler recorded the details of his coronation. Li Yuanhao knew that without books of their own, his people would have no past. Without a past, they could never claim to be equal to the Song.[2]

In 1038, he sent a letter to Song Renzong, demanding official Chinese recognition of his new status. The letter lists all of the reforms Li Yuanhao instituted in the Western Xia lands, including his creation of written language for the Tangut. It then gets to the point: "Now that the dress regulations have been completed," he writes, "the script put into effect, the rites and music made manifest, the vessels and implements prepared . . . I was enthroned as Shizu, Originator of Literature, Rooted in Might, Giver of Law, Founder of Ritual, Humane and Filial Emperor. My country is called Great Xia, and the reign era is called 'Heaven-Conferred Rites, Law, and Protracted Blessings.' I humbly look to Your Majesty the emperor, in your profound wisdom and perfection, whose benevolence extends to all things, to permit me to be invested as the 'ruler facing south' in this western land."[3]

The polite request covered over steely determination. Thirty years earlier, the Song emperor's father had been forced to recognize the Liao ruler as an emperor with status equal to himself, and now the Western Xia ruler wanted the same. Unlike the great dynasties of the past, the Song did not dominate the east. It was only one kingdom in a landscape of kingdoms; it was not notably more prosperous than its neighbors; but the Song emperor had something the northern and western kings did not. He had the sheen of millennia of tradition, and they wanted some of that gloss for themselves.

If he didn't yield it, they were ready to fight for it. Song Renzong declined to bestow the title of emperor on the western upstart, and in 1038, the Western Xia army invaded. Thirty years of peace had softened the Song border troops. One chronicler notes that less than half of the soldiers were still able to draw the heavy crossbows used in battle, and almost none of the officers or troops had combat experience.[4]

Between 1038 and 1042, the Western Xia overran the forts along the western frontier. Li Yuanhao advanced his men cautiously, not attempting to capture more of the difficult rocky terrain than he could defend. Slowly the western reaches of the Song were eaten away, and in 1042 the situation grew worse when the Liao to the north demanded another chunk of Song territory for themselves. Song Renzong offered to increase the annual tribute instead; this avoided a two-front war but drained the Song treasury even further.[5]

By 1044, he had decided to make peace. He still refused to recognize the Western Xia ruler as a real emperor, but he paid out yet more annual tribute to buy a truce. Li Yuanhao agreed to the compromise. Six years of fighting had stressed his own army, and even though he had failed to get the legitimization he craved, the money was an effective salve to his wounded personal pride.

The Song, meanwhile, had turned their attention back towards military matters. Apparently the war with the Western Xia had forced the Song generals to scramble for information; by 1044, the last year of the war, a band of scholars commissioned to put together a compendium on techniques of war had finished their work. The volume, *Wujing Zongyao*, describes a pump-powered flame-thrower that could hurl naphtha, the same "Greek fire" used by the defenders of Constantinople; it also explains how to make explosive black powder from coal, saltpeter, and sulfur, the first time in history that the formula for gunpowder appears in writing.

The purchased truce lasted for some time on both the northern and western borders, giving the Song time to rebuild their military might. Song Renzong raised taxes to pay for the tribute as well as a newly expanded national army. He also ordered new standards put into place for new army recruits. They would have to pass an eye exam, as well as tests in running, jumping, and shooting. This time, the temporary peace would be used to prepare for the next war.[6]

THE PEACE LASTED for almost fifty years. The Liao had earned official imperial recognition from the Song empire, along with cash payments; the Western Xia had received only the cash but had decided to be content.

And then another tribe, making the same journey from nomadic wanderings to settled empire, blew in from the north at the beginning of the twelfth century and swept down onto the settled kingdoms. They were the Jurchen, tribes who spoke a language distantly related to the Turkish tongues. They lived mostly on the wooded plains north of Goryeo, in the lands later called Manchuria; some of the western groups had come under the rule of Liao and were known as the "Civilized Jurchen," but the eastern bands were still free and wild. The Song and Liao courts called these the "Raw Jurchen," and they roamed beyond the control of either emperor.[7]

Late in the eleventh century, one of the eastern Jurchen clans, the Wanyan, began to conquer its Jurchen neighbors—the first clear step on the path to nationhood. Some of the Jurchen under attack fled south into Goryeo.

Since the days of its founder Wang Kon, the kingdom of Goryeo had declined to chase after the Song stamp of approval. It had fought its own border wars against the Liao, who made periodic attempts to expand into Goryeon territory, but a great border war in 1018 had shattered the Liao army, and since then the two countries had been more or less at peace. Until now, the nomadic Jurchen to the north had been more of an annoyance than a military threat: "The people of the northeast frontier frequently suffered from the Jurchen horsemen who came to invade and rob," remarks the contemporary chronicler Choe Seung-no. To keep them out, the eleventh-century kings of Goryeo built a Long Wall that stretched from the mouth of the Yalu river, over three hundred miles inland.[8]

The wall was effective against random wanderers, but it didn't stem the flood of refugees from other Jurchen tribes, fleeing from the ambitious Wanyan. When the Wanyan demanded that the refugees be returned, the Goryeon general Yun Kwan led a special army, "The Extraordinary Military Corps," north to fight against them.

Unlike the regular Goryeon army, which was largely made up of foot-soldiers, the Extraordinary Military Corps had a full division of cavalry, which was more effective against the mounted Jurchen. In 1107, the Extraordinary Military Corps pushed its way into Jurchen territory and built a series of defensive positions known as the Nine Forts in order to protect the northern territories.[9]

In 1115, the Wanyan clan of the Jurchen came under the rule of a younger brother named Akuta, and their fortunes began to change. Akuta realized the need for ceremonial kingship, for an established bureaucracy, for a history— for all the things that, time and time again, had turned wandering nomads into a settled state. Like every other aspiring king on the northern plain, he wanted the Song stamp of approval, but he was willing to work up to it. Instead he sent a message to the Liao emperor, demanding that the *Liao* extend the formal recognition that Akuta was a Great Holy and Enlightened Emperor. He wanted his clan to be known, from now on, by the Chinese name "Great Jin"; he intended to wear royal robes and ride in a jade-encrusted carriage, and (incidentally) he wanted the Liao to pay an annual tribute, almost as large as the tribute the Song paid to *them*.[10]

The Liao resisted, and the Jurchen attacked. With short-sighted enthusiasm, the Song emperor Huizong agreed to make an alliance *with* the Jurchen *against* the old northern Liao enemy. Song Huizong was not a military man; he had been on the throne since 1100 and spent much less time governing than he did building Taoist temples, endowing Taoist monasteries, and studying Taoist teachings.

In this he was encouraged by the flattery of a self-centered Taoist priest named Lin Lingsu, who assured the emperor that he was the incarnation of the supreme deity "Great Imperial Lord of Long Life." This convinced Huizong that he was indeed a Son of Heaven, possessor of the Divine Mandate; and he occupied his days with painting, poetry, tea ceremonies, and Taoist rituals.[11]

He was swayed into the alliance with the Jurchen when Akuta promised that after the joint conquest of the Liao, the Song could reclaim the southern reaches of the old Liao empire: this land had once been the Chinese "Sixteen Prefectures," and it had been in enemy hands for a century. Retaking the Prefectures would shore up the Divine Mandate with a real display of victory. So Huizong sent his army to help conquer the Liao, paying no mind to the expanding power of the Jurchen themselves. In 1122, the combined armies reached the Liao capital and took the emperor captive; the remains of the Liao army and a hundred thousand refugees fled west, away from the conquerors.[12]

But the Jurchen refused to hand over the Sixteen Prefectures. Akuta had died, and had been succeeded by his young brother, who took the Chinese name Jin Taizong; but probably neither brother had ever intended to follow through on the promise. Instead the Jurchen marched into Song territory, heading for the Song capital of Kaifeng.

Under Song Huizong's rule, the carefully built system of trained local militia had fallen to bits, and the Jurchen broke through the Song defenses with little difficulty. By the end of 1125 they had crossed the Yellow river and were in sight of the city.

Song Huizong, jolted out of his overconfidence, tried to escape from responsibility for the looming defeat by faking a stroke, abdicating, and ordering the royal robes placed on his heir, his twenty-five-year-old son, Qinzong. Qinzong refused to take on the thankless job; when the robes were draped on his shoulders, he pushed them off and told his father that to accept them would be disloyal and unfilial. Huizong, who was pretending that his right side was paralyzed, wrote a message with his left hand ordering his son to take up the Mandate. "He still strongly declined," says one account, so

> Huizong ordered the eunuchs to forcibly carry him to Blessed Tranquility Hall and put him on the throne. Qinzong was definitely unwilling to walk, so the eunuchs forcibly carried him. He struggled with them and passed out from holding his breath. After he recovered they resumed carrying him to the western chamber of Blessed Tranquillity Hall, where the grand councilors met and congratulated him.[13]

The Jurchen carried out their conquest of Kaifeng over several stages (demanding tribute, withdrawing, returning and demanding hostages, withdrawing), but by 1127 the game was over. The city was no longer able to hold out, and the Jurchen stormed its walls and began to steal treasure, food, animals, and women.

Song Qinzong, whose reign had not been one of courageous nobility, rounded up the daughters of the common people so that the Jurchen would rape them first, but the invaders soon broke into the houses of the nobility as well. The city was looted, burned, and then placed under enemy rule. Both Song Qinzong and his father were captured and taken, along with scores of other prisoners, back to the north. Huizong died in prison not long afterwards, but Qinzong lived for the next three decades in captivity.[14]

The Song era was over. Refugees from the Song court fled their city, taking with them Qinzong's younger half-brother Gaozong. They proclaimed him emperor in exile at Lin'an, far to the south. The Song had ended; the dynasty that would rule in the south for the next century was called the "Southern Song," but it was only a weak remnant of previous glories.*

Even worse, the northern land that now lay in Jurchen hands was the cradle of Chinese culture, the valley where the most honored of its divine kings

---

*The Song dynasty is sometimes known as the Northern Song, to differentiate it from the Southern Song. This can be misleading, since the "Northern Song" controlled both the northern and southern territories, so I have chosen to use simply "Song" for the dynasty that existed before 1127.

81.1: The Southern Song

had lived, the home of the great deeds that had made the ancient Chinese empire the envy of its nomadic neighbors. The poems of the Southern Song are filled with longing for the abandoned lands:

> I see their forts amid the forest when I gaze toward the Yellow River,
> The cloud of dust darkens the sky and the frost wind is bitter,
> The silence of the border region rends my heart,

wrote the poet Zhang Xiaoxiang.

> The beacon fires have been extinguished,
> the soldiers given rest . . .
> Yet I have heard that the old who were left behind in the central plains
> Constantly look toward the south
> Hoping to see the decorated imperial chariots.[15]

But the chariots never came. The Southern Song still claimed the Mandate of Heaven, but it had lost its physical connection to the place where the Mandate first descended. The history of the ancient emperors lay in the valley of the Yellow river; now that valley was in enemy hands.

TIMELINE 81

BYZANTIUM	RUS BULGARIA	TURKS	SONG CHINA	NORTH/WEST CHINA	GORYEO
Basil II (976–1025)	**Romanus** of Bulgaria (977–991)		Song Taizong (976–997)		
	Vladimir of the Rus (980–1015)		Song dynasty reunites China (979)		
				Li Deming of the Western Xia (982–1032)	**Liao Shengzong** of the Liao (982–1031)
Establishment of Varangian Guard (989)					
	Samuel of Bulgaria (997–1014)		Song Zhenzong (997–1022)		
		Nasir Khan of the Karakhanids (c. 998–1017)			
			Treaty of Chanyuan (1005)		
			Song Renzong (1022–1063)		
Constantine VIII (1025–1028) **Zoe** (1028–1050) **Romanos III** (1028–1034)					
Michael the Paphlagonian (1034–1041)				**Li Yuanhao** of the Western Xia (1032–1048)	
		Togrul (1038–1063)			
Michael V (1041–1042) **Constantine Monomachos** (1042–1055)			Truce with Western Xia		
Theodora (1055–1056) **Michael Gerontas** (1056–1057) **Isaac Comnenus** (1057–1059)					
Constantine X Doukas (1059–1067)		Capture of Baghdad			
		Alp Arslan (1064–1072)			
Romanos Diogenes (1068–1071)					
Michael VII (1071–1078)		Battle of Manzikert (1071)	Song Huizong (1100–1126) Extraordinary Military Corps invades Jurchen territory (1107)		
			Akuta of the Wanyan (1115–1123)		
			Fall of Liao (1122) **Jin Taizong** (1123–1134) Song Qinzong (1126–1127) Song Gaozong (1127–1162) Beginning of Southern Song		

— • —

Chapter Eighty-Two

Repentance at Canossa

Between 1060 and 1076,
Henry IV refuses to obey the pope,
gets himself excommunicated,
and is forced to stand barefoot in the snow pleading for mercy

IN 1060, THE CAPETIAN KING of Western Francia died and left his crown to his seven-year-old son Philip, a child incapable of halting the tide of private warfare that still surged back and forth across the Frankish lands. "Woe to thee, O land, when thy king is a child," contemporary chroniclers wrote, using the words of the book of Ecclesiastes to lament the disorder in the old Frankish lands.[1]

In Germany, another underage king ruled: Henry IV, now ten years old. His mother, who would rather have been a nun than the queen and regent for her son, avoided trouble with the noblemen of Germany by granting them power, and they ruled over their little independent duchies with the prickly defensiveness of minor kings. Right after Easter of 1062, the German archbishop Anno II, with the support of two powerful German counts, invited the young king to come and inspect a ship that had been outfitted particularly for his use. As soon as Henry stepped on board, the oarsmen cast off and whisked him away down the Rhine. The king had been kidnapped.

Twelve-year-old Henry dove into the river in an attempt to escape, but the water was cold and swift, and he nearly drowned before one of the conspirators dragged him back out. They took him to the city of Cologne, imprisoned him (safely and in luxury) in Anno's palatial archbishop's residence, and took over the rule of Germany.[2]

For three years, until Henry IV turned fifteen and could promise royal aid and support to anyone who might help him get his independence back, the archbishop and his henchmen struggled with each other for control of the country and of the king. Henry watched, waiting for his majority, becoming stronger, more mature, and more ruthless as the months ticked by.

No overarching rule of law could settle the wars between the Christian and Muslim armies farther east, but here, there was one institution that could appeal to all of the battling ambitious parties laying waste to the countryside. Despite the political meddling of a few of its more ambitious officials, the Christian church still preached its message of Christian brotherhood and loyalty to a kingdom not of the earth; the Christian church still claimed the allegiance of all kings and soldiers in the west.

In 1063, priests in the northern German city of Terouanne put together another set of regulations for the Peace and Truce of God. "These are the conditions which you must observe during the time of the peace which is commonly called the truce of God," the document began, "which begins with sunset on Wednesday and lasts until sunrise on Monday. During those four days and five nights no man or woman shall assault, wound, or slay another, or attack, seize, or destroy a castle, burg, or villa, by craft or by violence."[3]

Furthermore, the Peace would be observed during every day of Advent and Lent, as well as between the church feasts of Ascension and Pentecost—a schedule that made nearly three-quarters of the year off-limits for fighting. This was a lovely idea, but impractical, not to mention almost impossible to enforce. Still, the Peace of Terouanne brought into clearer view a growing tension in the kingdoms of the west: between the ideals of the kingdom of God and the kingdom of men, between the power of priests to enforce Christian behavior and the power of kings and warriors to do as they pleased.

It was a tension that became fully visible when Henry IV tired of his wife.

He had been betrothed, at the age of five, to the four-year-old Bertha of Turin, daughter of a prominent Italian nobleman. The marriage was celebrated when Henry IV turned fifteen, against Henry's own objections; he had never liked his intended wife, who seems to have been attractive enough but too shy and demure to appeal to the forceful adolescent Henry had become. Still, when Henry's advisors warned him that he might cause irreparable offense and damage to his prospects in Italy by cancelling the wedding, the king decided to go ahead.[4]

By 1069, he had concluded that his marriage was a mistake. He announced that he intended to seek a divorce from Bertha because he was simply unable to consummate the marriage. In an act of slightly overdue gallantry, he added that she was in no way at fault—which didn't ease her humiliation, but at least protected her from accusations of adultery.

The churchmen of Germany, putting their heads together, decided that this was too complicated a problem for them to rule on, and sent the request to Rome. There, Pope Alexander II absolutely refused to release Henry IV from his vows. "One who betrays the Christian faith by setting so pestilential an example," he sent back, by way of a special papal messenger, "will never be consecrated emperor."[5] The church of Rome had transferred its expectations of protection from the German king to the Normans of Italy, but the pope did not intend to give up his right to choose the next Holy Roman Emperor.

Henry IV, only eighteen, backed down. He withdrew his request for a divorce, and in the next years Bertha bore him a son and a daughter. But the sting of public reproof lingered; and Henry, who had been trained by a turbulent adolescence to be aggressive and uncompromising in demanding his own rights, did not forget that his will had been crossed.

In 1073, Alexander II died and the College of Cardinals elected a brilliant and severe archdeacon to replace him: Gregory VII, who came to the papacy determined to protect it from corruption and from reliance on swords and kings. He was deeply, irrevocably opposed to the idea that a layman, no matter how royal, could appoint any church official. That, he argued, was an act that would inevitably lead to corruption, to the sale of church offices, and to the domination of the emperor over St. Peter's heir. His view of his own God-given authority is laid starkly out in twenty-seven statements he put down on paper in March of 1075. The pope alone, he wrote, could appoint and remove bishops, call church councils, and authorize new church laws. The church of Rome had "never erred, and never will err till the end of time," and as its leader, the pope also had the right to depose emperors: "All princes," he concluded, "should kiss his feet."[6]

This was not an attractive idea to Henry IV, but since the beginning of Gregory VII's tenure, Henry had been preoccupied with putting down a serious rebellion in the duchy of Saxony. By the autumn of 1075, he had managed to temporarily suppress the revolt. This gave him time to consider Gregory's increasing power in Italy, which he reacted to in deed rather than word: he appointed new bishops to the bishoprics of Milan, Fermo, and Spoleto, taking for himself the exact authority that Gregory had claimed in his *Dictatus papae*.[7]

Gregory's reaction was measured and careful, and shows at least some hope that Henry IV would reconsider. In late December of 1075, he wrote the king a letter, offering to approve the royally chosen bishop of Milan and suggesting a roundabout and face-saving way for Henry IV to acknowledge his spiritual authority: the king should send away from his German court five of his advisors who had been excommunicated for their involvement in selling church offices. Faithful members of the Christian church were not supposed to associate with unrepentant sinners who had been excommunicated; Henry's willingness to exile these men would acknowledge that Gregory was still his spiritual father.[8]

A later account, written by Gregory himself, says that the pope sent this restrained letter by way of three papal envoys who were given the job of

82.1: *Penitential Journey of Henry IV*

delivering a much stronger verbal message. These men "secretly admonished him to do penance for his sins" and threatened that if he did not yield to the authority of the divine laws, "he should not only be excommunicated until he had made due satisfaction, but that he should also be deprived of his entire dignity as king without hope of recovery."[9]

Henry IV did not react well to threats, even private ones. In response, he summoned the excommunicated advisors and, on their counsel, convened an assembly of his court, several of the most powerful German princes, and two-thirds of the German bishops. The council met in the city of Worms in January of 1076, less than a month after Gregory VII's warning, and under Henry's direction agreed that two different letters should be written over the king's signature. One, sent to Rome, accused Gregory VII of seizing the papacy without due election, trampling on the rights of the bishops, and (as an extra touch) seducing an Italian noblewoman named Matilda. "Your accession was vitiated by gross perjuries," the letter read, "the church of God is exposed to the peril of severe storms by your misdeeds . . . you have besmirched your life and conduct by manifold disgrace. Accordingly, we renounce an obedience that we never promised you and will never show you."[10]

The second letter was longer, even more tabloid-like in its details, and circulated through Germany as a bit of royal propaganda justifying Henry's defiance of the pope. "Henry, king by the grace of God, to Hildebrand," the letter began, using Gregory VII's birth name and refusing to address him by the official name he had taken when he became pope:

> By your evil scheming you have sought to prise away from me the Italian kingdom. . . . You dared to rise up against me, the head, putting upon record what you very well know: to use your own words, that either you would die or else you would strip me of my soul and of my kingdom. . . . Every right to the papacy that you seem to have, I deny you; from the bishopric of the city whose patriciate is rightly mine by God's gift and by the sworn agreement of the Romans, I say—step down![11]

Gregory received the letter intended for Rome in mid-February of 1076. He and Henry IV were alike in one thing: he too disliked threats. On February 22, he announced that by the authority of St. Peter himself, the king was no longer part of the Christian church—an act with serious implications for Henry's secular power. "I absolve all Christians from the bond of any oath that they have made or shall make to him," he announced, "and I forbid anyone to serve him as king."[12]

Henry IV had overplayed his hand. With this official permission, the noblemen of Saxony—who had just barely been beaten into submission when the argument between king and pope broke out—once more rebelled. This time Henry IV was unable to overcome them. Many of the German aristocrats who had supported him in the last revolt were too nervous over Gregory VII's declaration to throw their weight behind the king this time around. By October of 1076, Henry IV could see that two choices lay in front of him: he could make amends with Gregory VII, or suffer through years of civil war which might well end in his forced removal from the throne.

The king chose immediate embarrassment over long-drawn-out humiliation. He collected his household, his wife Bertha, and his two-year-old son and heir Conrad, and with them began a penitential journey south through the Alps. The weather in the mountains crashed in on them: it was January, according to some chroniclers the worst winter in a hundred years, and the paths were covered with ice and snow. "Sometimes they crawled forwards on hands and feet," one account tells us, "sometimes they supported themselves on their guides, and sometimes, when they slipped on the icy ground, they fell a good way. . . . The horses were lowered with special machinery, or else dragged along with their legs tied together. In spite of this many were killed on the descent."[13]

Gregory VII, getting wind of the king's approach, thought that he was coming with an army and retreated to the fortress of Canossa, which had three walls around it. But when Henry IV appeared, it was as a penitent begging forgiveness. Gregory's own letter describing the king's approach says that he was barefoot, wearing sackcloth, and weeping, and that his self-humiliation moved everyone in the fortress: "He provoked all who were . . . there . . . to such great mercy and pitying compassion, that they interceded for him with many pleadings and tears," the pope wrote. "Indeed, some complained that we were showing, not the strictness of apostolic authority, but a cruelty that was reminiscent of a tyrant's inhumanity."[14]

Forced to forgive Henry IV as much by public pressure as by his own inclinations, Gregory VII agreed to restore the king's good standing. In return, Henry promised to recognize the pope's authority and to give up the practice of appointing his own bishops. A great reconciliation banquet followed. Henry sat at the table, silent and withdrawn, refusing to eat and drumming on the table with his fingers.[15]

He had managed to keep his crown, but his decision to repent had made one thing perfectly clear to the entire western world: when earthly and spiritual rulers clashed, earthly authority was the first to buckle.

TIMELINE 82

SONG CHINA	NORTH/WEST CHINA	GORYEO	WESTERN FRANCIA	GERMANY	ITALY	Roman Emperor
				Henry II (1002–1024)		
Treaty of Chanyuan (1005)						
					Pope Benedict VIII (1012–1024)	
						Henry II (1014–1024)
Song Renzong (1022–1063)				**Conrad II** (1024–1039)	Pope John XIX (1024–1032)	
						Conrad II (1027–1039)
	Li Yuanhao of the Western Xia (1032–1048)				Pope Benedict IX (1032–1045/1048)	
				Henry III (1039–1056)		
Truce with Western Xia						
					Pope Sylvester III (1045–1046)/ Pope Gregory VI (1045–1046) Pope Clement II (1046–1047)	
						Henry III (1046–1056)
					Pope Leo IV (1049–1054)	
					"Great Schism" of eastern and western churches (1054)	
				Henry IV (1056–1106)		
					Pope Nicholas II (1059–1061)	
			Philip (1060–1108)			
					Pope Alexander II (1061–1073) Pope Gregory VII (1073–1085)	
					Excommunication of Henry IV (1076)	
Song Huizong (1100–1126) Extraordinary Military Corps invades Jurchen territory (1107)						
Akuta of the Wanyan (1115–1123)						
Fall of Liao (1122) **Jin Taizong** (1123–1134) **Song Qinzong** (1126–1127) **Song Gaozong** (1127–1162) Beginning of Southern Song						

—

Chapter Eighty-Three

The Call

Between 1071 and 1095,
the Turks take Jerusalem away from the Fatimids of Egypt,
Henry IV forces the pope to crown him Holy Roman Emperor,
the emperor Alexius asks for help driving back the Turks,
and Pope Urban II summons a crusade

THE EMPEROR OF CONSTANTINOPLE was facing a combination of Turkish attack and domestic revolt—both less theologically complicated than Henry IV's problems, but equally damaging to royal power.

Romanos IV's defeat at the Battle of Manzikert was matched, in the same year, by defeats in Italy. In 1071, while the Byzantine armies struggled in Asia Minor, Robert Guiscard and his Normans had conquered the last Byzantine strongholds in Italy. The empire of Constantinople now lay up against the Black Sea, pushed into smaller and smaller territory by the expanding kingdoms of the west and the swelling Turkish power in the east.

The new senior emperor Michael VII was bookish and self-absorbed and paid little attention. "Nothing pleased him more than reading books," writes his tutor Michael Psellus with approval, but other chroniclers were less impressed: "While he spent his time on the useless pursuit of eloquence and wasted his energy on the composition of iambic and anapaestic verse (and they were very poor efforts indeed)," scoffed John Skylitzes, "he brought his empire to ruin." In 1074, Michael VII's uncle John Doukas led a rebellion against him; it was only quelled when Michael's general Alexius Comnenus hired soldiers from the Seljuq Turks to beef up the sparse troops still loyal to the crowned emperor.[1]

This required Byzantium to come to some sort of treaty with the Turks—which was a dangerous act indeed.

In 1073, Alp Arslan had been murdered by a prisoner he was interrogating, and his rule over the Turks went to his son Malik Shah. Malik Shah, only eighteen, began his sultanate with Ghaznavids strong on his east, the sultan of

Rum chafing for independence to the west, and Fatimid power reviving itself to the south. After losing the north of Syria to the Turks in 1070, the Fatimid caliphate in Egypt—which had been badly weakened by a six-year famine and mismanagement—had slowly begun to revive itself under the leadership of a general named Badr al-Jamali, who took control of the government in the name of the caliph and imposed a military dictatorship.[2]

Malik Shah fought hard to keep the Seljuq sultanate strong, and in most ways was triumphant. Necessity had forced Constantinople to suspend hostilities against the Turks; now Malik Shah threatened and tamed the sultan of Rum into temporary loyalty and reinforced the Ghaznavid border. Turkish armies, under the command of the general Atsiz ibn Abaq, pushed south all the way to Jerusalem, which up until now had been in the hands of the Fatimids of Egypt.

Atsiz and his soldiers laid siege to Jerusalem and forced the Fatimid defenders to surrender in 1073. Fatimid resistance in the city continued until 1077, but in that year Atsiz grew exasperated and massacred three thousand of its inhabitants—mostly Fatimid Arabs and Jews. This brought a final end to the Fatimid attempts to hold onto the city. It was now firmly under Malik Shah's overlordship.[3]

In Constantinople, Michael VII was less successful. The army in Asia Minor grew exasperated with his weakness and proclaimed their general Nikephoros Botaneiates emperor at the city of Nicaea. Nikephoros marched towards Constantinople, and Michael VII, realizing that he could not muster enough support to resist the army, promptly abdicated and entered a monastery. He left his wife, Maria, behind, and when Nikephoros Botaneiates arrived in the city, he married Maria and was crowned emperor as Nikephoros III.[4]

This brought only more trouble, and it was trouble that stretched all the way west to Italy.

Before his abdication, Michael VII had promised his four-year-old son, Constantine, in marriage to the daughter of the Norman adventurer Robert Guiscard, also known as Robert the Fox. This had been a desperate attempt by Michael VII to keep Guiscard from sailing east and attacking more Byzantine land after he had finished capturing the Byzantine territory in Italy. At the same time, Michael VII had put a large army under the command of his general Alexius Comnenus (the same general who had defeated his uncle John Doukas on his behalf) to prepare for a possible Norman invasion.

Now, against the wishes of his new wife, Nikephoros III disinherited her son and broke the betrothal to Guiscard's daughter. Guiscard immediately began to gear up for a massive invasion in revenge, while the empress Maria—distraught over her son's removal from the succession—appealed to the general Alexius to come and restore the little boy's rights.

Alexius Comnenus was at this point a vigorous soldier of thirty, the most powerful man in the empire, and Nikephoros III, decades older, had counted on his support. When Alexius instead accepted Maria's invitation and turned towards Constantinople, Nikephoros imitated his predecessor: he abdicated as soon as possible and got himself to a monastery before Alexius could enter the city with his soldiers. In 1081, Alexius was crowned emperor of Constantinople; less than a year later, Nikephoros died of old age in his monastery bed.

Alexius Comnenus kept faith with Maria and restored Constantine's position as co-emperor; but, ignoring Robert Guiscard's threats, he did not restore the Norman betrothal. Instead, he engaged his own young daughter Anna to the little boy, ensuring the succession for both Constantine and the Comnenus family.

This began a two-year war between the Normans of Italy, under Robert Guiscard's command, and the Byzantine army. "It was love of power that inspired Robert and never let him rest," wrote Alexius's daughter Anna, who served as her father's biographer. Anna is hardly an impartial witness, but there is no question that Guiscard hoped to add all of Byzantium to his empire. When he arrived at the Byzantine border, he had with him a monk who claimed to be the deposed Michael VII.

In Constantinople, it was widely believed that the man was an imposter, but Guiscard's attacks continued. "Alexius knew that the Empire was almost at its last gasp," Anna tells us. "The east was being horribly ravaged by the Turks; the west was in a bad condition, while Robert strained every nerve to put on the throne the pseudo-Michael who had taken refuge with him." Alexius was an intelligent commander, but the Norman army was stronger; it pushed steadily forward into Byzantine territory. At the same time, Malik Shah was threatening to invade from the other side.[5]

Alexius needed help, and he turned to Henry IV of Germany.

Henry IV had spent the years between 1077 and 1081 putting down another revolt in Saxony. The duke of Swabia, Rudolf, had managed to get himself declared rival king by the German aristocrats in Saxony and Bavaria. Three years of civil war between king and anti-king had followed.

At first, Pope Gregory VII had announced his neutrality in the fight, but by 1080, Gregory VII had decided that Rudolf would be a better German king, much more likely to yield ultimate control of the church to the pope. At the celebration of Easter, he again excommunicated Henry IV and announced that Rudolf was the rightful king of Germany.[6]

This decision was so clearly political in nature that most of the German bishops—even those who had sided with the pope during the last clash with Henry IV—rejected the excommunication as unlawful. So did a number of the Italian bishops. In May of 1080, right after the Easter excommunication,

Henry IV called his own synod. The loyal bishops called on Gregory VII to step down and elected the Italian archbishop Wibert of Ravenna to be pope in his place.

Henry IV planned to march down to Rome and install Wibert in St. Peter's seat by force, but first he had to finish the civil war in his own kingdom. On October 14, his army was defeated by the rebels in Saxony; but in the fighting Rudolf was severely wounded, his right hand cut off. Two days later he died from his injuries, and the revolt against Henry IV fell apart.[7]

Henry spent a few more months mopping up the resistance—months that Robert Guiscard spent ravaging the Byzantine countryside. Desperate to rid himself of the Normans so that he could turn around and deal with the Turks, Alexius sent messengers to Henry IV, requesting him to move his army into Italy sooner rather than later; Henry's invasion would force Robert to go back home and defend his Italian territory. "Although in other respects my affairs go well," the emperor wrote to the German king, "to a very small degree they are in disarray and confusion because of the actions of Robert." The casual wording was belied by the rest of the message: Alexius offered Henry IV the massive sum of 360,000 gold pieces to support the Italian campaign.[8]

Henry IV accepted, and in March of 1081 crossed over into Italy. Between 1081 and 1082 he attacked Rome three times, failing to breach the walls but coming closer and closer to conquest each time. Gregory VII sent desperate appeals to Robert Guiscard, over in Byzantium, but Guiscard was reluctant to abandon his invasion.

In his absence, Henry IV finally broke into the city of St. Peter. He entered Rome in June of 1083; Gregory VII walled himself up in a fortress on the west bank of the Tiber with his remaining supporters. For nearly a year, Henry IV worked to earn the loyalty of the Roman people, distributing gold liberally and slowly winning Gregory's followers over to his side. By March of 1084, he was able to convince the Roman priests to support him in deposing Gregory. On Palm Sunday, March 24, Wibert was proclaimed the new pope; a week later, on Easter Sunday, he crowned Henry IV as Holy Roman Emperor.* Henry was thirty-four years old and had spent nearly twenty years working towards this moment.[9]

Now Robert Guiscard finally and reluctantly returned to Italy, leaving his son Bohemund in charge of the Byzantine war. Henry IV heard of his approach and decided not to fight him. He and Wibert of Ravenna left Rome on May 21, three days before Guiscard's arrival.

Guiscard marched into the city as a deliverer, and was instead forced to

---

*Wibert took the papal name "Clement III," but is generally referred to as Antipope Clement III, since the later pope Paulino Scolari also took the name "Clement III" (1187–1191).

put down an immediate rebellion against his return, which he did with a fair amount of savagery. This restored the city to his control, but it made him so hated that he decided to retreat to the Norman lands in Italy, taking Gregory VII with him. The pope never returned to Rome; he died in 1085, on his deathbed absolving everyone he had excommunicated during his lifetime, "except Henry the so-called king and the archbishop of Ravenna."[10]

Robert Guiscard, preparing to sail back to Byzantium (his son Bohemund had immediately started losing battles), died from a fever two months later. He was seventy years old and left behind a reputation for conquest that lasted for centuries. Two hundred years later, the poet Dante placed him in the sphere of Mars along with Charlemagne and other great commanders, and wrote of the Byzantine soldiers who

> felt the thrust of painful blows
> when they fought hard against Robert Guiscard . . .
>   whose bones are still piled up
> at Ceperano.[11]

With Guiscard's death, the serious threat to the western borders of Byzantium came to an end.

But the Turkish threat to the east continued. Malik Shah's armies conquered Antioch, removing it from Byzantine control, and then pushed steadily into Asia Minor. As the Turks spread into Muslim land, they gradually adopted Islam; in the last years of his reign Malik Shah converted to the Shi'ite branch of the faith, the final step in making the Turks into a Muslim people.[12]

His death in 1092 did not bring an end to the Turkish threat, but it changed the Turkish alliance into a series of independent states. He left behind four sons and an ambitious brother, and as they fought over Malik Shah's domain, they fractured it into pieces. The Sultanate of Rum broke free under Malik Shah's former vassal, Kilij Arslan; Syria, Persia, Kirman (southern Persia), and Khorasan all separated from each other, each declaring itself a sovereign Turkish realm.

Seeing the opportunity to get back some of his conquered land in Asia Minor, Alexius Comnenus sent another message west, seeking more help for Byzantium. His old ally Henry IV was having difficulties: he was still king of Germany and Holy Roman Emperor, but the Lombards of northern Italy had rebelled against him, perhaps resenting the constant war Henry's feud with the pope had inflicted on them. Henry IV's declining power in Italy meant that his handpicked pope, Wibert of Ravenna, had also suffered from loss of authority; a new pope, Urban II, had been elevated in Rome in 1088.

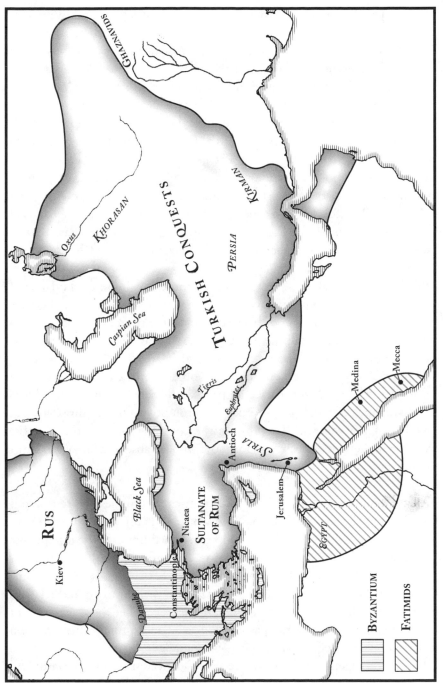

83.1: Turkish Conquests

Henry IV had no energy to spare for Constantinople, and Wibert of Ravenna had no power, so Alexius sent his envoys to Urban II instead. They asked the pope to send Italian soldiers east to help Alexius push back the Turkish invasion. This was a relatively simple request—Alexius needed mercenaries—but Urban II transformed it into something new.

He was on a tour through Italy and Western Francia, designed to demonstrate that the pope's authority—unlike the fractured authority of his predecessors—once again covered all of the Christian world.[13] Now he would demonstrate that the authority of St. Peter's heir stretched across the world.

In November of 1095, at Clermont in Western Francia, Urban II announced that it was not only time to help Byzantium in its battles against the Turks (as Alexius had asked), but also time to recapture Jerusalem from the hands of Muslims (something Alexius had not mentioned). "As most of you have heard," he announced, according to the Frankish chronicler Fulcher of Chartres,

> the Turks and Arabs . . . have occupied more and more of the lands of those Christians, and have overcome them in seven battles. They have killed and captured many, and have destroyed the churches and devastated the empire. If you permit them to continue thus for awhile with impurity, the faithful of God will be much more widely attacked by them. On this account I, or rather the Lord, beseech you as Christ's heralds to publish this everywhere and to persuade all people of whatever rank, foot-soldiers and knights, poor and rich, to carry aid promptly to those Christians and to destroy that vile race from the lands of our friends. I say this to those who are present, it is meant also for those who are absent. Moreover, Christ commands it.

All the Frankish noblemen who had been chafing under the restrictions of the Peace and Truce of God could now have something useful to do with their energy. "Let those who have been accustomed unjustly to wage private warfare against the faithful now go against the infidels," Urban II told his audience. "Let those who for a long time have been robbers, now become knights. Let those who have been fighting against their brothers and relatives now fight in a proper way against the barbarians. . . . Let those who go not put off the journey. . . . As soon as winter is over and spring comes, let them eagerly set out on the way with God as their guide."

Those who eagerly set out would receive the greatest possible reward: "All who die by the way, whether by land or by sea, or in battle against the pagans, shall have immediate remission of sins," Urban promised.[14] After the struggles of the last decades, Peter's heir had finally reasserted his authority—not only over the earthly world, but over the afterlife as well.

TIMELINE 83

WESTERN FRANCIA	GERMANY	ITALY	Roman Emperor	BYZANTIUM	TURKS
	Conrad II (1024–1039)	Pope John XIX (1024–1032)		Constantine VIII (1025–1028)	
			Conrad II (1027–1039)	Zoe (1028–1050) Romanos III (1028–1034)	
		Pope Benedict IX (1032–1045/1048)		Michael the Paphlagonian (1034–1041)	
					Togrul (1038–1063)
	Henry III (1039–1056)			Michael V (1041–1042) Constantine Monomachos (1042–1055)	
		Pope Sylvester III (1045–1046)/ Pope Gregory VI (1045–1046) Pope Clement II (1046–1047)			
			Henry III (1046–1056)		
		Pope Leo IV (1049–1054)			
		"Great Schism" of eastern and western churches (1054)			
	Henry IV (1056–1106)			Theodora (1055–1056) Michael Gerontas (1056–1057) Isaac Comnenus (1057–1059)	
		Pope Nicholas II (1059–1061)		Constantine X Doukas (1059–1067)	
Philip (1060–1108)					
		Pope Alexander II (1061–1073)			
					Alp Arslan (1064–1072)
				Romanos Diogenes (1068–1071) Michael VII (1071–1078)	Battle of Manzikert (1071)
					Malik Shah (1072–1092)
		Pope Gregory VII (1073–1084/1085) Excommunication of Henry IV (1076) Second excommunication of Henry IV (1080) Wibert of Ravenna (1080/1085–1100) Henry IV's conquest of Rome (1083)			Conquest of Jerusalem (1077)
				Nikephoros III (1078–1081) Alexius Comnenus (1081–1118)	
			Henry IV (1084–1106)		
		Pope Urban II (1088–1099)			
					Turkish empire fractures (1092) Kilij Arslan of Rum (1092–1107)
		Urban II summons the First Crusade (1095)			

Eighty-Four

Fighting for Jerusalem

Between 1095 and 1099,
Christian warriors from the west
set out on the First Crusade

"As soon as winter is over and spring is come," Pope Urban had told his audience; so in the cold months of late 1095 and early 1096, the quarrelsome aristocracy began to prepare for the journey east. The hope of heaven inspired many, but the chance to earn renown propelled others: "The first to sell his land and set out on the road to Jerusalem was Godfrey," writes Anna Comnena, "a very rich man, extremely proud of his noble birth, his own courage, and the glory of his family."[1]

Godfrey was a German nobleman, the duke of lower Lorraine. He was accompanied on crusade by his brothers Baldwin and Eustace, and the three siblings were followed in rapid succession by Robert Guiscard's son Bohemund, who left his father's Norman lands in Italy to answer the call with a smaller army; the Frankish duke Raymond of Toulouse, who brought ten thousand men with him; and Robert, the duke of Normandy. Robert, oldest son of William the Conqueror, had inherited Normandy at his father's death in 1087, while his younger brother William had become the second Norman king of England.

Scores of others travelled towards Constantinople, discrete bands of armed men all converging on a single point. The first to arrive, according to the twelfth-century account of William of Tyre, was Walter the Penniless, who (as his name suggests) was a Frankish nobleman too poor to hire a large army for himself. He was travelling through the old kingdom of Bulgaria in the early summer of 1096 when his small band of men, unpaid and starving, began to steal from the villages they passed. The Bulgarians retaliated by driving some of the robbers into a nearby church and setting it on fire. It was an unfortunate start to the first Crusade.[2]

Walter the Penniless arrived at Constantinople in mid-July with his remaining men and was given lodging by the emperor Alexius while they waited for the more prosperous dukes and their larger armies to arrive. But Raymond of

Toulouse and the others were still well behind them. The next army to arrive at Constantinople was a force of some thousands (contemporary accounts say forty thousand men or more, but are probably exaggerated) led by a cleric nicknamed "Peter the Little." On an earlier pilgrimage to Jerusalem, Peter had suffered "much ill-treatment at the hands of the Turks." He had returned to preach across the Frankish countryside that "all should depart from their homes [and] strive to liberate Jerusalem," and when Urban II had pronounced exactly the same message, Peter the Little had been delirious with joy.[3]

Later chroniclers would call Peter's army the "People's Crusade," as though it were made up of farmers and housewives. In fact, it had a full complement of soldiers; it just lacked high-profile aristocrats, who preferred to lead their own private armies. Peter and his troops arrived at Constantinople around August 1 and were welcomed in turn by the emperor, who then suggested that they move on across the Bosphorus Strait and camp near the Byzantine frontier while they awaited the rest of the crusader armies. Alexius was not anxious to add thousands of restless armed men to the population of Constantinople.[4]

The two forces, waiting in temporary quarters about twenty-five miles from the Turkish-held city of Nicaea, were soon joined by other random arrivals—bands of soldiers without experienced, forceful leadership. Bored crusaders, meeting no serious opposition, raided the Turkish countryside, and the mood of the camp shifted towards aggression. Before long, the entire leaderless force marched out and headed for Nicaea.

The sultan of Rum, Kilij Arslan, sent a detachment of his army out to swat the flies. "Of the twenty-five thousand foot soldiers and five hundred knights who had gone forth from the camp," writes William of Tyre, "there remained scarcely one who escaped either death or capture." Walter the Penniless was killed; Peter the Little escaped across the strait and begged the emperor for help. Alexius sent a Byzantine detachment back across the water, and the Turkish army, which was marching towards the camp to annihilate the rest of the ill-organized crusader force, sloped off and went back home.[5]

At this point Alexius was probably wondering what he had gotten himself into, but the arrival of the disciplined private armies of Bohemund, Raymond, and the others throughout the winter of 1096–1097 reassured him. However, the emperor had gotten a taste of the headstrong crusader mindset. He took precautions; as each duke arrived, Alexius asked him to swear an oath that "whatever cities, countries or forts he might in future subdue, which had in the first place belonged to the Roman Empire, he would hand over to the officer appointed by the emperor." This First Crusade, Alexius reminded them, was to be fought for the benefit of Byzantium, not for personal gain.[6]

In the spring of 1097, the united crusader forces poured across the straits into the Sultanate of Rum. They laid siege to Nicaea in mid-May and forced the city's surrender before the end of June. Accompanied by Byzantine troops under the command of Alexius's trusted general Taticius, the crusader army then marched southwards, towards the city of Jerusalem. One at a time, the Turkish-held cities fell to them: Smyrna, Ephesus, Philadelphia, Sardis.

The victories came to an abrupt halt at the city of Antioch.

With Godfrey, Bohemund, and Raymond of Toulouse in the lead, the crusaders laid siege to the city on October 21. Antioch was the strongest city in Syria; its ancient walls touched the Orontes river, allowing the defenders a constant supply of water and an easy way to resupply the city with food and arms; and the crusaders, although victorious, were weary from months of fighting. Most of them had never seen Antioch before, and they were unpleasantly startled by the city's defenses: "We found the city of Antioch very extensive," the Frankish nobleman Stephen of Blois wrote to his wife, "fortified with incredible strength and almost impregnable."

The siege dragged on and the nights began to grow colder. By December, the army had stripped the surrounding countryside bare of food and fuel. Provisions dwindled away. A party sent out to forage for food farther away encountered a Turkish detachment, which drove them back empty-handed. The horses, unaccustomed to such poor rations, were dying off; by January, fewer than two thousand mounts were left of the seventy thousand that had started off from Nicaea. "Day by day, the famine grew," writes William of Tyre. "In addition, the pavilions and tents in the camp had rotted. Thus, many who still had food perished because they could not endure the rigorous cold without protection. Floods of water fell in torrents so that both food and garments moulded and there was not a dry place where the pilgrims might lay their heads. . . . Pestilence broke out among the legions in the camp, so fatal that now there was scarcely room to bury the dead."[7]

Peter the Little, who had accompanied the army this far, deserted and tried to go home; he was hauled back by one of the captains, who forced him to swear that he would remain. In February, the Byzantine general Taticius yanked his men from camp and headed back towards Constantinople. Rumors of an approaching Muslim army disturbed the soldiers who remained.[8]

The possibility that the whole Crusade might fall apart at Antioch was growing ever more real. The city itself was in better shape than the camp; the contemporary Muslim account, written by the Syrian chronicler Ibn al-Qala-nisi, remarks that so much oil, salt, and other necessities went to Antioch by way of the river that it was actually cheaper to buy those staples in the besieged city than outside it. Meanwhile, crusaders who had already abandoned the cause were prospering. Godfrey's younger brother Baldwin had veered away from the main crusader army and gone to the independent city of Edessa, where the city's king had first employed him as a mercenary and then adopted him as son and heir; Stephen of Blois had announced that ill health required him to leave, and had gone with his men to more comfortable quarters on the Mediterranean coast.[9]

On March 4, the crusader outlook took a slight upswing when an English fleet docked on the Mediterranean coast about ten miles from the siege camp. The fleet had stopped at Constantinople for reprovisioning, and the emperor Alexius had ordered siege materials, tools, and workmen loaded onto the ships to be taken to Antioch. The fleet was commanded by none other than Edgar Atheling: the heir to the English throne who had surrendered to William the Conqueror at age fourteen. Now in his thirties, Edgar Atheling had already joined at least two failed wars. He had gone to Scotland in his late teens and had fought with the Scots in a fruitless rebellion against William the Conqueror, and ten years after that had joined a short-lived revolt against William's son and heir.

Now he was anchored on the Mediterranean shore, ready to aid in the conquest of Antioch. Raymond of Toulouse and Bohemund went together to bring the siege materials back to the camp; the crusaders built additional fortifications that blocked ships from refreshing Antioch's supplies from the river, and the city began to weaken.[10]

At last the defenders inside Antioch started to lose heart. Bohemund, who had a reputation for craftiness ("habitual rogue," Anna Comnena calls him), managed to talk one of the Turkish guards inside the city into a private deal. "Bohemund sent word that he would make him rich, with much honor," says the chronicle known as *Gesta Francorum*, "and [the guard] yielded to these words and promises, saying, 'At whatever hour he wishes, I will receive him.' "[11]

In the dark night of June 2, Bohemund's informant opened a postern gate, and Bohemund led his men into the city. They killed the guards at the large gate known as the Gate of the Bridge and threw it open from the inside. The rest of the crusader army flooded into Antioch. The frustration of the long siege burst out of them: "The victors roamed at will through places formerly inaccessible to them," writes William of Tyre, "and, maddened by lust of killing and greed for gain, they spared neither sex nor condition and paid no attention to age. . . . More than ten thousand citizens were slain that day; along the streets everywhere the corpses of the dead lay unburied."[12]

But despite the victory, the crusader army was soon in horrible straits. An enormous Muslim army, commanded by the Turkish general Kerbogha, had been dispatched by the Great Sultan of the Turks in Baghdad, and it arrived at Antioch just three days later. The crusaders swung the city's gates closed and gave thanks that they were not still in the siege camp outside, but they soon discovered that conditions inside the city were much worse than outside. Antioch was already empty of food; now it was stinking with corpses as well. Disease spread. The crusaders were reduced to digging up dead animals that had been buried weeks before so that they could eat the rotting flesh.[13]

In a desperate attempt to rally the crusaders, Bohemund ("a supreme mischief-maker," Anna Comnena adds) announced that God had sent a message of assurance and deliverance. It had come, he explained, to the peasant Peter Bartholomew, who was part of Raymond of Toulouse's entourage: the Holy Lance, the spear that had pierced the side of Jesus Christ during the Crucifixion, was inside the city. Peter Bartholomew had told the story to Raymond and to the bishop Adhemar, who had accompanied the army of Toulouse as a representative of the pope, and Raymond had believed him.

Adhemar, on the other hand, had called the story "nothing but words." However, he was willing to see whether the lance would actually be discovered. Bohemund took Peter Bartholomew, Raymond of Toulouse, and a handful of men into the church of St. Peter at Antioch, where they dug a pit in the place that Peter Bartholomew indicated. The pit was empty; Raymond of Toulouse, dejected, left the church, at which point Peter Bartholomew leaped into the pit and then climbed back out clutching the point of a spear.[14]

Raymond of Toulouse, a devout and honest man, apparently judged others by the yardstick he used to measure himself; he immediately embraced the discovery as genuine, and the bishop Adhemar chose to hold his tongue. The word spread through the crusader army, which took heart at this evidence of God's favor. On June 28, 1098, the crusaders charged out of Antioch with the "Holy Lance" in their midst and drove the Muslim army into retreat.

Antioch was now in crusader hands, but the city was never turned over to the emperor Alexius. Bohemund had sworn the oath without ever intending to keep it; now he claimed that since the surrender of the city had been arranged by him personally, the city had surrendered *to* him, and was now his. He intended to stay in Antioch as its prince. In this he was following the example of Godfrey's younger brother Baldwin, who had now inherited the rule of Edessa and was governing it as an independent Christian state: the County of Edessa. Bohemund would be prince of Antioch, ruler of a Christian kingdom in Syria.

Raymond of Toulouse disagreed with him sharply, and the two men quarrelled. In the end, Raymond separated himself from the decision to keep Antioch and left the city. He paid both Robert of Normandy (who was broke, by this time) and Bohemund's own nephew Tancred in gold to accompany him. Eventually, Godfrey and his men also followed Raymond from Antioch; Bohemund remained, flying his own flag above Antioch's walls.[15]

The remaining crusaders, led by Raymond of Toulouse, marched towards Jerusalem. Over fifty thousand men had crossed the Bosphorus Strait into Asia Minor at the beginning of the crusade; now fewer than fourteen thousand remained. Following the army was a throng of pilgrims who had been hoping to reach the holy city for almost three years now—"a helpless throng," William of Tyre says, "sick and feeble." On the way, the leading noblemen

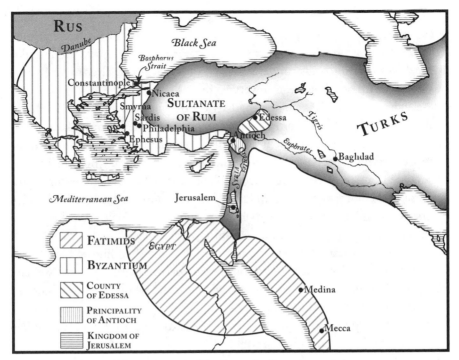

84.1: The Crusader States

in the army had demanded that Peter Bartholomew prove his claim to divine revelation; they forced him to undergo an ordeal by fire, walking through flame with the Holy Lance in his hand. Bartholomew had apparently begun to believe his own story. He was dreadfully burned and died after twelve days of agony, and the story of the Holy Lance quietly faded away.

The crusaders continued on towards Jerusalem. For a good cause, they could cope with being exhausted, outnumbered, sick, and hungry; but they objected to being manipulated.

The crusader army arrived at Jerusalem in early June of 1099. There they found a landscape as forbidding as Antioch's. The summer days were hot, and water was scarce; the Turks had plenty of time to stop up the springs and foul the wells near the city, so that the crusader army would have nothing to drink. Trees, buildings, and all possible sources of timber near the city walls had been levelled. The pack animals, deprived of water, died and a "pestilential stench . . . rose from their decaying bodies."[16]

But Jerusalem itself did not possess Antioch's frightening defenses, and the crusaders set doggedly to work. A siege camp was established around Jerusalem, and parties were sent far afield looking for wood. The attack on Jerusalem began on June 13. For three weeks, the crusaders battered the walls with ineffective siege machines built from twigs and brush.

When a fresh detachment of crusaders arrived by sea, Raymond of Toulouse directed that their ships be hauled aground and broken up for their wood. The siege towers built from the water-soaked timbers were rolled towards Jerusalem's walls; under cover of crusader arrow-fire, the northern moat was filled in. The siege towers were pushed over the newly laid dirt. "The fighters in the siege engines had set on fire sacks of straw and cushions stuffed with cotton," William of Tyre explains. "Fanned into a blaze by the north wind, these poured forth such dense smoke into the city that those who were trying to defend the wall could scarcely open their mouths or eyes. Bewildered and dazed by the torrent of black smoke, they abandoned the defense of the ramparts." The attackers lowered wooden bridges to the tops of the walls and stormed across them into the city. Antioch had taken seven months to conquer; Jerusalem, barely thirty days.[17]

Another massacre followed. "So terrible [was] the shedding of blood, that even the victors experienced sensations of horror and loathing," says William of Tyre. "No mercy was shown to anyone, and the whole place was flooded with the blood of the victims. Everywhere lay fragments of human bodies." Survivors were pulled from alleys, from closets, from cellars, and were killed by the sword or hurled from the walls.

The slaughter was in part the explosion of nearly two years of pent-up frustration with the heat, famine, disease, and misery of siege camps; in part, it was a calculated strategy to wipe out every trace of opposition. News had reached the crusaders that a Fatimid army was on its way from Egypt; the Fatimids, driven from Jerusalem by the Turks, were launching an attack to take it back.[18]

By the time the Fatimids arrived at Jerusalem's wall on August 12, the city was completely under crusader control. Godfrey led the crusader army out from the city's wall and drove the Egyptian army back without too much difficulty. The Egyptians retreated without mounting a second attack. Jerusalem had been taken; the goal of the First Crusade had been accomplished. Three Christian states, ruled by crusader nobles, now dotted the Muslim east: the County of Edessa, the Principality of Antioch, and the Kingdom of Jerusalem.

Raymond of Toulouse was the obvious choice to rule the conquered city of Jerusalem. Unlike Antioch, Jerusalem had not been a Byzantine city before its conquest by the Turks, so there was no obligation to hand it back to Alexius. But Raymond declined to accept the title of king; the slaughter had left a poor taste in his mouth.

He probably hoped to be offered the job again with another title, perhaps that of "count" or "governor." But like many good men, he was not particularly popular, and the second offer never came. Instead, Godfrey was offered the position and accepted it, ruling Jerusalem as its duke and protector.

T I M E L I N E 8 4

GERMANY NORMANDY	ENGLAND ITALY	Roman Emperor	CRUSADER BYZANTIUM TURKS STATES
			Togrul (1038–1063)
Henry III (1039–1056)	Harthacanute (1040–1042)		Michael V (1041–1042)
	Edward the Confessor (1042–1066)		Constantine Monomachos (1042–1055)
		Henry III (1046–1056)	
		Pope Leo IV (1049–1054)	
	"Great Schism" of eastern and western churches (1054)		Theodora (1055–1056)
Henry IV (1056–1106)			Michael Gerontas (1056–1057) Isaac Comnenus (1057–1059)
			Constantine X Doukas (1059–1067)
			Alp Arslan (1064–1072)
	Harold II (1066) **William the Conqueror** (1066–1087)		Romanos Diogenes (1068–1071) Michael VII
	Robert Guiscard gains control of southern Italy (1071)		(1071–1078) Battle of Manzikert (1071) **Malik Shah** (1072–1092)
	Pope Gregory VII (1073–1084/1085)		
Excommunication of Henry IV (1076)			Conquest of Jerusalem
			Nikephoros III (1077) (1078–1081)
Second excommunication of Henry IV (1080)	Wibert of Ravenna (1080/1085–1100)		Alexius Comnenus (1081–1118)
Henry IV's conquest of Rome (1083)		Henry IV (1084–1106)	
Robert of Normandy (1087–1106)	**William II** (1087–1100) Pope Urban II (1088–1099)		Turkish empire fractures (1092) **Kilij Arslan** of Rum (1092–1107)
	Urban II summons the First Crusade (1095)		
			Baldwin of Edessa (1098–1100) **Bohemund** of Antioch (1098–1111) **Godfrey** of Jerusalem (1099–1100)

Chapter Eighty-Five

Aftershocks

Between 1118 and 1129,
the ideal of crusade is written into law

IN SPAIN, Alfonso the Battler had been fighting for two decades against the Muslim Almoravids. This, as far as he was concerned, was also holy war. Recapturing Spain for Aragon-Navarre meant recapturing it for Christ, and it had been a long hard fight, complicated by his ongoing feud with his wife.

In 1118, a church council at Toulouse decreed that the capture of Zaragoza, the northernmost kingdom in the Almoravid realm, could be considered a crusade. This meant that helping to drive the Almoravid occupiers out of Zaragoza would be a righteous act, an accession of grace; one French account says that the pope himself promised forgiveness of sins to those willing to besiege the city.[1]

Alfonso had been trying to capture Zaragoza for at least four years. The additional energy provided by the council finally tipped the balance. Noblemen from the south of Western Francia brought their private armies to help out, and the realm fell to the Christian armies in the fall of 1118.

The energies of the First Crusade had spilled across the west all the way into Spain, and had shifted the balance of power back towards the Christian kings. The Almoravid power in Spain began to diminish. The Almoravid ruler, Ali ibn Yusuf, remained in Marrakesh; he treated Spain like a distant outpost, and the Almoravid soldiers stationed there were less and less inclined to fight to the death to keep their land.

Meanwhile, Alfonso the Battler wrote the crusader status of his Christian armies into church law by founding a series of military orders; soldiers who joined them earned the status of monks, full-time servants of God. The Confraternity of Belchite was formed in 1122 to defend one particular area, south of the Ebro river: "Having been touched by divine grace," Alfonso the Battler announced, in the order's charter, "we have established through our imperial authority a Christian knighthood and a brotherly army of Christians in Christ, in Spain at the castle which is called Belchite . . . so that they may serve God there, and thereafter for all the days of their lives subdue the pagans." Several other orders of Christian Knights followed, all devoted to keeping the Almoravids out of conquered territory.[2]

At the same time, military orders were springing up in the east. The first and most powerful began in Jerusalem, where Godfrey had governed the city for barely a year before dying of typhoid. The Frankish crusaders still in Jerusalem had invited his brother Baldwin of Edessa to come and be crowned as the king of Jerusalem; this was a step up from count of Edessa, so Baldwin handed Edessa over to a distant cousin (also named Baldwin) and made his way to Jerusalem.[3] He fought a series of battles over the next eighteen years and expanded the Kingdom of Jerusalem

85.1: Alfonso's Crusade

well past the city's borders; when he died in 1118, the same distant cousin who governed Edessa was crowned King Baldwin II of Jerusalem.

Now that the city was no longer in Turkish hands, more Christian pilgrims came to visit it; but all three crusader states were constantly under attack, and the journey was a perilous one. In 1119, the Frankish nobleman Hugh of Payens came to Jerusalem, searching for a way to better his soul. He decided that protecting pilgrims who were travelling unarmed from the coast to the city was a righteous mission, and over the next few years he recruited like-minded men to help him. They lived as monks: "not taking a wife," wrote the twelfth-century patriarch of Antioch, Michael the Syrian, "not bathing, having no personal possessions whatsoever, but having everything in common."

Like monks, they took vows of poverty, chastity, and obedience; unlike monks, they carried arms. Their services were so greatly appreciated by travellers to Jerusalem that King Baldwin II decided to make provision for them: he "granted them a temporary dwelling place in his own palace," says William of Tyre, "on the north side by the Temple of the Lord."[4] They took their name, the Knights Templar, from this dwelling place.*

---

*Although the crusaders and their chroniclers often speak of "the Temple," the Jewish temple destroyed in AD 70 had not been rebuilt. "Temple" sometimes refers to the mosque near the Dome of the Rock, and sometimes to the Dome itself.

In January 1129, Hugh of Payens travelled to the church council of Troyes to request formal recognition of his monastic order. The assembled churchmen approved of the order's purpose, and the great monastic reformer Bernard of Clairvaux took it upon himself to write the order's Rule. His Rule for the Knights Templar begins:

> I exhort you who, up until now, have embraced a secular knighthood in favor of humans only, and in which Christ was not the cause, to haste to associate yourself in perpetuity with the Order. . . . In this, the order of knighthood, which, despising love of justice, did not strive to defend the poor or churches (which was its duty), but to rob, despoil and kill, has flowered again and revived.[5]

This was exactly what Pope Urban II had hoped for: the redirection of violence into the paths of righteousness.

The founding of the military orders was the closing act in the drama begun by Constantine at the Milvian Bridge. Marching into Rome under the banner of the cross, he had taken a powerful and mysterious theology and bent it to his own purposes. It had promised unity; he needed unification. It had promised ultimate victory; he needed earthly victory, at once. It had promised an identity that transcended nationality and language; he needed to overcome nationalism. Most of all, he needed to convince his soldiers, the people of Rome, and the enemies who threatened him that he was driven by something higher and more noble than simple ambition.

Probably he needed to convince himself as well. Christianity gave Constantine freedom from guilt over his conquests, at the same time that it lent him the zeal he needed to pursue them. Seven hundred years later, the military orders did exactly the same thing for the men who joined them—and gave them a Rule to spell out precisely what they would gain. That marriage of spiritual gain and political power would shape the next five centuries; and the painful and protracted divorce between the two, the centuries after that.

TIMELINE 85

BYZANTIUM	TURKS	CRUSADER STATES	ALMORAVIDS	CHRISTIAN KINGDOMS
Theodora (1055–1056) Michael Gerontas (1056–1057) Isaac Comnenus (1057–1059)				
Constantine X Doukas (1059–1067)			Abu-Bakr of the Almoravids (1061–1087)	
	Alp Arslan (1064–1072)			Sancho II (the Strong) of Castile (1065–1072)
Romanos Diogenes (1068–1071)				
Michael VII (1071–1078) Battle of Manzikert (1071)	Malik Shah (1072–1092)			Alfonso VI (the Brave) of Castile and Leon (1072–1109)
Conquest of Jerusalem (1077) Nikephoros III (1078–1081)				
Alexius Comnenus (1081–1118)			Tashfin of the Almoravids (1087–1106)	
	Turkish empire fractures (1092) Kilij Arslan of Rum (1092–1107)			Establishment of El Cid's kingdom at Valencia (1094–1102)
		Baldwin of Edessa (1098–1100) Bohemund of Antioch (1098–1111) Godfrey of Jerusalem (1099–1100)		
				Alfonso the Battler of Aragon-Navarre (1104–1134)
			ibn Yusuf of the Almoravids (1106–1142)	
				Fall of Zaragoza (1118)
				Founding of the Confraternity of Belchite (1122)
				Recognition of the Knights Templar (1129)

Notes

Chapter One One Empire, Under God

1. The gory details are found in Lactantius, "Of the Manner in Which the Persecutors Died," chapter 44, in Philip Schaff, ed., *Ante-Nicene Fathers*, Vol. 7 (1896); and in Zosimus, *Historia Nova* (1814), book 2.
2. Zosimus, book 2.
3. Lactantius, "On the Manner in Which the Persecutors Died," chapter 49, in Schaff, *Ante-Nicene Fathers*, vol. 7.
4. Lactantius, *De Mortibus Persecutoram*, chapter 45, in *University of Pennsylvania, Dept of History: Translations and Reprints from the Original Sources of European History*, vol. 4:1 (1897), pp. 28–30.
5. Eusebius, *Life of Constantine*, 1.41, trans. Averil Cameron and Stuart G. Hall (1999), p. 86.
6. A. A. Vasiliev, *History of the Byzantine Empire, 324–1453*, vol. 1 (1952), p. 47.
7. Eusebius, *Life of Constantine*, 4.61; Vasiliev, pp. 48–49.
8. Chris Scarre, *Chronicle of the Roman Emperors* (1995), p. 215.
9. J. N. D. Kelly, *Early Christian Doctrines*, rev. ed. (1976), pp. 138–139.
10. Ignatius, *Letter to the Ephesians*, 7, in Philip Schaff, ed., *Ante-Nicene Fathers*, vol. 1 (1867).
11. Kelly, *Early Christian Doctrines*, p. 141.
12. Ibid., pp. 227–229.
13. Eusebius, *Life of Constantine*, 2.72.
14. Sozomen, *The Ecclesiastical History*, 4.16, in Philip Schaff and Henry Wace, eds., *A Select Library of the Nicene and Post-Nicene Fathers*, second series, Vol. 2 (1892).
15. Vasiliev, p. 54.
16. Vasiliev, p. 53.
17. Sozomen, *Ecclesiastical History*, 2.3, in Schaff and Wace, vol. 2.
18. Photius, *Epitome of the Ecclesiastical History of Philostorgius*, trans. Edward Walford (1860), 1.9.
19. Vasiliev, p. 59; Sozomen, *Ecclesiastical History*, 2.4, in Schaff and Wace, vol. 2.
20. Eusebius, *Life of Constantine*, 3.47.

Chapter Two Seeking the Mandate of Heaven

1. Luo Guanzhong, *Three Kingdoms*, trans. Moss Roberts (1991), pp. 922–924.
2. John MacGowan, *The Imperial History of China* (1897), p. 154.
3. Ibid., p. 155.
4. Guanzhong, p. 935.
5. C. P. Fitzgerald, *China* (1938), p. 255.
6. MacGowan, p. 160.
7. Ibid., p. 161.
8. Demetrius Charles Boulger, *The History of China*, vol. 1 (1972), pp. 134–135.
9. Franz Michael, *China through the Ages* (1986), p. 90; Ann Paludan, *Chronicle of the Chinese Emperors* (1998), p. 64; Rodney Leon Taylor, *The Religious Dimensions of Confucianism* (1990), p. 14.
10. Thomas J. Barfield, *The Perilous Frontier* (1989), p. 115.
11. Jacques Gernet, *A History of Chinese Civilization*, 2d ed., trans. J. R. Foster and Charles Hartman (1996), p. 187.

12. Marylin M. Rhie, *Early Buddhist Art of China and Central Asia*, vol. 2 (1999), p. 279.
13. MacGowan, p. 187; Barfield, p.117.
14. Gernet, p. 183.
15. Mohan Wijayaratna, *Buddhist Monastic Life*, trans. Claude Gransier and Steven Collins (1990), p. 3.
16. Michael, p. 101.
17. Kenneth Kuan Sheng Ch'en, *Buddhism in China* (1972), pp. 57–58; William Theodore de Bary et. al., *Sources of Chinese Tradition*, Vol. 1 (1963), p. xxi.

Chapter Three An Empire of the Mind

1. Ranbir Vohra, *The Making of India* (2001), p. 28.
2. K. A. Nilakanta Sastri, *A History of South India from Prehistoric Times to the Fall of Vijayanagari*, 3d ed. (1966), p. 92.
3. Romila Thapar, *Early India* (2002), p. 282.
4. Ibid., p. 283.
5. John Keay, *India* (2000), pp. 138–139.
6. Stanley Wolpert, *A New History of India*, 7th ed. (2004), p. 85.
7. Keay, p. 132.
8. Thapar, *Early India*, p. 280.
9. The Kalinga Edict, trans. by Romila Thapar, *Asoka and the Decline of the Mauryas*, 3d rev. ed. (1998), p. 255.
10. Thapar, *Early India*, p. 238.
11. Vasudev Vishnu Mirashi, *Literary and Historical Studies in Indology* (1975), pp. 119–121.
12. Thapar, *Early India*, p. 286; Keay, p. 142.
13. Faxian, *A record of Buddhistic kingdoms*, trans. James Legge (1886), pp. 42–43, 79.

Chapter Four The Persian Threat

1. Richard N. Frye, *The History of Ancient Iran* (1983), p. 309; Muhammed ibn Jarir al-Tabari, *The History of al-Tabari*, vol. 5 (1999), pp. 51–52.
2. al-Tabari, *History*, vol. 5, pp. 54–55.
3. Ibid., pp. 52–53.
4. T. D. Barnes, "Constantine and the Christians of Persia," *The Journal of Roman Studies*, 75 (1985), p. 132; also see Eusebius, *Life of Constantine*, 4.8
5. al-Tabari, *History*, vol. 5, p. 155.
6. Vahan M. Kurkjian, *A History of Armenia* (1958), pp. 119–120.
7. Schaff and Wace, *Select Library*, vol. 13, p. 244; Barnes, p. 128; Aphrahat, "Demonstration XXI: Of Persecution," in Schaff and Wace, *Select Library*, vol. 13, p. 519.
8. Barnes, p. 132; Eusebius, *Life of Constantine*, 4.56–57.
9. Scarre, p. 221; Eusebius, *Life of Constantine*, 4.75.
10. Frye, *The History of Ancient Iran*, p. 310.
11. Christopher S. Mackay, *Ancient Rome* (2004), p. 316.
12. Ibid., p. 317.
13. Frye, *History of Ancient Iran*, p. 310.
14. Ammianus Marcellinus, *The History of Ammianus Marcellinus*, (1982), vol. 1, 18.6.21–22.
15. Ibid., 18.8
16. Ibid., 19.3

Chapter Five **The Apostate**

1. Vasiliev, p. 69; Mackay, p. 320.
2. Vasiliev, p. 75.
3. Quoted in E. A. Thompson, *The Huns*, rev. Peter Heather (1999), p. 23.
4. Vasiliev, pp. 72–73.
5. al-Tabari, *History*, vol. 5, p. 59; Ammianus Marcellinus, *The History of Ammianus Marcellinus*, vol. 2 (1986), 23.5.10–11.
6. Ammianus, *History*, vol. 2 (1986), 25.3.15–23; Theodoret, *Church History*, 3.10, in Schaff and Wace, *Select Library*, vol. 3.
7. Ammianus, *History*, vol. 2, 25.5.4–6, 10.14–15; Mackay, p. 321.
8. al-Tabari, *History*, vol. 5, pp. 62–63.
9. Vasiliev, p. 78.
10. Ammianus II (1986), XXV.10.12–15.

Chapter Six **Earthquake and Invasion**

1. Zosimus, book 4; Theodoret, *Church History* 4.4, in Schaff and Wace, *Select Library*, vol. 3.
2. Ammianus Marcellinus, *The Later Roman Empire*, trans. Walter Hamilton (1986), 26.4.
3. Ibid.
4. Zosimus, book 4.
5. Vasiliev, p. 79; Socrates, *Church History*, 4.2, in Schaff and Wace, *Select Library*, vol. 2; Zosimus, book 4; Ammianus, *Later Roman Empire*, 26.5.
6. Gavin Kelly, "Ammianus and the Great Tsunami," *The Journal of Roman Studies*, (2004), p. 143.
7. Ammianus, *History*, vol. 2, 26.10.16–18.
8. Ammianus, *Later Roman Empire*, 26.4.
9. Socrates, *Church History*, 4.5 in Schaff and Wace, *Select Library*, vol. 2.
10. Kelly, "Ammianus and the Great Tsunami," p. 143; Libanius, "On Avenging Julian (Or. 24.14)," quoted in Kelly, p. 147.
11. "Letter of Auxentius," trans. Peter Heather and John Matthews, *The Goths in the Fourth Century* (1991), p. 138.
12. Gerhard Herm, *The Celts*, (1976), p. 226.
13. Quoted in Daithi O Hogain, *The Celts* (2003), p. 191.
14. Ibid., p. 205.
15. I. A. Richmond, *Roman Britain* (1955), p. 228.
16. O Hogain, p. 206.
17. Richmond, pp. 63–64.
18. Ammianus, *History*, vol. 3, 29.6.1.
19. Ibid., 29.6.5–6.
20. Ibid., 30.5.13–14.
21. Ibid., 30.6.3.
22. Ammianus, *Later Roman Empire*, pp. 412–415; Thompson, p. 26; Vasiliev, p. 86.
23. In Jordanes, *The Gothic History of Jordanes*, trans. Charles Christopher Mierow (1915), book 24.
24. Genesis 6:1–4.
25. Vasiliev, p. 86.
26. Ammianus, *History*, vol. 3, 31.8.6; Socrates, *Church History*, 4.38, in Schaff and Wace, *Select Library*, vol. 2.

Chapter Seven **Refounding the Kingdom**

1. *San-kuo chih* 30, trans. Michael C. Rogers, in Peter H. Lee et al., eds., *Sourcebook of Korean Civilization*, vol. 1 (1993), p. 17.
2. James Huntley Grayson, *Early Buddhism and Christianity in Korea* (1985), p. 19.
3. Chan Master Sheng Yen, *Zen Wisdom* (1993), p. 169; Ch'en, pp. 59–61.
4. Edward T. Ch'ien, "The Neo-Confucian Confrontation with Buddhism," *Journal of Chinese Philosophy*, 15 (1988), pp. 349–350; Ki-baik Lee, *A New History of Korea*, trans. Edward W. Wagner (1984), p. 38; Lee and deBary, p. 35.
5. Lee, *New History of Korea*, p. 37.
6. Grayson, *Early Buddhism and Christianity in Korea*, p. 26.
7. Lee, *New History of Korea*, p. 38; Lee and deBary (1993), p. 25; John Whitney Hall et al., *The Cambridge History of Japan* (1988), p. 361.

Chapter Eight **The Catholic Church**

1. Vasiliev, p. 79; Zosimus, book 4.
2. Gregory of Nyssa, "On the Divinity of the Son and of the Holy Spirit," In A. D. Lee, *Pagans and Christians in Late Antiquity* (2000), p. 110.
3. Sozomen, *Ecclesiastical History*, 7.4, in Schaff and Wace, *Select Library*, vol. 2.
4. Vasiliev, p. 80; Codex Theodosianus, 16.1–2, in Theodosius, *The Theodosian Codes and Novels and the Sirmondian Consititutions*, ed. Clyde Pharr, with Theresa Sherrer Davidson and Mary Brown Pharr (1952).
5. Sozomen, *Ecclesiastical History*, 7.12, in Schaff and Wace, *Select Library*, vol. 2.
6. Ibid.
7. Vasiliev, p. 87.
8. Scarre, p. 229.
9. Vasiliev, p. 81.

Chapter Nine **Excommunicated**

1. John Davies, *A History of Wales* (1993), p. 52.
2. O Hogain, pp. 206–207; Geoffrey of Monmouth, *The History of the Kings of Britain*, trans. Lewis Thorpe 1966), 9.2.
3. Zosimus, book 4.
4. al-Tabari *History*, p. 68.
5. Walter Pohl, "The Vandals: Fragments of a Narrative," in A. H. Merrills, ed., *Vandals, Romans and Berbers* (2004), p. 34; Paulus Orosius, *The Seven Books of History against the Pagans*, trans. Roy J. Defarrari (1964), p. 352.
6. Ambrose of Milan, *The Letters of St. Ambrose, Bishop of Milan*, trans. H. Walford (1881), letter 20; George Huntston Williams, "Christology and Church-State Relations in the Fourth Century (concluded)," *Church History*, 20:4 (1951), p. 5.
7. Sozomen, *Ecclesiastical History*, 7.13, in Schaff and Wace, *Select Library*, vol. 2.
8. Socrates, *Ecclesiastical History*, 5.14, in Schaff and Wace, *Select Library*, vol. 2; Orosius, book 7.
9. "The Memorial of Symmachus," in Ambrose of Milan, *Letters*, letter 7.
10. Ambrose of Milan, *Letters*, letter 8.
11. Sozomen, *Ecclesiastical History*, 7.25, in Schaff and Wace, *Select Library*, vol. 2.
12. Theodoret, *Church History*, 5.17, in Schaff and Wace, *Select Library*, vol. 3.
13. Vasiliev, p. 82.

Chapter Ten Cracked in Two

1. Orosius, book 7; Sozomon, *Ecclesiastical History*, 7.24 in Schaff and Wace, *Select Library*, vol. 2; Socrates, *Ecclesiastical History* 5.25, in Schaff and Wace, *Select Library*, vol. 12.
3. Finley Hooper, *Roman Realities* (1979), p. 536; Vasiliev, p. 90; Zosimus, book 5; J. B. Bury, *A History of the Later Roman Empire*, vol. 1 (1966), p. 62.
4. Roger Collins, *Early Medieval Europe, 300–1000*, 2d ed. (1999), p. 30.
5. Ibid., pp. 23–24, 39.
6. Bury, *History of the Later Roman Empire*, vol. 1, p. 64; Vasiliev, p. 91.
7. Claudian, "Against Rufinus," in *Claudian* (1922), trans. Maurice Platnauer, pp. 88–89.
8. Ibid., p. 88; Zosimus, book 5.
9. Zosimus, book 5.

Chapter Eleven The Sack of Rome

1. Henry Chadwick, *The Early Church* (1967), p. 169; Kelly, *Early Christian Doctrines*, pp. 13–14.
2. Augustine, *Confessions*, trans. Henry Chadwick (1998), 8.12.
3. Norman Cantor, *The Civilization of the Middle Ages* (1984), p. 51.
4. Kelly, *Early Christian Doctrines*, p. 410–411.
5. Philip Schaff, ed., *A Select Library of the Nicene and Post-Nicene Fathers*, vol. 4, first series (1889), p. 751.
6. Kelly, *Early Christian Doctrines*, p. 411.
7. Schaff, *Select Library*, vol. 4, p. 906.
8. Zosimus, book 5.
9. Procopius, *History of the Wars, Secret History, and Buildings*, trans. Averil Cameron (1967), I.2.
10. Ibid.
11. Claudian, *De Bello Gothico* 26.
12. Thomas Hodgkin, *Italy and Her Invaders* (1892), pp. 721–723.
13. O Hogain, p. 208; Collins, pp. 13, 25.
14. J. B. Bury, *History of the Later Roman Empire*, vol. 1, p. 113.
15. Ibid., p. 117; Collins, p. 14; Gregory of Tours, *The History of the Franks*, trans. Lewis Thorpe (1974), 2.8.
16. Zosimus, book 6.
17. Jerome, "Letter CXXVII," in Schaff and Wace, *Select Library*, vol. 6.

Chapter Twelve One Nature versus Two

1. Agathias, *The Histories*, trans. Joseph D. Frendo (1975), 4.26.8.
2. al-Tabari, *History*, vol. 5, p. 71.
3. Thompson, p. 35.
4. al-Tabari, *History*, vol. 5, p. 73.
5. Ibid., pp. 88–89.
6. Procopius, *History of the Wars, Secret History, and Buildings*, I.2.
7. Bury, *History of the Later Roman Empire*, vol. 1, p. 128.
8. George Ostrogorsky, *History of the Byzantine State*, rev. ed., trans. Joan Hussey (1969), p. 58.
9. Ugo Bianchi, "The Contribution of the Cologne Mani Codex to the Religio-Historical Study of Manicheism," in Mary Boyce, *Papers in Honour of Professor Mary Boyce* (1985), pp. 18–20.

Chapter Thirteen Seeking a Homeland

1. Jordanes, 30.157–158.
2. Ibid., 31.160.
3. Sozomen, *Ecclesiastical History*, 4.14, in Schaff and Wace, *Select Library*, vol. 2.
4. Collins, p. 25; O Hogain, p. 210.
5. J. M. Wallace-Hadrill, *The Long-Haired Kings and Other Studies in Frankish History* (1962), pp. 25–26; Orosius, book 7.
6. Peter Heather, *The Goths* (1996), pp. 148–149.

Chapter Fourteen The Gupta Decline

1. David Christian, *A History of Russia, Inner Asia and Mongolia* (1998), p. 248.
2. Procopius, *History of the Wars, Secret History, and Buildings*, book 3; Wilhelm Barthold, *An Historical Geography of Iran*, trans. Svat Soucek (1984), pp. 19–20; Thapar, *Early India*, p. 286.
3. Radha Kumud Mookerji, *The Gupta Empire* (1969), pp. 70, 74.
4. Sastri, *History of South India* (1966), p. 109.
5. D. K. Ganguly, *The Imperial Guptas and Their Times* (1987), pp. 108–109.
6. H. C. Ray, *The Dynastic History of Northern India (Early Mediaeval Period)*, 2d ed., vol. 1 (1973), p. xxxiii; Mookerji, p. 92; Thapar, *Early India*, p. 286; Hermann Kulke, *A History of India*, 4th ed. (2004), p. 90.
7. Keay, p. 102; Sastri, *History of South India*, p. 444.
8. Sastri, *History of South India*, p. 83.
9. Ibid., p. 117.
10. Michael, pp. 96–97.

Chapter Fifteen Northern Ambitions

1. MacGowan (1897), p. 201.
2. Ibid., p. 202.
3. Ibid., p. 208.
4. Gernet, pp. 175–176, 181.
5. Ibid., pp. 190–191.
6. Ch'en, p. 61.
7. Fabrizio Pregadio, *Great Clarity* (2005), p. 6.
8. Fitzgerald, *China*, p. 267.
9. MacGowan, p. 211.
10. Paludan, p. 219.
11. MacGowan, p. 214.

Chapter Sixteen The Huns

1. Jordanes, 24. pp. 86–87.
2. Ammianus, *Later Roman Empire*, 31.2; Thompson, pp. 48, 54.
3. Thompson, p. 68.
4. Jordanes, 35.181–182; Nestorius, *The Bazaar of Heracleides*, trans. G. R. Driver and Leonard Hodgson (1925), 2.2.
5. Leo the Great, "Letter XIV," in Schaff and Wace, *Select Library*, vol. 12.
6. Ostrogorsky, p. 59.
7. Thompson, p. 113.

8. Ibid., p. 116.
9. Priscus's account as preserved in Jordanes, 24.178–179.
10. Thompson, pp. 144–145.
11. J. B. Bury, "Just Grata Honoria," *The Journal of Roman Studies*, 9 (1919), p. 9.
12. Ibid.
13. Jordanes, 42.224.
14. Bury, *History of the Later Roman Empire*, vol. 1, p. 199.

Chapter Seventeen Attila

1. Gregory of Tours, 2.6.
2. Ian Wood, *The Merovingian Kingdoms, 450–751* (1994), p. 37.
3. Jordanes, book 38.
4. Hydatius, *The Chronicle of Hydatius and the Consularia Constantinopolitana*, trans. R. W. Burgess (1993), p. 101; Jordanes, book 40.
5. Jordanes, book 42.
6. Otto J. Maenchen-Helfen, *The World of the Huns* (1973), p. 141.
7. Ibid., p. 139; Hydatius, p. 103; Jordanes, book 43.
8. Ibid., book 49.

Chapter Eighteen Orthodoxy

1. Kelly *Early Christian Doctrines*, pp. 331, 339; Letter 28, "To Flavian, commonly called 'the Tome.'" in Schaff and Wace, *Select Library*, vol. 12.
2. Collins, p. 74.
3. Letter 93, "From the Synod of Chalcedon to Leo"; Letter 104, "Leo, the Bishop, to Marcian Augustus"; Letter 105, "To Pulcheria Augusta about the self-seeking of Anatolius"; Letter 106, "To Anatolius, Bishop of Constantinople, in rebuke of his self-seeking," all in Schaff and Wace, *Select Library*, vol. 12.
4. Yeghishe, *History of Vartan and the Armenian War*, 2d ed. (1952), pp. 4, 11.
5. Ibid., p. 75.
6. al-Tabari, *History*, vol. 5, p. 109.

Chapter Nineteen The High Kings

1. O Hogain, p. 211. Niall's exact dates are impossible to determine; he ruled in Ireland sometime between 390 and 455.
2. Tom Peete Cross and Clark Harris Slover, eds., *Ancient Irish Tales* (1936), p. 510.
3. Ibid., p. 512.
4. Patrick, *Confession*, in Joseph Cullen Ayer, *A Source Book for Ancient Church History* (1913), pp. 568–569; Bede, *Bede's Ecclesiastical History of the English People*, ed. Bertram Colgrave and R. A. B. Mynors (1969), 1.1.
5. Louise T. Moore et al., "A Y-Chromosome Signature of Hegemony in Gaelic Ireland." *The American Journal of Human Genetics*, 78 (Feb. 2006), pp. 334–338.
6. O Hogain, pp. 212–213.
7. Gildas, *The Ruin of Britain and Other Works*, trans. Michael Winterbottom (1978), 19.1.
8. O Hogain, pp. 214, 217 (O Hogain notes that "the sources . . . are confused and largely unreliable," making this a *probable* sequence of events); Gildas, 23.1.
9. Bede, 1.15; Gildas, 23.4.
10. Geoffrey of Monmouth, 6.10.

11. Gildas, 24.2–3.
12. Nennius, *History of the Britons*, 42, in J. A. Giles, *Old English Chronicles* (1908).
13. M. J. Swanton, trans. and ed., *The Anglo-Saxon Chronicle*, (1998), p. 13.

Chapter Twenty The End of the Roman Myth

1. C. D. Gordon, *The Age of Attila* (1960), p. 51.
2. Ibid., pp. 51–52; Bury, *History of the Later Roman Empire*, vol. 1, pp. 182–183.
3. Bury, *History of the Later Roman Empire*, vol. 1, p. 235.
4. Procopius, *History of the Wars and Buildings*, trans. H. B. Dewing, vol. 2 (1916), 3.25–26.
5. Bury, *History of the Later Roman* Empire, vol. 1, p. 237.
6. Procopius, *History of the Wars and Buildings*, trans. H. B. Dewing, Vol. 5 (1928), VII.4–13.
7. Hydatius (1993), p. 113.
8. Ibid., p. 115.
9. Collins, p. 33.
10. Sidonius Apollinaris, *Letters*, trans. O. M. Dalton (1915), 1.5.
11. O Hogain, p. 215.
12. Jordanes, 45.237–238.
13. Gordon, p. 122.
14. Jordanes, book 46, p. 119.

Chapter Twenty-One The Ostrogoths

1. Bury, *History of the Later Roman Empire*, vol. 1, pp. 230–231.
2. Ibid., p. 252.
3. Jordanes, 46.243.
4. Collins, p. 33; Bury, *History of the Later Roman Empire*, vol. 1, pp. 278–279.
5. John Moorhead, *Theoderic in Italy* (1992), pp. 16–17.
6. Ibid., pp. 19–20.
7. Anonymous Valensianus, quoted in Thomas S. Burns, *A History of the Ostrogoths* (1984), p. 72.
8. Moorhead, p. 30.
9. Ibid., pp. 73, 100–101, 140–142.
10. Moorhead, p. 60; Procopius, *History of the Wars and Buildings*, trans. H. B. Dewing, vol. 3 (1919), 5.2.
11. Gregory the Great, *The Dialogues of St. Gregory*, ed. Edmund G. Gardner (1911), 2.3.
12. Benedict, *The Holy Rule of St. Benedict*, trans. Boniface Verheyen, OSB (1949), prologue.
13. Gregory the Great, *The Dialogues* (1911), II.12.
14. Henry Bettenson and Chris Maunder, eds., *Documents of the Christian Church*, 3rd ed. (1999), p. 141.

Chapter Twenty-Two Byzantium

1. Joshua the Stylite, *The Chronicle of Joshua the Stylite*, trans. W. Wright (1882), 1.
2. Procopius, *History of the Wars and Buildings*, vol. 1 (1914), 1.3; Joshua the Stylite, 10–11.
3. Procopius, *History of the Wars and Buildings*, vol. 1, 1.4; al-Tabari, *History*, vol. 5, p. 111, 116; Joshua the Stylite, 11.
4. al-Tabari, *History*, vol. 5, pp. 128–129; Joshua the Stylite 18–19.
5. Mary Boyce, "On the Orthodoxy of Sasanian Zoroastrianism," *Bulletin of the School of Oriental and African Studies, University of London*, 59:1 (1996), p. 23.
6. Ehsan Yarshater, "Mazdakism," in Ehsan Yarshater, ed., *The Cambridge History of Iran*, vol. 3(2) (1983), p. 1019.

7. al-Tabari, *History*, vol. 5, p. 132; Procopius, *History of the Wars and Buildings*, vol. 1, 1.5.

8. Procopius, *History of the Wars and Buildings*, vol. 1, 1.5.

9. al-Tabari, *History*, vol. 5, p. 136; Procopius, *History of the Wars and Buildings*, vol. 1 (1914), 1.6.

10. Bury, *History of the Later Roman Empire*, vol. 1, p. 290.

11. Procopius, *History of the Wars and Buildings*, vol. 1, 1.7; Joshua the Stylite, 53.

12. Procopius, *History of the Wars and Buildings*, vol. 1, 1.10.

13. Samuel Hazzard Cross and Olgerd P. Sherbowitz-Wetzor, trans. and ed., *The Russian Primary Chronicle* (1953), p. 55; Bury, *History of the Later Roman Empire*, vol. 1, p. 294.

14. Evagrius Scholasticus, *Ecclesiastical History*, trans. E. Walford (1846), 38.

15. Timothy Gregory, *A History of Byzantium* (2005), pp. 121–123.

16. Geoffrey Greatrex, "The Nika Riot: A Reappraisal," *The Journal of Hellenic Studies*, 117 (1997), p. 64.

17. Procopius, *The Secret History*, trans. G. A. Williamson (1966), p. 73.

Chapter Twenty-Three Aspirations

1. Duan Wenjie, *Dunhuang Art* (1994), p. 127.

2. Gernet, pp. 192–193; J. A. G. Roberts, *The Complete History of China* (2003), pp. 68–69.

3. Joseph Needham et al., "Chemistry and Chemical Technology," in *Science and Civilization in China* vol. 3, part 3 (1976), p. 119.

4. Michael, pp. 96–97; W. Scott Morton and Charlton M. Lewis, *China*, 4th ed. (1995), pp. 77–78.

5. Richard Dawson, *Imperial China* (1972), p. 33.

6. Wong Kiew Kit, *The Art of Shaolin Kung Fu* (2002), p. 19.

7. Norman Kutcher, *Mourning in Late Imperial China* (1999), p. 93.

8. David A. Graff and Robin Higham, eds., *A Military History of China* (2002), p. 33; Roberts, p. 69; Dawson, p. 33.

9. MacGowan, p. 223.

10. Lee, *New History of Korea*, p. 40.

11. Ibid., pp. 38–40.

12. Ibid., p. 43; Keith Pratt, *Korea* (1999), p. 3.

13. Ilyon, *Samguk Yusa,* trans. Tae-hung Ha and Grafton K. Mintz (1972), pp. 67–68.

14. Lee and de Bary, pp. 72–73.

15. Ibid., pp. 77–78.

Chapter Twenty-Four Resentment

1. MacGowan, p. 225; Paludan, p. 72.

2. MacGowan, p. 225.

3. Ibid., pp. 226–227; Paludan, p. 73.

4. MacGowan, pp. 228–229.

5. MacGowan, p. 233; Fitzgerald, *China*, p. 279.

6. de Bary et al., p. 176.

7. MacGowan, p. 237.

8. Mark Elvin, *The Pattern of the Chinese Past* (1973), p. 47.

9. Graff and Higham (2002), p. 31.

10. Gernet, p. 175; Barfield, p. 124.

11. Barfield, p. 25.

12. Boulger, p. 163.

13. Roberts, p. 69.

Chapter Twenty-Five Elected Kings

1. Gregory of Tours, 2.18–19; Collins, p. 36.
2. Gregory of Tours, 2.27; Collins, p. 33.
3. Gregory of Tours, 2.30.
4. Ibid., 2.31.
5. Ibid., 2.37; Patrick J. Geary, *Before France and Germany* (1988), pp. 86–87.
6. Collins, pp. 36–37.
7. Geary, pp. 90–91.
8. Geoffrey of Monmouth, *History of the Kings of Britain*, trans. Lewis Thorpe (1966), 6.14.
9. Gildas; 25.3; William of Malmesbury, *Gesta Regum Anglorum*, vol. 1, trans. R. A. B. Mynors et al. (1998), 1.8; Bede, 1.16.
10. Swanton, pp. 14–15.
11. O Hogain, p. 216; Herm, p. 275.
12. Swanton, p. 15.
13. O Hogain, p. 216.
14. Herm, p. 277; O Hogain, p. 217. O Hogain suggests that Camlann may have been much farther north, on the western end of Hadrian's Wall, but Camelford in England is the traditional location.
15. J. M. Wallace-Hadrill, *Early Germanic Kingship in England and on the Continent* (1971), p. 14.
16. Collins, p. 43.

Chapter Twenty-Six Invasion and Eruption

1. Mookerji, pp. 119–120; Kulke, p. 90.
2. T. W. Rhys Davids, trans., *The Questions of King Milinda* (1890).
3. Charles Eliot, *Hinduism and Buddhism*, vol. 3 (1921), p. 198.
4. Thapar, *Early India*, p. 287.
5. Alexander Cunningham, *The Bhilsa Topes* (1854), p. 163.
6. Samuel Beal, trans., *Travels of Fah-hian and Sun-yung, Buddhist Pilgrims, from China to India (400 A.D. and 518 A.D.)*, (1969), p. 197.
7. Ganguly, *Imperial Guptas*, p. 120; Thapar, *Early India*, p. 287.
8. David Keys, *Catastrophe* (1999), pp. 254, 262–269. It is possible but not at all certain that Java and Sumatra were originally one connected land mass.
9. Ibid., pp. 5, 247, 251; Procopius, *History of the Wars and Buildings*, vol. 2 (1916), 4.14; Charles Cockell, *Impossible Extinction* (2003), p. 121.
10. Cassiodorus, *The Letters of Cassiodorus*, trans. Thomas Hodgkin (1886), pp. 518–520.
11. John Savino and Marie D. Jones, *Supervolcano*, (2007), p. 85.
12. Keys, p. 259.

Chapter Twenty-Seven The Americas

1. Keys, pp. 5, 189–190.
2. Richard E. W. Adams, *Ancient Civilizations of the New World* (1997), pp. 50–51.
3. Joyce Marcus, "The Origins of Mesoamerican Writing," *Annual Review of Anthropology*, 5 (1976), p. 37.
4. Ibid., pp. 39–40.
5. Elizabeth Hill Boone, *Cycles of Time and Meaning in the Mexican Books of Fate* (2007), p. 14.
6. Keys, pp. 186–87; Adams, pp. 43–44; George L. Cowgill, "State and Society at Teotihuacan, Mexico," *Annual Review of Anthropology*, 26 (1997), pp. 129–130.

7. Saburo Sugiyama, "Worldview Materialized in Teotihuacan, Mexico," *Latin American Antiquity*, 4:2 (1993), p. 105.
8. Richard Haly, "Bare Bones: Rethinking Mesoamerican Divinity," *History of Religions*, 31:3 (1992), pp. 280–281.
9. Ibid., p. 287.
10. Boone, p. 13.
11. Haly, p. 297; Keys, p. 193.
12. Rene Millon, "Teotihuacan: City, State and Civilization," in Victoria Reifler Bricker, ed., *Supplement to the Handbook of Middle American Indians*, vol. 1, pp. 235–238; Norman Yoffee, ed., *The Collapse of Ancient States and Civilizations* (1988), pp. 149ff; Keys, pp. 192–193, 197–198.
13. Ernesto Gonzalez Licon, *Vanished Mesoamerican Civilizations*, trans. Andrew Ellis (1991), pp. 81–83.
14. Ibid., p. 92.

Chapter Twenty-Eight Great and Holy Majesty

1. John J. Saunders, *A History of Medieval Islam* (1978), pp. 5–6.
2. Karen Armstrong, *Muhammad* (1993), p. 62.
3. Irfan Shahid, *Byzantium and the Arabs in the Sixth Century*, vol. 2, Part 1 (2002), pp. 2–3, 140; Hugh Kennedy, *The Prophet and the Age of the Caliphates*, 2d ed. (2004), p.17.
4. Alois Grillmeier, *Christ in Christian Tradition*, vol. 2, trans. O. C. Dean (1996), p. 306.
5. "The Letter of Simeon of Beth Arsham," quoted in Dionysius, *Chronicle*, part 3, trans. Witold Witakowski (1996), pp. 53–57, and in Stuart Munro-Hay, *The Quest for the Ark of the Covenant* (1996), pp. 60–62.
6. Procopius, *History of the Wars and Buildings*, vol. 1, 1.10; Saunders, *History of Medieval Islam*, p. 13; Armstrong *Muhammad*, p. 56; Grillmeier, p. 320.
7. Procopius, *Secret History*, 1.1–1.2, 9.15.
8. Ibid., 9.27–30.
9. James Stevenson, ed., *Creeds, Councils and Controversies* (1966), p. 337.
10. Severus of Al'Ashmunein, *History of the Patriarchs of the Coptic Church of Alexandria*, trans. B. Evetts (1904), Chapter 13; Antigone Samellas, *Death in the Eastern Mediterranean (50–600 A.D.)* (2002), p. 41 n. 77.
11. Fred Blume, trans., *Annotated Justinian Code* (2008), 5.4.
12. Gregory, pp. 124–126.
13. Blume, 1.14.
14. Ibid., 1.1.
15. Quoted in Sara Rappe, *Reading Neoplatonism* (2000), p. 197.

Chapter Twenty-Nine Pestilence

1. al-Tabari, *History*, vol. 5, pp. 148–149, 398.
2. Procopius, *Secret History*, 13.32.
3. Procopius, *History of the Wars and Buildings*, vol. 1, 1.24.
4. Bury, *History of the Later Roman Empire*, vol. 1, pp. 340–341.
5. Procopius, *History of the Wars and Buildings*, vol. 1, 1.24.
6. Ibid., 1.24.
7. Bury, *History of the Later Roman Empire*, vol. 1, pp. 344–345.
8. Procopius, *History of the Wars and Buildings*, vol. 7 (1940), 1.i.
9. Procopius, *History of the Wars and Buildings*, vol. 2, 3.20.
10. Pohl, "The Vandals," pp. 44–45; Collins, pp. 38–39.
11. Gregory, p. 121; Procopius, *History of the Wars and Buildings*, vol. 3, 5.3.

12. Cassiodorus, p. 444.

13. Gregory, p. 136; Bury, *History of the Later Roman Empire*, vol. 1, pp. 394–395.

14. Collins (1999), p. 198; Burns, pp. 206–207.

15. Procopius, *History of the Wars and Buildings*, vol. 3, 6.6.

16. al-Tabari, *History*, vol. 5, p. 158.

17. Ehsan Yarshater, ed., *The Cambridge History of Iran* (1983), p. 155.

18. al-Tabari *History*, vol. 5, pp. 157–158.

19. Yarshater, p. 155.

20. Procopius, *History of the Wars and Buildings*, vol. 1, 2.22.

21. Ibid., 2.13; William Rosen, *Justinian's Flea* (2007), p. 223.

22. Evagrius Scholasticus (1846), 29; Procopius, *History of the Wars and Buildings*, vol. 1, 2.23.

23. Bury, *History of the Later Roman Empire*, vol. 1, pp. 434–435.

24. Procopius, *History of the Wars and Buildings*, vol. 1, 2.27.

25. Eusebius, *Ecclesiastical History*, Books 1–5, trans. Roy J. Deferrari (1953), p. 82.

26. Procopius, *History of the Wars and Buildings*, vol. 1, 2:12; Evagrius Scholasticus, 27.

27. Procopius, *History of the Wars and Buildings*, vol. 1, 2.22; Evagrius Scholasticus 29; Rosen, pp. 222–223.

Chapter Thirty **The Heavenly Sovereign**

1. Lee, *New History of Korea*, p. 43.

2. Ibid., p. 46.

3. Robert Karl Reischauer, *Early Japanese History (c. 40 BC–AD 1167)*, part A (1967), pp. 8–9; Milton W. Meyer, *Japan*, 3d ed. (1993), p. 27.

4. Reischauer, p. 11.

5. Reischauer, p. 134; Richard Bowring, *The Religious Traditions of Japan, 500–1600* (2005), p. 15.

6. Lee, *New History of Korea*, pp. 44–47.

7. Reischauer, p. 134.

8. Bowring, pp. 40–41.

9. Joan R. Piggott, *The Emergence of Japanese Kingship* (1997), p. 75.

10. Reischauer, p. 138.

11. Reischauer, p. 139; Meyer, p. 33.

12. Kuroita-Katsumi, *Prince Shotoku and His Seventeen-Article Constitution* (1940), pp. 20–22.

Chapter Thirty-One **Reunification**

1. Yang Xuanzhi, "A Northerner's Defense of Northern Culture," in Patricia Ebrey, ed., *Chinese Civilization*, 2d ed., (1993), pp. 10–110.

2. MacGowan, pp. 240–241.

3. Paludan, p. 75.

4. Yan Zhitui, "Advice to His Sons," in Ebrey, pp. 110–111.

5. Arthur F. Wright, *The Sui Dynasty* (1978), pp. 57–58.

6. Quoted in ibid., p. 58.

7. Ibid., pp. 61–62.

8. Ibid., p. 63.

9. Ibid.

10. Paludan, p. 77.

11. Rayne Kruger, *All Under Heaven* (2003), pp. 184–186; Charles O. Hucker, *China's Imperial Port* (1975), p. 138.

12. Kruger, p. 189.

13. Ibid.; Roberts, p. 104.
14. Roberts, p. 82.

Chapter Thirty-Two The South Indian Kings

1. Thapar, *Early India*, p. 328; Benjamin Lewis Rice, *Mysore Inscriptions* (1983), p. 319.
2. Hermann Oldenberg, *The Religion of the Veda* (1988), p. 250; Wendy Doniger O'Flaherty, ed., *Textual Sources for the Study of Hinduism* (1990), pp. 15–17.
3. Rice, pp. 303, 305.
4. Pran Nath Chopra et al., *History of South India* (1979), p. 61.
5. Sachindra Kumar Maity, *Professor A. L. Basham, My Guruji and Problems and Perspectives of Ancient Indian History and Culture* (1997), p. 189.
6. Bana, *The Harsha Carita*, trans. Edward B. Cowell and F. W. Thomas (1968), chap. 4.
7. Wolpert, p. 94; Bana, chap. 8.
8. Karl J. Schmidt, *An Atlas and Survey of South Asian History* (1995), p. 29.
9. Maity, pp. 189–190; Rice, p. 322.
10. Thapar, *Early India*, p. 330.

Chapter Thirty-Three Two Emperors

1. Gwyn Jones, *A History of the Vikings* (1984), p. 25; Paul the Deacon, *History of the Lombards*, trans. William Dudley Foulke (1974), 1.2.
2. Burns, p. 214.
3. Gregory, p. 137.
4. Collins, pp. 43–48.
5. Michael M. Gunter, *The Kurds and the Future of Turkey* (1997), p. 7.
6. R. N. Frye, "The Political History of Iran under the Sasanians," in Yarshater, p. 156.
7. Bury, *History of the Later Roman Empire*, vol. 2, p. 33.
8. Paul the Deacon, 2.4.
9. Ibid., 1.27.
10. al-Tabari, *History*, vol. 5, pp. 149–150.
11. Saunders, *History of Medieval Islam*, p. 22; Armstrong, *Muhammad*, p. 58–59.
12. Saunders, p. 14; Thomas F. Cleary, trans., *The Essential Qu'ran* (1988), Surah 105.
13. Saunders, *History of Medieval Islam*, p. 14.
14. Bury, *History of the Later Roman Empire*, vol. 2, pp. 76–77.
15. Gregory, p. 150.
16. al-Tabari, *History*, vol. 5, pp. 156–161.

Chapter Thirty-Four The Mayors of the Palaces

1. Gregory of Tours, 4.27–28.
2. Venantius Fortunatus, *Venantius Fortunatus*, trans. Judith W. George (1995), p. 47.
3. Gregory of Tours, 4.51.
4. Frank Glessner Ryder, trans., *The Song of the Nibelungs* (1962), pp. 95–97, 188, 197.
5. Gregory of Tours, 8.9
6. Fredegar, *Fredegarii Chronicorum Liber Quartus cum Continuationibus*, trans. J. M. Wallace-Hadrill (1960), 4.17.
7. Ibid., 4.19.
8. Ibid., 4.30.
9. Ibid., 4.38.

10. Ibid., 4.42.
11. Geary, pp. 152–154.
12. Fredegar, 4.67.
13. Ibid., 4.85.
14. Ibid., *Continations* 1–2.
15. Geary, p. 180.

Chapter Thirty-Five Gregory the Great

1. Paul the Deacon, 2.28.
2. Ibid., 3.35.
3. Schaff and Wace, *Select Library*, vol. 12, p. 399.
4. Paul the Deacon, 3.24.
5. Schaff and Wace, *Select Library*, vol. 12, p. 420.
6. Epistle 1.3, in ibid., p. 532.
7. Jeffrey Richards, *The Popes and the Papacy in the Early Middle Ages, 476–752* (1979), p. 173.
8. Epistle 5.36, in Schaff and Wace, *Select Library*, vol. 12, p. 704.
9. Richards, p. 174.
10. Henry Mayr-Hartin, *The Coming of Christianity to Anglo-Saxon England* (1972), pp. 33–34.
11. Bede, 1.23; Gregory the Great, Epistle 5.51, in Schaff and Wace, *Select Library*, vol. 12, p. 753.
12. Bede, 1.25, 5.24.
13. Quoted in Fletcher, *The Barbarian Conversion* (1999), p. 115.
14. Bede, 1.26.
15. Epistle 8.30, in Schaff and Wace, *Select Library*, vol. 12, p. 815; Fletcher, *Barbarian Conversion*, p. 116.
16. Epistle 11.64, in Schaff and Wace, *Select Library*, vol. 13, p. 133.
17. Bede, 1.26.

Chapter Thirty-Six The Persian Crusade

1. al-Tabari, *History*, vol. 5, p. 298.
2. Theophylact Simocatta, *The History of Theophylact Simocatta*, trans. Michael Whitby and Mary Whitby (1986), 8.1–3
3. Frye, "Political History of Iran under the Sasanians," in Yarshater, pp. 163–165.
4. Gregory, p. 151.
5. Bury, *History of the Later Roman Empire*, vol. 2, pp. 126–128; Maurice, *Maurice's Strategikon*, trans. George T. Dennis (1984), 9.4.
6. Bury, *History of the Later Roman Empire*, vol. I, pp. 85–86.
7. Ibid., pp. 88–89.
8. Ibid., p. 92.
9. Theophanes the Confessor, *The Chronicle of Theophanes*, trans. Harry Turtledove (1982), p. 1.
10. Gregory the Great, Epistle 13.31, in Schaff and Wace, *Select Library*, vol. 13, p. 173.
11. Theophanes, *Chronicle* (1982), p. 3; Ostrogorsky, p. 84.
12. Theophanes, *Chronicle* (1982), p. 9.
13. Ibid., p. 10.
14. Fredegar 4.34.
15. Antiochus Strategos, "The Capture of Jerusalem by the Persians in 614 AD," trans. F. C. Conybeare, *English Historical Review*, 25 (1910), pp. 509–510.
16. Theophanes, *Chronicle* (1982), p. 12.
17. Bury, *History of the Later Roman Empire*, vol. 2, p. 219.
18. Quoted in ibid., p. 220.

19. Ibid., p. 223.
20. Theophanes, *Chronicle* (1982), pp. 13–14.
21. Ostrogorsky, pp. 100–101.
22. Theophanes, *Chronicle* (1982), p. 15.
23. Cross and Sherbowitz-Wetzor, p. 55.
24. Fredegar, 4.48.
25. Collins, pp. 118–119; Ostrogorsky, pp. 102–103.
26. Theodore the Syncellus, *Traduction et Commentaire de l'homélie écrite probablement par Théodore le Syncelle sur le siège de Constantinople en 626,* trans. Ferenc Makk (1975), 22.
27. Ostrogorsky, p. 103.
28. Theodore the Syncellus, 33.
29. Frye, *History of Ancient Iran,* p. 337.
30. Andreas N. Stratos, *Byzantium in the Seventh Century,* vol. 1 (1968), pp. 602–614.
31. al-Tabari, *History,* vol. 5, p. 678.
32. Theophanes, *Chronicle,* pp. 327–328.

Chapter Thirty-Seven **The Prophet**

1. Jerry Rogers et al., *Water Resources and Environmental History* (2004), p. 36.
2. Dionysius, p. 65.
3. Paul Dresch, *Tribes, Government, and History in Yemen* (1993), p. 6; Keys, pp. 60–62; *The Holy Qur'an,* trans. Abdullah Yusuf Ali (2000), Surah 34.15–16, 19.
4. Saunders, *History of Medieval Islam,* p. 22.
5. Ishaq, *The Life of Muhammad,* trans. A Guillaume (1997), p. 119.
6. Armstrong, *Muhammad,* pp. 58–59, 67–68, 94. I am indebted to Karen Armstrong for her insightful analysis of the differences between tribal and urban Arab society in the fifth and sixth centuries.
7. Marshall G. S. Hodgson, *The Venture of Islam,* vol. 1 (1974), pp. 149–150.
8. Ishaq, pp. 63, 73, 79.
9. Ibid., p. 84.
10. Ibid., p. 106.
11. Hodgson, *Venture of Islam,* vol. 1, p. 163.
12. *Holy Qur'an,* Surah 93; Ishaq, p. 112.
13. Ishaq, p. 119.
14. Ibid., p. 213.
15. Ibid., p. 221.
16. Ibid., p. 232.

Chapter Thirty-Eight **Tang Dominance**

1. John Curtis Perry and Bardwell L. Smith, eds., *Essays on T'ang Society* (1976), pp. 20–21.
2. Barfield, pp. 142–144.
3. Roberts, p. 82.
4. Barfield, p. 144.
5. Roberts, p. 105.
6. Barfield, p. 145.
7. Hucker, p. 141; René Grousset, *The Empire of the Steppes* (1970), p. 102.
8. Roberts, p. 106; A. Tom Grunfeld, *The Making of Modern Tibet,* rev. ed. (1996), p. 35.
9. Grunfeld, pp. 35–37; Roberts, pp. 105–107.
10. Michael, p. 111; Dora Shu-fang Dien, *Empress Wu Zetian in Fiction and in History* (2003), pp. 34–35.

11. Grousset, pp. 102–103.
12. C. P. Fitzgerald, *The Empress Wu* (1968), pp. 42–43.
13. Aston, *Nihongi* (1896), p. 191.
14. Aston, pp. 192–193.
15. Gary L. Ebersole, *Ritual Poetry and the Politics of Death in Early Japan* (1989), p. 231.
16. Carter J. Eckert et al., *Korea, Old and New* (1990), pp. 42–43.
17. Ibid., p. 43.

Chapter Thirty-Nine The Tribe of Faith

1. Armstrong, *Muhammad*, p. 154.
2. *Holy Qu'ran*, Surah 2.13; Martin Lings, *Muhammad* (1983), pp. 126–127.
3. Ishaq, pp. 235–236.
4. Ibid., p. 280.
5. Hodgson, *Venture of Islam*, vol. 1, pp. 174–175.
6. Ishaq, pp. 286–289.
7. Lings, pp. 136–137; *Holy Qu'ran*, Surah 2.217.
8. Lings, pp. 140–141.
9. Ishaq, p. 464.
10. Hodgson, *Venture of Islam*, vol. 1, pp. 194–195.
11. Barnaby Rogerson, *The Prophet Muhammad* (2003), pp. 207ff.
12. Saunders, *History of Medieval Islam*, pp. 139–140.
13. al-Tabari, *History*, vol. 14: *The Conquest of Iran*, trans. G. Rex Smith (1994), p. 114.
14. Kennedy, *Prophet and the Age*, pp. 55–56.
15. Saunders, *History of Medieval Islam*, p. 41.
16. al-Tabari, *History*, vol. 15, p. 86.
17. Bury, *History of the Later Roman Empire*, vol. 2, pp. 262–263.
18. al-Tabari, *History*, vol. 14, p. 114.
19. Bury, *History of the Later Roman Empire*, vol. 2, p. 235.
20. Vasiliev, p. 211.
21. Collins, p. 120.
22. Timothy Gregory, p. 171.
23. Bury, *History of the Later Roman Empire*, vol. 2, p. 287.
24. Paul the Deacon, 4.42.
25. al-Tabari, *History*, vol. 14, p. 77.

Chapter Forty Intersection

1. al-Tabari, *History*, vol. 14, p. 77.
2. Keay, p. 203.
3. al-Tabari, *History*, vol. 14, p. 77.
4. Ibid., p. 78.
5. Vincent Arthur Smith, *The Early History of India* (1904), p. 287.
6. Wolpert, p. 94; Gavin Flood, "The Saiva Traditions," in Gavin Flood, ed., *The Blackwell Companion to Hinduism* (2003), pp. 200–203; Harsha, *Nagananda*, trans. Palmer Boyd (1999), pp. 47–49.
7. Smith, pp. 290, 294.
8. Schmidt, p. 29.
9. Sastri, *History of South India*, pp. 115–116.
10. Kulke, p. 105.

Chapter Forty-One The Troubles of Empire

1. Kennedy, *Prophet and the Age*, p. 69.
2. Ibid., p. 70.
3. Collins, pp. 122–124.
4. al-Tabari, *History*, vol. 15, pp. 26–27.
5. Collins, p. 124; Bury, *History of the Later Roman Empire*, vol. 2, p. 288.
6. Theophanes, *Chronicle* (1982), p. 43.
7. al-Tabari, *History*, vol. 15, p. 22.
8. 'Abd al-Husain Zarrinkub, "The Arab Conquest of Iran and Its Aftermath," in R. N. Frye, ed., *The Cambridge History of Iran in Eight Volumes*, vol. 4(1975), p. 23; al-Tabari, vol. 15, p. 69.
9. Zarrinkub, pp. 24–25; al-Tabari, *History*, vol. 15, pp. 78–79.
10. al-Tabari, *History*, vol. 15, p. 63.
11. Kennedy, *Prophet and the Age*, p. 72; Collins, p. 121; Zarrinkub, p. 21.
12. al-Tabari, *History*, vol. 15, pp. 131, 138.
13. Ibid., pp. 141–142.
14. Ibid., pp. 188–189.
15. Ibid., p. 222.
16. Muhammad ibn al-Husayn Sharif al-Radi, *Nahjul Balagha*, trans. Mohammad Askari Jafery (1984), "Letter: To the Egyptians."
17. Kennedy, *Prophet and the Age*, p. 76.
18. Hodgson, *Venture of Islam*, pp. 214–215.
19. al-Radi, "A Reply to Mu'awiya's Letter."
20. Ibid., "A Letter to Mu'awiya."
21. Ibid., "To His Soldiers Before the Battle of Siffin."
22. Hodgson, *Venture of Islam*, vol. 1, p. 216.

Chapter Forty-Two Law and Language

1. Walter Pohl and Helmut Reimitz, *Strategies of Distinction* (1998), p. 58; Paul the Deacon, 4.42.
2. Pohl and Reimitz, p. 209.
3. Paul the Deacon, 5.6.
4. Ibid., 5.7.
5. Bury, *History of the Later Roman Empire*, vol. 2, p. 302.
6. Ibid., p. 303.
7. Collins (1999), pp. 124–125; Dineschandra Sircar, *Studies in the Geography of Ancient and Medieval India* (1971), p. 290.
8. Ostrogorsky, p. 124.
9. Bury, *History of the Later Roman Empire*, vol. 2, pp. 331–333.
10. Theophanes, *Chronicle* (1982), pp. 56–57.
11. Martin Sicker, *The Islamic World in Ascendancy* (2000), p. 23.
12. Theophanes, *Chronicle* (1982), p. 59.
13. Collins, p. 227.
14. Sicker, p. 24; Kennedy, *Prophet and the Age*, p. 98; Theophanes, *Chronicle* (1982), p. 64.
15. Collins, p. 228.

Chapter Forty-Three Creating the Past

1. David John Lu, *Japan* (1997), p. 27.
2. Piggott, p. 106; Lu, p. 27.
3. Piggott, pp. 83, 118–121.

4. Aston, p. 301.
5. Meyer, p. 37.
6. Michael, pp. 43–44, 113.
7. Meyer, pp. 44–45.
8. Piggott, pp. 1, 3.
9. Aston, pp. 110–111.

Chapter Forty-Four The Days of the Empress

1. Fitzgerald, *Empress Wu*, p. 88.
2. R. W. L. Guisso, *Wu Tse-T'ien and the Politics of Legitimization in T'ang China* (1978), p. 51.
3. Ibid., p. 52; Roberts, pp. 88–89.
4. Fitzgerald, *Empress Wu*, p. 116.
5. Ibid., pp. 127–128.
6. Ibid., pp. 135–136; Guisso, pp. 137–138.
7. Barfield, pp. 146–147.
8. Roberts, pp. 105–06.
9. Grousset, pp. 110–111; Roberts, p. 106.
10. Roberts, p. 90; Fitzgerald, *Empress Wu*, p. 163.
11. Guisso, p. 154; Michael, p. 111.
12. Michael, pp. 111–112; MacGowan, p. 309.
13. Michael, p. 112; Roberts, pp. 90–91.

Chapter Forty-Five Paths into Europe

1. Theophanes, *Chronicle* (1982), pp. 70–71.
2. Gregory, p. 111.
3. Theophanes, *Chronicle* (1982), pp. 72–73.
4. Collins, pp. 129–130.
5. Heather, pp. 284–285.
6. Collins, pp. 110–112.
7. Ibid., pp. 115–116.
8. Ibn Abd al-Hakam, *The History of the Conquest of Spain*, trans. John Harris Jones (1858), p. 22.
9. Bury, *History of the Later Roman Empire*, vol. 2, pp. 372–373, 382–383.
10. Sicker, p. 25; Bury, *History of the Later Roman Empire*, vol. 2, p. 401.
11. Theophanes, *Chronicle*, pp. 88–89.
12. Ibid., pp. 90–91.
13. Geary, p. 204.
14. Fredegar, p. 90.
15. Paul Fouracre, *The Age of Charles Martel* (2000), p. 88; Fredegar, p. 91.

Chapter Forty-Six The Kailasa of the South

1. Elliot and Dowson, *The History of India*, p. 405.
2. Ibid., pp. 119–120.
3. Ibid., pp. 170–172.
4. Sicker, p. 25; Keay, p. 185; Elliot and Dowson, p. 123.
5. Nau Nihal Singh, *The Royal Gurjars* (2003), p. 209.
6. Ibid., p. 210.
7. Ronald Inden, *Imagining India* (1992), p. 252.
8. Keay, pp. 200–201; Inden, pp. 257–258.

Chapter Forty-Seven Purifications

1. Sicker, p. 26.
2. Barfield, pp. 148–149.
3. "Epitome of the Iconoclastic Council of Constantinople, 754," in Schaff and Wace, *Select Library*, vol. 14, p. 543.
4. Eamon Duffy, *Saints & Sinners* (1997), p. 80.
5. Ostrogorsky, pp. 161–163.
6. Theophanes, *Chronicle* (1982), pp. 96–97.
7. Ibid., p. 97; St. John of Damascus, "First Apology," in *On the Divine Images: Three Apologies against Those Who Attack the Divine Images*, trans. David Anderson (1980), p. 31.
8. Theophanes, *Chronicle* (1982), p. 98.
9. Duffy, p. 82.
10. Collins, p. 230.
11. Jan T. Hallenbeck, *Pavia and Rome* (1982), p. 24.
12. Ibid., p. 25.
13. Ostrogorsky, p. 164; Theophanes, *Chronicle* (1982), p. 100.

Chapter Forty-Eight The Abbasids

1. Simon Franklin and Jonathan Shepard, *The Emergence of Rus, 750–1200* (1996), pp. 7–10.
2. Kevin Alan Brook, *The Jews of Khazaria*, 2d ed. (2006), p. 97; "The Letter of Joseph the King," in Jacob Rader Marcus, ed., *The Jew in the Medieval World*, rev. ed. (1999), pp. 227–228.
3. Kennedy (2004), *Prophet and the Age*, pp. 110–111.
4. al-Tabari, *History*, vol. 26, p. 72.
5. Kennedy, *Prophet and the Age*, p. 123.
6. Sicker, p. 27.
7. Ahmed ibn Mohammed al-Makkari, *The History of the Mohammedan Dynasties in Spain*, trans. Pascual de Gayangos (2002), pp. 95–96.
8. al-Tabari, *History*, vol. 27, pp. 172–174.
9. Arthur Wollaston, *The Sword of Islam* (1905), p. 130.
10. al-Tabari, *History*, vol. 28, p. 238; Sicker, p. 29.
11. M. A. Shaban, *Islamic History* (1976), p. 12.
12. Hodgson, *Venture of Islam*, vol. 1, pp. 286–287; al-Tabari, vol. 1, *History*, vol. 28, pp. 124ff; Shaban, p. 10.
13. Hodgson, *Venture of Islam*, vol. 1, p. 287.

Chapter Forty-Nine Charlemagne

1. Oliver J. Thatcher and Edgar Holmes McNeal, eds., *A Source Book for Medieval History* (1905), p. 102.
2. Fredegar (1960), 4.22.
3. Fredegar, 4.30; Joanna Story, ed., *Charlemagne* (2005), pp. 16–17; Einhard, "The Life of Charlemagne" 1.2, in Lewis Thorpe, trans., *Two Lives of Charlemagne* (1969).
4. Paul Edward Dutton, ed., *Carolingian Civilization* (1993), p. 11.
5. Slightly condensed from the *Clausula de unctione Pippini*, in Dutton, p. 12.
6. Fredegar, 4.38–39.
7. "The Donation of Constantine," in Dutton, pp. 14–19.
8. Einhard, "Life of Charlemagne" 3.18, in Thorpe.
9. J. M. Wallace-Hadrill, *The Barbarian West* (1962), p. 97.
10. Wallace-Hadrill, *Barbarian West* (1962), p. 97.

11. Einhard, "Life of Charlemagne" 2.6, in Thorpe.
12. Einhard, "Life of Charlemagne" 2.9–10, in Thorpe.
13. Charles Kenneth Scott-Moncrieff, trans., *The Song of Roland* (1920), p. 80.

Chapter Fifty The An Lushan Rebellion

1. Li Po, "A Farewell to Li Yun in the Xie Tiao Pavilion," in Xianyi Yang and Gladys Yang, trans., *Poetry and Prose of the Tang and Song* (1984), p. 31; Michael, p. 116.
2. Wang Wei, "Seeing Yuan the Second off on a Mission to Anxi," in Yang and Yang, p. 16; Roberts, p. 122.
3. Roberts, p. 92.
4. Li Po, "Fighting South of the City," in Yang and Yang, pp. 22–23.
5. Hans J. Van de Ven, *Warfare in Chinese History* (2000), pp. 132–133; Roberts, p. 103.
6. Roberts, p. 93.
7. Ibid.; Van de Ven, pp. 137–138.
8. Michael, p. 144; Bai Juyi, "Song of Eternal Sorrow," in Yang and Yang, pp. 111–115.
9. Charles D. Benn, *China's Golden Age* (2004), p. 10.
10. Van de Ven, p. 139.
11. Michael, p. 114; Roberts, p. 107.
12. Roberts, p. 108.
13. Lee, *New History of Korea*, p. 72; Roberts, pp. 110–111.
14. Michael, p. 114; Van de Ven, p. 144.

Chapter Fifty-One Imperator et Augustus

1. Theophanes, *Chronicle* (1982), p. 135.
2. Bury, *History of the Later Roman Empire*, vol. 2, pp. 478–479.
3. Sicker, p. 30.
4. Theophanes, *Chronicle* (1982), p. 141.
5. Derek Wilson, *Charlemagne* (2006), pp. 84–85.
6. J. M. Wallace-Hadrill, *The Frankish Church* (1983), pp. 413–414.
7. "Alcuin to Charlemagne," in Henry Morley and William Hall Griffin, *English Writers*, vol. 2 (1888), p. 165.
8. Theophanes, *Chronicle* (1982), pp. 146–147.
9. Ibid., p. 151.
10. Ibid., p. 153.
11. Ibid., p. 155.
12. Wallace-Hadrill, *Frankish Church*, pp. 220–223.
13. Wilson, p. 76.
14. Quoted in Wallace-Hadrill, *Frankish Church*, p. 186.
15. Quoted in Wilson, p. 77.
16. Notker the Stammerer, *Charlemagne* 27, in Thorpe, p. 125.
17. Wilson, p. 81; Wallace-Hadrill, *Barbarian West*, p. 109.
18. Quoted in Wilson, p. 81.
19. Theophanes the Confessor, *The Chronicle of Theophanes Confessor*, trans. Cyril Mango and Roger Scott (1997), p. 657.

Chapter Fifty-Two The New Sennacherib

1. al-Tabari, *History*, vol. 30, p. 100.
2. Sicker, p. 30.

3. Richard Hodges and David Whitehouse, *Mohammed, Charlemagne & the Origins of Europe* (1983), pp. 141, 158; Einhard, "Life of Charlemagne" 1.16, in Thorpe.
4. Collins, pp. 191–192.
5. Franklin and Shepard, p. 12.
6. Hugh Kennedy, *When Baghdad Ruled the Muslim World* (2005), p. 51.
7. Karsh, *Islamic Imperialism* (2006), p. 72.
8. Florin Curta, *Southeastern Europe in the Middle Ages* (2006), p. 147.
9. Curta, p. 149; Theophanes, *Chronicle of Theophanes Confessor* (1997), pp. 483–485.
10. Theophanes, *Chronicle of Theophanes Confessor* (1997), pp. 665–666.
11. Curta, pp. 149–150.
12. Theophanes, *Chronicle of Theophanes Confessor* (1997), p. 673.
13. Curta, p. 150.
14. Theophanes, *Chronicle of Theophanes Confessor* (1997), p. 679.
15. Wallace-Hadrill, *Barbarian West*, p. 112.
16. Theophanes, *Chronicle of Theophanes Confessor* (1997), p 685.
17. Ibid., p. 503.
18. Curta, p. 148.
19. Theophanes, *Chronicle of Theophanes Confessor* (1997), p. 686.
20. Dimitri Obolensky, *Byzantium and the Slavs* (1994), p. 40.

Chapter Fifty-Three Castle Lords and Regents

1. Jae-un Kang, *The Land of Scholars*, trans. Suzanne Lee (2006), p. 64.
2. Lee and de Bary, pp. 48–49.
3. Lee, *New History of Korea*, p. 84.
4. Lee, et al., *Sourcebook of Korean Civilization*, p. 122.
5. Kang, p. 232.
6. Lee, et al., *Sourcebook of Korean Civilization*, p. 133.
7. Lee, *New History of Korea*, p. 92.
8. Ibid., p. 93.
9. Lee, et al., *Sourcebook of Korean Civilization*, p. 220.
10. Lee, *New History of Korea*, p. 95.
11. Ibid., p. 96.
12. James Huntley Grayson, *Korea* (2002), pp. 57–58.
13. Reischauer, p. 216.
14. Meyer, p. 51.
15. Reischauer, p. 222; Meyer, p. 51.
16. Reischauer, pp. 232–233; Meyer, p. 54.
17. Meyer, p. 54; Karl F. Friday, *Hired Swords* (1992), pp. 74–75.
18. Piggott, p. 282; Reischauer, p. 249.
19. Peter Martin, *The Chrysanthemum Throne* (1997), p. 56.
20. Takie Sugiyama Lebra, *Above the Clouds* (1993), p. 35; Michele Marra, *The Aesthetics of Discontent* (1991), pp. 38–39.

Chapter Fifty-Four The Triumph of the Outsiders

1. Gernet, p. 266; Denis Twitchett et al., *The Cambridge History of China*, vol. 6 (1994), p. 7.
2. Roberts, p. 95; Van de Ven, p. 165.
3. MacGowan, pp. 329–331.
4. Chye Kiang Heng, *Cities of Aristocrats and Bureaucrats* (1999), pp. 20, 78–81.
5. Roberts, p. 107.

6. de Bary et al., p. 374.
7. Gernet, p. 267.
8. Roberts, p. 96.
9. Gernet, p. 267.
10. Quoted in Heng, p. 73.
11. Twitchett et al. (1994), p. 56.
12. MacGowan, pp. 338–339.
13. Ibid., pp. 339-340.
14. Twitchett et al. (1994), p. 10.
15. Roger Tennant, *A History of Korea* (1996), p. 67.
16. Ibid., pp. 67–68.
17. Lee et al., *Sourcebook of Korean Civilization*, p. 126.
18. Ibid., p. 126.
19. Tennant (1996), p. 68; Lee, *New History of Korea*, p. 98.
20. Lee, *New History of Korea*, p. 98; Tennant, pp. 68–69.
21. Lee, *New History of Korea*, p. 99; Tennant, p. 70.
22. Jong-gil Kim, *Among the Flowering Reeds* (2003), p. 32.
23. Tennant, pp. 69–70.
24. Lee et al. *Sourcebook of Korean Civilization* (1993), pp. 129, 261.
25. Tennant, pp. 70–71; Lee et al., *Sourcebook of Korean Civilization* (1993), p. 261.

Chapter Fifty-Five The Third Dynasty

1. al-Tabari, *History*, vol. 30, p. 335.
2. P. M. Holt, et al., eds. *The Cambridge History of Islam*, vol. 1 (1970), pp. 118–119.
3. al-Tabari, *History*, vol. 31, p. 23.
4. Ibid, pp. 48–51.
5. Ibid., pp. 152–153, 185–186.
6. Holt et al., pp. 119–123.
7. al-Tabari, *History*, vol. 32, pp. 131–134.

Chapter Fifty-Six The Vikings

1. Jones, *History of the Vikings*, pp. 25–26.
2. Louis Halphen, *Charlemagne and the Carolingian Empire*, trans. Giselle de Nie (1977), p. 97.
3. Wallace-Hadrill, *Early Germanic Kingship*, p. 114; Nithard's *Histories*, 2, in Bernhard Walter Scholz with Barbara Rogers, trans., *Carolingian Chronicles* (1970), p. 130.
4. Halphen, p. 158.
5. Scholz with Rogers, p. 131.
6. Ibid., p. 133.
7. Janet L. Nelson, trans., *The Annals of St. Bertin* (1991), p. 49.
8. "Engelbert at the Battle of Fontenoy," in Dutton, p. 364.
9. H. W. Carless Davis, *Charlemagne (Charles the Great)* (1925), p. 314.
10. Franklin and Shepard, p. 56.
11. P. H. Sawyer, *Kings and Vikings* (1982), p. 88; Pierre Riche, *The Carolingians*, trans. Michael Idomir Allen (1993), p. 192.
12. Riche, p. 197.
13. Franklin and Shepard, p. 9.
14. Ibid., p. 29.
15. Nelson, p. 44.
16. Franklin and Shepard, p. 40.

17. Ibid., pp. 55–56.
18. Photius, *The Homilies of Photius*, trans. Cyril Mango (1958), pp. 95–96.
19. Franklin and Shepard, p. 51.
20. Ibid., p. 58–59.

Chapter Fifty-Seven Long-Lived Kings

1. Dilip Kumar Ganguly, *Ancient India, History and Archaeology* (1994), p. 44; Rama Shankar Tripathi, *History of Kanauj* (1964), pp. 227–228.
2. Tripathi, pp. 232–234.
3. Sailendra Nath Sen, *Ancient Indian History and Civilization* (1988), p. 371.
4. R. C. Majumdar, *Ancient India* (1964), p. 367.
5. Kulke, p. 11.
6. Tripathi, pp. 239, 241.
7. Majumdar, p. 367; Tripathi, p. 243.
8. Majumdar, p. 404.

Chapter Fifty-Eight Foreign and Domestic Relations

1. From "The *Vita* of Methodius," in Deno John Geanakoplos, ed., *Byzantium* (1984), p. 348.
2. Ostrogorsky, p. 203.
3. Obolensky, p. 207.
4. P. M. Barford, *The Early Slavs* (2001), p. 221.
5. Nelson, p. 137.
6. Ostrogorsky, pp. 204–205.
7. Obolensky, p. 207; Barford, p. 222.
8. Vasiliev, p. 301.
9. Ibid., p. 304; Ostrogorsky, pp. 212–213.
10. Shaun Tougher, *The Reign of Leo VI (886–912)* (1997), p. 61.
11. Ibid., p. 62.

Chapter Fifty-Nine The Second Caliphate

1. Dominique Sourdel, *Medieval Islam* (1983), pp. 76–79; Seyyed Hossein Nasr, *Islamic Philosophy from Its Origin to the Present* (2006), p. 122.
2. Holt et al., p. 124; Sourdel, pp. 78–79.
3. Paul E. Walker, *Fatimid History and Ismaili Doctrine* (2008), 2.4
4. Holt et al., p. 125.
5. Ibid., pp. 125–126.
6. al-Tabari, *History*, vol. 34, translator's preface, pp. xi–xii.
7. al-Tabari, *History*, vol. 35, pp. 164–165.
8. Holt et al., p. 129.
9. S. D. Goitein, "On the Origin of the Term Vizier," *Journal of the American Oriental Society*, 81:4 (Sep.–Dec. 1961), pp. 425–426.

Chapter Sixty The Great Army of the Vikings

1. Quoted in Margaret Mahler, *A History of Chirk Castle and Chirkland* (1912), p. 202.
2. Magnus Magnusson, *Scotland* (2000), p. 40.
3. Collins, p. 194; Simeon of Durham, *The Historical Works of Simeon of Durham*, trans. J. Stevenson (1855), p. 487.

4. Bryan Sykes, *Saxons, Vikings, and Celts* (2006), p. 261; Snorri Sturluson, *Heimskringla*, trans. Erling Monsen (1932), p. 5; John Asser, *Asser's Life of King Alfred*, trans. Lionel Cecil Jane (1908), p. 41.
5. Bede, p. 299.
6. Seamus Heaney, *Beowulf* (2001), 2.175–179.
7. Sykes, p. 262.
8. Swanton, p. 68.
9. Ibid., p. 70; Simon Keynes and Michael Lapidge, trans., *Alfred the Great* (1983), p. 77.
10. Swanton, p. 71.
11. Keynes and Lapidge, p. 83.
12. Asser, p. 38.
13. Simeon of Durham, p. 476.
14. Keynes and Lapidge, p. 84.
15. John of Worcester, *The Chronicle of John of Worcester*, vol. 2: *The Annals from 450 to 1066*, trans. Jennifer Bray and P. McGurk (1995), p. 355.

Chapter Sixty-One Struggle for the Iron Crown

1. Eric Joseph Goldberg, *Struggle for Empire* (2006), p. 331.
2. Halphen, p. 319.
3. Ibid., p. 324.
4. Ibid., p. 327.
5. Quoted in Riche, p. 219.
6. Liudprand of Cremona, *The Complete Works of Liudprand of Cremona*, trans. Paolo Squatriti (2007), p. 67.
7. Ibid., p. 64.
8. Ibid., p. 69.
9. Constantine Porphyrogenitus, *De Administrando Imperio*, trans. R. J. H. Jenkins (1967), pp. 171–173.
10. Andras Rona-Tas, *Hungarians and Europe in the Early Middle Ages* (1999), pp. 336–337.

Chapter Sixty-Two Kampaku

1. Lebra, p. 35.
2. Reischauer, p. 270.
3. Sadaie Fujiwara and William Ninnis Porter, *A Hundred Verses from Old Japan* (1909), p. 12.
4. James S. De Benneville, *Saitō Mussashi-Bō Benkei* (1910), pp. 104–105; Meyer, p. 58.
5. Robert Borgen, *Sugawara No Michizane and the Early Heian Court* (1986), p. 176.
6. Reischauer, pp. 272–273.
7. Marra, p. 46.
8. Hall, et al., pp. 55–56; Borgen, p. 28.
9. Hall et al., p. 57; Borgen, pp. 208–209.
10. Reischauer, p. 279.
11. De Benneville, p. 106; Hall et al., p. 58.
12. Reischauer, p. 64.
13. Hall et al., pp. 59–60; Reischauer, pp. 287ff.
14. H. Paul Varley, *Warriors of Japan as Portrayed in the War Tales* (1994), p. 8.
15. Karl F. Friday, *Hired Swords* (1992), p. 10; Varley, pp. 144–145.
16. Friday, pp. 12–13; Varley, p. 145.

Chapter Sixty-Three **Basileus**

1. Tougher, *Reign of Leo VI*, p. 115.
2. Ibid., p. 117.
3. Arnold Toynbee, *Constantine Porphyrogenitus and His World* (1973), p. 13.
4. Lynda Garland, *Byzantine Empresses* (1999), p. 114.
5. Quoted in Garland, p. 115.
6. Vasiliev, p. 316.
7. Thomas Riha, ed., *Readings in Russian Civilization*, vol. 1 (1969), p. 2.
8. Steven Runciman, *The Emperor Romanus Lecapenus & His Reign* (1929), p. 44.
9. Ostrogorsky (1969), p. 261.
10. Leo the Deacon, *The History of Leo the Deacon* (2005), 7.7
11. Ostrogorsky, p. 263.
12. Liudprand of Cremona, p. 124.
13. Leo the Deacon, 7.7.
14. Liudprand of Cremona, p. 123.
15. Runciman, *Emperor Romanus Lecapenus & His Reign*, p. 61.
16. Ibid., p. 90, Romilly Jenkins, *Byzantium* (1987), pp. 242–243.
17. Runciman, *Emperor Romanus Lecapenus & His Reign*, p. 92.

Chapter Sixty-Four **The Creation of Normandy**

1. Liudprand of Cremona, p. 92.
2. Ibid., p. 94.
3. Riche, pp. 226–227.
4. *Gesta Normannorum Ducum*, vol. 1, trans. Elisabeth M. C. Van Houts (1992), p. 67.

Chapter Sixty-Five **The Kingdom of Germany**

1. Liudprand of Cremona, p. 75.
2. Josef Fleckenstein, *Early Medieval Germany*, trans. Bernard S. Smith (1978), pp. 108–110.
3. Ibid., p. 111; Liudprand of Cremona, p. 77.
4. Liudprand of Cremona, p. 85.
5. Fleckenstein, pp. 112–113.
6. Ibid., p. 116.
7. Liudprand of Cremona, pp. 89–90.
8. Ibid., p. 90.
9. Charles IV, *Autobiography of Emperor Charles IV and His Legend of St. Wenceslas*, trans. and ed. Balazs Nagy and Frank Schaer (2001), p. 185.
10. Ibid., p. 189.
11. Ibid., p. 193.

Chapter Sixty-Six **The Turn of the Wheel**

1. K. A. Nilakanta Sastri, *The Pandyan Kingdom* (1929), p. 81.
2. Ibid., p. 81.
3. Ibid., pp. 82, 99.
4. Ibid., p. 82.
5. Rice, p. 326.
6. Sen, p. 480; Sastri, *Pandyan Kingdom*, p. 100.
7. Karen Pechilis Prentiss, *The Embodiment of Bhakti* (1999), pp. 95–96.

8. Sastri, *Pandyan Kingdom*, p. 102.
9. Rice, p. 463.

Chapter Sixty-Seven The Capture of Baghdad

1. Karsh, p. 54.
2. Heinz Halm, *The Empire of the Mahdi* (1996), p. 173.
3. Ibid., pp. 175, 200–201.
4. Kennedy, *Prophet and the Age*, p. 314.
5. Archibald Ross Lewis, *The Development of Southern French and Catalan Society, 718–1050* (1965), pp. 70–71, 161.
6. W. Montgomery Watt, *A History of Islamic Spain* (1965), p. 40.
7. Ibid., p. 46.
8. Karsh, p. 62.
9. Franklin and Shepard, p. 64.
10. Kennedy, *Prophet and the Age*, p. 217; Karsh, p. 63.
11. Geoffrey L. Simons, *Iraq: From Sumer to Saddam* (1994), p. 161.
12. Kennedy, *Prophet and the Age*, pp. 194–195.
13. Peter Beaumont, *Drylands* (1993), pp. 126–127; Kennedy, *Prophet and the Age*, p. 197.

Chapter Sixty-Eight Three Kingdoms

1. Lee et al., *Sourcebook of Korean Civilization*, (1993), p. 261.
2. Lee, *New History of Korea* (1984), p. 101.
3. Lee et al., *Sourcebook of Korean Civilization*, p. 275.
4. Lee, *New History of Korea*, p. 103.
5. James B. Palais, *Confucian Statecraft and Korean Institutions* (1996), p. 214; Peter H. Lee et al., *Sources of Korean Tradition* (1997), p. 146.
6. Lee et al., *Sources of Korean Tradition*, pp. 146–147.
7. Lee et al., *Sourcebook of Korean Civilization*, p. 264.
8. Grousset, p. 128.
9. Ibid., pp. 570 n. 125, 129.
10. Ibid., p. 129.
11. MacGowan, p. 361.
12. Ibid.
13. Fitzgerald, *China*, p. 378.
14. MacGowan, p. 368.

Chapter Sixty-Nine Kings of England

1. Swanton, p. 104.
2. D. M. Hadley, *The Northern Danelaw* (2000), pp. 11–12.
3. William of Malmesbury, p. 207.
4. John of Worcester, *Chronicles*, vol. 2 (1995), p. 387.
5. Swanton, pp. 106, 108–109.
6. William of Malmesbury, p. 213.
7. Ibid., p. 233.
8. Ibid., p. 237.
9. Ibid., p. 237.
10. Ibid., p. 245.

11. John of Worcester, *Chronicles*, vol. 2, pp. 422–425; William of Malmesbury, pp. 239–241; Swanton, p. 118.

12. Jones, *History of the Vikings*, pp. 34–35, 45–46; Ornolfur Thorsson, ed., *The Sagas of the Icelanders: A Selection* (2001), p. 9.

13. Thorsson, p. 9.

14. Jones, *History of the Vikings*, p. 279.

15. Ibid., p. 95.

16. Thorsson, p. 81.

17. Sturluson, p. 104.

18. Ibid., p. 113.

19. Thorsson, p. 654.

20. Ibid., p. 655.

21. Sturluson, p. 140.

22. William of Malmesbury, p. 273.

23. John of Worcester, *Chronicles*, vol. 2, p. 425.

24. Sturluson, p. 141.

25. Ibid., pp. 214–215.

26. Henry of Huntingdon, *The Chronicle of Henry of Huntingdon*, trans. Thomas Forester (1853), p. 183.

27. Swanton, p. 135 n. 9.

28. Ian Howard, *Swein Forkbeard's Invasions and the Danish Conquest of England, 991–1017* (2003), pp. 62–63.

29. Swanton, p. 143.

30. Ibid., pp. 143–145; William of Malmesbury, pp. 302–303.

Chapter Seventy The Baptism of the Rus

1. Toynbee, pp. 10–11.

2. Mark Whittow, *The Making of Byzantium, 600–1025* (1996), pp. 321–322.

3. Ibn Fadlan, *Ibn Fadlan's Journey to Russia,* trans. Richard N. Frye (2005), pp. 64–65.

4. Ibid., pp. 68–70; Franklin and Shepard, pp. 44–45.

5. Jones, *History of the Vikings*, p. 260.

6. Cross and Sherbowitz-Wetzor, p. 68.

7. Leo the Deacon, p. 156.

8. Wladyslaw Duczko, *Viking Rus* (2004), pp. 214–215.

9. Toynbee, pp. 499–505; Whittow, pp. 258–259.

10. B. J. Kidd, *Documents Illustrative of the History of the Church*, vol. 3 (1920), p. 103.

11. Cross and Sherbowitz-Wetzor, p. 84.

12. Vasiliev, p. 302.

13. Leo the Deacon, pp. 58, 82.

14. Ostrogorsky, pp. 284–285.

15. Leo the Deacon, p. 83.

16. Ostrogorsky, pp. 284–285; Leo the Deacon, pp. 85–86.

17. Cross and Sherbowitz-Wetzor, p. 87. The chronology of these events is not entirely clear, but this is one of several plausible reconstructions. See also Whittow, pp. 260–261, and Ostrogorsky, pp. 292–293.

18. Leo the Deacon, pp. 136–141.

19. Ibid., p. 147.

20. Cross and Sherbowitz-Wetzor, p. 90.

21. Jones, *History of the Vikings*, pp. 262–263.

22. Cross and Sherbowitz-Wetzor, p. 113.

23. Ibid., pp. 97–98, 116
24. Ibid., p. 117.

Chapter Seventy-One The Holy Roman Emperor

1. Simon of Kéza, *Gesta Hungarorum*, trans. Lászlo Veszprémy and Frank Schaer (1999), p. 91.
2. Ibid., p. 93; Paul Lendvai, *The Hungarians*, trans. Ann Major (2003), pp. 27–28.
3. Uta-Renate Blumenthal, *The Investiture Controversy* (1988), p 39.
4. Thatcher and McNeal, pp. 116–117. The oath was actually taken in two parts, one recorded in 961 and the second in 962.
5. J. N. D. Kelly, *The Oxford Dictionary of Popes* (1986), pp. 126–127.
6. Susan Wood, *The Proprietary Church in the Medieval West* (2006), pp. 16–17.
7. Book of Acts 8:18–24.
8. Wood, p. 299.
9. Thatcher and McNeal, p. 118.
10. Kelly, *Oxford Dictionary of Popes*, p. 127.
11. Timothy Reuter and Rosamond McKitterick, eds., *The New Cambridge Medieval History*, vol. 3 (1999), p. 254.
12. Thietmar of Merseburg, *Ottonian Germany* (2001), pp. 126–127; Reuter and McKitterick, p. 255.
13. Thietmar of Merseburg, p. 149.
14. Ibid., p. 150; Gerd Althoff, *Otto III* (2003), pp. 33–34.
15. Althoff, pp. 38–39.
16. F. L. Ganshof, *Feudalism*, trans. Philip Grierson (1996), pp. 3–9.
17. Thatcher and McNeal, p. 412.
18. Blumenthal, p. 11.

Chapter Seventy-Two The Hardship of Sacred War

1. Keay, p. 204; Satish Chandra, *Medieval India* (2000), p. 17.
2. Sircar, pp. 290–291.
3. Quoted in Ray, p. 81.
4. Quoted in Keay, pp. 204–205.
5. Abu al-Nasr Muhammad ibn ʿAbd al-Jabbar al-Utbi, *Kitab-i-Yamini*, trans. James Reynolds (1858), pp. 23–24, 33.
6. Ibid., p. 39; Keay, p. 206.
7. Quoted in Elliot and Dowson, pp. 26–27; Chandra, p. 17.
8. Chandra, p. 18.
9. Ibid., p. 19.
10. Romesh Chunder Dutt, *A History of Civilisation in Ancient India* (2000), pp. 325–326.
11. Ibn Fadlan, pp. 37–38.
12. James Heitzman, *Gifts of Power* (1997), p. 6; Keay, p. 216; E. Hultzsch and H. Krishna Sastri, *Miscellaneous Inscriptions from the Tamil Country* (1899), "Tiruvalangadu Copper-Plates," v.84.
13. Pechilis Prentiss, pp. 100–101, 104.
14. Hultzsch and Sastri, "Tiruvalangadu Copper-Plates," v. 87, 96–97.
15. Ronald Findlay and Kevin H. O'Rourke, Power and Plenty (2007), p. 68; Hultzsch and Sastri, "Tiruvalangadu Copper-Plates," v.92.
16. Hultzsch and Sastri, "Tiruvalangadu Copper-Plates," v. 98, v.112.
17. Heitzman, pp. 6–10.
18. Sen, p. 44.

Chapter Seventy-Three Basil the Bulgar-Slayer

1. Michael Psellus, *Fourteen Byzantine Rulers*, trans. E. R. A. Sewter (1966), p. 27.
2. John Van Antwerp Fine, *The Early Medieval Balkans* (1983), p. 189.
3. Ostrogorsky, p. 301.
4. Psellus, pp. 31, 35.
5. Franklin and Shepard, pp. 162–163; Psellus, p. 35.
6. Psellus, p. 43.
7. Ibid., pp. 40, 43–44, 46.
8. Ostrogorsky, pp. 309–310; Curta, pp. 244–245.
9. Marshall G. S. Hodgson, *The Venture of Islam*, vol. 2 (1974), pp. 26–27.
10. Karen Armstrong, *Jerusalem* (1996), pp. 258–259.
11. Whittow, p. 381; Farhad Daftary, *A Short History of the Ismailis* (1998), pp. 101, 185.
12. R. J. Crampton, *A Concise History of Bulgaria* (1997), pp. 21–22.
13. Armstrong, Jerusalem, pp. 259–260; Hodgson, *Venture of Islam*, vol. 2 pp. 26–27.

Chapter Seventy-Four Defending the Mandate

1. Peter Lorge, *War, Politics and Society in Early Modern China* (2005), p. 32.
2. Karl F. Olsson, "The Structure of Power under the Third Emperor of Sung China" (1974) pp. 26–27.
3. Twitchett et al., p. 99.
4. Van de Ven, p. 185.
5. Twitchett et al., p. 99.
6. Peter Kees Bol, *"This Culture of Ours"* (1992), p. 55.
7. Lorge, pp. 33–34; Bol, pp. 51–52, 55.
8. Chuanjing Ding and Chu Djang, *A Compilation of Anecdotes of Sung Personalities*, trans. by Zhang Chu and Zhu Zhang (1989), p. 23.
9. Van de Ven, p. 189.
10. Jinsheng Tao, *Two Sons of Heaven* (1988), pp. 15–16.
11. Edward L. Davis, *Society and the Supernatural in Song China* (2001), p. 68.
12. Shepard Krech et al., *Encyclopedia of World Environmental History*, vol. 2 (2004), p. 602.
13. Paludan, p. 130.
14. Joseph Needham and Cunxun Qian, *Science and Civilization in China*, vol. 5 (1985), p. 97.

Chapter Seventy-Five The New Found Land

1. Thorsson, pp. 637–638.
2. Ibid., pp. 638–641.
3. Ibid., p. 639.
4. Ibid., pp. 644–645.
5. Ibid., p. 647.
6. Ibid., pp. 648, 670; Helge Ingstad and Anne Stine Ingstad, *The Viking Discovery of America* (2001), p. 48.
7. Alice Beck Kehoe, *America Before the European Invasions* (2002), p. 1.
8. Stuart J. Fiedel, *Prehistory of the Americas* (1987), pp. 152–153, 156–157; Kehoe, p. 102.
9. Fiedel, pp. 237, 254–257; Kehoe, pp. 175–177.
10. Kehoe, pp. 148–150; Fiedel, pp. 214–217.
11. Adams, p. 63.
12. Ibid., pp. 63–65.
13. Hans J. Prem, *The Ancient Americas* (1997), pp. 18–19; Robert J. Sharer and Sylvanus Griswold

Morley, *The Ancient Maya*, 5th ed. (1994), pp. 471–472; Nicholas J. Saunders, *Ancient Americas* (2004), p. 84.

14. Adams, p. 79; Saunders, *Ancient Americas*, p. 48.
15. H. B. Nicholson, *Topiltzin Quetzalcoatl* (2001), pp. 250–251.
16. Prem, pp. 21–22; Adams, pp. 68–69; Saunders, *Ancient Americas*, p. 79.
17. Nicholson, pp. 10–11.
18. Prem, p. 24; Adams, p. 73.
19. Adams, p. 75.

Chapter Seventy-Six Schism

1. James Muldoon, *Empire and Order* (1999), pp. 34–35.
2. Alexander Clarence Flick, *The Rise of the Mediaeval Church and Its Influence on the Civilisation of Western Europe from the First to the Thirteenth Century* (1909), p. 403.
3. Althoff, p.72.
4. Flick, p. 404; Althoff, pp. 73–79.
5. Kelly, *Oxford Dictionary of Popes*, pp. 27–28.
6. Slightly condensed from Thatcher and McNeal, pp. 119–120.
7. Thietmar of Merseburg, p. 187; Althoff, pp. 127–129.
8. Blumenthal, p. 42.
9. Ibid., p. 43.
10. Christopher Brooke, *Europe in the Central Middle Ages, 962–1154*, 2d ed. (1987), p. 227.
11. Robert Warrand Carlyle and A. J. Carlyle, *A History of Mediaeval Political Theory in the West* (1915), pp. 146, 164, 228; Brooke, p. 229.
12. Flick, p. 408.
13. Brooke, p. 231; Karle Hampe, *Germany under the Salian and Hohenstaufen Emperors*, trans. Ralph Bennett (1973), pp. 43–45.
14. Hampe, p. 47.
15. Stefan Weinfurter, *The Salian Century* (1999), p. 101.
16. Flick, p. 410; F. Donald Logan, *A History of the Church in the Middle Ages* (2002), pp. 102–103.
17. Thatcher and McNeal, pp. 121–122.
18. Ibid., p. 122.
19. Anna Comnena, *The Alexiad of Anna Comnena*, trans. E. R. A. Sewter (1969), 1.10–11
20. William of Apulia, "Gesta Roberti Wiscardi," book 2, in G. H. Pertz et al., *Chronica et annales aevi Salici* (1963).
21. Goffredo Malaterra, *The Deeds of Count Roger of Calabria and Sicily and of His Brother Duke Robert Guiscard*, trans. Kenneth Baxter Wolf (2005), book 1.
22. William of Apulia, book 2, in Pertz et al.
23. Henry Chadwick, *East and West* (2003), pp. 206–207, 211–213.
24. Horst Fuhrmann, *Germany in the High Middle Ages, c. 1050–1200*, trans. Timothy Reuter (1986), p. 55.

Chapter Seventy-Seven Danish Domination

1. Howard, pp. 126, 133.
2. Henry of Huntingdon, p. 192; Swanton, p. 145.
3. Henry of Huntingdon, p. 195.
4. Swanton, p. 152; William of Malmesbury, p. 317.
5. Swanton, p. 153.
6. John of Worcester, *Chronicles*, vol. 2, p. 503.
7. Swanton, pp. 157–159.

8. Ibid., p. 159.
9. Peter Rex, *Harold II* (2005), pp. 26–27; Swanton, p. 158.
10. *Encomium Emmae Reginae*, trans. Alistair Campbell (1998), p. xxxiv.
11. Swanton, p. 160.
12. Benjamin T. Hudson, *Prophecy of Berchán* (1996), pp. 223–224.
13. Swanton, pp. 160–162.

Chapter Seventy-Eight The Norman Conquest

1. David Howarth, *1066* (1977), p. 34; John of Worcester, *Chronicles*, vol. 2 p. 535.
2. William of Malmesbury, p. 353.
3. Henry of Huntingdon, p. 202; William of Malmesbury, p. 353.
4. Henry of Huntingdon, p. 202.
5. William of Malmesbury, p. 353; John of Worcester, *Chronicles*, vol. 2, pp. 570–571.
6. Howarth, pp. 67–68, 74–75.
7. Swanton, pp. 194–195.
8. Swanton, p. 196.
9. Howarth, pp. 127–129; Rex, pp. 217–219.
10. Howarth, pp. 134–135.
11. Henry of Huntingdon, p. 209.
12. Swanton, pp. 198–199.

Chapter Seventy-Nine The Kings of Spain

1. Watt, pp. 81–82; Abd Allah b. Buluggin, *The Tibyan*, trans. Amin T. Tibi (1986), p. 43.
2. Abd Allah b. Buluggin, p 43; Watt, p. 82.
3. Hugh Kennedy, "Muslim Spain and Portugal," in David Luscome and Jonathan Riley-Smith, eds., *The New Cambridge Medieval History*, vol. 4 (2004), p. 599.
4. Abd Allah b. Buluggin, p. 43.
5. Manuela Marin and Salma Khadra Jayyusi, *Handbuch der Orientalistik 12, Abt. 1, Bd.* (1992), p. 46.
6. Peter C. Scales, *The Fall of the Caliphate of Cordoba* (1994), p. 93; Marin and Jayyusi, p. 48.
7. Scales, pp. 2, 9, 99.
8. Anita George, *Annals of the Queens of Spain* (1850), pp. 52-53.
9. Pedro, King of Aragon, *The Chronicle of San Juan De La Peña*, trans. Lynn H. Nelson (1991), p. 14.
10. Simon Barton and R. A. Fletcher, *The World of El Cid* (2000), pp. 49–50.
11. Ibid., p. 101.
12. Ibid., p. 32.
13. Ibid., p. 103; trans., John Ormsby, *The Poem of the Cid*, (1879), p. 63.
14. Marín and Jayyusi, p. 61.
15. Roland Oliver and Brian M. Fagan, *Africa in the Iron Age, c. 500 BC to AD 1400* (1975), p. 160.
16. Oliver and Fagan, p. 160; David Robinson, *Muslim Societies in African History* (2004), pp. 39–40.
17. Oliver and Fagan, p. 161; Arie Schippers, *Spanish Hebrew Poetry and the Arab Literary Tradition* (1994), p. 331; Barton and Fletcher, p. 113.
18. Watt, p. 98.
19. Richard A. Fletcher, *The Quest for El Cid* (1990), p. 185; Barton and Fletcher, p. 147.
20. Bernard F. Reilly, *The Medieval Spains* (1993), p. 99; Luscome and Riley-Smith, p. 609; Marín and Jayyusi, pp. 64–65.
21. George, pp. 187–188; Reilly, p. 109.

Chapter Eighty The Arrival of the Turks

1. Psellus, pp. 53, 57.
2. Ibid., pp. 64–65.
3. Ibid., p. 81.
4. Shaun Tougher, "Byzantine Eunuchs: An Overview, with Special Reference to Their Creation and Origin," in Liz James, ed., *Women, Men, and Eunuchs* (1997), pp. 178–179.
5. Psellus, p. 93.
6. Ibid., p. 116.
7. Ibid., pp. 138–139.
8. Ibid., p. 155.
9. Ibid., p. 158.
10. Luscome and Riley-Smith, p. 230.
11. Grousset, p. 150.
12. Izz al-Din Ibn al-Athir, *The Annals of the Saljuq Turks*, trans. D. S. Richards (2002), pp. 67–68; Ibrahim Kafesoglu and Gary Leiser, *A History of the Seljuks* (1988), pp. 40–41.
13. Psellus, pp. 224–225.
14. Ibid., p. 300.
15. Archer Jones, *The Art of War in the Western World* (1987), p. 100.
16. Ibid., p. 101.
17. Psellus, pp. 365–366.

Chapter Eighty-One The Loss of the Song

1. Ruth W. Dunnell, *The Great State of White and High* (1996), p. 37.
2. Ibid., pp. 38–39.
3. Ebrey, pp. 140–141.
4. Lorge, p. 45.
5. Lorge, p. 46.
6. Gernet, pp. 310–311; Needham et al., pp. 93–94.
7. Twitchett et al., pp. 216, 219.
8. Lee et al., *Sourcebook of Korean Civilization*, p. 275; Lee, *New History of Korea*, p. 126.
9. Lee, *New History of Korea*, pp. 127–128.
10. Twitchett et al., p. 222.
11. Stephen Eskildsen, *The Teachings and Practices of the Early Quanzhen Taoist Masters* (2004), pp. 192–193.
12. Lorge , pp. 50–51.
13. David R. Olson and Michael Cole, *Technology, Literacy and the Evolution of Society* (2006), pp. 60–61.
14. Lorge, pp. 53–54.
15. Ebrey, p. 170.

Chapter Eighty-Two Repentance at Canossa

1. Fuhrmann, p. 52.
2. Ian S. Robinson, *Henry IV of Germany* (2000), p. 43.
3. Thatcher and McNeal, pp. 417–418.
4. Robinson, *Henry IV of Germany* (2000), pp. 110–111.
5. Ibid., p. 111.
6. R. W. Southern, *Western Society and the Church in the Middle Ages* (1970), p. 102; H. E. J. Cowdrey, *The Register of Pope Gregory VII, 1073–1085* (1998), p. 557.

7. Blumenthal, pp. 110–113; Cowdrey, pp. 130–131.

8. Cowdrey, pp. 133–134.

9. Ibid., p. 134.

10. Ibid., p. 137.

11. Ibid., p. 138.

12. Ibid., p. 141.

13. Fuhrmann, p. 65.

14. Ibid., p. 156.

15. Fuhrmann, pp. 65–66.

Chapter Eighty-Three **The Call**

1. Psellus, p. 369 and n. I, pp. 369–370; Ostrogorsky, pp. 347–348.

2. Saunders, *History of Medieval Islam*, pp. 149–150.

3. Armstrong, *Jerusalem*, pp. 268–269.

4. Ostrogorsky, pp. 348–349.

5. Comnena, 3.8–9.

6. Robinson, *Henry IV of Germany*, pp. 194–196.

7. Ibid., p. 204.

8. Comnena, 3.10.

9. Robinson, *Henry IV of Germany*, pp. 229–231.

10. Cowdrey, p. 446.

11. Dante, *Inferno*, trans. Allen Mandelbaum (1982), canto 28, lines 13–16.

12. Daftary, *A Short History of the Ismailis*, p. 125.

13. Thomas Asbridge, *The First Crusade* (2004), p. 32.

14. Thatcher and McNeal, pp. 513–517.

Chapter Eighty-Four **Fighting for Jerusalem**

1. Comnena, 10.5–6.

2. William of Tyre, *A History of Deeds Done Beyond the Sea*, vol. 1, trans. Emily Atwater Babcock and A. C. Krey (1976), pp. 98–99.

3. Comnena, 10.5.

4. Ibid., pp. 105–106; John France, *The Crusades and the Expansion of Catholic Christendom, 1000–1714* (2005), pp. 65–66.

5. William of Tyre, p. 109.

6. Comnena (1969), 10.9–10.

7. Asbridge, p. 158; France, pp. 76–77.

8. William of Tyre, pp. 214–215; France, p. 77.

9. Ibn Al-Qala nisi, *The Damascus Chronicle of the Crusades*, trans. Hamilton Gibb (2003), p. 43; Jean de Joinville and Geoffrey de Villehardouin, *Chronicle of the Crusades*, trans. M. R. B. Shaw, p. 8; Asbridge (2004), pp. 150–151; William of Tyre, pp. 239–240.

10. Steven Runciman, *A History of the Crusades*, vol. 1 (1951), pp. 227–228.

11. France, p. 79; Comnena, 10.11.

12. William of Tyre, p. 258.

13. Ibid., pp. 270–274.

14. William of Tyre, p. 281; Runciman, *History of the Crusades*, vol. 1, pp. 244–245.

15. France, p. 84.

16. William of Tyre, pp. 352–353; France, pp. 86–87.

17. William of Tyre, p. 368; France, pp. 88–89.

18. Ibn Al-Qala nisi, p. 48.

Chapter Eighty-Five **Aftershocks**

1. Clay Stalls, *Possessing the Land* (1995), p. 37.
2. Olivia Remie Constable, *Medieval Iberia* (1997), pp. 156–157.
3. Comnena, 9.8.
4. Malcolm Barber and A. K. Bate, eds., *The Templars* (2002), p. 27; William of Tyre, pp. 524–525.
5. Barber and Bate, p. 32.

Works Cited

Abd Allah b. Buluggin. *The Tibyan: Memoirs of Abd Allah B. Buluggin, Last Zirid Amir of Granada.* Trans. Amin T. Tibi. Leiden: Brill, 1986.

Adams, Richard E. W. *Ancient Civilizations of the New World.* Boulder, Colo.: Westview Press, 1997.

Agathias. *The Histories.* Trans. Joseph D. Frendo. *Corpus Fontium Historiae Byzantinae.* Vol. 2A. Series Berolinensis. Berlin: Walter De Gruyter, 1975.

al-Hakam, Ibn Abd. *The History of the Conquest of Spain.* Trans. John Harris Jones. New York: Burt Franklin, 1858.

al-Makkari, Ahmed ibn Mohammed. *The History of the Mohammedan Dynasties in Spain.* Trans. Pascual de Gayangos. London: Routledge, 2002.

al-Radi, Muhammad ibn al-Husayn Sharif. *Nahjul Balagha: Sermons, Letters, and Sayings of Imam Ali ibn Abu Talib.* Trans. Mohammad Askari Jafery. Elmhurst, N.Y.: Tahrike Tarsile Quran, 1984.

al-Tabari, Muhammad ibn Jarir. *The History of al-Tabari.* Bibliotheca Persica, ed. Ehsan Yar-Shater. Vol. 5: *The Sasanids, the Byzantines, the Lakhmids, and Yemen.* Trans. Clifford Edmund Bosworth. Albany: State University of New York Press, 1999.

———. *The History of al-Tabari.* Bibliotheca Persica, ed. Ehsan Yar-Shater. Vol. 14: *The Conquest of Iran.* Trans. G. Rex Smith. Albany: State University of New York Press, 1994.

———. *The History of al-Tabari.* Bibliotheca Persica, ed. Ehsan Yar-Shater. Vol. 15: *The Crisis of the Early Caliphate.* Trans. R. Stephen Humphreys. Albany: State University of New York Press, 1990.

———. *The History of al-Tabari.* Bibliotheca Persica, ed. Ehsan Yar-Shater. Vol. 26: *The Waning of the Umayyad Caliphate.* Trans. Carole Hillenbrand. Albany: State University of New York Press, 1989.

———. *The History of al-Tabari.* Bibliotheca Persica, ed. Ehsan Yar-Shater. Vol. 27: *The Abbasid Revolution.* Trans. John Alden Williams. Albany: State University of New York Press, 1985.

———. *The History of al-Tabari.* Bibliotheca Persica, ed. Ehsan Yar-Shater. Vol. 28: *Abbasid Authority Affirmed.* Trans. Jane Dammen McAuliffe. Albany: State University of New York Press, 1995.

———. *The History of al-Tabari.* Bibliotheca Persica, ed. Ehsan Yar-Shater. Vol. 30: *The Abbasid Caliphate in Equilibrium.* Trans. Clifford Edmund Bosworth. Albany: State University of New York Press, 1989.

———. *The History of al-Tabari.* Bibliotheca Persica, ed. Ehsan Yar-Shater. Vol. 31: *The War between Brothers.* Trans. Michael Fishbein. Albany: State University of New York Press, 1992.

———. *The History of al-Tabari.* Bibliotheca Persica, ed. Ehsan Yar-Shater. Vol. 32: *The Reunification of the Abbasid Caliphate.* Trans. C. E. Bosworth. Albany: State University of New York Press, 1987.

———. *The History of al-Tabari.* Bibliotheca Persica, ed. Ehsan Yar-Shater. Vol. 34: *Incipient Decline.* Trans. Joel L. Kraemer. Albany: State University of New York Press, 1989.

———. *The History of al-Tabari.* Bibliotheca Persica, ed. Ehsan Yar-Shater. Vol. 35: *The Crisis of the Abbasid Caliphate.* Trans. George Saliba. Albany: State University of New York Press, 1985.

Althoff, Gerd. *Otto III.* Trans. Phyllis G. Jestice. University Park: Pennsylvania State University Press, 2003.

al-Utbi, Abu al-Nasr Muhammad ibn 'Abd al-Jabbar. *Kitab-i-Yamini.* Trans. James Reynolds. London: Oriental Translation Fund of Great Britain and Ireland, 1858.

Ambrose of Milan. *The Letters of St. Ambrose, Bishop of Milan.* Trans. H. Walford. Oxford: James Parker, 1881.

Ammianus Marcellinus. *The History of Ammianus Marcellinus.* Vol. 1. Trans. John C. Rolfe. Cambridge, Mass.: Harvard University Press, 1982.

———. *The History of Ammianus Marcellinus.* Vol. 2 and 3. Trans. John C. Rolfe. Cambridge, Mass.: Harvard University Press, 1986.

———. *The Later Roman Empire (A.D. 354–378).* Trans. Walter Hamilton. New York: Penguin, 1986.

Antiochus Strategos. "The Capture of Jerusalem by the Persians in 614 AD," trans. F. C. Conybeare. *English Historical Review*, Vol. 25 (1910), pp. 502–517.

Armstrong, Karen. *Jerusalem: One City, Three Faiths.* New York: Alfred A. Knopf, 1996.

———. *Muhammad: A Biography of the Prophet.* San Francisco: HarperSanFrancisco, 1993.

Asbridge, Thomas. *The First Crusade: The Roots of the Conflict between Christianity and Islam.* Oxford: Oxford University Press, 2004.

Asser, John. *Asser's Life of King Alfred.* Trans. Lionel Cecil Jane. London: Chatto & Windus, 1908.

Aston, W. G., trans. *Nihongi: Chronicles of Japan from the Earliest Times to A.D. 697.* London: George Allen & Unwin, 1896.

Augustine. *Confessions.* Trans. Henry Chadwick. Oxford: Oxford University Press, 1998.

Ayer, Joseph Cullen. *A Source Book for Ancient Church History: From the Apostolic Age to the Close of the Conciliar Period.* New York: Charles Scribner's Sons, 1913.

Bacharach, Jere L. "The Dinar versus the Ducat." *International Journal of Middle East Studies*, Vol. 4, no. 1 (Jan. 1973), pp. 77–96.

Bana. *The Harsha Carita.* Trans. Edward B. Cowell and F. W. Thomas. Delhi: M. Banarsidass, 1968.

Barber, Malcolm, and A. K. Bate, eds. *The Templars: Selected Sources.* Manchester: Manchester University Press, 2002.

Barfield, Thomas J. *The Perilous Frontier: Nomadic Empires and China.* Oxford: Basil Blackwell, 1989.

Barford, P. M. *The Early Slavs: Culture and Society in Early Medieval Eastern Europe.* Ithaca, N.Y.: Cornell University Press, 2001.

Barnes, T. D. "Constantine and the Christians of Persia." *The Journal of Roman Studies*, Vol. 75 (1985), pp. 126–136.

Barthold, Wilhelm. *An Historical Geography of Iran.* Trans. Svat Soucek. Princeton, N.J.: Princeton University Press, 1984.

Barton, Simon, and R. A. Fletcher. *The World of El Cid: Chronicles of the Spanish Reconquest.* Manchester: Manchester University Press, 2000.

Beal, Samuel, trans. *Travels of Fah-Hian and Sung-Yun, Buddhist Pilgrims, from China to India (400 A.D. and 518 A.D.).* New York: Augustus M. Kelley, 1969.

Beaumont, Peter. *Drylands: Environmental Management and Development.* New York: Routledge, 1993.

Bede. *Bede's Ecclesiastical History of the English People.* Ed. Bertram Colgrave and R. A. B. Mynors. Oxford: Clarendon Press, 1969.

Benedict. *The Holy Rule of St. Benedict.* Trans. Boniface Verheyen, OSB. Atchison, Kans.: Abbey Student Press, 1949.

Benn, Charles D. *China's Golden Age: Everyday Life in the Tang Dynasty.* Oxford: Oxford University Press, 2004.

Bettenson, Henry, and Chris Maunder, eds. *Documents of the Christian Church.* 3d ed. Oxford: Oxford University Press, 1999.

Blume, Fred H. *Annotated Justinian Code.* Ed. Timothy Kearley. Laramie: University of Wyoming College of Law, 2008.

Blumenthal, Uta-Renate. *The Investiture Controversy: Church and Monarchy from the Ninth to the Twelfth Century.* Philadelphia: University of Pennsylvania Press, 1988.

Bol, Peter Kees. *"This Culture of Ours": Intellectual Transitions in T'ang and Sung China.* Stanford, Calif.: Stanford University Press, 1992.

Boone, Elizabeth Hill. *Cycles of Time and Meaning in the Mexican Books of Fate.* Austin: University of Texas Press, 2007.

Borgen, Robert. *Sugawara No Michizane and the Early Heian Court.* Harvard East Asian monographs, 120. Cambridge, Mass.: Council on East Asian Studies, Harvard University, 1986.

Boulger, Demetrius Charles. *The History of China.* Vol. 1. Rev. ed. Freeport, N.Y.: Books for Libraries Press, 1972.

Bowring, Richard. *The Religious Traditions of Japan, 500–1600.* Cambridge: Cambridge University Press, 2005.

Boyce, Mary. "On the Orthodoxy of Sasanian Zoroastrianism." *Bulletin of the School of Oriental and African Studies, University of London,* Vol. 59, no. 1 (1996), pp. 11–28.

———. *Papers in Honour of Professor Mary Boyce.* Leiden: E. J. Brill, 1985.

Brook, Kevin Alan. *The Jews of Khazaria.* 2d ed. New York: Rowman & Littlefield, 2006.

Brooke, Christopher. *Europe in the Central Middle Ages, 962–1154.* 2d ed. London: Longman, 1987.

Burns, Thomas S. *A History of the Ostrogoths.* Bloomington: Indiana University Press, 1984.

Bury, J. B. *A History of the Later Roman Empire: From Arcadius to Irene (395–800 AD).* Vol. 1 and 2. Amsterdam: Adolf M. Hakkert, 1966.

———. "Justa Grata Honoria." *The Journal of Roman Studies,* Vol. 9 (1919), pp. 1–13.

Cantor, Norman. *The Civilization of the Middle Ages.* New York: Harper Perennial, 1984.

Carlyle, Robert Warrand, and A. J. Carlyle. *A History of Mediaeval Political Theory in the West.* Edinburgh: W. Blackwood & Sons, 1915.

Cassiodorus. *The Letters of Cassiodorus.* Trans. Thomas Hodgkin. London: H. Frowde, 1886.

Chadwick, Henry. *The Early Church.* London: Penguin Books, 1967.

———. *East and West: The Making of a Rift in the Church: From Apostolic Times until the Council of Florence.* Oxford: Oxford University Press, 2003.

Chandra, Satish. *Medieval India: From Sultanat to the Mughals.* New Delhi: Har-Anand Publications, 2000.

Charles IV. *Autobiography of Emperor Charles IV and His Legend of St. Wenceslas.* Trans. and ed. Balazs Nagy and Frank Schaer. Budapest: Central European University Press, 2001.

Ch'en, Kenneth Kuan Sheng. *Buddhism in China: A Historical Survey.* Princeton, N.J.: Princeton University Press, 1972.

Ch'ien, Edward T. "The Neo-Confucian Confrontation with Buddhism: A Structural and Historical Analysis." *Journal of Chinese Philosophy,* Vol. 15 (1988), pp. 347–369.

Chopra, Pran Nath, T. K. Ravindran, and N. Subrahmanian. *History of South India.* New Delhi: S. Chand, 1979.

Christian, David. *A History of Russia, Inner Asia and Mongolia.* Oxford: Blackwell, 1998.

Claudian. *Claudian.* Trans. Maurice Platnauer. Cambridge, Mass.: Harvard University Press, 1922.

Cleary, Thomas F., trans. *The Essential Koran.* Edison, N.J.: Essential Book Sales, 1988.

Cockell, Charles. *Impossible Extinction: Natural Catastrophes and the Supremacy of the Microbial World.* Cambridge: Cambridge University Press, 2003.

Collins, Roger. *Early Medieval Europe, 300–1000.* 2d ed. New York: St. Martin's Press, 1999.

Comnena, Anna. *The Alexiad of Anna Comnena.* Trans. E. R. A. Sewter. New York: Penguin Books, 1969.

Constable, Olivia Remie. *Medieval Iberia: Readings from Christian, Muslim, and Jewish Sources.* Philadelphia: University of Pennsylvania Press, 1997.

Constantine Porphyrogenitus. *De Administrando Imperio.* Trans. R. J. H. Jenkins. Washington, D.C.: Dumbarton Oaks, 1967.

Cowdrey, H. E. J. *The Register of Pope Gregory VII, 1023–1085.* Oxford: Clarendon Press, 1998.

Cowgill, George L. "State and Society at Teotihuacan, Mexico." *Annual Review of Anthropology,* Vol. 26 (1997), pp. 129–161.

Crampton, R. J. *A Concise History of Bulgaria.* Cambridge: Cambridge University Press, 1997.

Cross, Samuel Hazzard, and Olgerd P. Sherbowitz-Wetzor, trans. and ed. *The Russian Primary Chronicle: Laurentian Text.* Cambridge, Mass.: Mediaeval Academy of America, 1953.

Cross, Tom Peete, and Clark Harris Slover, eds. *Ancient Irish Tales.* New York: Henry Holt, 1936.

Cunningham, Alexander. *The Bhilsa Topes: Buddhist Monuments of Central India.* Oxford: Oxford University Press, 1854.

Curta, Florin. *Southeastern Europe in the Middle Ages, 500–1250.* Cambridge: Cambridge University Press, 2006.

Daftary, Farhad. *A Short History of the Ismailis: Traditions of a Muslim Community.* Princeton, N.J.: M. Wiener, 1998.

Dante. *Inferno: The Divine Comedy.* Trans. Allen Mandelbaum. New York: Bantam Books, 1982.

Davids, T. W. Rhys, trans. *The Questions of King Milinda.* Delhi: Motilal Banarsidass, 1890.

Davies, John. *A History of Wales.* London: Penguin, 1993.

Davis, Edward L. *Society and the Supernatural in Song China.* Honolulu: University of Hawaii Press, 2001.

Davis, H. W. Carless. *Charlemagne (Charles the Great): The Hero of Two Nations.* Rev. ed. New York: Putnam, 1925.

Dawson, Richard. *Imperial China.* London: Hutchinson, 1972.

de Bary, William Theodore, Wing-tsit Chan, and Burton Watson, eds. *Sources of Chinese Tradition.* Vol. 1. New York: Columbia University Press, 1963.

De Benneville, James S. *Saitō Mussashi-Bō Benkei.* (Tales of the Wars of the Gempei). Yokohama: author, 1910.

de Joinville, Jean, and Geoffrey de Villehardouin. *Chronicle of the Crusades.* Trans. M. R. B. Shaw. New York: Penguin Books, 1963.

Dien, Dora Shu-fang. *Empress Wu Zetian in Fiction and in History: Female Defiance in Confucian China.* New York: Nova Science, 2003.

Ding, Chuanjing, and Chu Djang. *A Compilation of Anecdotes of Sung Personalities / Song Ren Yi Shi Hui Bian.* Jamaica, N.Y.: St. John's University Press, 1989.

Dionysius. *Chronicle: Known Also as the Chronicle of Zuqnin.* Part 3. Trans. Witold Witakowski. Liverpool: Liverpool University Press, 1996.

Dresch, Paul. *Tribes, Government, and History in Yemen.* Oxford: Clarendon Press, 1993.

Duczko, Wladyslaw. *Viking Rus: Studies on the Presence of Scandinavians in Eastern Europe.* Boston: Brill Academic, 2004.

Duffy, Eamon. *Saints & Sinners: A History of the Popes.* New Haven, Conn.: Yale University Press, 1997.

Dunnell, Ruth W. *The Great State of White and High: Buddhism and State Formation in Eleventh-Century Xia.* Honolulu: University of Hawaii Press, 1996.

Dutt, Romesh Chunder. *A History of Civilisation in Ancient India, Based on Sanskrit Literature.* New Delhi: Cosmo Publications, 2000.

Dutton, Paul Edward, ed. *Carolingian Civilization: A Reader.* Ontario: Broadview Press, 1993.

Ebersole, Gary L. *Ritual Poetry and the Politics of Death in Early Japan.* Princeton, N.J.: Princeton University Press, 1989.

Ebrey, Patricia, ed. *Chinese Civilization: A Sourcebook.* 2d ed. New York: Free Press, 1993.

Eckert, Carter J, Ki-baik Lee, Young Ick Lew, Michael Robinson, and Edward W. Wagner. *Korea, Old and New: A History*. Seoul: Ilchokak, 1990.

Eliot, Charles. *Hinduism and Buddhism: A Historical Sketch*. Vol. 3. London: Routledge & Kegan, 1921.

Elliot, Henry M., and John Dowson, eds. *The History of India, as Told by Its Own Historians*. Vol. 1. London: Trubner, 1867.

Elvin, Mark. *The Pattern of the Chinese Past*. Stanford, Calif.: Stanford University Press, 1973.

Encomium Emma Reginae. Trans. Alistair Campbell. Cambridge: Cambridge University Press, 1998.

Eskildsen, Stephen. *The Teachings and Practices of the Early Quanzhen Taoist Masters*. New York: State University of New York Press, 2004.

Eusebius. *Ecclesiastical History*. Books 1–5. Trans. Roy J. Deferrari. Washington, D.C.: Catholic University of America Press, 1953.

———. *Life of Constantine*. Trans. Averil Cameron and Stuart G. Hall. Oxford: Clarendon Press, 1999.

Evagrius Scholasticus. *Ecclesiastical History*. Trans. E. Walford. London: Samuel Bagster & Sons, 1846.

Fage, J. D., and Roland Anthony Oliver. *The Cambridge History of Africa*. Cambridge: Cambridge University Press, 1975.

Faxian. *A record of Buddhistic kingdoms, being an account by the Chinese monk Fā-hien of his travels in India and Ceylon (A.D. 399–414) in search of the Buddhist books of discipline*. Trans. James Legge. Oxford: Clarendon Press, 1886.

Fiedel, Stuart J. *Prehistory of the Americas*. Cambridge: Cambridge University Press, 1987.

Findlay, Ronald, and Kevin H. O'Rourke. *Power and Plenty: Trade, War and the World Economy in the Second Millennium*. Princeton, N.J.: Princeton University Press, 2007.

Fine, John Van Antwerp. *The Early Medieval Balkans: A Critical Survey from the Sixth to the Late Twelfth Century*. Ann Arbor: University of Michigan Press, 1983.

Fitzgerald, C. P. *China: A Short Cultural History*. London: D. Appleton-Century, 1938.

———. *The Empress Wu*. Vancouver: University of British Columbia, 1968.

Fleckenstein, Josef. *Early Medieval Germany*. Trans. Bernard S. Smith. Amsterdam: North-Holland, 1978.

Fletcher, Richard A. *The Barbarian Conversion: From Paganism to Christianity*. Berkeley: University of California Press, 1999.

———. *The Quest for El Cid*. New York: Knopf, 1990.

Flick, Alexander Clarence. *The Rise of the Mediaeval Church and Its Influence on the Civilisation of Western Europe from the First to the Thirteenth Century*. New York: B. Franklin, 1909.

Flood, Gavin. "The Saiva Traditions." In *The Blackwell Companion to Hinduism*, ed. Gavid Flood. Oxford: Blackwell, 2003.

Fouracre, Paul. *The Age of Charles Martel*. Essex, England: Pearson, 2000.

France, John. *The Crusades and the Expansion of Catholic Christendom, 1000–1714*. New York: Routledge, 2005.

Franklin, Simon, and Jonathan Shepard. *The Emergence of Rus, 750–1200*. New York: Longman, 1996.

Fredegar. *Fredegarii Chronicorum Liber Quartus cum Continuationibus*. Trans. J. M. Wallace-Hadrill. London: Thomas Nelson & Sons, 1960.

Friday, Karl F. *Hired Swords: The Rise of Private Warrior Power in Early Japan*. Stanford, Calif.: Stanford University Press, 1992.

Frye, R. N. "The Political History of Iran under the Sasanians." Pp. 116–180 in *The Cambridge History of Iran*. Vol. 3(1): *The Seleucid, Parthian and Sasanian Periods*, ed. Ehsan Yarshater. Cambridge: Cambridge University Press, 1983.

Frye, Richard N. *The History of Ancient Iran.* Munchen: C. H. Beck'sche Verlagsbuchhandlung, 1983.

Fuhrmann, Horst. *Germany in the High Middle Ages, c. 1050–1200.* Trans. Timothy Reuter. Cambridge: Cambridge University Press, 1986.

Fujiwara, Sadaie, and William Ninnis Porter. *A Hundred Verses from Old Japan; Being a Translation of the Hyaku-Nin-Isshiu.* Oxford: Clarendon Press, 1909.

Ganguly, D. K. *The Imperial Guptas and Their Times.* New Delhi: Shakti Malik, 1987.

Ganguly, Dilip Kumar. *Ancient India, History and Archaeology.* New Delhi: Abhinav, 1994.

Ganshof, F. L. *Feudalism.* Trans. Philip Grierson. Medieval academy reprints for teaching, 34. Toronto: University of Toronto Press, 1996.

Garland, Lynda. *Byzantine Empresses: Women and Power in Byzantium, AD 527–1204.* New York: Routledge, 1999.

Geanakoplos, Deno John, ed. *Byzantium: Church, Society, and Civilization Seen through Contemporary Eyes.* Chicago: University of Chicago Press, 1984.

Geary, Patrick J. *Before France and Germany: The Creation and Transformation of the Merovingian World.* Oxford: Oxford University Press, 1988.

Geoffrey of Monmouth. *History of the Kings of Britain.* Trans. Lewis Thorpe. New York: Penguin, 1966.

George, Anita. *Annals of the Queens of Spain, from the Period of the Conquest of the Goths down to the Reign of Her Present Majesty Isabel II, with the Remarkable Events That Occurred during Their Reigns, and Anecdotes of Their Courts.* New York: Baker & Scribner, 1850.

Gernet, Jacques. *A History of Chinese Civilization.* 2d ed. Trans. J. R. Foster and Charles Hartman. Cambridge: Cambridge University Press, 1996.

The Gesta Normannorum Ducum of William of Jumieges, Orderic Vitalis, and Robert of Torigni. Vol. 1: *Introduction and Books I–IV.* Trans. Elisabeth M. C. Van Houts. Oxford: Clarendon Press, 1992.

Gildas. *The Ruin of Britain and Other Works.* Trans. Michael Winterbottom. London: Phillimore, 1978.

Giles, J. A. *Old English Chronicles.* London: George Bell & Sons, 1908.

Goitein, S. D. "On the Origin of the Term Vizier." *Journal of the American Oriental Society,* Vol. 81, no. 4 (Sep.–Dec. 1961), pp. 425–426.

Goldberg, Eric Joseph. *Struggle for Empire: Kingship and Conflict under Louis the German, 817–876.* Ithaca, N.Y.: Cornell University Press, 2006.

Gordon, C. D. *The Age of Attila: Fifth-Century Byzantium and the Barbarians.* Ann Arbor: University of Michigan Press, 1960.

Graff, David A., and Robin Higham, eds. *A Military History of China.* Cambridge, Mass.: Westview Press, 2002.

Grayson, James Huntley. *Early Buddhism and Christianity in Korea: A Study in the Emplantation of Religion.* Leiden: E. J. Brill, 1985.

———. *Korea: A Religious History.* Rev. ed. New York: Routledge, 2002.

Greatrex, Geoffrey. "The Nika Riot: A Reappraisal." *The Journal of Hellenic Studies,* Vol. 117 (1997), pp. 60–86.

Gregory, Timothy. *A History of Byzantium.* Oxford: Blackwell, 2005.

Gregory the Great. *The Dialogues of St. Gregory.* Ed. Edmund G. Gardner. London: P. L. Warner, 1911.

Gregory of Tours. *The History of the Franks.* Trans. Lewis Thorpe. New York: Penguin Books, 1974.

Grillmeier, Alois. *Christ in Christian Tradition.* Vol. 2. Trans. O. C. Dean. New York: Continuum International, 1996.

Grousset, René. *The Empire of the Steppes: A History of Central Asia.* Trans. Naomi Walford. New Brunswick, N.J.: Rutgers University Press, 1970.

Grunfeld, A. Tom. *The Making of Modern Tibet*. Rev. ed. Armonk, N.Y.: M. E. Sharpe, 1996.

Guanzhong, Luo. *Three Kingdoms*. Trans. Moss Roberts. Berkeley: University of California Press, 1991.

Guisso, R. W. L. *Wu Tse-T'ien and the Politics of Legitimization in T'ang China*. Bellingham, Wash.: Western Washington University, 1978.

Gunter, Michael M. *The Kurds and the Future of Turkey*. New York: Macmillan, 1997.

Hadley, D. M. *The Northern Danelaw: Its Social Structure, c. 800–1100*. London: Leicester University Press, 2000.

Hall, John Whitney, Delmer M. Brown, and Kozo Yamamura. *The Cambridge History of Japan*. Cambridge: Cambridge University Press, 1988.

Hallenbeck, Jan T. *Pavia and Rome: The Lombard Monarchy and the Papacy in the Eighth Century*. Philadelphia, Penn.: American Philosophical Society, 1982.

Halm, Heinz. *The Empire of the Mahdi: The Rise of the Fatimids*. Leiden: E. J. Brill, 1996.

Halphen, Louis. *Charlemagne and the Carolingian Empire*. Trans. Giselle de Nie. Amsterdam: North-Holland, 1977.

Haly, Richard. "Bare Bones: Rethinking Mesoamerican Divinity." *History of Religions*, Vol. 31, no. 3 (Feb. 1992), pp. 269–304.

Hampe, Karl. *Germany under the Salian and Hohenstaufen Emperors*. Trans. Ralph Bennett. Totowa, N.J.: Rowman & Littlefield, 1973.

Harsha. *Nagananda*. Trans. Palmer Boyd. Cambridge, Ontario: In Parentheses Publications, 1999.

Heaney, Seamus. *Beowulf: A New Verse Translation*. New York: W. W. Norton, 2001.

Heather, Peter. *The Goths*. Oxford: Blackwell, 1996.

Heather, Peter, and John Matthews. *The Goths in the Fourth Century*. Liverpool: Liverpool University Press, 1991.

Heitzman, James. *Gifts of Power: Lordship in an Early Indian State*. Delhi: Oxford University Press, 1997.

Heng, Chye Kiang. *Cities of Aristocrats and Bureaucrats: The Development of Medieval Chinese City-scapes*. Honolulu: University of Hawaii Press, 1999.

Henry of Huntingdon. *The Chronicle of Henry of Huntingdon*. Trans. Thomas Forester. London: Henry G. Bohn, 1853.

Herm, Gerhard. *The Celts: The People Who Came Out of the Darkness*. New York: St. Martin's Press, 1976.

Hodges, Richard, and David Whitehouse. *Mohammed, Charlemagne & the Origins of Europe: Archaeology and the Pirenne Thesis*. Ithaca, N.Y.: Cornell University Press, 1983.

Hodgkin, Thomas. *Italy and Her Invaders*. Oxford: Clarendon Press, 1892.

Hodgson, Marshall G. S. *The Venture of Islam: Conscience and History in a World Civilization*. Vol. 1: *The Classical Age of Islam*. Chicago: University of Chicago Press, 1974.

———. *The Venture of Islam: Conscience and History in a World Civilization*. Vol. 2: *The Expansion of Islam in the Middle Periods*. Chicago: University of Chicago Press, 1974.

Holt, P. M., Ann K. S. Lambton, and Bernard Lewis, eds. *The Cambridge History of Islam*. Vol. 1. Cambridge: Cambridge University Press, 1970.

The Holy Qur'an. Trans. Abdullah Yusuf Ali. Hertfordshire, England: Wordsworth Editions, 2000.

Hooper, Finely. *Roman Realities*. Detroit: Wayne State University Press, 1979.

Howard, Ian. *Swein Forkbeard's Invasions and the Danish Conquest of England, 991–1017*. Suffolk, England: Boydell Press, 2003.

Howarth, David. *1066: The Year of the Conquest*. New York: Penguin Books, 1981.

Hucker, Charles O. *China's Imperial Past: An Introduction to Chinese History and Culture*. Stanford, Calif.: Stanford University Press, 1975.

Hudson, Benjamin T. *Prophecy of Berchán: Irish and Scottish High-Kings of the Early Middle Ages*. Westport, Conn.: Greenwood Press, 1996.

Hultzsch, E., and H. Krishna Sastri. *Miscellaneous Inscriptions from the Tamil Country*. South Indian inscriptions, Vol. 3. Madras: Printed by the superintendent, Gov't. Press [etc.], 1899.

Hydatius. *The Chronicle of Hydatius and the Consularia Constantinopolitana*. Trans. R. W. Burgess. Oxford: Clarendon Press, 1993.

Ibn al-Athīr, Izz al-Dīn. *The Annals of the Saljuq Turks: Selections from al-Kamil fi'l-Ta'rīkh of ʿIzz al-Dīn Ibn al-Athīr*. Trans. D. S. Richards. London: RoutledgeCurzon, 2002.

Ibn Al-Qala nisi. *The Damascus Chronicle of the Crusades*. Trans. Hamilton Gibb. Mineola, N.Y.: Dover, 2003.

Ibn Fadlan. *Ibn Fadlan's Journey to Russia: A Tenth-Century Traveler from Baghdad to the Volga River*. Trans. Richard N. Frye. Princeton, N.J.: Markus Wiener, 2005.

Ilyon. *Samguk Yusa: Legends and History of the Three Kingdoms of Ancient Korea*. Trans. Tae-hung Ha and Grafton K. Mintz. Seoul: Yonsei University Press, 1972.

Inden, Ronald. *Imagining India*. Oxford: Blackwell, 1992.

Ingstad, Helge, and Anne Stine Ingstad. *The Viking Discovery of America: The Excavation of a Settlement in L'Anse aux Meadows, Newfoundland*. New York: Checkmark Books, 2001.

Ishaq. *The Life of Muhammad: A Translation of Ishaq's Sirat Rasul Allah*. Trans. A. Guillaume. Karachi: Oxford University Press, 1997.

Jenkins, Romilly. *Byzantium: The Imperial Centuries, AD 610–1071*. Toronto: University of Toronto Press, 1987.

John of Worcester. *The Chronicles of John of Worcester*. Vol. 2: *The Annals from 450 to 1066*. Trans. Jennifer Bray and P. McGurk. Oxford: Clarendon Press, 1995.

———. *The Chronicles of John of Worcester*.

Jones, Archer. *The Art of War in the Western World*. Urbana: University of Illinois Press, 1987.

Jones, Gwyn. *A History of the Vikings*. Rev. ed. Oxford: Oxford University Press, 1984.

Jordanes. *The Gothic History of Jordanes*. Trans. Charles Christopher Mierow. Princeton, N.J.: Princeton University Press, 1915.

Joshua the Stylite. *The Chronicle of Joshua the Stylite*. Trans. W. Wright. Cambridge: Cambridge University Press, 1882.

Kafesoğlu, İbrahim, and Gary Leiser. *A History of the Seljuks: İbrahim Kafesoğlu's Interpretation and the Resulting Controversy*. Carbondale: Southern Illinois University Press, 1988.

Kang, Jae-eun. *The Land of Scholars: Two Thousand Years of Korean Confucianism*. Trans. Suzanne Lee. Paramus, N.J.: Homa & Sekey Books, 2006.

Karsh, Efraim. *Islamic Imperialism: A History*. New Haven, Conn.: Yale University Press, 2006.

Keay, John. *India: A History*. New York: Grove Press, 2000.

Kehoe, Alice Beck. *America Before the European Invasions*. London: Longman, 2002.

Kelly, Gavin. "Ammianus and the Great Tsunami." *The Journal of Roman Studies*, Vol. 94 (2004), pp. 141–167.

Kelly, J. N. D. *Early Christian Doctrines*. Rev. ed. San Francisco: Harper & Row, 1976.

———. *The Oxford Dictionary of Popes*. Oxford: Oxford University Press, 1986.

Kennedy, Hugh. *The Prophet and the Age of the Caliphates*. 2d ed. Harlow, England: Pearson Education, 2004.

———. *When Baghdad Ruled the Muslim World: The Rise and Fall of Islam's Greatest Dynasty*. Cambridge, Mass.: Da Capo Press, 2005.

Keynes, Simon, and Michael Lapidge, trans. *Alfred the Great: Asser's Life of King Alfred and Other Contemporary Sources*. New York: Penguin, 1983.

Keys, David. *Catastrophe: An Investigation into the Origins of the Modern World*. New York: Ballantine Books, 1999.

Kidd, B. J. *Documents Illustrative of the History of the Church*. Vol. 3. London: S.P.C.K., 1920.

Kim, Jong-gil. *Among the Flowering Reeds: Classic Korean Poems Written in Chinese*. Buffalo, N.Y.: White Pine, 2003.

Kit, Wong Kiew. *Art of Shaolin Kung Fu*. North Clarendon, Vt.: Tuttle, 2002.

Krech, Shepard, John Robert McNeill, and Carolyn Merchant. *Encyclopedia of World Environmental History*. New York: Routledge, 2004.

Kruger, Rayne. *All Under Heaven: A Complete History of China*. Chichester: John Wiley, 2003.

Kulke, Hermann. *A History of India*. 4th ed. New York: Routledge, 2004.

Kurkjian, Vahan M. *A History of Armenia*. New York: Armenian General Benevolent Union of America, 1958.

Kuroita-Katsumi. *Prince Shotoku and His Seventeen-Article Constitution*. Tokyo: Nippon Bunka Chuo Renmei, 1940.

Kutcher, Norman. *Mourning in Late Imperial China: Filial Piety and the State*. Cambridge: Cambridge University Press, 1999.

Lactantius. *De Mortibus Persecutorum*. Trans. O. F. Fritzsche. Pp. 28–30 in *University of Pennsylvania, Dept of History: Translations and Reprints from the Original Sources of European History*. Philadelphia: University of Pennsylvania Press, 1897. Vol. 4, no. 1.

Lebra, Takie Sugiyama. *Above the Clouds: Status Culture of the Modern Japanese Nobility*. Berkeley: University of California Press, 1993.

Lee, A. D. *Pagans and Christians in Late Antiquity: A Sourcebook*. New York: Routledge, 2000.

Lee, Ki-baik. *A New History of Korea*. Trans. Edward W. Wagner with Edward J. Shultz. Seoul: Ilchokak, 1984.

Lee, Peter H., Donald Baker, Yongho Ch'oe, Hugh H. W. Kang, and Han-Kyo Kim, eds. *Sourcebook of Korean Civilization*. Vol. 1: *From Early Times to the Sixteenth Century*. New York: Columbia University Press, 1993.

Lee, Peter H., Yongho Ch'oe, and William Theodore de Bary, eds. *Sources of Korean Tradition*. New York: Columbia University Press, 1997.

Lee, Peter H., and William Theodore de Bary, eds. *Sources of Korean Tradition*, Vol. 1: *From Early Times to the Sixteenth Century*. New York: Columbia University Press, 1993.

Lendvai, Paul. *The Hungarians: A Thousand Years of Victory in Defeat*. Trans. Ann Major. Princeton, N.J.: Princeton University Press, 2003.

Leo the Deacon. *The History of Leo the Deacon: Byzantine Military Expansion in the Tenth Century*. Trans. Alice-Mary Talbot and Denis F. Sullivan. Washington, D.C.: Dumbarton Oaks, 2005.

León Portilla, Miguel, and Earl Shorris, eds. *In the Language of Kings: An Anthology of Mesoamerican Literature—Pre-Columbian to the Present*. New York: W. W. Norton, 2001.

Lewis, Archibald Ross. *The Development of Southern French and Catalan Society, 718–1050*. Austin: University of Texas Press, 1965.

Licon, Ernesto Gonzalez. *Vanished Mesoamerican Civilizations: The History and Cultures of the Zapotecs and Mixtecs*. Trans. Andrew Ellis. Armonk, N.Y.: Sharpe Reference, 1991.

Lings, Martin. *Muhammad: His Life Based on the Earliest Sources*. Rochester, Vt.: Inner Traditions International, 1983.

Liudprand of Cremona. *The Complete Works of Liudprand of Cremona*. Trans. Paolo Squatriti. Washington, D.C.: Catholic University of America Press, 2007.

Logan, F. Donald. *A History of the Church in the Middle Ages*. New York: Routledge, 2002.

Lorge, Peter. *War, Politics and Society in Early Modern China, 900–1795*. New York: Routledge, 2005.

Lu, David John. *Japan: A Documentary History*. Armonk, N.Y.: M. E. Sharpe, 1997.

Luscome, David, and Jonathan Riley-Smith, eds. *The New Cambridge Medieval History*. Vol. 4. Cambridge: Cambridge University Press, 2004.

MacGowan, John. *The Imperial History of China*. London: Curzon Press, 1897.

Mackay, Christopher S. *Ancient Rome: A Military and Political History*. Cambridge: Cambridge University Press, 2004.

Maenchen-Helfen, Otto J. *The World of the Huns: Studies in Their History and Culture*. Berkeley: University of California Press, 1973.

Magnusson, Magnus. *Scotland: The Story of a Nation*. New York: Atlantic Monthly Press, 2000.

Mahler, Margaret. *A History of Chirk Castle and Chirkland: With a Chapter on Offa's Dyke*. London: G. Bell, 1912.

Maity, Sachindra Kumar. *Professor A. L. Basham, My Guruji and Problems and Perspectives of Ancient Indian History and Culture*. New Delhi: Abhinav, 1997.

Majumdar, R. C. *Ancient India*. Delhi: Motilal Banarsidass, 1964.

Malaterra, Goffredo. *The Deeds of Count Roger of Calabria and Sicily and of His Brother Duke Robert Guiscard*. Trans. Kenneth Baxter Wolf. Ann Arbor: University of Michigan Press, 2005.

Marcus, Jacob Rader, ed. *The Jew in the Medieval World: A Source Book, 315–1791*. Rev. ed. Cincinnati, Ohio: Hebrew Union College Press, 1999.

Marcus, Joyce. "The Origins of Mesoamerican Writing." *Annual Review of Anthropology*, Vol. 5 (1976), pp. 35–67.

Marín, Manuela, and Salma Khadra Jayyusi. *Handbuch der Orientalistik. Abt. 1, Bd 12, Der Nahe und Mittlere Osten: The Near and Middle East, the Legacy of Muslim Spain*. Leiden: Brill, 1992.

Marra, Michele. *The Aesthetics of Discontent: Politics and Reclusion in Medieval Japan*. Honolulu: University of Hawaii Press, 1991.

Martin, Peter. *The Chrysanthemum Throne: A History of the Emperors of Japan*. Honolulu: University of Hawaii Press, 1997.

Maurice. *Maurice's Strategikon: Handbook of Byzantine Military Strategy*. Trans. George T. Dennis. Philadelphia: University of Pennsylvania Press, 1984.

Mayr-Hartin, Henry. *The Coming of Christianity to Anglo-Saxon England*. London: Batsford, 1972.

Merrills, A. H. *Vandals, Romans and Berbers: New Perspectives on Late Antique North Africa*. Aldershot, England: Ashgate, 2004.

Meyer, Milton W. *Japan: A Concise History*. 3d ed. Lanham, Md.: Royman & Littlefield, 1993.

Michael, Franz. *China through the Ages: History of a Civilization*. Boulder, Colo.: Westview Press, 1986.

Millon, Rene. "Teotihuacan: City, State and Civilization." Pp. 235–238 in *Supplement to the Handbook of Middle American Indians*, vol. I, ed. Victoria Reifler Bricker. Austin: University of Texas Press, 1981.

Mirashi, Vasudev Vishnu. *Literary and Historical Studies in Indology*. Delhi: Motilal Banarasidass, 1975.

Mookerji, Radha Kumud. *The Gupta Empire*. Delhi: Motilal Banarsidass, 1969.

Moore, Louise T., Brian McEvoy, Eleanor Cape, Katharine Simms, and Daniel G. Bradley, "A Y-Chromosome Signature of Hegemony in Gaelic Ireland." *The American Journal of Human Genetics*, Vol. 78 (Feb. 2006), pp. 334–338.

Moorhead, John. *Theoderic in Italy*. Oxford: Clarendon Press, 1992.

Morley, Henry, and William Hall Griffin. *English Writers*. Vol. 2. New York: Cassell & Co., 1888.

Morton, W. Scott, and Charlton M. Lewis. *China: Its History and Culture*. 4th ed. New York: McGraw-Hill, 1995.

Muldoon, James. *Empire and Order: The Concept of Empire, 800–1800*. Houndmills, Basingstoke, Hampshire: Macmillan, 1999.

Munro-Hay, Stuart. *The Quest for the Ark of the Covenant: The True History of the Tablets of Moses*. London: I. B. Tauris, 1996.

Nasr, Seyyed Hossein. *Islamic Philosophy from Its Origin to the Present: Philosophy in the Land of Prophecy*. Albany: State University of New York Press, 2006.

Needham, Joseph, Ho Ping-Yu, and Lu Gwei-den. *Science and Civilisation in China*. Vol. 3, Part 3. Cambridge: Cambridge University Press, 1976.

Needham, Joseph, and Cunxun Qian. *Science and Civilisation in China*. Vol. 5: *Chemistry and Chemical Technology*. Part 1, *Paper and Printing*. Cambridge: Cambridge University Press, 1985.

Nelson, Janet L., trans. *The Annals of St. Bertin*. Manchester: Manchester University Press, 1991.

Nestorius. *The Bazaar of Heracleides*. Trans. G. R. Driver and Leonard Hodgson. Oxford: Clarendon Press, 1925.

Nicholson, H. B. *Topiltzin Quetzalcoatl: The Once and Future Lord of the Toltecs.* Boulder: University Press of Colorado, 2001.

Obolensky, Dimitri. *Byzantium and the Slavs.* Crestwood, N.Y.: St. Vladimir's Seminary Press, 1994.

O'Flaherty, Wendy Doniger, ed. *Textual Sources for the Study of Hinduism.* Chicago: University of Chicago Press, 1990.

O Hogain, Daithi. *The Celts: A History.* Woodbridge, England: Boydell Press, 2003.

Oldenberg, Hermann. *The Religion of the Veda.* Delhi: Motilal Banarsidass, 1988.

Oliver, Roland, and Brian M. Fagan. *Africa in the Iron Age, c. 500 BC to AD 1400.* Cambridge: Cambridge University Press, 1975.

Olson, David R., and Michael Cole. *Technology, Literacy and the Evolution of Society.* Mahwah, N.J.: Lawrence Erlbaum, 2006.

Olsson, Karl F. "The Structure of Power under the Third Emperor of Sung China: The Shifting Balance after the Peace of Shan-Yuan." Submitted dissertation. Chicago: University of Chicago, 1974.

Ormsby, John. *The Poem of the Cid: A Translation from the Spanish.* London: Longmans, Green, 1879.

Orosius, Paulus. *The Seven Books of History against the Pagans.* Trans. Roy J. Defarrari. Washington, D.C.: Catholic University of America Press, 1964.

Ostrogorsky, George. *History of the Byzantine State.* Rev. ed. Trans. Joan Hussey. New Brunswick, N.J.: Rutgers University Press, 1969.

Palais, James B. *Confucian Statecraft and Korean Institutions: Yu Hyongwon and the Late Choson Dynasty.* Seattle: University of Washington Press, 1996.

Paludan, Ann. *Chronicle of the Chinese Emperors.* London: Thames & Hudson, 1998.

Parfitt, Tudor. *The Road to Redemption: The Jews of the Yemen 1900–1950.* Boston, Mass.: Brill Academic, 1996.

Paul the Deacon. *History of the Lombards.* Trans. William Dudley Foulke. Philadelphia: University of Pennsylvania Press, 1974.

Pechilis Prentiss, Karen. *The Embodiment of Bhakti.* New York: Oxford University Press, 1999.

Pedro, King of Aragon. *The Chronicle of San Juan De La Peña: A Fourteenth-Century Official History of the Crown of Aragon.* Trans. Lynn H. Nelson. Philadelphia: University of Pennsylvania Press, 1991.

Pelikan, Jaroslav. *The Growth of Medieval Theology (600–1300).* Chicago: University of Chicago Press, 1978.

Perry, John Curtis, and Bardwell L. Smith, eds. *Essays on T'ang Society: The Interplay of Social, Political and Economic Forces.* Leiden: E. J. Brill, 1976.

Pertz, G. H., Georg Waitz, Rudolf Koepke, Ludwig Konrad Bethmann, Franz Friedrich Roger Wilmans, Wilhelm Wattenbach, Jan Kanty Szlachiowski, and Hugo de Sancta Maria. *Chronica et annales aevi Salici.* Stuttgart: Hiersemann, 1963.

Photius. *Epitome of the Ecclesiastical History of Philostorgius.* Trans. Edward Walford. London: Henry G. Bohn, 1860.

———. *The Homilies of Photius.* Trans. Cyril Mango. Cambridge, Mass.: Harvard University Press, 1958.

Piggott, Joan R. *The Emergence of Japanese Kingship.* Stanford, Calif.: Stanford University Press, 1997.

Plummer, Charles, and John Earle. *Two of the Saxon Chronicles Parallel.* Vol. 2. Oxford: Clarendon Press, 1899.

Pohl, Walter. "The Vandals: Fragments of a Narrative." In *Vandals, Romans and Berbers: New Perspectives on Late Antique North Africa,* ed. A. H. Merrills. Aldershot, England: Ashgate, 2004.

Pohl, Walter, and Helmut Reimitz. *Strategies of Distinction: The Construction of Ethnic Communities, 300–800.* Boston, Mass.: Brill Academic, 1998.

Pratt, Keith. *Korea: A Historical and Cultural Dictionary.* New York: RoutledgeCurzon, 1999.

Pregadio, Fabrizio. *Great Clarity: Daoism and Alchemy in Early Medieval China.* Palo Alto, Calif.: Stanford University Press, 2005.

Prem, Hanns J. *The Ancient Americas: A Brief History and Guide to Research.* Trans. Kornelia Kurbjuhn. Salt Lake City: University of Utah Press, 1997.

Procopius. *History of the Wars and Buildings.* Vol. 1: *History of the Wars,* Books I and II. Trans. H. B. Dewing. London: W. Heinemann, 1914.

———. *History of the Wars and Buildings.* Vol. 2: *History of the Wars,* Books III and IV. Trans. H. B. Dewing. London: W. Heinemann, 1916.

———. *History of the Wars and Buildings.* Vol. 3: *History of the Wars,* Books V and VI. Trans. H. B. Dewing. London: W. Heinemann, 1919.

———. *History of the Wars and Buildings.* Vol. 5: *History of the Wars,* Books VII and VIII. Trans. H. B. Dewing. London: W. Heinemann, 1928.

———. *History of the Wars and Buildings.* Vol. 7: *Buildings.* Trans. H. B. Dewing. London: W. Heinemann, 1940.

———. *History of the Wars, Secret History, and Buildings,* trans. Averil Cameron. New York: Twayne Publishers, 1967.

———. *The Secret History.* Trans. G. A. Williamson. New York: Penguin, 1966.

Psellus, Michael. *Fourteen Byzantine Rulers.* Trans. E. R. A. Sewter. New York: Penguin, 1966.

Rappe, Sara. *Reading Neoplatonism: Non-discursive Thinking in the Texts of Plotinus, Proclus, and Damascius.* Cambridge: Cambridge University Press, 2000.

Ray, H. C. *The Dynastic History of Northern India (Early Mediaeval Period).* Vol. 1, 2d ed. New Delhi: Munshiram Manoharlal, 1973.

Reilly, Bernard F. *The Medieval Spains.* Cambridge: Cambridge University Press, 1993.

Reischauer, Robert Karl. *Early Japanese History (c. 40 BC–AD 1167).* Part A. Gloucester, Mass.: Peter Smith, 1967.

Reuter, Timothy, and Rosamond McKitterick, eds. *The New Cambridge Medieval History.* Vol. 3. New York: Cambridge University Press, 1999.

Rex, Peter. *Harold II: The Doomed Saxon King.* Stroud, England: Tempus, 2005.

Rhie, Marylin M. *Early Buddhist Art of China and Central Asia.* Vol. 2. Leiden: Brill, 1999.

Rice, Benjamin Lewis. *Mysore Inscriptions.* New Delhi: Navrang, 1983.

Richards, Jeffrey. *The Popes and the Papacy in the Early Middle Ages, 476–752.* Boston: Routledge, 1979.

Riche, Pierre. *The Carolingians: A Family Who Forged Europe.* Trans. Michael Idomir Allen. Philadelphia: University of Pennsylvania Press, 1993.

Richmond, I. A. *Roman Britain.* Middlesex, England: Penguin Books, 1955.

Riha, Thomas, ed. *Readings in Russian Civilization.* Vol. 1. Chicago: University of Chicago Press, 1969.

Roberts, J. A. G. *The Complete History of China.* Gloucestershire, England: Sutton, 2003.

Robinson, David. *Muslim Societies in African History.* Cambridge: Cambridge University Press, 2004.

Robinson, Ian S. *Henry IV of Germany.* Cambridge: Cambridge University Press, 2000.

Rogers, Jerry, Glenn O. Brown, and Jurgen Garbrecht. *Water Resources and Environmental History.* Reston, Va.: American Society of Civil Engineers, 2004.

Rogerson, Barnaby. *The Prophet Muhammad: A Biography.* Mahway, N.J.: Hidden Spring, 2003.

Rona-Tas, Andras. *Hungarians and Europe in the Early Middle Ages: An Introduction to Early Hungarian History.* Budapest: Central European University Press, 1999.

Rosen, William. *Justinian's Flea: Plague, Empire, and the Birth of Europe.* New York: Viking, 2007.

Runciman, Steven. *The Emperor Romanus Lecapenus & His Reign: A Study of Tenth-Century Byzantium.* Cambridge: Cambridge University Press, 1929.

————. *A History of the Crusades*. Vol. 1: *The First Crusade and the Foundation of the Kingdom of Jerusalem*. Cambridge: Cambridge University Press, 1951.

Ryder, Frank Glessner. *The Song of the Nibelungs: A Verse Translation from the Middle High German*. Detroit, Mich.: Wayne State University Press, 1962.

St. John of Damascus. *On the Divine Images: Three Apologies against Those Who Attack the Divine Images*. Trans. David Anderson. Crestwood, N.Y.: St. Vladimir's Seminary Press, 1980.

Samellas, Antigone. *Death in the Eastern Mediterranean (50–600 A.D.): The Christianization of the East*. Tübingen: Mohr Siebeck, 2002.

Sastri, K. A. Nilakanta. *A History of South India from Prehistoric Times to the Fall of Vijayanagar*. 3d ed. Oxford: Oxford University Press, 1966.

————. *The Pandyan Kingdom: From the Earliest Times to the Sixteenth Century*. London: Luzac, 1929.

Saunders, John J. *A History of Medieval Islam*. New York: Routledge, 1978.

Saunders, Nicholas J. *Ancient Americas: The Great Civilisations*. Stroud, England: Sutton, 2004.

Savino, John, and Marie D. Jones. *Supervolcano: The Catastrophic Event That Changed the Course of Human History*. Franklin, N.J.: Career Press, 2007.

Sawyer, P. H. *Kings and Vikings: Scandinavia and Europe, AD 700–1100*. London: Methuen, 1982.

Scales, Peter C. *The Fall of the Caliphate of Cordoba: Berbers and Andalusis in Conflict*. Leiden: E. J. Brill, 1994.

Scarre, Chris. *Chronicle of the Roman Emperors*. London: Thames & Hudson, 1995.

Schaff, Philip, general ed. *Ante-Nicene Fathers*. Vol. 1: *The Apostolic Fathers, Justin Martyr, Irenaeus*. Trans. Alexander Roberts and James Donaldson, Edinburgh: T & T Clark, 1867.

————. *Ante-Nicene Fathers*. Vol. 7: *The Fathers of the Third and Fourth Centuries*. Trans. Alexander Roberts and James Donaldson. Edinburgh: T & T Clark, 1896.

————, general ed. *A Select Library of the Nicene and Post-Nicene Fathers*, first series. Vol. 4: *St. Augustin: The Writings against the Manichaeans and against the Donatists*. Trans. J. R. King. Edinburgh: T & T Clark, 1889.

Schaff, Philip, and Henry Wace, general eds. *A Select Library of the Nicene and Post-Nicene Fathers*, second series. Vol. 2: *Socrates and Sozomen*. Trans. A. C. Zenos and Chester D. Hartranft. New York: Christian Literature, 1892.

————. *A Select Library of the Nicene and Post-Nicene Fathers*, second series. Vol. 3: *Theodoret, Jerome, Gennadius, and Rufinus*. Trans. Blomfield Jackson, Ernest Richardson, and Henry Fremantle. New York: Christian Literature, 1892.

————. *A Select Library of the Nicene and Post-Nicene Fathers*, second series. Vol. 12: *Leo the Great and Gregory the Great*. Trans. Charles Lett Feltoe. New York: Christian Literature, 1892.

————. *A Select Library of the Nicene and Post-Nicene Fathers*, second series. Vol. 13: *Gregory the Great, Ephraim Syrus, Aphrahat*. Trans. James Barmby and John Gwynn. New York: Christian Literature, 1892.

————. *A Select Library of the Nicene and Post-Nicene Fathers*, second series. Vol. 14: *The Seven Ecumenical Councils of the Undivided Church*. Trans. H. Percival. New York: Christian Literature, 1892.

Schippers, Arie. *Spanish Hebrew Poetry and the Arab Literary Tradition: Arabic Themes in Hebrew Andalusian Poetry*. Leiden: E. J. Brill, 1994.

Schmidt, Karl J. *An Atlas and Survey of South Asian History*. Armonk, N.Y.: M. E. Sharpe, 1995.

Scholz, Bernhard Walter, with Barbara Rogers, trans. *Carolingian Chronicles*. Ann Arbor: University of Michigan Press, 1970.

Scott-Moncrieff, Charles Kenneth, trans. *The Song of Roland*. New York: E. P. Dutton, 1920.

Sen, Sailendra Nath. *Ancient Indian History and Civilization*. New Delhi: Wiley Eastern, 1988.

Severus of Al'Ashmunein. *History of the Patriarchs of the Coptic Church of Alexandria*, trans. B. Evetts. Paris: P. Fages, 1904.

Shaban, M. A. *Islamic History: A New Interpretation,* A.D. *750–1055 (A.H. 132–448).* Cambridge: Cambridge University Press, 1976.

Shahid, Irfan. *Byzantium and the Arabs in the Sixth Century.* Vol. 2, Part 1. Washington, D.C.: Dumbarton Oaks Research Library and Collection, 2002.

Sharer, Robert J., and Sylvanus Griswold Morley. *The Ancient Maya.* 5th ed. Stanford, Calif.: Stanford University Press, 1994.

Sheng Yen, Chan Master. *Zen Wisdom: Knowing and Doing.* Elmhurst, N.Y.: Dharma Drum, 1993.

Sicker, Martin. *The Islamic World in Ascendancy.* Westport, Conn.: Praeger, 2000.

Sidonius Apollinaris. *Letters.* Trans. O. M. Dalton. Oxford: Clarendon Press, 1915.

Simeon of Durham. *The Historical Works of Simeon of Durham.* Trans. J. Stevenson. In *The Church Historians of England,* Vol. 3, Part 2. London: Seeleys, 1855.

Simon of Kéza. *Gesta Hungarorum.* Trans. Lászlo Veszprémy and Frank Schaer. New York: Central European Press, 1999.

Simons, Geoffrey L. *Iraq: From Sumer to Saddam.* New York: St. Martin's Press, 1994.

Singh, Nau Nihal. *The Royal Gurjars: Their Contribution to India.* New Delhi: Anmol, 2003.

Sircar, Dineschandra. *Studies in the Geography of Ancient and Medieval India.* Delhi: Motilal Banarsidass, 1971.

Smith, Vincent Arthur. *The Early History of India.* Oxford: Clarendon Press, 1904.

Sourdel, Dominique. *Medieval Islam.* Boston, Mass.: Routledge, 1983.

Southern, R. W. *Western Society and the Church in the Middle Ages.* London: Penguin Books, 1970.

Stalls, Clay. *Possessing the Land: Aragon's Expansion into Islam's Ebro Frontier under Alfonso the Battler, 1104–1134.* Leiden: E. J. Brill, 1995.

Stevenson, James, ed. *Creeds, Councils and Controversies.* London: S.P.C.K., 1966.

Story, Joanna, ed. *Charlemagne: Empire and Society.* Manchester: Manchester University Press, 2005.

Stratos, Andreas N. *Byzantium in the Seventh Century.* Amsterdam: Adolf M. Hakkert, 1968.

Sturluson, Snorri. *Heimskringla: or, The Lives of the Norse Kings.* Trans. Erling Monsen. New York: D. Appleton, 1932.

Sugiyama, Saburo. "Worldview Materialized in Teotihuacan, Mexico." *Latin American Antiquity,* Vol. 4, no. 2 (Jun., 1993), pp. 103–129.

Swanton, M. J., trans. and ed. *The Anglo-Saxon Chronicle.* New York: Routledge, 1998.

Sykes, Bryan. *Saxons, Vikings, and Celts: The Genetic Roots of Britain and Ireland.* New York: W. W. Norton, 2006.

Tao, Jinsheng. *Two Sons of Heaven: Studies in Sung-Liao Relations.* Tucson: University of Arizona Press, 1988.

Taylor, Rodney Leon. *The Religious Dimensions of Confucianism.* Albany: State University of New York Press, 1990.

Tennant, Roger. *A History of Korea.* London: Keegan Paul, 1996.

Thapar, Romila. *Asoka and the Decline of the Mauryas.* 3d rev. ed. Oxford: Oxford University Press, 1998.

———. *Early India: From the Origins to AD 1300.* Berkeley, Calif.: University of California Press, 2002.

Thatcher, Oliver J., and Edgar Holmes McNeal, eds. *A Source Book for Medieval History.* New York: Scribners, 1905.

Theodore the Syncellus. *Traduction et Commentaire de l'homélie écrite probablement par Théodore le Syncelle sur le siège de Constantinople en 626.* Ed. Ferenc Makk and Leo Sternbach. Trans. Ferenc Makk. Szeged, Hungary: Acta Universitatis de Attila József Nominatae, 1975.

Theodosius. *The Theodosian Codes and Novels and the Simondian Constitutions.* Ed. Clyde Pharr, with Theresa Sherrer Davidson and Mary Brown Pharr. Princeton, N.J.: Princeton University Press, 1952.

Theophanes the Confessor. *The Chronicle of Theophanes*. Trans. Harry Turtledove. Philadelphia: University of Pennsylvania Press, 1982.

———. *The Chronicle of Theophanes Confessor*. Trans. Cyril Mango and Roger Scott. Oxford: Clarendon Press, 1997.

Theophylact Simocatta. *The History of Theophylact Simocatta: An English Translation with Introduction and Notes*. Trans. Michael Whitby and Mary Whitby. Oxford: Clarendon Press, 1986.

Thietmar of Merseburg. *Ottonian Germany: The Chronicon of Thietmar of Merseburg*. Trans. David A. Warner. Manchester: Manchester University Press, 2001.

Thompson, E. A. *The Huns*. Revised by Peter Heather. Oxford: Blackwell, 1999.

Thorpe, Lewis, trans. *Two Lives of Charlemagne: Einhard and Notker the Stammerer*. New York: Penguin, 1969.

Thorsson, Ornolfur, ed. *The Sagas of the Icelanders: A Selection*. New York: Penguin, 2001.

Tougher, Shaun. "Byzantine Eunuchs: An Overview, with Special Reference to Their Creation and Origin." Pp. 168–184 in *Women, Men, and Eunuchs: Gender in Byzantium*, ed. Liz James. London: Routledge, 1997.

———. *The Reign of Leo VI (886–912): Politics and People*. Leiden: Brill, 1997.

Toynbee, Arnold. *Constantine Porphyrogenitus and His World*. London: Oxford University Press, 1973.

Tripathi, Rama Shankar. *History of Kanauj: To the Moslem Conquest*. Delhi: Motilal Banarsidass, 1964.

Twitchett, Denis, Herbert Franke, and John K. Fairbank. *The Cambridge History of China*, Vol. 6: *Alien Regimes and Border States, 907–1368*. Cambridge: Cambridge University Press, 1994.

Van de Ven, Hans J. *Warfare in Chinese History*. Boston, Mass.: Brill Academic, 2000.

Varley, H. Paul. *Warriors of Japan as Portrayed in the War Tales*. Honolulu: University of Hawaii Press, 1994.

Vasiliev, A. A. *History of the Byzantine Empire, 324–1453*, Vol. 1. Madison: University of Wisconsin Press, 1952.

Venantius Fortunatus. *Venantius Fortunatus: Personal and Political Poems*. Trans. Judith W. George. Liverpool: Liverpool University Press, 1995.

Vohra, Ranbir. *The Making of India: A Historical Survey*. London: M. E. Sharpe, 2001.

Walker, Paul E. *Fatimid History and Ismaili Doctrine*. Burlington, Vt.: Ashgate, 2008.

Wallace-Hadrill, J. M. *The Barbarian West: The Early Middle Ages, A.D. 400–1000*. New York: Harper & Row, 1962.

———. *Early Germanic Kingship in England and on the Continent*. Oxford: Clarendon Press, 1971.

———. *The Frankish Church*. Oxford: Clarendon Press, 1983.

———. *The Long-Haired Kings and Other Studies in Frankish History*. London: Methuen, 1962.

Watt, W. Montgomery. *A History of Islamic Spain*. Edinburgh: Edinburgh University Press, 1965.

Weinfurter, Stefan. *The Salian Century: Main Currents in an Age of Transition*. Middle Ages series. Philadelphia: University of Pennsylvania Press, 1999.

Wenjie, Duan. *Dunhuang Art: Through the Eyes of Duan Wenjie*. Trans. Tan Chung. New Delhi: Abhinav, 1994.

Whittow, Mark. *The Making of Byzantium, 600–1025*. Berkeley: University of California Press, 1996.

Wijayaratna, Mohan. *Buddhist Monastic Life: According to the Texts of the Theravada Tradition*. Trans. Claude Grangier and Steven Collins. Cambridge: Cambridge University Press, 1990.

William of Malmesbury. *Gesta Regum Anglorum: The History of the English Kings*. Vol. 1. Trans. R. A. B. Mynors, R. M. Thomson, and M. Winterbottom. Oxford: Clarendon Press, 1998.

William of Tyre. *A History of Deeds Done beyond the Sea*. Vol. 1. Trans. Emily Atwater Babcock and A. C. Krey. New York: Octagon Books, 1976.

Williams, George Huntston. "Christology and Church-State Relations in the Fourth Century (concluded)." *Church History*, Vol. 20, no. 4 (Dec. 1951), pp. 3–26.

Wilson, Derek. *Charlemagne.* New York: Doubleday, 2006.

Wollaston, Arthur. *The Sword of Islam.* London: John Murray, 1905.

Wolpert, Stanley. *A New History of India.* 7th ed. Oxford: Oxford University Press, 2004.

Wood, Ian. *The Merovingian Kingdoms, 450–751.* London: Longman, 1994.

Wood, Susan. *The Proprietary Church in the Medieval West.* Oxford: Oxford University Press, 2006.

Wright, Arthur F. *The Sui Dynasty.* New York: Alfred A. Knopf, 1978.

Yang, Xianyi, and Gladys Yang, trans. *Poetry and Prose of the Tang and Song.* Beijing: Panda Books, 1984.

Yarshater, Ehsan, ed. *The Cambridge History of Iran.* Vol. 3(1): *The Seleucid, Parthian and Sasanian Periods.* Cambridge: Cambridge University Press, 1983.

———. "Mazdakism." Pp. 991–1024 in *The Cambridge History of Iran.* Vol. 3(2): *The Seleucid, Parthian and Sasanian Periods,* ed. Ehsan Yarshater. Cambridge: Cambridge University Press, 1983.

Yeghishe. *History of Vartan and the Armenian War.* 2d ed. New York: Delphic Press, 1952.

Yoffee, Norman, ed. *The Collapse of Ancient States and Civilizations.* Tucson: University of Arizona Press, 1988.

Zarrinkub, ʿAbd al-Husain. "The Arab Conquest of Iran and Its Aftermath." Pp. 1–56 in *The Cambridge History of Iran in Eight Volumes.* Vol. 4, ed. R. N. Frye. Cambridge: Cambridge University Press, 1975.

Zosimus. *Historia Nova.* Trans. anon. London: Green & Chaplin, 1814.

Permissions

Index

—

Page numbers in *italics* refer to illustrations and maps.

3179 1985